MOTOCOURSE

The World's Leading MotoGP & Superbike Annual

HAZLETON PUBLISHING

CONTENTS

chairman
RICHARD POULTER

editor
MICHAEL SCOTT

director
STEVEN PALMER

publisher
NICK POULTER

managing editor
ROBERT YARHAM

art editor
STEVE SMALL

business development manager
PETER MERCER

sales promotion
ANNALISA ZANELLA

results and statistics
KAY EDGE

chief photographers
GOLD & GOOSE
London, England
Telephone: (0)20-8870 1045
Fax: (0)20-8870 2234
E-mail: office@goldandgoose.com

MOTOCOURSE
2002–2003
is published by
Hazleton Publishing Ltd,
3 Richmond Hill,
Richmond, Surrey
TW10 6RE, England.

Colour reproduction by
Barrett Berkeley Ltd, London, England.

Printed in England by
Butler and Tanner Ltd,
Frome.

Hazleton Publishing Ltd is a member of
Profile Media Group Plc.

ISBN: 1-903135-13-3

Dust-jacket photograph:
MotoGP World Champion Valentino Rossi.

Title page photograph:
Superbike World Champion Colin Edwards
leads Troy Bayliss.

Both photographs: Gold & Goose

FOREWORD by Valentino Rossi	5
EDITOR'S INTRODUCTION	6
TOP TEN RIDERS OF 2002 by Michael Scott	10
STATE OF RACING by Michael Scott	18
DIFFERENT STROKES MotoGP technical review by Michael Scott	22
NEW ORDER Kevin Cameron assesses the new era of technical challenges for MotoGP bike designers	34
GRAND PRIX TEAMS AND RIDERS 2002 by Michael Scott	40
CULT FRICTION Michael Scott on Rossi, Biaggi and the cult of personality in MotoGP racing	46
2002 GRANDS PRIX	51
WORLD CHAMPIONSHIP RESULTS 2002 compiled by Kay Edge	148
SUPERBIKE WORLD CHAMPIONSHIP REVIEW by Gordon Ritchie	150
SUPERBIKE WORLD CHAMPIONSHIP POINTS TABLE compiled by Kay Edge	184
WORLD SUPERSPORT CHAMPIONSHIP REVIEW by Gordon Ritchie	186
ENDURANCE WORLD CHAMPIONSHIP REVIEW by Kel Edge	188
SIDECAR WORLD CHAMPIONSHIP REVIEW by John McKenzie	190
UNITED STATES RACING REVIEW by Paul Carruthers	192
ISLE OF MAN TT RACES REVIEW by Mac McDiarmid	196
BRITISH SUPERBIKES REVIEW by Gary Pinchin	200
MAJOR WORLDWIDE RESULTS compiled by Kay Edge	204

ACKNOWLEDGEMENTS

The Editor and staff of **MOTOCOURSE** wish to thank the following for their assistance in compiling the 2002–2003 edition: Marc Pétrier and Anne-Marie Gerber (FIM), Paul Butler (IRTA), Nick Harris and Eva Jirsenska (Dorna), Chuck Aksland, Jerry Burgess, Carlo Fiorani, Ali Forth, Lydia Guglielmi-Kirn, Iain Mackay, Randy Mamola, Tom O'Kane, Martin Port, Garry Taylor, Debbie van Zon, Rupert Williamson, Warren Willing, Jan Witteveen, as well as numerous colleagues and friends.

PHOTOGRAPHERS

Photographs in **MOTOCOURSE** 2002–2003 have been contributed by: Gold & Goose, Clive Challinor, Dave Collister, Dave Purves, Flick of the Wrist/Tom Hnatiw, Paterlini Giovanni Communication, Chris Sims-Fotomoto, Tom Riles.

DISTRIBUTORS

UNITED KINGDOM
J H Haynes & Co Ltd
Sparkford, Near Yeovil, Somerset
BA22 7JJ
Telephone: 01963 442030
Fax: 01963 440001

NORTH AMERICA
Motorbooks International
PO Box 1, 729 Prospect Avenue
Osceola, Wisconsin 54020, USA
Telephone: (1) 715 294 3345
Fax: (1) 715 294 4448

REST OF THE WORLD
Menoshire Ltd
Unit 13, 21 Wadsworth Road
Perivale, Middlesex UB6 7LQ
Telephone: 020 8566 7344
Fax: 020 8991 2439

MOTOCOURSE™
www.motocourse.com

foreword

To win four World Championships is like a dream. Especially to win the first four-stroke MotoGP championship, after winning the last 500 cc championship.

When I was young I used to admire the great racers — riders like Hailwood and Agostini. Later it was riders like Roberts, Rainey and Schwantz, and then Mick Doohan. Now I am proud that my name is also moving higher up the list as each year passes, with more wins and more championships.

Honda built us a very good bike for the first year of the new series. Where the other factories only tried to build a machine that would beat the old two-strokes, Honda set an altogether new goal. The RC211V was excellent. It won 14 out of 16 races.

I think I also got the best out of it, over the season. In this way I was able to win 11 times.

Maybe it looked easy, sometimes. That was not the case. The four-stroke is less difficult to set up and less challenging to ride than the two-stroke, and sometimes I missed my old NSR. But it is difficult in other ways. I had to learn different techniques, and also how to pace the race to suit the machine.

By the end of the year, when there were more Hondas and the other bikes had also improved, we had some very exciting close races. It was only a transitional year for the new class, but all the same I think there was some good racing for the fans.

Thinking back, one of the best moments was in Japan. We tested for two weeks before the first GP, working and working to find settings and so on. Then on race day it rained. I had also fallen off twice in practice — but I won the race. I realised then that the championship would be possible.

Next year it will be more difficult — certainly to win more than ten races will be very hard. My goal will not be to try to win more races than Doohan or anything like that. It will be to win the championship again.

My year would not have been possible without my great team — Jerry Burgess and the pit crew did a fantastic job for me. I must also thank everybody who gave me support, from sponsors through to my friends and family.

At the end of the year, I drove a rally car, and I expect soon to test an F1 car. People ask me if I plan to move to car racing. I am doing these things just to find out for myself what they are like. But my first passion is the same as always. It is motor cycles.

MOTOCOURSE also feels the passion for motor cycles above everything else. It is a beautiful book, and I am building a collection now with my picture on the front cover. My plan is that it will be there next year also!

Ciao

Photograph: Gold & Goose

by VALENTINO ROSSI

46

A GOOD START

Below: Sign of the times — at the third round at Jerez, the new four-stroke Hondas of Ukawa and Rossi pull away, two-stroke-mounted Alex Barros struggles grimly to keep in touch. His NSR was speeding towards extinction.
Photograph: Gold & Goose

RACING went through its biggest change in history in 2002. Evolution was firmly put to one side, and the rule-makers took control.

In the nick of time, it seems. Evolution under the previous rules had led to a blind two-stroke alley. What is more, it had also led to machines whose irrelevance to the real world was only rivalled by their similarity to one another. In spite of some good years, GP racing was going nowhere.

Switching to 990 cc four-stroke prototypes was a risky strategy. Perhaps they might not be fast enough to take over from the finely-honed 500s? Perhaps the promised factory support would not materialise? Although, since the factories had selected the engine size and written the rules, these questions answered themselves.

Another concern was more subtle.

Would Honda's senior role as industry leaders prove counterproductive? The spectre of total domination by Honda would preserve the worst of the old series, while bringing nothing much to the new one. And in the first part of the year, with Rossi winning every race, unless his team-mate Ukawa did so, this was an increasingly tangible worry. The other factories had shown willing so far. How long would they continue?

Thankfully, the latter part of the year brought encouragement. The Hondas weren't unbeatable, with Biaggi's Yamaha prevailing twice, and Gibernau's Suzuki coming close also in the wet in Portugal.

Even more encouragingly, when the numbers of the new Hondas rose from two to four in the final rounds, their closely matched performance led to some superb close battles. The new machines are clumsier than the old, and this makes their limits more accessible to more riders.

The transitional year went well, then; and the second year looks even better, with Ducati, Kawasaki and Proton joining Honda, Suzuki, Yamaha and Aprilia with redoubled numbers of four-strokes (no two-strokes are expected, unless Proton have a delay with their V5).

The gamble seems to have paid off, and the bounty is far-reaching. GP racing has been reintegrated into the overall pattern of world racing, correcting a mis-matched situation where the GPs were in an ever-more lofty and inaccessible ivory tower, and most national riders went on into production-based Superbike racing instead.

At the same time, the year confirmed another common tenet — that the same riders would be winning, no matter what the machines. Rossi had risen to pre-eminence the year before, his second in the premier class, and he won the last 500 title. Now he carried right on where he left off, winning the first MotoGP title as well.

Racing could go into the winter feeling pretty pleased with itself.

Yet there were still serious concerns. The four-strokes, even the relatively low-tuned first-generation four-strokes, had hiked costs by anywhere from 50 to 100 per cent. At the same time a worsening world financial climate had cut back on the amount of sponsorship money available.

This situation might get worse before it gets better — in 2006 tobacco sponsorship is due to stop, unless (as many expect) there is some stay of execution. And in spite of interest from elsewhere, notably telecommunications, tobacco still made up the bulk of sponsorship money in 2002 and will do again in 2003.

There's no room for complacency. But after the great plunge of 2002, there was every excuse for some quiet satisfaction.

Michael Scott
Wimbledon,
LONDON
November 2002

if the cap fits...

radial or radical?

Fact is Kawasaki invented the mid-weight supersports class way back when with the GPZ600R. Ever since, the competition have chased us hard and we've responded with some of the highest performing and most popular machines on the market under the mighty Ninja banner.

For 2003 we're carrying that banner higher than ever with the introduction of the eagerly awaited new ZX-6R. You can't mistake this for a run of the mill street bike 'cos it ain't. Right from the start, the designers produced a full-on track inspired focus for the 636cc fuel injected machine.

The result is not just a new generation of aggressive angular styling, but a top spec machine with more than it's

fair share of firsts. Radial front brakes make sense on a full-on racer so they appear on the ZX-6R. Upside-down front forks not only save more unsprung weight but add to precise handling characteristics so in they go.

Get on board and you won't be surprised to see a state-of-the-art tacho and speedometer along with the useful addition of a lap timer – as if we thought you could do without one! And if that still isn't "factory" enough for you, ask your franchised dealer about the availability of the limited edition ZX-6RR with slipper clutch, specially forged engine parts and adjustable swing arm pivot.

ZX-6R, you choose, they chase.

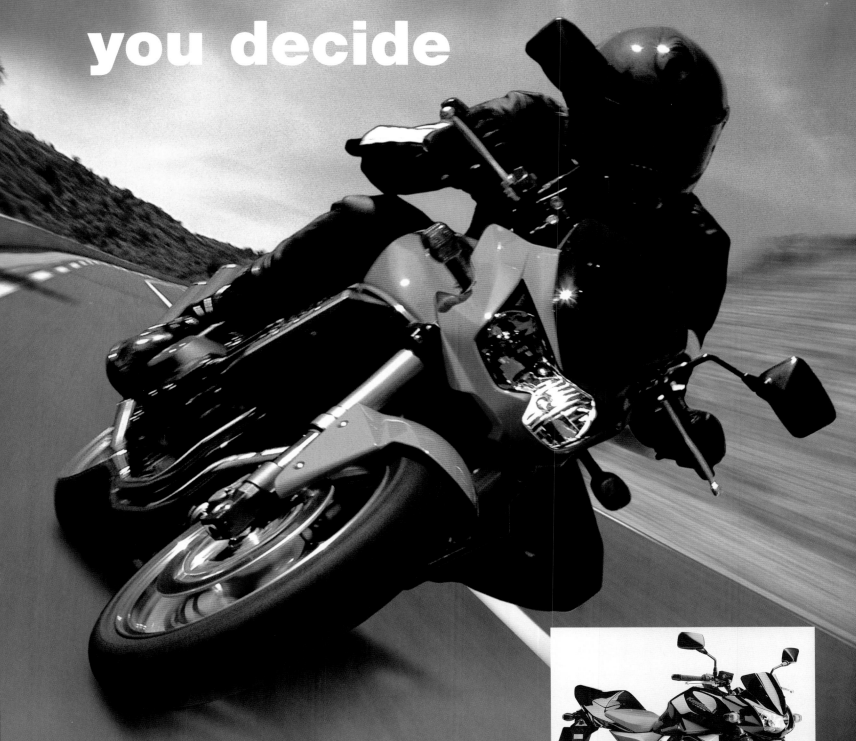

you decide

Zed Thou, a name from an illustrious past thrust into the future of today. You knew Kawasaki was proud of that whole sit up and beg, four pipe, DOHC heritage thing – now here's the physical evidence.

Yesterday's bad boy comes bang up to date with the Z1000 mixing urban warrior styling with a seductive streetfighter image. Sure the others have tried to rip off the Kawasaki naked aggression thing in the past – now we are back on top of the hill with the most radical mass produced super naked yet.

Bikini fairing with duel reflector beams, upside downies and six pot stoppers are what you get up front along with the trickest funky speedo and tacho console this side of F1.

Up back there are those four gold finished pipes and upswept tail with colour coded seat cover making this a solo or two up machine. Mix in a bored out ZX-9R mill and ultra trick EFi injection and the whole plot comes alive. Z1000, tough decisions were never this easy.

It might be easier if there were no choices in life – but it would sure be boring. Kawasaki's 2003 range is one of the most exciting in our history and is led by two stunning new machines, the ZX-6R and Z1000.

To get the flavour of the entire big K feel good factor, log on to www.kawasaki.co.uk, the 24/7 Kawasaki portal or visit your local authorised Kawasaki dealer.

Kawasaki
Let the good times roll.

1 VALENTINO

1 Valentino Rossi
2 Max Biaggi
3 Alex Barros
4 Jeremy McWilliams
5 Nobuatsu Aoki
6 Loris Capirossi
7 Marco Melandri
8 Daijiro Kato
9 Toni Elias
10 Arnaud Vincent

Photographs by Gold & Goose

ROSSI

Repsol Honda Team
2002 World Championship: 1st (MotoGP)
Race wins: 11
Pole positions: 7
Career GP wins: 50 (11 MGP, 13 500 cc, 14 250 cc, 12 125 cc)
World Championships: 4 (1 MGP, 1 500 cc, 1 250 cc, 1 125 cc)
Born: 16 February 1979, Urbino, Italy

VALENTINO Rossi's relatively downbeat finish to the year might have left enough of a question mark to give his rivals hope, but by then he'd already achieved every reasonable goal, and certainly proved repeatedly in 2002 that he was the best rider on the best bike. Again.

The best sportsmen have the gift of making excellence look easy. Rossi adds another dimension. He makes himself look lucky. He won in Britain, Germany, Portugal and Rio because other riders in front of him fell off. Even with the dictum 'you make your own luck', this seemed excessive.

Until Australia, where Barros outbraked him up the inside on the last lap, stealing the corner line and then running on straight under Rossi's front wheel. The Repsol rider missed him by inches. Luck? I don't think so.

Rossi missed his 'funny' two-stroke, and the strength of the competition from his own supposed Honda team-mates showed why: the four-stroke offers less of an edge for a rider to show exceptional ability. But if the bike was less of a challenge, Rossi was still the rider to master it first, and best.

Rossi has never had it as easy as this year. He faced tough opposition in each of his two years in the smaller classes, and last year on the two-stroke. This year he had a mechanical advantage. Seldom did any rider pose a serious challenge, unless he was also on a V5 Honda.

Rossi passed several more milestones — 355 points beating Doohan's 1997 record of 340; 50 personal GP wins, and 24 top-class wins put him equal with Rainey; only Schwantz, Lawson, Hailwood, Doohan and Agostini have won more. He is already, at the age of 23, among the giants of the sport.

'Next year, the title will be difficult,' said Rossi. 'For sure, it will be difficult to win ten or more races. But my goal isn't to win more races than Doohan or anything like that. It is the championship.'

WHAT a year Max Biaggi had. He started in high dudgeon, deeply dissatisfied with his new four-stroke and not minding who knew it. When it started going better a few races in, so did he, moving ahead of his team-mate with a couple of rostrum finishes. All the same, by the middle of the year he'd been dropped by Yamaha in favour of Checa.

This was some sort of a spur to the enigmatic Roman. From that point on he showed everything that had made him into such a great 250 champion, that had let him challenge Doohan for the title in his first 500 year, but that had shown only spasmodically during his four years with Yamaha.

Perhaps Max had more trouble than he expected adapting to the four-stroke — like many of his peers he had only ever raced two-strokes before. He would deny that, blaming the bike. And he had a point — the amount by which the Yamaha improved during the season showed that it was not too good to begin with.

His first win came when Rossi burned his tyres trying to stay in touch at Brno. Without that mechanical glitch, who knows how it would have come out? But his second, at Sepang, was achieved with no such provisos. Just a brilliant ride — smooth, accurate, sustained and just as aggressive as it needed to be.

Second overall was a just position. Max and the M1 were without question best of the rest. Next year he will be on equal equipment with deadly rival Rossi for the first time. If he can sustain the confidence and panache that he brought to the second half of 2002, it will be a confrontation to remember.

2 MAX BIAGGI

Marlboro Yamaha Team
2002 World Championship: 2nd (MotoGP)
Race wins: 2
Pole positions: 4
Career GP wins: 39 (2 MGP, 8 500 cc, 29 250 cc)
World Championships: 4 (250 cc)
Born: 26 June 1971, Rome, Italy

West Honda Pons

2002 World Championship: 4th (MotoGP)

Race wins: 2

Pole positions: 1

Career GP wins: 6 (2 MGP, 4 500 cc)

Born: 18 October 1970, São Paulo, Brazil

ALEX Barros is the living proof that practice makes perfect, and that age is no barrier to success. In his 13th premier-class season, the most experienced rider on the grids seemed to be getting the hang of this GP racing lark.

It wasn't only his two wins in the last four races that proved this endlessly surprising rider's growing strength. He'd produced some blistering rides on the two-stroke before that, forcing Rossi to dig very deep at Assen, and was a contender for victory in Germany.

Alex also had a headlong crash in Germany, taking out himself and Jacque. And he had a downbeat spell in the middle of the season, after returning from his annual trip to the Eight-Hour. In this way, and with his failed outbraking attack on Rossi in Australia, he showed he still has some flaws.

But he had also showed he still has the skill and determination to win races, taking two out of four chequered flags once he climbed on the four-stroke, as well as two lap records and one pole position. His skill and daring on the brakes have long been a hallmark, and it is particularly apposite to the new heavyweight four-strokes.

Barros racked up a record 151 consecutive starts in 2002, not missing a race since 1992. He has ridden factory bikes for Honda, Suzuki and Cagiva. Now he moves to a Yamaha for the first time. It will be fascinating to see if his splendid 2002 season was just an Indian summer, or if he really is still maturing.

3 ALEX **BARROS**

4 JEREMY **McWILLIAMS**

Proton Team KR

2002 World Championship: 14th (MotoGP)

Race wins: 0

Pole positions: 1

Career GP wins: 1 (250 cc)

Born: 4 April 1964, Carnmoney, Northern Ireland

AT last, Britain's top GP rider found his place in racing — the underdog racer with the underdog team. In the year that he turned 38, Kenny Roberts's Proton squad suited the veteran Ulsterman down to the ground.

With a deficit of 50 horsepower, maybe more, and almost always the slowest in a straight line by 10 or 15 mph, Jeremy had only one card in his hand: the three-cylinder lightweight's handling. Under braking and through the corners, nothing could touch it.

He made the most of it, not only gaining pole position in Australia but also qualifying on the front row in Rio as well. At both circuits he set the fastest-ever two-stroke lap, a record likely to stand. This was always his target, and most of the time his qualifying and race times would have made him a very serious contender last year.

It was all one year too late for the Proton, but the best shop window Jeremy could have asked for to display his talents and extraordinary determination. Next year, the new four-stroke will impose a different kind of test.

McWilliams has always had the talent, but has been knocking on the door of good teams for so long that he'd become somewhat tetchy about it. He mellowed a lot in 2002, but it didn't slow him down any.

5 NOBUATSU **AOKI**

McWILLIAMS dazzled with extraordinary lap times in practice, and by sheer grit and determination. Team-mate Nobu Aoki played the Proton game quite differently, and in the final analysis actually outperformed his team-mate. Concentrating on race performance, he out-pointed McWilliams in the championship, in spite of a series of mechanical failures, and a couple of times being knocked off by other riders. When he did finish, it was all but once in the top ten, and only once behind McWilliams.

This from a man who had been forgotten by racing the year before, obliged to take a year away tyre testing for Bridgestone after his early promise as a 250 GP winner and strong 500 debutant seemed to wither on the vine in three years with Suzuki.

The Bridgestone year was hugely productive for the eldest of three 'fireball' brothers. Developing all-new tyres on a Honda NSR obliged him to think deeply about tyre, chassis and suspension performance rather than about racing, and he learned a great deal.

When he was signed for Proton, cynics saw him as a piece of baggage that came along with the Bridgestone tyre contract. He surprised everybody with the strength and depth of his riding. And truly amazing angles of lean and corner speed, shown nowhere better than in his epic dice with Biaggi's much faster M1 Yamaha in Australia.

Proton Team KR	
2002 World Championship: 12th (MotoGP)	
Race wins: 0	
Pole positions: 0	
Career GP wins: 1 (250 cc)	
Born: 31 August 1971, Sumaga, Japan	

WE never did get to see what Loris might achieve on a four-stroke, but we certainly saw what he could do with a two-stroke, in a series of blistering practice laps that put him five times on the front row in the first seven races. Loris raced with distinction too, especially in the early part of the year, until a heavy crash at Assen spoiled probably his best chance yet.

Capirossi seems to attract misfortune in the same way Rossi evades it. Perhaps in his case it is just luck, but a number of races were spoiled by bad tyres or other problems, and temperament certainly plays a part in Capirossi's racing. In the end, he didn't deliver consistent results... but he did stand on the rostrum twice.

Sometimes unbeatable in the smaller classes, Loris has been gaining strength in the top class year by year, and in 2001 was consistently pushing Rossi and Biaggi. His greatest weakness in 2002 was knowing that he was already beaten, no matter how well he might have done in qualifying. This is a disheartening condition for any rider, especially a former triple World Champion.

Next year, he returns on the Ducati Desmosedici, with no excuses and everything to play for.

6 LORIS CAPIROSSI

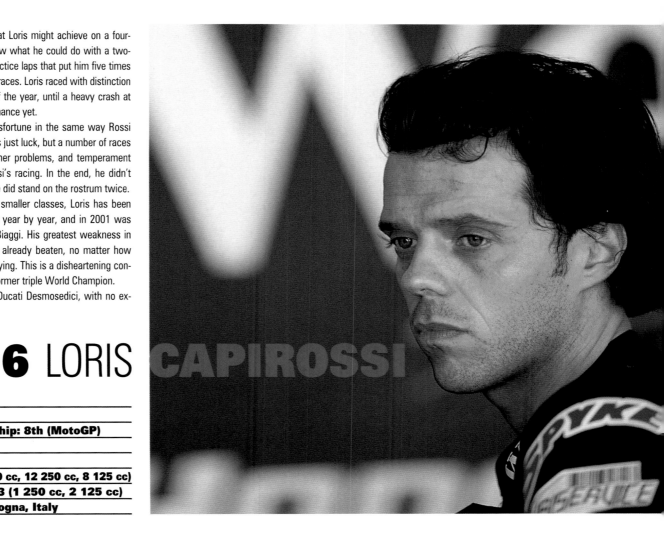

West Honda Pons	
2002 World Championship: 8th (MotoGP)	
Race wins: 0	
Pole positions: 0	
Career GP wins: 22 (2 500 cc, 12 250 cc, 8 125 cc)	
World Championships: 3 (1 250 cc, 2 125 cc)	
Born: 4 April 1973, Bologna, Italy	

MELANDRI'S misfortune, after an exciting second 250 season in 2001, winning his first race and finishing third overall, mixing it with the likes of Kato and Harada, was a lack of competition in 2002. Sure enough, Nieto ran him close in races and in the championship, but a sweep of six consecutive wins in the middle of the season meant Melandri clearly outclassed the Spaniard, and had a comfortable cushion even when he dropped a race with a breakdown at Sepang.

It wasn't his fault he wasn't pushed, but his status as youngest-ever 250 champion would be higher still if he'd had to work a bit harder.

Thus we must wait and see what Melandri is really made of. A precocious 125 talent in the wake of Rossi, he has lagged a little behind his illustrious predecessor, but made similar progress. Now he comes to the big class for 2003 on a Yamaha M1, to begin the next stage of the learning curve without ever having to submit to the harsh discipline of riding a 500 two-stroke.

Melandri is a well-rounded rider: intelligent, adaptable and fast. At least he has been so far. Mentored by Loris Reggiani, he seems to have all the ingredients to be outstanding. We haven't seen it yet, however.

7 MARCO MELANDRI

MS Aprilia Racing	
2002 World Championship: 1st (250 cc)	
Race wins: 9	
Pole positions: 2	
Career GP wins: 17 (10 250 cc, 7 125 cc)	
World Championships: 1 (250 cc)	
Born: 7 August 1982, Ravenna, Italy	

Fortuna Honda Gresini	
2002 World Championship: 7th (MotoGP)	
Race wins: 0	
Pole positions: 1	
Career GP wins: 17 (250 cc)	
World Championships: 1 (250 cc)	
Born: 4 July 1976, Saitama, Japan	

DID Kato flatter to deceive, or was he just a victim of circumstances? On his good days the 250 champion was astonishing, adapting to the double-size two-stroke as if it were barely any sort of a step at all, then doing the same on the four-stroke.

But there were too many bad days, and when it rained, or when the clutch started playing up, Kato was undone.

On the two-stroke, at least, all was not as it seemed. Kato had started testing on the Dunlops he knew so well, only for HRC to decree a (probably wise) switch to Michelin. This was indicative of his role.

After a striking second at Jerez, his results suffered. The reason was his role as chief tester for new parts for the

8 DAIJIRO KATO

NSR, and team insiders insisted this was spoiling his racing.

On a four-stroke at Brno, Kato was again awe-inspiring at first, less so later. And on both types he foundered at the really difficult tracks: Assen and Phillip Island.

Perhaps we expected too much after his towering performance on 250s, and serial success on a four-stroke at the Eight-Hour. It was, after all, still his first season in the class.

Taciturn to a fault, Kato is compact, composed and dedicated. And he's not an HRC favourite for nothing.

TONI Elias was the most exciting young prospect in the 125 class last year. He filled the same role in his first year on a 250. Race by race he grew stronger and more at ease with the factory Aprilia. He learned fast.

It wasn't so much his achievements in 2002, although they were impressive, including a superb win, selling Melandri a dummy at Motegi. It wasn't even that by the end of the year he was forced to defer to his team-mate Nieto when he could clearly have beaten him, to protect Nieto's championship chances.

It was the style with which he accomplished it all.

To describe the 19-year-old with the ever-ready toothy grin as 'Gung Ho' does him a disservice. The ex-motocrosser from Manresa outside Barcelona displays much more than courage and derring-do. He is also able to deploy tactics, persistence and racecraft, and to show fearsome aggression without actually riding dangerously.

Elias will start as favourite for next year's 250 title. After that, MotoGP beckons. With the potential to become Spain's Rossi, and all the heavyweight backing that implies, Elias is tipped for a very big future.

9 TONI ELIAS

Telefónica MoviStar Repsol YPF
2002 World Championship: 4th (250 cc)
Race wins: 1
Pole positions: 0
Career GP wins: 3 (1 250 cc, 2 125 cc)
Born: 26 March 1983, Manresa, Spain

10 ARNAUD VINCENT

ARNAUD Vincent is the exact opposite of most of his 125-class rivals. They are young teenagers, groomed for stardom, carefully mentored, well sponsored. He is a 27-year-old racing loner, who came GP racing relatively late, on his own resources. And triumphed in the hardest-fought championship of the year.

The Aprilia rider put together a very strong season, winning the first race in Japan and adding four more victories and a string of strong and above all reliable finishes: he scored points in every race, even at Motegi when his exhaust pipe split while a safe second. He soldiered on for 15th.

His trade mark — aside from an indomitable spirit — is late braking... very late braking. It stood him in good stead in the gangs of five or more often disputing the leading positions. He also rides very accurately in extreme circumstances, which is what you need on a 125 with no surplus of power.

Vincent personifies a more individual era of GP racing. From Nancy, he worked as a motor cycle mechanic to finance his racing — motocross until 20, then road racing. Three years later he was a GP racer of conspicuous determination. He is the first French 125 champion.

Imola Circuit Exalt Cycle Racing
2002 World Championship: 1st (125 cc)
Race wins: 5
Pole positions: 2
Career GP wins: 7 (125 cc)
Born: 30 September 1974 Nancy, France

we race.

Why do we race? So that you can ride the very best supersport machines in the world!
Running with an advanced new controlled filling die-cast Deltabox III frame and powered by a highly responsive in-line four-cylinder engine, the revolutionary new second-generation YZF-R6 is a showcase

yamaha-racing.com

You win.

for Yamaha's very latest race-bred technology.
And the same superior rideability and optimal balance that have made
the YZR–M1 a winner in MotoGP ensure that the remarkable new YZF–R6
and our legendary YZF–R1 deliver the most exhilarating and exciting
supersport performance.

YAMAHA
Touching Your Heart

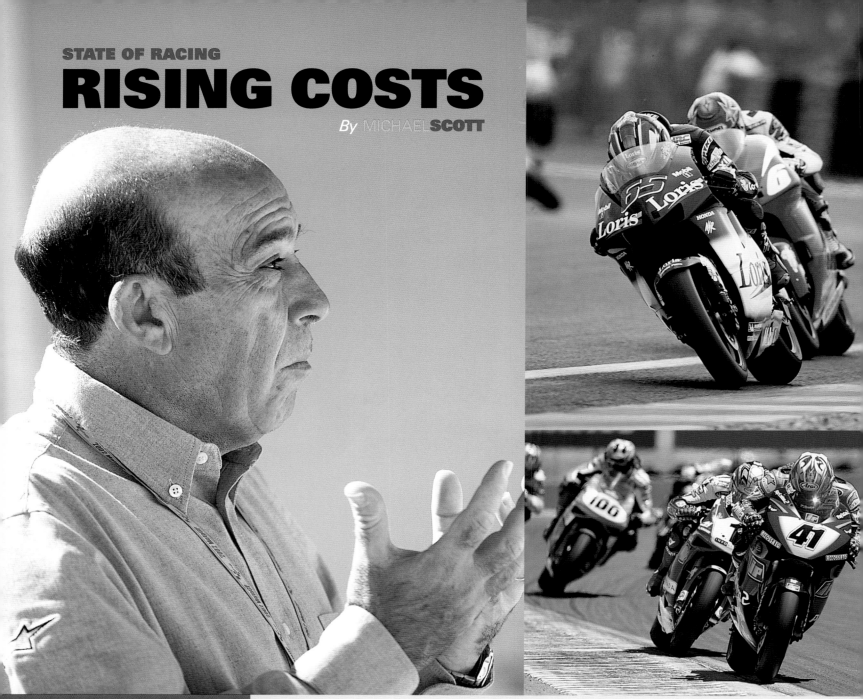

RISING COSTS

By MICHAEL**SCOTT**

Above: Dorna chief Carmelo Ezpeleta — 'I promise the franchise teams will survive.'

Right: Can this really be the British GP? Crowds packed Donington park to watch the new four-stroke GP racers.

Both photographs: Gold & Goose

BOOMING. Busting. Thriving. Struggling. Grand Prix racing — indeed world racing — garnered each of these adjectives during a pivotal year.

Of course, the MotoGP four-strokes were the decisive factor. Finally ushered in some years after conception, these were the bikes that changed everything. For the fans, for the riders, and for the future.

Perhaps the most important aspect is the way GP racing has been repositioned. For the past 25 years, the most important racing series had been travelling out on a side road with the two-strokes. It was a hell of a ride. Who can forget those untamed monsters of snappishness, so spirited that only the very finest and most daring riders and most gifted engineers could get the best out of them?

Motor cycling in general had long since taken another road. With the new four-strokes, GP racing rejoined that highway. Thanks to tradition, the federation, and most importantly the will of the manufacturers, it rejoined firmly in the van.

The new motor cycles will all inevitably give rise to supersports road versions — Honda's sonorous V5, the rorty V4 Suzuki, Yamaha's sophisticated M1, the gutsy Aprilia, the new V4 Ducati... This realignment alone lends huge importance to MotoGP.

The realignment in pure racing terms is as important. Suddenly, that small but mighty group of men who could tame two-strokes became irrelevant. Out-gunned and out-shouted in almost every department, the surviving two-strokes were little more than grid-fillers (though the Protons in particular made the most of it).

The new breed of four-stroke riders comprised the same men. This was not surprising. Talent will out. And although faster, the new four-strokes were much less precise than the two-strokes, at least in their first year, so they were notably easier to ride. This may change as competition forces the pace of development, but at first the 990s were, by comparison, great big softies. As former two-stroke tyrant Christian Sarron, now commentating for French TV, told *MOTOCOURSE*: 'They are really beautiful bikes... for girls.'

This opens up the top level of racing to a larger number of riders. The triangle just got broader.

More significantly, it opens a direct path from World Superbikes, where previously the two disparate machine types left a yawning gulf that some good four-stroke riders found impossible to cross. Now it's just a matter of moving up to a better four-stroke — with more power, less weight, better brakes. And more top-level rivals to race.

This worked first time out, with the two giants of SBK, Edwards and Bayliss, immediately taking what has become a short step. Many will follow. The same is true for national champions worldwide, also schooled on big four-strokes. New AMA champion Nicky Hayden has moved straight into a top factory ride, as Rossi's team-mate. He is reopening a well-blazed trail.

In the short term, this is a bitter blow for Superbikes, particularly since the factory support for MotoGP has been at the expense of the former top four-stroke series. In the longer term, however, Superbikes have a realistic and valuable place in world racing as a training ground for new riders, as well as a retirement home for older ones, who have many skills to pass on. After all, in a couple of years the production bikes from which Superbikes are derived will in any case be replicas of the GP machines.

The driving force for the change came mainly from the Japanese industry (Kawasaki will join Honda, Suzuki and Yamaha next year), with increasingly enthusiastic European support (Ducati and soon KTM will join Aprilia). The omens of Honda domination were clear in the first year, particularly when they promised there would be eight V5s on the grid in 2003. But not clear enough to discourage the opposition. We are in for an interesting decade or so of technical rivalry.

Dorna's new franchise structure, built roughly along F1 lines for the new class, was in for a blustery first year. The difficulties came from an outside world facing financial jitters and the possibility of war in the wake of the September 11 New York attack. Sponsorship money didn't exactly dry up, but it became much more scarce, at a time when overall leasing costs rose by 50 per cent or more. The chill struck particularly among the lower orders, while at press time Suzuki were yet to finalise a replacement for Telefónica MoviStar, who had filled Fortuna's gap with Honda. Fortuna had meanwhile replaced Marlboro at Yamaha, with Ducati making a pair with Ferrari for Marlboro in 2003.

Three franchise teams — West Honda Pons, Antena 3 d'Antin Yamaha, and Red Bull (WCM) Yamaha — lost their sponsorship entirely. The first-named was saved with a contra-deal with Pramac, whose one-year entry permit had expired, but who not only had backing and Honda motor cycles, but also Max Biaggi. The teams merged. D'Antin's fate is not clear, but he was expected to survive, possibly by splitting the franchise to run one Yamaha and another

Left: Battling over scraps — outgunned, two-stroke riders like Capirossi, Abe and Kato found themselves at a severe disadvantage almost everywhere.

Centre far left: Haga returned to Superbikes, here leading Bayliss and Hodgson. Next year he and Bayliss will be at the GPs.

Centre left: High expectations — Ducati's GP return next year reinforces manufacturer backing for the new series.

Below: And I love you too... Rossi remained MotoGP's greatest star attraction.
All photographs: Gold & Goose

Above: Alex Barros was simply sensational after switching from two-stroke to four-stroke. The new bikes offer more chances to more riders.

Below right: Phillip Island was one circuit that offered the two-strokes some fun — here McCoy's 500 Yamaha leads Aoki's three-cylinder Proton. Both will ride four-strokes next year.

Both photographs: Gold & Goose

In other respects, of course, a combination of Rossi fervour and MotoGP fever worldwide meant the series was thriving. Booming crowd attendances put the average over 16 GPs at more than 100,000 at each race (taken over three days); the biggest improvement came in Britain, where 58,716 race-day fans doubled the previous year's figure.

This brought some problems, crystalised in a menacing post-track invasion after the Italian GP at Mugello, where Abe was actually pulled off his bike, Ukawa's factory Honda suffered damage, and collisions with maddened spectators on the slow-down lap narrowly missed. This was in spite of extra fencing and a price hike, intended to keep numbers down in the Rossi–Biaggi axis. Racing is only the victim of its own success, of course, but this raised a frightening spectre of a serious accident, and much exercised the minds of the authorities without much resolution, except perhaps abandoning the slow-down lap altogether.

Race direction was exercised also by another major consideration... what to do about the interruptions posed when dry races turn wet. The current delays of half an hour or more simply don't work for TV, for obvious reasons. A number of alternatives were considered, including voluntary pit stops, compulsory pit stops, spare bikes set up for the wet, even pace cars, before a decision was reached to run flag-to-flag races next year, without stoppages, leaving decisions on tyres and pit stops to riders and teams. This met with fierce opposition, especially from the riders. Rossi was vocal. 'You must understand, with a slick tyre, just a drop of water and... whoosh.'

The idea was dropped, 'because for various reasons it was not acceptable to Dorna and the MSMA [manufacturers]', said Race Director Paul Butler. At press time, the GP commission was shortly to meet to discuss alternatives. Butler favoured the simpler — stick with the present stop–restart system, but compressed to a maximum of 20 minutes from the red flag (everyone in the pits, tyres changed, results confirmed) to a restart from a grid. Just like now, only quicker. A second involved race stoppage, then a rolling restart behind a pace car. MOTOCOURSE sees little advantage — except perhaps for pace-car sponsors BMW — in this added complication.

One more issue will be resolved next year — with a test case involving the cash-strapped WCM team. With entries but no motor cycles, there were two alternatives: a race-developed R1 Yamaha motor in a full race chassis, or a Ducati treated in much the same way by Italian tuners Pogipoloni. Both would conform to the currently rather loosely worded rules, if they have specially cast crankcases and some other engine parts. Production components are specifically forbidden, but not copies of production parts, which might be in a different material.

It would be a way of keeping the team alive, but hardly in keeping with the spirit of the prototype rules. Consider by contrast the case of Kenny Roberts and the Proton, who have undertaken an all-new one-off V5 racing motor to be ready for next season.

The acceptance or otherwise of a street-based racer for WCM will ultimately depend on the manufacturers' association MSMA, the architects of the new series. How they will respond remains to be seen.

paid-for Honda. WCM were in desperate straits, however, with no sponsors, motor cycles, or riders, after they had rather decently released Garry McCoy (to Kawasaki) and John Hopkins (to Suzuki). At press time, team boss Peter Clifford was not having much luck recruiting British riders, turned down by Steve Hislop and Michael Rutter. But Ezpeleta had, in an interview with MOTOCOURSE, indicated there would be a lifeline. Dorna would not provide WCM and other troubled franchise holders with direct financial support, he said, but would help with sponsorship or other backing 'from our resources. I promise you that WCM will survive. The franchise system is the strongest thing we have. We might have to make some adjustments, some allowances in the early years, but this is with general agreement.' It was, he pointed out, in all the franchise-holders' interests that the structure remain sound.

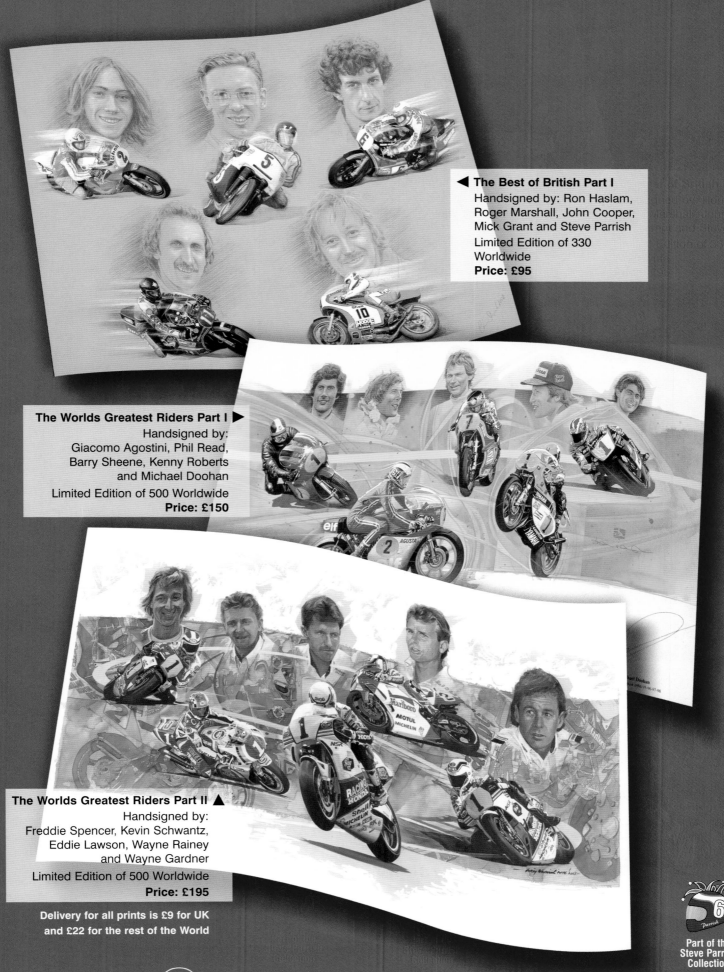

Five four-stroke motor cycles raced for the first time in 2002, and established a new order. From left: Honda RCV211, Kawasaki ZX-RR, Aprilia 'Cube', Suzuki GSV-R, Yamaha M1.
Photograph: Gold & Goose

DIFFERENT STROKES

By MICHAEL SCOTT

Right: King of the jungle — Honda's innovative V5 wiped the floor in the first four-stroke year, without needing much revision during the season.
Photograph: Gold & Goose

VALVE springs, valves — even; camshafts, fuel injection, slipper clutches, active electronic clutches, oil changes... There were lots of new things in the GP paddocks in 2002. But unless a rider crashed, one of them was not extra work for the mechanics. Overalled troops — a more dedicated group of engineers it would be hard to find anywhere — found themselves with time on their hands with the advent of the new four-stroke prototypes. Unless they had damage to repair.

For the ground troops, this was the greatest technical change, summed up in the plaintive comment of an HRC mechanic, at only the third race. 'With the two-stroke we'd use two cans of contact cleaner a race, almost, just because of the oil and tyre dust it chucked out. This year, we haven't even used a can yet.'

The reason was simple. Although not yet quite to the F1 pattern, engines came more or less sealed from the factory. They were run until they reached their service life (or blew up), and replaced.

Loaded with electronics, they were not really tunable, except by software adjustments, and these by and large came from the factories. With predictable throttle responses and broad torque curves, they also made less demand on chassis and tyres. Where it would often take three to four hour-long sessions to get a two-stroke's chassis and suspension fettled and the engine tuned and geared to best suit a particular track, the four-strokes were much more flexible.

For example, Honda introduced an all-new full-floating rear suspension system, with a linkage top and bottom rather than attached to the chassis at the top (creating space from the under-seat fuel tank). Never having tried it before, Rossi's famed crew chief and now eight-times title winner Jerry Burgess was eager to get its measure. 'It would've been wonderful to try it on the 500, so we knew what we were dealing with. With everything being so new it's hard to know the exact reason, but the bike seems terribly neutral. You can change the springs on the rear and change links — and not really change the character of the bike or make a better package that you can take to another race track. I'd like to be able to make it very bad or very good; we don't seem to be able to do that.'

A similar lack of sensitivity applied to other aspects of the machine as well. As Rossi said, the four-stroke was easy to ride fast: 'But it is much harder to make improvements. With the two-stroke, when you improve the settings or go for a really brave lap, you can improve your lap time by one or 1.5 seconds. With the four-stroke, you could work for a month and only find three- or four-tenths.'

Concerning the suspension, by the way, Burgess felt that the system was a weak point, adding unsprung weight and limiting performance, and that like other aspects of the machine, including the overall appearance, it had been chosen as much for marketing reasons as engineering (of which more anon). 'To me, the rear suspension is one of the areas we need to work on. Talking to HRC, it'll be on the bike next year, because a street bike's going to be coming out like that in the near future. Again, we're being led down an avenue that, until it starts costing us races, isn't going to be changed.'

The new four-strokes displayed a variety of approaches, but started out with a common canon. Horsepower was not really an issue: 990 cc meant it would be available in abundance — anywhere from 200 to 220 bhp. The limitation was not engine tuning, but the ability of the chassis and tyres to deal with it.

From the start, there was an atmosphere of secrecy... a reminder of an earlier pioneering period, when the Japanese factories were vying for supremacy with a plethora of new designs back in the Sixties.

Honda gave the appearance of being open, and did speak relatively freely about their all-new V5, although they did keep to themselves details like bore and stroke, compression ratio, valve angles and diameters and the exact rev ceiling. Yamaha by contrast (their fingers burned by their own gushing publicity over the previous 12 months) were guarded in the extreme. It was only late in the year, after considerable effort, that MOTOCOURSE was able to establish officially that the camshafts (uniquely) are chain-driven, and to establish for certain that the cylinder heads used Yamaha's trademark five valves per cylinder rather than the four that their F1 engine reverted to towards the end of its life.

There was still a wealth of interest in the new motors, which may be considered prototypes in the most literal sense, in that it is certain that all the manufacturers involved will offer for sale road bikes that closely resemble their GP fighters. This was most clearly illustrated by Honda, in several aspects. One was that overall control of the project was a joint effort between the racing wing HRC, and the central research and development department, where previous GP racers have been HRC's alone. In this case, the new bike was integrated from the start into the factory structure, whereby research and development works hand in glove with strategic product planning. We have already observed the suspension. Another aspect was the minimal Manga cartoon-influenced fairing and seat — clones to be seen at your local dealer shortly.

Eventually, perhaps inevitably, one type of engine will come to prevail, more favoured than the others under the rule structure, and the others will imitate. Until somebody has a better idea, or the rules are changed. In the first year, there was considerable variety. Bikes on the track ranged from three cylinders to five, configured in line or in vees. The V5 was of course the Honda, Suzuki designed a new V4, Yamaha stuck with a conventional in-line four, while Aprilia consulted Cosworth for their first in-line triple.

Two more bikes due next year fall into the same pattern, so that when the Proton is ready and racing there will be two V5s, while the Kawasaki reinforces the Yamaha in-line-four interpretation. The third, the Ducati Desmosedici, is somewhat different again in its deployment of a wider-angle V4; while KTM's proposed MotoGP prototype will also be a V4 of some type.

Aside from the switch to four-strokes, the biggest development in the year came from Michelin, with a second generation of 16.5-in. rear tyres. This was a big step forward, and had been developed in the Superbike programme. Grippier and longer lasting, the new S4 offered advantages to both two-strokes and four-strokes, and it was only towards the end of the season that Michelin acknowledged that they were starting to have to make special tyres for the heavier and more powerful MotoGP four-strokes: 'It is what we expected.' They also experimented further with dual-compound tyres.

But if Michelin's progress was impressive, so also was that of class newcomers Bridgestone, whose experience ran only to a single year of independent testing in 2001. Although they clearly lagged at the start of the year, and they lacked top-quality teams (the down-on-power Proton and one NSR Honda, ridden by Jurgen van den Goorbergh) they made rapid and consistent progress, and by the last races were hounding Michelin for grid and even mid-point race positions.

Dunlop had a dire season, by comparison, at least in MGP (once again they dominated the smaller classes). Their return with a full factory team, Suzuki, didn't last beyond the first two races, and Aprilia were expected to switch also to Michelin next year. Their handful of two-stroke riders fared only a little better.

The two-strokes were in any case largely irrelevant. The FIM acknowledged later in the season that they might have erred on the side of generosity in giving the four-strokes a 990 cc limit to be sure they were competitive with the two-strokes. Apart from a couple of desperate moments here and there, the four-strokes trounced them.

Above: Invincible partnership — Rossi celebrates with chief engineer Jeremy Burgess at Donington Park. It was Burgess's 100th GP win; Rossi's championship would be the Australian's eighth.
Photograph: Gold & Goose

MotoGP Weight Limits	
Two-stroke — 500 cc	
One or two cylinders	100 kg
Three cylinders	115 kg
Four cylinders	130 kg
Four-stroke — 990 cc	
Two or three cylinders	135 kg (Oval piston 145 kg)
Four or five cylinders	145 kg (Oval pistons 155 kg)
Six or more cylinders	155 kg

Top: Naked Honda shows its intricacy. Biggest break from convention was the fully floating rear suspension unit.

Above: The 75.5-degree V5 engine was in perfect balance.
Both photographs: Chris Sims-Fotomoto

Above right: Spartan bodywork offered little protection for the riders, but pointed the way forward for sports bike styling.
Photograph: Gold & Goose

HONDA

HRC continued development on their NSR two-stroke, if only for the first half of the season, with Kato the test pilot for sundry items including chassis and swing-arm variations. At the same time they supplied all their two-stroke teams with replicas of Rossi's title-winning NSR from last year. The riders took the bounty with mixed feelings. 'Now I can see how Rossi could win last year,' said Loris Capirossi, while team-mate Barros added: 'Compared with last year we can use one grade softer tyre for race distance.'

NSR development was finally abandoned mid-season, when factory rider Kato switched to a V5. Development on the V5 was by comparison rather static throughout the year. The big changes had come in two steps, last year after Rossi tested the first version after the Suzuka Eight-Hour, and then in the winter after his second tests at Jerez.

Burgess said: 'We gave them a list of about nine things, and they changed them.' One was wind pressure on the shoulders, which was improved but not solved during the year. There were matters of instrument positioning and such-like, but most crucially 'the initial power when you opened the throttle was way too much, so that had to be corrected.'

The result was easily the best MotoGP racer out of the box. By the end of the season, the RCV was under pressure, especially from Yamaha, but even then changes were confined to detail, apart from the introduction of a ram-air intake system mid-season, along with a slightly more free (and seemingly slightly louder) exhaust.

The RCV211 was a notably intricate and integrated design. The overall philosophy was to centralise the mass around the compact motor. The under-seat fuel tank was an important aspect, the rear suspension unit moved out of the way with a novel system operating it by linkage from above and below simultaneously.

The engine was the first V5 built for a motor cycle, and quite different from a narrow-angle monobloc car V5, although a very similar predecessor existed on paper for a range of modular engines designed for BSA-Triumph in the Seventies. HRC technicians were unaware of this, they said.

The RCV211 had three cylinders forward, two up. With five main bearings, the outer cylinder pairs ran on common big-end crankpins, like a pair of V-twins, with the central cylinder independent in between.

Exact crankshaft timing was never revealed, but could be calculated for the 75.5-degree motor. HRC disclosed that the outer cylinder pair had a 50 per cent balance factor, and that the middle cylinder did the rest in smoothing the engine without the need for a balance shaft. This information was enough for Proton engineer Tom O'Kane to calculate that with the two outer journals in alignment an interval of 104.5 degrees to the central journal would have this effect. 'Our V5 for next year is different,' he said. 'We want a more compact engine with a 60-degree vee angle, so as a result it will require a balance shaft.'

Bore and stroke were also not disclosed. Twin overhead camshafts are gear-driven with four valves per cylinder, while oiling is via a novel 'semi-dry sump' system. The crankcase is scavenged by a pump, the oil supply within the gearbox casing behind and below to eliminate drag on the crankshaft.

Downdraught induction has twin multi-hole injector nozzles operating in sequence. One is downstream of the throttle butterfly for low-range and mid-range throttle response, the other for wide-open operation. A refinement described by HRC was a prediction system taking into account the amount of fuel remaining in the intake ports and clinging to the inner surface of the ports, significantly improving rideability and fuel consumption.

Honda denied using traction control, although the machine did have the same three-position handlebar switch as the NSR, which allows the rider to select different power curve programs as a race progresses and tyres wear.

Aside from the fuel tank, under the seat and behind the engine, and thus requiring a pump, the rest of the motor cycle was conventional GP racer, with a twin-beam chassis that, said HRC, was more laterally flexible than the NSR chassis, but more torsionally rigid.

YAMAHA

The M1 suffered somewhat from over-enthusiastic pre-season publicity, and the factory retreated into secrecy while they worked to turn the disappointments of the pre-season tests and early races into the much stronger performance and pair of wins in the latter half of the season.

Even by then there remained much that was not known about a machine that appeared thoroughly conventional, with the chassis based closely on the YZR two-stroke twin beam, and the motor having links to the factory's roadgoing R1. It achieved the new level through clever and innovative detail engineering that took it beyond what appeared to be unambitious beginnings.

To be fair, the ambition was not lacking... just misplaced, at least according to Honda's clean-sheet-of-paper philosophy. Yamaha (and Suzuki) had taken a different approach, starting with their 500 two-stroke chassis dimensions, and then making an engine that would fit. To Honda fans, this compromised both designs from the outset.

The Yamaha espoused other quirky solutions. Apparently believing that horsepower simply wouldn't be an issue, they started with an engine undersized by (it is thought) some 40 or 50 cc. During the season, they would not reveal when, it was brought to the full 990 cc allowed. A new cylinder block was required, revealed project leader Ichiro Yoda.

Uniquely they also eschewed fuel injection in favour of carburettors, admittedly with some electronic controls, favouring the smoother throttle response offered by what is an instrument of response rather than initiation. At the factory, however, they were testing fuel injection in preparation for the next level of horsepower required: 'We need at least ten more, maybe 15. But it is never enough,' said Yoda.

Riders' complaints centred on handling and the chassis, with the lack of confidence in the front that both Biaggi and Checa suffered with the two-stroke seemingly worse. 'I usually brake all the way to the apex, but this bike won't allow that,' said Checa. Biaggi was also dismayed by the engine braking that ruined his corner entry.

Chassis work continued apace, with the first revision of the year coming at the very first race, and two more following. The most radical came at Mugello, and included a significant rearward shift in weight distribution by canting the cylinders more towards the upright. This required a bend in the main chassis spars.

The solution to the engine braking was comprehensive, innovative and elegant.

And three-fold. The first line of defence was a conventional ramp-type slipper clutch. When Biaggi complained it was not enough, Yamaha added a second layer to the system... an electronic add-on which operated the clutch hydraulics to add an element of control precision limited only by the software designer's imagination. It is an active clutch. The third was an engine run-on programme that operated on only one cylinder... reducing engine braking significantly without actually making the engine drive.

Finishing the season with a full 990 cc, the Yamaha used five valves per cylinder, with the twin overhead camshafts driven by a single-row chain. Power output and maximum revs were never divulged, but 220-plus and 15,000 to 16,000 rpm would be the bench-mark.

This page, clockwise from top left: **Yamaha M1 — bulbous bodywork was replaced with a more angular cowling mid-season; Yamaha team manager Geoff Crust; profusion of pipes and sensors shows how detail engineering turned M1 motor from conventional to competitive.**
All photographs: Gold & Goose

Bottom: **One of several chassis for the Yamaha — later versions had the cylinders closer to vertical.**
Photograph: Chris Sims-Fotomoto

SUZUKI

Suzuki planned to test their four-stroke during 2002, and then bring it out for 2003. Pressure from the riders as well as encouraging bench tests persuaded them to take the plunge directly. The bike was only a few months old when it surprised everyone by taking second in the opening GP.

That was a function of the weather. The project was put into different proportion in the upcoming races, and the first serious problem to solve was a surprise factory decision to switch to Dunlop tyres. The team was desperate to get back onto their long-standing Michelins, and by the third race they had done so.

The V4 was only rivalled by the Aprilia in terms of mellifluous exhaust note, and exuded a rather rough and ready charm compared with the sophisticated Honda. It was also almost competitive.

Almost was only enough to highlight several areas that needed attention, according to Roberts. These were wide-ranging, including the usual complaints about engine braking, which was particularly acute, said Kenny, 'because our engine has such a high compression ratio to try and make the power'. There was also a steady flow of evolutionary chassis, culminating in another version with promisingly revised geometry and stiffness ratios that was tested only after the season was over.

This was straightforward development, and overall the pattern was promising, with Roberts claiming a rostrum finish at Brazil and Gibernau coming within a few laps of winning in Portugal. Both of those were in wet conditions, however, and ultimate horsepower, and thus top speed, was another area where the new Suzuki was playing catch-up.

To Gibernau, the engine braking was the major issue. Again, it was addressed in several ways. The original version had a sprag clutch, offering a degree of slippage on the over-run that could be pre-set to different levels, but was not self-compensating like a ramp clutch. At the Portuguese GP Suzuki did bring a ramp clutch.

Roberts believed it had potential once optimum settings had been found, Gibernau found the cruder sprag more predictable. His other difficulty came from a fast idle programme initiated during downshifts to cut engine braking,

but he had several offs because the engine was still driving while he was trying to slow.

Although basically conventional, the GSV-R was Suzuki's first-ever high-performance V4 after a family of in-line fours. The vee layout offered certain advantages, notably being compact enough to fit into the RGV two-stroke chassis, although this was significantly altered by the time it made the circuit, including ducting through the main spar to feed the airbox beneath the tank.

The compact casings are also more rigid than an in-line four, but the biggest gain is lower internal friction, with only three main bearings instead of five. The included angle of 60 degrees meant the engine required a balance shaft, turning at crankshaft speed, which did (according to project leader Kunio Arase) introduce some frictional losses, but they were relatively negligible. In the early stages, this low-friction engine took time to achieve reliability.

Suzuki would not reveal the firing intervals between the paired cylinders, but Arase said: 'We considered several alternatives. Some believe a close firing order can increase rear tyre durability, some think a more even firing order has the same result. I think a lot depends on the technique of the individual rider. The major effect is to change the whole feeling of the engine, and especially the character of the engine braking.' These are areas also being explored by Ducati with their Desmosedici 90-degree V4.

Crankcases were revised once during the season, the major outward difference being the introduction of a drive for a remote starter motor. This made life easier for the mechanics. The sprag clutch had imposed a slightly Heath Robinson routine. To start with a rear-wheel roller the clutch had to be locked to prevent it slipping as designed. It was accessed by unclipping the lower fairing. Once the engine was running, the lock-up tool was removed, and the fairing refitted. Only then could the rider depart.

The engine is a wet-sump design, with gear-driven overhead camshafts and four valves per cylinder. Bore and stroke were not revealed. Induction is via twin-nozzle fuel injection, with an integrated ignition management programme.

Roberts was clear that while engine torque was good and the machine allowed him to spin the rear tyre at will, it was down on horsepower at the top end. Again, no figures were forthcoming. The target at the start of the season was 200 horsepower, which had been 'quite easily achieved' according to Arase, but it is likely that the motor still fell somewhat short of the Honda's 220 bhp.

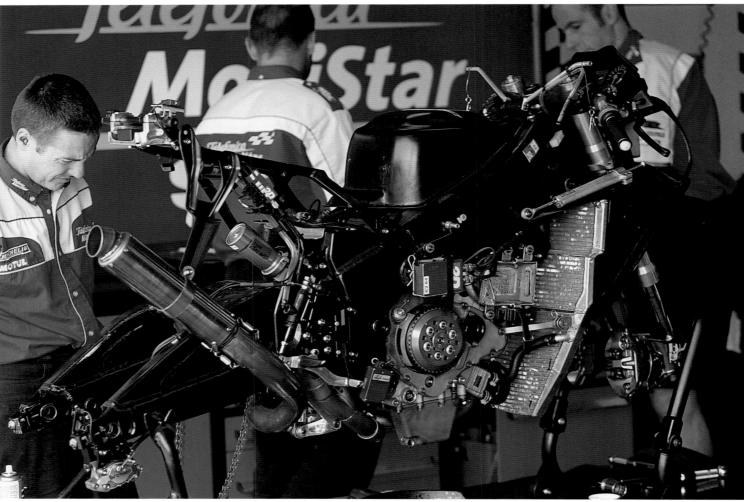

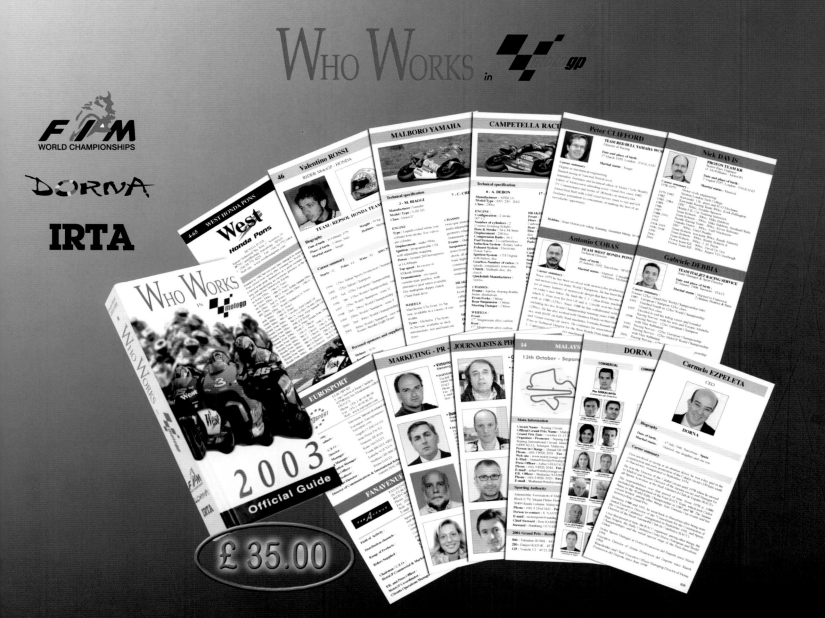

This page, anti-clockwise from top right: Aprilia Racing Director Jan Witteveen; Aprilia in profile — densely packed with machinery, the chassis followed Aprilia's usual fabricated box-section practice; massive swing-arm reflects robust construction required when 220 horsepower is unleashed; in-line triple had sweet exhaust note, abundant horsepower.

All photographs: Gold & Goose

APRILIA

The least well funded of the full-season four-strokes that started the year was in many ways the most adventurous. Aprilia had gone to Cosworth to develop an in-line three-cylinder engine, and not surprisingly the result included a hatful of F1 technology. Uniquely, the 'Cube' uses fly-by-wire throttle and pneumatic valves.

The throttle is in fact not quite to the F1 model, as Racing Director Jan Witteveen explained. 'The motor cycle regulation does not allow the throttle to be closed by ECU control: the throttle cable must operate the butterfly directly in that direction. This is to avoid the motor revving on in a crash, for example. But opening the twist-grip operates the butterflies through the computer, not the cable.'

Pneumatic valves had been used in the first version of the proposed Sauber GP motor, allowing revs up to 20,000 rpm. But they had been dropped early on, since steel springs could easily cope with the expected ceiling of 16,000 rpm. Witteveen agreed they were not necessary in the first version of the engine for the same reason — maximum revs were 15,000 rpm. 'But we are looking to the future, when we may need to use higher revs to make more power.'

Power, conspicuously, was not a shortcoming of the initial version of the machine, which ran for the first time only in January, making it a couple of months younger than the Suzuki. It was abundant, in far greater quantities than the squirming chassis and chattering Dunlop tyres could deal with. Riding the bike was always a big adventure for Regis Laconi, who when asked how it felt graphically mimed his arms getting stretched as he hung on for dear life under fly-me-to-the-moon acceleration. The Aprilia was the first of the four-strokes to top 200 mph, at Mugello.

Polish was lacking, and speed of development. Both were a direct function of budget limitations, particularly acute as Aprilia struggled to recover from a drastic slump in their backbone scooter sales. Limited funds meant that the motor cycle was 15 kg or more overweight because 'we were not able to use exotic materials. The engine casings are aluminium, but we would like to use magnesium,' said Witteveen. This particular component was improved during the summer break, with thinner castings. Lighter electronic control units were also part of a package that saved some five kilogrammes. Cash limitations also meant just one rider on the machine, severely limiting the amount of feedback available to engineers.

The three-cylinder motor has evenly spaced 120-degree crankshaft intervals, giving a sonorous scream to the exhaust note but also requiring a balance shaft. Four valves per cylinder are operated by gear-driven camshafts, closed pneumatically. Maximum power was given as 220 bhp at 14,500 rpm, though it pulled strongly, said Witteveen, from 9,000 rpm — a typically broad spread of power for the torquey 990 cc four-strokes.

The 'Cube' was the only full dry sump, with separate scavenge pumps for each crankcase. The ramp-type slipper clutch was by AP, in carbon.

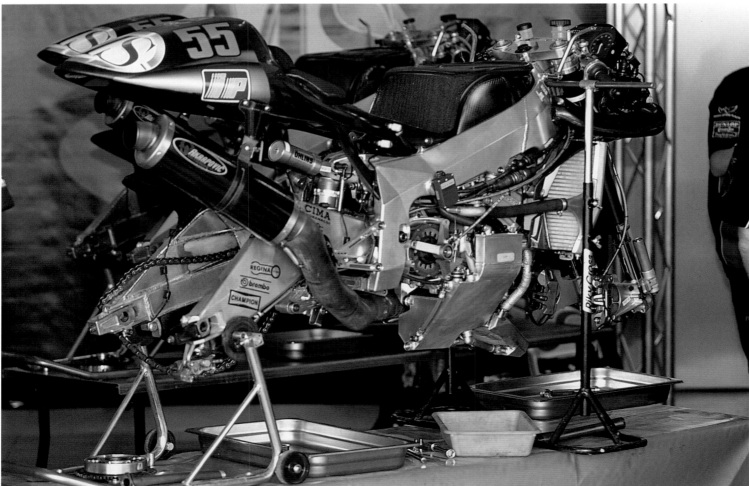

WORLD SUPER POWER

Cosworth's engines are at the forefront of every major motorsport championship in the world.

- FIA F1 WORLD CHAMPIONSHIP

- FIA WORLD RALLY CHAMPIONSHIP

- CART FEDEX CHAMPIONSHIP SERIES

- FIM WORLD SUPERBIKE CHAMPIONSHIP

- NASCAR

POWER BY
COSWORTH

Above right: Ducati's first public outing — Bayliss (on left) and test rider Guareschi rode machines at Valencia with different firing orders.
Both photographs: Gold & Goose

Below: Kawasaki chassis combined cast and fabricated sections.

Bottom: 'Edge design' curves made otherwise conventional Kawasaki look special.
Both photographs: Chris Sims-Fotomoto

NEWCOMERS

Two other four-strokes made an appearance during the year, from opposite ends of just about every spectrum. The first to appear was Ducati's keenly awaited Desmosedici V4, but that was static on a plinth at the Italian GP in June, and it was not until the final round in Valencia that the machine was seen and heard in action. By then, Kawasaki's Ninja ZX-RR had also arrived, and not only run but also raced, in the last four races as a wild card.

The Ducati conformed with the true prototype ideal — an all-new blue-sky design that was nonetheless very distinctively Ducati, with a 90-degree vee angle, and desmodromic valve gear in a steel trellis frame. They seriously considered sticking with their trademark 90-degree V-twin but decided that making the 220 bhp they believe will be necessary and taking advantage of the minimum weight limit would require expensive technology and materials. So they decided on a V4.

Intriguingly, they decided to simulate the widely spaced firing intervals of the V-twin by firing adjacent cylinders simultaneously — so the new bike was really two so-called L-twins siamesed together. They dubbed the motor Twin-

Pulse, but hedged their bets also with a Four-Pulse, with the cylinder pairs firing 360 degrees apart. The first motor sounded like a V-twin, the second like nothing else on earth, with a splendid ripping scream. As *MOTOCOURSE* went to press, new riders Bayliss and Capirossi were testing both types, with no decision made. 'Each rider might choose a different type, or perhaps different types for different circuits,' said Ducati Corse chief Claudio Domenicali, adding: 'The Twin-Pulse is more heavily stressed. Reliability might be an issue.'

The power target is 220 bhp, and a rev ceiling of 18,000 rpm was talked of — the highest revs ever for desmodromic valve gear.

Kawasaki's new war-horse came from the opposite direction — a road bike developed into a factory Superbike, and then taken a stage further to become the Ninja ZX-RR. Since technical lessons learned on this are likely to filter directly back to the road machines, does the lack of blue sky make it any less of a prototype?

The machine was developed in stages — first the 990 cc engine, using the Superbike bottom end and chassis, and fitted with carburettors at that stage, raced along with the GSV-R Suzukis as non-scoring entries in the All-Japan series (chalking up one win to Suzuki's several), ridden by ex-SBK pilot Yanagawa. The final machine used a similar chassis, with some thin-wall cast sections, but was 15 kg lighter overall; and the engine was now fuel-injected, with unique flat slides for the twin-nozzle system, instead of the butterflies used by others. The advantage is a clear bore at full throttle, and this was the most significant development, according to technical boss Shigetsu Takata.

More obvious was a bold new look at styling, under the guise of aerodynamics. An aggressive nose section was set off by a gigantic tail unit sporting 'edge' styling and drooping rearwards.

And as significant as anything at the Motegi launch or its subsequent four races was a comment by president Shinichi Marita, when asked what limits had been put on the budget for the project. 'We have to invest what is required and what is necessary,' he said.

The final new 2003 entry will be the Proton XM (Roman numerals for 990), a 60-degree V5 with fuel injection, four valves per cylinder and a balance shaft. 'At first I thought a three-cylinder engine would be the way to go, for the first two or three years,' said Roberts. 'But I don't want to be scratching for horsepower in a couple of seasons. I'm tired of watching our riders get overtaken on the straights.'

The Proton was due to begin testing by the end of this year, to be ready for the first race of 2003.

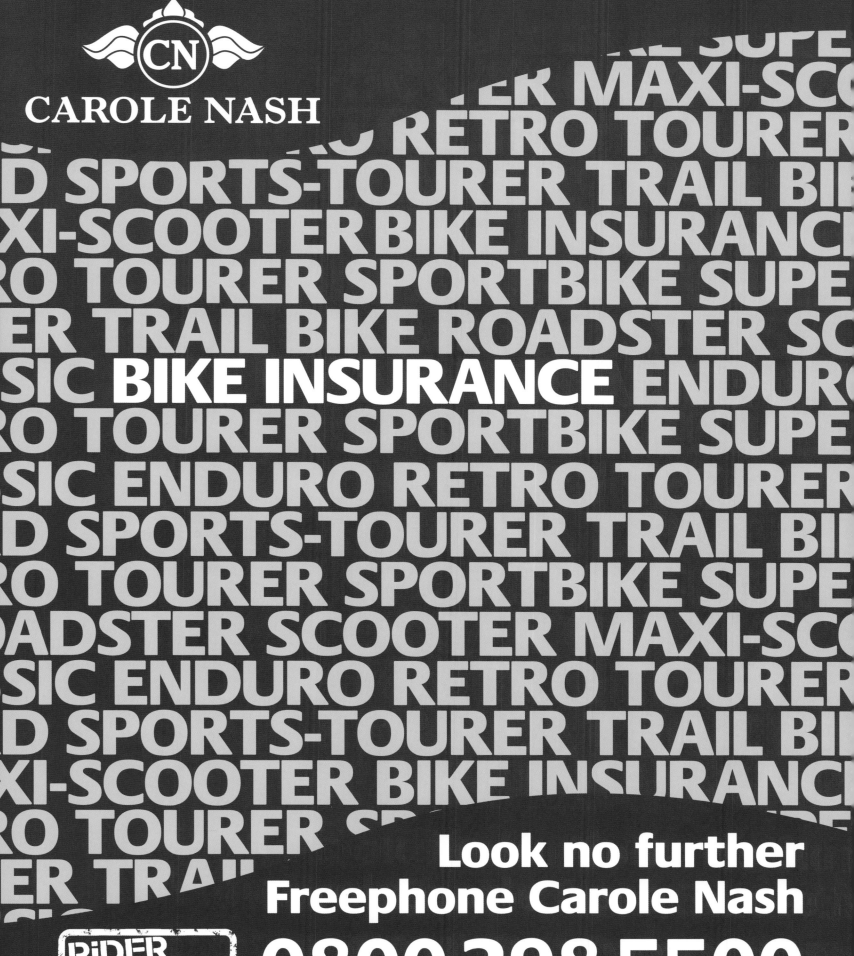

BIKE INSURANCE

Look no further
Freephone Carole Nash

0800 298 5500

Open 8-6.30 Mon-Fri 9-12 Sat Instant cover & free breakdown recovery on all policies. Calls may be recorded.
www.carolenash.com email: bikes@carolenash.com cars@carolenash.com
A member of the General Insurance Standards Council.
IRISH POLICIES AVAILABLE N. Ireland: 0800 298 5500 Ireland: Dublin 1800 298 550

TECHNICAL ESSAY
NEW ORDER

A new order of machines has opened up new opportunities to engineers. At the same time, developments in testing rigs and data acquisition have given them new tools. KEVIN CAMERON welcomes the new era . . .

New machines asked different questions of designers already grappling with sophisticated design problems. By the end of the season, various answers had led to more closely matched bikes. Here in Malaysia Barros's Honda leads eventual winner Biaggi's Yamaha, the Hondas of Kato, Ukawa and Rossi following on.
Photograph: Gold & Goose

THE 990 cc four-strokes have come and they have conquered. Before long, 500 two-strokes will be only a memory, joining other historical curiosities like the supercharged bikes of the pre-war era. New bikes bring with them new criteria of excellence. What might these be?

Four-strokes have already shown the value of torque that increases smoothly from zero — something that has never been possible in two-strokes despite their adoption of palliative technologies such as variable-height exhaust ports and electronic torque controls. Because four-stroke power is smooth from zero, it is possible to get the motor cycle under power earlier in turns. Because speed gained early in a turn exit is added to speed all the way down the next straight, smooth early power is equal in value to many extra horsepower on the top end. That, combined with the FIM's gift of doubled displacement, has made the new four-strokes very fast indeed.

Fast as they are, the new four-strokes face the usual racing problems of tyre chatter, lack of grip at high lean angles... brought about by lack of suspension or chassis compliance, and the coupling of handling ease to issues of vehicle mass and bulk. The faster they go, the more problems appear. Riders say, 'I live with chatter every day.'

Fortunately racing engineers now have some actual handling knowledge, as that field emerges from its cut-and-try past, into the beginnings of systematic analysis. In the early to mid-1990s, factory teams began to play with reduced chassis stiffness, and the occasional success showed something could be gained in this way. But when chassis are made significantly less stiff, they become flexible enough to display high-speed weave instability. Changes in chassis stiffness also caused tyre chatter to appear or disappear unpredictably. Chatter is the disturbing, rapid up-and-down bouncing of tyres (usually the front) — as Mick Grant noted long ago 'under conditions of high grip and heavy load'. Once chatter begins, the harder you try to accelerate, the less time the tyre spends on the ground, and the faster your machine heads for the outside. It was therefore clear that chassis stiffness and chatter were in some way linked as well.

During the late 1990s, attaining a good chassis/suspension/tyre set-up was compared with playing golf in complete darkness. You knew the cup was out there somewhere because some machines handled well — but there was no indication in which direction or how far that cup might be, and there were no reliable principles for finding it. Set-up was therefore to a large extent a game of blind iterations. Infallible wizards were in short supply.

Despite the mid-'90s discovery of the effects of swing-arm pivot height and swing-arm droop angle on whether a machine steered well or poorly during off-corner acceleration, many well-funded teams continued to struggle with this problem in the old ways. With poor swing-arm geometry, a machine would squat at the rear during acceleration, unweighting the front tyre enough to reduce its steering grip. The machine would run wide. The simple answer is to stop the squat with an over-stiff rear spring, resulting in hop and poor hook-up. Or to employ the only slightly less stone-age device of putting a kink in the rear suspension's rate curve, which simulates a stiff spring once the suspension has compressed sufficiently. Open-source material is now available to guide designers to better solutions.

Formula 1 car racing teams, their track testing limited by regulation, now test indoors on 'shaker' machines that can be programmed to closely simulate suspension motions on existing tracks, with instrumentation to provide predicted tyre grip data. Now motor cycle makers have begun to play with two-post shakers and with more advanced cornering simulator rigs. As the shaker's up-and-down frequency is swept upward from zero, you see one after another of the motor cycle's parts begin to vibrate. The front wheel oscillates rapidly forward and back, the seat back up and down. The amplitude of the motion increases as the shaker's frequency comes into step with the natural frequency of the vibrating part, then dies away as the applied frequency rises, and other parts in turn become excited. Making parts stiffer raises their natural frequency, and vice versa. This is why large-diameter male-slider forks are such a useful tool in the fight against front-end chatter; their natural bending frequency lies above the tyre bounce frequency. Another way to de-couple a chassis resonance is to change the mass of what is vibrating — that's why we've seen some hollow front axles filled with lead. Others — myself included — have seen chatter disappear upon adding the extra mass of a second front brake disc and caliper to a 250.

Because of this new appreciation, chassis stiffness is no longer discussed in terms of deflection per kilo of applied force, but rather in terms of oscillation frequency. Swing-arms are now appearing which are very deep vertically, but whose beams are laterally quite thin. Such a swing-arm strongly resists twisting deflections which lead to instability, but permits lateral flex as a supplementary suspension when the vehicle is at lean angles high enough to reduce the normal suspension's effectiveness. Will such a laterally flexible swing-arm be pro-chatter? It may be if the natural frequency of the wheel's mass, vibrating from side to side against the stiffness of the swing-arm, happens to be close to the tyre's bounce frequency. Then one motion reinforces the other. Fortunately, the swing-arm lateral frequency can be easily changed by adjusting the stiffness. The lower the stiffness, the lower the natural frequency of oscillation.

Four-stroke engines carry a high percentage of their weight above their pistons, in the form of tall cylinder heads filled with heavy equipment — cams, tappets and valves. Many GP engine architectures are now being explored — V5, V4, I-4, I-3. These contrast with the former two-stroke orthodoxy of V4s, and stimulate fresh discussion of what, if any, effect engine mass distribution may have upon handling and speed in manoeuvre. It may be that, as in F1, a single best configuration will quickly emerge. Or the present diversity may persist.

Comment has begun with Honda's comparison of its V5 RC211V engine to a sphere, with its mass concentrated within a small radius about its centre of gravity. An in-line engine such as Yamaha's I-4 M1 by contrast distributes its mass along a transverse line, in a suitcase-like shape. We are tempted to argue that as it is easier to change direction while carrying a 24-pound cannonball than while carrying a long ladder of equal weight, so a motor cycle powered by a sphere must change direction faster than one powered by a suitcase — either a wide in-line four, or a tall in-line triple. How can we test such thought experiments?

We already have some information from watching races. Based upon observation of four-stroke Superbikes, it is so far clear that engine architecture has been a less important determinant of handling quickness than steering geometry and longitudinal weight distribution. Kawasaki's in-line 750 has always been very quick in roll-over for turns, as a result of steering geometry that can be made so quick thanks to the forward location of engine mass (the damping that prevents front-wheel wobble comes from the size of the tyre footprint, which increases with the load carried by the tyre). The Ducati, with its engine mass further to the rear, cannot with stability adopt such quick steering and, despite its compact single-plane engine, the Ducati is notably slower in roll-over than the 'suitcase' Kawasaki in-line four. To add to our confusion, the Kawasaki has won only one World Superbike title to Ducati's many — despite these marked differences in engine architecture and steering quickness. Does this mean engine layout is unimportant? Certainly not — but on the evidence we have, the effects of engine shape are submerged in the 'background noise' created by other differences, not the least of which is the size of manufacturers' R&D budgets. An indifferent design, brilliantly exploited, can eclipse better designs, indifferently managed. If MotoGP evolves into an intensely competitive class, we may in time see engine architecture effects teased out to become important.

The mass properties of motor cycles — the rotational inertia they display around the three axes of rotation (yaw, pitch and roll) — are today accurately measured on oscillating stands. The vehicle is given freedom to rotate around one axis, restrained by springs. When it is set into oscillatory motion against the springs, its oscillation frequency is noted. By comparison with simple objects of easily calculated rotational inertia, that of the test motor cycle can be determined. Because rotation around the pitch or yaw axis involves large swinging motions of the wheels, which are the parts of the machine most distant from its centre of mass, it is unlikely that the much smaller effects of engine shape will strongly affect pitch or yaw inertia. It is mainly in roll, when the wheels tilt rather than swing, that engine shape has some importance.

In order for tyre chatter to occur, there must be an exciting force that drives the up-and-down bouncing motion, steadily adding energy to increase its amplitude. Most of this energy no doubt comes from the cyclic deformation of the tyre as its skips sideways across the track, driven by the engine's thrust. Some must also come from small imperfections in the tyre — out-of-round, out-of-balance, and force variation arising from invisible differences in carcase stiffness around the tyre. As a serendipitous benefit from new tyre manufacturing systems now coming into use, all of these imperfections are now being reduced by significant amounts. The result has been a reduction in the occurrence and severity of chatter. For many years, the holy grail of the tyre industry has been automation of the tyre building process. After many false starts over decades, build automation is now at hand. Previously, tyre carcase fabric had to be applied to a building drum by skilled persons — each piece precisely positioned. No matter how skilled we humans may be, each of us has a bad day from time to time. When the assembled components were finally placed in the steam-heated tyre curing mould, considerable movement of the fabric elements took place — occasionally resulting in mispositioned fabric, leading to force variation. The new manufacturing systems eliminate both human positioning error and much in-the-mould fabric motion.

Another source of handling progress is in damper design. For some years, sophistication has increased in the areas of washer stack selection and the shaping of fluid passages. Simple dampers suffer from 'valve transients' — short portions of the suspension stroke in which damping is inconsistent because damper valves take time to open or close. More advanced dampers — even those with beautifully ported valve bodies — can show momentary harshness as the mass of fluid in passages must be accelerated and decelerated. For a long time, it was considered the ultimate to be able to provide damping force directly proportional to suspension velocity. This has not been easy, for damper resistance naturally tends to increase exponentially with speed.

Now a long-obscured problem is being tackled. The goal of suspension is to allow the wheels to move up and down easily over road irregularities, isolating the vehicle from disturbances and protecting tyre grip from force spikes that cause sliding. Yet damping, in order to control particular unwanted motions, must oppose all motions. Better performance would result if a novel kind of frequency selective damper could damp only the undesired motions — such as the natural frequencies of vehicle pitch and heave, tyre chatter, and fork flexure. Otherwise the suspension would be left free to move, and no damping force would be added to the natural forces tending to break tyre grip. This frequency selectivity is not easy to achieve, but good progress is now being made in this direction.

New technical regulations have destroyed the old certainties, forcing a fresh review of all problems. New competitors have put more hands and minds at work on their solution. The passage of time has put new tools at the disposal of engineers. This will be fun.

Main picture: Steady torque curves increase corner exit speed. The Hondas of Ukawa and Rossi show how it's done in France, Rossi more upright but sliding more. He will soon overtake.

Above: Erv Kanemoto — one of the old-style two-stroke gurus who must now learn new tricks.

Right: Yamaha's massive chassis and deep-section swing-arm show continual work on stiffness ratios.

All photographs: Gold & Goose

Left: The down-on-power Protons offered superb handling to riders McWilliams (here in front) and Aoki. Corner speed was not enough to rival the four-strokes, however.

Above: Proton team owner Kenny Roberts (right) and team manager Chuck Aksland... pushing the boundaries of chassis technology.

Left: Last-minute advice for Ukawa.
All photographs: Gold & Goose

MICHELIN technology accelerated during 2002, leaving rival tyre manufacturers way behind in both MotoGP and World Superbike

Michelin has ruled bike racing's biggest world championships for many years now, but last season the French company upped the ante dramatically, achieving unprecedented domination of the new MotoGP World Championship and the World Super-bike Championship.

Michelin ruled both series, winning all 16 MotoGP events and scoring 25 victories from 26 races in World Superbike. Such superiority was all the more remarkable considering the new four-stroke-based MotoGP regulations that created the fastest, most powerful racing motor cycles the world has ever seen. Michelin responded to the MotoGP challenge with typical inventiveness, using its superior know-how to develop a new breed of tyre, designed specifi-cally to handle the 220-plus horsepower output of these amazing machines.

The S4-profile rear slick, developed from the 16.5-in. tyre that had revitalised the final two years of the 500 cc World Championship, was created to help MotoGP riders use the maximum mid-corner and corner-exit performance from their machines. MotoGP king Valentino Rossi (Repsol Honda Team RC211V-Michelin) won 11 races with the tyre and had nothing but praise for Michelin's efforts. 'Miche-lin has done great work this year,' declared the Ital-ian genius after securing Michelin's 11th consecutive premier-class World Championship and its 22nd in 27 years. 'The new four-strokes have been a big change, especially for the tyre companies who quickly realised that even their best 500 tyres wouldn't be enough. When we first tested the RCV in Europe in November 2001, the bike was so de-manding that we could only do five laps with 500 tyres. We realised that we needed more edge grip, because the four-stroke weighs 145 kilos, and all that weight presses through a tiny contact patch, and also more traction, because my bike already has 150 horsepower when you open the throttle at max-imum lean. When we tried the new S4 it was a big, big step forward.'

Former 500 World Champion Kenny Roberts (riding

MICHELIN TECHNOLOGY RULES THE WORLD

Top: Valentino Rossi, MotoGP Champion with 11 victories.

Max Biaggi (above) carried the Yamaha challenge.

Right: Michelin technicians take the track temperature.

the Telefónica Movistar Suzuki GSV-R-Michelin), who commenced 2002 with a rival tyre brand but quickly reverted to Michelin, was enraptured by the S4. 'The S4 is the biggest step I've ever had from a tyre,' said the Californian. 'It's the consistency, the turning, the feel and the grip — the tyre just feels so good and natural.'

The S4 takes the 16.5-in. concept a stage further — its trigonal profile giving a larger contact patch at high angles of lean for improved traction and feel, as well as cooler running for extended life. The result of this technology has been nothing short of stunning — the tyre's improved construction and design helped Michelin riders destroy lap and race records around the world, culminating in the season-ending Valencia GP where Alex Barros (West Honda Pons RC211V-Michelin) demolished the previous race record by an astonishing 65 seconds, an improvement of over two seconds per lap!

And despite two rival tyre companies contesting the MotoGP series, Michelin riders filled the top 11 places in the championship.

The story was the same in World Superbike, where Colin Edwards (Castrol Honda SP-2-Michelin) and Troy Bayliss (Ducati Infostrada 998-Michelin) fought an unforgettable season-long duel for the crown, leaving rival riders and tyre brands way behind at each and every round. The American and Australian ran away with series, sharing 25 wins between them, Edwards staging a remarkable late-season comeback to topple long-time series leader Bayliss at the final round at Imola. Their contest for the title delighted fans, who were amazed to see the pair happily hanging out in the paddock, then engaging in breathtaking, no-holds-barred battles on the track. Next year both Bayliss and Edwards move into MotoGP, with Michelin, of course...

Top row (left to right): A range of Michelin race tyres ready for action; Kenny Roberts and his Suzuki engineers in discussion with Michelin; The 'Texan Tornado' Colin Edwards using his Michelins to the max.

Below left: Superbike Superstars. Colin Edwards and Troy Bayliss shared 25 wins between them in a thrilling World Superbike championship battle.

RECENT MICHELIN WORLD CHAMPIONSHIP VICTORIES

500 GRANDS PRIX/MotoGP

1992	Wayne Rainey (Marlboro Team Roberts Yamaha-Michelin)
1993	Kevin Schwantz (Lucky Strike Suzuki-Michelin)
1994	Mick Doohan (Repsol Honda-Michelin)
1995	Mick Doohan (Repsol Honda-Michelin)
1996	Mick Doohan (Repsol Honda-Michelin)
1997	Mick Doohan (Repsol Honda-Michelin)
1998	Mick Doohan (Repsol Honda-Michelin)
1999	Alex Crivillé (Repsol YPF Honda-Michelin)
2000	Kenny Roberts (Telefónica Movistar Suzuki-Michelin)
2001	Valentino Rossi (Nastro Azzurro Honda-Michelin)
2002	Valentino Rossi (Repsol Honda Team-Michelin)

WORLD SUPERBIKE

1994	Carl Fogarty (Ducati-Michelin)
1995	Carl Fogarty (Ducati-Michelin)
1996	Troy Corser (Ducati-Michelin)
1997	John Kocinski (Castrol Honda-Michelin)
1998	Carl Fogarty (Ducati Performance-Michelin)
1999	Carl Fogarty (Ducati Performance-Michelin)
2000	Colin Edwards (Castrol Honda-Michelin)
2001	Troy Bayliss (Ducati Infostrada-Michelin)
2002	Colin Edwards (Castrol Honda-Michelin)

World Superbike Champion: Colin Edwards

MotoGP Champion: Valentino Rossi

Alex Barros (above) on the West Pons Honda and Repsol's Tohru Ukawa (left) were both MotoGP winners in 2002 on the Michelin-shod Honda RC211V.

The Michelin MotoGP team with Pierre Dupasquier (bottom left)

MICHELIN

Ukawa

GRAND PRIX TEAMS AND RIDERS

van den Goorbergh

Harada

MOTOGP

THE new MotoGP class started its transitional year with 20 full-time entrants. At the first race, two-strokes outnumbered the new 990s by 13:7, not counting wild cards. Fifteen rounds later, the balance had shifted, 12:8 in favour of the new bikes. A pivotal year.

The franchise system had needed some adjustment, following arguments with Honda, who wanted to run one-bike teams, and also following the late collapse of the proposed team run by Geoff Hardwick, previously sponsored by Shell Advance, who had a one-year slot for two riders. In the end, there were four teams with only one rider, three Hondas and one Aprilia — working adjustments forced by circumstances.

Hondas were thus outnumbered, with seven riders in five separate teams. Yamaha had four teams, two riders each, and eight motor cycles. The numbers were made up by two Suzukis, two Protons, and one Aprilia.

With the defending champion (although not the number one plate — he preferred as always 46) Honda's factory team was as last year, sponsored by Repsol and fielding Valentino Rossi (23 at the first race of the year) and Tohru Ukawa (28). Both started the season with full-factory RCV211 V5s, numbers swelled by the end of the year from two to four. Last year's Repsol team had numbered three: the casualty was 1999 champion Alex Criville, gently but firmly dropped by HRC in what would turn out to be a prescient decision.

The next senior team, by several measures, was another survivor from the year before: West-sponsored Honda Pons had the same two riders — Alex Barros (31) and Loris Capirossi (29), and the same bikes — NSR Honda two-strokes, although updated since the previous year's machine on which Rossi had won the title. For the last four races Pons also received one RC211V. He gave it to Barros — to great effect.

The next most senior team in HRC terms, however, was the Fortuna squad run by Fausto Gresini, with one rider — reigning 250 champion Daijiro Kato (25), making the final career step under close factory scrutiny.

The others were genuine satellite teams... Erv Kanemoto back from a year of Bridgestone tyre testing with those tyres on his yellow NSR, and Dutchman Jurgen van den Goorbergh (32) in the saddle. The other ex-Hardwick entry went (after some pressure from HRC) to Pramac, Italian importers of Honda industrial engines, with four-cylinder first-timer Tetsuya Harada (31), who was 250 champion in 1993 and would retire at the end of a disappointing season.

Checa

Jacque

Nakano

Abe

Riba

Yamaha also had considerable continuity. The central factory team was sponsored by Marlboro for a fourth consecutive year, and had the same two riders: Max Biaggi (30) and Carlos Checa (29). At first they rode the only four-stroke M1; again by the end of the year more had escaped the factory workshop for other teams.

The first to be thus gifted, for the last three races, was the French Tech 3 squad, which retained Gauloises sponsorship and the pair they had brought from the 250 class the year before... Olivier Jacque (28) and Shinya Nakano (24).

Only for the last two races did long-serving factory charger Norick Abe (26) finally have his increasingly plaintive requests heard, and he could swap his YZR two-stroke for an M1. The year had started with drama for the team, after d'Antin had achieved what some thought something of a coup, signing up Alex Criville for his second Yamaha. Criville, however, was far from fit, with a worsening of the suspected epilepsy that had troubled him from the beginning of 2000, possibly even before. He was a surprise absentee from pre-season tests, and scratched before the season began. By now somewhat desperate, former rider d'Antin hastily recruited Spaniard Pere Riba (32), taking him from 600 Supersports into GP racing, and the year began with a series of injuries that didn't let up. More often than not, his place was taken by José Luis Cardoso (27).

McCoy

Hopkins

Gibernau

Red Bull Yamaha were stuck with two-strokes all year, but their greater misfortune (aside from losing their sponsor) was further injury to top rider Garry McCoy (29). The Australian had been dominating pre-season tests when he broke his leg badly. The aftermath ruined his year; his place was taken at various times by Jean-Michel Bayle (33), and jobless ex-250 rider Alex Hofmann (21). The team also had a new teenage recruit, American Formula Xtreme champion John Hopkins (18), on the threshold of an impressive debut season.

The third Japanese factory, Suzuki, also arrived with a four-stroke, after a late decision to bring their new V4 out a year earlier than planned... certainly a better alternative for the riders than soldiering on with the two-stroke that had been soundly beaten the year before. They retained the backing of Telefónica MoviStar, and the same pair of riders, Kenny Roberts (28) and Sete Gibernau (29).

The final factory team represented the return to the class of Aprilia, with their own interpretation of the new four-stroke rules. This was a relatively small-scale effort with one rider — Frenchman Regis Laconi (26), who had run a knockabout but ultimately victorious Superbike season with the factory the year before.

The last team was determinedly two-stroke, by force of circumstances. Proton Team KR had no choice but to press on with their three-cylinder 500 cc lightweight, and complied with the two-bike regulations as well, doubling the size of their team with two new faces (new to Proton, that is), wily veteran Jeremy McWilliams (38) and former Honda and Suzuki rider, and more recently tyre tester, Nobuatsu Aoki (30). As it turned out, they should have done so a year earlier.

Roberts

Laconi

F. Nieto

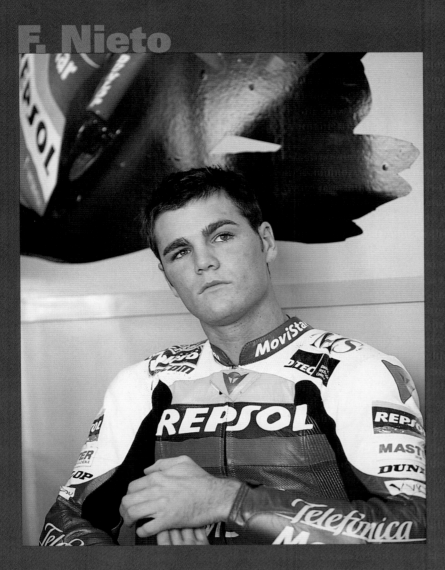

E VEN more than before, the strength of numbers came from Aprilia, in spite of cutting back their full factory team to just one. There were 14 of the Italian V-twins compared with six Hondas and four Yamahas, to make up a permanent strength of 24.

As ever the Aprilias ranged from Marco Melandri's full-factory machine, with MS sponsorship, to the lowliest privateer machine, with a wide range of variations in between. There are many ex-factory chassis and engine parts floating around to confuse the situation, but things were fairly clear cut at the top of the pile.

Melandri (19) was in his third year in the class, and his first as the top factory rider. There were two more full factory machines in the Telefónica Movi-Star-Repsol satellite team, where racing legend Angel Nieto hung over the pit wall to encourage his nephew Fonsi Nieto (23), and by the end of the season to slow down his precocious class rookie teammate Toni Elias (19), up from a blistering second season in the 125 class.

The next equipment level saw six riders with factory kits. Two to Campetella team-mates Frenchman Randy de Puniet (21), his star on the rise, and Spain's Alex Debon (26); two more to the Safilo Oxydo team — David Checa (21), younger brother of Carlos, and new teenage sensation Casey Stoner (16). Stoner is little known in his native Australia, having left the previous year to take advantage of Spanish racing regulations, which allowed him to go road racing a year earlier than in Australia. The last two kitted bikes went to ex-125 champ Roberto Locatelli (27), and the experienced nearly-man Franco Battaini (29).

Two Spanish rookies rode production Aprilias for the national team: Raul Jara (21) and Hector Faubel (18); plus German rookie Dirk Heidolf (25), low-grade standard-bearer for a nation's hopes of revival; and French rookie Hugo Marchand (20) joined Vincent Philippe (24) in the Scrab team, the older rider replaced mid-season by new boy Erwan Nigon (18).

Battaini

Faubel

Stoner

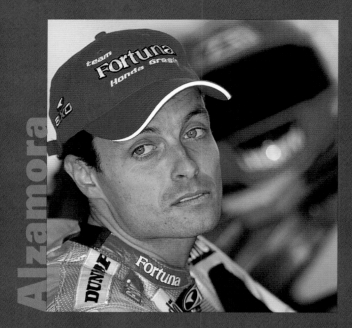

Alzamora

Rolfo

H. Aoki

Honda had just two factory NSR machines against the phalanx of Aprilias: now painted red and silver in Fortuna colours for the Gresini team. They retained Kato's old team-mate Emilio Alzamora (28), and replaced the departed champion with last year's best-of-the-rest of Aprilia riders, Roberto Rolfo (22) — from the frying pan into the fire, as it turned out.

This was to be a run-out year for the Aprilia-like twin-crank NSR, with future plans concentrating on development to the single-crank production RS, with factory backing in the form of upgrade parts for successful riders. This year saw a single development machine, named the RS250-W (for 'Works'), and ridden by ex-125 double champ Haruchika Aoki (26). This bike was run by the Dutch DeGraaf team, with a production machine for a second rider. Jarno Janssen (26) was the original entry, until he withdrew in the summer break. Dutch substitutes Henk van der Lagemaat (33) and Rob Filart (27) did the next two races before Czech Republic racer Jakub Smrz (19) crossed over from the 125 class to take over.

The Spanish Cibertel team signed the only two British riders in the class for a pair of RS Hondas, nominally with factory kits, although Jay Vincent (30) and Leon Haslam (18) found the bikes to be very much slower than required for any hope of anything but a handful of points.

Yamaha's top machines went to the turquoise Petronas-backed team, where Argentine rider Sebastian Porto (23) took over Naoki Matsudo's place alongside Malaysia's sole GP racer Shahrol Yuzy (26). Matsudo (28) moved to the Dark Dog Kurz Yamaha squad, with fellow-Japanese rider Taro Sekiguchi (26) his team-mate at first. He also quit after the summer break, and his place was taken by another Czech refugee from 125s — Jaroslav Hules (27).

J. Vincent

Haslam

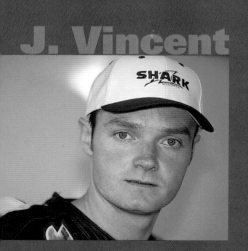

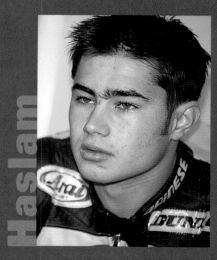

Porto

Matsudo

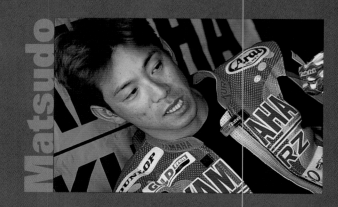

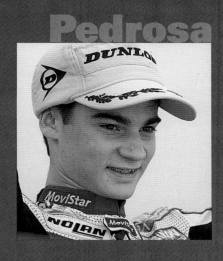

125cc

THE smallest class also had more shifts in population, for a variety of reasons. But the main players stayed put for the season, with Gilera and Derbi the only real factory machines, with a total of four. They were up against 14 Aprilias and 12 Hondas, plus two Italjets for a permanent entry of 32.

The factory Gilera was ridden for another season by defending champion Manuel Poggiali (19), with the identical Derbi again in the hands of Youichi Ui (29). Two more Gileras had been supplied to the Italian national team, for rookies Mattia Angeloni (18) and Michel Fabrizio (17).

The Aprilia hordes numbered some experienced riders and the usual crop of promising teenagers. The eventual champion was to be one of the former — Frenchman Arnaud Vincent (27); the most seasoned Aprilia rider was Italian Lucio Cecchinello (32), running his own Safilo Oxydo team with San Marino teenager Alex de Angelis (18) as his team-mate.

Italy provided a number of other Aprilia riders, including GP winner Simone Sanna (24), the diminutive Max Sabbatani (26), Gino Borsoi (28), and newcomers Alex Baldolini (17) and the fast but crash-prone Stefano Bianco (16).

Spain was well represented by ex-Derbi rider Pablo Nieto (21), now in his fifth season, and two fast youngsters, Angel Rodriguez (16) and 15-year-old Hector Barbera. Two others rode the Italian machines — German hope Steve Jenkner (25) and Welsh schoolboy Chaz Davies (15), who was the youngest rider at the start of the season, though others were to join as they passed their 15th birthdays.

Jaroslav Hules (27) started the season on an Aprilia, his place taken after the mid-point, when he moved to 250s, by former GP winner Ivan Goi (28) for a couple of races before 15-year-old Italian Marco Simoncello took over until the end of the year.

Honda's seasoned riders were Masao Azuma (31) and Nobbie Ueda (34), both from Japan. The young Turks were led by the Telefónica MoviStar Junior team of Daniel Pedrosa (16) and Joan Olivé (17), the only Spanish riders on the marque.

From Italy Mirko Giansanti (25) and rising star Andrea Dovizioso (16) rode stock Hondas, while Andrea Ballerini (28) took over the TSR machine from Ueda. Klaus Nöhles (25) was at first joined by Jarno Müller (23) before a mid-season melt-down saw Nöhles replaced by Gabor Talmacsi (20) — the Hungarian had started the season with Italjet, to the mutual dissatisfaction of both. Then Nöhles was brought back, and Talmacsi took Müller's place. A second Hungarian, Imre Toth (26) made his GP debut.

Jakub Smrz (19) had a similar bad start to the year, leaving his Elit team for the 250 class, his place taken by Swiss hope Thomas Luthi (15).

The last Honda newcomer was Finn Mika Kallio (19), on the Red Devil machine.

Italjet returned with Stefano Perugini (27) and at first Talmacsi, but he was replaced by British part-timer Leon Camier and eventually by Italian Christian Pistoni (21).

Poggiali

Pedrosa

Azuma

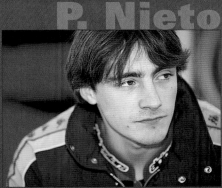

P. Nieto

Davies

Cecchinello

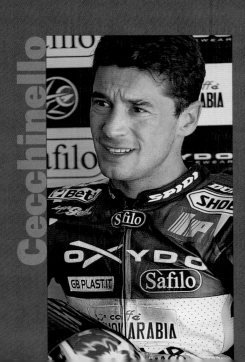

ROSSI versus BIAGGI

CULT FRICTION

By MICHAEL SCOTT

TO William Wordsworth, the gilding of springtime in the hills was laid on by nature — a host, a cloud of golden daffodils. It was different at Mugello. Many of the daffodils there were drunk.

Or just overcome perhaps with excitement, after watching the Big Yellow overtake the hated Red Devil at the ess-bend at their very feet. Either way, the army of Rossi fans, which must be numbered several thousand strong on this particular Sunday afternoon, led the charge through the fences as the chequered flag fell. By the time the riders arrived there again, they weren't playing to the crowd any more, but running right into them.

Mercifully, there were no serious consequences to what was potentially disastrous. Not in terms of injuries or damage, anyway. Unless you count a letter, both fulsome and strongly worded, from FIM president Francesco Zerbi, the main thrust of which seemed to be to condemn riders for inflaming the passions of the fans. 'It was inevitable,' wrote Zerbi. 'Motor cycling races have been also the victims of fanaticism and imbecility. Thus, as stadiums are often invaded, provoking material damages, now the tracks where the World Championships are held are also subject to the same evil. If... the invasion of a football stadium is serious, the invasion of a race track is even more serious. The invasions now take place while the riders are still racing on their bikes at very dangerous speeds.' Zerbi went on to exonerate the Mugello organisers and the FIM itself, but was less forgiving to showmanship among the riders: 'Perhaps it is nice to see Valentino or any other rider throw his racing clothes and his shoes to the public, but are we sure that this does not incite the public...'

It was addressed to all, but the real target was clear. Valentino Rossi had missed most of the fan-smash action, because he'd stopped earlier on to be booked by a pair of bogus policemen — another pre-arranged sally of theatrical wit from his ever-inventive and active fan club, who have been orchestrating post-race shows of one sort or another ever since Valentino was racing 125s. These displays break the rules, but Rossi has always been cavalier even when fined a few years ago. They were, he said, just having fun.

Yellow was not the only colour on the hillsides. The banks of red may not be as large, but were by no means inconsequential, and growing less so by the year. Max plays the game very differently from Rossi — brooding enigma to painted clown, but at the end of 2002 it definitely looked as though his approach was beginning to pay off. His image, of brave lone warrior, was improved when Yamaha 'let him go' (the public is funny like that), and then boosted still more when he immediately started to win races.

Two-man rivalry, of course, is the very stuff of great racing. The names echo down the roll of honour: Schwantz and Rainey, Lawson and Spencer, Roberts and Spencer, Hailwood and Agostini, Read and Agostini, Read and Hailwood, Read and Sheene, Read and Ivy. Indeed, Phil Read and almost everybody he rode against or with — the English rider (finally honoured this year in the Hall of Fame) was at serious loggerheads with anyone and everyone, on his way to preceding Rossi to 125, 250 and 500 World Championships. It was part of his racing recipe.

It is also part of Rossi's racing recipe, but he accomplishes it with such manifest charm that he has so far escaped the taint or even accusation of unsporting behaviour that many applied to the gamesmanship of Read and some other riders. In retrospect it is quite clear that he used Biaggi's strong image to build up his own, which is puzzling enough because with his gifts he hardly needed to do that. If there is an element of cynicism and orchestration in his well publicised enmity with Biaggi, nobody has divined it so far. Perhaps Rossi was merely carried along by circumstances.

Because the current Biaggi–Rossi axis has a momentum of its own, at a time when the cult of personality has become an even more powerful force than ever in all sports, including motor bike racing. There's an element of chicken and egg. Which came first, Rossi's engaging personality, or the cult that cleaves to it?

Either way, it has certainly gone out of control, and Rossi himself is something of a victim of his own success, not only as a racer but also as an accomplished player of the personality game. If he wanted to be famous, he might now not be so sure any more. He long since had to move away from his native Italy, at least from time to time: he maintains a home of sorts in London, where 'nobody knows who I am except in Italian restaurants', though that too is changing as his profile grows and grows.

'It is difficult, yes,' said Rossi. 'It is very hard to manage. It is impossible to do everything that everybody wants, and to manage the situation. But that is how it is. If I was in fifth place, for sure I wouldn't have this problem — so it is a good problem.'

His rivalry with Max has always been a cornerstone. As Biaggi said three years ago, when Rossi was about to join the top class: 'I was in 250 when Rossi rode 125, then in 500 when he rode 250. Now we will race against each other — but it feels as though he has been racing against me for years.'

This was a response to a consistent barrage of sniping from the younger rider, all lapped up and massaged (and to a large extent even fostered) by the Italian press over the years. A press that has always been a bit uneasy with Biaggi, who is (in anybody's language) something of a tricky and unpredictable customer, and who had collectively and individually been charmed from the earliest days by the impish, friendly and clearly hugely gifted Rossi. Making fun of Max rapidly went from a juvenile pastime to something of a national sport.

Whether Rossi regrets this now or not, he has backed off

Above: Full effort — Rossi prevailed more often than not in the actual racing.

Opposite page: Top of pile down under — Rossi flings his hat to the crowd in Australia after his 11th win in a season of record points.

Centre left: Enigmatic Max — his soulful look was always a counterpoint to Rossi's clowning.

Below: Always the main event. This time it's the Czech GP, and Max will go on to win.

All photographs: Gold & Goose

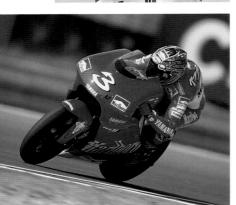

Top left: Biaggi held the winner's trophy only twice in 2002. This is at Sepang.

Top right: Rossi was always deadly serious in the saddle.

Above, from left: Biaggi in the bubble, Rossi in the sun; Max and the microphones.
All photographs: Gold & Goose

somewhat. As much as he is allowed to, with the topic never far from the Italian press's agenda. This interregnum is now over. When news broke that Max will be riding a Honda like Rossi's next year, the first questions were to Valentino about his reaction. 'For sure it will be funny. We raced together from 2000, and every time we had different bikes. And every time I win, he says it is because I have a Honda. This is an old problem for Honda riders basically, but especially for me with Biaggi. For sure next year if he is behind me, it will be because I have factory parts. He was the same with Doohan in 1998. But the mechanics and the other riders know the real situation. Honda has always in the past given very good bikes to non-factory riders... and Biaggi nearly won the championship in 1998 with a non-factory Honda. It was the same this year with Barros in Motegi.' (Where Barros beat Rossi, on a customer Honda.)

Over the years, the cult of personality has imbued all this bickering with an inflated sense of importance, fanned considerably by last year's brief post-race bout of physical violence after Rossi had just pipped Biaggi in Catalunya. The pair came to blows of a sort in a crowded vestibule on the way to the rostrum. After that, as usually, the tide of public sympathy went with Rossi.

By and large, Max has stayed somewhat aloof. Not without taking the odd chance of sniping of his own, of course, but the opportunities were more limited. It's hard when one of the most popular men in Italy is sniggering at you, and everyone else is joining in. There was a fine piece of Max-ness, however, after last year's catfight at Catalunya, after which (enjoined by their factory team staff) both men agreed to shake hands and preserve their silence on the details. 'It was not very nice,' said Max. 'He hit me when my hands were held down. But I don't want to talk about it.'

If there were signs that the tide was — if not turning, at least beginning to ebb during 2002 — Biaggi was quick to read them. Last year his obstinacy in the face of defeat ended up with him looking a bit silly after he had the same crash three times in the last handful of races, over-riding the Yamaha to the same inevitable conclusion. This year opened with the Yamaha clearly at a technical disadvantage to the Honda, and Max rode accordingly, declining to take risks to exceed its potential. Why had he not done that the year before? 'Because I was going for the championship. I needed to win races to keep it open,' he said.

This was in an exclusive interview with *MOTOCOURSE*, where Biaggi for the first time unburdened himself on his side of the public feuding. First, he spoke about the pressure from the press. 'In the paddock Rossi and Biaggi are the two big names. I don't want to take anything from Roberts and the others, but in the Italian press we are... up there. And it's normal if somebody gives a gun to a journalist to shoot they will shoot — they need to fill the column.'

Asked his response to Rossi's assertions about next year's battle, Biaggi said: 'You know, I have watched him — in year one he didn't win the first race; I did. He was with a factory team; I wasn't. He won two races — I also won two races. I was chasing the championship with the World Champion [Doohan] there; he didn't.

'When Rossi was much younger, he had a poster of me on his bedroom wall. He said this once, though not recently. Now he speaks badly about me all the time. There's some psychology there — some connection.

'I don't like to say too much about it. You know, if you don't like a person, you say it once or twice. You don't have to say it a million times.' He spoke about two incidents on TV this year, when Rossi had criticised once Biaggi and once Ukawa in post-race interviews, triggering a flood of hostile interactive e-mails to the station and (Biaggi claimed) a retraction by Rossi. This happened twice this year. Before people had an image of Rossi — that he is so nice, so sweet. Now there is a big change. I always said he's not what you see on television. I think people are beginning to realise this now.'

Biaggi's slow start to the season notwithstanding, the pair remained the main event, at least to the Italian media, and the armies of fans. They met in numbers again at venues other than Mugello during this last season, Brno being another track where the hillsides were painted with swathes of red and yellow. So far, the fervour has stopped short of open warfare, but sometimes one feels it can only be a matter of time.

Can it be stopped? Should it be stopped? The FIM president thinks it should, but it is hard to know exactly how. Biaggi was the top Italian rider when Rossi came on the scene. It's natural he should be a target. Rossi has now taken over that role, so it is natural that he should be Biaggi's target. And equally natural that the press should play up the feud, and that the fans should become polarised.

Trying to avoid the worst excesses of football fans is another matter. Increasingly heavy policing would seem to be the only answer, but we saw at Jerez what happens when the local force become a bit over-zealous — in taking up positions to prevent a track invasion by the crowd they invaded the track themselves, so that marshals held out yellow flags, and in the end affected the outcome of the race, admittedly only at the bottom end of the points table.

In the meantime, the rivalry remains in place, and the fact that both will at last be on the same kind of motor cycle only serves to spice it up still further. To the ultimate elevation of the spectacle. Next season should be a hell of a battle.

2002 GRANDS PRIX

JAPANESE GRAND PRIX 52

SOUTH AFRICAN GRAND PRIX 58

SPANISH GRAND PRIX 64

FRENCH GRAND PRIX 70

ITALIAN GRAND PRIX 76

CATALAN GRAND PRIX 82

DUTCH TT 88

BRITISH GRAND PRIX 94

GERMAN GRAND PRIX 100

CZECH GRAND PRIX 106

PORTUGUESE GRAND PRIX 112

RIO GRAND PRIX 118

PACIFIC GRAND PRIX 124

MALAYSIAN GRAND PRIX 130

AUSTRALIAN GRAND PRIX 136

VALENCIA GRAND PRIX 142

JAPANESE GP

SUZUKA

FIM WORLD CHAMPIONSHIP · ROUND 1

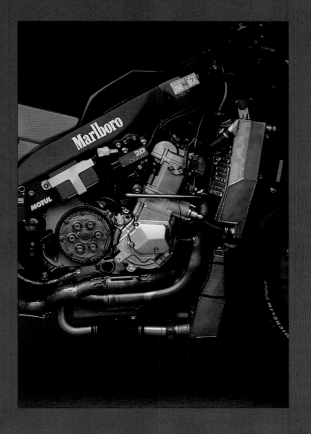

Left: **Look on my works, ye mighty, and despair. Honda's beautifully wrought V5 started as it would go on, by winning.**

Above: **Angular Yamaha was another good looker, after a long development programme.**

Right: **Cosworth-engined Aprilia was the newest four-stroke, and looked a lot more of a prototype.**

Below, from left: **The politest grid-girls in the world; practice was dry — race day wasn't; Rossi counts the number of times he fell off in practice.**

All photographs: Gold & Goose

THERE was no difficulty in feeling the history at Suzuka. The sound alone made it completely obvious; the atmosphere thick as the four-strokes blipped in pit lane, before the first free training on Friday morning. The soundtrack was immensely satisfying: from the shrill shriek of the Aprilia to the bold baritone of the Suzuki V4, by way of Honda's V5 — busy-sounding but disappointingly aurally unspectacular.

History prevailed, but in a different sense. As so often before, the weather turned nasty, making a splash-fest lottery of the first race of the new era, and elevating the usual strong Japanese wild cards to a pace-setting role. Rather more than this in the 250 race, where a pair of them ran away so far and so fast that it was hardly plausible when we learned afterwards that one — second-placed Daisaku Sakai — had run much of the race without sixth gear.

History, in this case, had puddles — and an intimate knowledge of their position and nature at the already technically difficult classic circuit (slightly altered this year to improve safety at a now-faster Dunlop Curve, and 38 metres shorter) paid the usual big dividends. In this way, mattress-haired Akira Ryo led two-thirds of the first MotoGP on a Suzuki that regular riders Roberts and Gibernau were darkly insisting was far from ready to race: Rossi cannily followed Ryo most of the way, taking the benefit of his local knowledge before going through to win, to fulfil at least one of the predictions. And vice versa, with big names like Biaggi and Roberts among eight MotoGP riders to add to a record total of 75 crashes in the weekend. Many people crashed twice, among them Melandri... and US rookie John Hopkins, who pitted for a new fairing after the second one, and finished the race five laps down, changing gear with his hand. Good enough for 12th: an impressive entry in his CV, and putting to shame fellow-Yamaha 500 two-stroke rider Jacque. The Frenchman had jumped the start to lead into turn one from the second row, and retired in a fit of pique after taking the resulting stop-and-go penalty, much dismaying his team, who had endured the hard life in Japan for two weeks (counting tests) to get him on the track. He threw away an easy eighth.

There were many surprises, after a pre-season test series that seemed to have answered too many questions. Rossi and the V5 had only met the rivals twice, and had dominated easily both times; come race weekend he was under pressure, some created by himself after two practice crashes, both triggered by over-confidence. The Yamaha M1 had been so disappointing — beaten twice by the two-strokes — that it had been dubbed 'Mission Impossible' by the pitiless Italian press. Now a new chassis took the project one step forward, and though the top speed was notably low for a four-stroke, both Biaggi and Checa challenged for pole, and Checa made the rostrum. (In fact, on the old chassis, since the new bike was set up for the dry, in line with off-target weather forecasts.)

Speed isn't everything, even with two fast straights, as the Aprilia illustrated. Clearly plenty powerful it was beaten on top end only by the three V5 Hondas, but the newest of the four-strokes had plenty of rough edges, and was never a threat. In the four-stroke/two-stroke battle, however, speed was more than enough. A comparison of data-logging speed traces by Suzuki's Warren Willing showed Roberts' 2001 two-stroke consistently one or two mph faster through the turns, but also illustrated how the four-stroke's extra 11 bhp grabbed it all back with interest as soon as the throttle was opened in any gear higher than third. Jacque reported after practice: 'It's like a V-twin 500 against a V4 — on the two-stroke you can't even stay in the draft,' while Abe had a similar experience in the race, crawling all over Ukawa in the bends and often passing him, only to be blown away twice a lap down the front and back straights. Demoralising, until his countryman obligingly fell off.

Renowned former racer and permanent technical director Jack Findlay had resigned, and his place was taken by Checa's former crew chief, New Zealander Mike Webb. His first strike, by happenstance, was against his former employers: Japanese scrutineers found that Yamaha's bulbous aerodynamic fairings exceeded the maximum width: frantic work with files removed the few millimetres as required from all but McCoy's bike, since the Australian preferred the older and smaller cowling. Honda also fell foul at the weigh-in. Bikes are put on the scales minus fuel tanks, with a two kilogram allowance. Not enough, said HRC, because our fuel pump is within the underseat tank, and the tank thus weighs more than two kg. Too bad, said the scrutineers. Luckily, the bike made the 143 kg minimum limit anyway.

If the Suzuki men were complaining about the bike, this was at least partly to avoid mentioning the far trickier matter of tyres. The switch to Dunlop had come from top factory level, much to the dismay of team, riders and (it later transpired) Dunlop's own racing squad. With good reason on all sides: returning to the class the newly Goodyear-owned company knew they would need time to catch up to Michelin, who had meanwhile upped the stakes with a new 16.5-in. rear with a larger rolling diameter and demonstrably better performance. Ryo's strong race showed that, at least in the wet, there wasn't much wrong with either tyres or bike, and it was plain to see that he was able to open the throttle significantly earlier than Rossi on the torquier but less predictable Honda. Poetic justice for Dunlop — but their relief was not to last much longer.

Spanish rookie Pere Riba, snaffled from World Supersport at the last minute to replace the soon-to-retire Alex Criville, had a bad start to his MotoGP career with a heavy crash on the first day, suffering shoulder fractures that ruled him out of the race.

MOTOGP RACE – 21 laps

Rossi's pre-season form led his compatriot Capirossi to say that he could win the championship with one hand tied behind his back. Was this true, he was asked before practice? 'I don't know. I try tomorrow,' he quipped. 'But not if it is my throttle and brake hand.' Over the next two days he kept both hands on the bars but still crashed twice, and by the end of practice Capirossi's two-stroke was on pole, as last year. Until one last effort by Rossi, helped by an unwitting tow down the back straight from deadly rival Biaggi, to take the top slot half a second faster than last year's time. 'He should buy me a pizza,' said Biaggi later.

Capirossi was second, with wild card Itoh alongside on his V5, painted in what looked very much like Honda production-bike colours. Part of the factory development team, the semi-retired former GP rider had one big advantage as the rain began after practice was over: he was the only person ever to have ridden the RCV in the wet.

Checa completed the first row, Biaggi led the second from Kato's two-stroke, the 250 champion having spoiled his debut with a first-day crash, blaming new Alpinestars boots that had been slippery on the footrest. Then came Ryo on the best Suzuki, with Jacque's two-stroke eighth.

The first practice session in anger had been promising for the year ahead, setting a new record for close times — the first dozen within a second of pole and a rather surprising mix of two-strokes and four-strokes. In the last 22 minutes pole had changed hands six times, with Capirossi, Biaggi and Checa all taking a turn before Rossi's last run.

Race-day rain should have stopped by 2 pm, according to the weather forecasters, but it was still falling steadily as the lights went green, and Jacque's old two-stroke leapt into the lead into the first corner. On the way out, the blue bike was simply swamped by an orchestral tide of torque, Itoh and Ryo surging ahead before they even reached the Esses, the pair swapping positions also so that the Suzuki — rawest of the new Japanese four-strokes — was in front, surprising everybody, including the team and factory staff. Later, Rossi would compliment not only rider but also the Suzuki's linear throttle response. 'I just couldn't get the power on as early as him,' he said.

Checa was fourth behind Jacque, but Rossi had also got away well, and

quickly passed the red four-stroke Yamaha, and then Jacque too by lap four.

Gibernau was also quick away, riding like a man possessed, pouncing on Checa in a daring move out of the hairpin on lap nine. He later explained his dramatic sliding technique — under brakes as well as power. 'My front tyre wasn't so good, and it was easier to slow the bike like that.'

Roberts's front tyre was even less good, after swapping on the line following vibration on the warm-up lap. He'd started off ninth, but was losing ground on lap seven when he crashed on the entry to Spoon Curve. 'It kept trying to tuck under, and eventually it did,' he explained. Biaggi, behind him, had also fallen earlier on the same lap, on the left before Dunlop, touching a white line. 'It was a stupid mistake, but easy to make because I was trying hard,' he said later.

Roberts had just suffered the indignity of being passed by the Proton of McWilliams, making the most of the conditions and the Bridgestone wets, with team-mate Aoki a little way back in pursuit. For the first three laps he had van den Goorbergh, on similar tyres, ahead of him. All the Bridgestone users had battled in practice, but the Dutchman had been fastest in the wet morning warm-up, and was revelling in the conditions until a front-end slide caught him out.

Gibernau was still charging, the lead within sight. On lap 11 he passed Itoh for third, with a decisive move into the hairpin, and quickly closed up on Rossi over the next three laps, the Suzuki skipping and sliding. Too quickly, as it turned out. Visibly faster than the Honda into the second Degner Curve, he lost the front and was down. It looked as though he had hit Rossi, and at first said that he'd had to brake mid-corner after the Italian had unexpectedly slowed. Later he revised his opinion, and took the blame himself.

Now Checa closed again, and on lap 13 the first four — Ryo, Rossi, Itoh and Checa — were covered by little more than 1.5 seconds. Some way back Ukawa and Abe were going back and forth, while McWilliams had set fastest lap so far on the Proton, and still had a chance of catching them. Then he settled back, mindful of a rear tyre that was going away, only to get caught out by a wet patch, crashing out of seventh with five laps left.

By lap 15, Rossi had learned what he needed from Ryo, and was pushing. The Suzuki rider didn't resist. 'I wanted Rossi to pass so I could see his race tactics. I was waiting and waiting, and he didn't come,' he said. The Honda finally slipped by under braking for the chicane, and now the pair of them started to force the pace, lap times dropping below 2m 20s a couple of times as they drew

away from Itoh and Checa. Two laps later, the gap was 1.6s. Then Itoh had a big slide in the Esses. 'I actually hit him and I thought we were both going to crash,' said Checa. In fact they both survived, the Spaniard now in third.

Ryo had a couple of stabs at Rossi onto the front straight, trying to use lapped riders to help, as well as his better corner exit speed. Valiant, but in the end to no avail. Checa and Itoh also stayed in that order, almost seven seconds adrift by the end.

Abe came next, then Barros and Aoki, who had settled for safety on the Proton after seeing both McWilliams and van den Goorbergh go down. 'I was the only Bridgestone rider left, so I wanted to be sure of finishing,' he said.

A lap behind, Laconi had gradually gained pace through the race in the Aprilia Cube's first outing in the wet, finishing comfortably ahead of Capirossi, Kato and Harada. It had been a dismal afternoon for the Italian, second on the grid but left on the line and almost last at the end of the first lap, with tyres that just couldn't find any grip. Kato had similar problems. 'I don't like racing in the wet, but this was worse than usual. I had no feeling from the bike,' he said.

McCoy had a pitiful weekend. Barely able to walk six weeks after his double right leg fracture and in extra pain because one of the fixing screws to the pin was coming loose, almost protruding from the skin, he was near the back when he crashed at the chicane. Game over.

Last finisher Hopkins was another four laps down after falling twice, fitting a new fairing, and plugging on. With only 12 finishers, last was a worthwhile result. And an object lesson to Jacque, who had rejoined ahead of Laconi after his stop-and-go, only to retire.

Below left: Ryo surprised everybody, and was properly pleased with second.

Below: Capirossi led the two-stroke resistance in practice.

Below right: Roberts had a lot on his mind — before and after the race.

Bottom: Ryo led Rossi like this for more than half the race. The champion was using him as an expert local guide.
All photographs: Gold & Goose

Right: **Surprise winner Miyazaki leads Sakai away from de Puniet.**

Below: **And they followed him all the way to the rostrum.**
All photographs: Gold & Goose

De Puniet was disputing third with Aoki, joined after half-distance by wild card Hiroshi Aoyama for a last-lap showdown. Only the Frenchman survived. Aoyama fell first, remounting for 12th in the well-spread field; Aoki was pushing through the chicane and the last right-hander until he crashed with barely 100 metres to go, his bike too badly damaged to rejoin.

Nieto had led the next gang from Alzamora, Porto and Matsudo. Three laps from the end he lost the rear and was flicked off, remounting hastily to recoup a few points. Six seconds back, wild card Choujun Kameya held off Rolfo's factory Honda, the Italian still struggling with the bike built around Kato. Debon was some way back, holding ninth from Battaini and rookie Elias.

There were just 16 finishers, with crashers including both fast-starting Haslam and team-mate Vincent, and Australian Casey Stoner.

125 cc RACE – 18 laps

A teeming start saw Jenkner race into the lead, pursued by Hules, and was almost ten seconds clear by lap ten. Then Jenkner slowed with a puncture (eventually finishing 15th), and one lap later Hules survived one moment at Degner only to crash finally a couple of corners later, into the Spoon.

Vincent had battled through for third, and now led, moving ahead of a to-and-fro gang. Giansanti forged through from a slow start to take control from Poggiali, Ueda and Sanna, Cecchinello dropping off the back. Now Giansanti started to take chunks out of Vincent's ten-second lead, halving it in two laps, with three to go.

The Frenchman got the message, but still had only three seconds in hand as they started the final lap. It was just enough for a fine victory. Giansanti and Poggiali were behind, Ueda surviving a high-speed trip through the dirt for a close fourth.

Sanna had lost touch, then wild card Aoyama held off Rodriguez, Perugini losing this group at the end with a last-lap moment that gifted eighth to pole-qualifier Pedrosa, ahead of Cecchinello after an off-track excursion of his own, and Borsoi. Perugini was 11th.

Crashers from a race with 37 starters and only 19 finishers included Sabbatani, Jarno Müller (twice), de Angelis, Bianco (also twice), Azuma, youngster Chaz Davies and the luckless Ui.

250 cc RACE – 19 laps

A familiar Suzuka scenario, local wild card riders galloping away through the spray while the regulars suffered various vicissitudes. Title favourite Melandri, for example, fell twice before being forced to retire; pole-starter Nieto fell once, but remounted for 13th.

Matsudo took off in front, wild card Daisaku Sakai on his heels, plus de Puniet and Aoki, who took over the lead on lap three. Sixth time round ex-GP racer, now wild card, Osamu Miyazaki took over, and never looked back. Sakai tagged on behind, and the pair of them pulled steadily away. Three laps from the end, Miyazaki pushed again, and by the finish he was almost seven seconds clear; Sakai, it transpired later, had lost sixth gear, and could only manage second.

Right: **Arnaud Vincent's win in the season-opener presaged a thrilling year for the determined Frenchman.**
Photograph: Gold & Goose

FIM WORLD CHAMPIONSHIP

SKYY VODKA
grand prix of
JAPAN

1 round

7 APRIL 2002

SUZUKA RACING CIRCUIT

First Curve • S curve • Degner Curve • Underpass • Hairpin • Spoon Curve • Chicane

CIRCUIT LENGTH: 3.617 miles/5.821 km

MotoGP

21 laps, 75.957 miles/122.241 km

Pos.	Rider (Nat.)	No.	Machine	Laps	Time & speed
1	Valentino Rossi (I)	46	Honda	21	49m 32.766s 91.983 mph/ 148.033 km/h
2	Akira Ryo (J)	33	Suzuki	21	49m 34.316s
3	Carlos Checa (E)	7	Yamaha	21	49m 41.119s
4	Shinichi Itoh (J)	72	Honda	21	49m 43.595s
5	Norick Abe (J)	6	Yamaha	21	49m 53.189s
6	Alex Barros (BR)	4	Honda	21	50m 05.025s
7	Nobuatsu Aoki (J)	9	Proton KR	21	50m 12.399s
8	Regis Laconi (F)	55	Aprilia	20	49m 40.232s
9	Loris Capirossi (I)	65	Honda	20	49m 44.518s
10	Daijiro Kato (J)	74	Honda	20	49m 48.895s
11	Tetsuya Harada (J)	31	Honda	20	50m 07.870s
12	John Hopkins (USA)	21	Yamaha	16	51m 42.424s
	Tohru Ukawa (J)	11	Honda	18	DNF
	Shinya Nakano (J)	56	Yamaha	17	DNF
	Jeremy McWilliams (GB)	99	Proton KR	16	DNF
	Sete Gibernau (E)	15	Suzuki	12	DNF
	Olivier Jacque (F)	19	Yamaha	12	DNF
	Kenny Roberts (USA)	10	Suzuki	6	DNF
	Max Biaggi (I)	3	Yamaha	6	DNF
	Jurgen van den Goorbergh (NL)	17	Honda	4	DNF
	Garry McCoy (AUS)	8	Yamaha	2	DNF
	Pere Riba (E)	20	Yamaha		DNS

Fastest lap: Rossi, 2m 19.105s, 93.606 mph/150.645 km/h (record).

Previous circuit record: Tohru Ukawa, J (Honda), 2m 06.805s, 103.357 mph/166.337 km/h (2001).

Event best maximum speed: Rossi, 195.9 mph/315.3 km/h (free practice no. 1).

Qualifying: 1 Rossi, 2m 04.226s; 2 Capirossi, 2m 04.409s; 3 Itoh, 2m 04.435s; 4 Checa, 2m 04.450s; 5 Biaggi, 2m 04.456s; 6 Kato, 2m 04.491s; 7 Ryo, 2m 04.746s; 8 Jacque, 2m 04.953s; 9 Nakano, 2m 05.098s; 10 Roberts, 2m 05.122s; 11 Ukawa, 2m 05.141s; 12 Abe, 2m 05.145s; 13 Barros, 2m 05.387s; 14 Gibernau, 2m 05.977s; 15 Aoki, 2m 06.094s; 16 Harada, 2m 06.112s; 17 McCoy, 2m 06.193s; 18 Hopkins, 2m 06.302s; 19 Laconi, 2m 06.379s; 20 van den Goorbergh, 2m 06.731s; 21 McWilliams, 2m 07.130s; 22 Riba, 2m 15.140s.

Fastest race laps: 1 Rossi, 2m 19.105s; 2 Ryo, 2m 19.219s; 3 Nakano, 2m 19.859s; 4 Barros, 2m 20.016s; 5 Gibernau, 2m 20.124s; 6 Checa, 2m 20.218s; 7 Itoh, 2m 20.327s; 8 Ukawa, 2m 20.596s; 9 Abe, 2m 20.669s; 10 McWilliams, 2m 20.732s; 11 Aoki, 2m 21.416s; 12 Jacque, 2m 21.985s; 13 Biaggi, 2m 22.722s; 14 Roberts, 2m 22.852s; 15 van den Goorbergh, 2m 23.487s; 16 Laconi, 2m 25.533s; 17 Capirossi, 2m 26.064s; 18 Hopkins, 2m 26.151s; 19 McCoy, 2m 26.462s; 20 Harada, 2m 26.959s; 21 Kato, 2m 27.064s.

World Championship: 1 Rossi, 25; 2 Ryo, 20; 3 Checa, 16; 4 Itoh, 13; 5 Abe, 11; 6 Barros, 10; 7 Aoki, 9; 8 Laconi, 8; 9 Capirossi, 7; 10 Kato, 6; 11 Harada, 5; 12 Hopkins, 4.

250 cc

19 laps, 68.723 miles/110.599 km

Pos.	Rider (Nat.)	No.	Machine	Laps	Time & speed
1	Osamu Miyazaki (J)	89	Yamaha	19	47m 09.454s 87.438 mph/ 140.718 km/h
2	Daisaku Sakai (J)	50	Honda	19	47m 16.395s
3	Randy de Puniet (F)	17	Aprilia	19	47m 38.474s
4	Emilio Alzamora (E)	7	Honda	19	47m 54.754s
5	Sebastian Porto (ARG)	9	Yamaha	19	47m 54.949s
6	Naoki Matsudo (J)	8	Yamaha	19	48m 04.179s
7	Choujun Kameya (J)	49	Honda	19	48m 10.026s
8	Roberto Rolfo (I)	4	Honda	19	48m 11.741s
9	Alex Debon (E)	6	Aprilia	19	48m 27.736s
10	Franco Battaini (I)	21	Aprilia	19	48m 28.831s
11	Toni Elias (E)	24	Aprilia	19	48m 40.935s
12	Hiroshi Aoyama (J)	92	Honda	19	48m 59.723s
13	Fonsi Nieto (E)	10	Aprilia	19	49m 05.459s
14	Hugo Marchand (F)	51	Aprilia	19	49m 16.124s
15	Raul Jara (E)	22	Aprilia	18	47m 13.919s
16	Roberto Locatelli (I)	15	Aprilia	18	47m 52.510s
	Haruchika Aoki (J)	11	Honda	18	DNF
	Leon Haslam (GB)	19	Honda	16	DNF
	Vincent Philippe (F)	25	Aprilia	14	DNF
	Marco Melandri (I)	3	Aprilia	13	DNF
	Jarno Janssen (NL)	41	Honda	9	DNF
	Shahrol Yuzy (MAL)	18	Yamaha	7	DNF
	Jay Vincent (GB)	12	Honda	4	DNF
	Taro Sekiguchi (J)	76	Yamaha	2	DNF
	Shinichi Nakatomi (J)	48	Honda	1	DNF
	Hector Faubel (E)	32	Aprilia	1	DNF
	Casey Stoner (AUS)	27	Aprilia	0	DNF
	David Checa (E)	42	Aprilia		DNS
	Dirk Heidolf (D)	28	Aprilia		DNQ

Fastest lap: Miyazaki, 2m 25.896s, 89.249 mph/143.633 km/h (record).

Previous circuit record: Daijiro Kato, J (Honda), 2m 08.658s, 101.868 mph/163.941 km/h (2001).

Event best maximum speed: Melandri, 168.2 mph/270.7 km/h (qualifying practice no. 1).

Qualifying: 1 Nieto, 2m 08.049s; 2 de Puniet, 2m 08.168s; 3 Melandri, 2m 08.579s; 4 Battaini, 2m 08.627s; 5 Debon, 2m 08.723s; 6 Alzamora, 2m 08.845s; 7 Porto, 2m 09.024s; 8 Miyazaki, 2m 09.177s; 9 Locatelli, 2m 09.205s; 10 Matsudo, 2m 09.692s; 11 Elias, 2m 09.930s; 12 Sakai, 2m 09.996s; 13 Aoyama, 2m 10.470s; 14 Rolfo, 2m 10.636s; 15 Stoner, 2m 10.675s; 16 Checa, 2m 10.837s; 17 Aoki, 2m 10.916s; 18 Yuzy, 2m 11.040s; 19 Nakatomi, 2m 11.084s; 20 Jara, 2m 11.127s; 21 Sekiguchi, 2m 11.281s; 22 Kameya, 2m 11.306s; 23 Philippe, 2m 11.601s; 24 Vincent, 2m 11.973s; 25 Haslam, 2m 12.212s; 26 Marchand, 2m 12.389s; 27 Janssen, 2m 12.492s; 28 Faubel, 2m 13.455s; 29 Heidolf, 2m 31.840s.

Fastest race laps: 1 Miyazaki, 2m 25.896s; 2 Sakai, 2m 26.118s; 3 Porto, 2m 27.850s; 4 de Puniet, 2m 27.963s; 5 Alzamora, 2m 28.007s; 6 Nieto, 2m 28.106s; 7 Aoki, 2m 28.204s; 8 Aoyama, 2m 28.282s; 9 Melandri, 2m 28.587s; 10 Haslam, 2m 28.790s; 11 Rolfo, 2m 28.943s; 12 Matsudo, 2m 29.138s; 13 Kameya, 2m 29.590s; 14 Elias, 2m 30.305s; 15 Debon, 2m 30.369s; 16 Locatelli, 2m 30.657s; 17 Battaini, 2m 31.190s; 18 Philippe, 2m 31.797s; 19 Janssen, 2m 31.812s; 20 Marchand, 2m 32.301s; 21 Yuzy, 2m 32.939s; 22 Vincent, 2m 33.510s; 23 Sekiguchi, 2m 34.342s; 24 Jara, 2m 34.692s; 25 Nakatomi, 2m 48.542s; 26 Faubel, 2m 55.587s.

World Championship: 1 Miyazaki, 25; 2 Sakai, 20; 3 de Puniet, 16; 4 Alzamora, 13; 5 Porto, 11; 6 Matsudo, 10; 7 Kameya, 9; 8 Rolfo, 8; 9 Debon, 7; 10 Battaini, 6; 11 Elias, 5; 12 Aoyama, 4; 13 Nieto, 3; 14 Marchand, 2; 15 Jara, 1.

125 cc

18 laps, 65.106 miles/104.778 km

Pos.	Rider (Nat.)	No.	Machine	Laps	Time & speed
1	Arnaud Vincent (F)	21	Aprilia	18	46m 22.971s 84.219 mph/ 135.538 km/h
2	Mirko Giansanti (I)	6	Honda	18	46m 24.135s
3	Manuel Poggiali (RSM)	1	Gilera	18	46m 25.529s
4	Noboru Ueda (J)	9	Honda	18	46m 26.450s
5	Simone Sanna (I)	16	Aprilia	18	46m 33.159s
6	Shuhei Aoyama (J)	66	Honda	18	46m 46.027s
7	Angel Rodriguez (E)	47	Aprilia	18	46m 46.624s
8	Daniel Pedrosa (E)	26	Honda	18	46m 56.459s
9	Lucio Cecchinello (I)	4	Aprilia	18	46m 57.256s
10	Gino Borsoi (I)	23	Aprilia	18	47m 10.275s
11	Stefano Perugini (I)	7	Italjet	18	47m 24.741s
12	Klaus Nöhles (D)	12	Honda	18	47m 29.035s
13	Joan Olivé (E)	25	Honda	18	47m 51.907s
14	Alex Baldolini (I)	19	Aprilia	18	47m 59.235s
15	Steve Jenkner (D)	17	Aprilia	18	48m 19.830s
16	Hector Barbera (E)	80	Aprilia	18	48m 34.565s
17	Mattia Angeloni (I)	31	Gilera	18	48m 37.135s
18	Imre Toth (H)	20	Honda	18	48m 40.075s
19	Suhathal Chaemsap (TH)	46	Honda	18	48m 58.612s
	Stefano Bianco (I)	33	Aprilia	15	DNF
	Toshihisa Kuzuhara (J)	65	Honda	14	DNF
	Jakub Smrz (CZ)	18	Honda	13	DNF
	Youichi Ui (J)	41	Derbi	12	DNF
	Chaz Davies (GB)	57	Aprilia	12	DNF
	Jaroslav Hules (CZ)	39	Aprilia	7	DNF
	Andrea Ballerini (I)	50	Honda	7	DNF
	Mika Kallio (SF)	36	Honda	7	DNF
	Masao Azuma (J)	5	Honda	6	DNF
	Andrea Dovizioso (I)	34	Honda	6	DNF
	Gabor Talmacsi (H)	8	Italjet	5	DNF
	Michel Fabrizio (I)	84	Gilera	5	DNF
	Jarno Müller (D)	10	Honda	5	DNF
	Hideyuki Ogata (J)	67	Honda	4	DNF
	Pablo Nieto (E)	22	Aprilia	3	DNF
	Alex de Angelis (RSM)	15	Aprilia	1	DNF
	Max Sabbatani (I)	11	Aprilia	0	DNF
	Akira Komuro (J)	68	Honda	0	DNF

Fastest lap: Bianco, 2m 30.798s, 86.348 mph/138.964 km/h (record).

Previous circuit record: Masao Azuma, J (Honda), 2m 15.353s, 96.830 mph/155.832 km/h (2001).

Event best maximum speed: Sabbatani, 145.6 mph/234.4 km/h (qualifying practice no. 1).

Qualifying: 1 Pedrosa, 2m 13.957s; 2 Nieto, 2m 14.424s; 3 Cecchinello, 2m 14.471s; 4 Borsoi, 2m 14.577s; 5 Azuma, 2m 14.659s; 6 Bianco, 2m 14.693s; 7 Poggiali, 2m 14.993s; 8 Jenkner, 2m 15.063s; 9 Hules, 2m 15.064s; 10 Sabbatani, 2m 15.092s; 11 Ueda, 2m 15.159s; 12 Ui, 2m 15.170s; 13 Rodriguez, 2m 15.336s; 14 Vincent, 2m 15.422s; 15 de Angelis, 2m 15.736s; 16 Kallio, 2m 15.957s; 17 Sanna, 2m 16.124s; 18 Olivé, 2m 16.281s; 19 Giansanti, 2m 16.343s; 20 Aoyama, 2m 16.696s; 21 Chaemsap, 2m 16.808s; 22 Smrz, 2m 17.044s; 23 Ogata, 2m 17.053s; 24 Müller, 2m 17.370s; 25 Dovizioso, 2m 17.403s; 26 Ballerini, 2m 17.486s; 27 Perugini, 2m 17.592s; 28 Barbera, 2m 17.745s; 29 Komuro, 2m 18.042s; 30 Nöhles, 2m 18.152s; 31 Talmacsi, 2m 18.153s; 32 Davies, 2m 18.231s; 33 Baldolini, 2m 18.445s; 34 Fabrizio, 2m 18.762s; 35 Toth, 2m 18.814s; 36 Kuzuhara, 2m 20.847s; 37 Angeloni, 2m 21.550s.

Fastest race laps: 1 Bianco, 2m 30.798s; 2 Giansanti, 2m 31.572s; 3 Jenkner, 2m 31.744s; 4 Poggiali, 2m 31.834s; 5 Ueda, 2m 31.867s; 6 Vincent, 2m 31.884s; 7 Hules, 2m 31.911s; 8 Sanna, 2m 32.470s; 9 Smrz, 2m 32.501s; 10 Pedrosa, 2m 32.683s; 11 Perugini, 2m 32.826s; 12 Aoyama, 2m 32.896s; 13 Rodriguez, 2m 33.152s; 14 Cecchinello, 2m 33.219s; 15 Azuma, 2m 33.472s; 16 Borsoi, 2m 33.660s; 17 Ballerini, 2m 33.859s; 18 Ui, 2m 34.087s; 19 Dovizioso, 2m 35.259s; 20 Nöhles, 2m 36.010s; 21 Fabrizio, 2m 36.235s; 22 Baldolini, 2m 36.626s; 23 Olivé, 2m 36.637s; 24 Kuzuhara, 2m 36.650s; 25 Barbera, 2m 36.942s; 26 Ogata, 2m 37.257s; 27 Angeloni, 2m 37.780s; 28 Toth, 2m 37.957s; 29 Kallio, 2m 38.166s; 30 Talmacsi, 2m 38.597s; 31 Davies, 2m 39.406s; 32 Chaemsap, 2m 39.810s; 33 Nieto, 2m 40.174s; 34 Müller, 2m 46.551s; 35 de Angelis, 2m 50.468s.

World Championship: 1 Vincent, 25; 2 Giansanti, 20; 3 Poggiali, 16; 4 Ueda, 13; 5 Sanna, 11; 6 Aoyama, 10; 7 Rodriguez, 9; 8 Pedrosa, 8; 9 Cecchinello, 7; 10 Borsoi, 6; 11 Perugini, 5; 12 Nöhles, 4; 13 Olivé, 3; 14 Baldolini, 2; 15 Jenkner, 1.

WELKOM

FIM WORLD CHAMPIONSHIP · ROUND 2

Above: Go!!!!!!!! It would have been Gauloises, but the GP had to find a new sponsor only days before the race.

Left: Melandri was in a field of his own for a lone 250 win.

Bottom far left: McWilliams was a threat, but the Protons were not yet reliable for their new pace.

Centre left: Capirossi's brave riding put his two-stroke among the front-row heavyweights.

Below left: Ukawa's win was a reward for persistence. It would be his last of the year.

Below: Garry McCoy was trying to ignore his leg injuries, but it was a losing battle.

All photographs: Gold & Goose

SOUTH AFRICAN GP

SUZUKA had shown the clear superiority of the four-strokes in both wet and dry. It was still too early to be completely sure, however, but if the two-strokes were ever going to get a chance to redress the balance, the battleground would have to be skewed in other ways. The second round provided such a chance. Literally.

For one, there was the nature of the track — very slow, very twisty. The 990s need some speed to show their real strength: we already knew that the corner speed of the lighter two-strokes is higher, and that in the bottom two gears they can accelerate at least as fast; and Welkom's straight is not particularly long. There was the unpredictable effect of the 4,400-ft altitude — though this might as easily favour the lower-tuned and less fussy four-strokes. In any case, if each type stood to lose some 15 per cent maximum power, the bigger engines would still be left with significantly more.

The real element of skew was the track surface. If it had been bumpy last year, it was even more so this, in spite of some resurfacing work. In the early hours of Saturday morning it became clear why. It was around 4 am when townsfolk and visitors alike were awoken by an earth tremor big enough to rattle the windows and awaken all the birds and animals, amid much squawking, barking, grunting and such like. Did the earth move for you too?

A regular event for Welkom — indeed, this gentle continental shrug is the reason why the gold-bearing reef is here close enough to the surface to be mined, and why the town is there at all, in the middle of an otherwise particularly featureless part of the high veld. But it does not bode well for the Phakisa Freeway, which each year looks more and more like a monumental folly, in spite of the manifest goodwill of the organisation. Erected by the provincial government four years before, the small-scale tri-oval banked part of the track has yet to be used in anger, and local pressmen who have driven on it at car launches report that it is also suffering badly from the shaky landscape, and it is now questionable whether it would be fit for racing, even if there was any racing to be done on it.

Another blow came from the central government, which unexpectedly and belatedly declined the so far virtually automatic waiver of legislation banning sporting tobacco sponsorship. Thus what had been on the calendar as the Gauloises Africa's GP lost its major sponsor, with just seven days to go before the start of practice.

More problems came during a farcical end to 125 qualifying. With two minutes left and everyone going for a time, the session was red-flagged after Azuma crashed, and his bike ended up in the middle of the track. This left just enough time after the restart to complete an out lap before the chequered flag, then one flying lap. Understandably the pack was rather keen to get going, setting off en masse when the marshals gave them the go-ahead in pit lane. To their surprise, halfway round they then came across the BMW safety car still circulating, an equally surprised Franco Uncini at the wheel. The flag had been shown prematurely, and the organisers were punished by a 10,000 Swiss francs fine. By this time, they were doubtless looking rather wistfully at a $10,000 dollar donation from an impromptu paddock collection, in support of a local charity for children stricken with Aids, in the HIV epidemic that is sweeping the country. They needed some charity on their own account too.

Anyway, the bikes did go out, on time, and it was interesting and educational to watch the way the different MotoGP versions did handle the bumps — the heavier four-strokes ploughing across them without getting so obviously out of shape, the two-strokes visibly thrown around more, but dancing across at an equally visible higher speed. It was an adventurous exercise for all, particularly early on in the lap, where the riders shut off to grab a left-hand apex before braking heavily for the first slow corner, right at the point where the road-racing track struck a seam where it crossed the banked oval. 'If the track continues to deteriorate at the same rate as over the past four years, it will be impossible to use next year,' said Jacque, whose feet were leaving the footrests there on fast laps; while Roberts quipped: 'I hear Honda's flying Ricky Carmichael in for final qualifying.'

The two-strokes were good in general: Capirossi singing an already familiar song about the hopelessness of his task, but still challenging strongly, leading practice on the first day; and Checa's popping and banging M1 Yamaha losing fourth place on the final lap to Kato's Honda. He was passed on the straight, and only narrowly held off Jacque's Yamaha two-stroke to the flag. He said later: 'His bike was faster than mine. That shows Yamaha what they need to do.' It was not quite that simple, since he'd also caught the visor of his helmet on the fairing as he ducked into the racing crouch, breaking his concentration — but the point was taken none the less.

The other drama concerned tyres, and the three-way battle in the top class. The Bridgestone runners were again gifted favourable conditions — their new rubber works well when it's wet or very hot, and glorious South African sunshine all weekend ensured the latter. Dunlop had responded to Michelin's new large-diameter 16.5-in. rear with a version of their own, but they came only in very restricted compounds, none of which was right, it seemed. The complaints of the Suzuki pair grew longer and louder, and their race performance seemed to prove it: Gibernau running off the track early on while disputing fifth, and eventually pitting to change the rear to finish plumb last; and Roberts stopping to change both tyres after running into dreadful handling problems. In fact, the cause was different, and the handling was even worse when he rejoined. The culprit, rather surprisingly, was a seizing steering damper. The stop in the pits had exposed the unit to even more heat off the V4 engine, and made it even stiffer. He retired.

In the scheme of things, it didn't make much difference. All weekend, messages were flying back and forth between Michelin in France, the factory race chiefs in Japan and the team. This would be Suzuki's last race on Dunlops.

Below: **Riba was hurt, and slow — and gave up the struggle to adapt to MotoGP pace.**

Bottom: **Clutch conundrum: Ukawa used the slipper clutch, Rossi was still using a stock one from his NSR. As a result, his wheels were out of line into as well as out of the turns.**
Both photographs: Gold & Goose

MOTOGP RACE – 28 laps

Suzuka's practice record was broken again, 19 out of 20 within 1.5 seconds, and only the injured Riba spoiling the picture, another 1.5 seconds down and struggling. By the second day Rossi and Capirossi were disputing pole, the four-stroke taking it by 32-thousandths, Ukawa third, and Biaggi making a late run for fourth. McCoy's two-stroke led row two, the Australian wrongly predicting that since he felt so much better, he didn't expect his injured leg to give him much trouble in the race. Roberts, Checa and Nakano completed the row, and an interesting mix of two- and four-strokes, with even the Protons on the pace — Aoki 11th, and McWilliams 16th, just 1.3 seconds down after challenging for pole on the first day. 'It's fun to be able to play with the big bikes,' he said.

The race was an ominous Honda benefit, albeit with a surprise winner, and Capirossi pushing the four-strokes hard for much of race distance, riding right on the very edge and only settling for third in the closing stages.

Rossi led away, shadowed by Ukawa and the heroic Capirossi, though by two-thirds distance the gap had grown to two seconds and he finally gave up the unequal struggle.

Rossi chose a softer tyre than Ukawa, and after 19 laps up front the gamble started to go wrong. He had already tried to escape, setting fastest lap; Ukawa responded with a new record of his own, and now looked steadier as Rossi started to suffer from wheelspin. And on lap 20, Ukawa was in front.

With three laps to go, Rossi reversed the positions. Now all he had to do was to hold on. But his tormentor could see his weakness, and wouldn't give up.

The last lap was a corker. Rossi left his braking late for one of the tight rights, slid out wide, and Ukawa pounced.

The champion attacked again into the last right, nosing ahead under braking. But he was sliding wide even as he did so, and on the exit Ukawa's tighter line and better grip saw him nip back ahead. At the end, he won by almost a second.

'It was just like our battles in the 250 class,' he beamed afterwards. Only with a different result.

Gibernau had started strongly to pass Roberts for fourth, fending off McCoy and Checa as his team-mate faded and eventually pitted for the first time. The Suzuki rider's run lasted seven laps, until Checa found his way past both of them and McCoy was leaning on him hard. A slide too far sent Gibernau off the track, to rejoin right at the back.

Checa had some clear air now, McCoy heading a two-stroke gang — Kato, Jacque, Barros, Abe and Nakano, nose to tail. Just like the good old days.

At two-thirds distance Jacque attacked Kato unsuccessfully, spurring his successor as 250 champion to greater efforts. At the same time McCoy was tiring and in pain, starting to drop backwards increasingly quickly.

Kato and Jacque now started closing on Checa, some 1.5 seconds ahead. By the last lap, they were on him, and Kato powered past to lead the four-stroke over the line.

The next trio were a couple of seconds adrift, Barros slipping to the back after running off line onto the slippery stuff. Then, with two laps to go, he hit one bump too many, and crashed out. Abe managed to fend off Nakano to the line.

By the finish, Biaggi's four-stroke had caught them up, but he complained that his problems with corner entry made overtaking too difficult to pass anyone except the slowing McCoy, who was tenth. Twenty long seconds behind came a still tentative V4 rookie van den Goorbergh, the only Bridgestone finisher. Harada was an unimpressive 13 seconds adrift, passing only Riba towards the end, the injured Spaniard hanging on to his rear wheel. Hopkins was a couple of seconds clear of Laconi, after an erratic ride with two off-track excursions; Gibernau finished 16th, a lap down, after pitting for a new rear.

McWilliams had a promising afternoon spoiled when his gearshift drum seized after five laps — he'd picked up three places (passing, among others, Biaggi) and was closing on Nakano when it happened; team-mate Aoki was looking for his own way past Biaggi when an oil leak sent him looping over the high side instead.

250 cc RACE – 26 laps

Battaini shaded a traffic-blocked Melandri for the second pole of his career, Rolfo's Honda and de Puniet completing the front row, knocking Nieto to fifth. Bright teenager Stoner was also on the second row, and the Australian took off in Melandri's wake, heading Locatelli and Rolfo, only to hit a big bump which sent him into a looping high-sider that he fought for what seemed like several seconds before succumbing.

Before long, Nieto and Battaini were moving forward, and the race settled for a spell — Melandri steadily pulling away, Locatelli a lonely second, then Battaini heading Nieto, de Puniet and Rolfo.

Towards half-distance, Battaini steadily closed up, de Puniet following on, Rolfo and Nieto dropping back. On lap 16, the race came alive. Battaini attacked Locatelli into a slow turn, the two touched and ran wide, and de Puniet dived through for three laps. Battaini hadn't given up, though, and he took him back to pull away for a safe second.

Behind, de Puniet's tyres were tired, and his wide lines gave Locatelli an opening on lap 22. By now Nieto was gaining speed as he burned off the fuel load, and was leaning on Rolfo. Both caught de Puniet, but Nieto wasn't to be stopped, setting fastest lap as he moved through to hound Locatelli. On the last lap, a hard pass pushed Locatelli wide, and both Nieto and Rolfo got by, de Puniet a little way back in sixth.

A long way back, Alzamora finally prevailed after what had been a big battle with the privateers. Porto was close behind, then Debon, Checa losing touch in tenth, well clear of Matsudo's Yamaha.

There were 17 finishers, Elias out of the points after a stop-and-go penalty for a jumped start.

125 cc RACE – 24 laps

Pedrosa was on pole again, and had gone quicker — that time disallowed by the red-flagged session; Cecchinello lost his front-row position for the same reason, while Vincent climbed up onto it, the only significant improvement after the restart.

Processional but tense, the first race saw a big group playing tactics and tyre preservation for the full distance. Pole-starter Pedrosa was the early leader, and then it went back and forth in a desultory fashion between Poggiali, Nieto and a couple of times Arnaud Vincent.

By the finish, there were still eight in the pack, and it was resolved on the last time round the twisting circuit, as Vincent's rather premature attack was firmly countered by Poggiali, with a well-judged first win of the year.

Vincent was second, then Pedrosa, after the misfortunate Nieto pushed slightly too hard one last time over the bumps, losing two places to take fifth behind Jenkner, a front-running presence throughout. Alex de Angelis was a close sixth, holding off Borsoi, who had caught up steadily. Sanna had dropped back by more than ten seconds at the finish.

Ui, Cecchinello, Smrz, Nöhles and Olivé were eliminated in a first-turn crash; Rodriguez crashed out after ten laps.

Above: Capirossi rode like a hero... and beat all the four-strokes, except the Hondas.

Left: At this time, Biaggi (with crew chief Fiorenzo Fanali) was still finding the Yamaha embarrassing.

Centre left: Battaini made the rostrum, and looked set for a revival in fortunes.

Below left: Tense procession: Pedrosa leads eventual 125 winner Poggiali, Nieto, Jenkner and Vincent.

All photographs: Gold & Goose

Left: Capirossi could be proud of third.

Below: Alex Debon... just another 250 rider who helped make Melandri's win that much easier.

Both photographs: Gold & Goose

Top left: Privateer 250s were left to bicker among themselves for the last points. Here Leon Haslam leads Dirk Heidolf and Jarno Janssen.

Above: Laconi's Aprilia was magnificently noisy, and usually frighteningly out of shape.

Right and above right: Mayhem — and a lucky escape, as Joan Olivé crashes in the thick of the 125 pack. Eventually four riders came down.

Below: The 250s blast away from the grid with Melandri in front and Casey Stoner (27) making an early impression.

All photographs: Gold & Goose

AFRICA'S
grand prix

round 2

21 APRIL 2002

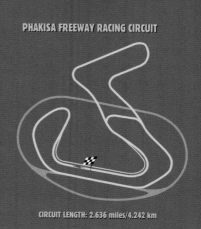

CIRCUIT LENGTH: 2.636 miles/4.242 km

MotoGP

28 laps, 73.808 miles/118.776 km

Pos.	Rider (Nat.)	No.	Machine	Laps	Time & speed
1	Tohru Ukawa (J)	11	Honda	28	44m 39.467s 99.159 mph/ 159.581 km/h
2	Valentino Rossi (I)	46	Honda	28	44m 40.399s
3	Loris Capirossi (I)	65	Honda	28	44m 47.726s
4	Daijiro Kato (J)	74	Honda	28	45m 06.429s
5	Carlos Checa (E)	7	Yamaha	28	45m 06.694s
6	Olivier Jacque (F)	19	Yamaha	28	45m 07.356s
7	Norick Abe (J)	6	Yamaha	28	45m 09.682s
8	Shinya Nakano (J)	56	Yamaha	28	45m 10.248s
9	Max Biaggi (I)	3	Yamaha	28	45m 23.263s
10	Garry McCoy (AUS)	8	Yamaha	28	45m 24.968s
11	Jurgen van den Goorbergh (NL)	17	Honda	28	45m 46.405s
12	Tetsuya Harada (J)	31	Honda	28	45m 59.027s
13	Pere Riba (E)	20	Yamaha	28	45m 59.324s
14	John Hopkins (USA)	21	Yamaha	28	46m 10.986s
15	Regis Laconi (F)	55	Aprilia	28	46m 12.192s
16	Sete Gibernau (E)	15	Suzuki	27	45m 09.539s
	Alex Barros (BR)	4	Honda	26	DNF
	Kenny Roberts (USA)	10	Suzuki	9	DNF
	Nobuatsu Aoki (J)	9	Proton KR	7	DNF
	Jeremy McWilliams (GB)	99	Proton KR	5	DNF

Fastest lap: Ukawa, 1m 34.834s, 100.059 mph/161.030 km/h (record).
Previous record: Valentino Rossi, I (Honda), 1m 35.508s, 99.354 mph/159.894 km/h (2001).
Event best maximum speed: Ukawa, 167.3 mph/269.3 km/h (free practice no. 2).
Qualifying: 1 Rossi, 1m 34.660s; 2 Capirossi, 1m 34.692s; 3 Ukawa, 1m 34.875s; 4 Biaggi, 1m 35.064s; 5 McCoy, 1m 35.378s; 6 Roberts, 1m 35.396s; 7 Checa, 1m 35.476s; 8 Nakano, 1m 35.508s; 9 Jacque, 1m 35.554s; 10 Gibernau, 1m 35.560s; 11 Aoki, 1m 35.695s; 12 van den Goorbergh, 1m 35.717s; 13 Barros, 1m 35.718s; 14 Kato, 1m 35.728s; 15 Abe, 1m 35.804s; 16 McWilliams, 1m 35.995s; 17 Hopkins, 1m 36.092s; 18 Laconi, 1m 36.161s; 19 Harada, 1m 36.164s; 20 Riba, 1m 37.623s.
Fastest race laps: 1 Ukawa, 1m 34.834s; 2 Rossi, 1m 34.960s; 3 Capirossi, 1m 35.256s; 4 Jacque, 1m 35.756s; 5 Kato, 1m 35.897s; 6 Nakano, 1m 35.950s; 7 Abe, 1m 35.959s; 8 Gibernau, 1m 35.997s; 9 McCoy, 1m 36.153s; 10 Checa, 1m 36.184s; 11 Barros, 1m 36.197s; 12 Roberts, 1m 36.282s; 13 Biaggi, 1m 36.387s; 14 Aoki, 1m 36.668s; 15 McWilliams, 1m 36.773s; 16 Laconi, 1m 36.816s; 17 Hopkins, 1m 37.118s; 18 van den Goorbergh, 1m 37.332s; 19 Harada, 1m 37.362s; 20 Riba, 1m 37.582s.
World Championship: 1 Rossi, 45; 2 Checa, 27; 3 Ukawa, 25; 4 Capirossi, 23; 5 Abe and Ryo, 20; 7 Kato, 19; 8 Itoh, 13; 9 Barros and Jacque, 10; 11 Aoki, Harada and Laconi, 9; 14 Nakano, 8; 15 Biaggi, 7; 16 Hopkins and McCoy, 6; 18 van den Goorbergh, 5; 19 Riba, 3.

250 cc

26 laps, 68.536 miles/110.292 km

Pos.	Rider (Nat.)	No.	Machine	Laps	Time & speed
1	Marco Melandri (I)	3	Aprilia	26	42m 52.922s 95.889 mph/ 154.319 km/h
2	Franco Battaini (I)	21	Aprilia	26	42m 55.884s
3	Fonsi Nieto (E)	10	Aprilia	26	42m 58.135s
4	Roberto Rolfo (I)	4	Honda	26	42m 59.212s
5	Roberto Locatelli (I)	15	Aprilia	26	42m 59.597s
6	Randy de Puniet (F)	17	Aprilia	26	43m 01.024s
7	Emilio Alzamora (E)	7	Honda	26	43m 15.493s
8	Sebastian Porto (ARG)	9	Yamaha	26	43m 17.093s
9	Alex Debon (E)	6	Aprilia	26	43m 21.083s
10	David Checa (E)	42	Aprilia	26	43m 29.183s
11	Naoki Matsudo (J)	8	Yamaha	26	43m 40.133s
12	Jay Vincent (GB)	12	Honda	26	43m 40.808s
13	Haruchika Aoki (J)	11	Honda	26	43m 46.028s
14	Dirk Heidolf (D)	28	Aprilia	26	43m 55.689s
15	Leon Haslam (GB)	19	Honda	26	43m 57.015s
16	Toni Elias (E)	24	Aprilia	26	44m 06.357s
17	Jarno Janssen (NL)	41	Honda	25	43m 22.163s
	Hector Faubel (E)	32	Aprilia	25	DNF
	Shahrol Yuzy (MAL)	18	Yamaha	25	DNF
	Raul Jara (E)	22	Aprilia	9	DNF
	Casey Stoner (AUS)	27	Aprilia	2	DNF
	Hugo Marchand (F)	51	Aprilia	1	DNF
	Vincent Philippe (F)	25	Aprilia	1	DNF
	Taro Sekiguchi (J)	76	Yamaha	0	DNF

Fastest lap: Nieto, 1m 37.860s, 96.966 mph/156.051 km/h.
Lap record: Marco Melandri, I (Aprilia), 1m 36.828s, 97.999 mph/157.714 km/h (2001).
Event best maximum speed: Debon, 152.4 mph/245.3 km/h (free practice no. 1).
Qualifying: 1 Battaini, 1m 37.604s; 2 Melandri, 1m 38.066s; 3 Rolfo, 1m 38.118s; 4 de Puniet, 1m 38.134s; 5 Nieto, 1m 38.185s; 6 Jara, 1m 38.542s; 7 Locatelli, 1m 38.546s; 8 Stoner, 1m 38.624s; 9 Debon, 1m 38.657s; 10 Matsudo, 1m 38.792s; 11 Alzamora, 1m 38.798s; 12 Porto, 1m 38.814s; 13 Aoki, 1m 38.943s; 14 Checa, 1m 39.152s; 15 Elias, 1m 39.165s; 16 Yuzy, 1m 39.465s; 17 Faubel, 1m 39.500s; 18 Haslam, 1m 39.578s; 19 Sekiguchi, 1m 39.716s; 20 Heidolf, 1m 39.764s; 21 Philippe, 1m 39.996s; 22 Vincent, 1m 40.094s; 23 Marchand, 1m 40.509s; 24 Janssen, 1m 40.792s.
Fastest race laps: 1 Nieto, 1m 37.860s; 2 Melandri, 1m 38.141s; 3 de Puniet, 1m 38.249s; 4 Rolfo, 1m 38.270s; 5 Battaini, 1m 38.337s; 6 Locatelli, 1m 38.474s; 7 Alzamora, 1m 38.644s; 8 Porto, 1m 38.744s; 9 Debon, 1m 38.959s; 10 Stoner, 1m 39.421s; 11 Faubel, 1m 39.474s; 12 Checa, 1m 39.501s; 13 Jara, 1m 39.521s; 14 Vincent, 1m 39.553s; 15 Elias, 1m 39.752s; 16 Aoki, 1m 39.772s; 17 Yuzy, 1m 39.893s; 18 Matsudo, 1m 39.963s; 19 Haslam, 1m 40.310s; 20 Heidolf, 1m 40.353s; 21 Janssen, 1m 41.020s; 22 Marchand, 1m 50.422s; 23 Philippe, 1m 50.777s.
World Championship: 1 Battaini and de Puniet, 26; 3 Melandri and Miyazaki, 25; 5 Alzamora, 22; 6 Rolfo, 21; 7 Sakai, 20; 8 Nieto and Porto, 19; 10 Matsudo, 15; 11 Debon, 14; 12 Locatelli, 11; 13 Kameya, 9; 14 Checa, 6; 15 Elias, 5; 16 Aoyama and Vincent, 4; 18 Aoki, 3; 19 Heidolf and Marchand, 2; 21 Haslam and Jara, 1.

125 cc

24 laps, 63.264 miles/101.808 km

Pos.	Rider (Nat.)	No.	Machine	Laps	Time & speed
1	Manuel Poggiali (RSM)	1	Gilera	24	41m 26.120s 91.604 mph/ 147.422 km/h
2	Arnaud Vincent (F)	21	Aprilia	24	41m 26.390s
3	Daniel Pedrosa (E)	26	Honda	24	41m 26.946s
4	Steve Jenkner (D)	17	Aprilia	24	41m 27.218s
5	Pablo Nieto (E)	22	Aprilia	24	41m 27.307s
6	Alex de Angelis (RSM)	15	Aprilia	24	41m 27.703s
7	Gino Borsoi (I)	23	Aprilia	24	41m 27.950s
8	Simone Sanna (I)	16	Aprilia	24	41m 38.959s
9	Masao Azuma (J)	5	Honda	24	41m 40.062s
10	Andrea Dovizioso (I)	34	Honda	24	41m 45.321s
11	Noboru Ueda (J)	9	Honda	24	41m 45.330s
12	Mika Kallio (SF)	36	Honda	24	42m 05.327s
13	Max Sabbatani (I)	11	Aprilia	24	42m 12.680s
14	Andrea Ballerini (I)	50	Honda	24	42m 19.830s
15	Michel Fabrizio (I)	84	Gilera	24	42m 19.988s
16	Mirko Giansanti (I)	6	Honda	24	42m 20.121s
17	Mattia Angeloni (I)	31	Gilera	24	42m 20.859s
18	Gabor Talmacsi (H)	8	Italjet	24	42m 21.006s
19	Jarno Müller (D)	10	Honda	24	42m 21.039s
20	Alex Baldolini (I)	19	Aprilia	24	42m 33.991s
21	Chaz Davies (GB)	57	Aprilia	24	42m 34.337s
22	Stefano Bianco (I)	33	Aprilia	24	42m 41.945s
23	Imre Toth (H)	20	Honda	24	43m 02.259s
24	Stefano Perugini (I)	7	Italjet	24	43m 09.575s
	Angel Rodriguez (E)	47	Aprilia	11	DNF
	Jaroslav Hules (CZ)	39	Aprilia	6	DNF
	Klaus Nöhles (D)	12	Honda	0	DNF
	Jakub Smrz (CZ)	18	Honda	0	DNF
	Joan Olivé (E)	25	Honda	0	DNF
	Lucio Cecchinello (I)	4	Aprilia	0	DNF
	Youichi Ui (J)	41	Derbi	0	DNF
	Hector Barbera (E)	80	Aprilia		DNS

Fastest lap: Poggiali, 1m 42.605s, 92.481 mph/148.834 km/h (record).
Previous record: Youichi Ui, J (Derbi), 1m 42.611s, 92.476 mph/148.826 km/h (2001).
Event best maximum speed: Poggiali, 131.1 mph/211.0 km/h (qualifying practice no. 2).
Qualifying: 1 Pedrosa, 1m 42.522s; 2 Poggiali, 1m 42.580s; 3 Nieto, 1m 42.588s; 4 Vincent, 1m 42.614s; 5 Cecchinello, 1m 42.852s; 6 Jenkner, 1m 42.975s; 7 Rodriguez, 1m 43.152s; 8 Borsoi, 1m 43.164s; 9 Hules, 1m 43.216s; 10 Bianco, 1m 43.219s; 11 Azuma, 1m 43.310s; 12 de Angelis, 1m 43.332s; 13 Olivé, 1m 43.502s; 14 Dovizioso, 1m 43.624s; 15 Sanna, 1m 43.677s; 16 Sanna, 1m 43.687s; 17 Ui, 1m 43.739s; 18 Müller, 1m 43.918s; 19 Kallio, 1m 43.944s; 20 Smrz, 1m 43.948s; 21 Giansanti, 1m 44.023s; 22 Sabbatani, 1m 44.078s; 23 Talmacsi, 1m 44.379s; 24 Perugini, 1m 44.518s; 25 Fabrizio, 1m 44.554s; 26 Barbera, 1m 44.725s; 27 Ballerini, 1m 44.975s; 28 Nöhles, 1m 44.979s; 29 Baldolini, 1m 45.499s; 30 Davies, 1m 45.577s; 31 Angeloni, 1m 45.831s; 32 Toth, 1m 46.736s.
Fastest race laps: 1 Poggiali, 1m 42.605s; 2 Sabbatani, 1m 42.687s; 3 Dovizioso, 1m 42.733s; 4 Bianco, 1m 42.742s; 5 Azuma, 1m 42.801s; 6 Pedrosa, 1m 42.808s; 7 de Angelis, 1m 42.817s; 8 Jenkner, 1m 42.892s; 9 Vincent, 1m 42.910s; 10 Nieto, 1m 42.919s; 11 Borsoi, 1m 42.933s; 12 Hules, 1m 43.127s; 13 Sanna, 1m 43.164s; 14 Ueda, 1m 43.167s; 15 Rodriguez, 1m 43.427s; 16 Kallio, 1m 43.461s; 17 Giansanti, 1m 43.950s; 18 Fabrizio, 1m 44.184s; 19 Müller, 1m 44.318s; 20 Talmacsi, 1m 44.336s; 21 Angeloni, 1m 44.386s; 22 Ballerini, 1m 44.648s; 23 Baldolini, 1m 44.781s; 24 Perugini, 1m 45.391s; 25 Davies, 1m 45.493s; 26 Toth, 1m 45.944s.
World Championship: 1 Vincent, 45; 2 Poggiali, 41; 3 Pedrosa, 24; 4 Giansanti, 20; 5 Sanna, 19; 6 Ueda, 18; 7 Borsoi, 15; 8 Jenkner, 14; 9 Nieto, 11; 10 Aoyama and de Angelis, 10; 12 Rodriguez, 9; 13 Azuma and Cecchinello, 7; 15 Dovizioso, 6; 16 Perugini, 5; 17 Kallio and Nöhles, 4; 19 Olivé and Sabbatani, 3; 21 Baldolini and Ballerini, 2; 23 Fabrizio, 1.

SPANISHGP

JEREZ

FIM WORLD CHAMPIONSHIP · ROUND 3

ROSSI resumed business as usual at Jerez. Or was it as usual? His race average time was a massive 24 seconds faster than his winning time last year, proving how the four-strokes have upped the pace. Then again, the top six at Jerez also beat last year's time — and four of them were on two-strokes just like the one he had used in 2001.

Statistics can be confusing. The track had been resurfaced, for one thing — it was smoother, but also more slippery, and the lap record was broken only in the top class. And Rossi had an easier run last year too — Biaggi crashing out and Capirossi taking an off-track adventure. This left only Abe to deal with — no problem.

The significance was Rossi's win, and that it might have been even faster. On the second lap in turn one he was hit hard from behind by Roberts's Suzuki, all but crashing. It dropped him from third to ninth, forcing a stirring recovery ride, at a track where the two-strokes were unexpectedly hard to beat in spite of the conspicuous advantage of the four-strokes down pit straight, one of only two places where the throttle is opened wide.

For 127,000 fans — Jerez now clearly outstrips Assen — it was the culmination of an eventful weekend laced with controversy. Biaggi had been black-flagged for the third time in his career, over-zealous police had invaded the track themselves trying to stop the spectators doing the same, earning a 15,000 Swiss francs fine for the organisers, and defending 125 champion Poggiali had been excluded for dangerous riding. But perhaps the most significant upset came in the three-way tyre wars, after Suzuki had dumped Dunlop just two races into the season.

The chain of events had begun at top factory level in Japan, where the decision to switch from their very long-standing dedication to the class-leading Michelins had last year dismayed riders and team... and also Dunlop, who knew full well that their return to the top class would not lead to overnight success. It was easy for them also to see the problems ahead. One was obvious: introducing another unknown element into the rush-job development of the GSV-R was a complication the team could have done without, and would doubtless say so. When the bike turned out to be much better than expected, and the tyres rather worse, at least at first, the ill-feeling was compounded... second in the wet at Suzuka had only flattered to deceive.

Frantic negotiation over the past fortnight had ended in a Suzuki U-turn, with Michelin in the driving seat. Doubtless 'original equipment' contracts for road bikes would ensue; in the meantime Michelin dictated a phased return to full partnership, not least to avoid upsetting their other MotoGP customers Honda and Yamaha, citing 'restricted production capacity' for a decision to supply Suzuki with 2001 tyres for the next 'three to five races', denying them the advantage of the latest large-diameter 16.5-in. tyres. Dunlop were obliged to take it on the chin; Roberts and Gibernau obliged to pronounce themselves pleased, which they did with sincerity. Indeed, the reason why Roberts hit Rossi was because he felt he had the machine combination to enable him to try hard, something he conspicuously avoids doing when things aren't right.

Track resurfacing was part of a major refit that wasn't quite finished. The pits themselves and some facilities had been upgraded, but much of the new building work was still in progress, including a spectacular circular VIP viewing platform over the start–finish straight, which remained windowless and empty; while race control was impressively equipped with closed-circuit TV monitoring, if little else. Everything that mattered was there, but all the same one wondered how Dorna would have reacted had a non-Spanish circuit been found in this condition at GP time.

The new $1-million Clinica Mobile was ready for an official launch, and the founder of the clinic, Dr Claudio Costa, also launched his autobiography at the same time. Proceeds of *Tears and triumph: my life in the Clinica Mobile* (published in Italian and English by Fucina srl of Milan) will go to the Clinica funds, and it will probably sell well, in spite of being extremely quirky — long on philosophical convolution and classical references, but short both on facts and clinical detail. One sentence might sum it up — Costa's grandiloquent description of a motor cycle: 'It is that animal part of the ancient centaur that safeguards our instincts and frees them to ride out and seek the answers to questions that torment us.'

Kenny Roberts had found an answer to the question that tormented him: what to do to stay in racing, revealing he had reached agreement with Proton for a MotoGP four-stroke next year. It would be 'a four- or five-cylinder', said Roberts slightly evasively, since they were already engaged on designing a V5. Which seemed an obvious choice, given the demonstrable superiority of the Honda, with four-cylinder merchants Yamaha and Suzuki still floundering somewhat, and the erratic three-cylinder Aprilia yet to convince that lighter weight and massive power are a successful combination. Although this truth was also possibly not true: racing boss Jan Witteveen confirmed that the bike was 'about 15 kg overweight. It would be very difficult to reach the minimum limit,' he told *MOTOCOURSE*. 'But we could very easily drop 10 kg, just by changing the materials. This is our first prototype: the casings are aluminium not magnesium, and we haven't used carbon-fibre. The priority is to develop the basics. It's also a matter of budget. Aprilia doesn't have the same money as Honda, and we are supporting racing programmes in 125 cc, 250 cc and Superbike as well as MotoGP.'

Alex Criville was at the track, to announce his retirement formally — he would not give details, but is thought to be suffering a form of epilepsy. Honda declined to lend him a bike for a lap of honour, which many thought churlish considering he had won them 15 500-class GPs and a championship; BMW filled the gap, with one of the open-topped circuit safety cars. Honda later made good, with a bike at Catalunya three races down the road, but remained the victims of some mirth when their grand new ex-Ferrari pit-wall structure was ordered removed minutes after having been erected. It exceeded the maximum width.

The quote of the meeting came from ex-500 GP winner Christian Sarron, visiting as a TV commentator for French EuroSport. Asked what he thought of the new four-strokes, he replied: 'They are really nice bikes. For girls.'

And the sign of the times came from new 125 entrant Jorge Lorenzo, obliged to miss the first day of qualifying because he was below the age limit. He turned 15 on Saturday, and celebrated by joining GP racing, qualifying 33rd. He displaced Welsh schoolboy Chaz Davies as the youngest rider in the World Championships.

Below: Ambushed by misfortune, Dunlop racing boss Jeremy Ferguson puts a brave face on the loss of the Suzuki team, and thinks about 250s instead. Photograph: Gold & Goose

Above: Happy 15th birthday came one day late for Jorge Lorenzo; he had to miss the first practice sessions.

Opposite page: An accident looking for a place... Barros (4) will outbrake Ukawa's faster Honda into turn one; behind, Roberts (10) is passing Kato (74), but on a collision course with Rossi.

Inset, anti-clockwise from left: Company for Carlos; victor Rossi side-saddles past riot police, who invaded the track on behalf of the capacity crowd; fans blow the trumpet for home winner Fonsi Nieto, on bike and on rostrum, with Uncle Angel and Rolfo. All photographs: Gold & Goose

MOTOGP · ROSSI · 250 cc · NIETO · 125 cc · CHECCHINELLO

MOTOGP RACE – 27 laps

The first all-Honda front row since 1998 was led again by Rossi, obliged to keep upping his pace by the chasing two-strokes; Barros just three-tenths down, then Capirossi and class rookie Kato, who had defeated Rossi here in pre-season tests.

Rossi led into the first corner, but his fuel-heavy four-stroke was no match for Barros's two-stroke, and he led lap one from Ukawa, Rossi, Kato and Roberts, who attacked Kato into turn one. Ill-advisedly. 'We need to improve our backshifting and clutch system before I can ride aggressively, and that was the perfect example. I braked pretty deep, the rear locked up, and I couldn't feel what gear I was in. I damn near took out Rossi, which was entirely my own fault,' he explained.

Roberts raised an arm in apology; Rossi narrowly stayed on the track, to resume the chase behind Biaggi, who had problems of his own. He'd crept forward on the startline, and though he'd stopped again it was still technically a jumped start. In the heat of the action of the next few laps, he missed the call-in for a stop-and-go penalty, leading inevitably to a black flag after six laps.

Ukawa blew past Barros second time down the back straight; on lap four Rossi did the same to Roberts to take third, and took two more to do it again to Barros, this time down the front straight.

Almost a quarter of the way into the race, Capirossi was quickly closing a two-second gap on the lead trio, while Kato had passed the slowing Roberts and was also closing. By half-distance, Ukawa led a group of five, from Rossi, Kato, Barros and Capirossi. Some way back, Checa was heading the next gang from Abe, Aoki (riding a blinder on the Proton, the heat favouring his Bridgestones) and Roberts, who had opted to settle for a safe finish on his less able tyres. A long way behind, slow-starting Gibernau was fending off McWilliams and Harada, with Laconi riding erratically behind them, then van den Goorbergh pressed by the feisty Hopkins. A disconsolate McCoy, who had qualified badly and was battling pain on the right-handers, was closing slowly.

Rossi said later his bike had been a handful when the fuel load was high, but now he was waiting his chance to pounce on Ukawa, and did so into turn one on lap 17, rapidly stretching away for a comfortable lead. Ukawa was under pressure from Kato, succumbing five laps later, the two-stroke then gaining ground at once. Barros was beginning to lose pace on worn-out tyres, and Capirossi took up the challenge, passing Ukawa for the first time into the final

hairpin on lap 24 to commence a desperate battle. Ukawa used his power to attack unsuccessfully into turn one, then Loris ran wide at the far hairpin and Tohru powered ahead on the exit. Loris attacked again at the last hairpin, but Ukawa accelerated narrowly past across the line... and so on and on. The issue was settled finally last time into the hairpin, where Ukawa successfully defended his line.

Barros was fifth, then Abe, relieved of the almost race-long frustration of crawling all over Checa's Yamaha in the turns only to be blown away on the straights when the red bike stuttered to a stop on the far side of the track with 'electrical trouble' while still disputing the position. 'It's better to break down on the last lap when you are sixth than when you are first,' he said philosophically.

Aoki had lost touch, then slowed on the last lap with fuel starvation on a low tank. He was still two seconds ahead of Roberts at the end. Then came Gibernau, Harada and Jacque — who had also jumped the start, but this time raced on after his stop-and-go. He had passed van den Goorbergh on the last lap, with both of them also getting by Laconi and McWilliams, his Proton suffering fuel starvation too, causing him to slow on the last lap, fearing a seize.

The order behind them on the road was McCoy, McWilliams, Hopkins and Laconi, but this was later altered by a controversial protest — McCoy and McWilliams at the back of it after being penalised five seconds apiece for passing Laconi under a yellow flag on the last lap (hung out because over-zealous police trying to prevent a crowd invasion had themselves come right up to the track-side). Since Laconi was very slow, and in fact stopped altogether soon after crossing the finish line, both were bitter. 'I was staring down his exhaust pipes... there was no way I could see the yellow flags,' said McCoy.

Nakano was well back, after falling early on and remounting; Riba had retired after two laps.

250 cc RACE – 26 laps

Battaini claimed pole by a clear half-second from Nieto and Melandri, with Porto's Yamaha upsetting the Aprilia party, and Rolfo's Honda fifth. Stoner had led at one point, ending an impressive seventh after his brakes failed and he crashed in the last session.

Melandri led away, but Nieto took over before the end of lap one, displaced from the third lap to the sixth by Locatelli. Close 250 racing had returned.

Above: Shiyozaki-san, long-time HRC engineer and head of the RCV211 V5 project, watches his baby win a third race in a row.

Top: Rossi, bottom left, recovers as Roberts waves an apology after their lap-two clash.

Both photographs: Gold & Goose

Battaini had moved to second by now, while Rolfo closed on the group steadily, and after Melandri had another lap up front the Italian moved ahead for a long spell in front of the brawling group. At the same time, Alzamora was closing gradually to make it a five-strong battle by lap 17. It would have been six, but de Puniet had fallen two laps earlier.

Nieto complained later that he'd again had trouble with a full fuel load, but as the end approached he was the fastest rider on the track, and easily outbraked Rolfo at the end of the back straight, the Italian settling for second as Nieto stretched away up front for his career-first win.

The battle for third went all the way to turn two on the penultimate lap. Melandri had displaced Battaini one turn before, but his compatriot fought back and they collided at the tight right. A disgruntled Melandri fell, Battaini ran across the gravel, and Alzamora could hardly belief his luck — the gift of third place at home in Spain.

Above left: Casey Stoner (16) had a strong ride to sixth, the youngest ever to score points in the 250 class.

Above: Pedrosa was a hero at home, but just missed the rostrum.

Left: A first ever win for Fonsi Nieto presaged a strong challenge for the 250 championship.

Below: Cecchinello leads Poggiali and de Angelis, who would later collide, with Vincent behind.

All photographs: Gold & Goose

Battaini got back on track ahead of Locatelli, who had lost touch with the group, and managed to fend him off to the finish. Then came Stoner, only five seconds back on an obviously slower bike... he'd been with the leaders earlier, then fended off Porto until the Argentine rider faded towards the end.

Debon had dropped even further back after running with this duo, but successfully defended eighth from Matsudo, with Elias another 11 seconds behind, just in front of Spanish rookie Hector Faubel. Aoki headed Yuzy, Bataille and Sekiguchi over the line in a close battle for the final points.

125 cc RACE – 23 laps

Pablo Nieto took his first-ever pole from Vincent and Poggiali, with de Angelis completing the front row. Poggiali was to lead until the final inches, fall, then cross the finish line tenth — but he won no points, and left the track clouded with controversy.

He had led away, with Jenkner taking over from laps six to 11, before slow starter Cecchinello caught up and moved to the front. He led until the finish. But there were six in the leading group, and lots of action to come as they tussled for position.

The worst of it happened on lap 21, on the way out of the double-right Angel Nieto corners near the end of the lap. De Angelis was in second; Poggiali wanted the position, and though he later claimed it was just a racing accident, it looked more like an assassination attempt as he came swerving across the track on the short straight and seemed to take his fellow San Marinan's front wheel out from under him. In fact his seat had jammed de Angelis's brake lever, but the effect was the same — a spectacular looping crash at high speed, from which de Angelis was very lucky to emerge without serious injury.

There was poetic justice to come, as Poggiali tried a hard pass on Cecchinello into the final hairpin for the last time. Instead he fell off, scrambling back to cross the line tenth. Sporting justice came after the race, when he was excluded for 'irresponsible riding'.

This left second to Vincent, half a second ahead of Jenkner for an all-Aprilia podium. Pedrosa had been with them, but was six seconds back at the finish, and five seconds ahead of the next group, headed by impressive Finnish rookie Mika Kallio from seasoned veterans Ui, Sanna and Azuma, with Olivé at the back of the group. Borsoi was a lonely tenth; Sabbatani headed the next gang.

MARLBORO SPANISH grand prix

round 3

5 MAY 2002

CIRCUITO DE JEREZ

Peluqui · Expo 92 · Angel Nieto · Michelin · Ducados · Dry Sack

CIRCUIT LENGTH: 2.748 miles/4.423 km

MotoGP

27 laps, 74.196 miles/119.421 km

Pos.	Rider (Nat.)	No.	Machine	Laps	Time & speed
1	Valentino Rossi (I)	46	Honda	27	46m 51.843s 95.004 mph/ 152.894 km/h
2	Daijiro Kato (J)	74	Honda	27	46m 53.033s
3	Tohru Ukawa (J)	11	Honda	27	46m 54.288s
4	Loris Capirossi (I)	65	Honda	27	46m 54.673s
5	Alex Barros (BR)	4	Honda	27	46m 55.960s
6	Norick Abe (J)	6	Yamaha	27	47m 10.360s
7	Nobuatsu Aoki (J)	9	Proton KR	27	47m 23.628s
8	Kenny Roberts (USA)	10	Suzuki	27	47m 25.719s
9	Sete Gibernau (E)	15	Suzuki	27	47m 30.605s
10	Tetsuya Harada (J)	31	Honda	27	47m 31.818s
11	Olivier Jacque (F)	19	Yamaha	27	47m 39.339s
12	Jurgen van den Goorbergh (NL)	17	Honda	27	47m 39.773s
13	John Hopkins (USA)	21	Yamaha	27	47m 42.092s
14	Regis Laconi (F)	55	Aprilia	27	47m 42.527s
15	Garry McCoy (AUS)	8	Yamaha	27	47m 45.136s
16	Jeremy McWilliams (GB)	99	Proton KR	27	47m 46.014s
17	Shinya Nakano (J)	56	Yamaha	27	48m 15.857s
	Carlos Checa (E)	7	Yamaha	26	DNF
	Pere Riba (E)	20	Yamaha	2	DNF
	Max Biaggi (I)	3	Yamaha		EXC

Fastest lap: Rossi, 1m 42.920s, 96.132 mph/154.710 km/h (record).

Previous record: Valentino Rossi, I (Honda), 1m 43.779s, 95.336 mph/153.429 km/h (2001).

Event best maximum speed: Ukawa, 171.9 mph/276.6 km/h (qualifying practice no. 2).

Qualifying: 1 Rossi, 1m 42.193s; 2 Barros, 1m 42.504s; 3 Capirossi, 1m 42.558s; 4 Kato, 1m 42.691s; 5 Checa, 1m 42.889s; 6 Ukawa, 1m 42.921s; 7 Biaggi, 1m 42.955s; 8 Jacque, 1m 43.047s; 9 Roberts, 1m 43.077s; 10 Abe, 1m 43.385s; 11 Harada, 1m 43.521s; 12 McWilliams, 1m 43.627s; 13 Gibernau, 1m 43.633s; 14 Nakano, 1m 43.784s; 15 Aoki, 1m 43.878s; 16 Hopkins, 1m 43.916s; 17 van den Goorbergh, 1m 44.142s; 18 McCoy, 1m 44.212s; 19 Laconi, 1m 44.597s; 20 Riba, 1m 45.575s.

Fastest race laps: 1 Rossi, 1m 42.920s; 2 Kato, 1m 43.111s; 3 Capirossi, 1m 43.363s; 4 Ukawa, 1m 43.446s; 5 Barros, 1m 43.568s; 6 Jacque, 1m 43.844s; 7 Abe, 1m 43.963s; 8 Checa, 1m 43.992s; 9 Roberts, 1m 44.191s; 10 Biaggi, 1m 44.395s; 11 Aoki, 1m 44.476s; 12 Nakano, 1m 44.507s; 13 McWilliams, 1m 44.641s; 14 Gibernau, 1m 44.737s; 15 McCoy, 1m 44.761s; 16 van den Goorbergh, 1m 44.828s; 17 Hopkins, 1m 44.885s; 18 Harada, 1m 44.943s; 19 Laconi, 1m 45.008s; 20 Riba, 1m 47.034s.

World Championship: 1 Rossi, 70; 2 Ukawa, 41; 3 Kato, 39; 4 Capirossi, 36; 5 Abe, 30; 6 Checa, 27; 7 Barros, 21; 8 Ryo, 20; 9 Aoki, 18; 10 Harada and Jacque, 15; 12 Itoh, 13; 13 Laconi, 11; 14 Hopkins and van den Goorbergh, 9; 16 Nakano and Roberts, 8; 18 Biaggi, Gibernau and McCoy, 7; 21 Riba, 3.

Left: Midway through the 250 race, and Rolfo leads from Melandri, Nieto, Locatelli and de Puniet, with Porto just coming into view.
Photograph: Gold & Goose

---

250 cc

26 laps, 71.448 miles/114.998 km

Pos.	Rider (Nat.)	No.	Machine	Laps	Time & speed
1	Fonsi Nieto (E)	10	Aprilia	26	46m 03.241s 93.094 mph/ 149.821 km/h
2	Roberto Rolfo (I)	4	Honda	26	46m 05.228s
3	Emilio Alzamora (E)	7	Honda	26	46m 08.596s
4	Franco Battaini (I)	21	Aprilia	26	46m 14.725s
5	Roberto Locatelli (I)	15	Aprilia	26	46m 15.223s
6	Casey Stoner (AUS)	27	Aprilia	26	46m 19.717s
7	Sebastian Porto (ARG)	9	Yamaha	26	46m 27.228s
8	Alex Debon (E)	6	Aprilia	26	46m 36.414s
9	Naoki Matsudo (J)	8	Yamaha	26	46m 36.714s
10	Toni Elias (E)	24	Aprilia	26	46m 47.252s
11	Hector Faubel (E)	32	Aprilia	26	46m 50.288s
12	Haruchika Aoki (J)	11	Honda	26	46m 51.824s
13	Shahrol Yuzy (MAL)	18	Yamaha	26	47m 04.338s
14	Eric Bataille (F)	34	Honda	26	47m 04.361s
15	Taro Sekiguchi (J)	76	Yamaha	26	47m 04.670s
16	Raul Jara (E)	22	Aprilia	26	47m 04.900s
17	Jay Vincent (GB)	12	Honda	26	47m 10.134s
18	Vincent Philippe (F)	25	Aprilia	26	47m 12.954s
19	Leon Haslam (GB)	19	Honda	26	47m 18.974s
20	Jarno Janssen (NL)	41	Honda	25	47m 49.697s
	Marco Melandri (I)	3	Aprilia	25	DNF
	Randy de Puniet (F)	17	Aprilia	15	DNF
	David Checa (E)	42	Aprilia	4	DNF
	Hugo Marchand (F)	51	Aprilia	3	DNF
	Dirk Heidolf (D)	28	Aprilia	0	DNF
	Luis Castro (E)	39	Yamaha		DNQ

Fastest lap: Nieto, 1m 45.243s, 94.010 mph/151.295 km/h.

Lap record: Daijiro Kato, J (Honda), 1m 44.444s, 94.729 mph/152.452 km/h (2001).

Event best maximum speed: Elias, 155.0 mph/249.5 km/h (free practice no. 2).

Qualifying: 1 Battaini, 1m 44.803s; 2 Nieto, 1m 45.268s; 3 Melandri, 1m 45.323s; 4 Porto, 1m 45.499s; 5 Rolfo, 1m 45.580s; 6 de Puniet, 1m 45.596s; 7 Stoner, 1m 45.648s; 8 Debon, 1m 45.694s; 9 Alzamora, 1m 45.915s; 10 Elias, 1m 46.170s; 11 Locatelli, 1m 46.253s; 12 Matsudo, 1m 46.293s; 13 Jara, 1m 46.502s; 14 Checa, 1m 46.545s; 15 Aoki, 1m 46.630s; 16 Sekiguchi, 1m 47.147s; 17 Faubel, 1m 47.173s; 18 Yuzy, 1m 47.241s; 19 Vincent, 1m 47.830s; 20 Janssen, 1m 48.022s; 21 Bataille, 1m 48.027s; 22 Marchand, 1m 48.068s; 23 Philippe, 1m 48.068s; 24 Haslam, 1m 48.248s; 25 Heidolf, 1m 48.972s; 26 Castro, 1m 54.539s.

Fastest race laps: 1 Nieto, 1m 45.243s; 2 Battaini, 1m 45.349s; 3 Alzamora, 1m 45.363s; 4 Rolfo, 1m 45.394s; 5 Melandri, 1m 45.494s; 6 Locatelli, 1m 45.586s; 7 de Puniet, 1m 45.688s; 8 Stoner, 1m 46.047s; 9 Porto, 1m 46.176s; 10 Debon, 1m 46.395s; 11 Aoki, 1m 46.568s; 12 Matsudo, 1m 46.703s; 13 Elias, 1m 46.790s; 14 Faubel, 1m 47.013s; 15 Sekiguchi, 1m 47.267s; 16 Checa, 1m 47.441s; 17 Bataille, 1m 47.453s; 18 Yuzy, 1m 47.492s; 19 Jara, 1m 47.681s; 20 Haslam, 1m 47.979s; 21 Vincent, 1m 48.010s; 22 Philippe, 1m 48.025s; 23 Marchand, 1m 48.605s; 24 Janssen, 1m 49.385s.

World Championship: 1 Nieto, 44; 2 Rolfo, 41; 3 Battaini, 39; 4 Alzamora, 38; 5 Porto, 28; 6 de Puniet, 26; 7 Melandri and Miyazaki, 25; 9 Debon, Locatelli and Matsudo, 22; 12 Sakai, 20; 13 Elias, 11; 14 Stoner, 10; 15 Kameya, 9; 16 Aoki, 7; 17 Checa, 6; 18 Faubel, 5; 19 Aoyama and Vincent, 4; 21 Yuzy, 3; 22 Bataille, Heidolf and Marchand, 2; 25 Haslam, Jara and Sekiguchi, 1.

---

125 cc

23 laps, 63.204 miles/101.729 km

Pos.	Rider (Nat.)	No.	Machine	Laps	Time & speed
1	Lucio Cecchinello (I)	4	Aprilia	23	42m 08.107s 90.012 mph/ 144.861 km/h
2	Arnaud Vincent (F)	21	Aprilia	23	42m 10.381s
3	Steve Jenkner (D)	17	Aprilia	23	42m 10.880s
4	Daniel Pedrosa (E)	26	Honda	23	42m 16.725s
5	Mika Kallio (SF)	36	Honda	23	42m 21.196s
6	Youichi Ui (J)	41	Derbi	23	42m 21.731s
7	Simone Sanna (I)	16	Aprilia	23	42m 23.288s
8	Masao Azuma (J)	5	Honda	23	42m 27.223s
9	Joan Olivé (E)	25	Honda	23	42m 27.292s
10	Gino Borsoi (I)	23	Aprilia	23	42m 32.300s
11	Max Sabbatani (I)	11	Aprilia	23	42m 42.617s
12	Hector Barbera (E)	80	Aprilia	23	42m 42.670s
13	Jakub Smrz (CZ)	18	Honda	23	42m 45.422s
14	Mirko Giansanti (I)	6	Honda	23	42m 46.057s
15	Andrea Ballerini (I)	50	Honda	23	42m 48.004s
16	Stefano Perugini (I)	7	Italjet	23	43m 05.800s
17	Noboru Ueda (J)	9	Honda	23	43m 12.042s
18	Michel Fabrizio (I)	84	Gilera	23	43m 12.066s
19	Stefano Bianco (I)	33	Aprilia	23	43m 12.078s
20	Gabor Talmacsi (H)	8	Italjet	23	43m 13.355s
21	Alex Baldolini (I)	19	Aprilia	23	43m 13.622s
22	Jorge Lorenzo (E)	48	Derbi	23	43m 19.468s
23	Mattia Angeloni (I)	31	Gilera	23	43m 21.224s
24	Chaz Davies (GB)	57	Aprilia	23	43m 26.014s
25	Alvaro Bautista (E)	51	Aprilia	23	43m 28.721s
26	Jarno Müller (D)	10	Honda	23	43m 31.281s
27	Imre Toth (H)	20	Honda	23	43m 58.299s
	Klaus Nöhles (D)	12	Honda	22	DNF
	Alex de Angelis (RSM)	15	Aprilia	21	DNF
	Andrea Dovizioso (I)	34	Honda	21	DNF
	Julian Simon (E)	52	Honda	14	DNF
	Pablo Nieto (E)	22	Honda	8	DNF
	Jaroslav Hules (CZ)	39	Aprilia	7	DNF
	Angel Rodriguez (E)	47	Aprilia	6	DNF
	Manuel Poggiali (RSM)	1	Gilera		EXC
	Ruben Catalan (E)	71	Aprilia		DNS

Fastest lap: Cecchinello, 1m 48.620s, 91.087 mph/146.591 km/h.

Lap record: Masao Azuma, J (Honda), 1m 48.385s, 91.285 mph/146.909 km/h (2001).

Event best maximum speed: Nieto, 138.0 mph/221.1 km/h (race).

Qualifying: 1 Nieto, 1m 49.018s; 2 Vincent, 1m 49.186s; 3 Poggiali, 1m 49.227s; 4 de Angelis, 1m 49.248s; 5 Jenkner, 1m 49.287s; 6 Cecchinello, 1m 49.494s; 7 Borsoi, 1m 49.786s; 8 Pedrosa, 1m 49.799s; 9 Sanna, 1m 49.831s; 10 Dovizioso, 1m 49.936s; 11 Ui, 1m 50.029s; 12 Olivé, 1m 50.074s; 13 Perugini, 1m 50.089s; 14 Rodriguez, 1m 50.130s; 15 Giansanti, 1m 50.157s; 16 Barbera, 1m 50.335s; 17 Kallio, 1m 50.541s; 18 Bianco, 1m 50.568s; 19 Azuma, 1m 51.054s; 20 Smrz, 1m 51.101s; 21 Ueda, 1m 51.104s; 22 Talmacsi, 1m 51.144s; 23 Sabbatani, 1m 51.306s; 24 Müller, 1m 51.632s; 25 Hules, 1m 51.777s; 26 Bautista, 1m 51.806s; 27 Nöhles, 1m 51.833s; 28 Davies, 1m 51.849s; 29 Simon, 1m 52.273s; 30 Ballerini, 1m 52.297s; 31 Baldolini, 1m 52.388s; 32 Fabrizio, 1m 52.661s; 33 Lorenzo, 1m 52.734s; 34 Angeloni, 1m 53.395s; 35 Toth, 1m 53.751s; 36 Catalan, 1m 53.885s.

Fastest race laps: 1 Cecchinello, 1m 48.620s; 2 Rodriguez, 1m 49.039s; 3 Vincent, 1m 49.140s; 4 Jenkner, 1m 49.176s; 5 de Angelis, 1m 49.233s; 6 Ui, 1m 49.286s; 7 Kallio, 1m 49.337s; 8 Pedrosa, 1m 49.348s; 9 Sanna, 1m 49.403s; 10 Nieto, 1m 49.417s; 11 Azuma, 1m 49.510s; 12 Bianco, 1m 49.513s; 13 Olivé, 1m 49.554s; 14 Barbera, 1m 49.585s; 15 Sabbatani, 1m 49.626s; 16 Dovizioso, 1m 49.766s; 17 Borsoi, 1m 49.786s; 18 Giansanti, 1m 50.116s; 19 Ballerini, 1m 50.237s; 20 Smrz, 1m 50.450s; 21 Perugini, 1m 50.785s; 22 Ueda, 1m 51.409s; 23 Baldolini, 1m 51.434s; 24 Fabrizio, 1m 51.456s; 25 Angeloni, 1m 51.526s; 26 Nöhles, 1m 51.561s; 27 Talmacsi, 1m 51.578s; 28 Davies, 1m 51.764s; 29 Bautista, 1m 51.788s; 30 Lorenzo, 1m 51.860s; 31 Simon, 1m 51.938s; 32 Müller, 1m 52.337s; 33 Hules, 1m 52.555s; 34 Toth, 1m 53.211s.

World Championship: 1 Vincent, 65; 2 Poggiali, 41; 3 Pedrosa, 37; 4 Cecchinello, 32; 5 Jenkner, 30; 6 Sanna, 28; 7 Giansanti, 22; 8 Borsoi, 21; 9 Ueda, 18; 10 Azuma and Kallio, 15; 12 Nieto, 11; 13 Aoyama, de Angelis, Olivé and Ui, 10; 17 Rodriguez, 9; 18 Sabbatani, 8; 19 Dovizioso, 6; 20 Perugini, 5; 21 Barbera and Nöhles, 4; 23 Ballerini and Smrz, 3; 25 Baldolini, 2; 26 Fabrizio, 1.

FRENCH GP

LE MANS

FIM WORLD CHAMPIONSHIP · ROUND 4

THE four-strokes have brought back more than musical exhausts... also the obsessive secrecy that was such a watchword to the Japanese companies in particular. When the bikes have been more or less the same as one another for more than 15 years, security was less obsessive. Not any longer...

Something was certainly different about the Yamahas when they arrived in France in flying form. First, they were visibly entering and thus leaving the corners better — the riders able to stamp down the gearbox without blipping the throttle and without the rear-wheel lock-up that had plagued them at earlier races. Second, they'd stopped sounding like World War Three every time the throttles were closed. No more embarrassing crepitations. Finally, they put up a very strong challenge to the Hondas.

The broad details were given freely enough. The upgrade was primarily electronic, had tested successfully at Mugello the week before, and had been directed at the crucial corner-entry phase. The key element was upgraded software for the two-stage slipper clutch, which supplements the usual centrifugal action with a hydraulic/electronic over-ride. This was intriguing enough: reading parameters including speed, front rear wheel speed, gear and throttle positions and even circuit location to measure out the degree of slippage required for the circumstances. The newly clean exhaust over-run was not a gift of fuel injection, as some suspected, but new carburettor electronics.

Real details were hard to come by, however. Since Yamaha were still coy about basics like cam drive and the exact capacity of the engine, greater intimacies were closely guarded. Clearly, however, the red bikes had achieved something of a breakthrough.

This cast a different light on some disparaging pre-event remarks by Rossi. Only Honda had really tackled the four-stroke problem, he opined, taking risks with fresh thinking and lots of new ideas. The others had aimed only at beating the 500 two-strokes... and it was not enough. 'The Suzuki is a good bike, and when they get the best tyres they will go faster,' he said, citing Ryo's better wet-weather throttle control at Suzuka as a revealing counterpoint to his Honda's biggest difficulty — too much power too soon. The Yamaha had impressed him less. 'They can improve — but I believe the ultimate potential of the M1 is only to stay with the two-strokes,' he said. This barb may not have been perfectly timed, while a very narrow victory in the rain-shortened GP undermined it still more.

Yamaha's spurt of development highlighted a four-stroke key — engine braking. Rossi also said that his tail-sliding corner entries were 'for show, not to go fast'; although Honda appeared to have avoided too much wheel-dragging without resorting to the same levels of electronics as Yamaha — in the climate of secrecy who could be sure of that? Another accomplished backer-in is Gibernau, especially in the wet, and the Suzuki team were fresh from wet testing at Michelin's track near Clermont Ferrand. Like Rossi, he pointed out that although it might look otherwise, backing in doesn't actually help you turn, and means 'it takes longer to get hooked up for a good exit'.

The threatened (or, for Suzuki, still on last year's rubber, promising) rain never came properly, only enough to shorten the main event by seven of 28 laps, leaving a substantial crowd rather short-changed. The consequences of the abbreviated afternoon were far-reaching. Urgent discussions resulted in a major policy change applied very abruptly mid-meeting three races down the road. The smaller classes were unaffected, but MotoGP races would have to run the requisite number of laps, with a restart, no matter how much of the distance had been completed.

The track was changed. From the Dunlop Bridge, the path of the 24-hour course into the Esses had been gently curved. The Bugatti circuit turns right off the section as before... but the previous slow U-turn had been replaced by a faster and more interesting corner. This one change had a significant effect, as was seen at Jerez some years ago, introducing a much-needed element of flow which reduced the former emphasis on drag-strip acceleration and braking, and helped both Roberts, with his best finish so far, and his father's Protons, at a track they'd been dreading. The change cut 125 metres from the lap, and marginally upped the average speed. Another small proof that, for motor cycles, faster corners invariably make for closer racing.

Kato was feeling the pinch of his position as HRC favourite, at the expense of the promise shown at the last race. He had experimental parts including a swing-arm and a different-spec motor, and when he crashed in the race, he enigmatically suggested afterwards that the bike had been rather hard to ride. Honda insiders gave a knowing nod. Mick Doohan regularly refused such testing requests point blank; Kato's status is different, and he was obliged to agree.

For the French, the big news was a comeback for Jean-Michel Bayle, whose GP career had run out of steam with injury in 1999, without coming even anywhere close to his heroic success levels on the dirt. The excitement was overblown, as at his debut in 1992, and was to prove short-lived.

For the rest, the important side of this story concerned the person he was replacing: Garry McCoy, who had finally cried enough after Friday morning's free practice, pulling out for the next few races to give his right leg a chance to heal once and for all. One can only imagine the level of pain that finally stopped him, after fighting through it at the previous three rounds. Neither team manager Clifford nor a series of worrying problems — a screw coming loose in Japan, agony in Spain, and now fresh X-rays that showed another screw had bent or even broken in situ — had been able to prevent this exemplary hero from having a go anyway. Which is, after all, his job. Not for the last time this season, the affair raised all sorts of questions about the probity of a medical system that fails to provide safeguards in this and other similar cases.

Something in the nature of concrete news at last from the MZ GP effort — but entirely negative. Contracted rider Cardoso had been 'temporarily released' to take the place of Riba in the Antena Yamaha team, and did not expect to be called back.

Lucio Cecchinello became the first person this year to take advantage of ship-to-shore radio rules allowing communication between pits and active rider. He used it to some effect in practice, finding it perfect for half the lap, useless for the rest. Some way to go yet... but the way the MotoGP race panned out, when they are working properly, it won't be before time.

Top: Never say die: McCoy gives it his all in practice, before conceding defeat.

Above: Bayle had tested the Red Bull Yamaha earlier in the year, and was hastily drafted in as a handy replacement.

Right: Kato was catching the leaders on his test-spec NSR, until it bit him.

Below: Red flags denied the crowd the climax of the big race. Never again, said the authorities.

Bottom: The eyes have it — Laconi survives yet another moment on the fast but wayward Aprilia.

Opposite page: Genius, clown and serial winner, Rossi acknowledges the adulation.
All photographs: Gold & Goose

Below: Roberts was half way to the tyres he wanted, but got his best result all the same.

Below centre left: Van den Goorbergh slugs it out with Nakano and Bayle for the last points on the table.

Below centre right: Aoki demonstrates the phenomenal cornering performance of the KR3 — Proton had dreaded the track, were surprised by a double top-ten finish.

Bottom: Abe took fourth and was top two-stroke, after yet another frustrating afternoon.
All photographs: Gold & Goose

MOTOGP RACE – 21 laps (from 28)

Practice was again hectic and close — discounting rusty Cardoso, the gap from full-house pole-man Rossi to 19th-placed rookie Hopkins was just 1.66 seconds. Checa was a meagre seven-hundredths slower, then Biaggi and Ukawa — the first-ever all-four-stroke MotoGP front row. Kato led row two from a surprised McWilliams and Capirossi.

For the first seven laps, a two-by-two parade up front resembled F1, pairs of team-mates reflecting the level of their machines. Rossi escorted Ukawa at the front, then Biaggi headed Checa, the Yamahas losing a few tenths each lap. The Suzukis hadn't joined the party, with Roberts tenth and Gibernau 11th.

Capirossi was fifth, heading Abe. Aoki had started well, and was briefly sixth — McWilliams was back in 15th on lap one after a slow getaway. Kato was soon moving forward from seventh, Roberts following on a couple of places behind, passing Nakano and then Aoki. But he couldn't match Kato's surge as the rookie found his rhythm, despatching Abe and then even Capirossi to start closing on the leaders.

At the same time, the pair of Yamahas started to close a gap that had never got bigger than 1.3 seconds.

The first big upset, on lap eight, came in the battle for tenth, where an on-form Harada had managed to get ahead of Nakano, only to run across the first part of the chicane at the end of the back straight. He rejoined, spraying gravel, and ricocheting off Nakano's Gauloises Yamaha straight into Jacque's identical bike. Harada survived for the moment, pitting, rejoining, then retiring. Nakano was left struggling with a bent handlebar; Jacque collected a gravel chip in his front hub, damaging the disc and putting him out of his home race.

That was not all. When the leaders came round, Checa was at the back of a close quartet, tucked in down the straight. He missed warning flags, and while the front three managed to avoid Harada's gravel, he didn't. Down he went.

By now, rain was more than threatening... actually spotting at some points. Lap times slowed accordingly by as much as two seconds, but Rossi blamed his own mistake rather than the surface after slowing on lap ten, balking Ukawa somewhat so that Biaggi was able to pounce on them both to lead. 'I tried to get away, but instead I had a big slide.'

Rossi was now third, and had another consideration: Kato was closing rapidly and would soon challenge. Then he also fell, from his hard-to-ride development NSR. Up front, Ukawa had surged past Biaggi on the start–finish straight, but the leading trio were glued together for six laps until Ukawa pushed again, and suddenly claimed a full second from Biaggi. It was lap 18 of a scheduled 28, not quite two-thirds distance, with conditions looking ever more threatening. The race might have to be stopped at any moment.

Rossi clearly understood the implications without needing special pit signals. He needed to be in front. Pretty soon, the lap-by-lap order might become

the final result. He'd been haunting Biaggi's rear wheel, and now moved inside at the end of the back straight to chase and close down on his team-mate rapidly enough to pass him on the tight corner before the back straight on the 21st lap. It was to prove crucial.

He led one more, then early on the 23rd slowed and raised his hand. Almost simultaneously the red flag came out in response to reports from marshals. The race was over, results were taken back two laps. And Rossi had won.

Who knows what another seven laps might have brought? Abe had already shot his bolt, closing impressively on Biaggi but then falling in line behind after a few half-hearted-looking attacks had been easily thwarted by the four-stroke's beefy acceleration.

Roberts was seven seconds behind in fifth, his best so far. For some time he'd been holding up Aoki, the Proton faster almost everywhere, the Suzuki claiming seniority and maintaining control by straight-line speed. Then the Japanese rider's Bridgestones gave up the ghost and he fell away, lucky that the race was stopped when it was. His tyres would not have gone very much further.

Capirossi had little fight in him, still shocked and depressed after a road accident in Italy in which an elderly cyclist had died, and was losing ground in seventh. 'I have not been myself, and I only wanted to finish,' he said later.

Barros was three seconds behind, his engine off song, ahead of Laconi after a brave run on the fast but wayward Aprilia, 17 seconds behind the leader in the bike's best dry finish. McWilliams was four seconds back, with rear tyre 'pulsing'; Hopkins was a best-yet 11th, after the satisfaction of over-taking the chatter-and-slide-troubled Gibernau's Suzuki. Nakano's bent Yamaha was pushing him; Bayle hard up behind, then van den Goorbergh dropping away with his own worn-out Bridgestone problems. Cardoso was six seconds back, 16th and last.

---

250 cc RACE – 26 laps

Nieto claimed his second pole of the season to head an all-Aprilia front row from de Puniet — who had crashed twice trying for a home-race pole — Locatelli and Melandri, who was battling pain from his Jerez foot injury. Elias and Stoner were two impressive faces on the second row.

Left: Line astern... the upgraded Yamahas are close together, Biaggi leading Checa, as they chase down the Hondas.

Bottom: Nieto and Melandri were inches apart, all the way to the flag.
Both photographs: Gold & Goose

Top right: De Puniet was thrilled to get his second podium of the season (and his career) at home.

Centre right: Locatelli was a continual annoyance to the leaders, but ultimately outpaced.

Bottom: Evergreen Lucio Cecchinello leads Poggiali, Borsoi, Pedrosa and the pack. He held the lead to the finish.

All photographs: Gold & Goose

Melandri led away, then Locatelli took the lead from laps three to ten. Nieto, de Puniet plus Stoner made five up front, until the Australian crashed out spectacularly, just as Battaini closed up to take his place, only to fall himself soon afterwards.

By half-distance, the leading four were spacing out, Melandri chasing Nieto as de Puniet and Locatelli lost ground slowly.

Two laps later, Melandri started to attack. He and Nieto between them set a series of fastest laps, with neither finding any advantage. Lap 25 saw Nieto slow to let Melandri past into the first slow right, only to dive back ahead at the next bend. He did the same thing at the back chicane. 'Neither of us wanted to lead onto the last lap,' said Nieto, who found himself in that position nevertheless. He managed to defend it, to win by less than a quarter of a second.

Six seconds behind, de Puniet did the same to Locatelli, who had also come back for a final attack.

Rolfo had been boxed on the early laps, and never got closer than five seconds to the last of the Aprilias. Had the race been a couple of laps longer he might have had trouble from Elias, who had a remarkable catch-up ride after colliding with Aoki in the early laps and dropping to 13th. He set third-fastest lap as he charged through, catching Alzamora with two laps to go, and easily despatching the factory Honda rider for a best-so-far sixth.

Porto had been with Alzamora, but was seven seconds behind at the finish; another eight seconds back, Debon came through to take ninth by inches from David Checa, himself narrowly ahead of Matsudo.

125 cc RACE – 24 laps

Poggiali was on pole, from Azuma, Pedrosa and Cecchinello, Vincent leading row two. Pedrosa led away, with the tight track keeping the pack close, while crashes and attrition whittled away at a nine-strong gang at half-distance.

Azuma led on lap four, then Poggiali took over for three more, but Cecchinello had a clear speed advantage on the front straight, and used it to seize control, staying there until the end in spite of a strong attack from Poggiali on the final lap.

A little before, Azuma had split the gang with a desperate move on Vincent, sending the Frenchman wide for a second time that race (earlier de Angelis had pushed him to seventh, speeding past then falling straight off).

Rodriguez fell out of the leading group too, with Ueda and Ui also crashing without quite getting there, Olivé and Sanna knocking each other down at the first chicane.

Azuma came back, with a final fling that took him over the kerb into the last corner and into third position, only to run wide on the exit, letting Pedrosa and Vincent back ahead, but managing to get to the flag narrowly before Pablo Nieto.

POLINI FRENCH grand prix

round 4

LE MANS – BUGATTI CIRCUIT

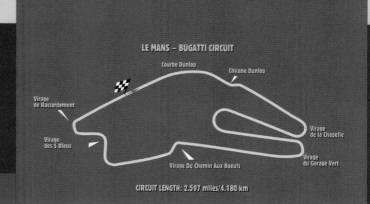

Courbe Dunlop
Chicane Dunlop
Virage de Raccordement
Virage de la Chapelle
Virage des 5 Bleus
Virage Du Chemin Aux Boeufs
Virage du Garage Vert

CIRCUIT LENGTH: 2.597 miles/4.180 km

19 MAY 2002

MotoGP

21 laps, 54.537 miles/87.780 km

Pos.	Rider (Nat.)	No.	Machine	Laps	Time & speed
1	Valentino Rossi (I)	46	Honda	21	34m 22.335s 95.211 mph/ 153.228 km/h
2	Tohru Ukawa (J)	11	Honda	21	34m 22.552s
3	Max Biaggi (I)	3	Yamaha	21	34m 22.939s
4	Norick Abe (J)	6	Yamaha	21	34m 24.036s
5	Kenny Roberts (USA)	10	Suzuki	21	34m 30.799s
6	Nobuatsu Aoki (J)	9	Proton KR	21	34m 32.547s
7	Loris Capirossi (I)	65	Honda	21	34m 34.772s
8	Alex Barros (BR)	4	Honda	21	34m 37.566s
9	Regis Laconi (F)	55	Aprilia	21	34m 39.490s
10	Jeremy McWilliams (GB)	99	Proton KR	21	34m 44.182s
11	John Hopkins (USA)	21	Yamaha	21	34m 47.456s
12	Sete Gibernau (E)	15	Suzuki	21	34m 48.254s
13	Shinya Nakano (J)	56	Yamaha	21	34m 48.562s
14	Jean-Michel Bayle (F)	18	Yamaha	21	34m 49.346s
15	Jurgen van den Goorbergh (NL)	17	Honda	21	34m 52.677s
16	José Luis Cardoso (E)	30	Yamaha	21	34m 58.909s
	Daijiro Kato (J)	74	Honda	11	DNF
	Olivier Jacque (F)	19	Yamaha	10	DNF
	Tetsuya Harada (J)	31	Honda	10	DNF
	Carlos Checa (E)	7	Yamaha	8	DNF
	Garry McCoy (AUS)	8	Yamaha		DNS

Fastest lap: Rossi, 1m 36.846s, 96.549 mph/155.380 km/h (record).

Previous circuit record: Max Biaggi, I (Yamaha), 1m 39.954s, 96.344 mph/155.051 km/h (2001).

Event best maximum speed: Biaggi, 184.5 mph/297.0 km/h (race).

Qualifying: 1 Rossi, 1m 36.046s; 2 Checa, 1m 36.122s; 3 Biaggi, 1m 36.193s; 4 Ukawa, 1m 36.223s; 5 Kato, 1m 36.349s; 6 McWilliams, 1m 36.507s; 7 Capirossi, 1m 36.515s; 8 Harada, 1m 36.525s; 9 Roberts, 1m 36.617s; 10 Nakano, 1m 36.714s; 11 Aoki, 1m 36.752s; 12 Abe, 1m 36.771s; 13 Jacque, 1m 36.785s; 14 Laconi, 1m 36.933s; 15 Barros, 1m 36.997s; 16 Gibernau, 1m 37.130s; 17 van den Goorbergh, 1m 37.186s; 18 Bayle, 1m 37.311s; 19 Hopkins, 1m 37.707s; 20 McCoy, 1m 38.235s; 21 Cardoso, 1m 38.261s.

Fastest race laps: 1 Rossi, 1m 36.846s; 2 Ukawa, 1m 36.879s; 3 Biaggi, 1m 37.065s; 4 Checa, 1m 37.165s; 5 Kato, 1m 37.291s; 6 Jacque, 1m 37.430s; 7 Nakano, 1m 37.476s; 8 Roberts, 1m 37.494s; 9 Abe, 1m 37.494s; 10 Capirossi, 1m 37.546s; 11 Harada, 1m 37.552s; 12 Aoki, 1m 37.842s; 13 Laconi, 1m 37.845s; 14 Gibernau, 1m 38.043s; 15 Barros, 1m 38.043s; 16 McWilliams, 1m 38.177s; 17 Bayle, 1m 38.336s; 18 van den Goorbergh, 1m 38.522s; 19 Hopkins, 1m 38.680s; 20 Cardoso, 1m 38.903s.

World Championship: 1 Rossi, 95; 2 Ukawa, 61; 3 Capirossi, 45; 4 Abe, 43; 5 Kato, 39; 6 Barros, 29; 7 Aoki, 28; 8 Checa, 27; 9 Biaggi, 23; 10 Ryo, 20; 11 Roberts, 19; 12 Laconi, 18; 13 Harada and Jacque, 15; 15 Hopkins, 14; 16 Itoh, 13; 17 Gibernau and Nakano, 11; 19 van den Goorbergh, 10; 20 McCoy, 7; 21 McWilliams, 6; 22 Riba, 3; 23 Bayle, 2.

250 cc

26 laps, 67.522 miles/108.680 km

Pos.	Rider (Nat.)	No.	Machine	Laps	Time & speed
1	Fonsi Nieto (E)	10	Aprilia	26	43m 41.140s 92.750 mph/ 149.266 km/h
2	Marco Melandri (I)	3	Aprilia	26	43m 41.392s
3	Randy de Puniet (F)	17	Aprilia	26	43m 47.571s
4	Roberto Locatelli (I)	15	Aprilia	26	43m 47.744s
5	Roberto Rolfo (I)	4	Honda	26	43m 52.667s
6	Toni Elias (E)	24	Aprilia	26	43m 54.297s
7	Emilio Alzamora (E)	7	Honda	26	43m 55.010s
8	Sebastian Porto (ARG)	9	Yamaha	26	44m 01.217s
9	Alex Debon (E)	6	Aprilia	26	44m 09.697s
10	David Checa (E)	42	Aprilia	26	44m 09.824s
11	Naoki Matsudo (J)	8	Yamaha	26	44m 10.032s
12	Taro Sekiguchi (J)	76	Yamaha	26	44m 16.288s
13	Shahrol Yuzy (MAL)	18	Yamaha	26	44m 16.484s
14	Hector Faubel (E)	32	Aprilia	26	44m 37.624s
15	Jay Vincent (GB)	12	Honda	26	44m 38.034s
16	Vincent Philippe (F)	25	Aprilia	26	44m 49.296s
17	Jarno Janssen (NL)	41	Honda	26	44m 49.530s
18	Dirk Heidolf (D)	28	Aprilia	26	44m 57.275s
19	Raul Jara (E)	22	Aprilia	26	44m 59.180s
20	Erwan Nigon (F)	36	Honda	25	44m 05.900s
	Thierry van den Bosch (F)	35	Aprilia	13	DNF
	Casey Stoner (AUS)	27	Aprilia	9	DNF
	Franco Battaini (I)	21	Aprilia	9	DNF
	Haruchika Aoki (J)	11	Honda	4	DNF
	Leon Haslam (GB)	19	Honda	2	DNF
	Yann Lussiana (F)	37	Honda		DNQ
	Samuel Aubry (F)	45	Honda		DNQ
	Herve Mora (F)	93	Aprilia		DNQ
	Hugo Marchand (F)	51	Aprilia		DNQ

Fastest lap: Melandri, 1m 39.648s, 93.834 mph/151.011 km/h (record).

Previous circuit record: Daijiro Kato, J (Honda), 1m 41.473s, 94.902 mph/152.730 km/h (2001).

Event best maximum speed: Elias, 159.4 mph/256.5 km/h (race).

Qualifying: 1 Nieto, 1m 38.903s; 2 de Puniet, 1m 39.391s; 3 Locatelli, 1m 39.506s; 4 Melandri, 1m 39.570s; 5 Elias, 1m 39.673s; 6 Battaini, 1m 39.811s; 7 Stoner, 1m 39.872s; 8 Aoki, 1m 40.233s; 9 Porto, 1m 40.234s; 10 Matsudo, 1m 40.340s; 11 Debon, 1m 40.450s; 12 Rolfo, 1m 40.666s; 13 Sekiguchi, 1m 40.791s; 14 Yuzy, 1m 40.910s; 15 Alzamora, 1m 40.928s; 16 Vincent, 1m 41.104s; 17 Checa, 1m 41.362s; 18 van den Bosch, 1m 41.629s; 19 Faubel, 1m 41.940s; 20 Philippe, 1m 42.080s; 21 Jara, 1m 42.187s; 22 Janssen, 1m 42.278s; 23 Heidolf, 1m 42.828s; 24 Nigon, 1m 43.582s; 25 Haslam, 1m 43.957s; 26 Lussiana, 1m 46.029s; 27 Aubry, 1m 46.051s; 28 Mora, 1m 46.608s; 29 Marchand, 1m 54.411s.

Fastest race laps: 1 Melandri, 1m 39.648s; 2 Nieto, 1m 39.663s; 3 Elias, 1m 40.090s; 4 Battaini, 1m 40.224s; 5 Rolfo, 1m 40.316s; 6 Alzamora, 1m 40.321s; 7 de Puniet, 1m 40.379s; 8 Locatelli, 1m 40.410s; 9 Stoner, 1m 40.706s; 10 Porto, 1m 40.718s; 11 Debon, 1m 40.850s; 12 Checa, 1m 40.916s; 13 Matsudo, 1m 40.962s; 14 Yuzy, 1m 41.157s; 15 Sekiguchi, 1m 41.172s; 16 Faubel, 1m 41.804s; 17 Vincent, 1m 41.917s; 18 Janssen, 1m 42.125s; 19 Aoki, 1m 42.259s; 20 Heidolf, 1m 42.560s; 21 van den Bosch, 1m 42.561s; 22 Jara, 1m 42.693s; 23 Philippe, 1m 42.702s; 24 Nigon, 1m 44.586s; 25 Haslam, 1m 49.497s.

World Championship: 1 Nieto, 69; 2 Rolfo, 52; 3 Alzamora, 47; 4 Melandri, 45; 5 de Puniet, 42; 6 Battaini, 39; 7 Porto, 36; 8 Locatelli, 35; 9 Debon, 29; 10 Matsudo, 27; 11 Miyazaki, 25; 12 Elias, 21; 13 Sakai, 20; 14 Checa, 12; 15 Stoner, 10; 16 Kameya, 9; 17 Aoki and Faubel, 7; 19 Yuzy, 6; 20 Sekiguchi and Vincent, 5; 22 Aoyama, 4; 23 Bataille, Heidolf and Marchand, 2; 26 Haslam and Jara, 1.

125 cc

24 laps, 62.328 miles/100.320 km

Pos.	Rider (Nat.)	No.	Machine	Laps	Time & speed
1	Lucio Cecchinello (I)	4	Aprilia	24	42m 09.029s 88.733 mph/ 142.802 km/h
2	Manuel Poggiali (RSM)	1	Gilera	24	42m 09.105s
3	Daniel Pedrosa (E)	26	Honda	24	42m 09.633s
4	Arnaud Vincent (F)	21	Aprilia	24	42m 09.894s
5	Masao Azuma (J)	5	Honda	24	42m 09.972s
6	Pablo Nieto (E)	22	Aprilia	24	42m 10.647s
7	Stefano Bianco (I)	33	Aprilia	24	42m 12.798s
8	Mika Kallio (SF)	36	Honda	24	42m 17.709s
9	Andrea Dovizioso (I)	34	Honda	24	42m 17.944s
10	Gino Borsoi (I)	23	Aprilia	24	42m 18.563s
11	Steve Jenkner (D)	17	Aprilia	24	42m 20.778s
12	Mirko Giansanti (I)	6	Honda	24	42m 29.281s
13	Max Sabbatani (I)	11	Aprilia	24	42m 41.111s
14	Klaus Nöhles (D)	12	Honda	24	42m 44.235s
15	Hector Barbera (E)	80	Aprilia	24	42m 58.555s
16	Andrea Ballerini (I)	50	Honda	24	43m 11.388s
17	Michel Fabrizio (I)	84	Gilera	24	43m 16.600s
18	Chaz Davies (GB)	57	Aprilia	24	43m 19.332s
19	Jorge Lorenzo (E)	48	Derbi	24	43m 20.027s
20	Gregory Lefort (F)	86	Aprilia	24	43m 20.508s
21	Mattia Angeloni (I)	31	Gilera	24	43m 45.362s
22	Imre Toth (H)	20	Honda	24	43m 50.063s
23	Jimmy Petit (F)	63	Honda	24	43m 51.546s
24	Gregory Leblanc (F)	85	Honda	23	42m 31.048s
25	Yohann Tiberio (F)	58	Honda	23	42m 31.180s
	Alex de Angelis (RSM)	15	Aprilia	11	DNF
	Jaroslav Hules (CZ)	39	Aprilia	11	DNF
	Simone Sanna (I)	16	Aprilia	10	DNF
	Joan Olivé (E)	25	Honda	10	DNF
	Alex Baldolini (I)	19	Aprilia	10	DNF
	Angel Rodriguez (E)	47	Aprilia	8	DNF
	Youichi Ui (J)	41	Derbi	8	DNF
	Gabor Talmacsi (H)	8	Italjet	5	DNF
	Noboru Ueda (J)	9	Honda	5	DNF
	Stefano Perugini (I)	7	Italjet	4	DNF
	Jakub Smrz (CZ)	18	Honda	0	DNF
	Vincent Braillard (CH)	59	Honda	0	DNF

Fastest lap: Azuma, 1m 44.259s, 89.684 mph/144.332 km/h (record).

Previous circuit record: Lucio Cecchinello, I (Aprilia), 1m 47.766s, 89.360 mph/143.811 km/h (2001).

Event best maximum speed: Vincent, 139.6 mph/224.6 km/h (race).

Qualifying: 1 Poggiali, 1m 44.002s; 2 Azuma, 1m 44.251s; 3 Pedrosa, 1m 44.257s; 4 Cecchinello, 1m 44.264s; 5 Vincent, 1m 44.389s; 6 de Angelis, 1m 44.403s; 7 Nieto, 1m 44.681s; 8 Borsoi, 1m 44.718s; 9 Rodriguez, 1m 44.798s; 10 Ui, 1m 45.055s; 11 Dovizioso, 1m 45.056s; 12 Sanna, 1m 45.114s; 13 Giansanti, 1m 45.235s; 14 Olivé, 1m 45.243s; 15 Hules, 1m 45.307s; 16 Jenkner, 1m 45.475s; 17 Ueda, 1m 45.538s; 18 Talmacsi, 1m 45.538s; 19 Sabbatani, 1m 45.695s; 20 Bianco, 1m 45.801s; 21 Kallio, 1m 45.807s; 22 Barbera, 1m 45.841s; 23 Davies, 1m 46.077s; 24 Ballerini, 1m 46.143s; 25 Smrz, 1m 46.235s; 26 Fabrizio, 1m 46.460s; 27 Nöhles, 1m 46.532s; 28 Perugini, 1m 46.534s; 29 Lorenzo, 1m 46.728s; 30 Baldolini, 1m 47.043s; 31 Lefort, 1m 47.084s; 32 Angeloni, 1m 47.780s; 33 Petit, 1m 48.473s; 34 Braillard, 1m 49.124s; 35 Toth, 1m 49.288s; 36 Tiberio, 1m 50.325s; 37 Leblanc, 1m 50.761s.

Fastest race laps: 1 Azuma, 1m 44.259s; 2 Borsoi, 1m 44.262s; 3 Vincent, 1m 44.353s; 4 de Angelis, 1m 44.385s; 5 Bianco, 1m 44.389s; 6 Pedrosa, 1m 44.414s; 7 Poggiali, 1m 44.519s; 8 Cecchinello, 1m 44.523s; 9 Kallio, 1m 44.630s; 10 Nieto, 1m 44.679s; 11 Dovizioso, 1m 44.726s; 12 Olivé, 1m 44.746s; 13 Ui, 1m 44.795s; 14 Sanna, 1m 44.871s; 15 Jenkner, 1m 44.911s; 16 Rodriguez, 1m 44.946s; 17 Hules, 1m 45.024s; 18 Sabbatani, 1m 45.129s; 19 Giansanti, 1m 45.259s; 20 Ueda, 1m 45.501s; 21 Talmacsi, 1m 45.686s; 22 Nöhles, 1m 45.748s; 23 Baldolini, 1m 46.112s; 24 Fabrizio, 1m 46.159s; 25 Barbera, 1m 46.219s; 26 Ballerini, 1m 46.723s; 27 Davies, 1m 46.794s; 28 Lefort, 1m 46.891s; 29 Perugini, 1m 46.896s; 30 Lorenzo, 1m 47.147s; 31 Angeloni, 1m 47.191s; 32 Toth, 1m 48.258s; 33 Petit, 1m 48.397s; 34 Tiberio, 1m 49.478s; 35 Leblanc, 1m 49.533s.

World Championship: 1 Vincent, 78; 2 Poggiali, 61; 3 Cecchinello, 57; 4 Pedrosa, 53; 5 Jenkner, 35; 6 Sanna, 28; 7 Borsoi, 27; 8 Azuma and Giansanti, 26; 10 Kallio, 23; 11 Nieto, 21; 12 Ueda, 18; 13 Dovizioso, 13; 14 Sabbatani, 11; 15 Aoyama, de Angelis, Olivé and Ui, 10; 19 Bianco and Rodriguez, 9; 21 Nöhles, 6; 22 Barbera and Perugini, 5; 24 Ballerini and Smrz, 3; 26 Baldolini, 2; 27 Fabrizio, 1.

ITALIAN GP

MUGELLO

FIM WORLD CHAMPIONSHIP · ROUND 5

THE adoration squads were out in force at Mugello, numbers and vehemence not visibly decreased by a 40 per cent price-hike meant to tame the crazy crowd. The object of their adoration, Vale, came up with the goods, including a piece of carefully orchestrated post-race theatre reminiscent of his most cheesily contrived early celebrations... two uniformed traffic policemen booked him after the race, for speeding, dangerous overtaking and riding without registration plates. Or something like that.

Rossi's amateur dramatics went further, his pit now equipped with a huge yellow armchair (until crew chief Jerry Burgess — tiring of the games and needing the space — unceremoniously threw it out after just one day), his helmet and leathers an Italian flag tribute. He was not the only one to play to the gallery. The most notable of the other racing thespians was Marco Melandri, who had scooped a tie-up with the just-released *Spiderman* movie, and was head-to-foot superhero, in red and blue. And won the race too.

Is this all too much? Maybe so, according to an open letter after the event, by FIM president Francesco Zerbi, deploring crowd-pleasing antics as irresponsible, in the wake of a near-disastrous post-race track invasion. Abe was actually pulled off his bike by a manic fan apparently trying to take his crash-helmet; Ukawa's Honda suffered bodywork damage, and several others reported near-misses at speed on a track awash with spectators on a fraught slow-down lap. They might disagree with Zerbi's opinion that they were more to blame than the organisers, who had, after all, installed a new $150,000 fence. So it must be the riders' fault. Perhaps it might be helpful if they were to slow down a bit, avoid close battles, and perhaps decide the result in advance, and parade around in that order?

Certainly, immoderate speed did not help an inflamed situation. And Mugello's straight, now the longest on the calendar (if you don't count the flat-out kink near the end) provided the first chance for the new four-strokes to stretch their legs beyond 200 mph, only recorded once before, by Shinichi Itoh's NSR Honda at Hockenheim in 1993. Laconi's Aprilia was the first, on Saturday afternoon, at 200.27 mph, with Ukawa's V5 Honda going 201.63 mph a little later. Biaggi's Yamaha also broke the barrier during the race with a tow, but Rossi's 199.52 mph was just short. It wasn't only top speed that was impressive either, with pole 1.3 seconds faster than last year.

And there's more to come. Not only was there hard news of Kawasaki's burgeoning MotoGP venture for 2003, but also the launch of the Ducati Sedici MotoGP. This drew a vast attendance on the eve of practice, where Ducati Corse MD Claudio Domenicali waxed lyrical about the 'Passion' involved in the exercise, before the bike was unveiled. It was promptly swamped by riders, photographers, press-men and the paddock hordes anxious for a first look. Much later that evening, the bike was still surrounded by photographers... but these were Suzuki engineers, taking digital pictures of design details, like the ultra-complex welding to the big exhaust collector rising under the seat.

The impact was undeniable. So also was the fact that the bike itself was on the rough-and-ready side. For one thing, notoriously, the tailpieces of the fairing underbelly were attached to the rear swing-arm. Some mistake, surely? But the bike was impressive nonetheless, with a bulky aerodynamic fairing and a distinctly Ducati look. The stranger was warmly welcomed.

Out in the real world, Yamaha's development of the M1 was at last gaining momentum. The big change here was a new chassis, which abandoned the straight-line steering head-to-swing-arm link, taking a dog-leg instead. This was in the interests of changing the balance; the engine had new crankcases and had the cylinders canted backwards where the chassis had previously been in the way. It was the fourth chassis update in the bike's development.

Not enough to ease the troubled mind of Max Biaggi, apparently, who threw a temper tantrum in the team's hospitality unit on Thursday night, charging staff and ramming the awning with his scooter in a dispute apparently concerning pasta. Max was clearly feeling the pressure. And not surprisingly. Quite apart from the difficulties of the current season — vying with renascent team-mate Checa for superiority while at the same time thoroughly eclipsed by the Rossi–Honda combination — Max was a central figure in a rider-market turmoil triggered by the Ducati's arrival. One strong rumour put Max on the bike, taking the Marlboro millions with him. On the other hand, there were plausible whispers that Ducati, mindful of Biaggi's propensity to blame the bike, wanted nothing to do with him, especially with an unproven machine to develop. Time would tell.

Two disturbing incidents in the smaller classes left some worrying questions about safety. Or was it three, the first being two-fold? This involved 16-year-old Casey Stoner, the bright Australian already known for being the youngest ever to score points in the 250 class, and secondly for a tendency to crash in spectacular fashion, usually on TV, never good for the reputation. In France he had broken his right scaphoid... a problematic and often incapacitating injury, dreaded by all motor cycle racers. Nothing daunted, Stoner went out for the first free practice. Here he discovered that the strength and feeling in his wrist were not all that they might be, and fell off again, suffering concussion.

In other sports, he would automatically be 'off games' for anything up to three weeks. In motor cycle GP racing, no such safeguard exists. He rode again in the afternoon, but that evening admitted he had been groggy. 'The brake markers seemed to move every lap,' he said. 'I was taking different lines all the time.' He thought then he'd probably call it a day. Next morning, however, he was ready to go again. Wrist pumped full of painkillers, he found another problem. 'I couldn't feel the throttle properly. I thought I was just rolling it on, but the data showed I opened it too far.' Another high-side, and another injury — a broken left-hand little finger. This time, he stayed down. Full marks for courage, of course, but once again what about the probity of a medical system that allowed him to be in that position?

The other incident was just a particularly nasty racing crash. The victim was little Max Sabbatani, in final 125 qualifying, whose right leg was trapped in the rear wheel as he and his bike tumbled through the gravel. Doctors feared amputation might be necessary, and his team mechanics had to be called to the scene to disassemble the bike enough for him to be untangled. Sabbatani made a rapid recovery from double compound fractures, however, and was back after missing only two more races.

Opposite: Webmaster Melandri did everything expected of a superhero.

Opposite inset left: Rossi was enthroned... but pragmatism soon turfed the armchair out of the pit.

Opposite inset right: Angry Abe remonstrates after being pulled off his bike — crowd invasion went beyond anything seen before.
All photographs: Gold & Goose

Above: Ton-up Gibernau celebrated his 100th GP start.

Top: The misfortunate Sabbatani, tangled with the wreckage, was extricated by his team mechanics.
Both photographs: Gold & Goose

Above: Capirossi wrestles with his wayward NSR — two-stroke riders regularly had to over-ride their machines to be in with a prayer.

Opposite: Biaggi was under pressure at home, and did the best his Yamaha could manage.

Below: The exhaust pipe orchestra strikes up, with Rossi the big bassoon. Biaggi, Ukawa and Checa give chase.

All photographs: Gold & Goose

MOTOGP RACE – 23 laps

Rossi had help from an unexpected quarter for his fifth pole in five races... he followed Aoki's Proton, borrowing corner speed from the agile lightweight, and in the last minutes slotted in more than half a second ahead of erstwhile poleman Biaggi, with 'my best ever practice lap'. Checa was third, then a banzai lap from Capirossi made a mixed front row again. The surprise of practice was Laconi's Aprilia, enjoying the benefit of the latest Dunlop qualifying tyres on the Italian company's test track, and heading row two.

Rossi gambled on a softer rear tyre, and took off in the lead from Checa and Biaggi, then Ukawa, Capirossi and by the end of lap one an aggressive Kenny Roberts, enjoying the 2002 front Michelins, though not yet the latest rear.

The Yamahas swapped back and forth for the next couple of laps, but by the fourth Biaggi was in second, and he and Rossi were moving away slightly while Checa was fending off Ukawa. Capirossi's soft rear was already past its best, and he was losing touch. Roberts was dropping back even faster, to succumb to Barros and then Aoki's Proton. One lap later, the ninth, he fell on the drop-off from the hill, locking the front while pushing too hard on the brakes to compensate for his deteriorating corner exits. 'Once it got hot, I lost the throttle connection to the back tyre. I was a sitting duck on the way out. My lap times aren't an indication of how hard I was trying. Crashing was.'

Aoki's strong run didn't last much longer, the motor seizing; while Gibernau had pitted after a charging first couple of laps from 18th on the grid into the top ten, only to get caught by the sliding rear under braking, running across the grass, rejoining at the back, then retiring in disgust. Kato crashed out a bit later, after a bad start, then working his way up almost to the top ten. He was suffering again from too much experimentation by HRC, rather than being allowed to settle down in the new class.

But the focus was on the two Italians up front. On lap seven Biaggi drafted past Rossi down the straight, without his rival trying to resist. Was he in trouble?

Obviously not, because he comfortably stayed with Max for the next six laps before slicing past in the middle of the downhill ess-bend, in front of the main army of his fans. He proceeded to pull away inexorably. No worries.

Ukawa and Checa were playing similar games a little way behind, but the balance was not so clearly tipped in the Honda's favour. It was certainly faster down the straight, which is where Ukawa took him for the first time on lap six, but Checa kept pushing and by lap 15 had got back in front firmly enough to finish the straight in the same position. He stayed there until the second-last lap; but power will out, and Ukawa used it to overtake, then fend off fierce attacks to cross the line just over a tenth ahead.

Barros closed relentlessly on his team-mate Capirossi, passing him soon after half-distance, and pulling steadily ahead. If he hadn't been held up in the early laps by Roberts, he said, he could have challenged the four-strokes. 'The time I lost was the gap between me and them,' he said. Capirossi was four seconds behind at the finish.

The loss of Roberts and then Aoki had broken up a big mid-field gang, but there were still several left — Laconi catching up from a bad start to trade blows with Harada, Jacque and Abe. Abe had escaped at the end; Laconi held off the two-strokes, with Nakano closing to within almost three seconds at the flag — he'd finished the first lap way at the back after a trip across the gravel halfway round.

Hopkins had a busy afternoon, stuck behind team-mate Bayle for the first eight laps, only getting past as Nakano came by. The rookie went with Nakano, and both passed the slowing McWilliams before his Proton also seized... he blamed lack of lubrication because he hadn't been able to use full throttle after the tyres faded, a real two-stroke quirk.

Bayle slowed radically towards the end, suffering from an arm-pump problem that brought his short-lived GP return to a premature end. Van den Goorbergh had been ahead of him, but also dropped right off the back, his Honda again punishing the Bridgestones beyond endurance. Riba crashed out unhurt.

Right: Melandri was unbeatable at home, but he had to work for it.

Below, from top: Wide flat-out at a wide, fast racetrack: Rolfo, Borsoi and Poggiali.
All photographs: Gold & Goose

250 cc RACE – 21 laps

Battaini took pole, in the undistinguished-looking 250 class, from Porto by a full half-second, the only rider in the top six not on an Aprilia, with rookie Elias third, Nieto fourth, Melandri leading the second row from Locatelli. Rolfo's Honda was way down in 14th.

Aprilia took the first six places in the race as well, after an all-Italian race-long three-way in arrears.

Melandri led away from the impressive Elias, with Locatelli, Battaini and Porto in tow. By lap three Elias was fourth and losing ground, while de Puniet was pushing Porto close behind, Locatelli and Melandri sharing the lead, Battaini poised behind.

By half-distance Elias had closed again, bringing de Puniet along until he made an overly ambitious attack into turn one, narrowly surviving and lucky to lose only half a second or so. Porto was dropping back, but still heading Nieto, slow off the line and in the early laps, but speeding up as the fuel load lightened to pass fast-starting Yuzy's Yamaha.

Up front Melandri was in control and Battaini prepared to risk all to reverse the situation. Over the limit in the first drop off the hill, he was out of the saddle and wild, narrowly missing his two companions and surely bound to crash. Instead he collected it again without running into the gravel, to rejoin a little way back.

This left third up for grabs. De Puniet had caught up again, and he and Elias changed places a couple of times, while Nieto started to close dramatically towards the finish, fastest man on the track as he started the last lap on de Puniet's back wheel. He outbraked him into turn one, then dived inside team-mate Elias five corners later, where Battaini had almost crashed, to force himself onto the rostrum. He was just half a second behind Locatelli, who was in turn even closer to Melandri.

Battaini was a lonely sixth, Porto three seconds behind.

Some way back, Rolfo had the frustration of having to pass Aoki's development production Honda on his off-form factory bike before a lonely ride to eighth. He'd also passed Yuzy as the Malaysian dropped back to ninth, where he managed to pip Checa after a long battle.

Three seconds back Alzamora took 11th after finally outdistancing Aoki. Debon went with him, but ran off on the last lap. Vincent Philippe led the next gang, with Matsudo and Vincent on his wheels for the final point. A little way back, Haslam got the worst of a three-way dice to avoid being last. Sekiguchi and Heidolf crashed out.

125 cc RACE - 20 laps

Poggiali claimed pole in the last seconds of practice, and the race win with even less time to spare, to make three home Italian winners after a heart-in-the-mouth race. The pack up front numbered 11 riders even at the finish, and seven of them had led for at least one lap.

Pedrosa was the first, then Poggiali, de Angelis, Jenkner, Cecchinello (pulling through strongly after finishing lap one 18th), Nieto and (for one lap) Ui.

The fast sweeping track kept them terrifyingly close, running into turn one three or more abreast, and crossing the finishing line in similar fashion.

Only one rider managed any sort of a breakaway — the increasingly strong Nieto, almost a second ahead on lap 13. Half a lap later he had a huge slide and a narrow escape, and was swallowed up again.

Nieto was back in front for the start of the final lap; Ui fifth. Poggiali's Gilera power put him ahead before turn one, while Nieto and Pedrosa lost time fighting each other. Over the line, Ui drafted past both of them to steal second.

A little gap by the end saw Borsoi head Cecchinello, de Angelis and Jenkner, with Vincent closing from a bad start to get through to ninth. Giansanti, Olivé and Barbera tangled in the first corner, and all fell; Rodriguez crashed out of the leading group.

CINZANO ITALIAN grand prix

5 round

2 JUNE 2002

CIRCUIT LENGTH: 3.259 miles/5.245 km

MotoGP

23 laps, 74.957 miles/120.635 km

Pos.	Rider (Nat.)	No.	Machine	Laps	Time & speed
1	Valentino Rossi (I)	46	Honda	23	43m 40.837s 102.964 mph/ 165.705 km/h
2	Max Biaggi (I)	3	Yamaha	23	43m 43.241s
3	Tohru Ukawa (J)	11	Honda	23	43m 52.126s
4	Carlos Checa (E)	7	Yamaha	23	43m 52.245s
5	Alex Barros (BR)	4	Honda	23	43m 56.208s
6	Loris Capirossi (I)	65	Honda	23	44m 00.847s
7	Norick Abe (J)	6	Yamaha	23	44m 07.284s
8	Regis Laconi (F)	55	Aprilia	23	44m 11.170s
9	Olivier Jacque (F)	19	Yamaha	23	44m 11.265s
10	Tetsuya Harada (J)	31	Honda	23	44m 11.596s
11	Shinya Nakano (J)	56	Yamaha	23	44m 14.999s
12	John Hopkins (USA)	21	Yamaha	23	44m 18.552s
13	Jean-Michel Bayle (F)	18	Yamaha	23	44m 58.640s
14	Jurgen van den Goorbergh (NL)	17	Honda	23	45m 00.637s
	Jeremy McWilliams (GB)	99	Proton KR	18	DNF
	Sete Gibernau (E)	15	Suzuki	14	DNF
	Nobuatsu Aoki (J)	9	Proton KR	9	DNF
	Daijiro Kato (J)	74	Honda	9	DNF
	Kenny Roberts (USA)	10	Suzuki	8	DNF
	Pere Riba (E)	20	Honda	1	DNF

Fastest lap: Ukawa, 1m 52.601s, 104.197 mph/167.689 km/h (record).

Previous record: Michael Doohan, AUS (Honda), 1m 53.342s, 103.516 mph/ 166.593 km/h (1998).

Event best maximum speed: Ukawa, 201.6 mph/324.5 km/h (qualifying practice no. 2).

Qualifying: 1 Rossi, 1m 51.258s; **2** Biaggi, 1m 51.837s; **3** Checa, 1m 52.086s; **4** Capirossi, 1m 52.107s; **5** Laconi, 1m 52.237s; **6** Jacque, 1m 52.345s; **7** Ukawa, 1m 52.434s; **8** Harada, 1m 52.532s; **9** Barros, 1m 52.630s; **10** Roberts, 1m 52.656s; **11** Aoki, 1m 52.740s; **12** McWilliams, 1m 52.751s; **13** Hopkins, 1m 52.923s; **14** Nakano, 1m 52.990s; **15** van den Goorbergh, 1m 53.040s; **16** Kato, 1m 53.120s; **17** Bayle, 1m 53.440s; **18** Gibernau, 1m 53.493s; **19** Abe, 1m 53.765s; **20** Riba, 1m 54.882s.

Fastest race laps: 1 Ukawa, 1m 52.601s; **2** Biaggi, 1m 52.996s; **3** Rossi, 1m 53.092s; **4** Checa, 1m 53.125s; **5** Capirossi, 1m 53.233s; **6** Roberts, 1m 53.513s; **7** Barros, 1m 53.829s; **8** Laconi, 1m 53.893s; **9** Kato, 1m 54.063s; **10** Aoki, 1m 54.068s; **11** Gibernau, 1m 54.118s; **12** Abe, 1m 54.126s; **13** Jacque, 1m 54.237s; **14** Harada, 1m 54.279s; **15** Nakano, 1m 54.380s; **16** Hopkins, 1m 54.535s; **17** McWilliams, 1m 54.583s; **18** Bayle, 1m 54.651s; **19** van den Goorbergh, 1m 55.258s; **20** Riba, 2m 04.817s.

World Championship: 1 Rossi, 120; **2** Ukawa, 77; **3** Capirossi, 55; **4** Abe, 52; **5** Biaggi, 43; **6** Barros and Checa, 40; **8** Kato, 39; **9** Aoki, 28; **10** Laconi, 26; **11** Jacque, 22; **12** Harada, 21; **13** Ryo, 20; **14** Roberts, 19; **15** Hopkins, 18; **16** Nakano, 16; **17** Itoh, 13; **18** van den Goorbergh, 12; **19** Gibernau, 11; **20** McCoy, 7; **21** McWilliams, 6; **22** Bayle, 5; **23** Riba, 3.

250 cc

21 laps, 68.439 miles/110.145 km

Pos.	Rider (Nat.)	No.	Machine	Laps	Time & speed
1	Marco Melandri (I)	3	Aprilia	21	40m 42.759s 100.864 mph/ 162.325 km/h
2	Roberto Locatelli (I)	15	Aprilia	21	40m 43.017s
3	Fonsi Nieto (E)	10	Aprilia	21	40m 43.479s
4	Toni Elias (E)	24	Aprilia	21	40m 44.223s
5	Randy de Puniet (F)	17	Aprilia	21	40m 44.477s
6	Franco Battaini (I)	21	Aprilia	21	40m 51.365s
7	Sebastian Porto (ARG)	9	Yamaha	21	40m 54.623s
8	Roberto Rolfo (I)	4	Honda	21	41m 00.007s
9	Shahrol Yuzy (MAL)	18	Yamaha	21	41m 11.240s
10	David Checa (E)	42	Aprilia	21	41m 11.249s
11	Emilio Alzamora (E)	7	Honda	21	41m 14.872s
12	Haruchika Aoki (J)	11	Honda	21	41m 17.529s
13	Vincent Philippe (F)	25	Aprilia	21	41m 34.596s
14	Naoki Matsudo (J)	8	Yamaha	21	41m 34.671s
15	Jay Vincent (GB)	12	Honda	21	41m 35.152s
16	Hector Faubel (E)	32	Aprilia	21	41m 39.871s
17	Raul Jara (E)	22	Aprilia	21	41m 39.957s
18	Leon Haslam (GB)	19	Honda	21	41m 40.496s
	Alex Debon (E)	6	Aprilia	20	DNF
	Dirk Heidolf (D)	28	Aprilia	18	DNF
	Jarno Janssen (NL)	41	Honda	2	DNF
	Hugo Marchand (F)	51	Aprilia	2	DNF
	Taro Sekiguchi (J)	76	Yamaha	1	DNF
	Casey Stoner (AUS)	27	Aprilia		DNS

Fastest lap: Nieto, 1m 54.812s, 102.191 mph/164.460 km/h.

Lap record: Shinya Nakano, J (Yamaha), 1m 54.462s, 102.503 mph/164.963 km/h (2000).

Event best maximum speed: Elias, 172.9 mph/278.3 km/h (qualifying practice no. 2).

Qualifying: 1 Battaini, 1m 54.344s; **2** Porto, 1m 54.818s; **3** Elias, 1m 54.838s; **4** Nieto, 1m 54.975s; **5** Melandri, 1m 55.080s; **6** Locatelli, 1m 55.095s; **7** Yuzy, 1m 55.647s; **8** de Puniet, 1m 55.657s; **9** Checa, 1m 56.068s; **10** Alzamora, 1m 56.252s; **11** Sekiguchi, 1m 56.276s; **12** Matsudo, 1m 56.283s; **13** Aoki, 1m 56.397s; **14** Rolfo, 1m 56.520s; **15** Debon, 1m 56.593s; **16** Jara, 1m 57.023s; **17** Vincent, 1m 57.493s; **18** Stoner, 1m 57.633s; **19** Philippe, 1m 57.974s; **20** Faubel, 1m 57.991s; **21** Haslam, 1m 58.216s; **22** Heidolf, 1m 58.236s; **23** Marchand, 1m 58.309s; **24** Janssen, 1m 59.031s.

Fastest race laps: 1 Nieto, 1m 54.812s; **2** Locatelli, 1m 55.328s; **3** Battaini, 1m 55.328s; **4** Elias, 1m 55.418s; **5** de Puniet, 1m 55.467s; **6** Melandri, 1m 55.565s; **7** Porto, 1m 55.925s; **8** Rolfo, 1m 56.080s; **9** Yuzy, 1m 56.398s; **10** Checa, 1m 56.411s; **11** Debon, 1m 56.719s; **12** Alzamora, 1m 56.786s; **13** Aoki, 1m 56.992s; **14** Vincent, 1m 57.345s; **15** Matsudo, 1m 57.494s; **16** Philippe, 1m 57.534s; **17** Jara, 1m 57.844s; **18** Faubel, 1m 57.977s; **19** Heidolf, 1m 58.057s; **20** Haslam, 1m 58.134s; **21** Marchand, 1m 59.779s; **22** Janssen, 2m 01.026s; **23** Sekiguchi, 2m 08.057s.

World Championship: 1 Nieto, 85; **2** Melandri, 70; **3** Rolfo, 60; **4** Locatelli, 55; **5** de Puniet, 53; **6** Alzamora, 52; **7** Battaini, 49; **8** Porto, 45; **9** Elias, 34; **10** Debon and Matsudo, 29; **12** Miyazaki, 25; **13** Sakai, 20; **14** Checa, 18; **15** Yuzy, 13; **16** Aoki, 11; **17** Stoner, 10; **18** Kameya, 9; **19** Faubel, 7; **20** Vincent, 6; **21** Sekiguchi, 5; **22** Aoyama, 4; **23** Philippe, 3; **24** Bataille, Heidolf and Marchand, 2; **27** Haslam and Jara, 1.

125 cc

20 laps, 65.180 miles/104.900 km

Pos.	Rider (Nat.)	No.	Machine	Laps	Time & speed
1	Manuel Poggiali (RSM)	1	Gilera	20	40m 20.019s 96.964 mph/ 156.048 km/h
2	Youichi Ui (J)	41	Derbi	20	40m 20.526s
3	Pablo Nieto (E)	22	Aprilia	20	40m 20.531s
4	Daniel Pedrosa (E)	26	Honda	20	40m 20.591s
5	Gino Borsoi (I)	23	Aprilia	20	40m 20.694s
6	Lucio Cecchinello (I)	4	Aprilia	20	40m 20.999s
7	Alex de Angelis (RSM)	15	Aprilia	20	40m 22.090s
8	Steve Jenkner (D)	17	Aprilia	20	40m 22.091s
9	Arnaud Vincent (F)	21	Aprilia	20	40m 22.228s
10	Andrea Ballerini (I)	50	Honda	20	40m 22.274s
11	Simone Sanna (I)	16	Aprilia	20	40m 22.451s
12	Andrea Dovizioso (I)	34	Honda	20	40m 24.066s
13	Masao Azuma (J)	5	Honda	20	40m 26.315s
14	Gioele Pellino (I)	53	Aprilia	20	40m 32.900s
15	Stefano Perugini (I)	7	Italjet	20	40m 56.144s
16	Michel Fabrizio (I)	84	Gilera	20	41m 00.249s
17	Gaspare Caffiero (I)	30	Honda	20	41m 03.429s
18	Chaz Davies (GB)	57	Aprilia	20	41m 03.736s
19	Alex Baldolini (I)	19	Aprilia	20	41m 22.897s
20	Jorge Lorenzo (E)	48	Derbi	20	41m 22.907s
21	Imre Toth (H)	20	Honda	20	41m 22.952s
22	Simone Corsi (I)	87	Honda	20	41m 54.938s
	Stefano Bianco (I)	33	Aprilia	16	DNF
	Jakub Smrz (CZ)	18	Honda	9	DNF
	Gabor Talmacsi (H)	8	Italjet	9	DNF
	Angel Rodriguez (E)	47	Aprilia	6	DNF
	Mattia Angeloni (I)	31	Gilera	4	DNF
	Marco Petrini (I)	54	Aprilia	4	DNF
	Joan Olivé (E)	25	Honda	0	DNF
	Mika Kallio (SF)	36	Honda	0	DNF
	Jaroslav Hules (CZ)	39	Aprilia	0	DNF
	Mirko Giansanti (I)	6	Honda	0	DNF
	Hector Barbera (E)	80	Aprilia	0	DNF
	Max Sabbatani (I)	11	Aprilia		DNS
	Klaus Nöhles (D)	12	Honda		DNS
	Noboru Ueda (J)	9	Honda		DNS

Fastest lap: Cecchinello, 1m 59.184s, 98.442 mph/158.427 km/h (record).

Previous record: Roberto Locatelli, I (Aprilia), 2m 00.029s, 97.749 mph/157.311 km/h (2000).

Event best maximum speed: Pedrosa, 147.1 mph/236.8 km/h (race).

Qualifying: 1 Poggiali, 1m 59.369s; **2** Pedrosa, 1m 59.409s; **3** de Angelis, 1m 59.536s; **4** Jenkner, 1m 59.636s; **5** Vincent, 1m 59.714s; **6** Borsoi, 1m 59.738s; **7** Smrz, 1m 59.740s; **8** Cecchinello, 2m 00.020s; **9** Sanna, 2m 00.190s; **10** Ballerini, 2m 00.285s; **11** Giansanti, 2m 00.312s; **12** Dovizioso, 2m 00.384s; **13** Perugini, 2m 00.559s; **14** Ui, 2m 00.602s; **15** Hules, 2m 00.625s; **16** Kallio, 2m 00.709s; **17** Sabbatani, 2m 00.775s; **18** Fabrizio, 2m 00.937s; **19** Azuma, 2m 00.990s; **20** Talmacsi, 2m 00.993s; **21** Pellino, 2m 01.027s; **22** Nöhles, 2m 01.028s; **23** Bianco, 2m 01.107s; **24** Olivé, 2m 01.311s; **25** Davies, 2m 01.338s; **26** Rodriguez, 2m 01.376s; **27** Petrini, 2m 01.887s; **28** Nieto, 2m 02.026s; **29** Angeloni, 2m 02.059s; **30** Ueda, 2m 02.103s; **31** Caffiero, 2m 02.147s; **32** Barbera, 2m 02.345s; **33** Lorenzo, 2m 02.728s; **34** Corsi, 2m 02.861s; **35** Toth, 2m 03.323s; **36** Baldolini, 2m 03.389s.

Fastest race laps: 1 Cecchinello, 1m 59.184s; **2** Nieto, 1m 59.368s; **3** Sanna, 1m 59.637s; **4** Pellino, 1m 59.637s; **5** Bianco, 1m 59.667s; **6** Borsoi, 1m 59.708s; **7** Ui, 1m 59.740s; **8** Vincent, 1m 59.745s; **9** Ballerini, 1m 59.755s; **10** Azuma, 1m 59.916s; **11** Pedrosa, 1m 59.956s; **12** de Angelis, 1m 59.975s; **13** Jenkner, 2m 00.006s; **14** Poggiali, 2m 00.062s; **15** Dovizioso, 2m 00.080s; **16** Perugini, 2m 00.096s; **17** Smrz, 2m 00.244s; **18** Fabrizio, 2m 00.410s; **19** Rodriguez, 2m 00.542s; **20** Davies, 2m 01.475s; **21** Talmacsi, 2m 01.575s; **22** Caffiero, 2m 01.617s; **23** Petrini, 2m 01.655s; **24** Angeloni, 2m 02.220s; **25** Toth, 2m 02.243s; **26** Lorenzo, 2m 02.542s; **27** Baldolini, 2m 02.599s; **28** Corsi, 2m 02.715s.

World Championship: 1 Poggiali, 86; **2** Vincent, 85; **3** Cecchinello, 67; **4** Pedrosa, 66; **5** Jenkner, 43; **6** Borsoi, 38; **7** Nieto, 37; **8** Sanna, 33; **9** Ui, 30; **10** Azuma, 29; **11** Giansanti, 26; **12** Kallio, 23; **13** de Angelis, 19; **14** Ueda, 18; **15** Dovizioso, 17; **16** Sabbatani, 11; **17** Aoyama and Olivé, 10; **19** Ballerini, Bianco and Rodriguez, 9; **22** Nöhles and Perugini, 6; **24** Barbera, 5; **25** Smrz, 3; **26** Baldolini and Pellino, 2; **28** Fabrizio, 1.

BARCELONA

FIM WORLD CHAMPIONSHIP · ROUND 6

MORE of the same, only different. And much faster. Although nominally the track with the longest straight of the year, the four-strokes didn't crack 200 mph down Montmelo's 1.4-km straight. But Rossi did set a race time a full 37 seconds faster than last year.

The sameness was Rossi's win. The differences were that this time he really had to work for it, and gave every appearance of being exhausted after the race. And that he hadn't, for the first time all year, qualified on pole. Perhaps the others were beginning to catch up at last.

Qualifying honours went to Biaggi's Yamaha, signifying the increasing fruitfulness of the high-intensity M1 programme, which they continued to prefer to keep secret; Suzuki also had a fresh round of upgrades to the hardware and the soft, in several senses, including Japanese GP hero Akira Ryo for the start of a wild-card spell on a third GSV-R, in factory colours, along with a full house of race department engineers. New crankcases reduced internal friction as well as offering a slot for a remote starter motor, ending the faintly embarrassing rigmarole of having to block out the slipper mechanism of the clutch to start up with the back-wheel roller. New engine management programming addressed the over-run phase by increasing idle speed to reduce engine braking. Small improvements, and almost negligible next to the acquisition at last of the S4 2002-version Michelin rear. Michelin had made them wait, nominally while upping production capacity but more of a political move to soothe ruffled feathers at Honda and Yamaha. Now the waiting was over at last, and Roberts had tested the tyres on the previous Monday at Mugello. He was ecstatic. 'It's the biggest leap forward since I switched to Michelins in 1998 [on the Modenas, from Dunlops],' said Roberts. 'We still have the same problems with the bike, mainly under braking and backshifting... but these tyres tend to mask them.'

New hardware — a 'wideline' chassis — also at Proton, where Roberts Senior disclosed the reason why. It was aimed at the next generation, the four-stroke, which he also revealed would be a V5, not unlike the Honda, but also not quite the same, with a narrower V-angle of 60 degrees. The choice of engine was simple logic, he would later say: the maximum number of cylinders within that weight bracket, and a deliberate move away from trying in vain to wring race wins from a low-powered lightweight. 'We know how to make a bike that has the highest corner speed, but I don't want our guys to be passed down the straights any more,' he said. As well as wide top rails, the chassis also had significant geometric differences, a 'different approach that I wanted to try after Kurtis rode the bike last year', said Roberts. The main difference was in stability, under brakes and mid-corner, working the tyres less, allowing easier line changes, and earlier throttle opening, said McWilliams, after he and Kenny had tested it at Almeria before Mugello. Some hard talking at a consolatory post-Mugello team party had persuaded Roberts to rush one version out for this race, rather than waiting until Donington, when bikes would be available for both riders. In spite of its early state of development (the team were obliged to machine up a different rear suspension link overnight on Friday) McWilliams stuck with it. 'We're treating it as something of a test — but already it's more consistent than the standard chassis, and it seems to have solved the pumping problem I've been having with the rear tyre,' he said.

The second race in Spain coincided with a carefully timed story in *El Mundo*, the large-circulation national daily, which was very hostile to Dorna, criticising their greed, 'looking for money in every pocket', and outlining the financial manoeuvring of three of the principal directors. The shock value was muted by the contents. There's nothing too surprising about businessmen trying to make a lot of money and pay as little tax as possible, and hints of other improprieties verging on race-fixing were only hints. All the same, Dorna were quick to excise the offending article from the sheaf of press-cutting copies routinely handed out to journalists. Barely a month later the reporter, Javier Olave, had left the paper after working there for several years. He had taken voluntary redundancy, but it all seemed a bit too coincidental not to start a fresh round of rumours of dark deeds at the top.

Alex Criville came back for another farewell: this time Honda came up with the parade-lap bike that they had denied him at Jerez — the NSR on which he had won the title. The ex-champion, Spain's most successful rider ever in the top class, was still tight-lipped about the exact reason for his retirement, but there was little doubt that he was suffering from a form of epilepsy. The vast crowd wished him well, and he returned the compliment in an emotional speech.

There were a few jobless riders in the paddock, in the unenviable role of ambulance-chasers. Johan Stigefelt was still hoping in vain, likewise Anthony West, who had come from Australia so he was at least on hand if something did come up. German Alex Hofmann was the lucky one, however, taking over McCoy's Red Bull Yamaha unexpectedly vacated by Bayle for a first-ever 500 ride.

After Mugello, and considering the size and enthusiasm of the crowd, concerns about a potential track invasion were allayed because the organisers had already installed an extra fence — making three in all — at the final bowl, where most of the crowd gathers. 'We will have to look at the situation on a track-by-track basis,' said race director Paul Butler. 'Phillip Island may be the best example. They encourage fans onto the track for the rostrum ceremony, but short-cut the slow-down lap to avoid any conflict.' The same system was adopted at Donington Park later in the season, in lieu of any investment in fences.

MOTOGP - ROSSI · 250 cc - MELANDRI · 125 cc - POGGIALI

Top left: Rossi had to work very hard for his win over Ukawa.

Bottom, from left: Goodbye again from Spain's only 500 champion — Alex Criville bade fans an emotional farewell; Kenny Roberts was delighted with the latest Michelins; Rookie Hopkins put his two-stroke on pole briefly; his pit crew and girlfriend Desirée Crossman were surprised and delighted.
All photographs: Gold & Goose

Below: Alex Barros gambled on a soft tyre, and it helped him to be top two-stroke.

Bottom left: Class first-timer Hofmann disputes last place with luckless rookie Riba.

Bottom right: Big and bouncy, Laconi's Aprilia had the legs to stay in front of McWilliams's hard-ridden Proton.

All photographs: Gold & Goose

MOTOGP RACE – 25 laps

Punishingly hot, practice was full of surprises and excitement, not least when John Hopkins put his Yamaha on pole with six minutes to go. This didn't last, in an epic final flurry, and he ended up sixth; highly impressive nevertheless. Biaggi was fastest, Checa falling off trying to match him; with Ukawa (faster than Rossi throughout) second, then Gibernau's Suzuki for the V4's first front row, and Rossi fourth.

The heat persisted on Sunday, but the pace didn't suffer. Ukawa led away from Checa and Biaggi, and on lap two Checa dived underneath the Honda and seized the lead. Rossi was fourth, but at the start of lap five he drafted past Biaggi down the long straight to dive ahead under braking. It was the beginning of the end for Max, forced to switch to his spare bike after his favourite broke in the morning, and still making last-minute setting adjustments on the startline. He was no longer a factor.

To the delight of almost 100,000 fans, Checa held the lead, with Rossi stuck behind Ukawa in spite of a new lap record. This carried on until half-distance, when Ukawa got a better drive off the last corner and surged past Checa on the straight. The Yamaha rider fought back under brakes to regain the lead; Ukawa had another go on the next long right over the hill, and prevailed for more than half a lap, until Checa outbraked him again at turn one.

The writing was on the wall, and Rossi was about to underline it. A little further round he outbraked Ukawa to shadow Checa until they reached turn one again, where he grabbed a lead that he would hold to the finish, under strong pressure all the way.

Ukawa did the same to Checa on lap 17, and now the Spaniard started to fade. Not Ukawa. His tyres — especially his front — were working better than Rossi's, and he pushed him constantly, holding tighter lines everywhere as Valentino continued with the lurid slides he'd been practising all weekend. But Rossi was man enough, and Ukawa was soundly if only narrowly beaten. 'It was a really hard race for the bike, the tyres — and for me. We changed so many settings over the weekend to find the best race set-up. I have to really thank my team,' he said.

Two Hondas, then two Yamahas, Checa slowing, Biaggi turning steadfast laps throughout but still almost four seconds behind, thanks to Checa's earlier pace.

It was all action behind. Roberts held a blocking fifth from Gibernau and Capirossi, until his team-mate slipped past on lap five. He said later Roberts's defensive riding had been holding him up, but he couldn't pull away, and two laps later Roberts was ahead again.

By now Barros had tagged on, but the quartet was soon a trio once more after Gibernau, drafting Roberts down the straight, missed his braking point for turn one, falling off unhurt.

It took Capirossi two laps to pass Roberts, Barros one more. Later, Roberts would take up a favourite topic — 'This is a hot, slippery track, and the throttle connection will determine your finishing position,' he said. Certainly the two-strokes were getting out of the corners faster.

Significantly enough, Barros had commented before practice: 'This year's NSR is so good we can use a grade softer tyre for the races.' That afternoon, he

had gone against Michelin's advice and fitted an even softer rear. It took him past Capirossi, who then had a major off-track excursion, rejoining behind Roberts, who had been dropping back after two-thirds distance. Capirossi was quickly past the Suzuki, finishing eight seconds behind Barros.

Behind this, a spirited 'Jacque Attack' mid-field on lap one had caused some mayhem. Attacking Abe, Jacque found himself overtaking on the inside kerb at the top of the first run up the hill. He survived by bouncing off Abe, but knocked him into Nakano, who cannoned off into van den Goorbergh. All three were down in a tangle, Nakano stretchered off with a bashed foot, Abe jumping back on, pitting, and rejoining to finish last.

Jacque, perhaps a little abashed, was alone until half-distance, when a threat from Aoki's Proton ended in the pits after crankshaft failure on lap two. This left Ryo to drop back into a gang comprising Hopkins, McWilliams, Laconi and Kato, the last-named fastest, soon to overtake them all and close steadily on Jacque, passing him on lap 21 and continuing to pull away at the finish.

Laconi led the remnants as long as his tyres could last; by lap nine Hopkins — using his equivalent Dunlops less severely than the lumbering Aprilia — took over, himself saved from a McWilliams attack by the way Ryo could always keep the Suzuki ahead of the Proton down the straights.

At the finish Ryo was just over a second behind Hopkins; McWilliams five seconds away, and Laconi another five, but overtaken at the end by Harada's Honda. Struggling rookie Riba was close, then Abe two laps down. Hofmann had been running with Riba until the last lap, but his bike stopped on the back straight and he did not finish.

Above: A fine race from Rolfo on last year's title-winning Honda saw the Italian hounding Nieto (10), and eventually beating him. De Puniet is close behind.

Below: Teenage aggression: Pedrosa dives underneath Poggiali to take the 125 race lead, but the latter's power prevailed in the end.

Both photographs: Gold & Goose

250 cc RACE – 23 laps

Aprilia took the top five slots in practice, Nieto almost half a second ahead of Melandri, Locatelli, de Puniet and Battaini, then Rolfo's Honda.

'Loca' was fastest away, but Melandri led into turn one, and two corners later Nieto forced Locatelli wide, and he and team-mate Elias both got by. Locatelli continued to lose places, then crashed out on lap six.

Nieto was pushing Melandri constantly, and Battaini was moving through after being initially repulsed by Elias, joining the leaders on lap six. Melandri's response was to up the pace, and gradually the first three stretched apart.

A little behind, Rolfo had recovered from a mediocre start, passing soon-to-retire Porto, then getting tangled with de Puniet, both moving forward. They too found Elias tough to overtake, with Rolfo cannily making the most of it to cut inside both of them to fourth. The Italian had escaped ahead by the time Elias's sliding rear tyre finally let de Puniet by, and was catching Battaini, and ahead on lap 15. His next target was Nieto, who later complained of a sliding front

tyre, but he managed to hold Rolfo at bay until de Puniet joined them. By the finish, Rolfo had prevailed for a fine second, Nieto was third from de Puniet, with Battaini too far behind to be any threat.

A ride as fine as any of these came from Australian teenager Stoner, his injuries no longer a serious problem. Left on the line at the start, he finished the first lap 19th, but was circulating at the same pace as the leaders, and picking up place after place, as well as the close company of one of his victims, Yuzy. Ninth by half-distance, he settled for a while, then observed that the trio four seconds ahead — Elias, Alzamora and Matsudo — were holding each other up. By lap 17, he and Yuzy were among them, and Stoner won the ensuing battle to the finish for a second sixth place, exhausted by the task of fending off Matsudo, Yuzy and Alzamora, Elias dropping back eight seconds in tenth, though well clear of the next pair, Aoki and Checa.

A second win in succession for Melandri saw Nieto's points lead shrink to six, and gave a feeling that a more natural order was soon to establish itself.

125 cc RACE – 22 laps

Poggiali won few new friends in Spain after his last outing ended in censure and disqualification, stealing pole from a hitherto ecstatic Pablo Nieto, then stealing the race from home hero Pedrosa in the run to the line. His win came by just 19-thousandths.

Pedrosa led for two laps from Ui, then Poggiali took over, only to run wide and drop to fifth behind an inspired Olivé and Jenkner, until the pair dropped back from a fierce pace.

By lap 11 Poggiali led again; three laps later Ui lost his place in the group with a high-side crash. So there were just the two, and the crowd roared as Pedrosa — faster through the twists — took the lead across the line for the last lap. Poggiali powered past by the end of the straight, but Pedrosa was poised, and pulled what seemed a master-stroke at the hairpin into the final bowl of right-handers leading to the finish line. He went into the last corner with a couple of lengths to spare, but either the Gilera was that much faster or Poggiali's timing that much better (and probably both), and the red bike sidled alongside on the exit to win by the narrowest of margins.

Jenkner was a lonely third; Olivé had fallen back into a five-strong battle, won by slow-starter Cecchinello, with Sanna also ahead of Olivé, then Bianco and Nieto, with impressive Finn Kallio losing the group only at the end, then hanging on to ninth by fending off the next gang, led by Giansanti. Borsoi, Dovizioso and Brannetti crashed together on the very first corner, Bautista a little further round on lap one; de Angelis survived one clash with Bianco only to crash properly a little later.

FIM WORLD CHAMPIONSHIP

CATALUNYA CIRCUIT — BARCELONA

MARLBORO
CATALAN
grand prix

round 6

16 JUNE 2002

Campsa
Repsol
Würth
La Caixa
Elf

CIRCUIT LENGTH: 2.937 miles/4.727 km

MotoGP

25 laps, 73.425 miles/118.175 km

Pos.	Rider (Nat.)	No.	Machine	Laps	Time & speed
1	Valentino Rossi (I)	46	Honda	25	44m 20.679s 99.354 mph/ 159.895 km/h
2	Tohru Ukawa (J)	11	Honda	25	44m 21.559s
3	Carlos Checa (E)	7	Yamaha	25	44m 29.210s
4	Max Biaggi (I)	3	Yamaha	25	44m 32.597s
5	Alex Barros (BR)	4	Honda	25	44m 43.061s
6	Loris Capirossi (I)	65	Honda	25	44m 50.775s
7	Kenny Roberts (USA)	10	Suzuki	25	44m 52.204s
8	Daijiro Kato (J)	74	Honda	25	44m 54.591s
9	Olivier Jacque (F)	19	Yamaha	25	44m 57.526s
10	John Hopkins (USA)	21	Yamaha	25	45m 12.259s
11	Akira Ryo (J)	33	Suzuki	25	45m 13.982s
12	Jeremy McWilliams (GB)	99	Proton KR	25	45m 18.264s
13	Tetsuya Harada (J)	31	Honda	25	45m 22.502s
14	Regis Laconi (F)	55	Aprilia	25	45m 23.681s
15	Pere Riba (E)	20	Yamaha	25	45m 25.402s
16	Norick Abe (J)	6	Yamaha	23	46m 04.367s
	Alex Hofmann (D)	66	Yamaha	24	DNF
	Sete Gibernau (E)	15	Suzuki	6	DNF
	Nobuatsu Aoki (J)	9	Proton KR	2	DNF
	Jurgen van den Goorbergh (NL)	17	Honda	0	DNF
	Shinya Nakano (J)	56	Yamaha	0	DNF

Fastest lap: Rossi, 1m 45.594s, 100.138 mph/161.156 km/h (record).
Previous record: Valentino Rossi, I (Honda), 1m 46.619s, 99.175 mph/159.607 km/h (2001).
Event best maximum speed: Ukawa, 197.1 mph/317.2 km/h (race).
Qualifying: 1 Biaggi, 1m 44.523s; 2 Ukawa, 1m 44.859s; 3 Gibernau, 1m 44.940s; 4 Rossi, 1m 44.950s; 5 Capirossi, 1m 45.133s; 6 Hopkins, 1m 45.148s; 7 Checa, 1m 45.253s; 8 Roberts, 1m 45.532s; 9 Barros, 1m 45.573s; 10 Nakano, 1m 45.750s; 11 Jacque, 1m 45.955s; 12 McWilliams, 1m 46.022s; 13 Laconi, 1m 46.057s; 14 van den Goorbergh, 1m 46.146s; 15 Kato, 1m 46.245s; 16 Abe, 1m 46.264s; 17 Ryo, 1m 46.280s; 18 Aoki, 1m 46.529s; 19 Hofmann, 1m 47.025s; 20 Harada, 1m 47.169s; 21 Riba, 1m 47.571s.
Fastest race laps: 1 Rossi, 1m 45.594s; 2 Checa, 1m 45.798s; 3 Ukawa, 1m 45.877s; 4 Biaggi, 1m 45.980s; 5 Gibernau, 1m 46.069s; 6 Roberts, 1m 46.179s; 7 Capirossi, 1m 46.292s; 8 Jacque, 1m 46.459s; 9 Barros, 1m 46.545s; 10 Kato, 1m 46.980s; 11 Abe, 1m 47.243s; 12 Ryo, 1m 47.371s; 13 Hopkins, 1m 47.536s; 14 Laconi, 1m 47.553s; 15 McWilliams, 1m 47.866s; 16 Riba, 1m 47.989s; 17 Harada, 1m 48.188s; 18 Hofmann, 1m 48.717s; 19 Aoki, 1m 53.057s.
World Championship: 1 Rossi, 145; 2 Ukawa, 97; 3 Capirossi, 65; 4 Biaggi and Checa, 56; 6 Abe, 52; 7 Barros, 51; 8 Kato, 47; 9 Jacque, 29; 10 Aoki, Laconi and Roberts, 28; 13 Ryo, 25; 14 Harada and Hopkins, 24; 16 Nakano, 16; 17 Itoh, 13; 18 van den Goorbergh, 12; 19 Gibernau, 11; 20 McWilliams, 10; 21 McCoy, 7; 22 Bayle, 5; 23 Riba, 4.

250 cc

23 laps, 67.551 miles/108.721 km

Pos.	Rider (Nat.)	No.	Machine	Laps	Time & speed
1	Marco Melandri (I)	3	Aprilia	23	41m 40.377s 97.266 mph/ 156.534 km/h
2	Roberto Rolfo (I)	4	Honda	23	41m 42.570s
3	Fonsi Nieto (E)	10	Aprilia	23	41m 43.066s
4	Randy de Puniet (F)	17	Aprilia	23	41m 43.327s
5	Franco Battaini (I)	21	Aprilia	23	41m 44.915s
6	Casey Stoner (AUS)	27	Aprilia	23	42m 03.478s
7	Naoki Matsudo (J)	8	Yamaha	23	42m 03.592s
8	Shahrol Yuzy (MAL)	18	Yamaha	23	42m 03.751s
9	Emilio Alzamora (E)	7	Honda	23	42m 04.963s
10	Toni Elias (E)	24	Aprilia	23	42m 11.098s
11	Haruchika Aoki (J)	11	Honda	23	42m 18.285s
12	David Checa (E)	42	Aprilia	23	42m 18.833s
13	Alex Debon (E)	6	Aprilia	23	42m 20.984s
14	Hugo Marchand (F)	51	Aprilia	23	42m 40.411s
15	Raul Jara (E)	22	Aprilia	23	42m 42.464s
16	Taro Sekiguchi (J)	76	Yamaha	23	42m 42.787s
17	Vincent Philippe (F)	25	Aprilia	23	42m 43.020s
18	Leon Haslam (GB)	19	Honda	23	42m 50.162s
19	Jay Vincent (GB)	12	Honda	23	42m 58.228s
20	Hector Faubel (E)	32	Aprilia	23	43m 10.490s
21	Dirk Heidolf (D)	28	Aprilia	23	43m 12.314s
22	Jarno Janssen (NL)	41	Honda	23	43m 28.174s
	Eric Bataille (F)	34	Honda	7	DNF
	Roberto Locatelli (I)	15	Aprilia	5	DNF
	Sebastian Porto (ARG)	9	Yamaha	4	DNF

Fastest lap: Battaini, 1m 48.063s, 97.850 mph/157.474 km/h.
Lap record: Valentino Rossi, I (Aprilia), 1m 47.585s, 98.285 mph/158.174 km/h (1998).
Event best maximum speed: Nieto, 168.1 mph/270.5 km/h (free practice no. 2).
Qualifying: 1 Nieto, 1m 47.315s; 2 Melandri, 1m 47.745s; 3 Locatelli, 1m 47.792s; 4 de Puniet, 1m 47.805s; 5 Battaini, 1m 47.817s; 6 Rolfo, 1m 48.058s; 7 Alzamora, 1m 48.444s; 8 Porto, 1m 48.447s; 9 Elias, 1m 48.598s; 10 Debon, 1m 48.721s; 11 Matsudo, 1m 48.737s; 12 Yuzy, 1m 48.772s; 13 Stoner, 1m 48.809s; 14 Aoki, 1m 48.938s; 15 Checa, 1m 49.249s; 16 Sekiguchi, 1m 49.314s; 17 Jara, 1m 49.370s; 18 Philippe, 1m 49.471s; 19 Marchand, 1m 50.084s; 20 Haslam, 1m 50.515s; 21 Vincent, 1m 50.907s; 22 Faubel, 1m 51.050s; 23 Janssen, 1m 51.204s; 24 Bataille, 1m 51.422s; 25 Heidolf, 1m 52.057s.
Fastest race laps: 1 Battaini, 1m 48.063s; 2 Melandri, 1m 48.078s; 3 Rolfo, 1m 48.136s; 4 de Puniet, 1m 48.145s; 5 Nieto, 1m 48.278s; 6 Alzamora, 1m 48.509s; 7 Elias, 1m 48.531s; 8 Locatelli, 1m 48.652s; 9 Matsudo, 1m 48.657s; 10 Stoner, 1m 48.717s; 11 Porto, 1m 48.815s; 12 Yuzy, 1m 48.980s; 13 Checa, 1m 49.421s; 14 Aoki, 1m 49.438s; 15 Debon, 1m 49.449s; 16 Faubel, 1m 50.159s; 17 Marchand, 1m 50.205s; 18 Philippe, 1m 50.314s; 19 Jara, 1m 50.337s; 20 Sekiguchi, 1m 50.485s; 21 Haslam, 1m 50.660s; 22 Vincent, 1m 50.752s; 23 Bataille, 1m 51.573s; 24 Janssen, 1m 51.768s; 25 Heidolf, 1m 51.955s.
World Championship: 1 Nieto, 101; 2 Melandri, 95; 3 Rolfo, 80; 4 de Puniet, 66; 5 Battaini, 60; 6 Alzamora, 59; 7 Locatelli, 55; 8 Porto, 45; 9 Elias, 40; 10 Matsudo, 38; 11 Debon, 32; 12 Miyazaki, 25; 13 Checa, 22; 14 Yuzy, 21; 15 Sakai and Stoner, 20; 17 Aoki, 16; 18 Kameya, 9; 19 Faubel, 7; 20 Vincent, 6; 21 Sekiguchi, 5; 22 Aoyama and Marchand, 4; 24 Philippe, 3; 25 Bataille, Heidolf and Jara, 2; 28 Haslam, 1.

125 cc

22 laps, 64.614 miles/103.994 km

Pos.	Rider (Nat.)	No.	Machine	Laps	Time & speed
1	Manuel Poggiali (RSM)	1	Gilera	22	41m 18.211s 93.869 mph/ 151.068 km/h
2	Daniel Pedrosa (E)	26	Honda	22	41m 28.230s
3	Steve Jenkner (D)	17	Aprilia	22	41m 28.099s
4	Lucio Cecchinello (I)	4	Aprilia	22	41m 33.608s
5	Simone Sanna (I)	16	Aprilia	22	41m 33.663s
6	Joan Olivé (E)	25	Honda	22	41m 33.478s
7	Stefano Bianco (I)	33	Aprilia	22	41m 33.760s
8	Pablo Nieto (E)	22	Aprilia	22	41m 34.429s
9	Mika Kallio (SF)	36	Honda	22	41m 40.973s
10	Mirko Giansanti (I)	6	Honda	22	41m 41.050s
11	Arnaud Vincent (F)	21	Aprilia	22	41m 41.278s
12	Andrea Ballerini (I)	50	Honda	22	41m 41.345s
13	Stefano Perugini (I)	7	Italjet	22	42m 01.556s
14	Jorge Lorenzo (E)	48	Derbi	22	42m 02.184s
15	Masao Azuma (J)	5	Honda	22	42m 05.400s
16	Jakub Smrz (CZ)	18	Honda	22	42m 05.544s
17	Gianluigi Scalvini (I)	32	Aprilia	22	42m 10.211s
18	Hector Barbera (E)	80	Aprilia	22	42m 29.569s
19	Mattia Angeloni (I)	31	Gilera	22	42m 29.699s
20	Alex Baldolini (I)	19	Aprilia	22	42m 39.814s
21	Jaroslav Hules (CZ)	39	Aprilia	22	42m 39.892s
22	Julian Simon (E)	52	Honda	22	42m 49.934s
23	Imre Toth (H)	20	Honda	22	42m 50.005s
24	Leon Camier (GB)	24	Italjet	21	42m 14.624s
	Chaz Davies (GB)	57	Aprilia	18	DNF
	Michel Fabrizio (I)	84	Gilera	14	DNF
	Youichi Ui (J)	41	Derbi	13	DNF
	Alex de Angelis (RSM)	15	Aprilia	13	DNF
	Angel Rodriguez (E)	47	Aprilia	4	DNF
	Gino Borsoi (I)	23	Aprilia	0	DNF
	Andrea Dovizioso (I)	34	Honda	0	DNF
	Alessandro Brannetti (I)	44	Honda	0	DNF
	Alvaro Bautista (E)	51	Aprilia	0	DNF
	Javier Machado (E)	55	Honda		DNQ

Fastest lap: Ui, 1m 51.443s, 94.882 mph/152.698 km/h (record).
Previous record: Stefano Perugini, I (Italjet), 1m 51.811s, 94.570 mph/152.196 km/h (2001).
Event best maximum speed: Borsoi, 145.8 mph/234.7 km/h (warm-up).
Qualifying: 1 Poggiali, 1m 51.216s; 2 Nieto, 1m 51.472s; 3 Jenkner, 1m 51.657s; 4 Pedrosa, 1m 51.667s; 5 Cecchinello, 1m 51.988s; 6 Ui, 1m 52.138s; 7 Lorenzo, 1m 52.143s; 8 Sanna, 1m 52.258s; 9 Borsoi, 1m 52.324s; 10 Kallio, 1m 52.343s; 11 Bianco, 1m 52.383s; 12 de Angelis, 1m 52.438s; 13 Azuma, 1m 52.565s; 14 Dovizioso, 1m 52.601s; 15 Hules, 1m 52.808s; 16 Giansanti, 1m 52.894s; 17 Perugini, 1m 52.899s; 18 Vincent, 1m 52.938s; 19 Ballerini, 1m 53.179s; 20 Fabrizio, 1m 53.306s; 21 Olivé, 1m 53.338s; 22 Davies, 1m 53.434s; 23 Scalvini, 1m 53.532s; 24 Smrz, 1m 53.736s; 25 Rodriguez, 1m 53.841s; 26 Simon, 1m 53.884s; 27 Barbera, 1m 54.286s; 28 Bautista, 1m 54.433s; 29 Angeloni, 1m 54.865s; 30 Brannetti, 1m 55.165s; 31 Toth, 1m 55.272s; 32 Baldolini, 1m 55.700s; 33 Camier, 1m 56.451s; 34 Machado, 1m 59.125s.
Fastest race laps: 1 Ui, 1m 51.443s; 2 Poggiali, 1m 51.484s; 3 Pedrosa, 1m 51.488s; 4 Jenkner, 1m 51.797s; 5 de Angelis, 1m 51.956s; 6 Olivé, 1m 52.020s; 7 Cecchinello, 1m 52.223s; 8 Sanna, 1m 52.383s; 9 Kallio, 1m 52.407s; 10 Nieto, 1m 52.411s; 11 Bianco, 1m 52.417s; 12 Giansanti, 1m 52.486s; 13 Vincent, 1m 52.634s; 14 Ballerini, 1m 52.676s; 15 Azuma, 1m 52.941s; 16 Davies, 1m 53.298s; 17 Lorenzo, 1m 53.415s; 18 Perugini, 1m 53.443s; 19 Fabrizio, 1m 53.494s; 20 Smrz, 1m 53.607s; 21 Barbera, 1m 53.636s; 22 Scalvini, 1m 53.697s; 23 Angeloni, 1m 54.186s; 24 Rodriguez, 1m 54.378s; 25 Baldolini, 1m 54.837s; 26 Hules, 1m 54.940s; 27 Simon, 1m 55.102s; 28 Toth, 1m 55.618s; 29 Camier, 1m 57.263s.
World Championship: 1 Poggiali, 111; 2 Vincent, 90; 3 Pedrosa, 86; 4 Cecchinello, 80; 5 Jenkner, 59; 6 Nieto, 45; 7 Sanna, 44; 8 Borsoi, 38; 9 Giansanti, 32; 10 Azuma, Kallio and Ui, 30; 13 Olivé, 20; 14 de Angelis, 19; 15 Bianco and Ueda, 18; 17 Dovizioso, 17; 18 Ballerini, 13; 19 Sabbatani, 11; 20 Aoyama, 10; 21 Perugini and Rodriguez, 9; 23 Nöhles, 6; 24 Barbera, 5; 25 Smrz, 3; 26 Baldolini, Lorenzo and Pellino, 2; 29 Fabrizio, 1.

DUTCH

ASSEN

FIM WORLD CHAMPIONSHIP · ROUND 7

WHEN a circuit is known as The Cathedral, you change it at your peril. At Assen, as so often before, they took a contrary view. To leave the circuit alone would have been at their peril. And this year the 35-million-Euro refit was finished.

The final change followed several schemes, and was the least damaging to the track itself, leaving most of it intact and losing only 22 metres of the longest lap of the year. Of course, it didn't please everybody. Nothing new in this. This was the fifth change since Assen's first races took place on the public roads in 1925. In 1926 already a shorter ten-mile loop was adopted; in 1955 the most recent layout was introduced, with a lap just short of five miles. Then, in 1984, the first loop was cut back by more than half, and the overall lap became 3.75 miles. On each occasion, you may be sure that people complained of the loss of particular favourite stretches.

The overall effect of the rebuild was impressive. The very restricted paddock had become extensive, all the new buildings were complete, the new pits excellent. The racers were concerned only with the circuit, and here a small miracle had been wrought to liberate the extra space. Where the classic fast zig-zag — the Veenslang — used to run across behind the paddock and onto the back straight, the whole section had been replicated a hundred or so metres further back. This zig and zag nature had been preserved, all the way to the now tighter Stekkenwal corner.

It's not that simple, of course. A track as subtle and as fast as this can't just be picked up and moved. The crucial difference was in the relative speeds of the new kinks. The old Veenslang had taken the 500s on a hugely demanding switchback through the gears from the Strubben horseshoe. The best riders sliced through smoothly at ever-increasing speed to tear onto the back straight (actually still curved) and gain a significant advantage; the pitfalls were many and hard to avoid: every really fast rider will remember at least one moment on the Veenslang.

The new kinks were further apart than before, and not only slower overall but also increasingly slow. The faster riders were having to gear down and even feather the brakes for the second right-hand kink, while there was relatively hard braking for the next left. It made a new and interesting challenge, entirely in character with Assen as a whole. But it was very different from the old and well-loved flat-out Veenslang. Although average speeds were barely affected, this had the interesting side-effect of reducing fuel consumption. The race had been shortened by one lap precisely because of fears the four-strokes would run out of fuel. The new layout made this reduction redundant.

Some liked it, some didn't, with Kenny Roberts Junior a lucid critic, on safety grounds. With Assen's endemically close racing, braking at such high speeds was dangerous, he averred. One slip or one touch and a rider (or two) might run straight, with or without his motor cycle... straight over the track where it loops back after the next kink, turning a private mishap into a multiple disaster. 'It would have been faster but safer if they'd just made it straight,' he said. Mercifully circumstances didn't combine in that way all weekend. McWilliams, riding the Proton, had a slant of his own. 'It won't be to everybody's taste, but it gets my vote. But then I've always liked dangerous circuits.'

Roberts had another issue, however, complaining the loss of the straight meant there was no place to relax. This was a serious matter to him, though he didn't mention why during an expansive press briefing on race eve ('I'm really enjoying racing again'). In fact Kenny had been suffering all season from 'arm pump-up', a variety of 'racer's wrist' that also afflicted (among many others) his father. This condition, relatively simply repaired by surgery, occurs when over-used forearm muscles develop more than the fascial sheath that contains them can bear. Use them hard — as on a racing motor cycle — and they pump up, causing severe pain and weakness. The extra weight of the four-stroke, as well as the obligation to blip in downshifts while braking, had made it worse... 'from the first test'. Kenny's plan was to tough it out, then quietly have the op in the summer break. That way, nobody need know until later. By now, however, the condition was deteriorating, and Assen — especially the new Assen — brought out the worst in it.

In the breaks in the usual hit-and-miss weather the riders concentrated on learning the new section and getting bikes and minds into the right settings. And by race day a political issue had distracted attention away from what was in any case now unchangeable. It was Rossi who led the protests after an unexpected announcement on the day before the race of a significant change in regulations, with immediate effect. Recent reluctant veteran of a pre-race film and photo-opportunity visit to a cheese factory (how symbolic), he fumed: 'They get us to do a whole lot of stupid things for the cameras, but when it is something as important as this, they don't even ask us. They're playing with our safety.'

The rule change was only for the MotoGP class, and abandoned the long-standing 'two-thirds-distance' rule... cut-off point for full results to be declared in a race stopped by changing weather. As at the French GP, where TV viewers and spectators were reckoned to have been short-changed. Okay for the smaller classes, but from now on, starting tomorrow, the two-thirds-distance rule would no longer apply to MotoGP. Races, no matter why stopped, would from now on restart until the full distance had been run.

This brought forth other spectres. Of perhaps a two-lap sprint, on a wet track, by hyped-up riders now packed dangerously together on the restart grid. As much as anything, the anger was for the insensitive timing and high-handedness of this major change in the regs, announced unexpectedly on the afternoon of final practice. Race director Paul Butler said: 'I don't see any safety problems,' but admitted it had all been a bit sudden: 'I expected this to take effect at the next race, but all the interested parties thought it should be brought in immediately.' Except, apparently, the riders.

All this in an interesting weekend — spiced up by the WCM Red Bull team getting everyone jagged up for a major announcement, then cancelling it at the last minute. 'The canapés were already on the tables,' said one wide-eyed staffer. At the same time, senior Moriwaki staff were also in the paddock. Sundry leaks and a bit of imagination put two and two together... and came up with eight. Eight RCV four-stroke Honda riders, that is, for next year: two for Rossi's HRC team and his partner, another pair for Gresini's Kato squad; and then two engine-only deals for Pons's team and WCM Red Bull. This last deal was rumoured to have been cooked up by HRC in conjunction with their Japanese allies Moriwaki, a chassis and tuning firm, and that's where Red Bull's chassis were coming from. This was followed by lots of 'can't confirm or deny' from various sources, and while it didn't necessarily all add up quite like that, the complexity of the whole affair did explain why Red Bull were summarily stopped from jumping the gun with such a far-reaching announcement.

Above: Rossi's fifth win in a row was celebrated with the usual adulation. By now he was already approaching god-like status.

Far left: Yamahas together again, but at this point of the season Checa (7) was getting more out of the M1 than Biaggi.

Centre left, above: Kenny Roberts Senior looks up to Junior; who would lead the race only to run into serious arm problems.

Centre left, below: Suzuki's heavy hitters — technical guru Warren Willing (left) and long-time team boss Garry Taylor.

Left: Melandri celebrates three in a row.

All photographs: Gold & Goose

Above: Alex Barros leads — his two-stroke was so fast through the changes of direction that only Rossi could go with him, while Roberts (10) would soon succumb to the Yamahas behind him.
Photograph: Gold & Goose

MOTOGP RACE – 19 laps

There was little time to learn the new subtleties of the circuit as well as fitting the four-strokes to Assen, with morning sessions truncated by bad weather. Rossi was back on pole, narrowly displacing Biaggi in the closing minutes. Roberts was third, his best yet, after more successful tests since Catalunya, then the top two-strokes, Capirossi on the front row, Barros only just off it. 'Just as I expected, we are close to the four-strokes here,' said Capirossi.

The rain held off as they lined up for the start, delayed by one-and-a-half hours to accommodate the football World Cup third-place play-off... and Biaggi took a flyer to lead into the first corner, only for Roberts to take over at the next, holding on as Rossi moved to second.

On lap three Barros, who had already flown past Ukawa and Capirossi, also pounced onto Biaggi on one corner entry, and then passed Rossi as well on the way out. Later on the same lap he swooped easily inside Roberts, to lead. One lap later and Roberts was starting to lose pace, dropping steadily to a lonely sixth, and Rossi was second. 'He and Max had a good pace, but when Barros came past he was in a different sport,' said Rossi later.

He stuck with Barros from then on, the pair taking 2.5 seconds directly from Ukawa, now ahead of both Yamahas. Capirossi had been in this group, but fell heavily at the start of lap five, suffering a broken arm and out of this and the next two races.

At the time, the four-stroke/two-stroke duel was fascinating. Rossi clearly had a speed advantage down the front straight, and drew easily alongside at one stage. But the two-stroke was clearly more agile through the twists, and Barros

was holding tight lines and eking out a little gap every time. Later, it had all the hallmarks of a cynical crowd-pleasing show by that old show-boater Rossi. With two laps left, he finally used everything his V5 had to offer, blasting past on the front straight and pulling away with great assurance. Later he complimented Barros's riding, and the Brazilian said he was pleased to have been the first two-stroke. Sadly, it all had a hollow ring.

Checa had most of the leading of the next trio, until Biaggi pounced on lap 12, only to drop back again with an error later on the same lap. Then he put a wheel on the grass at the first right-hander, surviving but losing touch. Ukawa hounded Checa to the end, and left his attack until the entry to the final chicane. He dived inside the Yamaha only to lose the front wheel, banging straight into the Spaniard. Ukawa fell, Checa didn't, making it across the gravel to rejoin for third, with Biaggi just three seconds adrift.

As Ukawa, helped by marshals, worked on push-starting his V5, Roberts was also approaching, but the Honda rider managed to fire up and wobble across the line less than a second before the healthy Suzuki made it. There had been some doubt as to whether the Honda was amenable to a bump start.

The other two-strokes had been hard at it. McWilliams led the next group, fending off a persistent Gibernau, through from behind. They exchanged places several times until Gibernau also touched the grass trying to tough it out under brakes for the chicane, slithering off and out. McWilliams now started to work on a four-second gap to Roberts when 'the gearbox just exploded'. His race was over.

Hopkins had been watching this, and now found himself well clear of the next group, where Aoki led Nakano, a struggling Abe gradually closing, an unexpectedly on-form Harada with him. Then Aoki was gone as well, his gearbox also failing.

Hopkins more than halved the gap on Roberts to cross the line only two seconds adrift while also keeping Nakano at bay. Then came Abe, while Harada had fallen back behind another group — Hofmann, van den Goorbergh and Kato, also locked in combat.

At the finish, van den Goorbergh pleased the home fans by passing Hofmann on the fast section for tenth, his best of the year so far, but Hofmann's 11th in only his second ever race on a 500 was highly creditable and secured an immediate invitation to jump off the Yamaha (McCoy was due back in England) and onto Capirossi's West Honda. Kato's close 12th demonstrated a continuing slump for the fancied 250 champion.

Harada was more than two seconds back, with Jacque all at sea with settings and well out of touch in 14th; Ryo cruising in almost a full lap behind. Laconi retired with electronic problems, and Riba pitted early.

Top right: Rossi is flanked by the heroic Barros and third-placed Checa.

Above: Japanese battle: Aoki gets the Proton on its side ahead of Nakano's Yamaha.

Left: Ukawa picks up his Honda. With only yards to the flag, he managed to bump-start it with the help of marshals, not an easy job with the new four-strokes.

Below left: McWilliams leads Harada (31), Hopkins (21) and frustrated four-stroker Gibernau, who crashed trying to find a way through.

All photographs: Gold & Goose

91

Right: Rolfo and Nieto lead the battle for the last 250 rostrum spot, from Locatelli, Porto and Aoki (11).

Below and below right: Pedrosa was a superb first-time winner, flanked on the rostrum by Poggiali and team-mate Olivé.

All photographs: Gold & Goose

250 cc RACE – 18 laps

Melandri was lucky enough to be fastest on the first day of practice, from de Puniet, Nieto and Elias, and stayed there as weather played havoc with the second day's timed session. Porto led row two, from Battaini, the amazing Stoner (who had challenged for pole) and Ralf Waldmann, a welcome return for the multiple GP winner, now jobless.

Another sprinkle of rain before the start mercifully came to nothing, and the race began on slicks with Elias surging into the early lead. Melandri didn't let it last beyond one lap, however, powering past for an almost undisturbed afternoon of class mastery.

The strongest challenge came from de Puniet, who had a brief tussle with Elias, then finally got ahead for good and closed down on the leader. Poised to attack on lap seven, he instead flicked sideways and flew over the high side.

Melandri was now unmolested for his third win in a row, Elias (who won his first 125 GP here last year) likewise for his first class rostrum.

A little way back, Rolfo was picking his way through a quartet comprising Nieto, struggling with bad settings and especially a full tank, Aoki and Porto, with Locatelli already losing touch by the time Rolfo got to the front on lap ten. Rolfo stretched away and closed on Elias, but the gap was too big.

Stoner had got away badly again, 18th on lap one, and was again moving through impressively with lap times rivalling the leaders. By half-distance he had closed on the trio disputing eighth: Battaini, Yuzy and Waldmann; and four laps later had picked his way through, even drawing away slightly towards the flag.

Debon was next, alone and 22 seconds adrift. Jara, Matsudo and Philippe took the final points, Checa missing out by less than a tenth in the final scramble.

Marchand and Faubel crashed out, Haslam retired to the pits, and Vincent was a distant 19th, feeling an increasingly severe need for speed.

125 cc RACE – 17 laps

First-time winner Pedrosa made no mistakes to head a teenage rostrum, starting from pole and leading from start to finish. A big gang behind had cut back to five by half-distance, with Cecchinello mainly in front, fast-starting Olivé playing an active role, Poggiali lurking menacingly, Vincent catching up to join in and Jenkner ever present.

On the final lap, Poggiali finally imposed the authority endowed by his very fast Gilera for second. Third, a career best by far, went to Pedrosa's team-mate Olivé, who refused to be bullied, and headed some tough riders: Vincent, Cecchinello and Jenkner, second to sixth covered by half a second.

There was an even bigger brawl for seventh, with rookie Mika Kallio consolidating his front-row start with some spirit until he crashed in the last-lap battle. The position went to Nieto by inches from Ui, de Angelis and Rodriguez. Dovizioso, Sanna, Borsoi and Azuma followed, with Talmacsi dropping back to claim the last point.

GAULOISES DUTCH TT

29 JUNE 2002

round 7

ASSEN RACING CIRCUIT

CIRCUIT LENGTH: 3.745 miles/6.027 km

MotoGP

19 laps, 71.155 miles/114.513 km

Pos.	Rider (Nat.)	No.	Machine	Laps	Time & speed
1	Valentino Rossi (I)	46	Honda	19	38m 49.425s 109.966 mph/ 176.973 km/h
2	Alex Barros (BR)	4	Honda	19	38m 51.658s
3	Carlos Checa (E)	7	Yamaha	19	38m 59.107s
4	Max Biaggi (I)	3	Yamaha	19	39m 02.733s
5	Tohru Ukawa (J)	11	Honda	19	39m 21.811s
6	Kenny Roberts (USA)	10	Suzuki	19	39m 22.703s
7	John Hopkins (USA)	21	Yamaha	19	39m 24.888s
8	Shinya Nakano (J)	56	Yamaha	19	39m 25.044s
9	Norick Abe (J)	6	Yamaha	19	39m 26.868s
10	Jurgen van den Goorbergh (NL)	17	Honda	19	39m 37.525s
11	Alex Hofmann (D)	66	Yamaha	19	39m 37.750s
12	Daijiro Kato (J)	74	Honda	19	39m 38.796s
13	Tetsuya Harada (J)	31	Honda	19	39m 41.183s
14	Olivier Jacque (F)	19	Yamaha	19	40m 01.215s
15	Akira Ryo (J)	33	Suzuki	19	42m 03.824s
	Nobuatsu Aoki (J)	9	Proton KR	11	DNF
	Jeremy McWilliams (GB)	99	Proton KR	8	DNF
	Sete Gibernau (E)	15	Suzuki	6	DNF
	Regis Laconi (F)	55	Aprilia	6	DNF
	Loris Capirossi (I)	65	Honda	4	DNF
	Pere Riba (E)	20	Yamaha	3	DNF

Fastest lap: Rossi, 2m 00.973s, 111.446 mph/179.355 km/h (record).

Previous circuit record: Kevin Schwantz, USA (Suzuki), 2m 02.443s, 110.510 mph/ 177.849 km/h (1991).

Event best maximum speed: Rossi, 160.1 mph/257.6 km/h (race).

Qualifying: 1 Rossi, 2m 01.691s; 2 Biaggi, 2m 01.716s; 3 Roberts, 2m 01.836s; 4 Capirossi, 2m 01.983s; 5 Barros, 2m 02.019s; 6 Checa, 2m 02.236s; 7 Harada, 2m 02.485s; 8 Ukawa, 2m 02.496s; 9 McWilliams, 2m 02.626s; 10 Hopkins, 2m 02.764s; 11 Laconi, 2m 03.167s; 12 Hofmann, 2m 03.187s; 13 Aoki, 2m 03.491s; 14 Nakano, 2m 03.516s; 15 van den Goorbergh, 2m 03.823s; 16 Gibernau, 2m 03.908s; 17 Kato, 2m 04.311s; 18 Riba, 2m 04.587s; 19 Abe, 2m 04.734s; 20 Jacque, 2m 05.161s; 21 Ryo, 2m 06.679s.

Fastest race laps: 1 Rossi, 2m 00.973s; 2 Ukawa, 2m 01.565s; 3 Barros, 2m 01.636s; 4 Checa, 2m 01.885s; 5 Biaggi, 2m 02.092s; 6 Nakano, 2m 02.676s; 7 Roberts, 2m 02.896s; 8 Harada, 2m 03.210s; 9 McWilliams, 2m 03.267s; 10 Capirossi, 2m 03.273s; 11 Abe, 2m 03.274s; 12 Laconi, 2m 03.425s; 13 Hopkins, 2m 03.507s; 14 Gibernau, 2m 03.563s; 15 Hofmann, 2m 03.816s; 16 Jacque, 2m 03.840s; 17 van den Goorbergh, 2m 03.939s; 18 Kato, 2m 03.974s; 19 Aoki, 2m 04.145s; 20 Riba, 2m 06.319s; 21 Ryo, 2m 06.663s.

World Championship: 1 Rossi, 170; 2 Ukawa, 108; 3 Checa, 72; 4 Barros, 71; 5 Biaggi, 69; 6 Capirossi, 65; 7 Abe, 59; 8 Kato, 51; 9 Roberts, 38; 10 Hopkins, 33; 11 Jacque, 31; 12 Aoki and Laconi, 28; 14 Harada, 27; 15 Ryo, 26; 16 Nakano, 24; 17 van den Goorbergh, 18; 18 Itoh, 13; 19 Gibernau, 11; 20 McWilliams, 10; 21 McCoy, 7; 22 Bayle and Hofmann, 5; 24 Riba, 4.

---

250 cc

18 laps, 67.410 miles/108.468 km

Pos.	Rider (Nat.)	No.	Machine	Laps	Time & speed
1	Marco Melandri (I)	3	Aprilia	18	37m 48.960s 106.955 mph/ 172.127 km/h
2	Toni Elias (E)	24	Aprilia	18	37m 53.917s
3	Roberto Rolfo (I)	4	Honda	18	37m 55.632s
4	Sebastian Porto (ARG)	9	Yamaha	18	38m 00.233s
5	Fonsi Nieto (E)	10	Aprilia	18	38m 03.125s
6	Haruchika Aoki (J)	11	Honda	18	38m 05.368s
7	Roberto Locatelli (I)	15	Aprilia	18	38m 12.912s
8	Casey Stoner (AUS)	27	Aprilia	18	38m 15.878s
9	Franco Battaini (I)	21	Aprilia	18	38m 16.415s
10	Shahrol Yuzy (MAL)	18	Yamaha	18	38m 16.438s
11	Ralf Waldmann (D)	26	Aprilia	18	38m 17.232s
12	Alex Debon (E)	6	Aprilia	18	38m 39.724s
13	Raul Jara (E)	22	Aprilia	18	38m 43.791s
14	Naoki Matsudo (J)	8	Yamaha	18	38m 46.916s
15	Vincent Philippe (F)	25	Aprilia	18	38m 48.180s
16	David Checa (E)	42	Aprilia	18	38m 48.217s
17	Taro Sekiguchi (J)	76	Yamaha	18	39m 17.958s
18	Jarno Janssen (NL)	41	Honda	18	39m 18.027s
19	Jay Vincent (GB)	12	Honda	18	39m 18.219s
20	Dirk Heidolf (D)	28	Aprilia	18	39m 29.707s
21	Peter Politiek (NL)	59	Honda	17	38m 03.083s
22	Jarno Boesveld (NL)	61	Aprilia	17	38m 10.063s
23	Gert Pieper (NL)	60	Aprilia	17	38m 28.516s
	Randy de Puniet (F)	17	Aprilia	7	DNF
	Leon Haslam (GB)	19	Honda	7	DNF
	Hector Faubel (E)	32	Aprilia	4	DNF
	Hugo Marchand (F)	51	Aprilia	2	DNF
	Emilio Alzamora (E)	7	Honda	2	DNF
	Thierry van den Bosch (F)	77	Aprilia		DNQ
	Jan Blok (NL)	58	Honda		DNQ

Fastest lap: Rolfo, 2m 04.824s, 108.008 mph/173.822 km/h (record).

Previous circuit record: Valentino Rossi, I (Aprilia), 2m 05.696s, 107.650 mph/ 173.246 km/h (1999).

Event best maximum speed: Locatelli, 155.3 mph/249.9 km/h (race).

Qualifying: 1 Melandri, 2m 04.520s; 2 de Puniet, 2m 04.596s; 3 Nieto, 2m 04.725s; 4 Elias, 2m 05.207s; 5 Porto, 2m 05.438s; 6 Battaini, 2m 05.581s; 7 Stoner, 2m 05.779s; 8 Waldmann, 2m 06.313s; 9 Locatelli, 2m 06.415s; 10 Philippe, 2m 06.435s; 11 Yuzy, 2m 06.579s; 12 Debon, 2m 06.657s; 13 Matsudo, 2m 06.832s; 14 Checa, 2m 06.888s; 15 Aoki, 2m 06.970s; 16 Janssen, 2m 07.255s; 17 Rolfo, 2m 07.294s; 18 Alzamora, 2m 07.391s; 19 Jara, 2m 07.535s; 20 Heidolf, 2m 08.835s; 21 Marchand, 2m 08.844s; 22 Haslam, 2m 09.080s; 23 Faubel, 2m 09.289s; 24 Vincent, 2m 09.415s; 25 Pieper, 2m 12.038s; 26 Sekiguchi, 2m 12.137s; 27 Boesveld, 2m 12.248s; 28 Politiek, 2m 12.353s; 29 van den Bosch, 2m 13.611s; 30 Blok, 2m 13.654s.

Fastest race laps: 1 Rolfo, 2m 04.824s; 2 Porto, 2m 04.840s; 3 de Puniet, 2m 04.964s; 4 Melandri, 2m 04.989s; 5 Elias, 2m 05.161s; 6 Nieto, 2m 05.281s; 7 Aoki, 2m 05.622s; 8 Yuzy, 2m 05.757s; 9 Stoner, 2m 05.825s; 10 Waldmann, 2m 05.945s; 11 Battaini, 2m 05.947s; 12 Locatelli, 2m 06.436s; 13 Philippe, 2m 06.678s; 14 Matsudo, 2m 06.876s; 15 Jara, 2m 07.188s; 16 Checa, 2m 07.204s; 17 Debon, 2m 07.686s; 18 Faubel, 2m 08.327s; 19 Vincent, 2m 08.360s; 20 Heidolf, 2m 08.480s; 21 Sekiguchi, 2m 08.594s; 22 Janssen, 2m 08.968s; 23 Marchand, 2m 11.868s; 24 Boesveld, 2m 12.920s; 25 Politiek, 2m 13.226s; 26 Pieper, 2m 13.297s; 27 Alzamora, 2m 15.129s; 28 Haslam, 2m 22.202s.

World Championship: 1 Melandri, 120; 2 Nieto, 112; 3 Rolfo, 96; 4 Battaini, 67; 5 de Puniet, 66; 6 Locatelli, 64; 7 Elias, 60; 8 Alzamora, 59; 9 Porto, 58; 10 Matsudo, 40; 11 Debon, 36; 12 Stoner, 28; 13 Yuzy, 27; 14 Aoki, 25; 15 Miyazaki, 25; 16 Checa, 22; 17 Sakai, 20; 18 Kameya, 9; 19 Faubel, 7; 20 Vincent, 6; 21 Jara, Sekiguchi and Waldmann, 5; 24 Aoyama, Marchand and Philippe, 4; 27 Bataille and Heidolf, 2; 29 Haslam, 1.

---

125 cc

17 laps, 63.665 miles/102.459 km

Pos.	Rider (Nat.)	No.	Machine	Laps	Time & speed
1	Daniel Pedrosa (E)	26	Honda	17	37m 31.974s 101.774 mph/ 163.790 km/h
2	Manuel Poggiali (RSM)	1	Gilera	17	37m 34.497s
3	Joan Olivé (E)	25	Honda	17	37m 34.690s
4	Arnaud Vincent (F)	21	Aprilia	17	37m 34.787s
5	Lucio Cecchinello (I)	4	Aprilia	17	37m 34.938s
6	Steve Jenkner (D)	17	Aprilia	17	37m 35.005s
7	Pablo Nieto (E)	22	Aprilia	17	37m 47.158s
8	Youichi Ui (J)	41	Derbi	17	37m 47.332s
9	Alex de Angelis (RSM)	15	Aprilia	17	37m 47.786s
10	Angel Rodriguez (E)	47	Aprilia	17	37m 48.104s
11	Andrea Dovizioso (I)	34	Honda	17	37m 49.102s
12	Simone Sanna (I)	16	Aprilia	17	37m 49.197s
13	Gino Borsoi (I)	23	Aprilia	17	37m 49.463s
14	Masao Azuma (J)	5	Honda	17	37m 51.046s
15	Gabor Talmacsi (H)	8	Honda	17	38m 00.571s
16	Jorge Lorenzo (E)	48	Derbi	17	38m 07.119s
17	Jaroslav Hules (CZ)	39	Aprilia	17	38m 11.240s
18	Andrea Ballerini (I)	50	Honda	17	38m 11.507s
19	Mirko Giansanti (I)	6	Honda	17	38m 11.746s
20	Hector Barbera (E)	80	Aprilia	17	38m 11.984s
21	Alex Baldolini (I)	19	Aprilia	17	38m 14.752s
22	Jakub Smrz (CZ)	18	Honda	17	38m 15.035s
23	Fabrizio Lai (I)	75	Honda	17	38m 23.785s
24	Chaz Davies (GB)	57	Aprilia	17	38m 31.478s
25	Shuhei Aoyama (J)	66	Honda	17	38m 38.831s
26	Mattia Angeloni (I)	31	Gilera	17	38m 46.495s
27	Imre Toth (H)	20	Honda	17	38m 52.531s
28	Leon Camier (GB)	24	Italjet	17	39m 18.280s
29	Stefano Bianco (I)	33	Aprilia	17	39m 18.622s
30	Adri den Bekker (NL)	89	Honda	17	39m 18.653s
31	Randy Gevers (NL)	60	Honda	17	39m 33.787s
32	Gerald Perdon (NL)	62	Honda	16	38m 18.594s
	Mika Kallio (SF)	36	Honda	16	DNF
	Michel Fabrizio (I)	84	Gilera	16	DNF
	Gianluigi Scalvini (I)	32	Aprilia	15	DNF
	Raymond Schouten (NL)	61	Honda	11	DNF
	Stefano Perugini (I)	7	Italjet	2	DNF

Fastest lap: Olivé, 2m 11.209s, 102.752 mph/165.363 km/h (record).

Previous circuit record: Noboru Ueda, J (Honda), 2m 13.225s, 101.566 mph/163.455 km/h (1999).

Event best maximum speed: Sanna, 138.9 mph/223.6 km/h (race).

Qualifying: 1 Pedrosa, 2m 11.882s; 2 Cecchinello, 2m 12.199s; 3 de Angelis, 2m 12.236s; 4 Kallio, 2m 12.519s; 5 Vincent, 2m 12.582s; 6 Poggiali, 2m 12.728s; 7 Rodriguez, 2m 12.859s; 8 Jenkner, 2m 12.867s; 9 Scalvini, 2m 12.910s; 10 Bianco, 2m 12.977s; 11 Nieto, 2m 13.071s; 12 Olivé, 2m 13.234s; 13 Azuma, 2m 13.452s; 14 Borsoi, 2m 13.548s; 15 Ui, 2m 13.610s; 16 Lorenzo, 2m 13.693s; 17 Ballerini, 2m 13.792s; 18 Sanna, 2m 13.855s; 19 Dovizioso, 2m 13.981s; 20 Talmacsi, 2m 14.074s; 21 Smrz, 2m 14.382s; 22 Baldolini, 2m 14.486s; 23 Hules, 2m 14.530s; 24 Barbera, 2m 14.883s; 25 Fabrizio, 2m 14.959s; 26 Lai, 2m 15.083s; 27 Davies, 2m 15.387s; 28 Toth, 2m 15.552s; 29 Giansanti, 2m 15.643s; 30 Angeloni, 2m 16.741s; 31 Aoyama, 2m 17.038s; 32 Camier, 2m 17.057s; 33 Schouten, 2m 17.797s; 34 Gevers, 2m 18.280s; 35 den Bekker, 2m 20.018s; 36 Perdon, 2m 21.692s; 37 Perugini, 2m 37.850s.

Fastest race laps: 1 Olivé, 2m 11.209s; 2 Jenkner, 2m 11.344s; 3 Nieto, 2m 11.401s; 4 Poggiali, 2m 11.536s; 5 Vincent, 2m 11.563s; 6 Pedrosa, 2m 11.735s; 7 Cecchinello, 2m 11.744s; 8 Ui, 2m 11.817s; 9 Sanna, 2m 11.869s; 10 Dovizioso, 2m 11.881s; 11 Kallio, 2m 11.977s; 12 Rodriguez, 2m 12.001s; 13 Scalvini, 2m 12.015s; 14 Bianco, 2m 12.118s; 15 de Angelis, 2m 12.134s; 16 Borsoi, 2m 12.146s; 17 Talmacsi, 2m 12.226s; 18 Azuma, 2m 12.311s; 19 Hules, 2m 13.031s; 20 Barbera, 2m 13.224s; 21 Lorenzo, 2m 13.311s; 22 Ballerini, 2m 13.360s; 23 Baldolini, 2m 13.369s; 24 Giansanti, 2m 13.374s; 25 Fabrizio, 2m 13.495s; 26 Smrz, 2m 13.560s; 27 Lai, 2m 13.574s; 28 Davies, 2m 14.328s; 29 Aoyama, 2m 14.579s; 30 Angeloni, 2m 15.517s; 31 Toth, 2m 15.618s; 32 den Bekker, 2m 17.388s; 33 Camier, 2m 17.414s; 34 Schouten, 2m 17.590s; 35 Gevers, 2m 18.058s; 36 Perdon, 2m 20.262s; 37 Perugini, 2m 27.695s.

World Championship: 1 Poggiali, 131; 2 Pedrosa, 111; 3 Vincent, 103; 4 Cecchinello, 91; 5 Jenkner, 69; 6 Nieto, 54; 7 Sanna, 48; 8 Borsoi, 41; 9 Ui, 38; 10 Olivé, 36; 11 Azuma and Giansanti, 32; 13 Kallio, 30; 14 de Angelis, 26; 15 Dovizioso, 22; 16 Bianco and Ueda, 18; 18 Rodriguez, 15; 19 Ballerini, 13; 20 Sabbatani, 11; 21 Aoyama, 10; 22 Perugini, 9; 23 Nöhles, 6; 24 Barbera, 5; 25 Smrz, 3; 26 Baldolini, Lorenzo and Pellino, 2; 29 Fabrizio and Talmacsi, 1.

BRITISH GP

DONINGTON

FIM WORLD CHAMPIONSHIP · ROUND 8

Opposite: If they all came to see Rossi, then they could go home satisfied. The biggest British GP crowd for ten years watched him win again.

Bottom right: TT fan Roberto Rolfo wore a yellow Joey Dunlop helmet as a tribute to the master of open-roads racing.
All photographs: Gold & Goose

ANYONE who took the day off on Friday in the hope of hearing all the new four-strokes for the first time was in for a disappointment — or a long wait, until Saturday. Unless they were there for the first three minutes of the first free training session, they would have to do without any Hondas. After that, both had gone.

Ukawa's departure was dramatic in the extreme. The latest of many distinguished victims of Donington's treacherous downhill Craner Curves, he didn't even complete a single lap on his sonorous V5, instead embarking on a series of flips that left the rider in poor condition and the bike comprehensively disassembled — the front wheel even shattered by one of a series of looping impacts that looked more like an air crash. He was out of the race, lucky that his worst injury was a fracture to his coccyx, since the cartwheeling bike had all but hit him twice.

Rossi went soon afterwards — also on his out lap, but at much lower speed at the final hairpin. He too landed heavily, suffering concussion and a minor fracture to his left thumb. He was out for the day, though he returned the next day with few visible signs of injury, and some inspired setting work from his team that gave him his seventh pole in eight races, followed by his seventh win, to secure a massive 87-point advantage after half the season.

Michelin immediately withdrew one of their latest dual-compound tyres that both had been using, showing admirable caution. Not misplaced, perhaps, in a weekend of many crashes... a total of 59 included many others from the top class, including: Roberts, Checa, Biaggi, Nakano, Gibernau, Kato, Hopkins and the luckless Riba, who broke his leg. The most telling comment came from the smallest class, and veteran victim Lucio Cecchinello. 'It's funny that IRTA [based in England] are very strict about parking, paddock and everything, and also about safety — but when you come here, the situation is very bad. They should renew this track. The number of crashes shows how dangerous it is.'

Not only the surface is overdue for renewal. After the failure of planning permission for a major revamp, the seediness and decline of Britain's GP venue since 1987 seemed all the more plain. Given the quality of the tracks and facilities at circuits such as Sepang, Valencia, Assen and even Brno, Donington now vies with Rio for general scuzziness. With the announcement just weeks later that both China and Malta were building new circuits, and hope to join the MotoGP party, and with no suitable replacements readily coming to mind, the future of the British round, on the calendar from the start as the Isle of Man TT, had seldom looked as bleak.

Those anticipating four-stroke auditory pleasures were rewarded with Rossi's return on Saturday, and more besides. The trumpeting blare of the Yamaha on the exit from the Melbourne Loop hairpin displayed an extraordinary variation not heard before: a flat-sounding misfire cutting in and out under full throttle. F1 fans recognised it immediately as some form of traction control, and though both Biaggi and Checa used it from time to time, it was not on all their bikes.

Clever, but sadly it was no use asking Yamaha for details, since they had clammed up completely over the course of a season that had begun with red faces after an overload of publicity for a bike that had fallen short of overblown expectations. At this halfway GP, it was clearly much improved: with a new chassis, the cleverest slipper clutch of all (an electronic/hydraulic affair), and a number of other signal improvements. Stricken with coyness, however, Yamaha had not yet even confirmed the cubic capacity or the method of valve drive, let alone the number of valves per cylinder or any but the vaguest electronic details.

Over at Proton, both riders now had the latest 'wideline' chassis, though in fact Aoki didn't like it. Of more interest was a leakage of details of the new V5 engine that Roberts had commissioned, and for which this chassis was ultimately being developed. It was no Honda copy, said Roberts, but a similarly logical interpretation of the same rules. Parallel evolution, if you like.

Lots of peripheral activity at what is still a key event, in spite of the poor surface and downmarket atmosphere. The most important was the huge revival of interest — a combination no doubt of Rossi Fever and MotoGP Fever — with a race-day crowd of 60,000 recalling the good old days, and more than three times the numbers of a couple of years ago. Records were broken at the annual Day of Champions as well, with the £100,000 mark exceeded for the first time — the top item being a set of leathers donated by Wayne Rainey, which went for £6,600, beating a set of Biaggi leathers by £800.

Respect for old heroes was reinforced by the latest (and some might think rather overdue) additions to the Hall of Fame: four-times 500 champion Geoff Duke and seven times 125, 250 and 500 champion Phil Read joined the lists. Read had the year before been joined by Rossi as the only champion in those three categories, and had a fine tribute to his successor. 'He reminds me of Mike Hailwood — not only with his talent, but in the fact that he puts a lot of fun and enjoyment into his racing.'

McCoy was back from his four-race absence, and signed during the weekend with Red Bull for next year, when he expected V5 Honda power. 'If you had to choose now, it would be a pretty good option,' he said. By the year's end, however, the dream was over. Team-mate Hopkins had circumvented the ban on pre-race testing here, as at some other circuits, by joining a track day, with Niall Mackenzie showing him the way round.

Mackenzie was on hand too, for the launch of his autobiography, in a good weekend for readers; the first English language biography of Rossi was also launched on the Saturday night; Jon Ekerold's autobiography had been released two weeks earlier.

Honda 250 factory rider Roberto Rolfo won new fans by wearing a Joey Dunlop replica helmet, and revealing: 'I love the Isle of Man, and would love to race there.' And down in the 125 class, Max Sabbatani made a welcome return, after missing just three races following his ghastly crash at Mugello.

MOTOGP RACE – 30 laps

Another epically close practice session saw Rossi snitch pole from Checa at the very last minute. Harada was a surprise third, enjoying the Dunlops-at-Donington effect after languishing all year so far; Barros took the last front-row position. The first four were covered by three-tenths, with 12 within the second; Biaggi led row two from Hopkins, McWilliams and Roberts.

Race day was clear and sunny, rewarding the unfamiliar crowd — the biggest for ten years.

Checa led away from Rossi, Biaggi and Roberts, who lost ground from the start. Barros was moving through from behind, passing Harada and Aoki, and then Roberts on lap five.

The pace of the leaders was fast, and they pulled away steadily. Rossi looked threatening from time to time, breaking Crafar's long-standing 1998 lap record fourth time round; Biaggi was just hanging on behind.

Soon after half-distance, on lap 18, Checa fell. It was on the way into the final hairpin, over the notorious bumps, and though he sprinted to the bike to rejoin, it was only to retire later on. 'I wasn't on the limit, but I held on to the brakes a little longer on that lap,' was his rueful comment.

From then on Rossi gradually pulled clear of Biaggi, in complete control on the edge of adhesion. A master at work, though he said: 'I don't know what would have happened if Checa hadn't fallen. I was quicker through the fast corners, but he was quicker through the last slow hairpins.' He had cut a full 20 seconds off his last-year's race average.

Biaggi had no answer, and a now-familiar complaint about the Yamaha's rather ponderous handling. 'I tried to pass Rossi early on, but the pace was too fast. My bike was losing agility through the fast corners. I just had to concentrate on finishing.'

Aoki passed Harada on lap nine, with Roberts, then Kato, Abe, Gibernau, Hopkins and Jacque close behind. McWilliams had been with them, only for a power valve to seize, for a retirement after six laps. Then Aoki's tyres started to fade still more, by when Abe had moved through to take over fourth. Kato and Gibernau were right with him, Hopkins and Jacque trading blows a little way back; Roberts continuing to drop away, his arm-pump problem almost crippling and his spirit sinking along with his position. After this race, he would fly directly back to the US for surgery.

Abe gained some clear air; on lap 22 Gibernau got to the front of his group, Jacque on his heels, diving past at the chicane with three laps left to secure fifth.

Kato followed, nursing a hand injury and a poorly set-up bike after his practice fall. Hopkins passed the fading Aoki for eighth on the last lap.

Nakano had an undistinguished race, ten seconds behind Aoki, and eight ahead of Harada, who had lost ground in an off-track excursion at the chicane.

McCoy was another four seconds back, happy enough to be able to finish after his long absence, and holding off wild card Ryo's Suzuki by less than a second. Then came Roberts, a similar distance ahead of van den Goorbergh.

Laconi was another seven-tenths behind after a typically erratic outing on the powerful but ill-handling Aprilia; Alex Hofmann, riding in place of Capirossi, was a further ten seconds adrift as he battled with fading tyres in his first race on the Honda — two weeks before he'd raced McCoy's Yamaha at Assen.

250 cc RACE – 27 laps

Nieto was on pole again from Melandri, who confidently blamed traffic for not being fastest; Porto's sweet-handling Yamaha was next, and then Alzamora after a Spanish muddle: Nieto had tried to give team-mate Elias a time-tow, but the Honda rider had slotted in behind him instead.

Porto led into the first corner — his first time ever up front — and rather surprisingly pulled a second clear of Nieto and Melandri over the first six laps, and maintained his lead for the next six. Then his back wheel locked abruptly going down the hill — and what he said later was a certain victory instead ended in seizure and angry retirement. It was his hundredth GP.

Nieto had made most of the running from Melandri, who took over finally shortly after half-distance. Rolfo was a little way behind, heading Aoki's RS-W Honda, Alzamora, Battaini and de Puniet. Battaini was on full form, and moved through to pounce on Rolfo on lap ten, less than two seconds behind the leaders. He gradually closed up until the 18th lap when he started to lose ground again, never having been quite close enough to challenge.

Elias had found neutral instead of second on the startline, and ended the first lap 14th and charging. By lap ten he was up to sixth, passing Aoki and de Puniet in the same lap, and closing on Rolfo, with Battaini in view ahead of that. He sliced past Rolfo on lap 15, and a gap of almost three seconds to Battaini then stretched as he was slowed by a backmarker. Nothing daunted, Elias tried even harder, to catch and pass Battaini on the final lap.

Up front, Nieto had been dogging Melandri, but when the Italian pushed again with four laps to go, he seemed to have nothing left, losing a second. Not so, however, and he set fastest lap as he closed again for a last-lap showdown. He outbraked Melandri into the chicane, and led down the hill to the penultimate hairpin. Melandri was on top of the situation, however. He dived firmly inside on the entry to the Melbourne Loop, and led round Goddards and across the line. Nieto realised he was beaten, and finished seven-tenths adrift.

Elias's second rostrum finish was by half a second from Battaini; Rolfo was a close fifth, de Puniet 15 seconds adrift, managing to stay ahead of Aoki quite comfortably.

Behind, Matsudo managed to fend off a closing Debon, who was in turn worried by Yuzy and Stoner inches behind, Alzamora dropping back from this battle to ward off Locatelli.

Sekiguchi was a distant 14th; Checa took the last point.

125 cc RACE – 26 laps

Poggiali was on pole, from Cecchinello, Pedrosa and Ui — the Japanese rider's first time on the front row since Brazil last year, in a troubled season but now at a favourite track.

Pedrosa led away, but first time round the final hairpin Ui dived inside, only to lose the place again down the next straight. Poggiali had a grandstand view, with Cecchinello, Azuma and Olivé in pursuit, heading the usual big pack.

Ui's revival didn't last, however, and he was soon slipping backwards. By lap six, the first four — Pedrosa, Cecchinello, Poggiali and Azuma — had broken free from the gang.

Preferring to control the pace, the veteran Cecchinello moved ahead round McLeans on the ninth lap, and stayed there, under extreme pressure, until Pedrosa went ahead again with four laps remaining.

By now, Vincent had worked his way through the pursuit pack and broken free to join the leaders, taking fourth from Azuma by half-distance.

The battle became frantic as the end drew near, with Vincent leading for the first time on lap 23, though never for long, and Cecchinello fighting back several times — until one lap later he paid the price of trying too hard, sliding off and out.

This gave the Frenchman a little breathing space, although Pedrosa had closed right up to within two-tenths over the line. He never did attack, however, being fully occupied in defending himself from the very persistent Poggiali.

Azuma had dropped out of contention by now, 13 seconds adrift at the finish and himself fending off the next group, with Jenkner heading Olivé, and de Angelis only two seconds behind. Then came Ui, another two seconds away, while Dovizioso held off Aoyama over the line.

Halfway through the year, and the title battle was spicing up somewhat, with Pedrosa closing on Poggiali, and Vincent chasing them both.

CINZANO BRITISH grand prix

round 8

14 JULY 2002

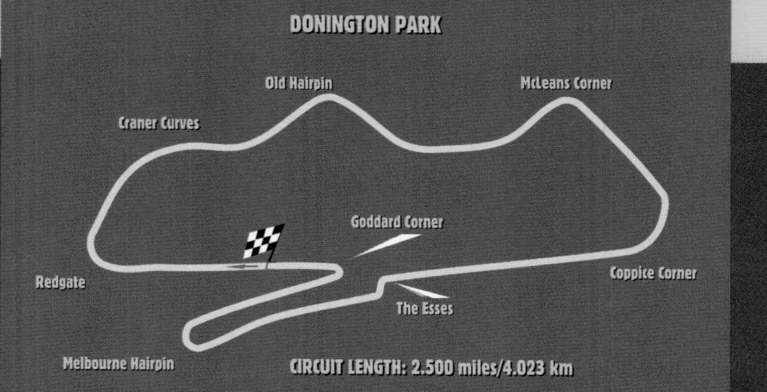
DONINGTON PARK
Old Hairpin
McLeans Corner
Craner Curves
Goddard Corner
Redgate
Coppice Corner
The Esses
Melbourne Hairpin
CIRCUIT LENGTH: 2.500 miles/4.023 km

MotoGP

30 laps, 75.000 miles/120.690 km

Pos.	Rider (Nat.)	No.	Machine	Laps	Time & speed
1	Valentino Rossi (I)	46	Honda	30	46m 32.888s 96.665 mph/ 155.567 km/h
2	Max Biaggi (I)	3	Yamaha	30	46m 35.259s
3	Alex Barros (BR)	4	Honda	30	46m 38.421s
4	Norick Abe (J)	6	Yamaha	30	46m 54.924s
5	Olivier Jacque (F)	19	Yamaha	30	47m 00.975s
6	Sete Gibernau (E)	15	Suzuki	30	47m 01.288s
7	Daijiro Kato (J)	74	Honda	30	47m 01.835s
8	John Hopkins (USA)	21	Yamaha	30	47m 04.385s
9	Nobuatsu Aoki (J)	9	Proton KR	30	47m 04.835s
10	Shinya Nakano (J)	56	Yamaha	30	47m 14.342s
11	Tetsuya Harada (J)	31	Honda	30	47m 22.346s
12	Garry McCoy (AUS)	8	Yamaha	30	47m 26.597s
13	Akira Ryo (J)	33	Suzuki	30	47m 27.368s
14	Kenny Roberts (USA)	10	Suzuki	30	47m 27.482s
15	Jurgen van den Goorbergh (NL)	17	Honda	30	47m 27.754s
16	Regis Laconi (F)	55	Aprilia	30	47m 28.413s
17	Alex Hofmann (D)	66	Honda	30	47m 38.789s
	Carlos Checa (E)	7	Yamaha	19	DNF
	Jeremy McWilliams (GB)	99	Proton KR	6	DNF
	Pere Riba (E)	20	Yamaha		DNS
	Tohru Ukawa (J)	11	Honda		DNS

Fastest lap: Rossi, 1m 32.247s, 97.555 mph/157.000 km/h (record).

Previous record: Simon Crafar, NZ (Yamaha), 1m 32.661s, 97.120 mph/156.298 km/h (1998).

Event best maximum speed: Rossi, 167.0 mph/268.8 km/h (race).

Qualifying: 1 Rossi, 1m 31.563s; 2 Checa, 1m 31.651s; 3 Harada, 1m 31.803s; 4 Barros, 1m 31.828s; 5 Biaggi, 1m 31.906s; 6 Hopkins, 1m 31.977s; 7 McWilliams, 1m 32.042s; 8 Roberts, 1m 32.123s; 9 van den Goorbergh, 1m 32.182s; 10 Aoki, 1m 32.361s; 11 Kato, 1m 32.408s; 12 Jacque, 1m 32.446s; 13 Abe, 1m 32.586s; 14 Ryo, 1m 32.707s; 15 Nakano, 1m 32.810s; 16 Laconi, 1m 32.861s; 17 Gibernau, 1m 33.055s; 18 McCoy, 1m 33.153s; 19 Hofmann, 1m 33.903s; 20 Riba, 1m 34.009s; 21 Ukawa .

Fastest race laps: 1 Rossi, 1m 32.247s; 2 Checa, 1m 32.300s; 3 Biaggi, 1m 32.376s; 4 Barros, 1m 32.614s; 5 Roberts, 1m 32.705s; 6 Hopkins, 1m 33.024s; 7 Harada, 1m 33.071s; 8 Kato, 1m 33.086s; 9 Aoki, 1m 33.125s; 10 Gibernau, 1m 33.248s; 11 Jacque, 1m 33.257s; 12 Abe, 1m 33.285s; 13 McWilliams, 1m 33.368s; 14 Nakano, 1m 33.578s; 15 Ryo, 1m 34.066s; 16 van den Goorbergh, 1m 34.081s; 17 Laconi, 1m 34.192s; 18 McCoy, 1m 34.223s; 19 Hofmann, 1m 34.518s.

World Championship: 1 Rossi, 195; 2 Ukawa, 108; 3 Biaggi, 89; 4 Barros, 87; 5 Abe and Checa, 72; 7 Capirossi, 65; 8 Kato, 60; 9 Jacque, 42; 10 Hopkins, 41; 11 Roberts, 40; 12 Aoki, 35; 13 Harada, 32; 14 Nakano, 30; 15 Ryo, 29; 16 Laconi, 28; 17 Gibernau, 21; 18 van den Goorbergh, 19; 19 Itoh, 13; 20 McCoy, 11; 21 McWilliams, 10; 22 Bayle and Hofmann, 5; 24 Riba, 4.

250 cc

27 laps, 67.500 miles/108.621 km

Pos.	Rider (Nat.)	No.	Machine	Laps	Time & speed
1	Marco Melandri (I)	3	Aprilia	27	42m 55.728s 94.333 mph/ 151.815 km/h
2	Fonsi Nieto (E)	10	Aprilia	27	42m 56.445s
3	Toni Elias (E)	24	Aprilia	27	42m 59.221s
4	Franco Battaini (I)	21	Aprilia	27	42m 59.662s
5	Roberto Rolfo (I)	4	Honda	27	43m 00.135s
6	Randy de Puniet (F)	17	Aprilia	27	43m 15.580s
7	Haruchika Aoki (J)	11	Honda	27	43m 17.498s
8	Naoki Matsudo (J)	8	Yamaha	27	43m 20.308s
9	Alex Debon (E)	6	Aprilia	27	43m 21.715s
10	Shahrol Yuzy (MAL)	18	Yamaha	27	43m 21.930s
11	Casey Stoner (AUS)	27	Aprilia	27	43m 27.349s
12	Emilio Alzamora (E)	7	Honda	27	43m 31.844s
13	Roberto Locatelli (I)	15	Aprilia	27	43m 41.067s
14	Taro Sekiguchi (J)	76	Yamaha	27	43m 41.266s
15	David Checa (E)	42	Aprilia	27	43m 53.204s
16	Jay Vincent (GB)	12	Honda	27	43m 56.523s
17	Leon Haslam (GB)	19	Honda	27	43m 59.702s
18	Dirk Heidolf (D)	28	Aprilia	27	44m 00.884s
19	Jarno Janssen (NL)	41	Honda	27	44m 15.130s
20	Hector Faubel (E)	32	Aprilia	27	44m 17.946s
21	Andrew Whittley (GB)	44	Aprilia	26	44m 16.135s
	Vincent Philippe (F)	25	Aprilia	26	DNF
	Raul Jara (E)	22	Aprilia	17	DNF
	Sebastian Porto (ARG)	9	Yamaha	12	DNF
	Hugo Marchand (F)	51	Aprilia	4	DNF
	Christopher Sansome (GB)	43	Honda		DNQ
	Jason Boyce (GB)	47	Honda		DNQ

Fastest lap: Nieto, 1m 34.411s, 95.319 mph/153.401 km/h.

Lap record: Daijiro Kato, J (Honda), 1m 34.096s, 95.638 mph/153.915 km/h (2001).

Event best maximum speed: Melandri, 148.0 mph/238.1 km/h (qualifying practice no. 1).

Qualifying: 1 Nieto, 1m 33.558s; 2 Melandri, 1m 33.810s; 3 Porto, 1m 34.035s; 4 Alzamora, 1m 34.159s; 5 Elias, 1m 34.360s; 6 Matsudo, 1m 34.399s; 7 Rolfo, 1m 34.748s; 8 Battaini, 1m 34.830s; 9 Sekiguchi, 1m 34.961s; 10 Aoki, 1m 34.965s; 11 Debon, 1m 35.001s; 12 de Puniet, 1m 35.092s; 13 Stoner, 1m 35.401s; 14 Locatelli, 1m 35.484s; 15 Yuzy, 1m 35.623s; 16 Checa, 1m 36.053s; 17 Janssen, 1m 36.267s; 18 Heidolf, 1m 36.453s; 19 Faubel, 1m 36.509s; 20 Haslam, 1m 36.526s; 21 Vincent, 1m 36.590s; 22 Philippe, 1m 36.626s; 23 Jara, 1m 36.795s; 24 Marchand, 1m 37.018s; 25 Whittley, 1m 40.011s; 26 Sansome, 1m 40.562s; 27 Boyce.

Fastest race laps: 1 Nieto, 1m 34.411s; 2 Elias, 1m 34.554s; 3 Melandri, 1m 34.624s; 4 Rolfo, 1m 34.713s; 5 Battaini, 1m 34.850s; 6 Porto, 1m 35.090s; 7 de Puniet, 1m 35.178s; 8 Aoki, 1m 35.381s; 9 Alzamora, 1m 35.437s; 10 Matsudo, 1m 35.491s; 11 Yuzy, 1m 35.545s; 12 Debon, 1m 35.576s; 13 Stoner, 1m 35.778s; 14 Sekiguchi, 1m 36.003s; 15 Locatelli, 1m 36.132s; 16 Checa, 1m 36.285s; 17 Vincent, 1m 36.423s; 18 Heidolf, 1m 36.583s; 19 Haslam, 1m 36.777s; 20 Faubel, 1m 36.897s; 21 Janssen, 1m 37.196s; 22 Jara, 1m 37.463s; 23 Philippe, 1m 37.610s; 24 Marchand, 1m 37.958s; 25 Whittley, 1m 40.936s.

World Championship: 1 Melandri, 145; 2 Nieto, 132; 3 Rolfo, 107; 4 Battaini, 80; 5 de Puniet and Elias, 76; 7 Locatelli, 67; 8 Alzamora, 63; 9 Porto, 58; 10 Matsudo, 48; 11 Debon, 43; 12 Aoki, 35; 13 Stoner and Yuzy, 33; 15 Miyazaki, 25; 16 Checa, 23; 17 Sakai, 20; 18 Kameya, 9; 19 Faubel and Sekiguchi, 7; 21 Vincent, 6; 22 Jara and Waldmann, 5; 24 Aoyama, Marchand and Philippe, 4; 27 Bataille and Heidolf, 2; 29 Haslam, 1.

125 cc

26 laps, 65.000 miles/104.598 km

Pos.	Rider (Nat.)	No.	Machine	Laps	Time & speed
1	Arnaud Vincent (F)	21	Aprilia	26	42m 57.387s 90.781 mph/ 146.098 km/h
2	Daniel Pedrosa (E)	26	Honda	26	42m 57.580s
3	Manuel Poggiali (RSM)	1	Gilera	26	42m 58.086s
4	Masao Azuma (J)	5	Honda	26	43m 10.869s
5	Steve Jenkner (D)	17	Aprilia	26	43m 11.030s
6	Joan Olivé (E)	25	Honda	26	43m 11.460s
7	Alex de Angelis (RSM)	15	Aprilia	26	43m 13.037s
8	Youichi Ui (J)	41	Derbi	26	43m 15.995s
9	Andrea Dovizioso (I)	34	Honda	26	43m 18.148s
10	Shuhei Aoyama (J)	66	Honda	26	43m 18.940s
11	Stefano Perugini (I)	7	Italjet	26	43m 38.625s
12	Andrea Ballerini (I)	50	Honda	26	43m 39.329s
13	Jorge Lorenzo (E)	48	Derbi	26	43m 43.851s
14	Fabrizio Lai (I)	75	Honda	26	43m 44.086s
15	Mirko Giansanti (I)	6	Honda	26	43m 50.203s
16	Chaz Davies (GB)	57	Aprilia	26	43m 53.648s
17	Simone Sanna (I)	16	Aprilia	26	44m 00.822s
18	Alex Baldolini (I)	19	Aprilia	26	44m 08.279s
19	Ivan Goi (I)	28	Aprilia	26	44m 14.390s
20	Imre Toth (H)	20	Honda	26	44m 29.682s
21	Christian Elkin (GB)	69	Honda	25	43m 15.463s
22	Christopher Martin (GB)	70	Honda	25	43m 15.794s
23	Mattia Angeloni (I)	31	Gilera	25	43m 40.454s
24	Leon Camier (GB)	24	Italjet	25	44m 37.369s
	Lucio Cecchinello (I)	4	Aprilia	23	DNF
	Mika Kallio (SF)	36	Honda	18	DNF
	Stefano Bianco (I)	33	Aprilia	16	DNF
	Guy Farbrother (GB)	90	Honda	15	DNF
	Gino Borsoi (I)	23	Aprilia	7	DNF
	Hector Barbera (E)	80	Aprilia	3	DNF
	Gabor Talmacsi (H)	8	Honda	3	DNF
	Angel Rodriguez (E)	47	Aprilia	3	DNF
	Michel Fabrizio (I)	84	Gilera	2	DNF
	Max Sabbatani (I)	11	Aprilia	0	DNF
	Pablo Nieto (E)	22	Aprilia	0	DNF
	Midge Smart (GB)	91	Honda	0	DNF

Fastest lap: Cecchinello, 1m 38.312s, 91.537 mph/147.314 km/h (record).

Previous record: Youichi Ui, J (Derbi), 1m 38.626s, 91.245 mph/146.845 km/h (2001).

Event best maximum speed: Jenkner, 130.3 mph/209.7 km/h (race).

Qualifying: 1 Poggiali, 1m 38.078s; 2 Cecchinello, 1m 38.216s; 3 Pedrosa, 1m 38.437s; 4 Ui, 1m 38.606s; 5 Borsoi, 1m 38.620s; 6 Olivé, 1m 38.646s; 7 de Angelis, 1m 38.692s; 8 Ballerini, 1m 38.758s; 9 Kallio, 1m 38.878s; 10 Azuma, 1m 38.893s; 11 Sanna, 1m 38.932s; 12 Lai, 1m 38.977s; 13 Dovizioso, 1m 38.978s; 14 Jenkner, 1m 38.991s; 15 Nieto, 1m 39.019s; 16 Vincent, 1m 39.035s; 17 Rodriguez, 1m 39.227s; 18 Perugini, 1m 39.273s; 19 Talmacsi, 1m 39.279s; 20 Aoyama, 1m 39.332s; 21 Lorenzo, 1m 39.519s; 22 Giansanti, 1m 39.638s; 23 Fabrizio, 1m 39.860s; 24 Davies, 1m 39.925s; 25 Bianco, 1m 39.987s; 26 Barbera, 1m 40.015s; 27 Sabbatani, 1m 40.752s; 28 Toth, 1m 40.921s; 29 Baldolini, 1m 40.997s; 30 Angeloni, 1m 41.003s; 31 Camier, 1m 41.296s; 32 Elkin, 1m 41.896s; 33 Goi, 1m 41.924s; 34 Martin, 1m 41.976s; 35 Farbrother, 1m 42.169s; 36 Smart, 1m 43.254s.

Fastest race laps: 1 Cecchinello, 1m 38.312s; 2 Vincent, 1m 38.333s; 3 Poggiali, 1m 38.388s; 4 Pedrosa, 1m 38.462s; 5 Azuma, 1m 38.788s; 6 de Angelis, 1m 38.795s; 7 Jenkner, 1m 38.866s; 8 Aoyama, 1m 38.880s; 9 Olivé, 1m 38.904s; 10 Borsoi, 1m 39.017s; 11 Kallio, 1m 39.142s; 12 Ui, 1m 39.149s; 13 Dovizioso, 1m 39.259s; 14 Ballerini, 1m 39.566s; 15 Lai, 1m 39.597s; 16 Perugini, 1m 39.786s; 17 Barbera, 1m 40.060s; 18 Sanna, 1m 40.084s; 19 Lorenzo, 1m 40.085s; 20 Davies, 1m 40.087s; 21 Giansanti, 1m 40.089s; 22 Baldolini, 1m 40.284s; 23 Talmacsi, 1m 40.515s; 24 Goi, 1m 40.688s; 25 Fabrizio, 1m 40.863s; 26 Bianco, 1m 40.978s; 27 Angeloni, 1m 41.408s; 28 Camier, 1m 41.422s; 29 Toth, 1m 41.625s; 30 Rodriguez, 1m 41.625s; 31 Elkin, 1m 42.316s; 32 Martin, 1m 42.667s; 33 Farbrother, 1m 43.797s.

World Championship: 1 Poggiali, 147; 2 Pedrosa, 131; 3 Vincent, 128; 4 Cecchinello, 91; 5 Jenkner, 80; 6 Nieto, 54; 7 Sanna, 48; 8 Olivé and Ui, 46; 10 Azuma, 45; 11 Borsoi, 41; 12 de Angelis, 35; 13 Giansanti, 33; 14 Kallio, 30; 15 Dovizioso, 29; 16 Bianco and Ueda, 18; 18 Ballerini, 17; 19 Aoyama, 16; 20 Rodriguez, 15; 21 Perugini, 14; 22 Sabbatani, 11; 23 Nöhles, 6; 24 Barbera and Lorenzo, 5; 26 Smrz, 3; 27 Baldolini, Lai and Pellino, 2; 30 Fabrizio and Talmacsi, 1.

GERMAN GP

SACHSENRING

FIM WORLD CHAMPIONSHIP · ROUND 9

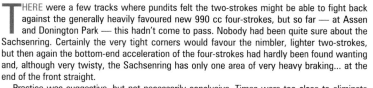

THERE were a few tracks where pundits felt the two-strokes might be able to fight back against the generally heavily favoured new 990 cc four-strokes, but so far — at Assen and Donington Park — this hadn't come to pass. Nobody had been quite sure about the Sachsenring. Certainly the very tight corners would favour the nimbler, lighter two-strokes, but then again the bottom-end acceleration of the four-strokes had hardly been found wanting and, although very twisty, the Sachsenring has only one area of very heavy braking... at the end of the front straight.

Practice was suggestive, but not necessarily conclusive. Times were too close to eliminate the lottery factor, with the closest-ever grid covering all 20 starters by 1.6 seconds, and pole changing hands three times in the final minute. Nonetheless, three out of four on the front row were two-strokes, with Jacque claiming his first-ever pole in the class. Rossi was battling to find the right set-up for once, with the best he could do to move up from ninth to sixth in the closing stages, while team-mate Ukawa was present but hurting after his heavy Donington tumble just the week before... but Rossi can never be ruled out. And though Suzuki were at sea with a new chassis and regular rider Roberts absent for arm surgery, the Yamahas were close, and Biaggi had only been toppled from pole by a tenth.

Sure enough, when the race came around, Rossi was there, leading with his usual assurance, if only by a narrow margin.

Then came his little slip. He made an error out on the back section, and was promptly pounced upon by Jacque and Barros. The two-strokes were in front, and clearly in control.

Many a slip? Barros only needed to make one. Seeing Jacque getting away triggered that old veil of red mist, closely followed by an absurdly over-ambitious braking attempt into the first corner. Coming from several bike lengths behind, there was never any chance that he would make it, but Jacque saw him coming and lifted to make room anyway. A piece of politeness that was rewarded by being knocked off, as the Brazilian Honda rider lost the front wheel and slid off, his bike skittling the erstwhile race leader.

So Rossi won again, his eighth victory in nine races, preserving the 100 per cent record of the four-strokes and of his dominant V5 Honda. The message was clear enough. It might have been possible for two-strokes to win at this most unusual circuit... but only if they didn't bump into each other.

It all contributed to a general mood of levity, with most people just wanting to get the weekend over so they could begin their holidays. Testing was allowed for the first couple of days, so that a few teams were staying on — but banned thereafter, at least at GP circuits, so holidaying was effectively compulsory.

The long break — the best part of five weeks — was well timed for recovering injury victims. Roberts had this in mind when he put his plans for arm surgery forward by a week to gain a longer time for recuperation. His place on the Suzuki, which had a new but not particularly successful chassis at this race, was taken by factory tester Yukio Kagayama, with his domestic team-mate Ryo on another wild-card ride. Capirossi was also gaining strength — his place taken once again by Alex Hofmann. Riba was substituted by Cardoso after his broken leg at Donington. Then Hopkins, who had been improving apace, fell heavily at the end of practice at the top of the hill — a pitfall that had also claimed Aoki that morning. The Japanese rider escaped unhurt, but Hopkins fractured a bone in his hand, and was out of the race.

Things would be a little different after the summer holiday. Most importantly, there would be one more V5 Honda to beat... and with HRC favourite Kato on board, this was bad news not only for the rivals, but also certainly for Ukawa and possibly for Rossi too — Kato had beaten him at pre-season tests at Jerez, riding a two-stroke NSR while Rossi essayed the V5. All of which fuelled speculation that perhaps Rossi wouldn't necessarily be hanging around for much longer. Having already revealed that bike racing was not the summit of his ambition and that he has a hankering for rallying, news broke that he had signed up for a drive in this year's Network Q Rally of Great Britain in mid-November. Rossi planned to drive a Peugeot for an Italian team.

Things would be different next year too, it was revealed, with Yamaha confirming that they would be losing the coveted Marlboro sponsorship at the end of this season. Marlboro made no comment, but it was to be assumed they would be joining Ducati's new GP effort, and it all contributed to increased speculation in what was already a sillier-than-usual silly season.

Some of it was worthwhile, some not. Few were able to take seriously word from MZ, whose factory is nearby, that they are progressing well with their proposed V4 four-stroke — especially since contracted test riders Ralf Waldmann and José Luis Cardoso were both present and riding for other people — Waldmann in another wild-card ride, Cardoso on Riba's Yamaha. More likely to be fruitful were rumblings from KTM, already recruiting for their proposed 125 entry next year, and also preparing a four-stroke, for 2004.

Finally, a delegation from China revealed news of their spectacular-sounding new circuit project. To be built in the shadow of the Great Wall, this will have seating for half a million, with tickets to be free of charge. Building would commence shortly, and this too would be ready for 2004. And ready to break all attendance records, right away.

Main picture: If only... early in the race, Barros and Jacque dispute the lead with the four-strokes losing ground — Biaggi briefly heading Rossi. Later, the two-strokes would rule themselves out.

Bottom, from left: Rossi fans howl at the Biaggi faction; Jacque's first class pole; Kagayama and Hofmann replaced injury victims Roberts and Capirossi.
All photographs: Gold & Goose

MOTOGP - ROSSI • 250 cc - MELANDRI • 125 cc - VINCENT

MOTOGP RACE – 30 laps

Jacque's first-ever class pole gave him the outside line for the run to the treacherous first corner, where they all funnel in while dropping from near top speed to first gear. Like all the rest, he would be trying everything to arrive ahead of what often turns out to be a rather destructive brawl.

The rain that had disrupted the 250 race was gone and track temperatures were high for the start, and it was Biaggi who led the scramble into turn one. He had changed his chassis settings again after the warm-up lap, and dropped back at once as he adjusted to them, with Ukawa taking the lead out of the twisty section, Barros, Jacque and Nakano heading Biaggi across the line at the end of lap one, then McWilliams and Abe before Rossi flashed past the pits.

Biaggi lost two more places on the next lap so that Rossi was on his tail and past him two laps later after the swoop down the hill, to surge past McWilliams down the straight.

Jacque had started to work on Barros, though his first pass was firmly reversed on lap five. Both picked past Ukawa before resuming battle, with Rossi now past everyone else and also past Ukawa after seven laps.

The front three stayed in the same order until after half-distance, the first ten still packed up close in a bellowing and shrieking mass, with Biaggi now regaining places, Checa with him, and McWilliams dropping away slightly in 11th, his corner speed falling as the tyres wore. Actually, he said later, that made it easier. 'Until then they were passing me so fast on the straights it was frightening, then I'd run up against them again in the corners. I nearly hit Biaggi once.'

By now also the two Telefónica MoviStar Suzukis had had a contretemps with Kato in his last two-stroke race. Kagayama had led the trio in tenth, but (Gibernau later said) was taking wild lines, riding 'from corner to corner rather than a 30-lap race'. McCoy also complained later about Kagayama's rough riding into the first corner.

Be this as it may, Kagayama was ahead of Kato and Gibernau when the more experienced Spaniard ran into the back of Kato, knocking him into Kagayama, after the Honda rider had slowed unexpectedly to avoid doing the same thing. It was a messy crash, but mercifully without serious injuries. By now, Cardoso was well out of the picture, after a stop-and-go for a jumped start, and Harada had pitted, complaining of a lack of grip.

Now Rossi started to attack, outbraking Jacque into the first corner, and Barros at the bottom of the hill after the back straight, just about the track's only two possibilities for passing. It was lap 19, and he crossed the line in his usual leading position, though with an unfamiliar close pack behind: Barros now second, then Jacque, Biaggi, Ukawa, Checa, Abe and Nakano, all within two seconds.

The last ten laps would be packed with drama, Jacque now seizing second and crawling all over Rossi through the twists, only to lose what he had gained on the straights, denying him the proximity for an outbraking attack. On lap 25, Rossi saved him the frustration, running wide himself on the sharp lefts on the way out of the very tight start of the lap. Jacque was right there, Barros also fast enough to take advantage.

Jacque started to inch away directly, a couple of lengths clear with three laps left. Barros couldn't bear it, since he felt he was faster than Jacque everywhere except on the straights. The consequence was his ruinous attack into turn one, and a gift win for Rossi.

Biaggi was a close second, inches ahead of Ukawa; Checa losing a little ground behind as he blocked Abe's every move. Abe didn't stop trying, which meant he wasn't protecting his own position when Nakano attacked on the last lap, gaining fifth in a high-risk move.

McWilliams was 13 seconds back at the end, in some danger from McCoy, whose last-lap lunge instead lured him into an error that gave Aoki the opening he'd been awaiting for much of the race, after picking through from 15th from a botched first corner.

Hofmann covered himself with glory fending off a persistent Ryo to the finish; van den Goorbergh and Cardoso a long way back in last.

What a way for Rossi to start his holiday.

250 cc RACE – 22 laps

Nieto's fifth pole followed domination of every session; Melandri was second from Locatelli and Rolfo, the quartet covered by half a second, and times behind were nowhere near as close as the big class. But the Spaniard got away slowly, finishing lap one down in seventh.

Rolfo led away in storming style, with Melandri and (for a short time) Matsudo in pursuit, Porto slotting into third on lap three. And that's how they carried on for 18 of the scheduled 29 laps.

Melandri seized the lead into the first corner on lap 19, and the two Italians

Opposite page, top: Rossi in the thick of it — the twisty track kept the bikes packed up close.

Opposite page, bottom: Sometimes you get lucky, some luck you make for yourself. Rossi benefited from both kinds in Germany.

Below: Melandri and Rolfo owned the 250 race.
All photographs: Gold & Goose

Right: Rolfo acknowledges the rain as Melandri bites the dust behind him.

Below: Nieto leads Matsudo... the Japanese rider couldn't sustain the pace.

Below centre: Steve Jenkner's podium came after he'd resisted a particularly brutal last-lap attack from Poggiali.

Bottom: Ui leads the second gang of 125 riders, from Kallio, Borsoi, Olivé and Giansanti.

All photographs: Gold & Goose

held the same positions — it was now Rolfo's turn to keep the pressure on. He dived past at the bottom of the hill on lap 23, but Melandri took the lead back again before they reached the main straight. It would clearly come to a last-lap showdown.

Or not, given that a rather insipid shower had sprinkled the track a little further round. A quarter of the way round lap 24 Melandri suddenly lost the front and fell, handing the lead to Rolfo. A worthless lead, however: the red flags came out at once, results were taken back to the end of lap 22, and Melandri was the winner. Luckless Rolfo could only shake his head, and regret never having the opportunity to put his last-lap plan into action, there being no last lap.

Lucky Melandri? Not really. For one thing, he was pretty battered by his fall; for another his team had been on top of the situation. 'We had a signal arranged, and when they saw rain coming they said: Push. That's when I passed Rolfo,' he said.

There had been a lively battle for fourth, after Matsudo faded, with Locatelli taking over and Nieto engaged with de Puniet, before the Frenchman ran off the track once, and shortly afterwards crashed out with a big high-sider.

By lap eight, Nieto was with Locatelli, and took two laps to get past. They carried on in that order until the premature finish, much too far behind Porto to think about catching him.

After 15 laps, Matsudo had fallen into the clutches of Elias and Battaini, with the Italian leading the group briefly, then Elias taking over and Matsudo behind him at the race finish, the three still locked in combat.

Waldmann had battled through the next gaggle, and had moved a couple of seconds clear of Debon and Yuzy, with Aoki at the back of the group when he crashed heavily. Then came a seven-strong scrum disputing the last points, in the closest battle of a typically rather downbeat 250 race. By luck, German rookie Dirk Heidolf was in front of the two British team-mates Haslam

and Vincent, Checa and Sekiguchi on the crucial 22nd lap, the last-named missing a point by half a second. Jara had been with them, but had lost touch by then.

125 cc RACE – 27 laps

Vincent was on pole by a full half-second from Poggiali, and the Frenchman led fellow front-row starters Sanna and de Angelis, plus Rodriguez, away. Poggiali was slow off the line, and overwhelmed into the first corner, finishing lap one 15th.

Vincent held a narrow lead from de Angelis, Sanna dropping back steadily after losing second on lap four. It was a two-man show, with de Angelis attacking on the last lap on the second-last corner, but running wide into the final bend, giving Vincent the chance to dive inside and block him on the exit. Flawless tactics, with de Angelis content enough with his first podium.

Jenkner and Pedrosa had caught Sanna, and also Nieto on lap ten. By then, Poggiali had worked his way through the mid-field pack, and closed a gap of four seconds at an impressive rate of a second a lap.

Jenkner made most of the running, with Pedrosa taking over with ten laps remaining. Poggiali had pushed through by now, and one lap later was ahead of the Honda rider, who then dropped to the back of the group, blaming sliding tyres.

The rest scrapped it out, Nieto and Jenkner getting back ahead of Poggiali with four laps left, but Nieto then making a little slip to lose not only third, but also fourth to Poggiali, who mounted a fearsome attack on Jenkner on the run to the line, almost forcing him onto the grass as he veered across the track.

Sanna was sixth, then Pedrosa. Ui led the next battling group, from Kallio, Borsoi, Olivé and Giansanti, the next trio — Dovizioso, Rodriguez and Azuma — taking the last points.

CINZANO
GERMAN
grand prix

21 JULY 2002

round 9

SACHSENRING GRAND PRIX CIRCUIT

CIRCUIT LENGTH: 2.302 miles/3.704 km

MotoGP

30 laps, 69.060 miles/111.120 km

Pos.	Rider (Nat.)	No.	Machine	Laps	Time & speed
1	Valentino Rossi (I)	46	Honda	30	43m 32.783s 95.135 mph/ 153.105 km/h
2	Max Biaggi (I)	3	Yamaha	30	43m 33.513s
3	Tohru Ukawa (J)	11	Honda	30	43m 33.883s
4	Carlos Checa (E)	7	Yamaha	30	43m 35.113s
5	Shinya Nakano (J)	56	Yamaha	30	43m 35.526s
6	Norick Abe (J)	6	Yamaha	30	43m 35.563s
7	Jeremy McWilliams (GB)	99	Proton KR	30	43m 48.221s
8	Nobuatsu Aoki (J)	9	Proton KR	30	43m 51.763s
9	Garry McCoy (AUS)	8	Yamaha	30	43m 52.052s
10	Alex Hofmann (D)	66	Honda	30	44m 07.316s
11	Akira Ryo (J)	33	Suzuki	30	44m 07.375s
12	Jurgen van den Goorbergh (NL)	17	Honda	30	44m 18.187s
13	José Luis Cardoso (E)	30	Yamaha	30	44m 49.243s
	Olivier Jacque (F)	19	Yamaha	27	DNF
	Alex Barros (BR)	4	Honda	27	DNF
	Regis Laconi (F)	55	Aprilia	25	DNF
	Tetsuya Harada (J)	31	Honda	16	DNF
	Yukio Kagayama (J)	51	Suzuki	10	DNF
	Daijiro Kato (J)	74	Honda	10	DNF
	Sete Gibernau (E)	15	Suzuki	10	DNF
	John Hopkins (USA)	21	Yamaha		DNS

Fastest lap: Rossi, 1m 26.226s, 96.091 mph/154.644 km/h (record).

Previous record: Shinya Nakano, J (Yamaha), 1m 26.808s, 95.447 mph/153.607 km/h (2001).

Event best maximum speed: Biaggi, 173.3 mph/278.9 km/h (qualifying practice no. 1).

Qualifying: 1 Jacque, 1m 25.758s; 2 Nakano, 1m 25.838s; 3 Biaggi, 1m 25.875s; 4 Barros, 1m 25.956s; 5 Ukawa, 1m 25.991s; 6 Rossi, 1m 25.992s; 7 McWilliams, 1m 26.067s; 8 McCoy, 1m 26.095s; 9 Kato, 1m 26.105s; 10 Checa, 1m 26.118s; 11 Kagayama, 1m 26.232s; 12 Gibernau, 1m 26.387s; 13 Aoki, 1m 26.502s; 14 Hopkins, 1m 26.551s; 15 Abe, 1m 26.555s; 16 Laconi, 1m 26.648s; 17 Harada, 1m 26.686s; 18 van den Goorbergh, 1m 26.790s; 19 Hofmann, 1m 27.034s; 20 Cardoso, 1m 27.262s; 21 Ryo, 1m 27.305s.

Fastest race laps: 1 Rossi, 1m 26.226s; 2 Biaggi, 1m 26.370s; 3 Nakano, 1m 26.397s; 4 Ukawa, 1m 26.460s; 5 Jacque, 1m 26.513s; 6 Barros, 1m 26.527s; 7 Abe, 1m 26.618s; 8 Checa, 1m 26.643s; 9 Kagayama, 1m 26.715s; 10 McWilliams, 1m 26.861s; 11 Aoki, 1m 26.927s; 12 Gibernau, 1m 26.997s; 13 McCoy, 1m 27.127s; 14 Kato, 1m 27.191s; 15 Hofmann, 1m 27.236s; 16 Harada, 1m 27.397s; 17 Ryo, 1m 27.399s; 18 Laconi, 1m 27.452s; 19 Cardoso, 1m 27.628s; 20 van den Goorbergh, 1m 27.913s.

World Championship: 1 Rossi, 220; 2 Ukawa, 124; 3 Biaggi, 109; 4 Barros, 87; 5 Checa, 85; 6 Abe, 82; 7 Capirossi, 65; 8 Kato, 60; 9 Aoki, 43; 10 Jacque, 42; 11 Hopkins and Nakano, 41; 13 Roberts, 40; 14 Ryo, 34; 15 Harada, 32; 16 Laconi, 28; 17 van den Goorbergh, 23; 18 Gibernau, 21; 19 McWilliams, 19; 20 McCoy, 18; 21 Itoh, 13; 22 Hofmann, 11; 23 Bayle, 5; 24 Riba, 4; 25 Cardoso, 3.

250 cc

22 laps, 50.644 miles/81.488 km

Pos.	Rider (Nat.)	No.	Machine	Laps	Time & speed
1	Marco Melandri (I)	3	Aprilia	22	32m 12.725s 94.314 mph/ 151.784 km/h
2	Roberto Rolfo (I)	4	Honda	22	32m 12.906s
3	Sebastian Porto (ARG)	9	Yamaha	22	32m 14.875s
4	Fonsi Nieto (E)	10	Aprilia	22	32m 21.196s
5	Roberto Locatelli (I)	15	Aprilia	22	32m 28.290s
6	Toni Elias (E)	24	Aprilia	22	32m 42.268s
7	Naoki Matsudo (J)	8	Yamaha	22	32m 42.582s
8	Franco Battaini (I)	21	Aprilia	22	32m 42.615s
9	Ralf Waldmann (D)	26	Aprilia	22	32m 51.378s
10	Alex Debon (E)	6	Aprilia	22	32m 53.258s
11	Shahrol Yuzy (MAL)	18	Yamaha	22	32m 54.956s
12	Dirk Heidolf (D)	28	Aprilia	22	33m 12.714s
13	Leon Haslam (GB)	19	Honda	22	33m 13.029s
14	Jay Vincent (GB)	12	Honda	22	33m 13.159s
15	David Checa (E)	42	Aprilia	22	33m 13.294s
16	Taro Sekiguchi (J)	76	Yamaha	22	33m 13.736s
17	Raul Jara (E)	22	Aprilia	22	33m 15.576s
18	Hector Faubel (E)	32	Aprilia	22	33m 37.308s
19	Max Neukirchner (D)	53	Honda	21	32m 20.869s
	Vincent Philippe (F)	25	Aprilia	19	DNF
	Haruchika Aoki (J)	11	Honda	15	DNF
	Randy de Puniet (F)	17	Aprilia	14	DNF
	Hugo Marchand (F)	51	Aprilia	11	DNF
	Thierry van den Bosch (F)	77	Aprilia	10	DNF
	Nico Kehrer (D)	54	Honda	8	DNF
	Emilio Alzamora (E)	7	Honda	6	DNF
	Jarno Janssen (NL)	41	Honda	4	DNF
	Casey Stoner (AUS)	27	Aprilia	1	DNF
	Christian Gemmel (D)	52	Honda	1	DNF

Fastest lap: Rolfo, 1m 27.234s, 94.981 mph/152.857 km/h.

Lap record: Marco Melandri, I (Aprilia), 1m 27.233s, 94.982 mph/152.859 km/h (2001).

Event best maximum speed: Melandri, 150.9 mph/242.9 km/h (qualifying practice no. 2).

Qualifying: 1 Nieto, 1m 26.874s; 2 Melandri, 1m 27.171s; 3 Locatelli, 1m 27.445s; 4 Rolfo, 1m 27.446s; 5 Battaini, 1m 27.566s; 6 Porto, 1m 27.613s; 7 de Puniet, 1m 27.669s; 8 Debon, 1m 27.775s; 9 Elias, 1m 27.865s; 10 Matsudo, 1m 27.943s; 11 Aoki, 1m 28.138s; 12 Stoner, 1m 28.278s; 13 Alzamora, 1m 28.359s; 14 Waldmann, 1m 28.591s; 15 Philippe, 1m 29.064s; 16 Heidolf, 1m 29.067s; 17 Yuzy, 1m 29.072s; 18 Haslam, 1m 29.104s; 19 Vincent, 1m 29.290s; 20 Checa, 1m 29.489s; 21 Jara, 1m 29.525s; 22 Janssen, 1m 29.672s; 23 Marchand, 1m 29.735s; 24 van den Bosch, 1m 29.794s; 25 Sekiguchi, 1m 29.925s; 26 Faubel, 1m 29.936s; 27 Gemmel, 1m 30.251s; 28 Neukirchner, 1m 30.379s; 29 Kehrer, 1m 32.623s.

Fastest race laps: 1 Rolfo, 1m 27.234s; 2 Melandri, 1m 27.338s; 3 Porto, 1m 27.457s; 4 Nieto, 1m 27.620s; 5 Locatelli, 1m 27.892s; 6 Matsudo, 1m 28.088s; 7 de Puniet, 1m 28.093s; 8 Battaini, 1m 28.344s; 9 Elias, 1m 28.390s; 10 Yuzy, 1m 28.817s; 11 Waldmann, 1m 28.890s; 12 Debon, 1m 28.991s; 13 Aoki, 1m 29.200s; 14 Alzamora, 1m 29.250s; 15 Heidolf, 1m 29.380s; 16 Vincent, 1m 29.518s; 17 Checa, 1m 29.663s; 18 Haslam, 1m 29.734s; 19 Jara, 1m 29.809s; 20 Sekiguchi, 1m 29.900s; 21 van den Bosch, 1m 30.205s; 22 Philippe, 1m 30.256s; 23 Marchand, 1m 30.517s; 24 Faubel, 1m 30.521s; 25 Janssen, 1m 30.878s; 26 Neukirchner, 1m 31.510s; 27 Stoner, 1m 32.685s; 28 Kehrer, 1m 34.197s; 29 Gemmel, 2m 00.326s.

World Championship: 1 Melandri, 170; 2 Nieto, 145; 3 Rolfo, 127; 4 Battaini, 88; 5 Elias, 86; 6 Locatelli, 78; 7 de Puniet, 76; 8 Porto, 74; 9 Alzamora, 63; 10 Matsudo, 57; 11 Debon, 49; 12 Yuzy, 38; 13 Aoki, 35; 14 Stoner, 33; 15 Miyazaki, 25; 16 Checa, 24; 17 Sakai, 20; 18 Waldmann, 12; 19 Kameya, 9; 20 Vincent, 8; 21 Faubel and Sekiguchi, 7; 23 Heidolf, 6; 24 Jara, 5; 25 Aoyama, Haslam, Marchand and Philippe, 4; 29 Bataille, 2.

125 cc

27 laps, 62.154 miles/100.008 km

Pos.	Rider (Nat.)	No.	Machine	Laps	Time & speed
1	Arnaud Vincent (F)	21	Aprilia	27	40m 40.023s 91.684 mph/ 147.551 km/h
2	Alex de Angelis (RSM)	15	Aprilia	27	40m 40.131s
3	Steve Jenkner (D)	17	Aprilia	27	40m 50.018s
4	Manuel Poggiali (RSM)	1	Gilera	27	40m 50.019s
5	Pablo Nieto (E)	22	Aprilia	27	40m 50.183s
6	Simone Sanna (I)	16	Aprilia	27	40m 56.041s
7	Daniel Pedrosa (E)	26	Honda	27	40m 56.849s
8	Youichi Ui (J)	41	Derbi	27	41m 03.944s
9	Mika Kallio (SF)	36	Honda	27	41m 04.027s
10	Gino Borsoi (I)	23	Aprilia	27	41m 04.286s
11	Joan Olivé (E)	25	Honda	27	41m 04.830s
12	Mirko Giansanti (I)	6	Honda	27	41m 04.881s
13	Andrea Dovizioso (I)	34	Honda	27	41m 20.563s
14	Angel Rodriguez (E)	47	Aprilia	27	41m 20.718s
15	Masao Azuma (J)	5	Honda	27	41m 20.966s
16	Klaus Nöhles (D)	12	Honda	27	41m 28.852s
17	Jorge Lorenzo (E)	48	Derbi	27	41m 28.879s
18	Gabor Talmacsi (H)	8	Honda	27	41m 29.204s
19	Alex Baldolini (I)	19	Aprilia	27	41m 41.972s
20	Chaz Davies (GB)	57	Aprilia	27	41m 43.148s
21	Hector Barbera (E)	80	Aprilia	27	41m 49.293s
22	Max Sabbatani (I)	11	Aprilia	27	41m 49.733s
23	Michel Fabrizio (I)	84	Gilera	27	41m 50.127s
24	Ivan Goi (I)	28	Aprilia	27	42m 04.915s
25	Imre Toth (H)	20	Honda	27	42m 04.963s
26	Thomas Luthi (CH)	77	Honda	27	42m 08.907s
27	Mattia Angeloni (I)	31	Gilera	27	42m 11.384s
28	Dario Giuseppetti (D)	72	Honda	27	42m 11.650s
29	Claudius Klein (D)	73	Honda	27	42m 12.315s
30	Patrick Unger (D)	92	Honda	27	42m 12.407s
31	Jascha Büch (D)	74	Honda	26	41m 01.293s
32	Matej Smrz (CZ)	76	Honda	26	41m 01.512s
33	Manuel Mickan (D)	93	Honda	26	41m 09.406s
	Stefano Perugini (I)	7	Italjet	15	DNF
	Andrea Ballerini (I)	50	Honda	14	DNF
	Lucio Cecchinello (I)	4	Aprilia	13	DNF
	Christian Pistoni (I)	42	Italjet	7	DNF

Fastest lap: Jenkner, 1m 29.486s, 92.591 mph/149.011 km/h (record).

Previous record: Lucio Cecchinello, I (Aprilia), 1m 30.371s, 91.684 mph/147.551 km/h (2001).

Event best maximum speed: Borsoi, 129.9 mph/209.2 km/h (race).

Qualifying: 1 Vincent, 1m 29.097s; 2 Poggiali, 1m 29.606s; 3 Sanna, 1m 29.607s; 4 de Angelis, 1m 29.626s; 5 Cecchinello, 1m 29.629s; 6 Nieto, 1m 29.668s; 7 Jenkner, 1m 29.770s; 8 Pedrosa, 1m 29.916s; 9 Rodriguez, 1m 29.958s; 10 Kallio, 1m 30.119s; 11 Ui, 1m 30.123s; 12 Borsoi, 1m 30.270s; 13 Dovizioso, 1m 30.353s; 14 Talmacsi, 1m 30.356s; 15 Olivé, 1m 30.431s; 16 Giansanti, 1m 30.657s; 17 Baldolini, 1m 30.640s; 18 Sabbatani, 1m 31.055s; 19 Lorenzo, 1m 31.060s; 20 Perugini, 1m 31.077s; 21 Azuma, 1m 31.125s; 22 Nöhles, 1m 31.390s; 23 Davies, 1m 31.561s; 24 Giuseppetti, 1m 31.855s; 25 Fabrizio, 1m 31.968s; 26 Toth, 1m 32.068s; 27 Ballerini, 1m 32.069s; 28 Goi, 1m 32.386s; 29 Barbera, 1m 32.387s; 30 Klein, 1m 32.399s; 31 Unger, 1m 32.624s; 32 Mickan, 1m 32.657s; 33 Luthi, 1m 32.889s; 34 Angeloni, 1m 33.036s; 35 Büch, 1m 33.571s; 36 Pistoni, 1m 33.628s; 37 Smrz, 1m 33.687s.

Fastest race laps: 1 Jenkner, 1m 29.486s; 2 de Angelis, 1m 29.717s; 3 Vincent, 1m 29.806s; 4 Poggiali, 1m 29.884s; 5 Pedrosa, 1m 29.887s; 6 Nieto, 1m 29.904s; 7 Sanna, 1m 30.077s; 8 Cecchinello, 1m 30.089s; 9 Ui, 1m 30.311s; 10 Borsoi, 1m 30.397s; 11 Olivé, 1m 30.429s; 12 Giansanti, 1m 30.445s; 13 Kallio, 1m 30.481s; 14 Azuma, 1m 30.571s; 15 Dovizioso, 1m 30.774s; 16 Rodriguez, 1m 30.810s; 17 Talmacsi, 1m 30.939s; 18 Davies, 1m 30.975s; 19 Baldolini, 1m 31.024s; 20 Lorenzo, 1m 31.284s; 21 Nöhles, 1m 31.443s; 22 Ballerini, 1m 31.468s; 23 Fabrizio, 1m 31.641s; 24 Sabbatani, 1m 31.771s; 25 Perugini, 1m 31.876s; 26 Goi, 1m 31.911s; 27 Barbera, 1m 32.035s; 28 Luthi, 1m 32.072s; 29 Toth, 1m 32.460s; 30 Unger, 1m 32.558s; 31 Klein, 1m 32.615s; 32 Giuseppetti, 1m 32.640s; 33 Angeloni, 1m 32.677s; 34 Büch, 1m 33.283s; 35 Smrz, 1m 33.393s; 36 Pistoni, 1m 33.649s; 37 Mickan, 1m 33.963s.

World Championship: 1 Poggiali, 160; 2 Vincent, 153; 3 Pedrosa, 140; 4 Jenkner, 96; 5 Cecchinello, 91; 6 Nieto, 65; 7 Sanna, 58; 8 de Angelis, 55; 9 Ui, 54; 10 Olivé, 51; 11 Borsoi, 47; 12 Azuma, 46; 13 Giansanti and Kallio, 37; 15 Dovizioso, 32; 16 Bianco and Ueda, 18; 18 Ballerini and Rodriguez, 17; 20 Aoyama, 16; 21 Perugini, 14; 22 Sabbatani, 11; 23 Nöhles, 6; 24 Barbera and Lorenzo, 5; 26 Smrz, 3; 27 Baldolini, Lai and Pellino, 2; 30 Fabrizio and Talmacsi, 1.

BRNO

FIM WORLD CHAMPIONSHIP · ROUND 10

CZECH GP

Main picture: Brno specialist Biaggi leads two Hondas — Rossi and Kato. By the end, there was only one left.

Far left, top: Californian surgeon Art Ting shows off his handiwork — curing arm pump-up problems on both of Kenny Roberts Junior's arms.

Far left, bottom: Look on my works — part two: HRC showed off their naked V5, and promised at least eight for next year.

Centre: Ukawa survived a big race-morning crash to make the rostrum again.

Left: Soon-to-be ex-Yamaha rider Biaggi at last broke the spell of Rossi and the RCV for his first win of 2002.
All photographs: Gold & Goose

How important is testing? Vital, obviously. Not only to get the motor cycle right, but also to get the rider tuned in to its peculiarities. These MotoGP prototypes are, after all, the fastest and most challenging racing motor cycles in the world. Aren't they?

Not, apparently, if your name is Daijiro Kato, with or without the 'h'.

Testing was banned in the summer break, after the end of July. Some teams had stayed on in Germany: Kanemoto's Bridgestone-shod Honda outfit found a way round it by bringing in last year's tyre-tester Shinichi Itoh for a runaround at Brno, while regular rider Jurgen van den Goorbergh obeyed the rules and stayed out of the saddle.

Kato's holiday included a nice relaxing break winning the Suzuka Eight-Hour (again), then a 'fitting session' for the RCV four-stroke at Honda's factory test circuit at Tochigi... too small and too tight for any high-speed or serious testing. Just a matter of getting him comfortable, he insisted, which mainly involved some extra seat padding behind the diminutive rider. (And, suggested MCN's cartoonist 'Sprocket', an HRC factory ladder to help him climb on board.)

It is as much a measure of the motor cycle as the man that the little Japanese rider was on the pace after three laps, and challenging for pole from his eighth. And as if that wasn't depressing enough for those unlucky enough not to have a V5, HRC had some more news at Brno. Next year there will be at least eight RCVs on the grid, comprising three factory bikes, five production versions, and possibly two more with Moriwaki chassis. This was announced at a well-attended HRC press conference in the paddock, where HRC MD Koiji Nakajima vouchsafed: 'It was not our original intention to dominate this series, but to develop it.'

On the available evidence, it seemed that domination was about to become complete, and that any riders not able to acquire one of these exemplary machines might as well not even bother turning up. But that, of course, was before Max Biaggi and Yamaha inflicted the first-ever defeat on the V5.

Actually it was a tyre failure that stopped Rossi from even trying to win, and the post mortem continued for several weeks, with Michelin finally suggesting that the Honda used its tyres harder than the other four-strokes. 'We don't have a tyre problem. Michelin do,' growled team boss Jeremy Burgess. Only later did it emerge that clutch trouble had sent the tyre south. All interesting news for Dunlop, who have suffered similarly in the past, but who celebrated their 100th consecutive 250-class win on the same day.

With the Czech Republic still mopping up after catastrophic floods, GP racing started again with a vengeance at Brno. In the dry, and as if there wasn't a world outside, because what was going on in the paddock was already of consuming interest.

The four-strokes all benefited from the break. Honda's changes included a new ram-air intake system, with the fairing modified with ear-piece intakes each side below the handlebars. In fact, only Ukawa used the system; Rossi kept the bigger fairing but disconnected the airways, and Kato had the earlier version. The carbon rear exhaust can was also replaced with titanium, supposedly to allow greater flow to match the intakes, but sadly not releasing much more noise.

Suzuki had a new chassis as well as detail changes such as revised engine mapping, but were wrong-footed when they were delayed by Czech customs at Prague airport. The new units arrived after practice had begun, on payment of a hefty deposit, only in time to be used for day two. Since, as team manager Taylor said, 'these things seldom work straight out of the box', this cost them set-up time, with serious consequences for Roberts at least.

Aprilia had shaved off 5 kg with a raft of changes, including lighter electronics, revised engine casings and other trimmings that didn't really show.

Yamaha had the most obvious change — apart from yet another new chassis: completely revised bodywork that replaced the bulbous streamliner with sharp modern styling and a reduced frontal area. It also revealed their previously hidden ram-air intake, a letter-box slot made of pliable plastic, so that when the forks compress under braking the front mudguard actually squeezes it shut. Since the throttle is closed, this has no effect on performance; meanwhile the intake is sited at the area of maximum pressure, where air is dammed under the fairing nose.

At least one rider had important physical modifications — Kenny Roberts displayed fresh scars on his forearms, where fasciotomy surgery had relieved the muscle sheaths to stop an arm-pump problem that had troubled him, he said, for many years. 'I've been training on the ranch in California, and in terms of endurance I can do things that I've never been able to do before on the 600 singles,' he said. 'Riding 500s it was always possible to find a way round the problem, but the four-stroke is heavier and you have to blip the throttle under braking. I had problems from the first test, and at Assen they started to get bad. After Donington, I was destroyed.'

Two contrasting vignettes from practice: Laconi's Aprilia died near the bottom of the hill. It was his better bike, he said later, and he elected to push it all the way back to the pits. 'Nobody even helped me,' he said wistfully. Another was Pablo Nieto, who crashed his 125 Aprilia near the end of the session. Desperate to pick up his spare, he commandeered a bicycle and pedalled back to the pits, looking more than faintly ridiculous as he entered pit lane, still helmeted, with officials trying in vain to stop him.

Ukawa crashed heavily in race-morning warm-up, when he found a false neutral on the last corner, then the bike jumped into first. Luckily, his existing injuries were not made worse.

Finally, the paddock was struck by bad news from Australia. Barry Sheene disclosed that he was suffering from cancer, sending shock waves round those who had known him and even raced against him in the Seventies.

Right: Gibernau was on cracking form for his best race of the year.

Below: Four-stroke first-timer Kato challenged for pole and race victory. Was the bike really that good, or was it the rider? Barros would prove the point three races later.

Both photographs: Gold & Goose

MOTOGP RACE – 22 laps

Max stole pole from Kato in the closing minutes by less than a tenth — using the old chassis for its greater familiarity. Rossi had been at sea on the first day, but closed right up on Kato, though running out of time for a late-session run; McCoy was back in a big way, fastest two-stroke and on the front row; Capirossi's two-stroke led row two from Checa, fast rookie Hopkins and Ukawa... the first seven all inside last year's pole time.

The two Yamahas led away; Rossi passed Checa for second by the first left; Kato and Ukawa were close. Behind there was a confusion of swerving and avoiding action at the first and second corners, with McCoy, Nakano and McWilliams the big losers. McCoy finished the first lap 16th, McWilliams 17th. Nakano didn't, falling on the first run down the hill trying to regain ground.

Kato was third by the end of lap one, the first three starting to move away from Checa and Ukawa after only three laps. Checa had been fiddling with settings on the new chassis right up to warm-up, and it still wasn't right. Sure enough, Ukawa was by on lap five and Capirossi started to press hard, though ultimately in vain.

Hopkins, fast away, was already troubled by a radiator leak that would put him in the pits after 12 laps, and was holding up Abe and the pack. By lap four both Suzukis were ahead of the stricken Red Bull Yamaha. Roberts was soon to slow, bad set-up worsening a tyre chunking problem. Gibernau was on a charge, closing a 1.6-second gap to Capirossi in three laps, diving inside aggressively and taking just two more laps to pass Checa, then closing on Ukawa straight away. He attacked him vigorously, but the Honda's greater power and speed made it a hopeless task, and with five laps to go he started to fall away backwards, with sliding tyres.

By now, Ukawa was third. Until half-distance, the leading trio had played follow-my-leader. Then Biaggi upped the pace, gaining a half-second gap on lap 13. Rossi responded, closing up and even showing Max his front wheel now and then, perhaps hoping for a repeat of last year, when this triggered a crash from his deadly rival.

Then it was suddenly all over. On lap 16 at the bottom of the hill Rossi slowed, looking at the back of his Honda as Kato swept past. TV replays showed that something had broken on the run down the hill, shards of carbon fibre flying off the back of the bike. It was the rear hugger, smashed by the disintegrating tyre. Rossi pitted for a new one, but was so far behind there was little point in continuing.

Kato was already 1.5 seconds behind Biaggi, his own rear tyre sliding as the Yamaha rider pushed on steadily to win by 2.8 seconds. Ukawa was safe in third, Gibernau likewise in fourth, and ditto Checa and Capirossi.

The racing came among the remainder, with McWilliams providing the excitement as he scythed through from the back in one of the rides of his life on a bike more than 10 mph down on speed, although on the 'best yet' Bridgestone tyres. 'The only place I could pass was in the middle of the "ess" bends — I had a few close calls,' he said later. He'd passed one or two riders almost every lap in the first half of the race, and was pulling clear of a desultory scrap between Roberts and Abe, though the five-second gap to Capirossi was too much for him to deal with. Sadly, none of this was seen on TV, the cameras instead following the sterile trio up front.

Abe was a lonely eighth, with Roberts slowing more towards the end. 'Every time I opened the throttle the bike would snap sideways,' he explained. Barros and Jacque caught him easily by the end, consigning him to 11th; van den Goorbergh was some way back, then McCoy, who had never recovered from his first-corner problems, blaming tyres that didn't work right. 'I thought I was making some headway three laps in, but after that there was nothing I could do. I couldn't carry any corner speed,' he said.

Ryo was way back in 14th, Harada even further behind, fending off Laconi by a tenth, with wild card Sylvain Guintoli another ten seconds adrift on the third Gauloises Yamaha. Aoki crashed out on lap 12, his different style not working with the Bridgestones.

250 cc RACE – 20 laps

Nieto led every session, while 'flu-stricken Melandri was second, Porto third and Locatelli fourth, times close and Rolfo's re-cowled and rather different-looking factory Honda on row two and threatening.

It was a race of sporadic excitement. Elias led away from Porto; by lap two Nieto, Melandri and Rolfo were ahead of this pair and opening a gap.

Rolfo was at last enjoying some parity of performance, and took the lead on lap six, with the two Aprilias content to wait behind until there were five laps left.

Now Nieto attacked, but he underestimated Rolfo's speed and determination, and ran wide and off line. This gave Melandri his chance to slip into second. Two corners later, Nieto tried to get it back, and instead ran off into the grass, for a big save, managing to regain the track in fifth, some 3.5 seconds behind Elias and Porto.

Now there were just two, and Melandri shadowed Rolfo until, with only two laps to go, he outbraked with apparent ease into the first corner. Rolfo wasn't for being beaten now, and rather uncharacteristically started taking big risks to regain the lead. A slide on the last corner didn't deter him; an even bigger one

half a lap later ended his race, his front wheel sliding away and the silver bike low-siding into the gravel.

Now Elias and Porto were battling for second, with Porto able to benefit from the young Spaniard running into tyre trouble and move ahead as Nieto closed up with impressive speed. On the last lap, he was just 1.5 seconds behind his team-mate, but if he expected any after-you from the younger Telefónica MoviStar Repsol rider there was none forthcoming, and Fonsi finished the lap two-tenths off the rostrum.

Yuzy was on form, battling Locatelli in a scrap behind Porto in the early laps, until he fell off, a frequent occurrence. De Puniet was behind, not quite on terms.

Stoner was again the mid-fielder to watch: picking his way steadily from 15th on lap one, taking only three laps to work his way through a batch comprising Aoki, Battaini, Checa and Matsudo. On lap ten he was closing rapidly on de Puniet, and a couple later he was ahead, the Frenchman following behind as he closed on double practice crasher Locatelli. By the finish the young Australian was ahead of the Italian, but not quite able to match Nieto's final charge.

On the last lap Checa and Battaini collided, the former rejoining for 18th, Battaini out, leaving eighth and ninth to Matsudo and Aoki, separated by inches.

The next battle was between David Garcia, replacing the convalescing Alzamora on the second factory Honda, wild card Waldmann and Briton Jay Vincent. They finished in that order. Another 13 seconds back, Alex Debon snitched 13th from Dirk Heidolf, with a lone Raul Jara taking the last point.

125 cc RACE – 19 laps

De Angelis claimed his first pole by a quarter of a second, ahead of Sanna, Pedrosa and Poggiali — two Aprilias, one Honda and one Gilera on the front row — with Jenkner, Cecchinello, Nieto and Vincent close behind. A close race with a big leading group would be guaranteed — youth versus experience on a wide track allowing each full expression. They went at it to the end, with experience taking the honours by just two-tenths.

Sanna led away, but Pedrosa and Vincent finished lap one ahead of a brawl. Two laps later an eight-strong group had broken away, Vincent now leading.

Olivé was the first to go, running off-line down the hill and high-siding on the dirtier surface on lap seven. On lap eight Nieto also fell, while Borsoi joined briefly to bring the numbers back up to seven.

Young teenager Hector Barbera got in front to lead his first GP on the 14th and 15th tours, but never across the line. Cecchinello had taken that role, losing it to Vincent on the penultimate lap.

Cecchinello took it back into the first corner, while behind him the scramble intensified as they approached the final fast chicane. Vincent took a sweeping line, aiming to attack the leader. Instead, it gave Pedrosa just enough room to dive inside. Barbera held off Poggiali; Jenkner, Sanna and de Angelis were close behind; Borsoi four seconds adrift.

Kallio fended off Talmacsi, leaving Azuma trailing; Bianco stayed on to hold 13th from Giansanti and Sabbatani.

Poggiali's losing streak saw his points lead dwindle to just two over Vincent.

Above: Wild card Waldmann leads David Garcia (replacing convalescent Alzamora on the factory Honda) and British privateer Jay Vincent — they crossed the line within half a second, with Garcia in front.

Below: Typically close 125 racing, with the lead changing several times a lap — here Cecchinello heads de Angelis, Vincent, Poggiali, Pedrosa and Sanna.

Below left: Youth, experience and determination personified — Pedrosa, Cecchinello and Vincent on the rostrum.
All photographs: Gold & Goose

Right: Porto had another strong race at a track where handling means as much as ultimate horsepower.

Main picture: But Melandri was unbeatable, with or without the opposition of Rolfo.
Both photographs: Gold & Goose

GAULOISES CZECH grand prix

round 10

25 AUGUST 2002

CIRCUIT LENGTH: 3.357 miles/5.403 km

MotoGP

22 laps, 73.854 miles/118.866 km

Pos.	Rider (Nat.)	No.	Machine	Laps	Time & speed
1	Max Biaggi (I)	3	Yamaha	22	44m 36.498s 99.344 mph/ 159.879 km/h
2	Daijiro Kato (J)	74	Honda	22	44m 39.253s
3	Tohru Ukawa (J)	11	Honda	22	44m 44.096s
4	Sete Gibernau (E)	15	Suzuki	22	44m 48.387s
5	Carlos Checa (E)	7	Yamaha	22	44m 50.527s
6	Loris Capirossi (I)	65	Honda	22	44m 54.758s
7	Jeremy McWilliams (GB)	99	Proton KR	22	45m 01.338s
8	Norick Abe (J)	6	Yamaha	22	45m 03.070s
9	Alex Barros (BR)	4	Honda	22	45m 05.239s
10	Olivier Jacque (F)	19	Yamaha	22	45m 05.654s
11	Kenny Roberts (USA)	10	Suzuki	22	45m 09.418s
12	Jurgen van den Goorbergh (NL)	17	Honda	22	45m 15.168s
13	Garry McCoy (AUS)	8	Yamaha	22	45m 21.642s
14	Akira Ryo (J)	33	Suzuki	22	45m 28.430s
15	Tetsuya Harada (J)	31	Honda	22	45m 38.669s
16	Regis Laconi (F)	55	Aprilia	22	45m 38.736s
17	Sylvain Guintoli (F)	50	Yamaha	22	45m 49.963s
	Valentino Rossi (I)	46	Honda	20	DNF
	John Hopkins (USA)	21	Yamaha	12	DNF
	Nobuatsu Aoki (J)	9	Proton KR	11	DNF
	Shinya Nakano (J)	56	Yamaha	0	DNF
	Pere Riba (E)	20	Yamaha		DNS

Fastest lap: Kato, 2m 00.605s, 100.212 mph/161.276 km/h (record).

Previous record: Valentino Rossi, I (Honda), 2m 01.461s, 99.506 mph/160.140 km/h (2001).

Event best maximum speed: Biaggi, 182.4 mph/293.6 km/h (qualifying practice no. 2).

Qualifying: 1 Biaggi, 1m 59.646s; 2 Kato, 1m 59.740s; 3 Rossi, 1m 59.997s; 4 McCoy, 2m 00.129s; 5 Capirossi, 2m 00.146s; 6 Checa, 2m 00.186s; 7 Hopkins, 2m 00.241s; 8 Ukawa, 2m 00.485s; 9 Gibernau, 2m 00.567s; 10 Barros, 2m 00.619s; 11 Nakano, 2m 00.659s; 12 McWilliams, 2m 00.674s; 13 van den Goorbergh, 2m 00.835s; 14 Aoki, 2m 00.985s; 15 Jacque, 2m 01.058s; 16 Abe, 2m 01.239s; 17 Harada, 2m 01.435s; 18 Laconi, 2m 01.494s; 19 Roberts, 2m 01.582s; 20 Ryo, 2m 02.085s; 21 Guintoli, 2m 03.054s; 22 Riba, 2m 04.329s.

Fastest race laps: 1 Kato, 2m 00.605s; 2 Biaggi, 2m 00.718s; 3 Rossi, 2m 00.758s; 4 Ukawa, 2m 00.909s; 5 Checa, 2m 01.066s; 6 Gibernau, 2m 01.264s; 7 Capirossi, 2m 01.366s; 8 McWilliams, 2m 01.624s; 9 Roberts, 2m 01.997s; 10 Abe, 2m 02.006s; 11 Barros, 2m 02.128s; 12 Aoki, 2m 02.131s; 13 Hopkins, 2m 02.152s; 14 McCoy, 2m 02.171s; 15 Jacque, 2m 02.184s; 16 van den Goorbergh, 2m 02.334s; 17 Ryo, 2m 02.907s; 18 Laconi, 2m 03.116s; 19 Harada, 2m 03.461s; 20 Guintoli, 2m 04.246s.

World Championship: 1 Rossi, 220; 2 Ukawa, 140; 3 Biaggi, 134; 4 Checa, 96; 5 Barros, 94; 6 Abe, 90; 7 Kato, 80; 8 Capirossi, 75; 9 Jacque, 48; 10 Roberts, 45; 11 Aoki, 43; 12 Hopkins and Nakano, 41; 14 Ryo, 36; 15 Gibernau, 34; 16 Harada, 33; 17 Laconi and McWilliams, 28; 19 van den Goorbergh, 27; 20 McCoy, 21; 21 Itoh, 13; 22 Hofmann, 11; 23 Bayle, 5; 24 Riba, 4; 25 Cardoso, 3.

---

250 cc

20 laps, 67.140 miles/108.060 km

Pos.	Rider (Nat.)	No.	Machine	Laps	Time & speed
1	Marco Melandri (I)	3	Aprilia	20	41m 41.572s 96.628 mph/ 155.508 km/h
2	Sebastian Porto (ARG)	9	Yamaha	20	41m 48.595s
3	Toni Elias (E)	24	Aprilia	20	41m 49.707s
4	Fonsi Nieto (E)	10	Aprilia	20	41m 49.879s
5	Casey Stoner (AUS)	27	Aprilia	20	41m 52.894s
6	Randy de Puniet (F)	17	Aprilia	20	41m 53.208s
7	Roberto Locatelli (I)	15	Aprilia	20	41m 58.560s
8	Naoki Matsudo (J)	8	Yamaha	20	42m 02.556s
9	Haruchika Aoki (J)	11	Honda	20	42m 02.574s
10	David Garcia (E)	84	Honda	20	42m 11.831s
11	Ralf Waldmann (D)	26	Aprilia	20	42m 11.929s
12	Jay Vincent (GB)	12	Honda	20	42m 12.377s
13	Alex Debon (E)	6	Aprilia	20	42m 25.164s
14	Dirk Heidolf (D)	28	Aprilia	20	42m 25.713s
15	Raul Jara (E)	22	Aprilia	20	42m 32.085s
16	Erwan Nigon (F)	36	Aprilia	20	42m 43.797s
17	Leon Haslam (GB)	19	Honda	20	42m 45.630s
18	David Checa (E)	42	Aprilia	20	42m 57.091s
19	Henk van den Lagemaat (NL)	29	Honda	20	43m 46.862s
20	Gabor Rizmayer (H)	63	Honda	19	41m 56.003s
	Franco Battaini (I)	21	Aprilia	19	DNF
	Hector Faubel (E)	32	Aprilia	19	DNF
	Roberto Rolfo (I)	4	Honda	18	DNF
	Jaroslav Hules (CZ)	13	Yamaha	15	DNF
	Shahrol Yuzy (MAL)	18	Yamaha	10	DNF
	Vladimir Castka (SLK)	64	Yamaha	4	DNF
	Hugo Marchand (F)	51	Aprilia	0	DNF
	Radomil Rous (CZ)	62	Honda		DNS
	Roger Heierli (CH)	65	Honda		DNQ

Fastest lap: Melandri, 2m 04.039s, 97.438 mph/156.811 km/h.

Lap record: Marco Melandri, I (Aprilia), 2m 03.836s, 97.598 mph/157.069 km/h (2001).

Event best maximum speed: Stoner, 157.5 mph/253.5 km/h (race).

Qualifying: 1 Nieto, 2m 03.037s; 2 Melandri, 2m 03.563s; 3 Porto, 2m 03.711s; 4 Locatelli, 2m 03.919s; 5 Battaini, 2m 03.957s; 6 Rolfo, 2m 04.051s; 7 Elias, 2m 04.266s; 8 Matsudo, 2m 04.311s; 9 de Puniet, 2m 04.537s; 10 Waldmann, 2m 04.583s; 11 Debon, 2m 05.241s; 12 Aoki, 2m 05.252s; 13 Yuzy, 2m 05.415s; 14 Vincent, 2m 05.654s; 15 Checa, 2m 05.681s; 16 Jara, 2m 05.754s; 17 Garcia, 2m 05.941s; 18 Marchand, 2m 06.135s; 19 Haslam, 2m 06.188s; 20 Stoner, 2m 06.441s; 21 Faubel, 2m 06.454s; 22 Heidolf, 2m 06.572s; 23 Nigon, 2m 06.882s; 24 Hules, 2m 07.322s; 25 van den Lagemaat, 2m 08.905s; 26 Castka, 2m 09.143s; 27 Rizmayer, 2m 09.543s; 28 Rous, 2m 10.916s; 29 Heierli, 2m 12.699s.

Fastest race laps: 1 Melandri, 2m 04.039s; 2 Rolfo, 2m 04.316s; 3 Nieto, 2m 04.382s; 4 Locatelli, 2m 04.496s; 5 Elias, 2m 04.526s; 6 Yuzy, 2m 04.587s; 7 Checa, 2m 04.756s; 8 Porto, 2m 04.759s; 9 de Puniet, 2m 04.842s; 10 Stoner, 2m 04.844s; 11 Battaini, 2m 04.951s; 12 Aoki, 2m 05.214s; 13 Waldmann, 2m 05.297s; 14 Garcia, 2m 05.376s; 15 Matsudo, 2m 05.409s; 16 Vincent, 2m 05.612s; 17 Heidolf, 2m 05.933s; 18 Faubel, 2m 06.001s; 19 Debon, 2m 06.395s; 20 Jara, 2m 06.510s; 21 Hules, 2m 06.929s; 22 Nigon, 2m 07.033s; 23 Haslam, 2m 07.136s; 24 van den Lagemaat, 2m 09.617s; 25 Rizmayer, 2m 11.019s; 26 Castka, 2m 11.574s.

World Championship: 1 Melandri, 195; 2 Nieto, 158; 3 Rolfo, 127; 4 Elias, 102; 5 Porto, 94; 6 Battaini, 88; 7 Locatelli, 87; 8 de Puniet, 86; 9 Matsudo, 65; 10 Alzamora, 63; 11 Debon, 52; 12 Stoner, 44; 13 Aoki, 42; 14 Yuzy, 38; 15 Miyazaki, 25; 16 Checa, 24; 17 Sakai, 20; 18 Waldmann, 17; 19 Vincent, 12; 20 Kameya, 9; 21 Heidolf, 8; 22 Faubel and Sekiguchi, 7; 24 Garcia and Jara, 6; 26 Aoyama, Haslam, Marchand and Philippe, 4; 30 Bataille, 2.

---

125 cc

19 laps, 63.783 miles/102.657 km

Pos.	Rider (Nat.)	No.	Machine	Laps	Time & speed
1	Lucio Cecchinello (I)	4	Aprilia	19	41m 18.287s 92.659 mph/ 149.121 km/h
2	Daniel Pedrosa (E)	26	Honda	19	41m 18.489s
3	Arnaud Vincent (F)	21	Aprilia	19	41m 18.565s
4	Hector Barbera (E)	80	Aprilia	19	41m 18.781s
5	Manuel Poggiali (RSM)	1	Gilera	19	41m 18.782s
6	Steve Jenkner (D)	17	Aprilia	19	41m 19.004s
7	Simone Sanna (I)	16	Aprilia	19	41m 19.188s
8	Alex de Angelis (RSM)	15	Aprilia	19	41m 19.596s
9	Gino Borsoi (I)	23	Aprilia	19	41m 23.866s
10	Mika Kallio (SF)	36	Honda	19	41m 25.378s
11	Gabor Talmacsi (H)	8	Honda	19	41m 25.647s
12	Masao Azuma (J)	5	Honda	19	42m 32.613s
13	Stefano Bianco (I)	33	Aprilia	19	42m 32.632s
14	Mirko Giansanti (I)	6	Honda	19	41m 35.277s
15	Max Sabbatani (I)	11	Aprilia	19	41m 36.393s
16	Klaus Nöhles (D)	12	Honda	19	41m 36.473s
17	Youichi Ui (J)	41	Derbi	19	41m 40.628s
18	Stefano Perugini (I)	7	Italjet	19	41m 40.695s
19	Thomas Luthi (CH)	77	Honda	19	41m 40.729s
20	Jorge Lorenzo (E)	48	Derbi	19	41m 59.335s
21	Andrea Dovizioso (I)	34	Honda	19	41m 59.495s
22	Gioele Pellino (I)	53	Aprilia	19	42m 02.305s
23	Robbin Harms (DK)	88	Honda	19	42m 08.494s
24	Mattia Angeloni (I)	31	Gilera	19	42m 08.659s
25	Michel Fabrizio (I)	84	Gilera	19	42m 08.738s
26	Imre Toth (H)	20	Honda	19	42m 08.987s
27	Marco Simoncelli (I)	37	Aprilia	19	42m 09.033s
28	Igor Kalab (CZ)	49	Honda	19	42m 09.847s
29	Dario Giuseppetti (D)	72	Honda	19	42m 25.615s
30	Matej Smrz (CZ)	76	Aprilia	19	43m 05.672s
	Lukas Pesek (CZ)	56	Honda	15	DNF
	Andrea Ballerini (I)	50	Honda	13	DNF
	Pablo Nieto (E)	22	Aprilia	7	DNF
	Joan Olivé (E)	25	Honda	6	DNF
	Christian Pistoni (I)	42	Italjet	5	DNF
	Chaz Davies (GB)	57	Aprilia		DNS

Fastest lap: Cecchinello, 2m 08.903s, 93.761 mph/150.894 km/h (record).

Previous record: Youichi Ui, J (Derbi), 2m 09.416s, 93.390 mph/150.296 km/h (2000).

Event best maximum speed: Pedrosa, 138.9 mph/223.6 km/h (race).

Qualifying: 1 de Angelis, 2m 08.746s; 2 Sanna, 2m 08.992s; 3 Pedrosa, 2m 09.000s; 4 Poggiali, 2m 09.105s; 5 Jenkner, 2m 09.244s; 6 Cecchinello, 2m 09.307s; 7 Nieto, 2m 09.406s; 8 Vincent, 2m 09.506s; 9 Barbera, 2m 09.514s; 10 Borsoi, 2m 09.563s; 11 Talmacsi, 2m 09.612s; 12 Olivé, 2m 09.713s; 13 Ui, 2m 09.862s; 14 Kallio, 2m 10.061s; 15 Bianco, 2m 10.163s; 16 Perugini, 2m 10.223s; 17 Nöhles, 2m 10.240s; 18 Luthi, 2m 10.267s; 19 Azuma, 2m 10.317s; 20 Giansanti, 2m 10.340s; 21 Dovizioso, 2m 10.602s; 22 Sabbatani, 2m 10.763s; 23 Ballerini, 2m 10.852s; 24 Simoncelli, 2m 11.117s; 25 Pesek, 2m 11.241s; 26 Pellino, 2m 11.487s; 27 Lorenzo, 2m 11.987s; 28 Fabrizio, 2m 12.150s; 29 Harms, 2m 12.199s; 30 Davies, 2m 12.348s; 31 Toth, 2m 12.569s; 32 Pistoni, 2m 12.761s; 33 Giuseppetti, 2m 12.814s; 34 Smrz, 2m 13.120s; 35 Angeloni, 2m 13.598s; 36 Kalab, 2m 13.873s.

Fastest race laps: 1 Cecchinello, 2m 08.903s; 2 Jenkner, 2m 08.956s; 3 Barbera, 2m 09.017s; 4 de Angelis, 2m 09.043s; 5 Poggiali, 2m 09.091s; 6 Nieto, 2m 09.226s; 7 Sanna, 2m 09.256s; 8 Pedrosa, 2m 09.335s; 9 Vincent, 2m 09.366s; 10 Olivé, 2m 09.392s; 11 Kallio, 2m 09.417s; 12 Azuma, 2m 09.441s; 13 Borsoi, 2m 09.551s; 14 Bianco, 2m 09.585s; 15 Nöhles, 2m 09.691s; 16 Luthi, 2m 09.838s; 17 Talmacsi, 2m 09.942s; 18 Giansanti, 2m 09.986s; 19 Sabbatani, 2m 10.005s; 20 Ballerini, 2m 10.015s; 21 Perugini, 2m 10.115s; 22 Ui, 2m 10.220s; 23 Pellino, 2m 10.925s; 24 Dovizioso, 2m 11.087s; 25 Lorenzo, 2m 11.490s; 26 Simoncelli, 2m 11.587s; 27 Fabrizio, 2m 11.634s; 28 Pesek, 2m 11.646s; 29 Kalab, 2m 11.749s; 30 Angeloni, 2m 11.774s; 31 Harms, 2m 11.780s; 32 Toth, 2m 11.796s; 33 Giuseppetti, 2m 11.976s; 34 Smrz, 2m 13.705s; 35 Pistoni, 2m 13.859s.

World Championship: 1 Poggiali, 171; 2 Vincent, 169; 3 Pedrosa, 160; 4 Cecchinello, 116; 5 Jenkner, 106; 6 Sanna, 67; 7 Nieto, 65; 8 de Angelis, 63; 9 Borsoi and Ui, 54; 11 Olivé, 51; 12 Azuma, 50; 13 Kallio, 43; 14 Giansanti, 39; 15 Dovizioso, 32; 16 Bianco, 21; 17 Barbera and Ueda, 18; 19 Ballerini and Rodriguez, 17; 21 Aoyama, 16; 22 Perugini, 14; 23 Sabbatani, 12; 24 Nöhles and Talmacsi, 6; 26 Lorenzo, 5; 27 Smrz, 3; 28 Baldolini, Lai and Pellino, 2; 31 Fabrizio, 1.

PORTUGUESE GP

FIM WORLD CHAMPIONSHIP · ROUND 11

Suzuki caught up with the rest of the MotoGP bikes at Portugal. At last, they too had a ramp slipper clutch. The fall-out was riveting — one of the blue Telefónica bikes came close enough to winning the race; the other was a season-best fourth. Funnily enough, it had nothing to do with the clutch. Or possibly it did.

The reason why Gibernau led from the second to almost the end of the fourth-last lap was because he was having one of those days, as at Valencia last year, when he was unbeatable in the wet. Because the weather was dire, and conditions treacherous in the extreme — with no less than 54 race crashes, 29 in the 125 class, six of them more than once. Gibernau even had Rossi beaten. The Honda rider was closing, but the gap was still 3.6 seconds with four laps to go, and all he could do was keep the pressure on.

Then it was all over. Changing direction up the hill his back wheel lost grip, slid sideways, and Gibernau was spat into the sand. As in Germany (and at Donington, though in rather more promising circumstances), lucky old Rossi inherited the lead when a rider fell off in front of him.

It wasn't the clutch that let him lead, said Gibernau, but it was the clutch that fetched him down, while the bike wasn't even leaned over. While obviously potentially better than the sprag clutch, it was still in its very early stages and wasn't set right — erratic all race long, and this time it dragged too much and caught him out.

Roberts, by contrast, praised it. Maybe there was still a long way to go, not least in getting the chassis and engine set differently to respond to its different performance. But it was progress. He rode to a cautious fourth, prepared to try a little harder than so far this year, obviously, but still not to stick his neck out. 'This bike is still very young, and it's not to the point where it feels part of me, and me part of it,' he explained.

Wet tracks, however, are riders' tracks, and that is why fully wet races are almost always interesting and unpredictable. It was certainly the case at Estoril, where blustery but dry practice gave way to sweeping Atlantic squalls on Sunday morning, some of cloudburst proportions. If the big class was a nail-biter, the smaller classes were even more fraught.

And, in the case of the 250s, historic. Only twice before in history has a rider fallen off while leading, re-mounted, and gone on to win the race. The first was Mike Hailwood at the Isle of Man in 1965, slipping off the MV at Sarah's Cottage, and rather cheating by push-starting down the hill, against the flow of traffic. The second was Ralf Waldmann, at a sodden Suzuka in 1995. 'Waldie' had crashed his 250 and got going again without even losing the lead.

Nobody had done it with such style as Fonsi Nieto, though. He slipped off at one of the uphill chicanes, but kept hold of the handlebars to keep the engine running. Whether deliberately (as he later said) or by accident (as it appeared), he neglected to declutch, so when he tried to pick the bike up the spinning wheel triggered a spectacular 360-degree horizontal spin for bike and rider. A prone pirouette, if you like. Or a ground-level doughnut. Amazingly, he gathered it all up without losing the engine and pointing in the right direction, and jumped back, seventh but losing barely ten seconds. By the end, he'd taken them all back again, and was fending off a late charge by Melandri to take a classic win.

Team-mate Elias had an even more colourful race — falling off three times, and still finishing in the points, albeit three laps behind. Nobody was quite sure if anybody had ever done that before. Elias, who ran much of the race with only one footpeg, was sure he never wanted to do it again.

The 125 race was a minor epic — Arnaud Vincent taking the points lead after leading most of the race, losing it to Sanna with three corners left, then getting it back in the last turn. This fine racing was a reward after a weekend of uncertainty, where weather-struck practice went ahead against a background of intensifying and in most cases increasingly fruitless gossip. In an environment stricken with money worries — too many bikes and teams, not enough sponsors (or riders) — things were getting urgent.

Who would go where? And who would pay? Would Telefónica MoviStar stay with Suzuki or take Gibernau to Honda? Was Fortuna off to pick up Yamaha's bills? Had Max signed for Honda? Who would ride the Kawasaki? Were Red Bull boss Dieter Mateschitz's paddock threats to pull out to be taken seriously? Was Nicky Hayden coming to Yamaha?

Rumours with the ring of truth in the morning had been turned upside down by events the same afternoon. Some of the above would turn out to have legs, but for the present they just contributed to an unsettled feeling, exacerbated by the thought of the gruelling forthcoming flyaway season, with four continents in five weekends.

It was a relief to be able to talk about tyres... Michelin revealing that for the first time they had brought a different spec of tyre especially for the four-strokes. This followed the Brno failure, and acknowledged that the four-strokes make heavier demands on the rubber than the lighter and less powerful two-strokes, in spite of their gentle power delivery. According to race boss Nicolas Goubert: 'It is what we expected, as the four-strokes start pushing each other and the other bikes are becoming more competitive with Honda. They are not near the limit on horsepower, and can easily make more. With the two-strokes, already on the limit, we were just refining the product. The four-strokes are pushing us into new areas.'

In between testing the stronger new tyres, as the weather allowed, riders however were in huddles with their managers, or spying to see who went into which team motorhome, and how their faces looked when they came out again.

MOTOGP - ROSSI • 250 cc - NIETO • 125 cc - VINCENT

MOTO**GP** RACE – 28 laps

Rain spoiled Saturday plans, with a brief dry window at the very end of the second session. Checa was readiest, for his first pole on the M1. Kato was alongside, after two test days at Valencia on the V5 more than doubled his experience on the four-stroke; then Rossi and Barros, on a first-day time, with Biaggi leading row two, McWilliams alongside. And warm-up was wet enough to hunt for settings on a streaming track.

They all funnelled into the slow first corner without drama, though Jacque and Riba fell off later in the lap on the final chicane, close together but independently, while pole-starter Checa was boxed up in 12th. Rossi was in front first time over the line, taking over from Barros, with Roberts, then Gibernau taking fifth from McWilliams as they ran into the first corner again. A man on a mission.

At the end of that lap Gibernau was third, and next time round he'd puddle-surfed past Rossi and was pulling away from a field already depleted by watery problems: Aoki's engine had seized, McWilliams crashed after similar problems with ingested spray, remounting at the back.

Gibernau had a second on Rossi after lap four, and was still pulling steadily ahead at two- or three-tenths a lap. Barros had dropped back; Roberts in third was cautious, giving way to Ukawa on lap six, who promptly splashed past Rossi as well, then seemingly delaying his team-mate as Gibernau built a margin of six seconds after 12 laps.

Now Rossi moved past Ukawa, and the chase was on. 'I'd found my rhythm,' said the Italian later. 'But Sete had another idea.' Rossi did close bit by bit, but not fast enough. He was running out of time, and at the end of lap 24 Gibernau had 3.6 seconds in hand and seemed in control. Instead, he crashed before finishing the lap, landing heavily, and leaving the track in an ambulance, his collarbone dislocated. 'I'd been having trouble with the clutch from the start, and it was getting worse. Maybe it was the rain. Now I closed the throttle and the back wheel just locked.'

It was hard to say whether Rossi had triggered the crash. Team boss Burgess thought so, describing Rossi's gifted win as the best pressure ride he'd ever seen. Certainly he hadn't given up on an apparently hopeless task. 'I'm not sure if I could have caught Sete. I think not. It is very easy to make a small error and pay a big price in these conditions. Sete did. I feel sorry for him,' said the winner.

Behind this, Checa had been recovering the ground he'd lost with wheelspin in the first three gears off the start, and was pulling through at a quickening pace. He passed the soon-to-crash Laconi for seventh by lap three, and was ahead of both Biaggi and Barros one lap later, pulling clear to close a gap of three seconds on Roberts. By lap 11 he was with him, taking fourth a lap later to close down on Ukawa. The Honda was a bit harder, but four laps later he was ahead of him as well, pulling clear by the time he was promoted to second, his best result of the year; Ukawa was third and Roberts fourth.

Biaggi, again using the previous chassis, was busy fending off Barros to the end, finally losing the battle on the last lap.

Drama galore behind in the conditions, though not much close racing. Hopkins had been ahead of Abe in seventh until he aquaplaned off into the gravel, staying wheels down to finish 15 seconds adrift. McWilliams had pushed through to ninth, well ahead of Harada and McCoy, still battling to find his race form. Nakano had also fallen, and remounted for 12th, the last finisher.

Van den Goorbergh had retired early, a slick-shift problem causing a misfire; then Aoki seized. Laconi slipped off with 25 laps to go, Capirossi likewise three laps later, and Kato also from a lowly position at the back, showing a somehow welcome weakness in his first wet four-stroke ride.

250 cc RACE – 26 laps

The improving Porto's first pole came by four-tenths after a battle with Melandri. 'At tracks where power is not so important, the Yamaha works well,' he said. Nieto was third, with Rolfo completing the first row.

The rain redoubled as they lined up to start. De Puniet pulled out on the line; Rolfo led the cloud of spray down the hill, displaced by Nieto a couple of corners later. But Rolfo had been judged as having jumped the start, and would be called in for a stop-and-go penalty, complaining bitterly all the while. In fact, video evidence showed that he hadn't crossed the line, but he had been rolling when the lights went green. Enough for the decision to stick. 'It was in any case irrevocable. I could have won,' said the Italian later.

Wet specialist Matsudo was ahead at the start of lap two, lapping two seconds a lap faster than the next best, with almost eight seconds in hand by lap six. Rolfo's demotion promoted Battaini to second, Aoki and Nieto close, then a growing gap to a cautious Melandri, whose position was under threat from Briton Jay Vincent, inspired by the opportunity the conditions offered.

A big slide halved Matsudo's lead on lap seven, but he maintained the gap ahead of a field riven by dramatic events, with riders falling off, recovering, and speeding up only to slow down again.

On lap 13, Nieto passed Battaini, only to fall and spin a little later on. He rejoined in seventh, still less than 12 seconds behind Matsudo. Battaini also fell after just three more laps, remounting to crash once again and retire. Then Aoki, second on lap 16, was also down and out.

At the same time, Vincent had found a way past Melandri, who had slowed him in the corners, but was in third for half a lap before he also fell.

Nieto was forging through, past Locatelli and Porto, then also Melandri one lap later, the 17th. He took four laps to halve a 13-second gap to Matsudo, who felt the pressure, surviving one slide only to crash heavily under brakes on lap 22, dreams of a first victory shattered.

Thus Nieto led again, with Melandri five seconds adrift and the rain still sheeting down. The gap was closing, and Nieto raised his hand a couple of times hoping the race would be stopped. It wasn't, and Melandri was a second behind as they started the last lap. But for a disobliging back-marker he might have won, though he was still just over half a second behind at the flag, breaking a six-race run of victories.

Left: Checa on a charge towards second — Ukawa (11) is his last victim.

Below: Nieto celebrates breaking a six-race run of wins for 250 rival Melandri.

Bottom: Matsudo was set to run away with the 250 race, as Nieto and Debon (6) are left behind. The Japanese rider's first win was snatched away by circumstances.

All photographs: Gold & Goose

Above: Melandri is under pressure from Jay Vincent's private Honda, Alzamora leading the pursuit. The Briton finally passed the factory bike, only to fall off.

Right: Teenage newcomer Jorge Lorenzo was just one of 23 125 riders to fall off in 29 separate incidents — a record.

Below: Vincent holds Sanna at bay — all the way to the flag.
All photographs: Gold & Goose

Porto's caution was rewarded by third; Rolfo had stormed through to fourth after rejoining in 13th on lap seven. He was 23 seconds behind the leader, after losing 30-odd in the penalty. He might indeed have won.

Haslam's seventh was a career best, but with mixed feelings; he might have done better still if he had not fallen and remounted early on. Checa and Heidolf (ninth) were the last riders on the same lap as the leader, with only 13 finishers and points for all... even Elias, soldiering on with what was left of his bike.

Stoner retired from an unequal battle. Others to fall included Yuzy (twice), Debon, Nigon and Bataille.

125 cc RACE – 24 laps

Pedrosa took a fourth pole, two-tenths ahead of Poggiali and Ui redux, both enjoying long-awaited upgrades to the Gilera/Derbi stable. Jenkner completed row one; Finnish rookie Kallio was fifth, his best so far.

The track was damp, and Poggiali fell on the sighting lap, pitting to swap bikes, to start from the back of the grid.

Talmacsi led away, but Vincent took over on lap two, with Jenkner close, Sanna pushing through to sixth. Olivé had crashed on lap two, the first of a record number of 29 crashes involving 23 riders, with many remounting to try again more than once... Ueda actually fell twice on the same lap, thereafter retiring.

Poggiali was 17th after one lap, and moving through rapidly as the carnage went on.

Among the leaders, de Angelis was next, getting back on only to crash out again later; then Ui, out of the race; then Cecchinello, rejoining at the back. Then Giansanti, Fabrizio, Angeloni, Barbera, Perugini, Borsoi... and many others.

It made Vincent look even more impressive, with Jenkner in second, then Sanna closing up after following Talmacsi for a while, until the Hungarian also slithered off.

With four laps to go Poggiali was up to fourth, almost 20 seconds adrift. Then he too crashed out.

The leading trio stayed close together, then Sanna consigned Jenkner to third with two laps left, the German narrowly staying on the track after the encounter, losing touch.

On the last lap, Sanna seized the lead at the last chicane, then ran into the final bend in fourth gear instead of third. That pushed him wide; Vincent was ready to dive inside to win.

Nieto was a distant fourth, Azuma another ten seconds back. Cecchinello pulled through to sixth; Borsoi was four seconds adrift, then Kallio, all three having fallen during the race, Cecchinello and Borsoi twice each. Pedrosa, who finished tenth, fell only once. Chaz Davies was four seconds behind in 11th, opening his points score with an impressively steady ride.

FIM WORLD CHAMPIONSHIP

MARLBORO
PORTUGUESE
grand prix

ESTORIL CIRCUIT

round **11**

CIRCUIT LENGTH: 2.599 miles/4.182 km

8 SEPTEMBER 2002

MotoGP

28 laps, 72.772 miles/117.096 km

Pos.	Rider (Nat.)	No.	Machine	Laps	Time & speed
1	Valentino Rossi (I)	46	Honda	28	54m 12.962s 80.522 mph/ 129.588 km/h
2	Carlos Checa (E)	7	Yamaha	28	54m 35.162s
3	Tohru Ukawa (J)	11	Honda	28	54m 37.182s
4	Kenny Roberts (USA)	10	Suzuki	28	54m 53.794s
5	Alex Barros (BR)	4	Honda	28	54m 55.671s
6	Max Biaggi (I)	3	Yamaha	28	54m 57.026s
7	Norick Abe (J)	6	Yamaha	28	56m 01.974s
8	John Hopkins (USA)	21	Yamaha	28	56m 16.063s
9	Jeremy McWilliams (GB)	99	Proton KR	27	54m 33.830s
10	Tetsuya Harada (J)	31	Honda	27	55m 01.691s
11	Garry McCoy (AUS)	8	Yamaha	27	55m 15.117s
12	Shinya Nakano (J)	56	Yamaha	27	55m 21.518s
	Sete Gibernau (E)	15	Suzuki	24	DNF
	Daijiro Kato (J)	74	Honda	7	DNF
	Loris Capirossi (I)	65	Honda	6	DNF
	Regis Laconi (F)	55	Aprilia	3	DNF
	Nobuatsu Aoki (J)	9	Proton KR	2	DNF
	Jurgen van den Goorbergh (NL)	17	Honda	2	DNF
	Olivier Jacque (F)	19	Yamaha	0	DNF
	Pere Riba (E)	20	Yamaha	0	DNF

Fastest lap: Rossi, 1m 52.302s, 83.300 mph/134.059 km/h.
Lap record: Loris Capirossi, I (Honda), 1m 40.683s, 92.914 mph/149.530 km/h (2001).
Event best maximum speed: Rossi, 190.9 mph/307.3 km/h (qualifying practice no. 2).
Qualifying: 1 Checa, 1m 39.793s; **2** Kato, 1m 39.868s; **3** Rossi, 1m 39.984s; **4** Barros, 1m 40.112s; **5** Biaggi, 1m 40.147s; **6** McWilliams, 1m 40.308s; **7** Capirossi, 1m 40.315s; **8** Ukawa, 1m 40.509s; **9** Gibernau, 1m 40.747s; **10** van den Goorbergh, 1m 40.771s; **11** Aoki, 1m 40.814s; **12** Roberts, 1m 40.965s; **13** Abe, 1m 40.969s; **14** Laconi, 1m 41.032s; **15** Hopkins, 1m 41.092s; **16** McCoy, 1m 41.169s; **17** Nakano, 1m 41.231s; **18** Harada, 1m 41.463s; **19** Jacque, 1m 41.535s; **20** Riba, 1m 43.782s.
Fastest race laps: 1 Rossi, 1m 52.302s; **2** Gibernau, 1m 52.476s; **3** Checa, 1m 53.463s; **4** Ukawa, 1m 54.548s; **5** Barros, 1m 55.180s; **6** Roberts, 1m 55.293s; **7** Biaggi, 1m 55.323s; **8** McWilliams, 1m 57.211s; **9** Abe, 1m 57.237s; **10** Hopkins, 1m 57.390s; **11** Nakano, 1m 58.069s; **12** McCoy, 1m 58.255s; **13** Capirossi, 1m 58.951s; **14** Harada, 1m 59.192s; **15** Laconi, 2m 02.191s; **16** Kato, 2m 02.590s; **17** Aoki, 2m 02.924s; **18** van den Goorbergh, 2m 06.189s.
World Championship: 1 Rossi, 245; **2** Ukawa, 156; **3** Biaggi, 144; **4** Checa, 116; **5** Barros, 105; **6** Abe, 99; **7** Kato, 80; **8** Capirossi, 75; **9** Roberts, 58; **10** Hopkins, 49; **11** Jacque, 48; **12** Nakano, 45; **13** Aoki, 43; **14** Harada, 39; **15** Ryo, 36; **16** McWilliams, 35; **17** Gibernau, 34; **18** Laconi, 28; **19** van den Goorbergh, 27; **20** McCoy, 26; **21** Itoh, 13; **22** Hofmann, 11; **23** Bayle, 5; **24** Riba, 4; **25** Cardoso, 3.

250 cc

26 laps, 67.574 miles/108.732 km

Pos.	Rider (Nat.)	No.	Machine	Laps	Time & speed
1	Fonsi Nieto (E)	10	Aprilia	26	53m 58.901s 75.095 mph/ 120.854 km/h
2	Marco Melandri (I)	3	Aprilia	26	53m 59.585s
3	Sebastian Porto (ARG)	9	Yamaha	26	54m 06.243s
4	Roberto Rolfo (I)	4	Honda	26	54m 22.477s
5	Roberto Locatelli (I)	15	Aprilia	26	54m 48.135s
6	Emilio Alzamora (E)	7	Honda	26	54m 59.529s
7	Leon Haslam (GB)	19	Honda	26	55m 35.535s
8	David Checa (E)	42	Aprilia	26	55m 38.451s
9	Dirk Heidolf (D)	28	Aprilia	26	56m 11.641s
10	Hector Faubel (E)	32	Aprilia	25	54m 02.669s
11	Raul Jara (E)	22	Aprilia	25	54m 06.465s
12	Erwan Nigon (F)	36	Aprilia	25	54m 41.563s
13	Toni Elias (E)	24	Aprilia	23	54m 55.925s
	Gregory Lefort (F)	57	Aprilia	23	DNF
	Shahrol Yuzy (MAL)	18	Yamaha	22	DNF
	Naoki Matsudo (J)	8	Yamaha	21	DNF
	Franco Battaini (I)	21	Aprilia	20	DNF
	Casey Stoner (AUS)	27	Aprilia	19	DNF
	Haruchika Aoki (J)	11	Honda	17	DNF
	Jay Vincent (GB)	12	Honda	17	DNF
	Eric Bataille (AND)	34	Honda	7	DNF
	Alex Debon (E)	6	Aprilia	6	DNF
	Jaroslav Hules (CZ)	13	Yamaha	2	DNF
	Randy de Puniet (F)	17	Aprilia		DNS
	Rob Filart (NL)	30	Honda		DNQ

Fastest lap: Nieto, 2m 00.120s, 77.879 mph/125.334 km/h.
Lap record: Daijiro Kato, J (Honda), 1m 42.285s, 91.458 mph/147.188 km/h (2001).
Event best maximum speed: Elias, 169.2 mph/272.3 km/h (qualifying practice no. 1).
Qualifying: 1 Porto, 1m 41.708s; **2** Melandri, 1m 42.097s; **3** Nieto, 1m 42.325s; **4** Rolfo, 1m 42.353s; **5** Battaini, 1m 42.430s; **6** Elias, 1m 42.451s; **7** Alzamora, 1m 42.591s; **8** Matsudo, 1m 42.652s; **9** de Puniet, 1m 42.916s; **10** Debon, 1m 43.259s; **11** Locatelli, 1m 43.272s; **12** Yuzy, 1m 43.607s; **13** Stoner, 1m 43.671s; **14** Haslam, 1m 43.796s; **15** Aoki, 1m 43.829s; **16** Hules, 1m 44.003s; **17** Bataille, 1m 44.140s; **18** Vincent, 1m 44.167s; **19** Checa, 1m 44.243s; **20** Nigon, 1m 45.043s; **21** Heidolf, 1m 45.047s; **22** Faubel, 1m 45.171s; **23** Jara, 1m 45.833s; **24** Lefort, 1m 46.543s; **25** Filart, 1m 49.680s.
Fastest race laps: 1 Nieto, 2m 00.120s; **2** Battaini, 2m 00.803s; **3** Matsudo, 2m 00.955s; **4** Aoki, 2m 01.068s; **5** Rolfo, 2m 01.237s; **6** Porto, 2m 01.462s; **7** Melandri, 2m 02.152s; **8** Vincent, 2m 02.172s; **9** Elias, 2m 02.351s; **10** Locatelli, 2m 02.672s; **11** Yuzy, 2m 02.869s; **12** Alzamora, 2m 03.057s; **13** Lefort, 2m 03.227s; **14** Haslam, 2m 03.516s; **15** Checa, 2m 04.055s; **16** Heidolf, 2m 04.464s; **17** Faubel, 2m 05.081s; **18** Bataille, 2m 05.491s; **19** Jara, 2m 05.794s; **20** Nigon, 2m 06.026s; **21** Stoner, 2m 06.387s; **22** Debon, 2m 10.900s; **23** Hules, 2m 11.084s.
World Championship: 1 Melandri, 215; **2** Nieto, 183; **3** Rolfo, 140; **4** Porto, 110; **5** Elias, 105; **6** Locatelli, 98; **7** Battaini, 88; **8** de Puniet, 86; **9** Alzamora, 30 Matsudo, 65; **11** Debon, 52; **12** Stoner, 44; **13** Aoki, 42; **14** Yuzy, 38; **15** Checa, 32; **16** Miyazaki, 25; **17** Sakai, 20; **18** Waldmann, 17; **19** Heidolf, 15; **20** Faubel and Haslam, 13; **22** Vincent, 12; **23** Jara, 11; **24** Kameya, 9; **25** Sekiguchi, 7; **26** Garcia, 6; **27** Aoyama, Marchand, Nigon and Philippe, 4; **31** Bataille, 2.

125 cc

24 laps, 62.376 miles/100.368 km

Pos.	Rider (Nat.)	No.	Machine	Laps	Time & speed
1	Arnaud Vincent (F)	21	Aprilia	24	49m 05.300s 76.229 mph/ 122.678 km/h
2	Simone Sanna (I)	16	Aprilia	24	49m 06.167s
3	Steve Jenkner (D)	17	Aprilia	24	49m 07.900s
4	Pablo Nieto (E)	22	Aprilia	24	49m 53.820s
5	Masao Azuma (J)	5	Honda	24	50m 03.272s
6	Lucio Cecchinello (I)	4	Aprilia	24	50m 15.335s
7	Gino Borsoi (I)	23	Aprilia	24	50m 19.982s
8	Mika Kallio (SF)	36	Honda	24	50m 33.294s
9	Thomas Luthi (CH)	77	Honda	24	50m 44.743s
10	Daniel Pedrosa (E)	26	Honda	24	50m 55.819s
11	Chaz Davies (GB)	57	Aprilia	24	50m 59.825s
12	Christian Pistoni (I)	42	Italjet	23	49m 16.373s
13	Marco Simoncelli (I)	37	Aprilia	23	50m 29.152s
14	Julian Simon (E)	52	Honda	23	50m 29.216s
	Andrea Dovizioso (I)	34	Honda	22	DNF
	Manuel Poggiali (RSM)	1	Gilera	20	DNF
	Stefano Bianco (I)	33	Aprilia	20	DNF
	Noboru Ueda (J)	9	Honda	18	DNF
	Michel Fabrizio (I)	84	Gilera	16	DNF
	Mattia Angeloni (I)	31	Gilera	15	DNF
	Imre Toth (H)	20	Honda	13	DNF
	Hector Barbera (E)	80	Aprilia	9	DNF
	Alex Baldolini (I)	19	Aprilia	8	DNF
	Stefano Perugini (I)	7	Italjet	7	DNF
	Gabor Talmacsi (H)	8	Honda	6	DNF
	Jorge Lorenzo (E)	48	Derbi	6	DNF
	Andrea Ballerini (I)	50	Honda	6	DNF
	Klaus Nöhles (D)	12	Honda	6	DNF
	Mirko Giansanti (I)	6	Honda	4	DNF
	Alex de Angelis (RSM)	15	Aprilia	4	DNF
	Max Sabbatani (I)	11	Aprilia	4	DNF
	Youichi Ui (J)	41	Derbi	3	DNF
	Joan Olivé (E)	25	Honda	1	DNF
	Pedro Monteiro (P)	78	Honda		DNQ
	Joao Pinto (P)	79	Honda		DNQ
	Filipe Costa (P)	94	Yamaha		DNQ

Fastest lap: Jenkner, 2m 01.050s, 77.281 mph/124.371 km/h.
Lap record: Youichi Ui, J (Derbi), 1m 46.329s, 87.980 mph/141.590 km/h (2001).
Event best maximum speed: Borsoi, 147.0 mph/236.6 km/h (qualifying practice no. 1).
Qualifying: 1 Pedrosa, 1m 46.664s; **2** Poggiali, 1m 46.872s; **3** Ui, 1m 47.113s; **4** Jenkner, 1m 47.113s; **5** Kallio, 1m 47.320s; **6** Sanna, 1m 47.373s; **7** Giansanti, 1m 47.502s; **8** Cecchinello, 1m 47.510s; **9** Vincent, 1m 47.562s; **10** de Angelis, 1m 47.566s; **11** Talmacsi, 1m 47.573s; **12** Olivé, 1m 47.794s; **13** Bianco, 1m 47.962s; **14** Barbera, 1m 48.055s; **15** Borsoi, 1m 48.220s; **16** Ueda, 1m 48.242s; **17** Ballerini, 1m 48.408s; **18** Dovizioso, 1m 48.452s; **19** Fabrizio, 1m 48.457s; **20** Azuma, 1m 48.492s; **21** Nieto, 1m 48.527s; **22** Nöhles, 1m 48.571s; **23** Angeloni, 1m 48.746s; **24** Sabbatani, 1m 48.866s; **25** Lorenzo, 1m 48.873s; **26** Baldolini, 1m 48.919s; **27** Simon, 1m 49.036s; **28** Perugini, 1m 49.310s; **29** Luthi, 1m 49.360s; **30** Davies, 1m 49.661s; **31** Toth, 1m 49.743s; **32** Simoncelli, 1m 50.338s; **33** Pistoni, 1m 51.600s; **34** Monteiro, 1m 56.425s; **35** Pinto, 1m 57.631s; **36** Costa, 1m 59.190s.
Fastest race laps: 1 Jenkner, 2m 01.050s; **2** Vincent, 2m 01.055s; **3** Bianco, 2m 01.303s; **4** Sanna, 2m 01.340s; **5** Cecchinello, 2m 01.559s; **6** Poggiali, 2m 01.584s; **7** Barbera, 2m 02.114s; **8** Dovizioso, 2m 02.233s; **9** Nieto, 2m 02.241s; **10** Azuma, 2m 02.320s; **11** Borsoi, 2m 02.345s; **12** Ueda, 2m 02.761s; **13** Baldolini, 2m 02.956s; **14** Kallio, 2m 03.065s; **15** Luthi, 2m 03.130s; **16** Talmacsi, 2m 03.135s; **17** Perugini, 2m 03.175s; **18** Pedrosa, 2m 03.468s; **19** de Angelis, 2m 03.497s; **20** Ui, 2m 03.548s; **21** Lorenzo, 2m 04.264s; **22** Angeloni, 2m 04.851s; **23** Nöhles, 2m 04.994s; **24** Davies, 2m 05.154s; **25** Fabrizio, 2m 05.228s; **26** Ballerini, 2m 05.237s; **27** Giansanti, 2m 05.284s; **28** Pistoni, 2m 05.314s; **29** Toth, 2m 06.191s; **30** Simoncelli, 2m 08.186s; **31** Simon, 2m 08.222s; **32** Olivé, 2m 11.824s; **33** Sabbatani, 2m 12.497s.
World Championship: 1 Vincent, 194; **2** Poggiali, 171; **3** Pedrosa, 166; **4** Cecchinello, 126; **5** Jenkner, 122; **6** Sanna, 87; **7** Nieto, 78; **8** Borsoi and de Angelis, 63; **10** Azuma, 61; **11** Ui, 54; **12** Kallio and Olivé, 51; **14** Giansanti, 39; **15** Dovizioso, 32; **16** Bianco, 21; **17** Barbera and Ueda, 18; **19** Ballerini and Rodriguez, 17; **21** Aoyama, 16; **22** Perugini, 14; **23** Sabbatani, 12; **24** Luthi, 7; **25** Nöhles and Talmacsi, 6; **27** Davies and Lorenzo, 5; **29** Pistoni, 4; **30** Simoncelli and Smrz, 3; **32** Baldolini, Lai, Pellino and Simon, 2; **36** Fabrizio, 1.

RIOGP

FIM WORLD CHAMPIONSHIP · ROUND 12

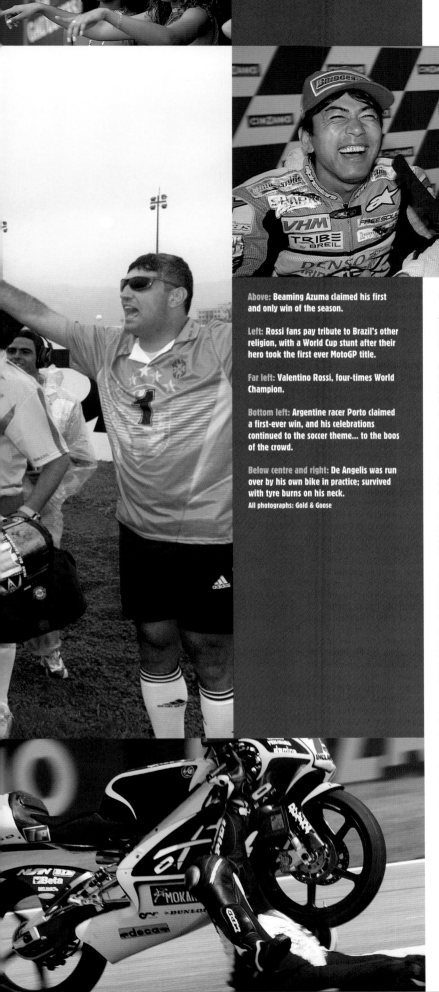

Above: Beaming Azuma claimed his first and only win of the season.

Left: Rossi fans pay tribute to Brazil's other religion, with a World Cup stunt after their hero took the first ever MotoGP title.

Far left: Valentino Rossi, four-times World Champion.

Bottom left: Argentine racer Porto claimed a first-ever win, and his celebrations continued to the soccer theme... to the boos of the crowd.

Below centre and right: De Angelis was run over by his own bike in practice; survived with tyre burns on his neck.
All photographs: Gold & Goose

T HE Rio GP is one out of the loop. The longest-surviving Latin American race shares with Assen the distinction of running on Saturday, for similar reasons of religion. In Holland, old-style Calvinism set tradition long before the World Championships began in 1949; in Brazil it's football, to which Sundays are devoted (discovered when the race was run on a Saturday, to ease a travel schedule to Motegi, and the crowd was doubled).

The track is uniquely both nice and horrid: great width makes sterile-looking turns into broad sweepers offering a variety of lines, rewarding creative riders; dreadful bumps then punish them severely. It is all too easy to go into a corner a foot or so off line, only to have the front wheel shaken out of your hands. Then, before you can recover control, you are off the sticky patch and onto the dirt, so it's often too late to do anything about it.

Then, just to make sure it was really tricky, it rained on race day. Rossi's historic first MotoGP championship, gained with a tenth canny victory this year, took place under lowering skies and in clouds of spray. It was another example of how Rossi weaves skill into luck, and how his judgement was once again shown to be the most superior in difficult conditions. But it took Carlos Checa to prove it.

Funnily enough, last year's Rio GP was also wet, and also between Rossi and Checa, on their respective NSR and YZR two-strokes. Fraught to the end, the race was finally decided in Rossi's favour, with ill-placed back-marker Anthony West blocking any chance Checa might have had to retaliate.

This year saw Checa shine again, and his light dulled again, after what can only be described as an extraordinary afternoon. Having qualified fifth at a favourite circuit, Checa made the fundamental error of having the bike in neutral when the lights went green. Everyone else left at speed; he was lucky not to be hit. Then he nearly spun out as he stomped it into gear and gave it heaps. Only another contretemps (Gibernau knocking Kato and Aoki off at turn one, Laconi and Cardoso also involved) meant he wasn't last at the end of the first lap.

Checa was 11 seconds behind after two laps, but riding like a man possessed. Roberts redux led half the race then Rossi took over, Checa meanwhile scything through, riding high and lapping one and sometimes almost two seconds quicker than the leaders. He arrived, said Rossi, 'from another planet'.

The howling Yamaha took half a lap to overtake the surprised champion, diving inside under braking at the end of the long back straight. Checa was still gaining ground as he heeled it into the next right-hand bend. And the bike just kept right on heeling...

Checa was the fall guy in more senses than one. He'd already shown his capacity for misfortune in practice, falling on something spilled by Ukawa's Honda on the first day, then stopping out on track with a smoky engine blow-up of his own on the second. It was unfortunately timed, because the Yamaha camp was already in a state of crisis, and the pratfalls of Carlos just made the edifice seem all the more insecure.

Eight weeks before, in a bold sweep, they'd dumped Biaggi, keeping Carlos their favoured choice, and were already head-hunting US Bright Boy Nicky Hayden. They had received (explained Yamaha Motor Racing's MD Lin Jarvis to *MOTOCOURSE* at Rio) a written commitment for the deal. It seems that they dallied in turning intent into contract, and in the interim Hayden won the US AMA title. This activated a prior clause in Hayden's Honda contract, of which Yamaha were not aware. Now Honda had a first option, as long as they were to match any outside offer. They exercised it. Thus this favoured rookie dumped a similar deal with Yamaha for a reputedly well-paid full factory Honda ride for 2003. This left Jarvis little to do but to feel badly used, and to threaten legal action against Hayden's management team, 'because in Yamaha's mind, the manner in which negotiations proceeded was neither correct nor to the appropriate professional standards we expect.'

By now, even people close to the team were beginning to wonder out loud at Yamaha's thinking, dumping the almost immaculate though uncomfortably outspoken (and not very companionable) Max in favour of the seldom-faster firecracker Spaniard. Rio's race added weight: Max had followed Checa in the surge past Roberts, but stayed inside the limit for a clean and contained second place, and from here on his season would improve dramatically even as Checa's continued to deteriorate.

The prodigal Max had been smiling before the race, as the Pramac team proudly announced they had signed him up for three years to ride a Honda. The little matter of not having a franchise for an entry was forgotten for the moment, as people considered the prospect of Biaggi face to face with Rossi on more or less equal machinery. On the opposite outer edge, three teams with franchises but no money... Red Bull Yamaha, who had now signed both McCoy and Hopkins, but also lost their main sponsor, with the Moriwaki deal fast coming to pieces. Antena 3 Yamaha were in a similar plight; likewise Honda Pons, with West to leave bike racing.

At least more bikes were becoming available, with Yamaha confirming that they would have two extra M1 four-strokes for the Gauloises riders Nakano and Jacque for the last three races — to the unexpectedly outspoken dismay of their faithful servant Norick Abe, who has ridden for the factory since 1994 and won three GPs. As this year's top two-stroke Yamaha rider in the championship, with consistently the best race and finish record, he was 'disappointed and surprised' that he hadn't been the first to try the new monster.

But these are complex times of shifting loyalties in racing — echoed at Suzuki, where technical guru Warren Willing was an unexpected Rio absentee. Regarded by many as the architect of Roberts's championship in 2000, the Australian ex-racer had been increasingly sidelined with the arrival of the four-stroke (like all the factories Suzuki keep the engine within their own hands), and it was an open secret that he was off to join KTM to help prepare them for their four-stroke entry in 2004. Not with any more of our inside information, said Suzuki.

Above: Fastest-ever two-stroke rider McWilliams went flying after cold weather made his engine seize.

Above right: Checa closes on Biaggi and Roberts. Soon the order would be reversed.
Both photographs: Gold & Goose

MOTOGP RACE – 24 laps

As in South Africa, it's debatable whether heavier bikes are better at ironing out the bumps, or whether they get thrown around more. The long straight played to the 990s, but the many high-speed corners favoured the two-strokes to an unexpected degree, with two out of four on the front row.

Biaggi had pole from Rossi, but the champion-elect only dislodged the Proton by three-and-a-half hundredths, with McWilliams's corner attacks overcoming a 20-mph top-speed disadvantage for the fastest ever two-stroke lap... half a tenth faster than an on-the-edge McCoy. Times were close, the first 19 within 1.77 seconds.

Checa was left flailing on the line; Gibernau was caught out again by the Suzuki's back-shifting problem (a software program keeps driving the engine) and Kato was down and out. Aoki was bruised and sent way off into the grass, the last to rejoin; Laconi and Cardoso were also off the track.

Roberts had taken a flyer from row four, trailing Rossi by turn three, while Biaggi, McWilliams, Ukawa, van den Goorbergh and Barros formed up behind. Second time into turn two, Roberts dived underneath Rossi, cautious in the slippery conditions. Ukawa also pushed inside McWilliams, but fell soon afterwards, failing to restart his V5 to rejoin. This was crucial to both Rossi and Biaggi: if Ukawa had been on the rostrum Rossi would have needed one more race to secure his title, while Biaggi had the chance to take second place on points. Both were informed by their pits, and Biaggi especially responded by going for position.

McWilliams was losing power because his engine was running too cold. At the start of lap five, lying fifth, the cold triggered a seize as he tipped it into the first corner, and his race ended in the gravel.

Barros had passed him by then, but was losing ground to the four-strokes. Up front, Rossi was in familiar mode, following comfortably and frequently pushing alongside with a 20 km/h speed advantage on the straight. Roberts would firmly close the door, Biaggi watching a little way behind. This went on until half-distance.

Checa had been setting one fastest lap after another, 15th on lap one, 12th one lap later, ninth on lap three... and so on. On lap seven he slashed past Barros

to take fourth, still 11.3 seconds adrift of Biaggi; six laps later he was less than two seconds behind.

Rossi was not aware of this threat, but made his own decision to take the lead at the end of lap 14. 'Behind Kenny, when the rain got heavier I couldn't see the track.'

Half a lap later Roberts got the shock of his life as both Biaggi and Checa came flying past him on the back straight. Checa pushed past Biaggi one lap later to set about Rossi. The Spaniard tailed him onto the long back straight, dived past him under brakes at the end of it, and was still leading as they ran into the next right-hander. He never made the exit.

'I was amazed at how fast I caught the leaders, and I took the lead because it was easier for visibility. I went into the corner the same as always. I was concentrating on the front grip — but the back let go. I don't know why,' he said later. It transpired that he had gone down two gears instead of one.

From then on, Biaggi kept Rossi honest, and they finished just 1.6 seconds apart.

Roberts dropped back, keeping enough in hand for his first four-stroke rostrum, Barros still out of touch at the flag. Behind, Jacque had led Abe, but after missing most of warm-up his wet settings weren't quite on, and when Capirossi caught up from a poor start the Japanese rider moved ahead, Capirossi following. By the finish, Capirossi had finally managed to prevail over Abe, and Jacque was dropping away.

Gibernau had been picking his way through but was still troubled with back-shift blues, passing a fading van den Goorbergh for an eventual eighth with ten laps to go. The Dutchman faced last-laps pressure from Laconi as well, until the Frenchman hit a puddle and fell.

McCoy was another eight seconds adrift, blaming a leaking visor that filled with water every time anyone came past in the early laps, then a sliding front tyre when he could see where he was going. Cardoso cruised to 11th, Aoki 30 seconds back, never really recovering from the painful collision with Gibernau. Slowcoach Harada was a lap behind, ahead only of Hopkins, who had fallen and remounted to finish in the points... something of a trademark for the upbeat rookie.

Rossi's race had been superb. His title was now unassailable. It had been a remarkable year. And it wasn't over yet.

250 cc RACE – 22 laps

A mad final flurry put five riders within six-hundredths; de Puniet taking a first pole from Porto, Elias and Melandri, with Nieto on row two. A wet-dry-wet race threw in a level of confusion that spread them all out again.

Porto rose above it all in unprecedented fashion, charging away to lead the first lap by 2.6 seconds, more than doubling it on the second, and ten seconds ahead after seven laps. In a class of his own, he stayed there all the way to the flag. It was his first win in 105 attempts, the first for an Argentine since 1962 — and in neighbouring Brazil it earned him boos from the crowd.

Elias led the early pursuit, but by lap two wet-specialist Matsudo was second — only to be called in for a stop-and-go for a jumped start.

Now Rolfo took over, from Melandri, de Puniet, Elias, Battaini, Alzamora, Stoner, Vincent and Nieto, all jammed up close and trading places. Vincent was out on lap five, the luckless Briton's big chance gone with a seized engine.

As the track dried towards half-distance, Melandri took over from Rolfo, Elias losing touch with a run onto the grass, Battaini taking over his chase role.

Behind this Nieto and Stoner had been engaged, with de Puniet dropping back and then crashing out. As the rain began again on lap 13, Nieto was working on a three-second gap to Elias, Stoner following.

Now Nieto's softer suspension settings were working better. He was soon past Elias and could see title rival Melandri, 2.3 seconds ahead and getting closer. Then it all went wrong. He slid off and his bike was destroyed in the gravel trap, stopping a 20-race run of finishes in the points, and dealing a death blow to his title hopes. His distress as he stomped off was plain to see.

Porto and Rolfo were safe now; Battaini slacking off at the finish. Melandri was happy with safe points for fourth, two seconds ahead of Elias and Stoner a delighted sixth.

Alzamora was a distant seventh, the vengeful Matsudo an angry eighth; his last victim was former team-mate Yuzy, narrowly ahead of the battling Haslam and Hules, disputing tenth. With Locatelli pitting, and Marchand, Aoki and Debon crashing out, there were just 17 finishers.

125 cc RACE – 21 laps

Poggiali claimed a clear 125 pole, a quarter of a second ahead of title rival Vincent, both knocking an on-form Talmacsi down.

Soft rain all but stopped, the well-drained track was damp rather than wet, and soon patchily dry. This favoured those who had chosen drier tyres.

Talmacsi led away, but by lap two Vincent was past, Cecchinello and Poggiali close behind the Hungarian... and Pedrosa 16th and about to crash, seriously damaging his title chances.

Rising teenager Barbera was with the leaders, as was Swiss youngster Luthi, until he crashed after four laps, lying fourth.

By half-distance, Vincent and Poggiali had opened up a significant lead, Nieto ahead of Talmacsi, and Barbera dropping away.

It was a real fight, Poggiali several times passing Vincent into the first corner, only for the positions to be reversed again two corners later. Then, at two-thirds distance, it started raining again, and those with the deeper grooves and softer rubber began to benefit.

Azuma had picked his way through from 12th on lap one to fifth and then third, heading Talmacsi, Perugini and Nieto. Lapping better than two seconds a lap quicker than the leaders, it took Azuma three laps to consume a 6.7-second gap, and as the rain redoubled on lap 19 he took a lead he would hold to the end.

Poggiali seemed to have won the battle for second, but on the last lap Vincent drafted by on the straight and held him at bay to the flag. Talmacsi was a lone fourth, then Nieto and Perugini. Behind them Derbi second-stringer Lorenzo held off Mika Kallio, through from 20th on the first lap.

Ui and Jenkner both crashed out, the latter rejoining, but out of the points.

Below: Ueda's waterproofs billow as he leads Angeloni, Olivé and Simoncelli.

Bottom: Azuma had the right tyres for the job in changing conditions in the 125 race.
Both photographs: Gold & Goose

CINZANO
RIO
grand prix

round 12

21 SEPTEMBER 2002

AUTODROMO DE JACAREPAGUA NELSON PIQUET

CIRCUIT LENGTH: 3.065 MILES/4.933 KM

MotoGP

24 laps, 73.560 miles/118.392 km

Pos.	Rider (Nat.)	No.	Machine	Laps	Time & speed
1	Valentino Rossi (I)	46	Honda	24	49m 09.516s 89.789 mph/ 144.502 km/h
2	Max Biaggi (I)	3	Yamaha	24	49m 11.190s
3	Kenny Roberts (USA)	10	Suzuki	24	49m 28.280s
4	Alex Barros (BR)	4	Honda	24	49m 34.275s
5	Loris Capirossi (I)	65	Honda	24	49m 41.870s
6	Norick Abe (J)	6	Yamaha	24	49m 43.876s
7	Olivier Jacque (F)	19	Honda	24	49m 53.766s
8	Sete Gibernau (E)	15	Suzuki	24	50m 06.666s
9	Jurgen van den Goorbergh (NL)	17	Honda	24	50m 19.503s
10	Garry McCoy (AUS)	8	Yamaha	24	50m 27.127s
11	José Luis Cardoso (E)	30	Aprilia	24	50m 30.353s
12	Nobuatsu Aoki (J)	9	Proton KR	24	51m 00.290s
13	Tetsuya Harada (J)	31	Honda	23	49m 15.451s
14	John Hopkins (USA)	21	Yamaha	23	50m 44.086s
	Regis Laconi (F)	55	Aprilia	22	DNF
	Carlos Checa (E)	7	Yamaha	16	DNF
	Jeremy McWilliams (GB)	99	Proton KR	4	DNF
	Shinya Nakano (J)	56	Yamaha	3	DNF
	Tohru Ukawa (J)	11	Honda	1	DNF
	Daijiro Kato (J)	74	Honda	0	DNF

Fastest lap: Checa, 1m 59.827s, 92.089 mph/148.203 km/h.

Lap record: Tadayuki Okada, J (Honda), 1m 51.928s, 98.588 mph/158.662 km/h (1997).

Event best maximum speed: Rossi, 196.1 km/h/315.6 km/h (qualifying practice no. 1).

Qualifying: 1 Biaggi, 1m 50.568s; 2 Rossi, 1m 50.827s; 3 McWilliams, 1m 50.862s; 4 McCoy, 1m 50.927s; 5 Checa, 1m 50.978s; 6 Kato, 1m 51.066s; 7 Jacque, 1m 51.160s; 8 van den Goorbergh, 1m 51.197s; 9 Ukawa, 1m 51.211s; 10 Aoki, 1m 51.287s; 11 Abe, 1m 51.476s; 12 Capirossi, 1m 51.481s; 13 Nakano, 1m 51.517s; 14 Hopkins, 1m 51.624s; 15 Barros, 1m 51.670s; 16 Roberts, 1m 51.753s; 17 Laconi, 1m 51.820s; 18 Gibernau, 1m 51.994s; 19 Harada, 1m 52.339s; 20 Cardoso, 1m 52.747s.

Fastest race laps: 1 Checa, 1m 59.827s; 2 Capirossi, 2m 01.437s; 3 Roberts, 2m 01.466s; 4 Biaggi, 2m 01.578s; 5 Rossi, 2m 01.581s; 6 Barros, 2m 01.820s; 7 Abe, 2m 02.052s; 8 Jacque, 2m 02.638s; 9 Gibernau, 2m 02.777s; 10 Laconi, 2m 03.649s; 11 van den Goorbergh, 2m 03.652s; 12 Cardoso, 2m 03.998s; 13 McCoy, 2m 04.055s; 14 Hopkins, 2m 04.993s; 15 Aoki, 2m 05.042s; 16 McWilliams, 2m 06.029s; 17 Harada, 2m 07.205s; 18 Nakano, 2m 07.957s; 19 Ukawa, 2m 12.931s.

World Championship: 1 Rossi, 270; 2 Biaggi, 164; 3 Ukawa, 156; 4 Barros, 118; 5 Checa, 116; 6 Abe, 109; 7 Capirossi, 86; 8 Kato, 80; 9 Roberts, 74; 10 Jacque, 57; 11 Hopkins, 51; 12 Aoki, 47; 13 Nakano, 45; 14 Gibernau and Harada, 42; 16 Ryo, 36; 17 McWilliams, 35; 18 van den Goorbergh, 34; 19 McCoy, 32; 20 Laconi, 28; 21 Itoh, 13; 22 Hofmann, 11; 23 Cardoso, 8; 24 Bayle, 5; 25 Riba, 4.

250 cc

22 laps, 67.430 miles/108.526 km

Pos.	Rider (Nat.)	No.	Machine	Laps	Time & speed
1	Sebastian Porto (ARG)	9	Yamaha	22	47m 01.307s 86.047 mph/ 138.479 km/h
2	Roberto Rolfo (I)	4	Honda	22	47m 15.421s
3	Franco Battaini (I)	21	Aprilia	22	47m 17.119s
4	Marco Melandri (I)	3	Aprilia	22	47m 28.305s
5	Toni Elias (E)	24	Aprilia	22	47m 30.840s
6	Casey Stoner (AUS)	27	Aprilia	22	47m 33.175s
7	Emilio Alzamora (E)	7	Honda	22	47m 46.680s
8	Naoki Matsudo (J)	8	Yamaha	22	48m 12.631s
9	Shahrol Yuzy (MAL)	18	Yamaha	22	48m 15.094s
10	Leon Haslam (GB)	19	Honda	22	48m 16.785s
11	Jaroslav Hules (CZ)	13	Yamaha	22	48m 18.022s
12	David Checa (E)	42	Aprilia	22	48m 52.151s
13	Erwan Nigon (F)	36	Aprilia	22	49m 00.024s
14	Dirk Heidolf (D)	28	Aprilia	22	49m 13.347s
15	Jakub Smrz (CZ)	96	Honda	21	47m 10.097s
16	Raul Jara (E)	22	Aprilia	21	47m 36.122s
17	Hector Faubel (E)	32	Aprilia	21	47m 39.443s
	Fonsi Nieto (E)	10	Aprilia	15	DNF
	Randy de Puniet (F)	17	Aprilia	14	DNF
	Hugo Marchand (F)	51	Aprilia	14	DNF
	Alex Debon (E)	6	Aprilia	12	DNF
	Roberto Locatelli (I)	15	Aprilia	12	DNF
	Jay Vincent (GB)	12	Honda	4	DNF
	Eric Bataille (AND)	34	Honda	1	DNF
	Haruchika Aoki (J)	11	Honda	1	DNF

Fastest lap: Porto, 2m 04.661s, 88.518 mph/142.456 km/h.

Lap record: Valentino Rossi, I (Aprilia), 1m 54.230s, 96.601 mph/155.465 km/h (1999).

Event best maximum speed: Melandri, 164.9 mph/265.4 km/h (qualifying practice no. 2).

Qualifying: 1 de Puniet, 1m 53.939s; 2 Porto, 1m 53.959s; 3 Elias, 1m 53.961s; 4 Melandri, 1m 53.970s; 5 Nieto, 1m 54.002s; 6 Locatelli, 1m 54.429s; 7 Matsudo, 1m 54.492s; 8 Debon, 1m 54.881s; 9 Rolfo, 1m 54.936s; 10 Battaini, 1m 55.013s; 11 Alzamora, 1m 55.242s; 12 Stoner, 1m 55.490s; 13 Yuzy, 1m 55.576s; 14 Hules, 1m 55.610s; 15 Nigon, 1m 56.053s; 16 Vincent, 1m 56.172s; 17 Haslam, 1m 56.221s; 18 Checa, 1m 56.256s; 19 Aoki, 1m 56.337s; 20 Marchand, 1m 56.509s; 21 Bataille, 1m 56.787s; 22 Faubel, 1m 57.046s; 23 Smrz, 1m 57.143s; 24 Heidolf, 1m 57.271s; 25 Jara, 1m 57.612s.

Fastest race laps: 1 Porto, 2m 04.661s; 2 Rolfo, 2m 04.862s; 3 Elias, 2m 05.017s; 4 Melandri, 2m 05.221s; 5 Battaini, 2m 05.303s; 6 Nieto, 2m 06.077s; 7 Stoner, 2m 06.280s; 8 Alzamora, 2m 06.779s; 9 de Puniet, 2m 06.802s; 10 Matsudo, 2m 07.305s; 11 Debon, 2m 07.942s; 12 Yuzy, 2m 07.954s; 13 Vincent, 2m 08.569s; 14 Hules, 2m 08.598s; 15 Marchand, 2m 08.717s; 16 Haslam, 2m 08.777s; 17 Locatelli, 2m 08.795s; 18 Heidolf, 2m 09.307s; 19 Nigon, 2m 09.922s; 20 Checa, 2m 10.044s; 21 Smrz, 2m 10.397s; 22 Faubel, 2m 10.658s; 23 Jara, 2m 11.595s; 24 Bataille, 2m 16.678s; 25 Aoki, 2m 18.131s.

World Championship: 1 Melandri, 228; 2 Nieto, 183; 3 Rolfo, 160; 4 Porto, 135; 5 Elias, 116; 6 Battaini, 104; 7 Locatelli, 98; 8 de Puniet, 86; 9 Alzamora, 82; 10 Matsudo, 73; 11 Stoner, 54; 12 Debon, 52; 13 Yuzy, 45; 14 Aoki, 42; 15 Checa, 36; 16 Miyazaki, 25; 17 Sakai, 20; 18 Haslam, 19; 19 Heidolf and Waldmann, 17; 21 Faubel, 13; 22 Vincent, 12; 23 Jara, 11; 24 Kameya, 9; 25 Nigon and Sekiguchi, 7; 27 Garcia, 6; 28 Hules, 5; 29 Aoyama, Marchand and Philippe, 4; 32 Bataille, 2; 33 Smrz, 1.

125 cc

21 laps, 64.365 miles/103.593 km

Pos.	Rider (Nat.)	No.	Machine	Laps	Time & speed
1	Masao Azuma (J)	5	Honda	21	46m 28.675s 83.097 mph/ 133.731 km/h
2	Arnaud Vincent (F)	21	Aprilia	21	46m 30.380s
3	Manuel Poggiali (RSM)	1	Gilera	21	46m 30.435s
4	Gabor Talmacsi (H)	8	Honda	21	46m 37.852s
5	Pablo Nieto (E)	22	Aprilia	21	46m 55.271s
6	Stefano Perugini (I)	7	Italjet	21	47m 01.420s
7	Jorge Lorenzo (E)	48	Derbi	21	47m 02.825s
8	Mika Kallio (SF)	36	Honda	21	47m 03.163s
9	Klaus Nöhles (D)	12	Honda	21	47m 05.316s
10	Lucio Cecchinello (I)	4	Aprilia	21	47m 09.056s
11	Alex de Angelis (RSM)	15	Aprilia	21	47m 09.290s
12	Gino Borsoi (I)	23	Aprilia	21	47m 10.103s
13	Andrea Dovizioso (I)	34	Honda	21	47m 10.283s
14	Simone Sanna (I)	16	Aprilia	21	47m 10.305s
15	Hector Barbera (E)	80	Aprilia	21	47m 13.822s
16	Andrea Ballerini (I)	50	Aprilia	21	47m 18.560s
17	Stefano Bianco (I)	33	Aprilia	21	47m 25.735s
18	Steve Jenkner (D)	17	Aprilia	21	47m 42.623s
19	Christian Pistoni (I)	42	Italjet	21	47m 42.736s
20	Mirko Giansanti (I)	6	Honda	21	47m 46.170s
21	Marco Simoncelli (I)	37	Aprilia	21	47m 52.215s
22	Joan Olivé (E)	25	Honda	21	47m 52.734s
23	Michel Fabrizio (I)	84	Gilera	21	47m 54.864s
24	Thomas Luthi (CH)	77	Honda	21	47m 57.900s
25	Noboru Ueda (J)	9	Honda	21	48m 01.077s
26	Dario Giuseppetti (D)	72	Honda	21	48m 13.766s
27	Mattia Angeloni (I)	31	Gilera	21	48m 21.294s
28	Imre Toth (H)	20	Honda	21	48m 30.226s
29	Chaz Davies (GB)	57	Aprilia	21	48m 32.938s
	Youichi Ui (J)	41	Derbi	12	DNF
	Daniel Pedrosa (E)	26	Honda	2	DNF
	Alex Baldolini (I)	19	Aprilia	1	DNF

Fastest lap: Azuma, 2m 10.065s, 84.840 mph/136.537 km/h.

Lap record: Mirko Giansanti, I (Honda), 1m 59.368s, 92.443 km/h/148.773 km/h (2000).

Event best maximum speed: Ballerini, 141.6 mph/227.9 km/h (qualifying practice no. 1).

Qualifying: 1 Poggiali, 1m 57.888s; 2 Vincent, 1m 58.141s; 3 Talmacsi, 1m 58.298s; 4 de Angelis, 1m 58.307s; 5 Cecchinello, 1m 58.405s; 6 Jenkner, 1m 58.527s; 7 Nieto, 1m 58.552s; 8 Pedrosa, 1m 58.858s; 9 Kallio, 1m 59.062s; 10 Barbera, 1m 59.079s; 11 Borsoi, 1m 59.116s; 12 Ui, 1m 59.174s; 13 Giansanti, 1m 59.289s; 14 Lorenzo, 1m 59.331s; 15 Sanna, 1m 59.424s; 16 Olivé, 1m 59.424s; 17 Dovizioso, 1m 59.469s; 18 Azuma, 1m 59.556s; 19 Perugini, 1m 59.594s; 20 Bianco, 1m 59.714s; 21 Nöhles, 1m 59.760s; 22 Ueda, 1m 59.993s; 23 Ballerini, 2m 00.022s; 24 Luthi, 2m 00.032s; 25 Simoncelli, 2m 00.310s; 26 Fabrizio, 2m 00.952s; 27 Toth, 2m 01.618s; 28 Davies, 2m 01.842s; 29 Angeloni, 2m 02.085s; 30 Pistoni, 2m 02.225s; 31 Giuseppetti, 2m 03.316s; 32 Baldolini, 2m 03.949s.

Fastest race laps: 1 Azuma, 2m 10.065s; 2 Poggiali, 2m 10.549s; 3 Perugini, 2m 10.599s; 4 Nieto, 2m 10.614s; 5 Vincent, 2m 10.809s; 6 Cecchinello, 2m 11.235s; 7 Talmacsi, 2m 11.381s; 8 Luthi, 2m 11.422s; 9 Barbera, 2m 11.441s; 10 Nöhles, 2m 11.454s; 11 Bianco, 2m 11.530s; 12 Borsoi, 2m 11.764s; 13 Ballerini, 2m 11.865s; 14 Kallio, 2m 11.890s; 15 Giansanti, 2m 11.897s; 16 Lorenzo, 2m 11.980s; 17 Jenkner, 2m 12.168s; 18 Ui, 2m 12.180s; 19 Sanna, 2m 12.339s; 20 Dovizioso, 2m 12.340s; 21 Fabrizio, 2m 12.548s; 22 de Angelis, 2m 13.063s; 23 Pistoni, 2m 13.268s; 24 Simoncelli, 2m 13.480s; 25 Olivé, 2m 13.622s; 26 Ueda, 2m 14.345s; 27 Davies, 2m 14.498s; 28 Giuseppetti, 2m 14.562s; 29 Toth, 2m 14.612s; 30 Angeloni, 2m 14.871s; 31 Pedrosa, 2m 17.545s; 32 Baldolini, 2m 29.178s.

World Championship: 1 Vincent, 214; 2 Poggiali, 187; 3 Pedrosa, 164; 4 Cecchinello, 132; 5 Jenkner, 122; 6 Nieto and Sanna, 89; 8 Azuma, 86; 9 de Angelis, 68; 10 Borsoi, 67; 11 Kallio, 59; 12 Ui, 54; 13 Olivé, 51; 14 Giansanti, 39; 15 Dovizioso, 35; 16 Perugini, 24; 17 Bianco, 21; 18 Barbera and Talmacsi, 19; 20 Ueda, 18; 21 Ballerini and Rodriguez, 17; 23 Aoyama, 16; 24 Lorenzo, 14; 25 Nöhles, 13; 26 Sabbatani, 12; 27 Luthi, 7; 28 Davies, 5; 29 Pistoni, 4; 30 Simoncelli and Smrz, 3; 32 Baldolini, Lai, Pellino and Simon, 2; 36 Fabrizio, 1.

Main picture: Porto was in a class of his own on the Yamaha.

Inset: The Argentine rider ran away from the start.

Both photographs: Gold & Goose

MOTEGI

FIM WORLD CHAMPIONSHIP · ROUND 13

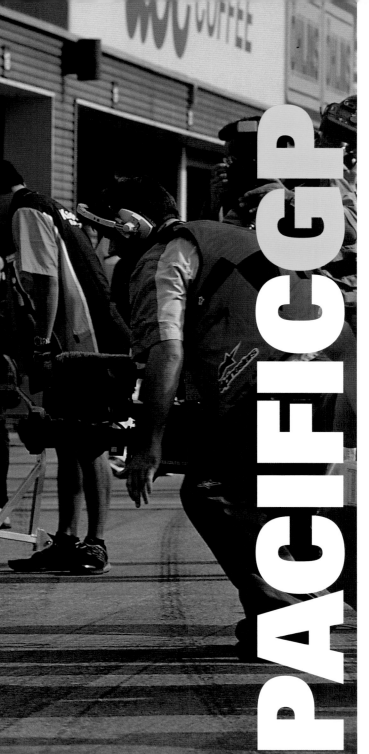

PACIFIC GP

THE four-stroke era had begun in Japan, at Suzuka. The second visit to Japan of the year, this time to the far-away flyaway Motegi, marked another beginning, with three new and very significant additions.

One was Kawasaki, toe in the water with their ugly-duck new green 990 Ninja. A modest enough beginning, rather spoiled by an oil leak in the race that sprayed following competitors (yes, there were a few behind Yanagawa) before getting on the back tyre and dumping him heavily enough to put him out for the rest of the year.

Then there was Yamaha's first wild card of the year — factory man Yoshikawa. The greater significance was that his bike was the first M1 to race with fuel injection rather than carburettors.

The third: the provision of a fourth V5 Honda, the first to go to a non-factory rider in a satellite team: to Alex Barros in the West Pons squad. And that was significant enough for the apparently ever-improving veteran to ride the pants off Rossi and the factory bikes and win, in only his third day on an over-the-counter machine.

There's always more than meets the eye, of course, quite apart from the fact that, with the title won, it's understandable if Rossi's urgency was on holiday. The real culprit was clutch problems, that spoiled Rossi's finesse, troubled Ukawa as well, and ruled Kato out of the race early. The same problems, it now emerged, had contributed to Rossi's rear tyre failure at Brno, and for similar reasons. Honda's first race mechanical failure highlighted how clutches are currently the most crucial aspect of the new four-stroke technology.

Like Brno but worse, Motegi has a number of corners where the bikes slow all the way down from a high gear to second or even first. Piling down through the box, the slipper clutches do their business — modulating engine braking by slipping. Slipping, however, creates heat; heat creates expansion. And expansion plays havoc with clutch clearances, making it grab, bind and snatch, so that on-the-limit riding becomes extremely difficult. In this way, Honda's own track at Motegi highlighted a chink in their armour.

Yamaha's clever active clutch system seemed to cope; Suzuki's new ramp-type slipper was troublesome enough for Gibernau to revert to the earlier non-self-compensating sprag clutch on Saturday morning — no more predictable, but at least familiar. Roberts persevered, his mind on forcing the pace of development now for next year's bike. 'We're able to get the bike to do things it couldn't do before. Not all of them are good. But it's progress,' he said.

Words that meant that Roberts had plighted his troth again to Suzuki — terms agreed for two more years, contract still to be finalised. This was not hugely surprising, but took a possible name off the Yamaha list to replace Max. Now another American hove into view: new Superbike champion Colin Edwards, deeply miffed at Hayden's factory Honda for just one AMA title while he got nothing after two world titles.

The silly season just got sillier. At least one thing seemed sure: Barros to Kawasaki. Even his team-mate Loris Capirossi was talking about that — or at least his manager Carlo Pernat was, in an angry outburst at HRC for steering the new V5 to Barros. 'Okay, Loris has signed for Ducati next year. But Barros has signed for Kawasaki, and HRC didn't even give consideration to Capirossi.' Sure enough, in the coming weeks, this would turn out to be not true.

You want certainties? One is that Kawasaki have a long way to go. Another is that their starting point is definitely in touch. Especially considering the words of president Shinichi Marita at the pre-race launch. Asked about the budget limits, he replied: 'We are prepared to spend as much as it takes.' The bike that qualified more than two seconds behind pole had only been completed the previous month, and had run just five test-track days. Before that, the basic engine had been race-developed in the Superbike chassis. As well as the extra weight, it ran with carburettors. The Ninja ZX-RR was all new, close to the GP minimum weight, and running the only flat-slide (rather than butterfly) fuel injection in the pack. It sounded good, with more bass notes than its sister Superbike. And it looked all new, with rather strange styling — an aggressively beaky fairing set off a treat by an extraordinarily large seat unit, as if high-speed pizza delivery might be a secondary role.

The value of any aerodynamic contribution did not seem of much significance, though the top speed was not bad: 13th overall, 12 km/h slower than Ukawa's pace-setting Honda, and faster than the Aprilia and Gibernau's Suzuki. More basic issues are to be solved, and the bike was obviously a handful. Trailing the throttle into the turns would lead to such spectacular fishtail slides that Yanagawa frequently abandoned the attempt, declutching to freewheel to the apex, Doohan style. It was a handful on the way out too, and he complained of overly sudden throttle response from the new injection. For a first attempt, and putting the oil leak, the crash and the injury to the chief test rider to the back of one's mind, it wasn't a bad first showing.

But will being close to this year's pack be enough? Perhaps not, if one is to take the words of HRC chief Kanezawa-san seriously. *MOTOCOURSE* asked him about vague rumours that Honda are to build a V6 to replace their V5. He agreed enthusiastically. 'We have drawn a six. And I would like to build it for next year.' This was stunning, and though he tried to fudge the issue with some more engineer's chat, about the desire to experiment, and the need to consider all types of engine, even a single, he had perhaps deliberately tossed a tantalising challenge into the air.

MOTOGP - BARROS • 250 cc - ELIAS • 125 cc - PEDROSA

Above: New kid on the block... Yanagawa rolls the Kawasaki out for its first practice gallop.

Far left: And he's down. This crash was in qualifying: a heavier fall in the race put him out for the rest of the year.

Left: Wild card Yoshikawa was riding a fuel-injected M1 — the bike's first public outing. Probably.

Right: It took Alex Barros three days to learn how to win on the new Honda.
All photographs: Gold & Goose

Above: **See how they run. The four-strokes of Barros, Rossi and Kato lead Capirossi in the early stages, Biaggi and Ukawa chase behind, then the Suzukis of Roberts and Gibernau lead Checa.**
Photograph: Gold & Goose

MOTOGP RACE – 24 laps

Motegi is a track of medium-speed corners and drag-strip straights. Everyone knew the four-strokes would be fast, and on only the first day of qualifying slide-happy Kato set a time 0.8 seconds inside last year's pole. On Saturday the main players ran into various problems — Kato slid a bit too far and crashed, Rossi was uncharacteristically searching for set-up, Biaggi's better bike (now on the latest chassis for the first time) had electrical problems — and Kato's flyer was still enough for his first pole in the class. Biaggi was fractionally slower, then a superhuman effort by the angry Capirossi put his NSR two-stroke third by seven-thousandths, ahead of Checa as well as his four-stroke-blessed team-mate Barros, who led the second row.

Laconi started from the pit lane after his Aprilia declined to fire for the warm-up lap. Capirossi led into turn one, but he was quickly overwhelmed by Rossi, Barros and Kato's V5 power, with Biaggi looming behind, and Ukawa, soon to follow Max past fast-starting Roberts.

Gibernau now locked on behind his team-mate, but not for long — blowing up in a cloud of smoke on the sixth lap.

Kato and Barros traded blows until lap five, when the Brazilian dived inside Rossi under braking before the first underpass. One lap later Kato followed suit, and resumed his vigorous attacks on Barros. Then he slowed suddenly at the bottom of the last hill, running wide to cruise to the pits — the first and worst fried Honda clutch of the afternoon.

Capirossi was still hanging on; a little way back Ukawa was following Biaggi when it was the Yamaha's turn to give off a smoky plume, and retire. A strange one. He'd gone for a soft mixed-compound front (a wilful choice, said Michelin), and the harder-compound centre strip had delaminated, cutting a radial slice out of the mudguard.

Up front Barros led, Rossi still looking fairly nonchalant as he slid the Honda into and out of the turns. In fact, he was close to the limit on an increasingly difficult motor cycle, while Barros was comfortably nursing his tyres. On lap 19, he seemed to let Rossi through (though he denied it); two laps later Rossi fish-tailed wide on the difficult downhill entry to the right at the bottom of the final drop. Barros was through again, and Rossi starting to look flustered, although still just half a second adrift as they started the last lap.

Barros decided 'now was the time to take risks'. As the factory Honda rider battled with poor settings and a dodgy clutch, he unleashed the full potential of his over-the-counter version to set fastest lap of the race on his final lap — a new record. Roundly beaten by 1.6 seconds, Rossi was obliged to lapse into philosophical humour. 'Every time I race with him, he f***s me. I really hope he goes to Kawasaki next year.'

Ukawa never came close to catching Capirossi; nor Checa the Japanese rider. He finally found his way past Roberts on lap eight, but — his confidence drained — he pulled away only slowly. Roberts kept on steadily, safely clear of Abe, whose hands were full with a persistent Jacque, who finally attacked on the last lap to reverse the order past the flag. It was his last two-stroke ride of the year.

250 cc RACE – 23 laps

Surprise. This dull circuit yielded an all-action 250 thriller, best race of a dour season — largely due to the dazzling riding of Toni Elias, rewarded with his first victory in the class. Today, he looked set for the top.

Nieto had taken pole from Melandri by a tenth; de Puniet alongside, and then one of those Japanese really wild cards: factory-backed Takahashi, on the same development RS250-W as Aoki.

De Puniet's luck ran out with a breakdown on the warm-up lap; he started from the pit lane instead of the front row then ran off the track on lap two while trying to catch up, retiring angrily.

Melandri led Nieto into turn one, and the stop-and-start circuit meant it took a few laps for the running order to settle. By the sixth Nieto was a second adrift of Melandri, with team-mate Elias hungry to pass; Alzamora was fourth, with Takahashi poised, then a growing gap to Battaini, Porto and Rolfo.

Elias finally took second on lap eight, and Takahashi followed him past a couple of corners later, Nieto later complaining of being short of revs and power. Melandri's lead was up to two seconds and he was looking comfortably in control. Little did he know...

By half-distance they were on him. The Aprilias were faster, but the Honda had them on the corners, and Takahashi dived inside Elias with apparent ease

Above: Kato was out of luck for his first home four-stroke GP.

Left: Wild card Takahashi gained a rostrum third at a first attempt for Honda.

Below: Nieto leads, but he's slowing up Elias and Takahashi in pursuit. Alzamora is out of touch behind.
All photographs: Gold & Goose

The Protons filled the top ten, Aoki finally prevailing over McWilliams, who was troubled by a stiff gearshift. Another good result at a track that suited the KR3 the least.

Hopkins and Harada had headed the Kawasaki from the start, with Yoshikawa's injected M1 behind it, as well as van den Goorbergh and McCoy.

By lap six Laconi had barged his way from the back and was lining up the Kawasaki when he and those behind found themselves riding blind in a mist of oil. Van den Goorbergh had just removed his last tear-off visor, and missed his braking point as a result. Shortly afterwards, and if only through a glass darkly, they saw the big green tail unit flick sideways, precipitating the little Japanese rider into a heavy high-sider that left him with a fractured pelvis.

Hopkins held 11th, pulling a frustrated train, until lap 19, when he finally succumbed to Laconi, and soon afterwards also Yoshikawa. Van den Goorbergh also picked up the pace now, passing both Harada and Hopkins with three laps to go, then quickly catching and passing Yoshikawa's M1 as well on the final lap. At the end, he had succumbed again to the M1's straight-line speed, but along with the Proton double top ten it was a demonstration of rapid improvement by their Bridgestone tyres.

Nakano and McCoy trailed in, the first never finding good settings and happy to park the two-stroke, McCoy dropping to the back with a choked motor after the start. He copped the Kawasaki spray, then ran into tyre trouble that left him gripless mid-corner.

Right: Audacious and confident, this is how Elias beat Melandri for his first 250 GP win.

Below: Pedrosa put himself back in the picture with a convincing 125 win.

Bottom: Early in the race, Pedrosa leads Vincent, Dovizioso, Poggiali and the rest.

All photographs: Gold & Goose

running onto the back straight on lap 15, successfully holding him off at the end of it to harry Melandri. Elias was waiting for his moment. Three laps later he put a really aggressive pass on him, then forced the pace until this unexpected Honda threat finally wilted.

Elias again waited for his moment, closing right up to Melandri only as they started a thrilling final lap. His first attack came at the corner before the first underpass, diving underneath only to run wide on the exit, so Melandri came out in front again. He did it again half a lap later, with the same result. That should have been it, really, but his 125 rivals know that Elias is not one to give up.

Through the second underpass, he was inches behind. Melandri held it tight into the penultimate left, expecting Elias to try to push through inside under braking. Instead the audacious Spaniard went round the outside, with just enough speed and space to mount the block into the second part of the corner instead. The race was won.

'I tried to close all the holes,' said Melandri afterwards. 'But I was also thinking about the championship.'

Takahashi was safe in third, with Nieto narrowly fending off Alzamora for fourth. By the finish, Rolfo had caught right up, with Battaini holding seventh two seconds adrift, Porto close behind. Another 13 seconds back was the lone Locatelli; then Debon beat race-long rival Aoyama for tenth.

Wild card Nakasuga held off Aoki's Honda; another Yamaha wild card, Ryuji Yokoe, was 14th, with Hules taking the last point.

Three races to go, and Melandri had a 52-point lead. Surely not much could go wrong now?

125 cc RACE – 21 laps

Pedrosa's fifth pole survived Poggiali's late attack by just over a tenth; points-leader Vincent was on the far end of the front row, the other side of Jenkner.

It was Vincent who led the first lap, Pedrosa taking over firmly on the second to eke out a steady gap that was over eight seconds by the finish.

Motegi had the opposite effect on this usually close class, and the pursuit was spread out, Poggiali and Jenkner disputing third a couple of seconds behind Vincent.

With two laps to go, it all went wrong for the Frenchman. Vincent slowed, climbing out of the seat to try and see what was wrong with his bike as one by one his pursuers came past. His exhaust was coming to pieces, and all he could do was soldier on to salvage one point.

Minimal excitement behind: Dovizioso was third at the end of lap one but flew off in a massive high-side as he started the second. This left Barbera with Poggiali in the early stages, the youngster then dropping behind Jenkner to find himself among Nieto and Cecchinello. The last-named retired, while Nieto pulled clear for fourth.

Kallio lost this group for a lonely sixth; Borsoi came through for seventh; Olivé held off Lorenzo's Derbi for eighth, with wild card and ex-GP veteran Hideyuki Nakajoh a close tenth.

De Angelis crashed out while battling with Kallio; Sanna pitted to retire.

Vincent's misfortune cut his lead over Poggiali to just eight points, with Pedrosa coming back into the picture. This one would go to the wire.

FIM WORLD CHAMPIONSHIP

GAULOISES PACIFIC grand prix

round 13

6 OCTOBER 2002

TWIN RING MOTEGI

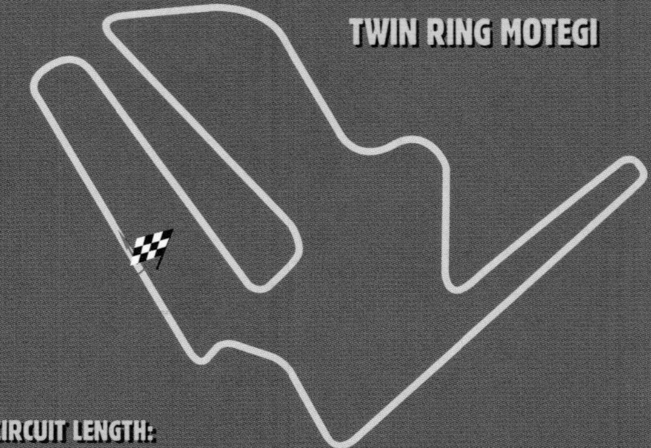

CIRCUIT LENGTH: 2.983 miles/4.801 km

MotoGP

24 laps, 71.592 miles/115.224 km

Pos.	Rider (Nat.)	No.	Machine	Laps	Time & speed
1	Alex Barros (BR)	4	Honda	24	44m 18.913s 96.938 mph/ 156.006 km/h
2	Valentino Rossi (I)	46	Honda	24	44m 20.554s
3	Loris Capirossi (I)	65	Honda	24	44m 26.585s
4	Tohru Ukawa (J)	11	Honda	24	44m 37.033s
5	Carlos Checa (E)	7	Yamaha	24	44m 43.949s
6	Kenny Roberts (USA)	10	Suzuki	24	44m 48.114s
7	Olivier Jacque (F)	19	Yamaha	24	44m 51.815s
8	Norick Abe (J)	6	Yamaha	24	44m 52.200s
9	Nobuatsu Aoki (J)	9	Proton KR	24	44m 54.862s
10	Jeremy McWilliams (GB)	99	Proton KR	24	44m 56.268s
11	Regis Laconi (F)	55	Aprilia	24	45m 07.952s
12	Wataru Yoshikawa (J)	45	Yamaha	24	45m 08.094s
13	Jurgen van den Goorbergh (NL)	17	Honda	24	45m 08.502s
14	John Hopkins (USA)	21	Yamaha	24	45m 10.984s
15	Tetsuya Harada (J)	31	Honda	24	45m 11.093s
16	Shinya Nakano (J)	56	Yamaha	24	45m 19.398s
17	Garry McCoy (AUS)	8	Yamaha	24	45m 21.145s
	Max Biaggi (I)	3	Yamaha	15	DNF
	Daijiro Kato (J)	74	Honda	8	DNF
	Akira Yanagawa (J)	48	Kawasaki	6	DNF
	Sete Gibernau (E)	15	Suzuki	5	DNF
	Pere Riba (E)	20	Yamaha		DNS

Fastest lap: Barros, 1m 49.947s, 97.679 mph/157.199 km/h (record).

Previous record: Valentino Rossi, I (Honda), 1m 50.591s, 97.110 mph/156.283 km/h (2000).

Event best maximum speed: Ukawa, 179.1 mph/288.2 km/h (warm-up).

Qualifying: 1 Kato, 1m 49.052s; 2 Biaggi, 1m 49.162s; 3 Capirossi, 1m 49.169s; 4 Checa, 1m 49.224s; 5 Barros, 1m 49.492s; 6 Rossi, 1m 49.530s; 7 Ukawa, 1m 49.755s; 8 Roberts, 1m 49.859s; 9 Jacque, 1m 50.160s; 10 McWilliams, 1m 50.171s; 11 Gibernau, 1m 50.208s; 12 Laconi, 1m 50.306s; 13 Aoki, 1m 50.342s; 14 Abe, 1m 50.533s; 15 McCoy, 1m 50.702s; 16 Hopkins, 1m 50.849s; 17 Nakano, 1m 50.954s; 18 Yanagawa, 1m 51.234s; 19 Yoshikawa, 1m 51.278s; 20 van den Goorbergh, 1m 51.863s; 21 Harada, 1m 51.908s; 22 Riba, 1m 53.131s.

Fastest race laps: 1 Barros, 1m 49.947s; 2 Rossi, 1m 50.055s; 3 Capirossi, 1m 50.243s; 4 Kato, 1m 50.407s; 5 Biaggi, 1m 50.492s; 6 Ukawa, 1m 50.670s; 7 Checa, 1m 50.853s; 8 Gibernau, 1m 50.952s; 9 Roberts, 1m 50.981s; 10 Yoshikawa, 1m 51.306s; 11 Jacque, 1m 51.438s; 12 Abe, 1m 51.464s; 13 McWilliams, 1m 51.465s; 14 van den Goorbergh, 1m 51.538s; 15 Aoki, 1m 51.550s; 16 Harada, 1m 51.756s; 17 Hopkins, 1m 51.845s; 18 Laconi, 1m 51.971s; 19 Yanagawa, 1m 52.113s; 20 McCoy, 1m 52.221s; 21 Nakano, 1m 52.344s.

World Championship: 1 Rossi, 290; 2 Ukawa, 169; 3 Biaggi, 164; 4 Barros, 143; 5 Checa, 127; 6 Abe, 117; 7 Capirossi, 102; 8 Roberts, 84; 9 Kato, 80; 10 Jacque, 66; 11 Aoki, 54; 12 Hopkins, 53; 13 Nakano, 45; 14 Harada, 43; 15 Gibernau, 42; 16 McWilliams, 41; 17 van den Goorbergh, 37; 18 Ryo, 36; 19 Laconi, 33; 20 McCoy, 32; 21 Itoh, 13; 22 Hofmann, 11; 23 Cardoso, 8; 24 Bayle, 5; 25 Riba and Yoshikawa, 4.

250 cc

23 laps, 68.609 miles/110.423 km

Pos.	Rider (Nat.)	No.	Machine	Laps	Time & speed
1	Toni Elias (E)	24	Aprilia	23	43m 52.991s 93.813 mph/ 150.977 km/h
2	Marco Melandri (I)	3	Aprilia	23	43m 53.166s
3	Yuki Takahashi (J)	72	Honda	23	43m 57.422s
4	Fonsi Nieto (E)	10	Aprilia	23	44m 01.191s
5	Emilio Alzamora (E)	7	Honda	23	44m 01.803s
6	Roberto Rolfo (I)	4	Honda	23	44m 02.817s
7	Franco Battaini (I)	21	Aprilia	23	44m 04.819s
8	Sebastian Porto (ARG)	9	Yamaha	23	44m 05.717s
9	Roberto Locatelli (I)	15	Aprilia	23	44m 19.158s
10	Alex Debon (E)	6	Aprilia	23	44m 25.227s
11	Hiroshi Aoyama (J)	92	Honda	23	44m 25.369s
12	Katsuyuki Nakasuga (J)	71	Yamaha	23	44m 32.374s
13	Haruchika Aoki (J)	11	Honda	23	44m 32.638s
14	Ryuji Yokoe (J)	70	Yamaha	23	44m 34.377s
15	Jaroslav Hules (CZ)	13	Yamaha	23	44m 39.943s
16	Naoki Matsudo (J)	8	Yamaha	23	44m 45.170s
17	Casey Stoner (AUS)	27	Aprilia	23	44m 45.654s
18	Shahrol Yuzy (MAL)	18	Yamaha	23	44m 47.110s
19	Jay Vincent (GB)	12	Honda	23	44m 47.756s
20	Dirk Heidolf (D)	28	Aprilia	23	44m 52.073s
21	David Checa (E)	42	Aprilia	23	44m 52.491s
22	Hector Faubel (E)	32	Aprilia	23	45m 14.649s
23	Erwan Nigon (F)	36	Aprilia	23	45m 27.397s
24	Jakub Smrz (CZ)	96	Honda	23	45m 42.916s
	Tekkyu Kayoh (J)	68	Yamaha	19	DNF
	Hugo Marchand (F)	51	Aprilia	12	DNF
	Leon Haslam (GB)	19	Honda	12	DNF
	Raul Jara (E)	22	Aprilia	9	DNF
	Randy de Puniet (F)	17	Aprilia	3	DNF
	Noboyuki Ohsaki (J)	69	Yamaha	0	DNF

Fastest lap: Elias, 1m 53.392s, 94.711 mph/152.423 km/h.

Lap record: Shinya Nakano, J (Yamaha), 1m 52.253s, 95.673 mph/153.970 km/h (2000).

Event best maximum speed: Elias, 156.6 mph/252.1 km/h (free practice no. 2).

Qualifying: 1 Nieto, 1m 52.389s; 2 Melandri, 1m 52.490s; 3 de Puniet, 1m 53.043s; 4 Takahashi, 1m 53.666s; 5 Elias, 1m 53.667s; 6 Porto, 1m 53.701s; 7 Alzamora, 1m 54.066s; 8 Rolfo, 1m 54.067s; 9 Battaini, 1m 54.080s; 10 Debon, 1m 54.125s; 11 Yuzy, 1m 54.135s; 12 Matsudo, 1m 54.457s; 13 Aoyama, 1m 54.468s; 14 Ohsaki, 1m 54.516s; 15 Kayoh, 1m 54.562s; 16 Yokoe, 1m 54.566s; 17 Locatelli, 1m 54.721s; 18 Hules, 1m 54.765s; 19 Nakasuga, 1m 54.970s; 20 Aoki, 1m 55.009s; 21 Stoner, 1m 55.051s; 22 Vincent, 1m 55.349s; 23 Marchand, 1m 55.569s; 24 Checa, 1m 55.671s; 25 Heidolf, 1m 55.723s; 26 Haslam, 1m 55.999s; 27 Faubel, 1m 56.602s; 28 Smrz, 1m 56.741s; 29 Nigon, 1m 56.767s; 30 Jara, 1m 57.944s.

Fastest race laps: 1 Elias, 1m 53.392s; 2 Melandri, 1m 53.512s; 3 Takahashi, 1m 53.682s; 4 Rolfo, 1m 53.978s; 5 Alzamora, 1m 54.105s; 6 Nieto, 1m 54.216s; 7 Porto, 1m 54.322s; 8 Battaini, 1m 54.464s; 9 Kayoh, 1m 54.723s; 10 Locatelli, 1m 54.774s; 11 Stoner, 1m 54.908s; 12 Hules, 1m 54.934s; 13 Yuzy, 1m 54.946s; 14 Matsudo, 1m 54.952s; 15 Yokoe, 1m 55.004s; 16 Nakasuga, 1m 55.026s; 17 Aoyama, 1m 55.050s; 18 Debon, 1m 55.130s; 19 Aoki, 1m 55.285s; 20 Vincent, 1m 55.547s; 21 Heidolf, 1m 55.782s; 22 Marchand, 1m 55.899s; 23 Checa, 1m 55.903s; 24 Haslam, 1m 56.386s; 25 de Puniet, 1m 56.540s; 26 Faubel, 1m 56.728s; 27 Nigon, 1m 56.798s; 28 Smrz, 1m 57.360s; 29 Jara, 1m 59.369s.

World Championship: 1 Melandri, 248; 2 Nieto, 196; 3 Rolfo, 170; 4 Porto, 143; 5 Elias, 141; 6 Battaini, 113; 7 Locatelli, 105; 8 Alzamora, 93; 9 de Puniet, 86; 10 Matsudo, 73; 11 Debon, 58; 12 Stoner, 54; 13 Aoki and Yuzy, 45; 15 Checa, 36; 16 Miyazaki, 25; 17 Sakai, 20; 18 Haslam, 19; 19 Heidolf and Waldmann, 17; 21 Takahashi, 16; 22 Faubel, 13; 23 Vincent, 12; 24 Jara, 11; 25 Aoyama and Kameya, 9; 27 Nigon and Sekiguchi, 7; 29 Garcia and Hules, 6; 31 Marchand, Nakasuga and Philippe, 4; 34 Bataille and Yokoe, 2; 36 Smrz, 1.

125 cc

21 laps, 62.643 miles/100.821 km

Pos.	Rider (Nat.)	No.	Machine	Laps	Time & speed
1	Daniel Pedrosa (E)	26	Honda	21	41m 43.377s 90.090 mph/ 144.986 km/h
2	Manuel Poggiali (RSM)	1	Gilera	21	41m 51.448s
3	Steve Jenkner (D)	17	Aprilia	21	41m 52.078s
4	Pablo Nieto (E)	22	Aprilia	21	41m 58.802s
5	Hector Barbera (E)	80	Aprilia	21	42m 07.942s
6	Mika Kallio (SF)	36	Honda	21	42m 12.961s
7	Gino Borsoi (I)	23	Aprilia	21	42m 16.484s
8	Joan Olivé (E)	25	Honda	21	42m 18.297s
9	Jorge Lorenzo (E)	48	Derbi	21	42m 19.427s
10	Hideyuki Nakajoh (J)	97	Honda	21	42m 19.824s
11	Shuhei Aoyama (J)	66	Honda	21	42m 23.433s
12	Youichi Ui (J)	41	Derbi	21	42m 28.040s
13	Michel Fabrizio (I)	84	Gilera	21	42m 33.076s
14	Mirko Giansanti (I)	6	Honda	21	42m 33.449s
15	Arnaud Vincent (F)	21	Aprilia	21	42m 36.085s
16	Takashi Yasuda (J)	95	Honda	21	42m 43.609s
17	Stefano Bianco (I)	33	Aprilia	21	42m 43.925s
18	Masao Azuma (J)	5	Honda	21	42m 45.118s
19	Max Sabbatani (I)	11	Aprilia	21	42m 47.492s
20	Stefano Perugini (I)	7	Italjet	21	42m 50.508s
21	Gabor Talmacsi (H)	8	Honda	21	42m 50.547s
22	Andrea Ballerini (I)	50	Aprilia	21	42m 51.158s
23	Imre Toth (H)	20	Honda	21	42m 54.936s
24	Chaz Davies (GB)	57	Aprilia	21	43m 04.488s
25	Klaus Nöhles (D)	12	Honda	21	43m 10.447s
26	Alex Baldolini (I)	19	Aprilia	21	43m 16.407s
27	Noboru Ueda (J)	9	Honda	21	43m 32.176s
28	Mattia Angeloni (I)	31	Gilera	19	43m 32.165s
	Toshihisa Kuzuhara (J)	65	Honda	20	DNF
	Lucio Cecchinello (I)	4	Aprilia	18	DNF
	Simone Sanna (I)	16	Aprilia	13	DNF
	Alex de Angelis (RSM)	15	Aprilia	10	DNF
	Akira Komuro (J)	68	Honda	6	DNF
	Dario Giuseppetti (D)	72	Honda	6	DNF
	Christian Pistoni (I)	42	Italjet	4	DNF
	Andrea Dovizioso (I)	34	Honda	1	DNF
	Hideyuki Ogata (J)	67	Honda	0	DNF

Fastest lap: Pedrosa, 1m 58.354s, 90.741 mph/146.033km/h (record).

Previous record: Roberto Locatelli, I (Aprilia), 1m 58.816s, 90.388 mph/145.465 km/h (2000).

Event best maximum speed: Nieto, 124.3 mph/200.0 km/h (warm-up).

Qualifying: 1 Pedrosa, 1m 58.026s; 2 Poggiali, 1m 58.139s; 3 Jenkner, 1m 58.688s; 4 Vincent, 1m 58.745s; 5 Dovizioso, 1m 58.944s; 6 Cecchinello, 1m 59.002s; 7 Nieto, 1m 59.155s; 8 Barbera, 1m 59.407s; 9 Borsoi, 1m 59.650s; 10 Ogata, 1m 59.867s; 11 Azuma, 1m 59.907s; 12 Lorenzo, 1m 59.914s; 13 Ui, 1m 59.977s; 14 Fabrizio, 1m 59.990s; 15 Bianco, 2m 00.036s; 16 Sanna, 2m 00.040s; 17 Kallio, 2m 00.049s; 18 Giansanti, 2m 00.053s; 19 de Angelis, 2m 00.059s; 20 Sabbatani, 2m 00.079s; 21 Aoyama, 2m 00.122s; 22 Olivé, 2m 00.210s; 23 Ueda, 2m 00.472s; 24 Yasuda, 2m 00.556s; 25 Talmacsi, 2m 00.791s; 26 Nakajoh, 2m 00.838s; 27 Kuzuhara, 2m 00.843s; 28 Giuseppetti, 2m 00.874s; 29 Nöhles, 2m 01.007s; 30 Perugini, 2m 01.084s; 31 Angeloni, 2m 01.288s; 32 Ballerini, 2m 01.547s; 33 Komuro, 2m 02.324s; 34 Toth, 2m 02.356s; 35 Davies, 2m 02.408s; 36 Pistoni, 2m 02.783s; 37 Baldolini, 2m 03.056s.

Fastest race laps: 1 Pedrosa, 1m 58.354s; 2 Vincent, 1m 58.397s; 3 Poggiali, 1m 58.493s; 4 Jenkner, 1m 58.542s; 5 Cecchinello, 1m 58.941s; 6 Barbera, 1m 59.022s; 7 Nieto, 1m 59.037s; 8 Borsoi, 1m 59.403s; 9 de Angelis, 1m 59.516s; 10 Kallio, 1m 59.607s; 11 Nakajoh, 1m 59.715s; 12 Olivé, 1m 59.777s; 13 Aoyama, 1m 59.886s; 14 Lorenzo, 1m 59.970s; 15 Giansanti, 2m 00.078s; 16 Ui, 2m 00.348s; 17 Sanna, 2m 00.429s; 18 Fabrizio, 2m 00.548s; 19 Angeloni, 2m 00.591s; 20 Talmacsi, 2m 00.675s; 21 Toth, 2m 00.869s; 22 Sabbatani, 2m 00.878s; 23 Perugini, 2m 00.888s; 24 Yasuda, 2m 00.961s; 25 Bianco, 2m 00.979s; 26 Azuma, 2m 01.055s; 27 Nöhles, 2m 01.110s; 28 Ueda, 2m 01.119s; 29 Kuzuhara, 2m 01.147s; 30 Ballerini, 2m 01.287s; 31 Davies, 2m 01.530s; 32 Baldolini, 2m 02.133s; 33 Komuro, 2m 02.458s; 34 Giuseppetti, 2m 02.558s; 35 Pistoni, 2m 04.246s; 36 Dovizioso, 2m 05.727s.

World Championship: 1 Vincent, 215; 2 Poggiali, 207; 3 Pedrosa, 191; 4 Jenkner, 138; 5 Cecchinello, 132; 6 Nieto, 102; 7 Sanna, 89; 8 Azuma, 86; 9 Borsoi, 76; 10 Kallio, 69; 11 de Angelis, 68; 12 Olivé, 59; 13 Ui, 58; 14 Giansanti, 41; 15 Dovizioso, 35; 16 Barbera, 30; 17 Perugini, 24; 18 Aoyama, Bianco and Lorenzo, 21; 21 Talmacsi, 19; 22 Ueda, 18; 23 Ballerini and Rodriguez, 17; 25 Nöhles, 13; 26 Sabbatani, 12; 27 Luthi, 7; 28 Nakajoh, 6; 29 Davies, 5; 30 Fabrizio and Pistoni, 4; 32 Simoncelli and Smrz, 3; 34 Baldolini, Lai, Pellino and Simon, 2.

SEPANG

FIM WORLD CHAMPIONSHIP · ROUND 14

Left: Great racing, not many fans... Biaggi leads Barros and the squabbling Rossi and Ukawa past Sepang's massive but deserted stands.

Bottom left: Biaggi scored a superb second win of the year.

Below: 'Frankly stupid': Kenny Roberts shows off a model of next year's Proton V5.

Below centre: Teenage whiz-kid Casey Stoner was invincible in a fierce kart race.

Bottom: Pitt made his GP debut, gained the new Kawasaki's first finish.
All photographs: Gold & Goose

MIDWAY point for the long-haul trio, Malaysia obliged with the usual steamy weather and the ever-present threat of tropical storms. There was a change in the weather on the ground. At Motegi, numbers had been equal. Here, for the first time, four-strokes outnumbered two-strokes: four Hondas; four Yamahas — with Nakano and Jacque getting their first bites; three Suzukis — Ryo was there as a wild card; one Aprilia; one Kawasaki; 13 MotoGP machines up against nine 500s. A sign of the times indeed.

The profusion of the new led to mixed results, and at least one epiphany. Malaysia marked the first time that Rossi's RCV211 V5 Honda was beaten in a straight fight by a motor cycle other than another RCV. Biaggi and the red Yamaha produced one of those immaculate performances that marks this remarkable rider at his best. He was almost unbeatable, after typically steady progress through practice culminating in a characteristic sprint at the close that nearly secured pole, followed by an inch-perfect race. Checa by comparison qualified fifth and raced to seventh, never happy with the settings, and behind brand-new M1 rider Nakano. Max had a point to prove, and wasn't he doing it well? Being sacked by Yamaha had not only brought out the best in his riding, but was now also enhancing his image and popularity as well. A nice irony.

And where was Rossi? Where indeed. Tangled up in an unseemly brawl for second, unable to escape from Ukawa and Barros. Every time he got ahead he'd be nailed again under brakes, and there were several incidences of club-racer-like over-enthusiasm where Rossi would try to gain one place, only to lose one by running in too fast. Could he have challenged Max? We would never know. Because to challenge him, first he had to get there.

Three Hondas tripping over each other was a comforting sight for rivals still coming to terms with the daunting news that there will be eight of the almost unbeaten V5s on the grid next year. If this is what happens when you get a crowd of them, then bring on some more. In a strange way, having more Hondas might give rivals more chance rather than less.

The reason, according to Rossi's famous crew chief Jerry Burgess, is that the V5s are all so very closely matched. The bikes are not sensitive instruments like the old two-strokes, and there's little scope for engineers to find hidden tweaks, or to discover a way to give their riders something a little different that they can use to advantage. They all go more or less the same anyway. This leaves only one overtaking opportunity: under brakes. An area where Alex Barros has long excelled. It may be that he is lacking in all-round skills compared with Rossi, but the four-stroke Honda had given him a bike where this single strength counts for a lot.

Malaysia posed another conundrum. Back in pre-season tests, in very similar conditions and without the benefit of lots of other bikes sweeping the track and laying fresh rubber on the racing line, Rossi had set a lap time of 2m 03.6s. Now, half a season later, his best practice time was 2m 05.19s, and Barros's pole 2m 04.487s. Rossi blamed braking performance because of the troublesome slipper clutch, though it was hard to think why.

Last year, the Petronas Sauber made its appearance at Sepang. The GP project had since sunk almost without trace, reborn instead as the Team Foggy Superbike. This year, the new V5 four-stroke Proton, the next Malaysian challenger, made its appearance, albeit only in the form of a scale model of the engine. There was still a long way to go to a complete running motor cycle, obviously, and Kenny Roberts made no bones about it. 'Trying to do what we're trying to do in the time available is quite frankly stupid,' he said, at the ceremonial unveiling at the Proton cars factory. The engine looked rather large, as did the Sauber when it first appeared, with induction ports taped over mysteriously; the programme was for it to be bench-tested by the end of November and track-tested possibly in December, to be ready for the first race of 2003. An ambitious time-scale for an ambitious project, but nonetheless to be taken seriously, an illustration of what a force Kenny's Banbury-based engineering company has become, in six years of learning from scratch and in public how to build an effective racing motor cycle from nothing but dreams.

Another of next year's new boys, a little further advanced, took a step backwards. Perhaps. Kawasaki were bereft of the ZZ-RR's test rider Yanagawa after his heavy Motegi spill, and drafted in GP novice Andrew Pitt to take his place on the green thing. Pitt (24) won the Supersport World Championship for team manager Eckl in 2001, and was somewhat wide-eyed about the way the GP machine 'just keeps on pulling' in top gear. He was also off the pace, but improved consistently and was never in danger of not qualifying. Bad handling at Motegi had been traced to a frame breakage, so now it was reinforced, with an all-new chassis due a week later in Australia.

Among the fun and games was a pre-race go-kart contest that was rather revealing, if only for the way tooth-and-nail rivals Rossi and Biaggi bumped into each other often enough to spoil each other's race completely. And also, perhaps, for the talents of the victor, teenager Casey Stoner, who blitzed practice, started from the back of the grid, and came through to win convincingly.

Yet it is Rossi who is destined for four wheels, with further confirmation in Malaysia of imminent tests for his factory-backed Peugeot for the post-season Rally of Great Britain. Surely his performance in the bike race had nothing to do with getting bored with two wheels?

Finally, a flag-man's error messed up the 125 race. Perhaps over-excited by the thrilling contest, he showed the chequered flag to back-markers instead of the leaders, still rounding the hairpin. At that point, title contender Poggiali fell off — but the rules are clear, said race director Paul Butler. 'There was no protest, but we had no option but to take results from the previous lap.' (And to fine the organisers 10,000 Swiss francs.) This reinstated Poggiali in fourth, and it was only through luck that it didn't in the end affect the outcome of the most delicately balanced championship of all.

MOTOGP - BIAGGI • 250 cc - NIETO • 125 cc - VINCENT

Below: A crucial moment: Biaggi is sweeping into the final hairpin, but Rossi's bid to outbrake Barros will fail, putting them both out of touch.

Bottom: Black lines and an exhaust-pipe orchestra as four-strokes outnumber two-strokes for the first time: Barros leads from Biaggi, Kato, Ukawa and Rossi.

Both photographs: Gold & Goose

MOTOGP RACE – 21 laps

Biaggi was sure he had pole, but he didn't realise he had Barros following on to stop the clock a fraction quicker. 'He should buy me a pizza,' he said. 'A pizza. Caviar — anything you like,' responded Barros, following up his race win and lap record in his first four-stroke ride with pole for his second. Kato was third, stiff and sore after another crash on the first day, going too far with a corner-entry slide; then another superhuman effort from Capirossi, still angry at being passed over for the four-stroke. 'The two-strokes are competitive for most of the lap, but on the last two straights you lose half a second,' he said.

McWilliams on the slower Proton measured his loss at a full second, 'and I am only seven-tenths off pole. That says it all,' he said. He had Checa and Ukawa ahead on row two, and a disgruntled Rossi behind, after his team got the timing wrong for once for an end-of-session flyer. 'I am not happy with the way we are working,' he said.

Barros led Biaggi, with Kato and Ukawa then Rossi and Checa after one lap, McWilliams 18th after bogging on the line with a grabbing clutch. Rossi passed Ukawa into the last hairpin only to run wide on the exit — a sign of troubles to come.

Two laps later he tried again into turn one, doing the same to drop behind Ukawa and Checa, taking another lap to repass the Yamaha. Progress was difficult, though Ukawa took advantage of an error from Kato, then Rossi passed them both. But he was desperate and they were delaying one another, the leaders now two seconds clear after six laps, Kato losing the group as Rossi and Ukawa closed a bit on Barros, just over a second adrift at half-distance.

Now Barros made a slip, and Biaggi closed up, then took the lead against fierce opposition at the start of lap 12. This bickering let the other two Hondas close the gap finally, and at the end of lap 13 a second covered the first four.

Into the final hairpin next time and Rossi ran wide, taking Barros

with him and letting Ukawa through. Barros was generous in his comment: 'It's part of racing. I would have done the same to him.' Biaggi was now clear, and over the next four laps he pulled out more than two seconds, while Ukawa repulsed Rossi's every attempt to get past, earning an angry rebuke later. The champion finally managed to get by on lap 19, and he halved the lead next time round. It was not enough, and Biaggi claimed the win.

Barros also finally passed Ukawa, with Kato a lone fifth, and Nakano likewise in sixth.

Capirossi had dropped back rapidly from seventh on lap one. Nakano took over, Roberts on his back wheel, but unable to get by the faster and better-balanced M1. Nakano was getting the feeling, speeding up after half-distance to catch Checa, diving underneath to pull away gradually on lap 14.

Roberts couldn't pass Checa, with Capirossi keeping the pressure on close behind.

Ryo had delayed the next gang, with Abe managing to swap positions by half-distance, though unable to escape. The Protons had been close, McWilliams passing Aoki after four laps then bringing him along, van den Goorbergh following. On lap 18 Aoki seized mid-corner, slowing van den Goorbergh so he lost touch as the Japanese rider pulled off the track.

Gibernau had a fresh engine after a warm-up blow-up, and the settings weren't spot on, with software making the idle speed too high so the bike was pushing into the turns. On lap three this pushed him onto the grass, dropping him to the back, to pick his way through the slower two-strokes to 15th, promoted one place when Harada retired.

His victims were mostly battling with sliding Dunlops. McCoy led the group throughout for the last point, while Cardoso (on Michelins) finally prevailed over Laconi and Hopkins, who had slipped off and remounted. Pitt circulated steadily well out of touch for the new Kawasaki's first finish; Jacque's four-stroke debut had been brief, high-siding out on lap four. Harada retired.

Biaggi's second win took him past Ukawa to second overall, the next-best goal for the season.

Left: Fonsi and Toni — the finishing order was settled by team instructions.

Below left: 'I have to say very very thank you.' Elias accepts Nieto's heartfelt gratitude for the gift of a win.

Below: Vincent smoked everybody in an unexpectedly abbreviated 125 race.

Bottom: The battle for the last 125 points — Dovizioso chases Nöhles. Lorenzo, Borsoi and Giansanti chase him.
All photographs: Gold & Goose

250 cc RACE – 20 laps

Nieto had only one option left to save his slender title chances. He had to win every remaining race. Accordingly he defeated Melandri for pole by the impressive margin of almost half a second. First-day leader Elias was third, Locatelli completing the front row, Battaini leading the second, Aprilias filling the first five slots before Rolfo's Honda.

Elias led away, but Nieto flew past a couple of bends later and started to work on building up an impressive lead, with Melandri third as the field streamed towards the end of the first lap. Then the points leader slowed dramatically at the start of the last straight, waving a leg in warning to those behind, crossing the line 14th. He cruised one more lap, then pitted and watched disconsolately as mechanics diagnosed an electronic failure. No points for Marco.

This was an unexpected gift for Nieto, who made the most of it, more than three seconds clear after two laps, as Rolfo got ahead of Elias for a couple of laps. The young Spaniard regained second on lap four, and rapidly began to pull away from the Honda to close on team-mate Nieto.

He certainly looked as though he could pass him at any moment, but then again Nieto was obviously aware from team discussions prior to the race that Elias had been instructed to stay behind. This instruction was reinforced at half-distance with a signal reading: 'Toni — P2 OK.'

Rolfo did close slightly to within 1.5 seconds, but had dropped away somewhat again at the finish, never a serious threat in another processional 250 race.

Some way behind there was a good battle for fourth, Porto's Petronas-sponsored Yamaha enjoying support from the small crowd as he held off de Puniet and Battaini, Matsudo hanging on behind until almost half-distance.

This trio swapped back and forth, de Puniet leading as they began the last lap, then Battaini and Porto, who was waiting his moment to dive past both of them in one corner, hanging on to fourth to the finish, with Battaini now fifth.

Matsudo managed to stay clear of the next battle, between Yuzy, pulling out all the stops at home, and Alzamora, who had escaped a scrap with Checa to tag on behind the fast-starting Malaysian. With three laps to go he pushed past, but Yuzy fought back, finally narrowly beaten by the more powerful factory Honda.

Checa was followed by Stoner after another trademark charge through the mid-field. Twentieth at the end of lap one, he picked

his way through steadily, 12th by half-distance, then passing Aoki to finish well ahead in 11th.

Locatelli had got away well, but dropped back behind Stoner to get into a big battle with Jay Vincent, who had earlier been trading blows with Alzamora. Vincent was three seconds behind the Italian at the finish, with Hules taking the last point.

Melandri's rare breakdown all but halved his lead, but with two races to go he was still 27 points clear. Even with one more non-finish he would still be ahead — and surely nobody would have that much bad luck.

125 cc RACE – 18 laps

Pedrosa had a heavy crash in the final session, stretchered away to be consigned from first to third on the grid, with Vincent grabbing a big margin and Poggiali second. Jenkner completed the first row, increasingly impressive Spanish youngster Barbera led row two.

Pedrosa was back again on Sunday, hurting but still keen, and led away, with Vincent taking over before half a lap was completed. A big gang went with him, and after 11 laps of hanging on for grim death a little slide dropped the Frenchman to fourth in a six-strong leading group.

Cecchinello took over at first, but Pedrosa dived inside into the final hairpin to cross the line ahead, only for Cecchinello to do the same to him next lap, and also Vincent, up to second by dint of the most daring late braking imaginable. One lap later he regained a lead he held to the end, still under severe pressure.

Jenkner and Nieto lost touch by the end, but the remaining four were fighting tooth and nail — Poggiali taking sweeping lines, then almost colliding with Pedrosa and running wide to drop to fourth as they started the final lap.

Now Pedrosa slipped past Cecchinello on the final straight, and pushed Vincent all the way to the flag, Cecchinello close behind. Poggiali had one last card — a desperate late-braking lunge into the final hairpin that instead pitched him over and into the gravel. This left fourth to Nieto... until the decision to take the results from the previous lap because of the flag-man's error. This reshuffled Cecchinello and Pedrosa, but more importantly reinstated Poggiali in fourth. A very lucky man.

Kallio took control of the next group from Barbera with three laps to go, Azuma dropping away at the finish. De Angelis and Sanna were spaced out behind, Ui a lonely 12th.

And Vincent, thanks to circumstances, was only 20 points ahead of Poggiali.

Friends disunited: Barros (above) radiates joy after another strong ride on the four-stroke; team-mate Capirossi (left) simmers at being left on the outclassed two-stroke.
Both photographs: Gold & Goose

FIM WORLD CHAMPIONSHIP

GAULOISES
MALAYSIAN
grand prix

13 OCTOBER 2002

round **14**

SEPANG

CIRCUIT LENGTH: 3.447 miles/5.548 km

MotoGP

21 laps, 72.387 miles/116.508 km

Pos.	Rider (Nat.)	No.	Machine	Laps	Time & speed
1	Max Biaggi (I)	3	Yamaha	21	44m 01.592s 98.660 mph/ 158.778 km/h
2	Valentino Rossi (I)	46	Honda	21	44m 02.134s
3	Alex Barros (BR)	4	Honda	21	44m 03.164s
4	Tohru Ukawa (J)	11	Honda	21	44m 03.830s
5	Daijiro Kato (J)	74	Honda	21	44m 10.067s
6	Shinya Nakano (J)	56	Yamaha	21	44m 24.592s
7	Carlos Checa (E)	7	Yamaha	21	44m 25.952s
8	Kenny Roberts (USA)	10	Suzuki	21	44m 26.301s
9	Loris Capirossi (I)	65	Honda	21	44m 29.261s
10	Norick Abe (J)	6	Yamaha	21	44m 43.403s
11	Akira Ryo (J)	33	Suzuki	21	44m 44.195s
12	Jeremy McWilliams (GB)	99	Proton KR	21	44m 47.353s
13	Jurgen van den Goorbergh (NL)	17	Honda	21	44m 49.908s
14	Sete Gibernau (E)	15	Suzuki	21	45m 02.862s
15	Garry McCoy (AUS)	8	Yamaha	21	45m 14.688s
16	José Luis Cardoso (E)	30	Yamaha	21	45m 17.095s
17	Regis Laconi (F)	55	Aprilia	21	45m 23.105s
18	John Hopkins (USA)	21	Yamaha	21	45m 44.276s
19	Andrew Pitt (AUS)	84	Kawasaki	21	45m 49.748s
	Nobuatsu Aoki (J)	9	Proton KR	18	DNF
	Tetsuya Harada (J)	31	Honda	11	DNF
	Olivier Jacque (F)	19	Yamaha	3	DNF

Fastest lap: Biaggi, 2m 04.925s, 99.344 mph/159.878 km/h (record).
Previous record: Valentino Rossi, I (Honda), 2m 06.618s, 98.015 mph/157.740 km/h (2001).

Event best maximum speed: Ukawa, 191.0 mph/307.4 km/h (qualifying practice no. 2).

Qualifying: 1 Barros, 2m 04.487s; 2 Biaggi, 2m 04.536s; 3 Kato, 2m 04.680s; 4 Capirossi, 2m 04.785s; 5 Checa, 2m 05.031s; 6 Ukawa, 2m 05.106s; 7 McWilliams, 2m 05.170s; 8 Rossi, 2m 05.188s; 9 McCoy, 2m 05.400s; 10 van den Goorbergh, 2m 05.671s; 11 Abe, 2m 05.800s; 12 Roberts, 2m 05.911s; 13 Aoki, 2m 06.061s; 14 Harada, 2m 06.148s; 15 Gibernau, 2m 06.362s; 16 Nakano, 2m 06.451s; 17 Jacque, 2m 06.580s; 18 Ryo, 2m 06.635s; 19 Hopkins, 2m 06.857s; 20 Laconi, 2m 07.126s; 21 Cardoso, 2m 08.028s; 22 Pitt, 2m 09.106s.

Fastest race laps: 1 Biaggi, 2m 04.925s; 2 Barros, 2m 05.064s; 3 Rossi, 2m 05.116s; 4 Ukawa, 2m 05.118s; 5 Kato, 2m 05.428s; 6 Checa, 2m 05.689s; 7 Roberts, 2m 06.122s; 8 Nakano, 2m 06.166s; 9 Capirossi, 2m 06.184s; 10 Ryo, 2m 06.715s; 11 Abe, 2m 06.844s; 12 van den Goorbergh, 2m 07.016s; 13 McWilliams, 2m 07.099s; 14 Aoki, 2m 07.163s; 15 Jacque, 2m 07.182s; 16 Gibernau, 2m 07.515s; 17 Harada, 2m 07.715s; 18 Cardoso, 2m 07.994s; 19 Hopkins, 2m 08.005s; 20 McCoy, 2m 08.156s; 21 Laconi, 2m 08.260s; 22 Pitt, 2m 09.983s.

World Championship: 1 Rossi, 310; 2 Biaggi, 189; 3 Ukawa, 182; 4 Barros, 159; 5 Checa, 136; 6 Abe, 123; 7 Capirossi, 109; 8 Roberts, 92; 9 Kato, 91; 10 Jacque, 66; 11 Nakano, 55; 12 Aoki, 54; 13 Hopkins, 53; 14 McWilliams, 45; 15 Gibernau, 44; 16 Harada, 43; 17 Ryo, 41; 18 van den Goorbergh, 40; 19 Laconi and McCoy, 33; 21 Itoh, 13; 22 Hofmann, 11; 23 Cardoso, 8; 24 Bayle, 5; 25 Riba and Yoshikawa, 4.

250 cc

20 laps, 68.940 miles/110.960 km

Pos.	Rider (Nat.)	No.	Machine	Laps	Time & speed
1	Fonsi Nieto (E)	10	Aprilia	20	43m 28.624s 95.150 mph/ 153.129 km/h
2	Toni Elias (E)	24	Aprilia	20	43m 29.036s
3	Roberto Rolfo (I)	4	Honda	20	43m 31.571s
4	Sebastian Porto (ARG)	9	Yamaha	20	43m 36.534s
5	Franco Battaini (I)	21	Aprilia	20	43m 37.205s
6	Randy de Puniet (F)	17	Aprilia	20	43m 37.330s
7	Naoki Matsudo (J)	8	Yamaha	20	43m 47.779s
8	Emilio Alzamora (E)	7	Honda	20	43m 51.083s
9	Shahrol Yuzy (MAL)	18	Yamaha	20	43m 51.318s
10	David Checa (E)	42	Aprilia	20	43m 57.974s
11	Casey Stoner (AUS)	27	Aprilia	20	44m 05.126s
12	Haruchika Aoki (J)	11	Honda	20	44m 08.640s
13	Roberto Locatelli (I)	15	Aprilia	20	44m 15.182s
14	Jay Vincent (GB)	12	Honda	20	44m 18.417s
15	Jaroslav Hules (CZ)	13	Yamaha	20	44m 25.824s
16	Jakub Smrz (CZ)	96	Honda	20	44m 31.542s
17	Leon Haslam (GB)	19	Honda	20	44m 31.574s
18	Dirk Heidolf (D)	28	Aprilia	20	44m 31.993s
19	Hugo Marchand (F)	51	Aprilia	20	44m 41.769s
	Erwan Nigon (F)	36	Aprilia	14	DNF
	Hector Faubel (E)	32	Aprilia	9	DNF
	Alex Debon (E)	6	Aprilia	8	DNF
	Raul Jara (E)	22	Aprilia	6	DNF
	Marco Melandri (I)	3	Aprilia	2	DNF

Fastest lap: Nieto, 2m 08.858s, 96.311 mph/154.998 km/h (record).
Previous record: Daijiro Kato, J (Honda), 2m 08.920s, 96.265 mph/154.923 km/h (2001).

Event best maximum speed: Nieto, 160.9 mph/259.1 km/h (qualifying practice no. 2).

Qualifying: 1 Nieto, 2m 08.067s; 2 Melandri, 2m 08.518s; 3 Elias, 2m 09.017s; 4 Locatelli, 2m 09.330s; 5 Battaini, 2m 09.584s; 6 Rolfo, 2m 09.618s; 7 de Puniet, 2m 09.774s; 8 Porto, 2m 09.928s; 9 Debon, 2m 10.077s; 10 Stoner, 2m 10.162s; 11 Checa, 2m 10.216s; 12 Yuzy, 2m 10.358s; 13 Alzamora, 2m 10.560s; 14 Matsudo, 2m 10.600s; 15 Aoki, 2m 11.004s; 16 Heidolf, 2m 11.483s; 17 Marchand, 2m 11.550s; 18 Vincent, 2m 11.930s; 19 Faubel, 2m 12.179s; 20 Haslam, 2m 12.475s; 21 Hules, 2m 12.592s; 22 Nigon, 2m 12.607s; 23 Smrz, 2m 13.090s; 24 Jara, 2m 13.230s.

Fastest race laps: 1 Nieto, 2m 08.858s; 2 Elias, 2m 09.253s; 3 de Puniet, 2m 09.471s; 4 Rolfo, 2m 09.515s; 5 Porto, 2m 09.802s; 6 Battaini, 2m 09.982s; 7 Matsudo, 2m 10.054s; 8 Alzamora, 2m 10.238s; 9 Yuzy, 2m 10.664s; 10 Debon, 2m 10.855s; 11 Checa, 2m 10.884s; 12 Stoner, 2m 10.942s; 13 Vincent, 2m 11.226s; 14 Locatelli, 2m 11.330s; 15 Aoki, 2m 11.457s; 16 Hules, 2m 11.792s; 17 Heidolf, 2m 12.117s; 18 Smrz, 2m 12.223s; 19 Haslam, 2m 12.314s; 20 Marchand, 2m 12.382s; 21 Faubel, 2m 12.432s; 22 Nigon, 2m 12.945s; 23 Jara, 2m 15.248s; 24 Melandri, 2m 20.328s.

World Championship: 1 Melandri, 248; 2 Nieto, 221; 3 Rolfo, 186; 4 Elias, 161; 5 Porto, 156; 6 Battaini, 124; 7 Locatelli, 108; 8 Alzamora, 101; 9 de Puniet, 96; 10 Matsudo, 82; 11 Stoner, 59; 12 Debon, 58; 13 Yuzy, 52; 14 Aoki, 49; 15 Checa, 42; 16 Miyazaki, 25; 17 Sakai, 20; 18 Haslam, 19; 19 Heidolf and Waldmann, 17; 21 Takahashi, 16; 22 Vincent, 14; 23 Faubel, 13; 24 Jara, 11; 25 Aoyama and Kameya, 9; 27 Hules, Nigon and Sekiguchi, 7; 30 Garcia, 6; 31 Marchand, Nakasuga and Philippe, 4; 34 Bataille and Yokoe, 2; 36 Smrz, 1.

125 cc

18 laps, 62.046 miles/99.864 km

Pos.	Rider (Nat.)	No.	Machine	Laps	Time & speed
1	Arnaud Vincent (F)	21	Aprilia	18	40m 32.656s 91.829 mph/ 147.785 km/h
2	Lucio Cecchinello (I)	4	Aprilia	18	40m 32.934s
3	Daniel Pedrosa (E)	26	Honda	18	40m 33.001s
4	Manuel Poggiali (RSM)	1	Gilera	18	40m 33.469s
5	Pablo Nieto (E)	22	Aprilia	18	40m 36.303s
6	Steve Jenkner (D)	17	Aprilia	18	40m 38.944s
7	Mika Kallio (SF)	36	Honda	18	40m 45.676s
8	Hector Barbera (SF)	80	Aprilia	18	40m 45.684s
9	Masao Azuma (J)	5	Honda	18	40m 45.911s
10	Alex de Angelis (RSM)	15	Aprilia	18	40m 54.150s
11	Simone Sanna (I)	16	Aprilia	18	40m 57.865s
12	Youichi Ui (J)	41	Derbi	18	41m 03.167s
13	Joan Olivé (E)	25	Honda	18	41m 09.204s
14	Klaus Nöhles (D)	12	Honda	18	41m 18.639s
15	Andrea Dovizioso (I)	34	Honda	18	41m 19.091s
16	Mirko Giansanti (I)	6	Honda	18	41m 19.122s
17	Mattia Angeloni (I)	31	Gilera	18	41m 19.757s
18	Noboru Ueda (J)	9	Honda	18	41m 20.346s
19	Gino Borsoi (I)	23	Aprilia	18	41m 20.380s
20	Jorge Lorenzo (E)	48	Derbi	18	41m 20.735s
21	Thomas Luthi (CH)	77	Honda	18	41m 55.310s
22	Imre Toth (H)	20	Honda	18	41m 55.377s
23	Alex Baldolini (I)	19	Aprilia	18	41m 55.523s
24	Dario Giuseppetti (D)	72	Honda	18	41m 55.702s
25	Chaz Davies (GB)	57	Aprilia	18	42m 08.670s
26	Michel Fabrizio (I)	84	Gilera	18	42m 09.448s
	Christian Pistoni (I)	42	Italjet	16	DNF
	Joshua Waters (AUS)	83	Honda	15	DNF
	Gabor Talmacsi (H)	8	Honda	6	DNF
	Marco Simoncelli (I)	37	Aprilia	5	DNF
	Andrea Ballerini (I)	50	Aprilia	3	DNF
	Max Sabbatani (I)	11	Aprilia	2	DNF
	Stefano Bianco (I)	33	Aprilia	1	DNF
	Stefano Perugini (I)	7	Italjet	1	DNF

Fastest lap: Cecchinello, 2m 13.919s, 92.671 mph/149.140 km/h (record).
Previous record: Youichi Ui, J (Derbi), 2m 14.961s, 91.956 mph/147.989 km/h (2001).

Event best maximum speed: Bianco, 139.9 mph/225.1 km/h (warm-up).

Qualifying: 1 Vincent, 2m 13.563s; 2 Poggiali, 2m 13.998s; 3 Pedrosa, 2m 14.075s; 4 Jenkner, 2m 14.110s; 5 Barbera, 2m 14.381s; 6 Ui, 2m 14.638s; 7 Cecchinello, 2m 14.690s; 8 Sabbatani, 2m 14.711s; 9 Azuma, 2m 14.717s; 10 Nieto, 2m 14.736s; 11 Nöhles, 2m 14.977s; 12 Bianco, 2m 15.250s; 13 Ballerini, 2m 15.281s; 14 Kallio, 2m 15.320s; 15 Giansanti, 2m 15.350s; 16 Olivé, 2m 15.364s; 17 Dovizioso, 2m 15.427s; 18 Angeloni, 2m 15.621s; 19 de Angelis, 2m 15.726s; 20 Borsoi, 2m 15.743s; 21 Fabrizio, 2m 16.015s; 22 Sanna, 2m 16.316s; 23 Talmacsi, 2m 16.443s; 24 Lorenzo, 2m 16.499s; 25 Perugini, 2m 16.534s; 26 Ueda, 2m 17.380s; 27 Simoncelli, 2m 17.719s; 28 Toth, 2m 18.088s; 29 Giuseppetti, 2m 18.213s; 30 Luthi, 2m 18.381s; 31 Davies, 2m 18.968s; 32 Baldolini, 2m 18.986s; 33 Pistoni, 2m 21.121s; 34 Waters, 2m 21.470s.

Fastest race laps: 1 Cecchinello, 2m 13.919s; 2 Pedrosa, 2m 13.925s; 3 Jenkner, 2m 13.927s; 4 Poggiali, 2m 14.135s; 5 Kallio, 2m 14.195s; 6 Vincent, 2m 14.199s; 7 Azuma, 2m 14.407s; 8 Nieto, 2m 14.526s; 9 de Angelis, 2m 14.526s; 10 Barbera, 2m 14.534s; 11 Sanna, 2m 14.805s; 12 Ballerini, 2m 15.177s; 13 Sabbatani, 2m 15.387s; 14 Olivé, 2m 15.523s; 15 Ui, 2m 15.704s; 16 Borsoi, 2m 15.943s; 17 Lorenzo, 2m 16.042s; 18 Giansanti, 2m 16.119s; 19 Ueda, 2m 16.172s; 20 Angeloni, 2m 16.244s; 21 Dovizioso, 2m 16.355s; 22 Talmacsi, 2m 16.360s; 23 Nöhles, 2m 16.390s; 24 Simoncelli, 2m 16.843s; 25 Fabrizio, 2m 17.262s; 26 Luthi, 2m 18.288s; 27 Giuseppetti, 2m 18.316s; 28 Toth, 2m 18.520s; 29 Baldolini, 2m 18.522s; 30 Davies, 2m 18.744s; 31 Waters, 2m 20.583s; 32 Pistoni, 2m 20.889s; 33 Bianco, 2m 26.335s; 34 Perugini, 2m 28.309s.

World Championship: 1 Vincent, 240; 2 Poggiali, 220; 3 Pedrosa, 207; 4 Cecchinello, 152; 5 Jenkner, 148; 6 Nieto, 113; 7 Sanna, 94; 8 Azuma, 93; 9 Kallio, 78; 10 Borsoi, 76; 11 de Angelis, 74; 12 Olivé and Ui, 62; 14 Giansanti, 41; 15 Barbera, 38; 16 Dovizioso, 36; 17 Perugini, 24; 18 Aoyama, Bianco and Lorenzo, 21; 21 Talmacsi, 19; 22 Ueda, 18; 23 Ballerini and Rodriguez, 17; 25 Nöhles, 15; 26 Sabbatani, 12; 27 Luthi, 7; 28 Nakajoh, 6; 29 Davies, 5; 30 Fabrizio and Pistoni, 4; 32 Simoncelli and Smrz, 3; 34 Baldolini, Lai, Pellino and Simon, 2.

PHILLIP ISLAND

AUSTRALIAN GP

FIM WORLD CHAMPIONSHIP · ROUND 15

THE old 500s were coming to the end of their last chances now. Once again, nobody had been quite sure just what would happen when the two-strokes met the four-strokes at Phillip Island. The doubt was even more palpable after practice, with an all-two-stroke front row for the first time all year, and the last in history.

The splendid seaside circuit (rather worryingly offered for sale shortly before the race) is fast, with a significant straight — only the second circuit after Mugello where the new 990s breached 200 mph. More importantly there are only two slow corners, both of which lead into other turns rather than onto straights, so the acceleration advantage of the big bikes was offset by the better braking and higher corner speed of the 500s. To a huge extent, Jeremy McWilliams's sleek little triple two-stroke Proton was the slowest bike down the straight, with a weekend's best of 186.6 mph, with Rossi's Honda fastest at 201.01. Yet the veteran Ulsterman qualified on pole.

It was Jeremy's third at the track, the first ever for the only independent bike in GP racing. Alongside him were McCoy's Yamaha, Aoki's Proton and van den Goorbergh's NSR, representing the full range of surviving two-strokes. New four-stroke convert Abe might have looked askance at this, had he not already been carried away after a very heavy tumble from the M1 on the second morning; likewise Jacque and Nakano, similarly struggling in 16th and 17th on an admittedly tight grid.

Remarkably, all the occupants of the front row were 30 or over. There was another common factor, underlined by the absence of Capirossi's NSR from the front ranks. For the first time anyone could remember (even GP statistician Dr Martin Raines was unable to put a date on it) not one of the front-row qualifiers was on Michelin tyres. Both Protons and van den Goorbergh were on Bridgestones, McCoy on Dunlops.

Did this mean Michelin were at last under serious threat? Maybe so in the future, if Bridgestone continue with their rate of improvement in their second season in the class. More to the point, it meant that all their riders were for once disadvantaged by the French company's refusal to bring special soft qualifying tyres. 'We prefer for our teams to set the bikes up on race tyres,' sniffed a spokesman, but if things carry on like this the policy might change.

The race of course was different. Those 990s are great big bullies when they get in a pack, but recollections of the Australian GP will always be enhanced by the memory of Aoki in particular harrying Max Biaggi throughout the race. The Proton was passed every time down the straight, making it imperative for Aoki to get ahead as soon as possible thereafter, with some highly daring riding and quite extraordinary angles of lean. 'I must have been like a fly to Max, but it was what I had to do,' he explained happily afterwards, while team boss Roberts came out with the quote of the weekend. 'It's like when your dog gets real old and sick, and you have to take her to the vet to be put down. And in the car, she gets all frisky. That's what our bike's doing.'

The weather is always precarious and reliably cold at Phillip Island, and while the rain stayed away when the bikes were running, an icy wind gusting up to almost 30 mph at times was ever-present. It caused all the usual problems, and provoked some varied reactions, especially to the question of how to reduce the effect of crosswinds, generating significant and very variable lift on the leaning machines. To drill or not to drill was the question. Aprilia are always keen on holey fairings, and there were plenty of them. At Suzuki Gibernau preferred to leave his bike intact, but Roberts commissioned major surgery, with chunks cut out of the front of the lower flanks. He seemed reassured, but rather worryingly the radical butchery had no effect on maximum speed, which must give the designers pause for thought. There was a similar disparity at Proton. McWilliams wanted holes, Aoki insisted that suspension settings were the way to get over the problem. Large and small holes were drilled on Jeremy's fairing, concentrating on upper and lower surfaces, and he summed it up clearly enough: 'I have no idea if it really helps, but I think I can feel the effect, so it's psychologically better anyway.'

Abe's awaited four-stroke debut saw him on the same fuel-injected machine ridden by Yoshikawa at Motegi, and while potentially faster than the carburetted bikes it was obviously a bit of a struggle. He blamed rider error rather than the erratic responses for his very fast crash, which damaged both machine and rider enough to rule them out of the race.

Barry Sheene was a welcome presence in the paddock, looking gaunt after some weeks on a severe diet regime, the first step in his one-man fight against cancer, but chirpy as ever, on 'light duties' for the Channel Ten TV coverage, and showing his son Freddie round the paddock. Given a special place in the parade of open-top cars that take the drivers round on race morning, Sheene got a bigger ovation from the 40,000-strong crowd than Rossi.

Australia was for once relatively short of home heroes — McCoy providing an attenuated last hurrah with trouble in the race, Casey Stoner hardly known at home, having left Australia to go road racing before he'd reached the national minimum age limit. Brendan Clarke, who'd come to 500 GPs last year as a schoolboy to ride the V-twin Honda previously used by Leon Haslam, had hoped to provide some excitement as a wild card in the 250 class, arranging a reasonably competitive Aprilia to be delivered from Germany. Alas, the best-laid plans... shipping delays meant the bike cleared customs in Australia the day after the race.

The GP coincided with a day of national mourning for victims of the terrorist bombing attack in Bali the week before, with more than 100 Australians among the victims. A minute's silence was observed ten minutes before the main race.

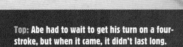

Top: Abe had to wait to get his turn on a four-stroke, but when it came, it didn't last long.

Above: The Proton pair — Aoki congratulates team-mate McWilliams after he'd blitzed the last-ever two-stroke pole position.

Left: Barry Sheene was in the pits, on form, and enjoying the adulation of the fans.

Opposite page: Rossi reasserted his authority with his first win since taking the title three races ago.

Below: Bike city at Australia's race of the year.
All photographs: Gold & Goose

MOTOGP RACE — 27 laps

Barros, making a record 150th consecutive GP start, turned 32 on the first day of practice, making him old enough for the front row. But he was not fast enough, in spite of being the top four-stroke, leading row two from Ukawa, Rossi and Biaggi. His comment was pithy: 'The front row... is a mirage. They all used chewing-gum tyres.' And pole man McWilliams concurred somewhat, after a 'rather ragged' lap put him there. 'The race will be tough. We get eaten down the straight. It might be a contact sport tomorrow.'

Barros led away again, the Hondas of Rossi and Ukawa behind, then van den Goorbergh and McCoy carrying the two-stroke banner.

The expected close race up front didn't materialise: Barros led comfortably, Rossi sometimes more than a second behind, but both more than five seconds clear after eight laps. After ten, Rossi started to develop his race, closing up comfortably enough then running with the black V5, sometimes pulling alongside at the end of the straight. He pounced into turn one on the 23rd lap, but he wasn't able to escape, with Barros taking his turn to push and probe. He was still right there as they started the last lap.

Then came the crucial move. Rossi led into Honda Hairpin, but Barros saw just enough room inside to go for a block pass. Leaving his braking even later than the champion, he ran alongside and then ahead as they approached the apex. But Barros never made it. Still too fast, he picked the bike up and took to the escape road.

Was it luck or skill that allowed Rossi to follow his usual line, missing his erstwhile rival's back wheel by what looked like inches? Let's just call it superlative judgement and race maturity, and he went on to score a significant personal milestone — his 50th GP victory. They were so far ahead that Barros was able to U-turn and rejoin without losing second place.

No such comfort behind. The first group comprised Ukawa,

250 cc RACE — 25 laps

The race that decided the title was between just two men. Nieto's ninth pole came at the end of a slow-paced 250 practice, with Melandri just two-tenths away. Porto was close; Elias was fourth, but somewhat downbeat after a high-speed crash on Saturday. Two rows back, Leon Haslam was tenth, his best-yet qualifying.

Elias led away, but Melandri was ahead by the end of the lap, and halfway round the next Elias let Nieto past. From then on the rivals pulled steadily away, Nieto making the occasional attack, only for Melandri to pass him straight back. The Italian wasn't up for being managed, or forced into any error.

After the midway point, Nieto tried other tactics, passing firmly then trying to get away. Again, it was in vain. Melandri could follow his every move.

With three to go, Nieto let him past again, dogging his tracks. 'I didn't want to lead the start of the last lap,' he explained. He held off his final attack until after Honda Hairpin, pushing past into the next turn, Siberia, overlooking the sea. Melandri forced straight back past into the next right, then Nieto led into the next left. The Spaniard led the final dive down the hill into the tight MG corner. The last hard braking of the lap was enough for Melandri to dive inside firmly, the power of his factory Aprilia enough to thwart Nieto's attempt to draft past over the line. He won the title like a champion, the youngest ever in the 250 class.

The battle for third also lasted to the very finish. Rolfo had caught and passed Elias after four laps, with Porto logging on directly. Locatelli might have made the trio a quartet, but he slid off on lap six. After half-distance, Elias lost touch; Porto just stuck there and waited until the last lap before pouncing on the Honda for a fifth podium finish in the last seven races.

De Puniet had passed Battaini, and the pair closed quickly on Elias. The Frenchman got ahead but also fell victim to a last-lap pass; Battaini was a couple of seconds back. Checa had escaped from his group, with Debon following on. Stoner was four seconds adrift after an up-and-down home GP. He'd been caught and passed by Aoki and Hules, locked in combat, but managed to close up again and escape for tenth.

Alzamora was a lone and lacklustre 13th, ahead of a furious privateer battle. Vincent had crashed out of the thick of it at MG, lucky not to cause a major pile-up. Matsudo beat Yuzy over the line, with Heidolf, Smrz and Haslam inches behind, but out of the points.

Above: Grim-faced, Nieto joins new 250 champion Melandri on the box.

Opposite page: Two-strokes were cannon fodder for the four-strokes on the straight. Here Ukawa leads van den Goorbergh's two-stroke Honda, Kato catching up fast, followed by McCoy, Roberts and the rest.

Opposite page, bottom left: Biaggi and Aoki — their battle was spectacular, even if the final result was predestined.

Bottom: Melandri in control, ahead of Elias and Nieto.

All photographs: Gold & Goose

Kato and van den Goorbergh, with the four-strokes galloping away down the straight, the flying Dutchman passing Kato straight back in the first corner or two. He never did get ahead of Ukawa, and significantly enough Kato led over the line pretty much every time. Including the 27th, consigning van den Goorbergh to a year's-best fifth. It was an object lesson in the ultimate value of horsepower.

McCoy and Roberts lost touch early, but remained close, Roberts lacking the drive and control he needed to use his extra speed. By lap six, Biaggi and Aoki had got past a soon-to-fade Gibernau, and latched on behind, joined after one-third distance also by Jacque.

McCoy was leading the group on lap 13, but pitted next time round for a new rear tyre, the first one having proved wanting. The same tyre then saw him do his fastest laps of the race. 'The first must have been the bad one in the batch,' he said.

By now, Aoki was measuring himself off Biaggi, and was to lead him over the line on four occasions in their sustained battle. 'Many risks, very hard riding,' said Aoki later. It took them two laps to get past Roberts, and to pull away ahead, with the inevitable final result. Horsepower again.

Jacque had meantime been shadowing Roberts, lining up to pass him over the line (just as he'd won the 250 title here two years previously), and succeeding again.

McWilliams had a frustrating afternoon. Slow off the line from pole, he was 14th on lap one and charging through when trouble from his still-cool carbon brakes saw him run off at Honda Hairpin. He rejoined last, and set furious lap times close to those of the leaders as he pulled through to tenth.

His last victim had been the still off-form Checa; then Nakano, Gibernau, Harada and Cardoso for the final points. Hopkins had been with them, but again slipped off and remounted, just in time to repass Pitt's Kawasaki over the line by two-hundredths. Capirossi was an early retirement, likewise Laconi and wild card Itoh.

Right: Body language speaks volumes in the 125 battle — Pedrosa heads de Angelis, Poggiali, Vincent and Sanna, Cecchinello obscured.

Below: Another reshuffle, and now Poggiali heads Cecchinello, Pedrosa, Sanna and Vincent.
Both photographs: Gold & Goose

125 cc **RACE — 23 laps**

Vincent wasn't even in the top ten in practice, until the closing minutes, when he zipped into second, next to rival Poggiali. De Angelis and Jenkner completed row one; Pedrosa was battling ill-handling, on row three.

A group of nine led away at a good pace, with Olivé and Dovizioso getting left behind after six laps. The remaining seven laid on a fearsome spectacle — three- and four-abreast into corners, drafting on the straights, the lead swapping back and forth.

Pedrosa was the first leader, then Sanna and Poggiali, with Cecchinello taking over for a long spell. Vincent led for the one and only time over the line at the halfway point, but his bike was plainly lacking top speed, and he was having to ride like the devil. Then Cecchinello took control.

De Angelis, a consistent challenger, slowed and pulled off with eight laps left; soon afterwards Nieto had caught up to take his place, and he was among those challenging for the lead on the last lap.

Poggiali's bike was fast, his tactics strong. He pounced on Cecchinello with half a lap to go, and held on to the finish. Nieto was third.

Vincent's group seemed out of touch, but a cavalier last lap brought him back and he was just short of drafting past Nieto over the line. Pedrosa had come with him, the first five crossing the line in less than six-tenths of a second. Whew.

Sanna slowed towards the finish, but was well clear of Jenkner, who had in turn escaped from Azuma, Olivé and Dovizioso.

One more race would settle the title. Vincent still led and Pedrosa's chances were spent, but Poggiali's fourth at Malaysia and a fine win here had brought him to within just eight points.

FIM WORLD CHAMPIONSHIP

SKYY VODKA AUSTRALIAN grand prix

round 15

20 OCTOBER 2002

PHILLIP ISLAND

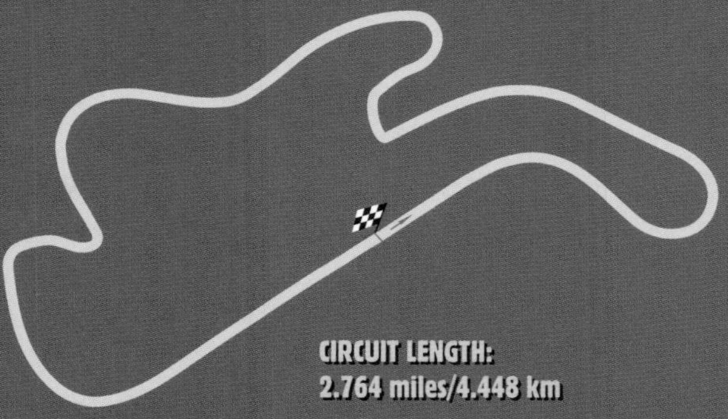

CIRCUIT LENGTH:
2.764 miles/4.448 km

MotoGP

27 laps, 74.628 miles/120.096 km

Pos.	Rider (Nat.)	No.	Machine	Laps	Time & speed
1	Valentino Rossi (I)	46	Honda	27	42m 02.041s 106.519 mph/ 171.426 km/h
2	Alex Barros (BR)	4	Honda	27	42m 11.823s
3	Tohru Ukawa (J)	11	Honda	27	42m 13.175s
4	Daijiro Kato (J)	74	Honda	27	42m 13.368s
5	Jurgen van den Goorbergh (NL)	17	Honda	27	42m 13.455s
6	Max Biaggi (I)	3	Yamaha	27	42m 22.978s
7	Nobuatsu Aoki (J)	9	Proton KR	27	42m 24.546s
8	Olivier Jacque (F)	19	Yamaha	27	42m 28.683s
9	Kenny Roberts (USA)	10	Suzuki	27	42m 28.733s
10	Jeremy McWilliams (GB)	99	Proton KR	27	42m 34.035s
11	Carlos Checa (E)	7	Yamaha	27	42m 36.604s
12	Sete Gibernau (E)	15	Suzuki	27	42m 40.868s
13	Shinya Nakano (J)	56	Yamaha	27	42m 47.459s
14	Tetsuya Harada (J)	31	Honda	27	42m 54.583s
15	José Luis Cardoso (E)	30	Yamaha	27	42m 54.806s
16	John Hopkins (USA)	21	Yamaha	27	43m 14.210s
17	Andrew Pitt (AUS)	84	Kawasaki	27	43m 14.237s
18	Garry McCoy (AUS)	8	Yamaha	26	42m 02.526s
	Shinichi Itoh (J)	72	Honda	11	DNF
	Regis Laconi (F)	55	Aprilia	10	DNF
	Loris Capirossi (I)	65	Honda	2	DNF
	Norick Abe (J)	6	Yamaha		DNS

Fastest lap: Rossi, 1m 32.233s, 107.877 mph/173.612 km/h (record).

Previous record: Kenny Roberts, USA (Suzuki), 1m 32.743s, 107.284 mph/ 172.657 km/h (1999).

Event best maximum speed: Rossi, 201.0 mph/323.5 km/h (qualifying practice no. 1).

Qualifying: 1 McWilliams, 1m 31.919s; 2 McCoy, 1m 32.325s; 3 Aoki, 1m 32.477s; 4 van den Goorbergh, 1m 32.509s; 5 Barros, 1m 32.572s; 6 Ukawa, 1m 32.592s; 7 Rossi, 1m 32.849s; 8 Biaggi, 1m 32.889s; 9 Capirossi, 1m 32.918s; 10 Kato, 1m 32.927s; 11 Laconi, 1m 32.927s; 12 Roberts, 1m 33.116s; 13 Itoh, 1m 33.160s; 14 Hopkins, 1m 33.424s; 15 Gibernau, 1m 33.433s; 16 Nakano, 1m 33.471s; 17 Jacque, 1m 33.565s; 18 Harada, 1m 33.572s; 19 Pitt, 1m 33.842s; 20 Checa, 1m 33.848s; 21 Cardoso, 1m 34.447s; 22 Abe, 1m 35.317s.

Fastest race laps: 1 Rossi, 1m 32.233s; 2 Barros, 1m 32.377s; 3 McCoy, 1m 32.877s; 4 Kato, 1m 33.015s; 5 van den Goorbergh, 1m 33.016s; 6 Ukawa, 1m 33.116s; 7 Jacque, 1m 33.152s; 8 McWilliams, 1m 33.203s; 9 Biaggi, 1m 33.264s; 10 Aoki, 1m 33.291s; 11 Roberts, 1m 33.491s; 12 Gibernau, 1m 33.519s; 13 Itoh, 1m 33.795s; 14 Checa, 1m 33.819s; 15 Harada, 1m 33.829s; 16 Nakano, 1m 33.961s; 17 Laconi, 1m 34.055s; 18 Cardoso, 1m 34.274s; 19 Hopkins, 1m 34.351s; 20 Pitt, 1m 34.864s; 21 Capirossi, 1m 35.495s.

World Championship: 1 Rossi, 335; 2 Biaggi, 199; 3 Ukawa, 198; 4 Barros, 179; 5 Checa, 141; 6 Abe, 123; 7 Capirossi, 109; 8 Kato, 104; 9 Roberts, 99; 10 Jacque, 74; 11 Aoki, 63; 12 Nakano, 58; 13 Hopkins, 53; 14 McWilliams and van den Goorbergh, 51; 16 Gibernau, 48; 17 Harada, 45; 18 Ryo, 41; 19 Laconi and McCoy, 33; 21 Itoh, 13; 22 Hofmann, 11; 23 Cardoso, 9; 24 Bayle, 5; 25 Riba and Yoshikawa, 4.

250 cc

25 laps, 69.100 miles/111.200 km

Pos.	Rider (Nat.)	No.	Machine	Laps	Time & speed
1	Marco Melandri (I)	3	Aprilia	25	39m 44.293s 104.327 mph/ 167.898 km/h
2	Fonsi Nieto (E)	10	Aprilia	25	39m 44.300s
3	Sebastian Porto (ARG)	9	Yamaha	25	39m 50.059s
4	Roberto Rolfo (I)	4	Honda	25	40m 00.335s
5	Toni Elias (E)	24	Aprilia	25	40m 03.210s
6	Randy de Puniet (F)	17	Aprilia	25	40m 03.278s
7	Franco Battaini (I)	21	Aprilia	25	40m 05.642s
8	David Checa (E)	42	Aprilia	25	40m 23.875s
9	Alex Debon (E)	6	Aprilia	25	40m 30.523s
10	Casey Stoner (AUS)	27	Aprilia	25	40m 34.938s
11	Haruchika Aoki (J)	11	Honda	25	40m 39.561s
12	Jaroslav Hules (CZ)	13	Yamaha	25	40m 39.581s
13	Emilio Alzamora (E)	7	Honda	25	40m 51.684s
14	Naoki Matsudo (J)	8	Yamaha	25	40m 53.858s
15	Shahrol Yuzy (MAL)	18	Yamaha	25	40m 54.266s
16	Dirk Heidolf (D)	28	Aprilia	25	40m 54.563s
17	Jakub Smrz (CZ)	96	Honda	25	40m 54.661s
18	Leon Haslam (GB)	19	Honda	25	40m 55.259s
19	Hector Faubel (E)	32	Aprilia	25	41m 09.534s
20	Russell Holland (AUS)	79	Yamaha	24	40m 07.758s
	Raul Jara (E)	22	Aprilia	19	DNF
	Jay Vincent (GB)	12	Honda	16	DNF
	Roberto Locatelli (I)	15	Aprilia	5	DNF
	Erwan Nigon (F)	36	Aprilia	3	DNF
	Hugo Marchand (F)	51	Aprilia		DNS
	Mark Stanley (AUS)	81	Honda		DNQ
	Earl Lynch (AUS)	80	Yamaha		DNQ
	Peter Taplin (AUS)	78	Honda		DNQ

Fastest lap: Melandri, 1m 34.072s, 105.769 mph/170.218 km/h.

Lap record: Valentino Rossi, I (Aprilia), 1m 33.556s, 106.352 mph/171.157 km/h (1999).

Event best maximum speed: Melandri, 173.9 mph/279.9 km/h (qualifying practice no. 1).

Qualifying: 1 Nieto, 1m 33.904s; 2 Melandri, 1m 34.096s; 3 Porto, 1m 34.336s; 4 Elias, 1m 34.507s; 5 de Puniet, 1m 34.554s; 6 Battaini, 1m 34.773s; 7 Hules, 1m 35.347s; 8 Debon, 1m 35.487s; 9 Rolfo, 1m 35.590s; 10 Haslam, 1m 35.628s; 11 Alzamora, 1m 35.787s; 12 Checa, 1m 35.866s; 13 Stoner, 1m 35.916s; 14 Locatelli, 1m 36.092s; 15 Aoki, 1m 36.198s; 16 Matsudo, 1m 36.486s; 17 Vincent, 1m 36.519s; 18 Yuzy, 1m 36.939s; 19 Faubel, 1m 37.342s; 20 Nigon, 1m 37.560s; 21 Heidolf, 1m 37.642s; 22 Smrz, 1m 37.840s; 23 Marchand, 1m 37.883s; 24 Jara, 1m 38.149s; 25 Holland, 1m 38.529s; 26 Stanley, 1m 41.439s; 27 Lynch, 1m 41.765s; 28 Taplin, 1m 43.144s.

Fastest race laps: 1 Melandri, 1m 34.072s; 2 Nieto, 1m 34.237s; 3 Rolfo, 1m 34.527s; 4 Porto, 1m 34.857s; 5 Locatelli, 1m 35.189s; 6 de Puniet, 1m 35.213s; 7 Elias, 1m 35.253s; 8 Battaini, 1m 35.531s; 9 Checa, 1m 35.792s; 10 Stoner, 1m 36.207s; 11 Debon, 1m 36.250s; 12 Hules, 1m 36.408s; 13 Aoki, 1m 36.466s; 14 Alzamora, 1m 36.747s; 15 Matsudo, 1m 36.782s; 16 Heidolf, 1m 36.792s; 17 Vincent, 1m 36.955s; 18 Yuzy, 1m 37.065s; 19 Smrz, 1m 37.068s; 20 Haslam, 1m 37.275s; 21 Holland, 1m 37.746s; 22 Faubel, 1m 37.794s; 23 Jara, 1m 38.272s; 24 Nigon, 1m 38.541s.

World Championship: 1 Melandri, 273; 2 Nieto, 241; 3 Rolfo, 199; 4 Elias and Porto, 172; 6 Battaini, 133; 7 Locatelli, 108; 8 de Puniet, 106; 9 Alzamora, 104; 10 Matsudo, 84; 11 Debon and Stoner, 65; 13 Aoki, 54; 14 Yuzy, 53; 15 Checa, 50; 16 Miyazaki, 25; 17 Sakai, 20; 18 Haslam, 19; 19 Heidolf and Waldmann, 17; 21 Takahashi, 16; 22 Vincent, 14; 23 Faubel, 13; 24 Hules and Jara, 11; 26 Aoyama and Kameya, 9; 28 Nigon and Sekiguchi, 7; 30 Garcia, 6; 31 Marchand, Nakasuga and Philippe, 4; 34 Bataille and Yokoe, 2; 36 Smrz, 1.

125 cc

23 laps, 63.572 miles/102.304 km

Pos.	Rider (Nat.)	No.	Machine	Laps	Time & speed
1	Manuel Poggiali (RSM)	1	Gilera	23	38m 09.028s 99.976 mph/ 160.895 km/h
2	Lucio Cecchinello (I)	4	Aprilia	23	38m 09.280s
3	Pablo Nieto (E)	22	Aprilia	23	38m 09.338s
4	Arnaud Vincent (F)	21	Aprilia	23	38m 09.442s
5	Daniel Pedrosa (E)	26	Honda	23	38m 09.603s
6	Simone Sanna (I)	16	Aprilia	23	38m 13.643s
7	Steve Jenkner (D)	17	Aprilia	23	38m 24.889s
8	Masao Azuma (J)	5	Honda	23	38m 29.572s
9	Joan Olivé (E)	25	Honda	23	38m 29.861s
10	Andrea Dovizioso (I)	34	Honda	23	38m 30.196s
11	Andrea Ballerini (I)	50	Aprilia	23	38m 36.040s
12	Stefano Perugini (I)	7	Italjet	23	38m 40.673s
13	Youichi Ui (J)	41	Derbi	23	38m 41.414s
14	Hector Barbera (E)	80	Aprilia	23	38m 47.075s
15	Mirko Giansanti (I)	6	Honda	23	38m 47.145s
16	Gabor Talmacsi (H)	8	Honda	23	38m 47.310s
17	Max Sabbatani (I)	11	Aprilia	23	39m 03.632s
18	Klaus Nöhles (D)	12	Honda	23	39m 05.717s
19	Mattia Angeloni (I)	31	Gilera	23	39m 05.889s
20	Alex Baldolini (I)	19	Aprilia	23	39m 06.169s
21	Noboru Ueda (J)	9	Honda	23	39m 06.176s
22	Chaz Davies (GB)	57	Aprilia	23	39m 36.706s
23	Imre Toth (H)	20	Honda	23	39m 40.625s
24	Dario Giuseppetti (D)	72	Honda	23	39m 40.881s
25	Joshua Waters (AUS)	83	Honda	22	38m 53.918s
26	Peter Holmes (AUS)	64	Honda	22	39m 16.064s
27	Jeremy Crowe (AUS)	82	Honda	22	39m 40.288s
	Jorge Lorenzo (E)	48	Derbi	18	DNF
	Michel Fabrizio (I)	84	Gilera	18	DNF
	Alex de Angelis (RSM)	15	Aprilia	15	DNF
	Mika Kallio (SF)	36	Honda	14	DNF
	Thomas Luthi (CH)	77	Honda	7	DNF
	Gino Borsoi (I)	23	Aprilia	6	DNF
	Christian Pistoni (I)	42	Italjet	6	DNF
	Stefano Bianco (I)	33	Aprilia	0	DNF
	Marco Simoncelli (I)	37	Aprilia	0	DNF
	Tim Inkster (AUS)	81	Honda		DNQ

Fastest lap: Pedrosa, 1m 37.983s, 101.547 mph/163.424 km/h (record).

Previous record: Marco Melandri, I (Honda), 1m 38.118s, 101.407 mph/163.199 km/h (1999).

Event best maximum speed: Cecchinello, 151.1 mph/243.2 km/h (qualifying practice no. 1).

Qualifying: 1 Poggiali, 1m 38.632s; 2 Vincent, 1m 38.889s; 3 de Angelis, 1m 38.903s; 4 Jenkner, 1m 38.926s; 5 Cecchinello, 1m 39.223s; 6 Nieto, 1m 39.296s; 7 Sanna, 1m 39.334s; 8 Bianco, 1m 39.369s; 9 Dovizioso, 1m 39.498s; 10 Pedrosa, 1m 39.618s; 11 Kallio, 1m 39.632s; 12 Ballerini, 1m 39.685s; 13 Perugini, 1m 39.709s; 14 Ui, 1m 39.868s; 15 Borsoi, 1m 39.960s; 16 Olivé, 1m 40.076s; 17 Azuma, 1m 40.326s; 18 Simoncelli, 1m 40.335s; 19 Barbera, 1m 40.715s; 20 Talmacsi, 1m 40.985s; 21 Sabbatani, 1m 40.998s; 22 Lorenzo, 1m 41.059s; 23 Fabrizio, 1m 41.071s; 24 Giansanti, 1m 41.138s; 25 Nöhles, 1m 41.415s; 26 Ueda, 1m 41.613s; 27 Angeloni, 1m 41.716s; 28 Baldolini, 1m 41.884s; 29 Davies, 1m 42.417s; 30 Toth, 1m 42.862s; 31 Luthi, 1m 43.039s; 32 Waters, 1m 44.031s; 33 Giuseppetti, 1m 44.322s; 34 Pistoni, 1m 44.437s; 35 Holmes, 1m 45.444s; 36 Crowe, 1m 45.513s; 37 Inkster, 1m 54.543s.

Fastest race laps: 1 Pedrosa, 1m 37.983s; 2 Vincent, 1m 38.040s; 3 Nieto, 1m 38.239s; 4 Poggiali, 1m 38.330s; 5 Cecchinello, 1m 38.443s; 6 de Angelis, 1m 38.490s; 7 Sanna, 1m 38.517s; 8 Olivé, 1m 38.666s; 9 Jenkner, 1m 38.673s; 10 Perugini, 1m 39.195s; 11 Azuma, 1m 39.238s; 12 Dovizioso, 1m 39.250s; 13 Talmacsi, 1m 39.443s; 14 Ballerini, 1m 39.461s; 15 Kallio, 1m 39.677s; 16 Giansanti, 1m 39.868s; 17 Barbera, 1m 39.883s; 18 Borsoi, 1m 40.074s; 19 Ui, 1m 40.105s; 20 Fabrizio, 1m 40.345s; 21 Nöhles, 1m 40.525s; 22 Baldolini, 1m 40.579s; 23 Ueda, 1m 40.591s; 24 Lorenzo, 1m 40.637s; 25 Angeloni, 1m 40.693s; 26 Sabbatani, 1m 40.723s; 27 Davies, 1m 41.806s; 28 Giuseppetti, 1m 41.861s; 29 Toth, 1m 41.908s; 30 Waters, 1m 42.045s; 31 Luthi, 1m 42.531s; 32 Pistoni, 1m 43.637s; 33 Holmes, 1m 45.022s; 34 Crowe, 1m 46.684s.

World Championship: 1 Vincent, 253; 2 Poggiali, 245; 3 Pedrosa, 218; 4 Cecchinello, 172; 5 Jenkner, 157; 6 Nieto, 129; 7 Sanna, 104; 8 Azuma, 101; 9 Kallio, 78; 10 Borsoi, 76; 11 de Angelis, 74; 12 Olivé, 69; 13 Ui, 65; 14 Dovizioso and Giansanti, 42; 16 Barbera, 40; 17 Perugini, 28; 18 Ballerini, 22; 19 Aoyama, Bianco and Lorenzo, 21; 22 Talmacsi, 19; 23 Ueda, 18; 24 Rodriguez, 17; 25 Nöhles, 15; 26 Sabbatani, 12; 27 Luthi, 7; 28 Nakajoh, 6; 29 Davies, 5; 30 Fabrizio and Pistoni, 4; 32 Simoncelli and Smrz, 3; 34 Baldolini, Lai, Pellino and Simon, 2.

Left: Barros gets a drenching from defeated rivals Rossi and Biaggi, after a second win in four races.

Below, from top: A capacity crowd put more than 120,000 in the grandstands for the third GP in Spain; Arnaud Vincent — proud and worthy first French 125 champion; Pitt claimed first points for Kawasaki.

Bottom, left to right: New boys in town — Nicky Hayden with mentor Mick Doohan, Colin Edwards, and Troy Bayliss demonstrating his new GP Ducati.

All photographs: Gold & Goose

VALENCIA GP

SPAIN is different. Even from itself. This was clear at a spectacular race-eve ceremony, in the cramped town square of nearby Cheste. A ceremonial burning of effigies, to be precise... but not (as elsewhere) of hated enemies, in the usual way. This was 'la Falla', a very Valencian tradition, wherein the effigies are little short of art works in their own right, and the subjects are heroes rather than villains.

It was sponsors Telefónica MoviStar who commissioned a noted practitioner of the art to make not just caricatures of their 2002 riders — Roberts, Gibernau, Nieto, Elias, Pedrosa and Olivé — but also team managers, all surmounted by a giant model of a racing bike. The whole thing stood two or more storeys high, and as the crowd pressed in to see the stars themselves floodlit on the balcony, it went up at a speed not far short of explosive, singeing eyebrows and driving the pressing multitude back.

It was also a farewell party. The sponsors announced their plans during the weekend to move from Suzuki to the Gresini Honda team, with Kato joined by Gibernau on V5 Hondas. They were expected also to continue backing 250 runners Nieto and Elias, but there was no word on the future of the junior team.

This was another part of the long-muddled jigsaw that was taking shape almost as the hours passed at the last race of the year, although contract terms meant some announcements had to wait until Monday morning.

A significant influx of Americans included AMA 250 champion Chuck Sorensen on a wild-card ride, and Kurtis Roberts, networking. Also present and correct, both Colin Edwards and Nicky Hayden, the latter for a 'Howdy Pardner' visit, flying home without testing, the former fighting to restrain himself from confirming that he will ride the Aprilia next year, with Haga his team-mate. Yamaha were biting their tongues, Monday being the day they could confirm Melandri for the factory team, now Fortuna-sponsored; and Barros would be replacing Nakano at Gauloises. Kawasaki also had to wait before announcing they had signed Garry McCoy; Suzuki a bit longer to confirm they had recruited John Hopkins to replace Gibernau, the other rider who had already signed for the now sponsorless WCM team. It was likewise confirmed that Pramac would be joining forces with Sito Pons, with a berth for a second rider on V5 Hondas. Meanwhile KTM announced their immediate entry to the 125 class, and into MotoGP with a V4 in 2005, though there were whispers that the original 2004 target date might see wild-card and other rides.

And Ducati were there, for a race-day public debut of two versions of their Desmosedici V4, outwardly identical, and looking more lithe and stylish on the move than the rather bulbous bodywork that had appeared on a plinth at Mugello. Ridden by Bayliss and tester Guareschi, each bike had a very different sound. Troy's bike had the twin-pulse crankshaft timing, with adjacent cylinders firing simultaneously to replicate not only the power delivery of their 90-degree V-twin, but also the bass-dominated sound. Guareschi's bike was timed for the cylinders to fire 360 degrees apart, and had a snarling howl to chill the blood. They had yet to decide which was the more effective layout, Ducati Corse boss Claudio Domenicali told *MOTOCOURSE*, but the twin-pulse put the engine under more stress, with potentially greater reliability problems.

Over the next three days most of them went testing too: Barros matching his lap time after switching to the Yamaha, but falling off; Capirossi and Bayliss both close on the Desmo Dukes; Gibernau enjoying the uncomplicated feeling of the V5, and so on.

Never before had a new season begun so intensely, so soon after the end of the old one.

Meanwhile, WCM were casting about for replacement riders, including an offer to British Superbike Champion Steve Hislop. How so, without bikes or backing? Because, as Dorna boss Ezpeleta told *MOTOCOURSE* quite unequivocally, although Dorna would not support the troubled franchise-holders financially, they would help with sponsorship or other support 'from our resources. I promise you that WCM will survive,' he said, and the franchise structure with it. 'The franchise system is the biggest value that we have.'

But we get ahead of ourselves. There was a final race to be run, and a last title won. And the smallest class had provided a fine season, full of courage and dastardly deeds. Poggiali's Spanish disqualification for dangerous riding put him in the latter category, thrusting the (relatively) chivalrous loner Arnaud Vincent into the other more noble role, in the eyes of many. The Malaysian contretemps seemed grossly unfair, working in Poggiali's favour this time; but it certainly made for an exciting climax. Pedrosa won his home race, but Vincent's steadfast ride to second meant that he left the field of combat as champion. Natural justice, it seemed, had prevailed; and if attaching floppy rabbit ears to his helmet hardly dignified the occasion, Vincent was a popular winner.

The race marked the end for two distinguished Japanese riders, both 1993 250 champion Tetsuya Harada and long-standing 125 hero Nobbie Ueda confirming this would be their last race. Ueda won the first of 13 GPs at his first attempt in 1991, and was a pioneer of a new breed of multilingual international Japanese riders.

The race brought Kawasaki's first points, the reward for being among only 14 finishers — and nor was Pitt last.

The casualties had started uncomfortably early, when Checa once again messed up on the startline. In Rio he hadn't put the bike in gear, here he stalled it. He was on the second row; by the time the unsighted Cardoso reached him from the fifth row he was doing all of 70 or 80 mph, and rammed him directly from behind. It was one of the worst types of accident, and though Checa stomped off in chagrin, Cardoso slumped awfully limply by the pit wall as the race went on, debris still on the track. Amazingly, he was badly bruised and winded but not otherwise hurt, and later came out to watch the end of the race.

MOTOGP - BARROS • 250 cc - MELANDRI • 125 cc - PEDROSA

Above: Barros stretches them — Rossi and Biaggi in pursuit.

Photograph: Gold & Goose

MOTOGP RACE – 30 laps

Testing here at the start of the year, the two-strokes had outpaced the M1 Yamaha to such an extent that Biaggi had dubbed it 'an embarrassment'. A measure of progress, then, as his vanquisher McCoy went even faster, but Biaggi far outranked the YZR to put the M1 on pole. It was at Barros's expense, with Kato third, and then McCoy.

Checa led row two from Rossi (no fan of a bad-luck track) and Ukawa, the Spaniard hoping for a home revival: instead more opprobrium after his misfortune on the startline. McWilliams closed the second row.

Barros was leading again, from Biaggi, Rossi and Kato as they blasted past the accident scene for the first time, Nakano fifth but already losing ground. One lap later, Rossi was second... and the leading quartet carried on to cross the finish line in the same order, not without high tension and a few changes on the way. Rossi was usually within a second or less of Barros, and after half-distance was starting to push, showing his front wheel under braking and running very close. Towards the end of lap 16 Barros left a little too much room through an ess-bend, and Rossi was leading. He'd done it on purpose, said Barros, and he promptly found a better drive out of the last corner to move ahead again at the end of the front straight.

Rossi was still poised as they started the last lap; Barros outbraked him into the first corner... but he was in too hot, and ran right to the edge of the kerb on the exit. Rossi pulled alongside;

Barros again waited and waited before braking for the next sharp left. This time it came off. He had the line, seized the apex, and went on to beat Rossi fair and square for a second time in four races.

'We worked, but we did not work well,' said Rossi, looking tired. 'But Alex got faster from Friday onwards.'

Biaggi was inexplicably slower than in practice, he said, but his target was a safe finish for second overall, and he got that, with Kato and rival Ukawa trailing in behind.

Nakano dropped to sixth, where he first had to block the persistent McCoy, until the two-stroke defender was called into the pits for a jumped start. Now Gibernau was pressing the Yamaha, but he didn't last long either, running on at turn one with his all-too-familiar difficulty in getting the Suzuki stopped. He managed to avoid falling as he sped across the gravel, rejoining right at the back, continuing only because he couldn't face his team with a non-finish in his last ride. 'They deserved better,' he said.

That was on lap six, and now Roberts started to catch the Japanese rider, closing to within a second before the tyres went down and he started to fall away again. Capirossi was also closing fast, and was past Roberts on lap 19, only to slide off a few turns later. Now the Suzuki started to catch the Yamaha once more. 'I was using different gears and it improved my lap time,' explained Roberts. 'I was getting the taste of passing him and planning for the last lap' when his engine blew up instead.

At the start of the second lap Laconi had run into Aoki at turn one, taking both down and out and leaving McWilliams alone. He gradually closed up on Jacque, losing ground after Capirossi had

blown by, and the Proton was ahead by half-distance, leaving Jacque involved with Abe and van den Goorbergh. Then McWilliams slowed as he ran into chatter and slide problems and the trio caught up. Van den Goorbergh went with McWilliams as he dug a little deeper to move away again. On the last lap the Dutch rider pounced to take the honour of first two-stroke in almost certainly the type's last GP.

Jacque held off Abe; Hopkins was 18 seconds back and complaining of sliding tyres, followed by Pitt's Kawasaki, with Gibernau a lap adrift and Harada 14th after a trip to the pits, last in his final race. Wild card Garcia retired from a position in the points, suffering arm-pump problems before half-distance.

Second was Rossi's best-ever finish at Valencia; and racked up a record points score of 355 for the season.

Above: Thank you, and good night — Biaggi bids farewell to race engineer Fiorenzo Fanali after his last race for Yamaha.

Left: Family portrait — the Barros clan.
Both photographs: Gold & Goose

145

Right: Melandri leads the pack at the start of the 250 race.

Below: An emotional Vincent took the 125 title after a season of constant tension.

Bottom: De Angelis leads Barbera in a teenage frenzy.

All photographs: Gold & Goose

250 cc RACE – 27 laps

Melandri took pole on a Friday time, the crowded track taking the blame for a general dearth of improvement on Saturday. De Puniet ran him close, with Porto alongside and Alzamora finding some home-track stimulus for his second front row this year, with fellow local rider Debon leading row two.

The race was rather dull, the capacity Spanish crowd obliged to watch Melandri moving straight into the lead and staying there all the way to the finish.

Elias had been second and losing ground from the start, but when he gave way to let team-mate Nieto through to attack after four laps, the older rider was in no better state, and fell off another four laps later, close in front of Elias. 'Second was out of the question for me today,' he explained later.

Porto had been fourth at the end of lap one, but broke down before finishing another lap, and the next along were the two NSR Hondas, Rolfo leading Alzamora.

Behind them, de Puniet had come through from a mediocre start, first passing by Matsudo and Debon, and then Locatelli, but he couldn't get close to the Hondas.

On the last lap, Alzamora finally moved on Rolfo, going underneath him under brakes at the first hairpin, to the joy of the packed grandstands. Alas he ran wide on the exit of the turn, and Rolfo went straight back past, to lead him over the line by two-tenths. Alzamora was still on the rostrum, though, for the first time since Jerez, at the other end of the season.

De Puniet was 15 seconds back, then Locatelli, finally seeing off a determined Checa by a couple of tenths. A little way behind, Battaini prevailed over Matsudo and Debon.

Elias? His bike had gone onto one cylinder with eight laps to go, and he'd been dropping back rapidly, lucky to be still tenth at the flag, four seconds ahead of Yuzy. 'I was riding a 125,' he said later.

Aoki beat Stoner this time, Vincent close behind. US champ Sorensen found the pace of the world class impressive, qualifying and finishing last, a lap down.

The only change of significance in the championship was that rookie of the year Elias took fourth overall from non-scorer Porto — by exactly the six points he scored here.

125 cc RACE – 25 laps

The front row could hardly have been closer for the final showdown, Pedrosa taking pole ahead of Poggiali, Nieto and Vincent. With another eight riders within a second, a tough race was guaranteed. But only two men really mattered.

Vincent was in a determined frame of mind, and led away for a blistering first lap, taking three-quarters of a second out of Pedrosa. But the Spanish teenager closed up through Valencia's demented loops and waited two laps before taking the lead.

The pair had already broken away from a brawl, led by Barbera. This was a blow for Poggiali, in the thick of it. He needed to finish at least two places ahead of Vincent. A desperate bid to get ahead took him in too hot, and he lost six places running wide to recover.

Vincent now needed only to finish, and he was happy to follow the neat-riding Pedrosa as they eked tenths from the pack behind. De Angelis took over for a spell, Barbera, Jenkner, Nieto and Borsoi up close. By halfway, Poggiali had worked to the front of the next group, heading Sabbatani, Olivé, Sanna and Cecchinello, but was three seconds adrift of the five-strong battle for third. He never did catch up, though Borsoi came backwards to meet him to promote him to seventh.

Up front, Vincent shadowed the blue Honda, never really trying to overtake, and as Pedrosa crossed the line to claim a third win of the year, he was just one-tenth behind. Job done.

The others brawled to the end, Nieto pushing through over the last few laps to snitch the final rostrum spot by three-tenths from de Angelis, Jenkner less than a tenth behind.

Barbera had also dropped back, while Poggiali had broken free, but he was still eight-tenths behind over the line. Practice crasher Cecchinello overcame pain to move through to eighth, from Olivé, Borsoi and Sabbatani.

Nobbie Ueda crashed out of his last race after three laps, from 23rd position; Ui also crashed out.

FIM WORLD CHAMPIONSHIP

CIRCUITO DE LA COMUNITAT VALENCIANA

MARLBORO
VALENCIA
grand prix

round 16

3 NOVEMBER 2002

CIRCUIT LENGTH: 2.489 miles/4.005 km

MotoGP

30 laps, 74.670 miles/120.150 km

Pos.	Rider (Nat.)	No.	Machine	Laps	Time & speed
1	Alex Barros (BR)	4	Honda	30	47m 22.404s 94.557 mph/ 152.174 km/h
2	Valentino Rossi (I)	46	Honda	30	47m 22.634s
3	Max Biaggi (I)	3	Yamaha	30	47m 37.617s
4	Daijiro Kato (J)	74	Honda	30	47m 44.908s
5	Tohru Ukawa (J)	11	Honda	30	47m 57.569s
6	Shinya Nakano (J)	56	Yamaha	30	48m 12.573s
7	Jurgen van den Goorbergh (NL)	17	Honda	30	48m 26.218s
8	Jeremy McWilliams (GB)	99	Proton KR	30	48m 27.483s
9	Olivier Jacque (F)	19	Yamaha	30	48m 30.716s
10	Norick Abe (J)	6	Yamaha	30	48m 30.716s
11	John Hopkins (USA)	21	Yamaha	30	48m 48.645s
12	Andrew Pitt (AUS)	84	Kawasaki	30	48m 49.831s
13	Sete Gibernau (E)	15	Suzuki	29	47m 30.217s
14	Tetsuya Harada (J)	31	Honda	29	48m 52.938s
	Kenny Roberts (USA)	10	Suzuki	24	DNF
	Loris Capirossi (I)	65	Honda	19	DNF
	David Garcia (E)	29	Proton KR	13	DNF
	Garry McCoy (AUS)	8	Yamaha	6	DNF
	Nobuatsu Aoki (J)	9	Proton KR	1	DNF
	Regis Laconi (F)	55	Aprilia	1	DNF
	José Luis Cardoso (E)	30	Yamaha	0	DNF
	Carlos Checa (E)	7	Yamaha	0	DNF

Fastest lap: Barros, 1m 33.873s, 95.436 mph/153.590 km/h (record).

Previous record: Alex Criville, E (Honda), 1m 36.085s, 93.239 mph/150.054 km/h (2000).

Event best maximum speed: Kato, 191.9 mph/308.9 km/h (race).

Qualifying: 1 Biaggi, 1m 33.211s; 2 Barros, 1m 33.584s; 3 Kato, 1m 33.641s; 4 McCoy, 1m 33.794s; 5 Checa, 1m 33.815s; 6 Rossi, 1m 33.855s; 7 Ukawa, 1m 34.053s; 8 McWilliams, 1m 34.139s; 9 Nakano, 1m 34.177s; 10 Gibernau, 1m 34.242s; 11 Jacque, 1m 34.276s; 12 Capirossi, 1m 34.280s; 13 Laconi, 1m 34.480s; 14 Roberts, 1m 34.525s; 15 van den Goorbergh, 1m 34.536s; 16 Aoki, 1m 34.579s; 17 Hopkins, 1m 35.044s; 18 Pitt, 1m 35.107s; 19 Garcia, 1m 35.186s; 20 Abe, 1m 35.333s; 21 Cardoso, 1m 35.337s; 22 Harada, 1m 35.606s.

Fastest race laps: 1 Barros, 1m 33.873s; 2 Rossi, 1m 34.157s; 3 Biaggi, 1m 34.409s; 4 Kato, 1m 34.641s; 5 Ukawa, 1m 35.042s; 6 Capirossi, 1m 35.234s; 7 Roberts, 1m 35.326s; 8 Jacque, 1m 35.337s; 9 Nakano, 1m 35.342s; 10 Gibernau, 1m 35.376s; 11 McCoy, 1m 35.804s; 12 McWilliams, 1m 35.994s; 13 van den Goorbergh, 1m 36.053s; 14 Abe, 1m 36.083s; 15 Hopkins, 1m 36.400s; 16 Harada, 1m 36.573s; 17 Pitt, 1m 36.784s; 18 Garcia, 1m 36.852s; 19 Aoki, 1m 44.626s; 20 Laconi, 1m 44.973s.

Final World Championship points: see pages 148–149.

250 cc

27 laps, 67.203 miles/108.135 km

Pos.	Rider (Nat.)	No.	Machine	Laps	Time & speed
1	Marco Melandri (I)	3	Aprilia	27	43m 57.812s 91.701 mph/ 147.579 km/h
2	Roberto Rolfo (I)	4	Honda	27	44m 02.130s
3	Emilio Alzamora (E)	7	Honda	27	44m 02.350s
4	Randy de Puniet (F)	17	Aprilia	27	44m 16.026s
5	Roberto Locatelli (I)	15	Aprilia	27	44m 19.802s
6	David Checa (E)	42	Aprilia	27	44m 19.985s
7	Franco Battaini (I)	21	Aprilia	27	44m 24.567s
8	Naoki Matsudo (J)	8	Yamaha	27	44m 24.721s
9	Alex Debon (E)	6	Aprilia	27	44m 24.727s
10	Toni Elias (E)	24	Aprilia	27	44m 30.192s
11	Shahrol Yuzy (MAL)	18	Yamaha	27	44m 34.106s
12	Haruchika Aoki (J)	11	Honda	27	44m 40.691s
13	Casey Stoner (AUS)	27	Aprilia	27	44m 40.701s
14	Jay Vincent (GB)	12	Honda	27	44m 42.754s
15	Hector Faubel (E)	32	Aprilia	27	44m 45.160s
16	Jaroslav Hules (CZ)	13	Yamaha	27	44m 45.661s
17	Leon Haslam (GB)	19	Honda	27	45m 04.662s
18	Angel Rodriguez (E)	74	Aprilia	27	45m 18.088s
19	Dirk Heidolf (D)	28	Aprilia	27	45m 22.301s
20	Erwan Nigon (F)	36	Aprilia	27	45m 25.671s
21	Chuck Sorensen (USA)	90	Aprilia	26	44m 23.367s
	Jakub Smrz (CZ)	96	Honda	26	DNF
	Raul Jara (E)	22	Aprilia	15	DNF
	Fonsi Nieto (E)	10	Aprilia	7	DNF
	Eric Bataille (F)	34	Honda	4	DNF
	Hugo Marchand (F)	51	Aprilia	2	DNF
	Sebastian Porto (ARG)	9	Yamaha	1	DNF
	Luis Castro (E)	39	Yamaha		DNQ

Fastest lap: Melandri, 1m 36.784s, 92.566 mph/148.970 km/h.

Lap record: Shinya Nakano, J (Yamaha), 1m 36.398s, 92.937 mph/149.567 km/h (2000).

Event best maximum speed: Melandri, 162.2 mph/261.1 km/h (qualifying practice no. 2).

Qualifying: 1 Melandri, 1m 35.885s; 2 de Puniet, 1m 35.979s; 3 Porto, 1m 36.415s; 4 Alzamora, 1m 36.459s; 5 Debon, 1m 36.552s; 6 Nieto, 1m 36.593s; 7 Rolfo, 1m 36.635s; 8 Elias, 1m 36.769s; 9 Battaini, 1m 36.827s; 10 Stoner, 1m 36.971s; 11 Checa, 1m 37.097s; 12 Locatelli, 1m 37.099s; 13 Yuzy, 1m 37.355s; 14 Matsudo, 1m 37.425s; 15 Faubel, 1m 37.656s; 16 Aoki, 1m 37.783s; 17 Marchand, 1m 38.351s; 18 Vincent, 1m 38.395s; 19 Hules, 1m 38.644s; 20 Smrz, 1m 38.691s; 21 Haslam, 1m 38.741s; 22 Heidolf, 1m 38.787s; 23 Nigon, 1m 38.839s; 24 Bataille, 1m 39.460s; 25 Jara, 1m 39.649s; 26 Rodriguez, 1m 39.911s; 27 Sorensen, 1m 41.533s; 28 Castro, 1m 43.580s.

Fastest race laps: 1 Melandri, 1m 36.784s; 2 Nieto, 1m 36.888s; 3 Elias, 1m 36.972s; 4 Alzamora, 1m 37.206s; 5 Rolfo, 1m 37.283s; 6 de Puniet, 1m 37.430s; 7 Battaini, 1m 37.561s; 8 Checa, 1m 37.704s; 9 Locatelli, 1m 37.738s; 10 Yuzy, 1m 37.830s; 11 Debon, 1m 37.870s; 12 Matsudo, 1m 37.879s; 13 Vincent, 1m 38.397s; 14 Aoki, 1m 38.457s; 15 Stoner, 1m 38.464s; 16 Faubel, 1m 38.521s; 17 Hules, 1m 38.588s; 18 Bataille, 1m 38.880s; 19 Smrz, 1m 38.908s; 20 Heidolf, 1m 39.133s; 21 Haslam, 1m 39.150s; 22 Rodriguez, 1m 39.688s; 23 Marchand, 1m 39.737s; 24 Nigon, 1m 39.843s; 25 Jara, 1m 41.045s; 26 Sorensen, 1m 41.657s; 27 Porto, 1m 42.628s.

Final World Championship points: see pages 148–149.

125 cc

25 laps, 62.225 miles/100.125 km

Pos.	Rider (Nat.)	No.	Machine	Laps	Time & speed
1	Daniel Pedrosa (E)	26	Honda	25	42m 13.044s 88.420 mph/ 142.299 km/h
2	Arnaud Vincent (F)	21	Aprilia	25	42m 13.144s
3	Pablo Nieto (E)	22	Aprilia	25	42m 15.748s
4	Alex de Angelis (RSM)	15	Aprilia	25	42m 16.113s
5	Steve Jenkner (D)	17	Aprilia	25	42m 16.180s
6	Hector Barbera (E)	80	Aprilia	25	42m 21.085s
7	Manuel Poggiali (RSM)	1	Gilera	25	42m 21.896s
8	Lucio Cecchinello (I)	4	Aprilia	25	42m 24.923s
9	Joan Olivé (E)	25	Honda	25	42m 25.081s
10	Gino Borsoi (I)	23	Aprilia	25	42m 27.801s
11	Max Sabbatani (I)	11	Aprilia	25	42m 28.211s
12	Andrea Ballerini (I)	50	Aprilia	25	42m 31.516s
13	Stefano Bianco (I)	33	Aprilia	25	42m 31.558s
14	Simone Sanna (I)	16	Aprilia	25	42m 31.848s
15	Gabor Talmacsi (H)	8	Honda	25	42m 36.738s
16	Mika Kallio (SF)	36	Honda	25	42m 36.770s
17	Andrea Dovizioso (I)	34	Honda	25	42m 36.826s
18	Masao Azuma (J)	5	Honda	25	42m 37.002s
19	Mirko Giansanti (I)	6	Honda	25	42m 37.154s
20	Michel Fabrizio (I)	84	Gilera	25	43m 07.394s
21	Klaus Nöhles (D)	12	Honda	25	43m 11.619s
22	Jorge Lorenzo (E)	48	Derbi	25	43m 11.960s
23	Alvaro Bautista (E)	51	Aprilia	25	43m 12.330s
24	Thomas Luthi (CH)	77	Honda	25	43m 23.065s
25	Imre Toth (H)	20	Honda	25	43m 23.199s
26	Ruben Catalan (E)	71	Aprilia	25	43m 29.169s
27	Dario Giuseppetti (D)	72	Honda	25	43m 29.182s
28	Chaz Davies (GB)	57	Aprilia	25	43m 33.102s
29	Vincent Braillard (CH)	59	Honda	24	43m 49.093s
	Stefano Perugini (I)	7	Italjet	22	DNF
	Mattia Angeloni (I)	31	Gilera	20	DNF
	Julian Simon (E)	52	Honda	18	DNF
	Alex Baldolini (I)	19	Aprilia	13	DNF
	Youichi Ui (J)	41	Derbi	10	DNF
	Christian Pistoni (I)	42	Italjet	9	DNF
	Chris Peris (CAN)	98	Aprilia	9	DNF
	Noboru Ueda (J)	9	Honda	3	DNF
	Marco Simoncelli (I)	37	Aprilia	3	DNF

Fastest lap: Jenkner, 1m 40.252s, 89.364 mph/143.817 km/h (record).

Previous record: Youichi Ui, J (Derbi), 1m 40.631s, 89.027 mph/143.275 km/h (2000).

Event best maximum speed: Cecchinello, 140.5 mph/226.1 km/h (race).

Qualifying: 1 Pedrosa, 1m 39.426s; 2 Poggiali, 1m 39.547s; 3 Nieto, 1m 39.590s; 4 Vincent, 1m 39.600s; 5 de Angelis, 1m 39.819s; 6 Barbera, 1m 39.916s; 7 Jenkner, 1m 40.000s; 8 Borsoi, 1m 40.058s; 9 Ballerini, 1m 40.190s; 10 Kallio, 1m 40.322s; 11 Talmacsi, 1m 40.337s; 12 Olivé, 1m 40.421s; 13 Sabbatani, 1m 40.506s; 14 Dovizioso, 1m 40.565s; 15 Sanna, 1m 40.602s; 16 Ui, 1m 40.611s; 17 Giansanti, 1m 40.676s; 18 Cecchinello, 1m 40.989s; 19 Azuma, 1m 41.136s; 20 Bianco, 1m 41.138s; 21 Ueda, 1m 41.412s; 22 Simon, 1m 41.416s; 23 Angeloni, 1m 41.441s; 24 Simoncelli, 1m 41.460s; 25 Fabrizio, 1m 41.511s; 26 Lorenzo, 1m 41.566s; 27 Perugini, 1m 41.720s; 28 Bautista, 1m 41.746s; 29 Baldolini, 1m 41.879s; 30 Nöhles, 1m 41.888s; 31 Davies, 1m 42.408s; 32 Catalan, 1m 42.632s; 33 Toth, 1m 42.691s; 34 Giuseppetti, 1m 42.758s; 35 Luthi, 1m 42.861s; 36 Pistoni, 1m 44.581s; 37 Braillard, 1m 45.878s; 38 Peris, 1m 46.223s.

Fastest race laps: 1 Jenkner, 1m 40.252s; 2 de Angelis, 1m 40.392s; 3 Pedrosa, 1m 40.413s; 4 Vincent, 1m 40.433s; 5 Nieto, 1m 40.629s; 6 Borsoi, 1m 40.676s; 7 Barbera, 1m 40.686s; 8 Poggiali, 1m 40.771s; 9 Sabbatani, 1m 40.800s; 10 Cecchinello, 1m 40.825s; 11 Sanna, 1m 40.902s; 12 Olivé, 1m 40.945s; 13 Giansanti, 1m 40.953s; 14 Bianco, 1m 41.058s; 15 Dovizioso, 1m 41.068s; 16 Ballerini, 1m 41.172s; 17 Azuma, 1m 41.197s; 18 Talmacsi, 1m 41.322s; 19 Kallio, 1m 41.429s; 20 Fabrizio, 1m 42.006s; 21 Ui, 1m 42.030s; 22 Nöhles, 1m 42.107s; 23 Perugini, 1m 42.117s; 24 Angeloni, 1m 42.149s; 25 Lorenzo, 1m 42.292s; 26 Bautista, 1m 42.443s; 27 Toth, 1m 42.695s; 28 Simon, 1m 42.707s; 29 Luthi, 1m 42.836s; 30 Simoncelli, 1m 43.050s; 31 Catalan, 1m 43.070s; 32 Davies, 1m 43.077s; 33 Giuseppetti, 1m 43.180s; 34 Baldolini, 1m 43.199s; 35 Ueda, 1m 43.261s; 36 Pistoni, 1m 44.757s; 37 Peris, 1m 47.372s; 38 Braillard, 1m 47.535s.

Final World Championship points: see pages 148–149.

RESULTS 2002

Photograph: Gold & Goose

MotoGP

Position	Rider	Nationality	Machine	Japan	South Africa	Spain	France	Italy	Catalunya	Netherlands	Great Britain	Germany	Czech Republic	Portugal	Rio	Pacific	Malaysia	Australia	Valencia	Points total
1	Valentino Rossi	I	Honda	25	20	25	25	25	25	25	25	25	–	25	25	20	20	25	20	355
2	Max Biaggi	I	Yamaha	–	7	–	16	20	13	13	20	20	25	10	20	–	25	10	16	215
3	Tohru Ukawa	J	Honda	–	25	16	20	16	20	11	–	16	16	16	–	13	13	16	11	209
4	Alex Barros	BR	Honda	10	–	11	8	11	11	20	16	–	7	11	13	25	16	20	25	204
5	Carlos Checa	E	Yamaha	16	11	–	–	13	16	16	–	13	11	20	–	11	9	5	–	141
6	Norick Abe	J	Yamaha	11	9	10	13	9	–	7	13	10	8	9	10	8	6	–	6	129
7	Daijiro Kato	J	Honda	6	13	20	–	–	8	4	9	–	20	–	–	–	11	13	13	117
8	Loris Capirossi	I	Honda	7	16	13	9	10	10	–	–	–	10	–	11	16	7	–	–	109
9	Kenny Roberts	USA	Suzuki	–	–	8	11	–	9	10	2	–	5	13	16	10	8	7	–	99
10	Olivier Jacque	F	Yamaha	–	10	5	–	7	7	2	11	–	6	–	9	9	–	8	7	81
11	Shinya Nakano	J	Yamaha	–	8	–	3	5	–	8	6	11	–	4	–	–	10	3	10	68
12	Nobuatsu Aoki	J	Proton KR	9	–	9	10	–	–	–	–	7	8	–	–	4	7	–	9	63
13	Jurgen van den Goorbergh	NL	Honda	–	5	4	1	2	–	6	1	4	4	–	7	3	3	11	9	60
14	Jeremy McWilliams	GB	Proton KR	–	–	–	6	–	4	–	–	9	9	7	–	6	4	6	8	59
15	John Hopkins	USA	Yamaha	4	2	3	5	4	6	9	8	–	–	8	2	2	–	–	5	58
16	Sete Gibernau	E	Suzuki	–	–	7	4	–	–	–	10	–	13	–	8	–	2	4	3	51
17	Tetsuya Harada	J	Honda	5	4	6	–	6	3	3	5	–	1	6	3	1	–	2	2	47
18	Akira Ryo	J	Suzuki	20	–	–	–	–	5	1	3	5	2	–	–	–	5	–	–	41
19 =	Regis Laconi	F	Aprilia	8	1	2	7	8	2	–	–	–	–	–	5	–	–	–	–	33
19 =	Garry McCoy	AUS	Yamaha	–	6	1	–	–	–	–	4	7	3	5	6	–	1	–	–	33
21	Shinichi Itoh	J	Honda	13	–	–	–	–	–	–	–	–	–	–	–	–	–	–	–	13
22	Alex Hofmann	D	Yamaha	–	–	–	–	–	–	5	–	6	–	–	–	–	–	–	–	11
23	José Luis Cardoso	E	Yamaha	–	–	–	–	–	–	–	–	3	–	5	–	–	1	–	–	9
24	Jean-Michel Bayle	F	Yamaha	–	–	–	2	3	–	–	–	–	–	–	–	–	–	–	–	5
25 =	Andrew Pitt	AUS	Kawasaki	–	–	–	–	–	–	–	–	–	–	–	–	–	–	4	–	4
25 =	Pere Riba	E	Yamaha	–	3	–	–	–	1	–	–	–	–	–	–	–	–	–	–	4
25 =	Wataru Yoshikawa	J	Yamaha	–	–	–	–	–	–	–	–	–	–	–	–	–	4	–	–	4

250cc

Position	Rider	Nationality	Machine	Japan	South Africa	Spain	France	Italy	Catalunya	Netherlands	Great Britain	Germany	Czech Republic	Portugal	Rio	Pacific	Malaysia	Australia	Valencia	Points total
1	Marco Melandri	I	Aprilia	–	25	–	20	25	25	25	25	25	25	20	13	20	–	25	25	298
2	Fonsi Nieto	E	Aprilia	3	16	25	25	16	16	11	20	13	13	25	–	13	25	20	–	241
3	Roberto Rolfo	I	Honda	8	13	20	11	8	20	16	11	20	–	13	20	10	16	13	20	219
4	Toni Elias	E	Aprilia	5	–	6	10	13	6	20	16	10	16	3	11	25	20	11	6	178
5	Sebastian Porto	ARG	Yamaha	11	8	9	8	9	–	13	–	16	20	16	25	8	13	16	–	172
6	Franco Battaini	I	Aprilia	6	20	13	–	10	11	7	13	8	–	–	16	9	11	9	9	142
7	Emilio Alzamora	E	Honda	13	9	16	9	5	7	–	4	–	10	9	11	8	3	16	–	120
8=	Randy de Puniet	F	Aprilia	16	10	–	16	11	13	–	10	–	10	–	–	10	10	13	–	119
8=	Roberto Locatelli	I	Aprilia	–	11	11	13	20	–	9	3	11	9	11	–	7	3	–	11	119
10	Naoki Matsudo	J	Yamaha	10	5	7	5	2	9	2	8	9	8	–	8	–	9	2	8	92
11	Alex Debon	E	Aprilia	7	7	8	7	–	3	4	7	6	3	–	–	6	–	7	7	72
12	Casey Stoner	AUS	Aprilia	–	–	10	–	–	10	8	5	–	11	–	10	–	5	6	3	68
13	David Checa	E	Aprilia	–	6	–	6	6	4	–	1	1	–	8	4	–	6	8	10	60
14=	Haruchika Aoki	J	Honda	–	3	4	–	4	5	10	9	–	7	–	–	3	4	5	4	58
14=	Shahrol Yuzy	MAL	Yamaha	–	–	3	3	7	8	6	6	5	–	–	7	–	7	1	5	58
16	Osamu Miyazaki	J	Yamaha	25	–	–	–	–	–	–	–	–	–	–	–	–	–	–	–	25
17	Daisaku Sakai	J	Honda	20	–	–	–	–	–	–	–	–	–	–	–	–	–	–	–	20
18	Leon Haslam	GB	Honda	–	1	–	–	–	–	–	–	3	–	9	6	–	–	–	–	19
19=	Dirk Heidolf	D	Aprilia	–	2	–	–	–	–	–	–	4	2	7	2	–	–	–	–	17
19=	Ralf Waldmann	D	Aprilia	–	–	–	–	–	–	5	–	7	5	–	–	–	–	–	–	17
21=	Yuki Takahashi	J	Honda	–	–	–	–	–	–	–	–	–	–	–	–	16	–	–	–	16
21=	Jay Vincent	GB	Honda	–	4	–	1	1	–	–	–	2	4	–	–	2	–	2	–	16
23	Hector Faubel	E	Aprilia	–	–	5	2	–	–	–	–	–	–	6	–	–	–	–	1	14
24=	Jaroslav Hules	CZ	Yamaha	–	–	–	–	–	–	–	–	–	–	–	5	1	1	4	–	11
24=	Raul Jara	E	Aprilia	1	–	–	–	–	1	3	–	–	1	5	–	–	–	–	–	11
26=	Hiroshi Aoyama	J	Honda	4	–	–	–	–	–	–	–	–	–	–	–	5	–	–	–	9
26=	Choujun Kameya	J	Honda	9	–	–	–	–	–	–	–	–	–	–	–	–	–	–	–	9
28=	Erwan Nigon	F	Aprilia	–	–	–	–	–	–	–	–	–	–	4	3	–	–	–	–	7
28=	Taro Sekiguchi	J	Yamaha	–	–	1	4	–	–	–	2	–	–	–	–	–	–	–	–	7
30	David Garcia	E	Honda	–	–	–	–	–	–	–	–	–	6	–	–	–	–	–	–	6
31=	Hugo Marchand	F	Aprilia	2	–	–	–	–	2	–	–	–	–	–	–	–	–	–	–	4
31=	Katsuyuki Nakasuga	J	Yamaha	–	–	–	–	–	–	–	–	–	–	–	–	–	4	–	–	4
31=	Vincent Philippe	F	Aprilia	–	–	–	3	–	1	–	–	–	–	–	–	–	–	–	–	4
34=	Eric Bataille	F	Honda	–	2	–	–	–	–	–	–	–	–	–	–	–	–	–	–	2
34=	Ryuji Yokoe	J	Yamaha	–	–	–	–	–	–	–	–	–	–	–	–	2	–	–	–	2
36	Jakub Smrz	CZ	Honda	–	–	–	–	–	–	–	–	–	–	–	1	–	–	–	–	1

125cc

Position	Rider	Nationality	Machine	Japan	South Africa	Spain	France	Italy	Catalunya	Netherlands	Great Britain	Germany	Czech Republic	Portugal	Rio	Pacific	Malaysia	Australia	Valencia	Points total
1	Arnaud Vincent	F	Aprilia	25	20	20	13	7	5	13	25	25	16	25	20	1	25	13	20	273
2	Manuel Poggiali	RSM	Gilera	16	25	–	20	25	25	20	16	13	11	–	16	20	13	25	9	254
3	Daniel Pedrosa	E	Honda	8	16	13	16	13	20	25	20	9	20	6	–	25	16	11	25	243
4	Lucio Cecchinello	I	Aprilia	7	–	25	25	10	13	11	–	–	25	10	6	–	20	20	8	180
5	Steve Jenkner	D	Aprilia	1	13	16	5	8	16	10	11	16	10	16	–	16	10	9	11	168
6	Pablo Nieto	E	Aprilia	–	11	–	10	16	8	9	–	11	–	13	11	13	11	16	16	145
7	Simone Sanna	I	Aprilia	11	8	9	–	5	11	4	–	10	9	20	2	–	5	10	2	106
8	Masao Azuma	J	Honda	–	7	8	11	3	1	2	13	1	4	11	25	–	7	8	–	101
9	Alex de Angelis	RSM	Aprilia	–	10	–	–	9	–	7	9	20	8	–	5	–	6	–	13	87
10	Gino Borsoi	I	Aprilia	6	9	6	6	11	–	3	–	6	7	9	4	9	–	–	6	82
11	Mika Kallio	SF	Honda	–	4	11	8	–	7	–	–	7	6	8	8	10	9	–	–	78
12	Joan Olivé	E	Honda	3	–	7	–	–	10	16	10	5	–	–	8	3	7	7	7	76
13	Youichi Ui	J	Derbi	–	–	10	–	20	–	8	8	8	–	–	–	4	4	3	–	65
14	Hector Barbera	E	Aprilia	–	–	4	1	–	–	–	–	13	–	1	11	8	2	10	–	50
15	Mirko Giansanti	I	Honda	20	–	2	4	–	6	–	1	4	2	–	–	2	–	1	–	42
16	Andrea Dovizioso	I	Honda	–	6	–	7	4	–	5	7	3	–	–	3	–	1	6	–	42
17	Stefano Perugini	I	Italjet	5	–	–	–	1	3	–	5	–	–	–	10	–	–	4	–	28
18	Andrea Ballerini	I	Aprilia	–	2	1	–	6	4	–	4	–	–	–	–	–	–	5	4	26
19	Stefano Bianco	I	Aprilia	–	–	–	9	–	9	–	–	–	3	–	–	–	–	–	3	24
20=	Shuhei Aoyama	J	Honda	10	–	–	–	–	–	6	–	–	–	–	5	–	–	–	–	21
20=	Jorge Lorenzo	E	Derbi	–	–	–	–	2	–	3	–	–	–	9	7	–	–	1	–	21
22	Gabor Talmacsi	H	Honda	–	–	–	–	–	1	–	5	–	13	–	–	–	1	–	–	20
23	Noboru Ueda	J	Honda	13	5	–	–	–	–	–	–	–	–	–	–	–	–	–	–	18
24=	Angel Rodriguez	E	Aprilia	9	–	–	–	–	6	–	2	–	–	–	–	–	–	–	–	17
24=	Max Sabbatani	I	Aprilia	–	3	5	3	–	–	–	–	1	–	–	–	–	–	–	5	17
26	Klaus Nöhles	D	Honda	4	–	–	2	–	–	–	–	–	–	7	–	2	–	–	–	15
27	Thomas Luthi	CH	Honda	–	–	–	–	–	–	–	–	–	–	7	–	–	–	–	–	7
28	Hideyuki Nakajoh	J	Honda	–	–	–	–	–	–	–	–	–	–	–	6	–	–	–	–	6
29	Chaz Davies	GB	Aprilia	–	–	–	–	–	–	–	–	–	–	5	–	–	–	–	–	5
30=	Michel Fabrizio	I	Gilera	–	1	–	–	–	–	–	–	–	–	–	3	–	–	–	–	4
30=	Christian Pistoni	I	Italjet	–	–	–	–	–	–	–	–	–	–	–	4	–	–	–	–	4
32=	Marco Simoncelli	I	Aprilia	–	–	–	–	–	–	–	–	–	–	–	3	–	–	–	–	3
32=	Jakub Smrz	CZ	Honda	–	–	3	–	–	–	–	–	–	–	–	–	–	–	–	–	3
34=	Alex Baldolini	I	Aprilia	2	–	–	–	–	–	–	–	–	–	–	–	–	–	–	–	2
34=	Fabrizio Lai	I	Honda	–	–	–	–	–	–	–	2	–	–	–	–	–	–	–	–	2
34=	Gioele Pellino	I	Aprilia	–	–	–	–	–	2	–	–	–	–	–	–	–	–	–	–	2
34=	Julian Simon	E	Honda	–	–	–	–	–	–	–	–	–	–	–	2	–	–	–	–	2

WORLD SUPERBIKE RACING AT THE CROSSROADS

IT may have only been a two-horse race but the horses were the finest thoroughbreds, from the traditional SBK winners Honda and Ducati, and the riders were the last two World Champions in their own right, Colin Edwards (2000) and Troy Bayliss (2001).

As the balance of race wins between all SBK rivals narrowed to the monochrome spectrum of black or white/Edwards or Bayliss (with only one fiery intermission of the 'Technicolor' Makoto Tamada at Sugo breaking the sequence), the statistics at least start to tell the story of 2002 better than a surfeit of words ever could.

- Bayliss and Edwards were on Michelins, only Tamada gave Dunlop a win all year.
- No four-cylinder rider got on a podium, never mind won a race.
- Bayliss took 13 of his 14 race wins before Laguna Seca.
- Edwards scored nine of his 11 wins from Laguna onwards.
- Edwards took 14 non-winning podiums, while Bayliss took only eight.
- Edwards scored no finish lower than fourth and had a straight 25 race podiums, easily a record.
- Bayliss had one DNF, Edwards none.
- Edwards was the first westerner since the mid-Nineties to win at Sugo.
- Edwards and Bayliss demolished the previous best points scores in a season, both bursting through the 500-point barrier even before the last race of the year.
- Edwards took a record nine consecutive wins at season end, another SBK record.

Moving from the objective to the subjective, it all ended magnificently, with a classic showdown and a subsequent feel-good factor right off the scale. All a far air-horn blast or vee-twin boom from the way the series looked early in the year. With Bayliss cleaning up, scoring double wins at will and his main rival Edwards seemingly helpless to stop him on 90 per cent of occasions, the season looked to be all over by mid-point.

Add in the fact that no one else could reach the class of either top man, and the whole she-bang was spiralling into a dull and soggy abyss, just as MotoGP was exploding in new-found four-stroke sound and glory.

SBK is now at yet another of its many crossroads, stripped of some of its main talents — man and metallic — and facing a thus-far losing battle to make all the factories stick with it until the blanket 1,000 cc limit comes in for the 2004 season, when its relevance to the bike-buying public increases again.

The season's monumental Ben Hur-style climax, on the historic Emilia-Romagna Circus Maximus of Imola, may have salvaged a lacklustre season in the memory of most, but until Edwards's remarkable persistence started to pay off in wins, it all looked pretty thin and wan.

All change at SBK central for next year and how many times have we heard that? Too many for some of the factories it appears in the short term, so roll on 2004.

By GORDON**RITCHIE**

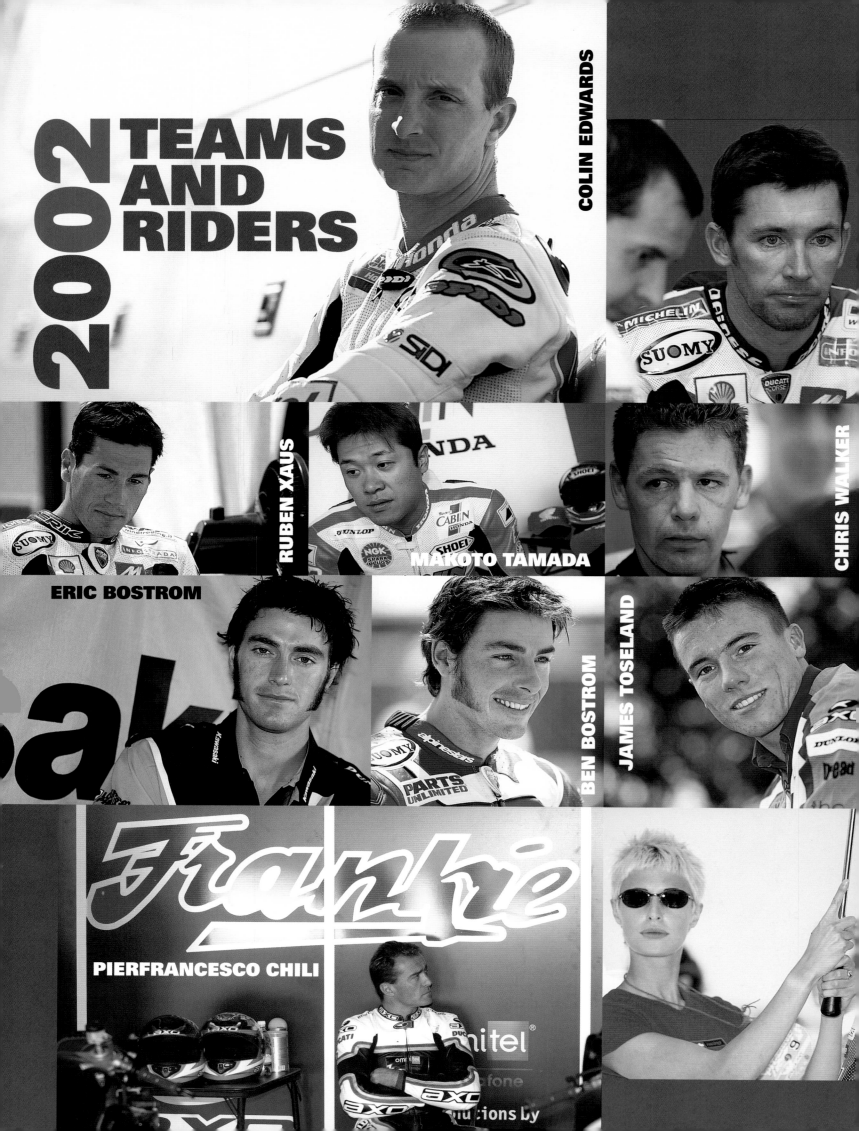

2002 TEAMS AND RIDERS

COLIN EDWARDS

RUBEN XAUS

MAKOTO TAMADA

CHRIS WALKER

ERIC BOSTROM

BEN BOSTROM

JAMES TOSELAND

PIERFRANCESCO CHILI

Frankie

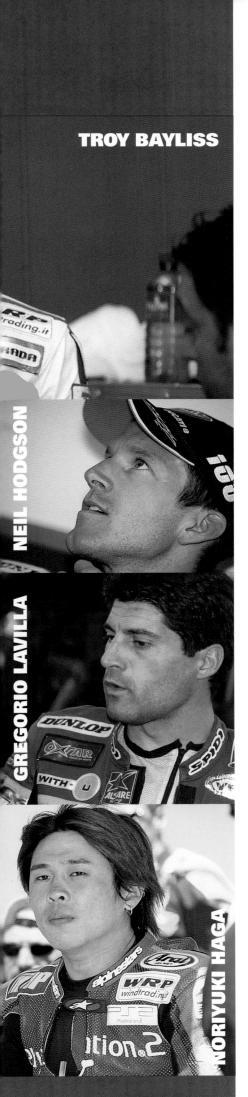

TROY BAYLISS

NEIL HODGSON

GREGORIO LAVILLA

NORIYUKI HAGA

No Yamaha again; Honda, Suzuki and Aprilia factory presence cut to one rider apiece; no Bimota, no Mondial, no Team Foggy machine and most importantly — it bears repeating — no Yamaha again. It was a consistent drop of strength in depth almost across the spectrum for SBK in 2002, and it showed on the grid. Half a production line of good privateer Ducatis filled some gaps but, compared to 2001, the entry was a tad emaciated.

Playstation 2 FGF Aprilia

All change at the coal-face for Aprilia's latest anthracite-coloured challenger. A new FGF acronym hinted at the new status of the team, using full factory equipment in a semi-autonomous outfit run by the previous year's ruling family in the Aprilia pit garage, the Guidottis — Fabrizio, Giacomo and Francesco.

A single-rider team was a disappointment to many, who saw it as some kind of admission of defeat before they had even started, but due to financial constraints, one man it had to be.

The talented but ultimately flawed Noriyuki Haga was always going to be a high-profile, high-risk appointee on a big vee-twin, after spending virtually an entire career on fours and the odd two-stroke.

The gamble didn't quite pay off, with only seven podium finishes on a bike which could claim no huge disadvantages — other than tyre supplier — compared to the Honda or Ducatis.

Benelli Sport

It was one of those years for lone rider Peter Goddard and the three-cylinder Benelli. Missing the season start with problems that had persisted throughout the first half-year of its existence in 2001 was an indication of where it was all going.

Even when they did show up, Goddard never quite overcame the machine's lack of pace to qualify for Superpole, ending the season on a dull note when the machine broke and crashed at home in Imola. They scored points, but the experiment thus far was too little budget, a couple of seasons too late.

Ducati Infostrada

Troy Bayliss and Ruben Xaus were a good-on-paper pairing, especially as Xaus had broken his duck of wins the year previously and Bayliss was a hot favourite to carry on where he left off — before breaking his collarbone at Imola at least.

After winter testing Ducati's choices were still deemed good, with Bayliss really on it. When Xaus wasn't off it he too was on it, although his reputation for crashing would come back to haunt his pre-season dreams.

A mid-season change of sponsor logo, after Wind bought out Infostrada, added some extra colour to the most stable and yet passionate team in the paddock.

The all-new bikes looked pretty much the same as the old ones and, as usual, appeared to smell of victory just sitting still.

Ducati L&M

It looked like Bostrom was a sure thing to challenge the top men on a near-level footing, but with the Dunlops outgripped by Michelin from first to last, and Bostrom unable to come to terms with the even more peaky 2003 Testastretta, he slumped. All that worked for him in 2001 worked against him in 2002, and each race day he disintegrated further as a serious force.

Castrol Honda

Down to one, but in the minds of many, including a forthright Edwards, he frequently felt like a lone gunman anyway, with his most recent team-mates being one stage removed from unwitting patsy status.

The consistent, then astonishingly consistent, and then just plain brilliant performances of Edwards also proved that he had a near-flawless bike and team in 2002, possibly for the first time. Credit should therefore also go to Crew Chief Adrian Gorst and team manager Neil Tuxworth.

Kawasaki Racing Team

All change for the Kawasaki team in 2002, in terms of the riders, the suspension supplier — but not the results. The latter went downhill, a natural result of even better vee-twins for the works and privateer riders.

The riders, Chris Walker and Hitoyasu Izutsu, struggled with injury, illness, and the realisation that it was only a one-year deal anyway, as Kawasaki started work on their MotoGP effort. Everyone tried their best, were occasionally

rewarded with everything but a podium, and even had some positive media exposure when occasional entrant Eric Bostrom came out of the West to play on four occasions.

Team Suzuki Alstare Corona Extra

Another single-rider team taking a few steps back from the abyss that the previous year had offered them. The chasm between the twins and fours made no difference to Kawasaki refugee Gregorio Lavilla, as he swapped the old 'Kwak' for the equally uncompetitive new Suzuki. Lavilla found the same result, tenth overall, and no podiums.

GSE Racing/HM Plant Ducati

Back again as one identical unit for the most part, the HM Plant team brought their knowledge, sometimes hard won in 2001, to bear in efficient fashion for both Neil Hodgson and James Toseland in 2002. Their personal best season performances (on Dunlops remember) were rewards of a kind, but Michelin riders crushed any hopes of a win for Hodgson.

Darrell Healey (Team Principal) and disciplinarian team manager Colin Wright run a tight ship, and again were given the best non-2002 factory kit by Ducati Corse.

OTHER NOTABLE TEAMS

DFX Pirelli Ducati Team
Steve Martin was back again, joined by former Aprilia rider, and the original test pilot on the Aprilia Mille project, Alessandro Antonello.

Ducati NCR
The legendary Pierfrancesco Chili was the lead troubadour in Stefano Caracchi's band of Axo-sponsored wandering desmo minstrels, making sweet and booming vee-twin music, and even a podium finish, by year-end. Accompanying Antipodean protégé Broc Parkes dressed in different clothes, supplied by Parmalat Australia, and had some sweet results at the end of the year.

Team Pedercini
Eponymously operated by top privateer Lucio, it became a three-rider effort in 2002, with the addition of Marco Borciani and Stefano Foti, although Pedercini was still the top jockey.

Pacific Team
Thierry Mulot, veteran of many a campaign, was the chosen rider in 2002, but once more the small team found life tough on a 2000-spec machine and didn't do a full season.

JM SBK Team
Jiri Mrkyvka's team, still running a 1999 machine, had several mechanical problems and was thus ditched from the last round by the scrutineers on safety grounds.

Spaziotel Racing Team
Juan Borja's latest port of call was sponsored by Italian phone money, and it was enough for 2002-spec customer Testastrettas, giving Borja a best of seventh in the rain at Silverstone.

Rumi Castrol Honda
Not to be confused with the big boys at the posh end of the points table, the near-stock VTR of Heckles was regularly one of the slowest things through the radar traps, and Mark and his machine parted company on several occasions, trying to make up for it.

White Endurance Team
Bertrand Stey and Yann Gyger were perennial back-markers, and replacements were called in on occasion, including Jeronimo Vidal and Thierry Mulot.

Kawasaki Bertocchi
Mauro Sanchini and Ivan Clementi were in action for the long-standing team, scoring points during some spirited rides against the much-improved customer Ducatis.

Both Honda and Ducati got serious again — Ducati at the beginning of the season and Honda towards the end — as the stakes got higher for each of the SBK biggies. Changes took place in other areas for other manufacturers, but nothing like as comprehensively as with the usual SBK big two, as the results showed.

Clockwise from bottom left: Ducati completely revamped the 999 cc Testastretta, claiming 188 horsepower for Bayliss's multi-victorious Desmo; Honda's 175-horsepower SP2 was already good — revised mid-year, it gained at least five horsepower, and gave Edwards everything he needed; Kawasaki's ZX7-RR was the dinosaur of the paddock — still fast, but not fast enough — this is Walker's machine; Haga's personal play station — but his lead-footed technique took the blame for the Mille's imperfect reliability record; a view of which Colin Edwards eventually tired: the back of the factory Ducati.
All photographs: Gold & Goose

APRILIA

For a bike with a good record of reliability since its appearance in 1999, the Aprilia Mille went about ruining it quite successfully even before the testing season had finished. It improved into the race season but there were still some high-profile DNFs.

Reasons were brought forward, such as the lack of direct factory control this year, the exit of long-term project engineering boss Giuseppe Bernicchia, an ambitious winter of power redeployment and (probably the most likely answer) the heavy down-change boot of Noriyuki Haga, accustomed to just stamping down the gears on high-revving fours and GP two-strokes.

Putting out over 170 bhp at over 13,000 rpm the unique 60° vee-twin is no longer the most over-square motor on the grid, and was also seldom the outright fastest, as Ducati then Honda made inroads in those areas.

It also got heavier for some reason, despite the ultra-light OZ wheels, at 164 kg.

Having reached some kind of limit in its present guise, maybe there will be a replacement or a more comprehensive engine redesign in its near future.

BENELLI

The Tornado Tre 900, the only triple in the championship, was little changed from the 2001 version, in terms of architecture and internals, at least in matters that made any difference to the machine's top speed and acceleration.

According to sources in the team, new power-up components, sourced from the team's own resources, were ignored for the season, and the claimed 170-plus bhp at 13,000 rpm was somewhat whimsical. Funky design that it is, the Benelli delivered power in a 270° firing format, in a 1-3-2 order. Each cylinder was a booming 88 mm x 49.2 mm in dimension.

A version of a Marelli EFI system was used to tame the Benelli's already-tame power delivery, with two injectors per cylinder fitted.

The claimed dry weight of 162 kg, exactly on the limit, was also called into question.

It wasn't all bad, with Goddard continually praising the handling characteristics of the semi-tubular/semi-cast alloy chassis, which allowed him to fight riders on faster bikes at the slower tracks.

DUCATI

Few expected Ducati would comprehensively revamp their new-for-2001 Testastretta factory bikes, but the 998F02 (code for a 2002 factory machine) was completely re-designed.

Growing from 998 cc to 999 cc (in readiness for the all-new 999 road-bike model in 2003) thanks to a whopping 104 mm x 58.8 mm bore and stroke, the claimed horsepower for the latest 'desmo' was a thundering 188 bhp at 12,500 rpm.

Single-injector throttle bodies replaced the twin- or three-injector types, with the new Magneti Marelli MF3S units proving finicky to set up for some.

Brembo 290 or 330 mm rotors were this year's brake options and, remarkably, the bike was still not claimed to be right on the 162 kg minimum weight limit, by 2 kg.

The 2001-spec F01s of the HM Plant team had a claimed 175 bhp on tap at 12,000 rpm and weighed in at 165 kg with oil and water. Most other teams used Testastretta customer-spec engines, leading to an improvement of power output and rideability for the mid-pack Ducati runners.

HONDA

A game of two halves for Honda, with the VTR1000SP2 changing spec from the Oschersleben race onwards, thanks to Suzuka Eight-Hour race enhancements. Another 999 cc, 100 mm x 63.6 mm engine, the original version produced a claimed 175 bhp at 12,000 rpm.

The main mid-season changes ran to a completely new twin silencer exhaust system, a new engine specification giving four or five bhp throughout the range, a more efficient lubrication system, new combustion chamber profiles, cam profiles, and fitment of the smaller of the two homologated throttle bodies, the 62 mm versions, not the 64 mm. The rev-ceiling was no higher than the 12,000 of the existing machine, but the extra power came from a larger peak torque figure, as yet undisclosed.

Chassis-wise, the SP2's revised engine mounts gave Edwards more feel from the rear, with less rigidity in some areas a deliberate design parameter.

KAWASAKI

Still running carburettors, the ZX-7RR was an impressive museum piece, but a museum piece all the same.

Putting out 171 bhp at the rear tyre at 15,200 rpm the Kawasaki gets easier to ride every year, yet further outclassed by the big vee-twins.

With the arrival of Öhlins fan Hitoyasu Izutsu, and long-time Swedish suspension rider Chris Walker, the team reverted to the same make of suspension as the majority of their rivals, foregoing the financially more expedient WP supplier.

The 41 mm Keihin carbs stayed, when all others are now fuel injected, and the engine architecture of 73 mm x 44.7 mm remained constant.

The T-Rex of the class, it could still bite hard on the speed-trap figures, but even its previous advantage in that area went by the wayside in the year the twins really did take over the SBK world.

SUZUKI

Smaller in bore than the Kawasaki the Suzuki relied on the same-size 42 mm throttle bodies and fuel injection system as its 2001 version.

Its 749 cc engine came with a 72 mm x 46 mm bore and stroke, which could rev the purple and yellow peril beyond 15,000 rpm. No claimed power this year, but 180 bhp or so, depending on spec, would be fair for the occasionally fast GSX-R.

The main change in the machine's appearance was the WP front and rear suspension, which followed Lavilla over from Kawasaki. Massive 51 mm USD forks, all in aluminium, made no significant improvement in the results. Suzuki went its own way with brakes as well, running Tokico calipers.

Another bike that didn't make the weight limit, the GSX-R tipped the scales at 166 kg, a strange figure after a year of development and refinement.

Looks like this was the last year for the GSX-R750, and it was a whimperingly quiet one, its finicky nature partly to blame.

PETRONAS FP1

Didn't get a start after failing to reach the first homologation stage, but was tested at the end of the year in any case.

The radical triple, with the injected induction system at the front and exhausts exiting to the rear features several unusual design features, and a striking set of visuals.

TORNADO'S RETURN

WHEREVER Colin Edwards sees out his career, SBK or MotoGP, on Japanese or Italian equipment, a lot of people (and the odd international corporation) should wave him off on an ocean of gratitude.

The current management of SBK really should, for single-handedly turning the 2002 season, one of snooze-inducing predictability and waning public interest for much of the year, into an intense nail-biting run to the flag.

Michelin should, and have, said thanks for Edwards doing days and days of extra-curricular testing to make it their most bumper SBK season ever, and for picking out the tyres for Ducati's requirements as well.

Honda and HRC, more than anybody, should be lauding Edwards from the rooftops, the Texas Tornado having given them their second World Superbike Championship of the millennium, making it two out of three since their first decision to take on Ducati on a level footing with a vee-twin. Also the fact that Edwards did half the work in winning Honda a back-to-back brace of all-important Suzuka Eight-Hour races should not be passed over.

Passed over... now there is an interesting phrase. One that Colin Edwards has felt the cold shoulder of more than once. Especially since he arrived on planet SBK, and certainly since he took his first World Championship in 2000.

An AMA 250 cc champion at 19, an often-injured AMA and global Superbike slow-burner until he got his hands on a Honda RC45 in 1998, Edwards was not natural championship material in those days.

Even his first World Championship win, in a year when he proved to be Honda's lone road-racing World Champion, was only convincing during the last few rounds, on what was seen as the best bike and tyre combo in the class.

So you can see why his dream of being a 500 GP rider was only a possibility, not a sure-fire thing in those days.

His second place in last year's title, under an avalanche of Ducatis and a certain Troy Bayliss, was an even better performance than his championship-winning year, but still no GP contract came forth.

This year, Edwards has grown out of all recognition to those who saw him as only fleetingly competitive in the late Nineties.

In 2002, his legendary vat of self-confidence still appeared to be overflowing as he lined up on the grid, even after the 14 races Troy Bayliss had won with grinding regularity on his way to what was an almost assured crown.

Edwards's belief that he could still win only wobbled once. After race one at Laguna, in which he placed a disappointed third, his thoughts were negative for the first time. 'To finish third was soul-destroying,' summed up his state of mind well enough.

Temporarily at least, because a mere couple of hours later Edwards had returned to sharp focus, beaten Bayliss into second and started an epic journey into SBK legend.

His nine-in-a-row race wins, following on from 16 straight podiums, made him champion in the most unlikely way possible. He had his rival Bayliss to thank for tripping and falling at Assen, but Edwards's fault-free season of 26 points scores, none lower than fourth, was simply awe-inspiring.

The frequent record-breaking lap and race pace of the championship campaign was another factor which made Edwards's performance all the more remarkable — especially as it was achieved with no sudden extra 40 bhp to shave off most of the tenths of a second in lap time either, unlike the MotoGP lads.

Equipped with a more fulsome power curve and other small but significant aids to riding pleasure on his revised-spec VTR, Edwards was given a welcome boost in his late-season races, as he and Bayliss fought out their game of nerves to its astonishing climax. Edwards's belief in his ability to win, his persistence in the face of a dream even his own team thought impossible at one stage, has become a textbook lesson for any would-be champions, in any sporting endeavour.

As if Edwards's character and commitment had not been reinforced with granite frequently enough in public, we need only remember he was also HRC's lone SBK representative, with no team-mates to try and squeeze points off the other guy weekend after weekend.

He may chew tobacco, speak his mind more often than is the norm in the GP paddock and occasionally cuss during interviews like he was in a Texas bar room, but as a hard-working team-player, as a rider who needs no external motivation — as a hardcore racer — Colin Edwards is now the finished, polished, consistently rapid article.

At the time of going to press MotoGP finally beckons, with Aprilia signing him up after near misses with both Honda and Yamaha.

That it has taken him this long to get noticed may be merely a part of MotoGP's regular bouts of unhealthy and incestuous introspection, but anyone not considering Edwards as maybe at least the next best thing to their current number one rider in the premier class is simply not paying enough attention.

Or as his great 2002 rival Bayliss has gone on record as saying, when Edwards's long-term employers apparently passed him over for one of their numerous 2003 season RC211V rides (on his favoured Michelins at least), 'What's wrong with those guys? Are they stupid?'

Above: Bayliss shares the first of many 2002 rostrum moments with daughter Abbey.

Above right: Nitro Nori couldn't be acid with two second places on his SBK return.

Right: Walker, unable to blink due to Bell's palsy, showed true courage, won points.

All photographs: Gold & Goose

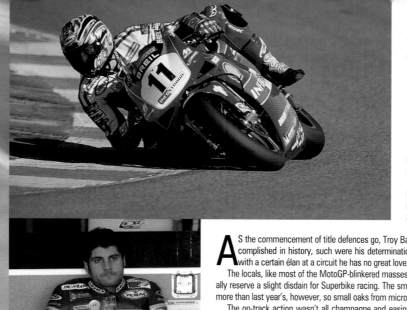

Left: The pressure was on Xaus, and eventually he succumbed.

Opposite page: Bayliss leads Bostrom and Haga; Edwards is still in touch.

All photographs: Gold & Goose

Above: Gregorio Lavilla was encouraged by an eighth place in the first race; disappointed after a collision with James Toseland in the second.

Below: Now you see them... Team Foggy Petronas was launched, Hayden and Corser flanking SBK hero Fogarty. They had riders, livery, but no motor bikes. They'd be on track by Monza, said Fogarty.

Bottom: Benelli had a motor cycle, but kept it covered. They missed the opening rounds awaiting more power.

All photographs: Gold & Goose

A S the commencement of title defences go, Troy Bayliss's 2002 effort must rank as one of the most accomplished in history, such were his determination, confidence and sheer pace — all demonstrated with a certain élan at a circuit he has no great love for. One weekend down, 50 points in the bank.

The locals, like most of the MotoGP-blinkered masses in Spain, generally prefer Vale in Valencia, and usually reserve a slight disdain for Superbike racing. The smallish crowd of 41,000 (weekend) was still healthily more than last year's, however, so small oaks from micro acorns do seem to grow.

The on-track action wasn't all champagne and easing off on the final laps for the dominant Bayliss, because he almost messed his blotter when he was a tad too aggressive on the final corner (an early warning that his driven mentality can sometimes get the better of him). Any criticism of the champ would have been churlish, however, because he simply stomped them all, right into the red Iberian dust, overcoming a sighting lap scare (when he had to hop onto his second bike for race two), and scoring the all-important double win. What more do you want from your heroes? Perfection?

If you were double second-place finisher in round one and yet had missed out on a lot of testing in the winter, after a semi-disastrous defection across Checkpoint Carlos into MotoGP the previous season, you would be a happy man on 10 March. Returning SBK prodigal son Noriyuki Haga was certainly happy with a pair of podiums — almost as happy as Aprilia themselves.

Race two was shortened due to gravel from a crash polluting the racing line, making it a 20-lapper, not the scheduled 23, but it was still no contest.

Ben Bostrom (third in race one on his Ducati L&M 998 F02) could only manage fourth in the second leg and was disgruntled with the fact that he felt that his factory missile was a damp squib compared to Bayliss's big red rocket. Difficult to see why, when he took the new lap record on lap six of race two, with a 1m 35.306s.

Colin Edwards (Castrol Honda), the other American in the field, was third in the second race, swapping places with Bostrom after race one, the pair going joint third in the early-season table.

If the locals had come to see anybody, it was their own 'traccas' firework-in-waiting, Ruben Xaus (Ducati Infostrada). Fifth in the first event and crashing while closing in on the leaders in race two, he went home a chastened, if no less excitable racer.

Neil Hodgson (HM Plant Ducati) filled the fifth slot in the second race, having been sixth in race one. He was seriously miffed after the opener, but still left the day fifth overall in the championship battle, at a circuit he says was left over from an episode of Mickey's Mousketeers.

In Superbike racing full time for the first time, Hitoyasu Izutsu gave the Kawasaki Racing Team an encouraging pair of results, with a seventh in race one and sixth in the second. In an increasingly segregated society, consisting of the 'Have Got Twins' and the 'Have Not Got Twins, ' this wasn't as shabby as it might have been.

Chris Walker was a slugging seventh in race two, despite suffering the lasting effects of Bell's palsy.

Inspection report after the first day of school? The favourite playground game was unquestionably 'Beat the Top Ducati Rider' in order to win the championship, just like the GP boys have always got to beat the top Honda rider to win theirs. Even if we now live in a world of similar strokes for different folks, some things obviously never change.

Round 1 VALENCIA, Spain
10 March, 2.489-mile/4.005-km km circuit

Race 1 23 laps, 57.247 miles/92.115 km

Pl. Name, Nat. (Machine)	No.	Time & speed	Laps
1 Troy Bayliss, AUS (Ducati)	1	36m 51.963s	23
		93.155 mph/149.918 km/h	
2 Noriyuki Haga, J (Aprilia)	41	36m 55.139s	23
3 Ben Bostrom, USA (Ducati)	155	36m 55.279s	23
4 Colin Edwards, USA (Honda)	2	36m 55.990s	23
5 Ruben Xaus, E (Ducati)	11	37m 00.673s	23
6 Neil Hodgson, GB (Ducati)	100	37m 06.408s	23
7 Hitoyasu Izutsu, J (Kawasaki)	14	37m 07.858s	23
8 Gregorio Lavilla, E (Suzuki)	10	37m 22.778s	23
9 Pierfrancesco Chili, I (Ducati)	7	37m 22.783s	23
10 Chris Walker, GB (Kawasaki)	9	37m 23.559s	23
11 Juan Borja, E (Ducati)	33	37m 23.630s	23
12 James Toseland, GB (Ducati)	52	37m 28.233s	23
13 Alessandro Antonello, I (Ducati)	30	37m 31.935s	23
14 Lucio Pedercini, I (Ducati)	19	37m 35.765s	23
15 Broc Parkes, AUS (Ducati)	12	37m 38.615s	23
16 Marco Borciani, I (Ducati)	20	37m 39.535s	23
17 Steve Martin, AUS (Ducati)	99	37m 40.830s	23
18 Ivan Clementi, I (Kawasaki)	36	38m 15.961s	23
19 Mauro Sanchini, I (Kawasaki)	46	38m 17.806s	23
20 Thierry Mulot, F (Ducati)	69	38m 28.476s	23
21 Mark Heckles, GB (Honda)	5	37m 16.270s	22

DNF: Yann Gyger, CH (Honda) 70, 12 laps; Serafino Foti, I (Ducati) 28, 12 laps; Bertrand Stey, F (Honda) 68, 3 laps.

Fastest lap: Bayliss, 1m 35.639s, 93.674 mph/150.754 km/h (record).

Race 2 20 laps, 49.780 miles/80.100 km

Pl. Name, Nat. (Machine)	No.	Time & speed	Laps
1 Troy Bayliss, AUS (Ducati)	1	32m 03.384s	20
		93.158 mph/149.923 km/h	
2 Noriyuki Haga, J (Aprilia)	41	32m 04.562s	20
3 Colin Edwards, USA (Honda)	2	32m 05.669s	20
4 Ben Bostrom, USA (Ducati)	155	32m 08.528s	20
5 Neil Hodgson, GB (Ducati)	100	32m 20.766s	20
6 Hitoyasu Izutsu, J (Kawasaki)	14	32m 29.194s	20
7 Chris Walker, GB (Kawasaki)	9	32m 35.121s	20
8 Juan Borja, E (Ducati)	33	32m 36.591s	20
9 Steve Martin, AUS (Ducati)	99	32m 41.085s	20
10 James Toseland, GB (Ducati)	52	32m 41.595s	20
11 Lucio Pedercini, I (Ducati)	19	32m 44.323s	20
12 Marco Borciani, I (Ducati)	20	32m 45.224s	20
13 Ivan Clementi, I (Kawasaki)	36	33m 03.127s	20
14 Serafino Foti, I (Ducati)	28	33m 03.415s	20
15 Mauro Sanchini, I (Kawasaki)	46	33m 09.494s	20
16 Thierry Mulot, F (Ducati)	69	33m 28.008s	20
17 Bertrand Stey, F (Honda)	68	33m 37.544s	20

DNF: Mark Heckles, GB (Honda) 5, 18 laps; Pierfrancesco Chili, I (Ducati) 7, 9 laps; Gregorio Lavilla, E (Suzuki) 10, 8 laps; Yann Gyger, CH (Honda) 70, 8 laps; Ruben Xaus, E (Ducati) 11, 7 laps; Alessandro Antonello, I (Ducati) 30, 6 laps.

Fastest lap: Bostrom, 1m 35.306s, 94.002 mph/151.281 km/h (record).

Superpole: Bayliss, 1m 34.814s, 94.489 mph/152.066 km/h.

Previous record: Troy Corser, AUS (Aprilia), 1m 36.128s, 93.198 mph/149.988 km.h (2001).

Championship points: 1 Bayliss, 50; 2 Haga, 40; 3 Bostrom and Edwards, 29; 5 Hodgson, 21; 6 Izutsu, 19; 7 Walker, 15; 8 Borja, 13; 9 Xaus, 11; 10 Toseland, 10; 11 Lavilla, 8; 12 Chili, Martin and Pedercini, 7; 15 Borciani, 4.

Right: Bayliss and Edwards in a formation to become familiar; Haga, Hodgson and Bostrom following on.

Below: Xaus made it to the rostrum twice.
Both photographs: Gold & Goose

Above centre: Haga — was he rough, or was the Aprilia fragile?

Right: Edwards kept the pressure on... it was all he could do.
All photographs: Gold & Goose

WORLD SUPERBIKE CHAMPIONSHIP · ROUND 2

Above: Mid-field battle — Walker keeps the Kawasaki ahead of the Ducatis of Pedercini, Martin and Antonello.

Left: Bayliss and home fan — he kept them all happy.
Both photographs: Gold & Goose

N O one had ever won the first four SBK races of any season, not even the previous Ducati legends Doug Polen and Carl Fogarty. Someone, or something had always got in their way. Nothing blocked the path of Troy Bayliss on home tarmac, however, not even the close interest paid in him by Superpole winner Colin Edwards.

In fairness, Bayliss had to work for his supremacy after Edwards put in the fastest laps of both races and looked like a real challenger for two wins.

Relative tyre performance had as much to do with the result as anything else, with Ducati once more proving that their system of testing almost all possible rear Michelin options, irrespective of rider hunches or previous data, usually pays dividends. A methodical Italian approach? A bizarre concept, but effective.

After leading for much of the races Edwards missed a gear to allow Bayliss past on one occasion, but differential pace was the real reason for Bayliss's wins — especially on the last half-dozen laps, when the Honda had already used up its rear Michelin in the near-50°C track temperatures.

The initially fast Ruben Xaus, the third and last factory-supplied Michelin rider, found himself third and no better in each race, an early sign that Michelin's assertion that they had ploughed more resources and experience into their SBK tyre programme was not an empty boast. They had certainly found some extra vulcanicity from somewhere, because the best Dunlop riders, Bostrom (fourth and fifth) and Hodgson (fifth and fourth) were respectively 21 and 18 seconds adrift of Bayliss. That was almost a second a lap, and an ominous sign of things to come for Dunlop. And Pirelli.

Whether Haga is too aggressive for the delicate Aprilia, or the Aprilia was operating too close to the limit of reliability anyway was an imponderable many considered at length after Phillip Island. Whatever the cause, Aprilia's pre-season fragility returned in any case, with Haga out with brake problems in race one, and an off-the-pace sixth in race two.

Haga's countryman Hitoyasu Izutsu had been quietly impressive on his four-cylinder Kawasaki again, a bike of advanced years and the 'wrong' tyre supplier. Not to say engine configuration in these days of the 180 bhp twin. Sixth in race one, Izutsu crashed in race two, one of a fair few to fall at the base of the tricky MG corner.

A war of attrition between James Toseland and Gregorio Lavilla in each race put Lavilla seventh in race one and eighth in race two, with Toseland his mirror image each time.

The second factory Kawasaki rider in the field, Chris Walker, had a subdued ride in each outing, scoring a brace of ninth places, working hard to overcome his frozen face muscles and keep sweat out of his unblinking left eye.

Ducati privateers Juan Borja and Lucio Pedercini took a tenth-place finish each, with Borja top 12 in the opener. Mark Heckles, the rookie in Superbike, used a better-class-of-customer 'Mich' to score his first points in race two; payback for overcoming the agony of a huge high-side in practice.

In fact, everyone was suffering some kind of internal seizure at Phillip Island, the pain coming from the same source — Bayliss fever. It was laying everybody else low, but taking the originator to new and untested levels of excellence. People were already starting to talk of the championship's being completed by Brands Hatch, plus absolute record point scores and the like. With Bayliss 31 points ahead after only four races, the feeling was completely understandable, especially in his native Australia.

South Africa, though, now that was going to be different — or so said Edwards.

Round 2 PHILLIP ISLAND, Australia
24 March, 2.762-mile/4.445-km circuit
2 x 22 laps, 60.764 miles/97.790 km

Race 1

Pl. Name Nat. (Machine)	No.	Time & speed Laps
1 Troy Bayliss, AUS (Ducati)	1	34m 30.102s 22
		105.671 mph/170.061 km/h
2 Colin Edwards, USA (Honda)	2	34m 32.571s 22
3 Ruben Xaus, E (Ducati)	11	34m 40.162s 22
4 Ben Bostrom, USA (Ducati)	155	34m 51.234s 22
5 Neil Hodgson, GB (Ducati)	100	34m 51.320s 22
6 Hitoyasu Izutsu, J (Kawasaki)	14	35m 08.025s 22
7 Gregorio Lavilla, E (Suzuki)	10	35m 08.111s 22
8 James Toseland, GB (Ducati)	52	35m 11.240s 22
9 Chris Walker, GB (Kawasaki)	9	35m 20.981s 22
10 Lucio Pedercini, I (Ducati)	19	35m 31.648s 22
11 Marco Borciani, I (Ducati)	20	35m 36.470s 22
12 Juan Borja, E (Ducati)	33	35m 40.282s 22
13 Steve Martin, AUS (Ducati)	99	35m 46.709s 22
14 Alessandro Antonello, I (Ducati)	30	35m 47.983s 22
15 Mauro Sanchini, I (Kawasaki)	46	35m 48.026s 22
16 Mark Heckles, GB (Honda)	5	35m 49.332s 22

DNF: Ivan Clementi, I (Kawasaki) 36, 21 laps; Broc Parkes, AUS (Ducati) 12, 12 laps; Pierfrancesco Chili, I (Ducati) 7, 12 laps; Serafino Foti, I (Ducati) 28, 10 laps; Noriyuki Haga, J (Aprilia) 41, 9 laps; Bertrand Stey, F (Honda) 68, 4 laps; Alistair Maxwell, AUS (Kawasaki) 17, 0 laps.

Fastest lap: Edwards, 1m 33.383s, 106.479 mph/171.361 km/h.

Race 2

Pl. Name Nat. (Machine)	No.	Time & speed Laps
1 Troy Bayliss, AUS (Ducati)	1	34m 35.633s 22
		105.390 mph/169.608 km/h
2 Colin Edwards, USA (Honda)	2	34m 38.105s 22
3 Ruben Xaus, E (Ducati)	11	34m 45.315s 22
4 Neil Hodgson, GB (Ducati)	100	34m 54.546s 22
5 Ben Bostrom, USA (Ducati)	155	34m 54.577s 22
6 Noriyuki Haga, J (Aprilia)	41	34m 55.206s 22
7 James Toseland, GB (Ducati)	52	35m 08.589s 22
8 Gregorio Lavilla, E (Suzuki)	10	35m 08.634s 22
9 Chris Walker, GB (Kawasaki)	9	35m 08.718s 22
10 Juan Borja, E (Ducati)	33	35m 37.515s 22
11 Alessandro Antonello, I (Ducati)	30	35m 39.836s 22
12 Mauro Sanchini, I (Kawasaki)	46	35m 42.860s 22
13 Broc Parkes, AUS (Ducati)	12	35m 43.195s 22
14 Mark Heckles, GB (Honda)	5	35m 43.427s 22
15 Ivan Clementi, I (Kawasaki)	36	35m 45.036s 22
16 Bertrand Stey, F (Honda)	68	34m 40.919s 21
17 Alistair Maxwell, AUS (Kawasaki)	17	35m 28.989s 21

DNF: Hitoyasu Izutsu, J (Kawasaki) 14, 16 laps; Marco Borciani, I (Ducati) 20, 15 laps; Lucio Pedercini, I (Ducati) 19, 11 laps; Pierfrancesco Chili, I (Ducati) 7, 8 laps; Steve Martin, AUS (Ducati) 99, 7 laps; Serafino Foti, I (Ducati) 28, 6 laps.

Fastest lap: Edwards, 1m 33.700s, 106.117 mph/170.779 km/h.

Superpole: Edwards, 1m 32.767s, 107.185 mph/172.497 km/h.

Lap record: Troy Corser, AUS (Ducati), 1m 33.019s, 106.894 mph/172.029 km/h (1999).

Championship points: 1 Bayliss, 100; 2 Edwards, 69; 3 Bostrom, 53; 4 Haga, 50; 5 Hodgson, 45; 6 Xaus, 43; 7 Izutsu and Walker, 29;
9 Toseland, 27; 10 Lavilla, 25; 11 Borja, 23; 12 Pedercini, 13; 13 Antonello and Martin, 10; 15 Borciani, 9.

Above: Ben Bostrom in thoughtful pose as a difficult season stretched ahead.

Right: Edwards was in flying form for a record Superpole.

Far right: Pit-lane walkabout pleased South African race fans.
All photographs: Gold & Goose

Top left: Haga was enjoying his return to stardom.

Opposite page: Bayliss kisses the kerb — he had to work for the double.

Left: Xaus displayed a permanently rumbustious riding style.

Below left: Six out of six, and Bayliss was already looking invincible.

All photographs: Gold & Goose

AFTER three-times Kyalami race-winner Colin Edwards won Superpole (at an absolute record pace of 1m 41.321s) and 2001 winner Ben Bostrom was in equally fine qualifying mettle, the result of SBK's latest African adventure did not look like a foregone conclusion on Saturday night. With Noriyuki Haga also a previous Kyalami race winner (before being excluded for doping infringements) it really looked like we were going to have the first multi-rider scrap of the year. And no Troy Bayliss disappearing act to spoil the party.

There were indeed some excellent fights, in the early sections only, but despite the excitement of some forceful elbow-to-elbow combat, the wins both gravitated toward Bayliss once more.

Six out of six, and 45 points clear of an otherwise excellent Edwards. This was becoming a red brick wall of Bayliss and Ducati domination, especially as Xaus proved to be on double-podium form, taking a third and then a second place. A disastrous Superpole had put him on row three, eliciting some audacious overtakes and burned-up tyres before the end of the 25-lap races.

Bayliss's immaculate displays were hindered only by the attention of the other factory men for short periods of each race, although some of the action was spectacular in the extreme. Haga was in elbow-barging mood, Xaus an avenging red devil as he made up places, Edwards smooth yet determined as ever.

In race one Edwards was the nearest challenger, four seconds down at the flag, although Haga had led until he dropped back and then crashed, thanks to a broken engine, at the entrance to Nashua. His dramatic day continued when he was struck by a bird while leading on lap one of the second race, but he dropped back to finish sixth. The luckless wildfowl virtually exploded on his crash helmet, sending a smokescreen of feathers into the chasing pack, with Bayliss the main man affected by this gift from the skies. Haga did, however, take a new lap record in race two, at 1m 42.178s.

The Dunlop-supplied Ducati riders, Ben Bostrom and Neil Hodgson, swapped fourth and fifth places, with Bostrom in the ascendancy in race one.

Hitoyasu Izutsu merely proved that the fours do not like Kyalami better than anywhere else, and a pair of seventh places may as well have been a single 14th for a factory rider. Izutsu had a lonely race in the first event, a more frantic one in race two, overcoming Toseland, ahead in race one.

Pierfrancesco Chili failed to start either race, after he clashed with Ruben Xaus in morning warm-up, breaking his left collarbone when he was spat off his machine under braking.

The tortuous curves of Kyalami, one of the better layouts in the great scheme of World Championship tracks, proved to be a great test for all, but even the previous ringmasters had to give best to the lion in the Ducati encampment. Another new world conquered, another even-split Michelin/Dunlop track annexed by the French.

Round 3 KYALAMI, South Africa

7 April, 2.649-mile/4.263-km circuit

2 x 25 laps, 66.225 miles/106.575 km

Race 1

Pl. Name Nat. (Machine)	No.	Time & speed	Laps
1 Troy Bayliss, AUS (Ducati)	1	43m 01.781s	25
		92.340 mph/148.607 km/h	
2 Colin Edwards, USA (Honda)	2	43m 05.900s	25
3 Ruben Xaus, E (Ducati)	11	43m 08.317s	25
4 Ben Bostrom, USA (Ducati)	155	43m 13.764s	25
5 Neil Hodgson, GB (Ducati)	100	43m 18.605s	25
6 James Toseland, GB (Ducati)	52	43m 31.325s	25
7 Hitoyasu Izutsu, J (Kawasaki)	14	43m 39.161s	25
8 Chris Walker, GB (Kawasaki)	9	43m 49.079s	25
9 Juan Borja, E (Ducati)	33	43m 56.353s	25
10 Marco Borciani, I (Ducati)	20	43m 56.822s	25
11 Broc Parkes, AUS (Ducati)	12	44m 20.069s	25
12 Serafino Foti, I (Ducati)	28	44m 31.713s	25
13 Mauro Sanchini, I (Kawasaki)	46	43m 06.408s	24
14 Bertrand Stey, F (Honda)	68	43m 10.744s	24

DNF: Noriyuki Haga, J (Aprilia) 41, 17 laps; Lucio Pedercini, I (Ducati) 19, 12 laps; Gregorio Lavilla, E (Suzuki) 10, 12 laps; Jiri Mrkyvka, CZ (Ducati) 23, 8 laps; Steve Martin, AUS (Ducati) 99, 6 laps; Alessandro Antonello, I (Ducati) 30, 1 lap; DNS: Mark Heckles, GB (Honda) 5; Pierfrancesco Chili, I (Ducati) 7.

Fastest lap: Haga, 1m 42.197s, 93.311 mph/150.169 km/h (record).

Race 2

Pl. Name Nat. (Machine)	No.	Time & speed	Laps
1 Troy Bayliss, AUS (Ducati)	1	42m 57.014s	25
		92.511 mph/148.882 km/h	
2 Ruben Xaus, E (Ducati)	11	42m 59.687s	25
3 Colin Edwards, USA (Honda)	2	43m 03.404s	25
4 Neil Hodgson, GB (Ducati)	100	43m 03.788s	25
5 Ben Bostrom, USA (Ducati)	155	43m 06.368s	25
6 Noriyuki Haga, J (Aprilia)	41	43m 08.997s	25
7 Hitoyasu Izutsu, J (Kawasaki)	14	43m 24.674s	25
8 James Toseland, GB (Ducati)	52	43m 25.890s	25
9 Chris Walker, GB (Kawasaki)	9	43m 37.795s	25
10 Juan Borja, E (Ducati)	33	43m 40.269s	25
11 Gregorio Lavilla, E (Suzuki)	10	43m 43.392s	25
12 Lucio Pedercini, I (Ducati)	19	43m 53.429s	25
13 Marco Borciani, I (Ducati)	20	43m 58.815s	25
14 Broc Parkes, AUS (Ducati)	12	44m 15.014s	25
15 Serafino Foti, I (Ducati)	28	44m 30.178s	25
16 Mauro Sanchini, I (Kawasaki)	46	43m 20.047s	24
17 Bertrand Stey, F (Honda)	68	43m 21.563s	24
18 Jiri Mrkyvka, CZ (Ducati)	23	43m 22.313s	24

DNF: Alessandro Antonello, I (Ducati) 30, 14 laps; Steve Martin, AUS (Ducati) 99, 4 laps; DNS: Pierfrancesco Chili, I (Ducati) 7; Mark Heckles, GB (Honda) 5.

Fastest lap: Haga, 1m 42.178s, 93.328 mph/150.197 km/h (record).

Superpole: Edwards, 1m 41.321s, 94.117 mph/151.467 km/h.

Previous record: Ben Bostrom, USA (Ducati), 1m 42.928s, 92.648 mph/149.102 km/h (2001).

Championship points: 1 Bayliss, 150; 2 Edwards, 105; 3 Xaus, 79; 4 Bostrom, 77; 5 Hodgson, 69; 6 Haga, 60; 7 Izutsu, 47; 8 Toseland, 45; 9 Walker, 44; 10 Borja, 36; 11 Lavilla, 30; 12 Borciani, 18; 13 Pedercini, 17; 14 Parkes, 11; 15 Antonello and Martin, 10.

SUGO

WORLD SUPERBIKE CHAMPIONSHIP · ROUND 4

Above: Neil Hodgson — ahead of Bayliss twice, and on the rostrum once.

Above right: Tamada was once again the man to beat in Japan. Edwards did so, once.

Right: Team boss Tady Okada — ex-GP winner and SBK rider — joins winner Tamada on the rostrum, with Edwards (left) and Hodgson.
All photographs: Gold & Goose

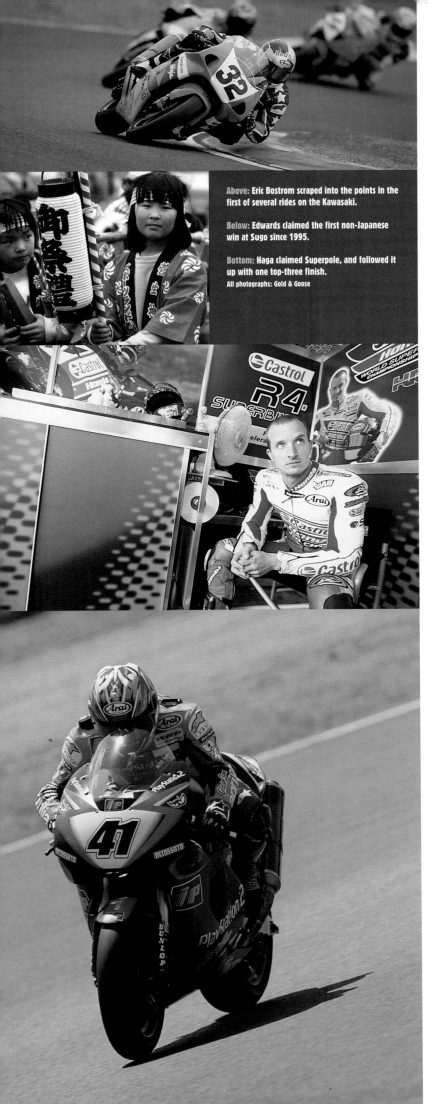

Above: Eric Bostrom scraped into the points in the first of several rides on the Kawasaki.

Below: Edwards claimed the first non-Japanese win at Sugo since 1995.

Bottom: Haga claimed Superpole, and followed it up with one top-three finish.
All photographs: Gold & Goose

THE run of six wins for Troy Bayliss came to a Honda-inspired end at Sugo, and thus he failed to match the seven-in-a-row record of Doug Polen. He wasn't moaning about it, and with good reason, because his relative performance when compared to the previous season's Sugo weekend was more than remarkable. Placing 13th and 15th in 2001, he was a more competitive fifth and fourth this year.

All the Western riders had a similar upturn in fortunes; with Colin Edwards's first race win being the best performance from a non-Japanese rider since 1995. It was his own first race win since 'Oschers' in 2001.

It was also the first Michelin win in a long time at this most Dunlop of recent SBK tracks. (It came as no surprise to many to find out that Edwards had tested for Michelin at Sugo in the winter, explaining a lot of the improvements for all three 'Mich' riders.)

Normal Nippon/Dunlop service was resumed in race two, when the double winner from 2001, Makoto Tamada, ripped away to his third Sugo SBK win in four goes, and it did look even more suspiciously like his earlier second place was something of a sandbagging effort, allowing Edwards to hold him off in the final stages of the 25-lap contest.

Sugo was further proof that SBK racing had not stood still in the winter months, with Noriyuki Haga and then Tamada setting new lap records at yet another track, and the race records comfortably beaten — underlining Edwards's assertion that the championship was getting tougher, even if there sometimes appeared to be only two men in it. In Superpole, Haga failed to go faster than the previous record, but he did score what was only his second career Superpole win.

A couple of minor pieces of history at Sugo, then, some with a wide-ranging significance for the overall championship battle, as Edwards clawed back Bayliss's lead to 24 points after his first and second places.

Neil Hodgson started what was to become a quite familiar groundhog position: third on points over a weekend and, in most instances, better than the rest of the SBK herd, albeit some distance behind the Michelin race. In race one he was fourth, race two third, but in the championship he was already a mighty 76 points adrift of Bayliss.

Cool track temperatures of 25°C made tyre choice a strange one for all the riders at Sugo in any case, but colder still was the challenge from the usually numerous white-hot local wild-card riders. Other than Tamada, the highest-placed local All-Japan contestant proved to be ex-Kawasaki Superbike institution, Akira Yanagawa, sixth in both races. An inscrutable development this season, which lent itself to the idea that SBK really was tougher after all.

Haga, third and fifth, was again competent, Xaus ninth and then again a crasher, Ben Bostrom seventh on two occasions, somehow managing to drown in four-cylinder machines when the twins in general had complete mastery of all the top positions. Chopping rim sizes between races smacked of desperation, never a welcome presence in any pit box.

Tamada's new lap record stands at 1m 29.108s, and was set geriatrically far along the timeline of the race, on the 17th lap of 25.

Eric Bostrom, on the first of his supposedly few Kawasaki SBK rides, was 13th and 14th, but with Hitoyasu Izutsu out with a broken wrist in warm-up, he would get a fair few more cracks of the world whip. And maybe some more of the top riders would get a bite at a race win?

Round 4 SUGO, Japan
21 April, 2.322-mile/3.737-km circuit
2 x 25 laps, 58.050 miles/93.425 km

Race 1

Pl.	Name Nat. (Machine)	No.	Time & speed	Laps
1	Colin Edwards, USA (Honda)	2	37m 24.515s	25
			93.109 mph/149.845 km/h	
2	Makoto Tamada, J (Honda)	42	37m 24.676s	25
3	Noriyuki Haga, J (Aprilia)	41	37m 29.001s	25
4	Neil Hodgson, GB (Ducati)	100	37m 36.770s	25
5	Troy Bayliss, AUS (Ducati)	1	37m 45.828s	25
6	Akira Yanagawa, J (Kawasaki)	49	37m 47.392s	25
7	Ben Bostrom, USA (Ducati)	155	37m 47.776s	25
8	Wataru Yoshikawa, J (Yamaha)	43	37m 50.874s	25
9	James Toseland, GB (Honda)	52	37m 53.597s	25
10	Takeshi Tsujimura, J (Yamaha)	45	37m 54.863s	25
11	Chris Walker, GB (Kawasaki)	9	37m 55.537s	25
12	Gregorio Lavilla, E (Suzuki)	10	38m 06.876s	25
13	Eric Bostrom, USA (Kawasaki)	32	38m 07.883s	25
14	Juan Borja, E (Ducati)	33	38m 08.649s	25
15	Yuichi Takeda, J (Honda)	48	38m 08.787s	25
16	Lucio Pedercini, I (Ducati)	19	38m 41.742s	25
17	Steve Martin, AUS (Ducati)	99	38m 44.488s	25
18	Ivan Clementi, I (Kawasaki)	36	38m 49.028s	25
19	Kenichiro Nakamura, J (Honda)	47	38m 57.712s	25
20	Mauro Sanchini, I (Kawasaki)	46	37m 24.677s	24
21	Mark Heckles, GB (Honda)	5	37m 51.570s	24

DNF: Ruben Xaus, E (Ducati) 11, 17 laps; Broc Parkes, AUS (Ducati) 12, 8 laps; Alessandro Antonello, I (Ducati) 30, 4 laps; Marco Borciani, I (Ducati) 20, 1 lap; DNS: Hitoyasu Izutsu, J (Kawasaki) 14.

Fastest lap: Haga, 1m 29.175s, 93.742 mph/150.863 km/h (record).

Race 2

Pl.	Name Nat. (Machine)	No.	Time & speed	Laps
1	Makoto Tamada, J (Honda)	42	37m 26.628s	25
			93.022 mph/149.704 km/h	
2	Colin Edwards, USA (Honda)	2	37m 29.925s	25
3	Neil Hodgson, GB (Ducati)	100	37m 30.097s	25
4	Troy Bayliss, AUS (Ducati)	1	37m 30.308s	25
5	Noriyuki Haga, J (Aprilia)	41	37m 34.084s	25
6	Akira Yanagawa, J (Kawasaki)	49	37m 36.190s	25
7	Ben Bostrom, USA (Ducati)	155	37m 39.361s	25
8	Wataru Yoshikawa, J (Yamaha)	43	37m 47.325s	25
9	Ruben Xaus, E (Ducati)	11	37m 54.849s	25
10	Takeshi Tsujimura, J (Yamaha)	45	37m 55.163s	25
11	James Toseland, GB (Ducati)	52	38m 00.052s	25
12	Gregorio Lavilla, E (Suzuki)	10	38m 00.550s	25
13	Chris Walker, GB (Kawasaki)	9	38m 01.249s	25
14	Eric Bostrom, USA (Kawasaki)	32	38m 05.189s	25
15	Juan Borja, E (Ducati)	33	38m 13.500s	25
16	Yuichi Takeda, J (Honda)	48	38m 15.735s	25
17	Marco Borciani, I (Ducati)	20	38m 36.813s	25
18	Lucio Pedercini, I (Ducati)	19	38m 38.131s	25
19	Ivan Clementi, I (Kawasaki)	36	38m 41.360s	25
20	Steve Martin, AUS (Ducati)	99	38m 42.822s	25
21	Kenichiro Nakamura, J (Honda)	47	38m 58.150s	25
22	Mauro Sanchini, I (Kawasaki)	46	37m 32.159s	24

DNF: Mark Heckles, GB (Honda) 5, 17 laps; Broc Parkes, AUS (Ducati) 12, 5 laps; DNS: Alessandro Antonello, I (Ducati) 30; Hitoyasu Izutsu, J (Kawasaki) 14.

Fastest lap: Tamada, 1m 29.108s, 93.812 mph/150.976 km/h (record).

Superpole: Haga, 1m 28.806s, 94.132 mph/151.490 km/h.

Previous record: Makoto Tamada, J (Honda), 1m 29.522s, 93.378 mph/150.278 km/h (2001).

Championship points: 1 Bayliss, 174; 2 Edwards, 150; 3 Hodgson, 98; 4 Bostrom, 95; 5 Haga, 87; 6 Xaus, 86; 7 Toseland, 57; 8 Walker, 52; 9 Izutsu, 47; 10 Tamada, 45; 11 Borja, 39; 12 Lavilla, 38; 13 Yanagawa, 20; 14 Borciani, 18; 15 Pedercini, 17.

Above: Goddard and the Benelli joined the party — but Monza is no track for anyone at a power disadvantage.

Right: Bayliss, Hodgson and Edwards in the early stages... Neil thought he'd won after the other two cut the chicane.

Main picture: Battle in the park: Hodgson, Edwards and Chili chase double-winner Bayliss.
All photographs: Gold & Goose

166

Below: Hodgson contemplates his best-of-the-rest Dunlop-shod Ducati.

Below centre: Bostrom's Ducati season was strangely worse than his last.

Below left and right: Monza snapshots: glamour is in the eye of the beholder.

Bottom right: Chili thought he'd made the podium at home, but was wrong.

All photographs: Gold & Goose

MONZA

For Neil Hodgson, like most riders, Monza is special. ('The long fast straights are like no other track, with people hanging over the wall, it's a beautiful place.') Everybody loves it, and why not, because it's a genuine grand-daddy of a circuit, where machine speed is important, rider speed more so, and an ability to react to some dramatic changes of velocity, from flat out to Mickey-Mouse slow and back again, is a necessary part of any rider's box of tricks.

And tricks there were at Monza, according to the aforesaid Hodgson. A pre-race memo had been circulated to the riders warning them about the risk of a ten-second penalty for anyone who cut the modified first chicane.

Sure enough, in race one no less a deity than Bayliss outbraked himself, ran across the slip road and re-joined. He lost time, as did Colin Edwards, but nonetheless, the erstwhile off-piste pairing caught and re-passed first Pierfrancesco Chili and then new leader Hodgson.

Convinced Bayliss would be docked time, Hodgson just sat behind his slipstream on the last lap, waiting to collect the silverware for the win. With no penalty applied, Hodgson screeched into pit lane, threw a five-second fit in the winner's circle and then shrugged his shoulders, unhappy about it but acknowledging that Bayliss was the fastest man in the race, setting a new lap record on lap 14 of 18, 1m 47.434s.

Chili, for his part, relegated to fourth by Edwards, nursed his wrath with a visor-up, head-shaking ride down pit lane, filtering past winner's circle in disgust, where he felt he should have been.

James Toseland rose to new heights with his fifth place, well ahead of factory boy Xaus, suffering from his Sugo hand injury.

There was some classic action in each race, with the leaders passing and re-passing out of the slipstream, banging on the brakes and seemingly sliding past at will. Only Bayliss's slight advantage on speed, and his determination to take another double, gave him a two seconds-plus gap over Edwards, Haga (out in race one with another mechanical failure) and a fourth-place Hodgson, who had a blowing exhaust, losing him some vital Monza horsepower.

A whopping 20 seconds back came the blue and purple 750 cc four of Gregorio Lavilla, having what would turn out to be his best race of the year. Not slow his Suzuki, just slow off the corners.

Xaus, the survivor of a monumental high-side exiting Ascari in the warm-up, was a crasher yet again (eight practice and race offs in only five rounds) leaving local Ducati privateer Lucio Pedercini sixth in the second leg.

Toseland and Chili both fell at the same point of the first chicane, and neither was to complete the second race, despite picking up, dusting off and going on.

The day belonged to Bayliss and his re-branded rolling billboard of a Ducati, and both were adored in time-honoured fashion by the *Tifosi*.

But rider of the day went to the unrecognisably hard and determined Neil Hodgson, who is learning to speak his mind like another Lancastrian Ducati rider. 'I was seriously closing 50 yards on the brakes and the second and third riders should be embarrassed with the result. My bike was like a 600 out of the turns.'

Eric Bostrom was back, replacing the injured Izutsu, and the American was fazed only a tad by the monumental Monza, taking ninth and seventh, and taking them more expeditiously than his brother Ben, a retiree and then a mere ninth in the second race.

Ten races, eight wins for Bayliss, and 38 points from Bayliss to Edwards.

Round 5 MONZA, Italy
12 May, 3.600-mile/5.793-km circuit
2 x 18 laps, 64.800 miles/104.274 km

Race 1

Pl. Name Nat. (Machine)	No.	Time & speed	Laps
1 Troy Bayliss, AUS (Ducati)	1	32m 34.429s	18
		119.347 mph/192.070 km/h	
2 Neil Hodgson, GB (Ducati)	100	32m 34.688s	18
3 Colin Edwards, USA (Honda)	2	32m 35.005s	18
4 Pierfrancesco Chili, I (Ducati)	7	32m 40.851s	18
5 James Toseland, GB (Ducati)	52	32m 53.289s	18
6 Ruben Xaus, E (Ducati)	11	33m 01.957s	18
7 Gregorio Lavilla, E (Suzuki)	10	33m 12.693s	18
8 Alessandro Antonello, I (Ducati)	30	33m 13.071s	18
9 Eric Bostrom, USA (Kawasaki)	32	33m 13.174s	18
10 Steve Martin, AUS (Ducati)	99	33m 30.611s	18
11 Juan Borja, E (Ducati)	33	33m 38.839s	18
12 Mauro Sanchini, I (Kawasaki)	46	34m 03.080s	18
13 Alessandro Valia, I (Ducati)	50	34m 09.286s	18
14 Peter Goddard, AUS (Benelli)	6	34m 13.297s	18
15 Mark Heckles, GB (Honda)	5	34m 13.328s	18
16 Cristian Caliumi, I (Ducati)	93	32m 43.562s	17
17 Ivan Clementi, I (Kawasaki)	36	32m 49.929s	17
18 Thierry Mulot, F (Ducati)	69	32m 52.815s	17

DNF: Chris Walker, GB (Kawasaki) 9, 15 laps; Marco Borciani, I (Ducati) 20, 15 laps; Serafino Foti, I (Ducati) 28, 13 laps; Lucio Pedercini, I (Ducati) 19, 11 laps; Ben Bostrom, USA (Ducati) 155, 11 laps; Broc Parkes, AUS (Ducati) 12, 8 laps; Paolo Blora, I (Ducati) 113, 8 laps; Noriyuki Haga, J (Aprilia) 41, 2 laps; Bertrand Stey, F (Honda) 68, 1 lap.

Fastest lap: Bayliss, 1m 47.434s, 120.619 mph/194.117 km/h (record).

Race 2

Pl. Name Nat. (Machine)	No.	Time & speed	Laps
1 Troy Bayliss, AUS (Ducati)	1	32m 51.693s	18
		118.302 mph/190.388 km/h	
2 Colin Edwards, USA (Honda)	2	32m 53.919s	18
3 Noriyuki Haga, J (Aprilia)	41	32m 53.960s	18
4 Neil Hodgson, GB (Ducati)	100	32m 53.984s	18
5 Gregorio Lavilla, E (Suzuki)	10	33m 13.537s	18
6 Lucio Pedercini, I (Ducati)	19	33m 13.651s	18
7 Eric Bostrom, USA (Kawasaki)	32	33m 14.026s	18
8 Broc Parkes, AUS (Ducati)	12	33m 26.178s	18
9 Ben Bostrom, USA (Ducati)	155	33m 26.235s	18
10 Chris Walker, GB (Kawasaki)	9	33m 26.315s	18
11 Steve Martin, AUS (Ducati)	99	33m 34.441s	18
12 Serafino Foti, I (Ducati)	28	33m 52.791s	18
13 Mauro Sanchini, I (Kawasaki)	46	33m 59.235s	18
14 Ivan Clementi, I (Kawasaki)	36	34m 10.312s	18
15 Alessandro Valia, I (Ducati)	50	34m 13.618s	18
16 Paolo Blora, I (Ducati)	113	34m 15.381s	18
17 Peter Goddard, AUS (Benelli)	6	34m 28.798s	18
18 Mark Heckles, GB (Honda)	5	34m 07.447s	17

DNF: Juan Borja, E (Ducati) 33, 15 laps; Marco Borciani, I (Ducati) 20, 12 laps; Alessandro Antonello, I (Ducati) 30, 9 laps; Pierfrancesco Chili, I (Ducati) 7, 6 laps; Cristian Caliumi, I (Ducati) 93, 6 laps; James Toseland, GB (Ducati) 52, 5 laps; Thierry Mulot, F (Ducati) 69, 5 laps; Bertrand Stey, F (Honda) 68, 4 laps; Ruben Xaus, E (Ducati) 11, 2 laps.

Fastest lap: Bayliss, 1m 48.570s, 119.357 mph/192.086 km/h.

Superpole: Hodgson, 1m 47.913s, 120.084 mph/193.256 km/h.

Previous record: Colin Edwards, USA (Honda), 1m 48.913s, 118.981 mph/191.481 km/h (2001).

Championship points: 1 Bayliss, 224; 2 Edwards, 186; 3 Hodgson, 131; 4 Haga, 103; 5 B. Bostrom, 102; 6 Xaus, 96; 7 Toseland, 68; 8 Lavilla and Walker, 58; 10 Izutsu, 47; 11 Tamada, 45; 12 Borja, 44; 13 Pedercini, 27; 14 E. Bostrom and Martin, 21.

SILVERSTONE

F Monza was affected by controversy then Silverstone was simply awash with the stuff. It was even more awash with water, great oceans of it, standing in sheets on the track and making the grip treacherous in the extreme.

For the first ever SBK visit to Silverstone (owned by SBK's parent company Octagon, unlike the Donington circuit it replaced on the calendar) it was a poor welcome, especially considering the song and dance SBK made about being at Britain's vaunted full F1 Grand Prix track — all five kilometres of it.

The first race was actually only some ten minutes away from being cancelled, due to the adverse weather. A reduction in the rains for a period convinced the officials that racing life could continue apace. The first race should never have been run according to some, and it featured Troy Bayliss, the fastest rider on show again, falling twice, once taking Colin Edwards on to the grass with him and once tipping off all on his own. He was lapping a margin of four seconds faster than anyone else at the time so two crashes was probably an inevitable outcome.

His Royal Australian majesty getting on again was deemed far from fair by some because (curiously) the cut-out mechanism on his machine, designed to stop the engine in the event of a crash, failed to work on either occasion, causing protests and much ill feeling. It was, after all, a safety issue. Nonetheless, the hyper-aggressive Bayliss remounted to take an eventual fifth place.

The winner, for the second time in 2002, was Colin Edwards, running even smoother than the surface of the many small ponds on the edges of the tarmac, and faster than the rain could fall in the early stages. Haga and Hodgson had an occasionally high-risk game of water wrestling, giving the locals some distraction from the miserable conditions. Hodgson even ran off the track at the super-fast last corner, doing the virtual full length of the main straight on the grass, all at well over 100 mph.

After realising Haga had the better set-up Hodgson slowed somewhat, and the Japanese thus splashed home second, with old stager Pierfrancesco Chili fourth.

A great ride from Mark Heckles, on an underpowered Honda VTR, gave him sixth behind Bayliss, the best result he could have hoped for in any circumstance.

Edwards survived a scare on the warm-up lap for the second outing, when his machine slipped from under him on one of Luffield's walking-pace corners in the wet. A broken left footpeg and the handy intervention of Honda's unique electric starter got him going again, in time to regain composure for the start.

Having to give best to Edwards and co. in the first running, Bayliss scored his ninth race win in 12 attempts in the second race, earning a 5,000 Swiss francs fine for 'a gesture prejudicial to the sport', as he made an unmistakable 'up yours' with arms and fingers towards pit lane.

As it transpired, Edwards took second, Ruben Xaus third, and the top four-cylinder finish of the season so far went to Chris Walker, who took a popular fourth for Kawasaki. Rising local star Shane Byrne ripped his way to the top five holding off Hodgson on the way, packing the off-podium places with Brits.

Silverstone lost Bayliss some ground but it was nonetheless an unmissable sign that he was going to go for race wins no matter what. Edwards, a morale-boosting winner in race one, chipped away at Bayliss some more, moving to within 29 points.

Round 6 SILVERSTONE, Great Britain
26 May, 3.165-mile/5.094-km circuit
2 x 20 laps, 63.300 miles/101.880 km

Race 1

Pl. Name Nat. (Machine)	No.	Time & speed	Laps
1 Colin Edwards, USA (Honda)	2	43m 27.508s	20
		87.401 mph/140.658 km/h	
2 Noriyuki Haga, J (Aprilia)	41	43m 34.866s	20
3 Neil Hodgson, GB (Ducati)	100	44m 00.498s	20
4 Pierfrancesco Chili, I (Ducati)	7	44m 19.106s	20
5 Troy Bayliss, AUS (Ducati)	1	44m 22.230s	20
6 Mark Heckles, GB (Honda)	5	44m 28.636s	20
7 Ben Bostrom, USA (Ducati)	155	44m 30.139s	20
8 Ruben Xaus, E (Ducati)	11	44m 40.033s	20
9 Shane Byrne, GB (Ducati)	55	44m 42.734s	20
10 James Toseland, GB (Ducati)	52	44m 51.178s	20
11 Eric Bostrom, USA (Kawasaki)	32	44m 56.126s	20
12 Michael Rutter, GB (Ducati)	54	44m 56.352s	20
13 Peter Goddard, AUS (Benelli)	6	45m 02.106s	20
14 Chris Walker, GB (Kawasaki)	9	45m 27.802s	20
15 Mauro Sanchini, I (Kawasaki)	46	43m 38.250s	19
16 Dean Ellison, GB (Ducati)	56	44m 47.562s	19

DNF: Ivan Clementi, I (Kawasaki) 36, 18 laps; Steve Hislop, GB (Ducati) 53, 10 laps; Glen Richards, GB (Kawasaki) 57, 9 laps; Broc Parkes, AUS (Ducati) 12, 9 laps; Gregorio Lavilla, E (Suzuki) 10, 8 laps; Serafino Foti, I (Ducati) 28, 8 laps; Juan Borja, E (Ducati) 33, 7 laps; Lucio Pedercini, I (Ducati) 19, 3 laps; Alessandro Antonello, I (Ducati) 30, 3 laps; Marco Borciani, I (Ducati) 20, 1 lap.

Fastest lap: Bayliss, 2m 05.551s, 90.759 mph/146.063 km/h (record).

Race 2

Pl. Name Nat. (Machine)	No.	Time & speed	Laps
1 Troy Bayliss, AUS (Ducati)	1	41m 20.474s	20
		91.877 mph/147.862 km/h	
2 Colin Edwards, USA (Honda)	2	41m 25.383s	20
3 Ruben Xaus, E (Ducati)	11	41m 37.130s	20
4 Chris Walker, GB (Kawasaki)	9	42m 18.909s	20
5 Shane Byrne, GB (Ducati)	55	42m 21.540s	20
6 Neil Hodgson, GB (Ducati)	100	42m 32.455s	20
7 Juan Borja, E (Ducati)	33	42m 35.886s	20
8 Ben Bostrom, USA (Ducati)	155	42m 37.796s	20
9 James Toseland, GB (Ducati)	52	42m 45.360s	20
10 Noriyuki Haga, J (Aprilia)	41	43m 01.781s	20
11 Pierfrancesco Chili, I (Ducati)	7	43m 15.792s	20
12 Broc Parkes, AUS (Ducati)	12	43m 18.242s	20
13 Alessandro Antonello, I (Ducati)	30	43m 20.834s	20
14 Gregorio Lavilla, E (Suzuki)	10	41m 27.499s	19
15 Peter Goddard, AUS (Benelli)	6	41m 29.601s	19
16 Eric Bostrom, USA (Kawasaki)	32	41m 34.591s	19
17 Jiri Mrkvyka, CZ (Ducati)	23	41m 35.236s	19
18 Ivan Clementi, I (Kawasaki)	36	42m 09.828s	19
19 Steve Martin, AUS (Ducati)	99	42m 35.550s	19

DNF: Lucio Pedercini, I (Ducati) 19, 17 laps; Glen Richards, GB (Kawasaki) 57, 13 laps; Serafino Foti, I (Ducati) 28, 13 laps; Mauro Sanchini, I (Kawasaki) 46, 9 laps; Michael Rutter, GB (Ducati) 54, 7 laps; Mark Heckles, GB (Honda) 5, 5 laps; Marco Borciani, I (Ducati) 20, 4 laps; Dean Ellison, GB (Ducati) 56, 1 lap; Steve Hislop, GB (Ducati) 53, 1 lap.

Fastest lap: Bayliss, 2m 02.145s, 93.290 mph/150.136 km/h (record).

Superpole: Bayliss, 1m 47.729s, 105.774 mph/170.227 km/h.

Previous record: no previous race.

Championship points: 1 Bayliss, 260; 2 Edwards, 231; 3 Hodgson, 157; 4 Haga, 129; 5 Xaus, 120; 6 B. Bostrom, 119; 7 Toseland, 81; 8 Walker, 73; 9 Lavilla, 60; 10 Borja, 53; 11 Izutsu, 47; 12 Tamada, 45; 13 Chili, 38; 14 Pedercini, 27; 15 E. Bostrom, 26.

Above: Smoothness and control paid big dividends for Edwards in the first race.

Top left: Massive crowds did not shrink from the rain.

Top centre: Michael Rutter leads Hodgson and Walker in an all-British splash-fest.

Top right: Bayliss's first spill nearly took Edwards down as well.

Far left: Atrocious conditions for motor cycle racing.

Left: Haga leads Edwards and Hodgson into Copse.

All photographs: Gold & Goose

LAUSITZ

SBK SUPERBIKE
WORLD CHAMPIONS

GERMAN ROUN
EUROSPEEDWAY LAU
8,9 JUNE 2002

WORLD SUPERBIKE CHAMPIONSHIP · ROUND 7

Far left: Hodgson looks for fans: the vastness of the Lausitzring is daunting.

Left: Bayliss (centre) and Edwards (left) were dominant, with Xaus finding form for two third places. It was a fifth double win for Bayliss.

Below: Supersub Alex Hofmann took over the spare Kawasaki; later he would do similar duty in GPs.

Below centre: Bostrom rediscovered some form, even leading one race.

Bottom: Xaus lived up to his promise after recent setbacks.

Bottom left: Haga leads Bostrom and Chili, with Toseland (52) in the background.
All photographs: Gold & Goose

THE biggest, most expensive palette in SBK ironically features the least colour and texture on the track itself, just one of the reasons why all the riders come for the points, not the pleasure.

Bayliss, again a double winner, found it a punishing place, as he had to work hard in race one, describing it as possibly the hardest of his life, as Xaus and Edwards steeled themselves to the task in even more determined mood than usual. He was pushed to lap-record pace in the opener, with a 1m 39.704s, illustrating how hard his task really was in the first German race of the year.

It was a three-man weekend without a doubt, with Xaus coming back to full form, especially in race two. Criticised by his team-mate for block passing, Xaus nonetheless proved his speed and aggression (setting the fastest lap in race two), albeit 'only' taking two thirds to Edwards's brace of second-place finishes. Longer gearing choices than Bayliss and seeming front tyre abuse started to take its toll, plus the suspicion of Ducati clutch problems in the second.

Xaus was fortunate in another respect to score his second podium, saving a sure crash, elbow on the deck and all, right under Edwards's nose.

It rained in practice at Lausitz, but race day was miraculously dry, a relief to everyone with an interest in seeing some real racing — especially after the curious track surface was wet for most of the weekend in 2001.

Bayliss's wins constituted his fifth double of the year, and having finished no lower than fifth in any race he was back to 39 points ahead of Edwards, who once more had no answer to the red rocketeer in the final laps.

Ben Bostrom and Noriyuki Haga swapped fourth- and fifth-place finishes, with Bostrom taking the higher position in race two. He was actually the early leader in the second race, until the whirlwind of Bayliss blew past him for keeps.

Pierfrancesco Chili proved to be the fastest privateer rider, taking his NCR 998RS Ducati to a pair of lonely but assured sixth places.

Chris Walker's rear wheel hub sheared on the startline and the English rider from the German team struggled through the second race to finish ninth. Lavilla's Suzuki was eighth behind Toseland in race one and crashed out of race two.

Hodgson failed to finish race one after a second-lap crash, and despite restarting was retired by his team on lap 12. Finishing eighth behind his team-mate in the second race put the cap on a dismal day for him and Dunlop.

Another race, another Michelin benefit.

With Eric Bostrom on AMA Superbike duty, German rider Alex Hofmann was drafted into the Kawasaki Racing Team, and he had an assured and competent, if not very competitive, SBK debut, scoring 15th- and 13th-place finishes as the latest stand-in for regular rider Izutsu.

Bayliss's performances once more proved to be ultimately peerless, but in Edwards Honda nonetheless had a superb stalking horse. He knew he couldn't live with the Ducati in most conditions, but he had been towering above the others just as surely as Bayliss had been on tiptoes over him.

Round 7 LAUSITZ, Germany
9 June, 2.650-mile/4.265-km circuit
2 x 24 laps, 63.600 miles/102.360 km

Race 1

Pl. Name Nat. (Machine)	No.	Time & speed	Laps
1 Troy Bayliss, AUS (Ducati)	1	40m 06.073s	24
		95.164 mph/153.152 km/h	
2 Colin Edwards, USA (Honda)	2	40m 06.724s	24
3 Ruben Xaus, E (Ducati)	11	40m 25.039s	24
4 Noriyuki Haga, J (Aprilia)	41	40m 29.555s	24
5 Ben Bostrom, USA (Ducati)	155	40m 33.893s	24
6 Pierfrancesco Chili, I (Ducati)	7	40m 41.715s	24
7 James Toseland, GB (Ducati)	52	40m 46.587s	24
8 Gregorio Lavilla, E (Suzuki)	10	40m 53.169s	24
9 Steve Martin, AUS (Ducati)	99	40m 53.600s	24
10 Lucio Pedercini, I (Ducati)	19	41m 15.525s	24
11 Broc Parkes, AUS (Ducati)	12	41m 15.696s	24
12 Marco Borciani, I (Ducati)	20	41m 18.979s	24
13 Alessandro Antonello, I (Ducati)	30	41m 31.170s	24
14 Mauro Sanchini, I (Kawasaki)	46	41m 39.424s	24
15 Alexander Hofmann, D (Kawasaki)	66	41m 42.338s	24
16 Serafino Foti, I (Ducati)	28	40m 20.497s	23
17 Mark Heckles, GB (Honda)	5	40m 45.645s	23
18 Ivan Clementi, I (Kawasaki)	36	40m 50.965s	23
19 Thierry Mulot, F (Honda)	69	40m 53.367s	23

DNF: Juan Borja, E (Ducati) 33, 18 laps; Peter Goddard, AUS (Benelli) 6, 18 laps; Neil Hodgson, GB (Ducati) 100, 11 laps; Jiri Mrkyvka, CZ (Ducati) 23, 9 laps; Chris Walker, GB (Kawasaki) 9, 0 laps.

Fastest lap: Bayliss, 1m 39.704s, 95.689 mph/153.996 km/h (record).

Race 2

Pl. Name Nat. (Machine)	No.	Time & speed	Laps
1 Troy Bayliss, AUS (Ducati)	1	40m 09.633s	24
		95.024 mph/152.926 km/h	
2 Colin Edwards, USA (Honda)	2	40m 11.283s	24
3 Ruben Xaus, E (Ducati)	11	40m 14.698s	24
4 Ben Bostrom, USA (Ducati)	155	40m 23.596s	24
5 Noriyuki Haga, J (Aprilia)	41	40m 29.665s	24
6 Pierfrancesco Chili, I (Ducati)	7	40m 38.599s	24
7 James Toseland, GB (Ducati)	52	40m 41.013s	24
8 Neil Hodgson, GB (Ducati)	100	40m 47.976s	24
9 Chris Walker, GB (Kawasaki)	9	41m 03.885s	24
10 Lucio Pedercini, I (Ducati)	19	41m 12.154s	24
11 Steve Martin, AUS (Ducati)	99	41m 12.428s	24
12 Marco Borciani, I (Ducati)	20	41m 13.843s	24
13 Alexander Hofmann, D (Kawasaki)	66	41m 29.370s	24
14 Mauro Sanchini, I (Kawasaki)	46	41m 33.398s	24
15 Peter Goddard, AUS (Benelli)	6	41m 33.958s	24
16 Serafino Foti, I (Ducati)	28	41m 45.381s	24
17 Mark Heckles, GB (Honda)	5	41m 51.207s	24

DNF: Alessandro Antonello, I (Ducati) 30, 19 laps; Broc Parkes, AUS (Ducati) 12, 19 laps; Juan Borja, E (Ducati) 33, 14 laps; Ivan Clementi, I (Ducati) 36, 8 laps; Thierry Mulot, F (Honda) 69, 7 laps; Gregorio Lavilla, E (Suzuki) 10, 1 lap; DNS: Jiri Mrkyvka, CZ (Ducati) 23.

Fastest lap: Xaus, 1m 39.679s, 95.712 mph/154.034 km/h (record).

Superpole: Bayliss, 1m 39.395s, 95.986 mph/154.475 km/h.

Previous record: Troy Bayliss, AUS (Ducati), 1m 40.599s, 94.837 mph/152.626 km/h (2001).

Championship points: 1 Bayliss, 310; 2 Edwards, 271; 3 Hodgson, 165; 4 Haga, 153; 5 Xaus, 152; 6 B. Bostrom, 143; 7 Toseland, 99; 8 Walker, 80; 9 Lavilla, 68; 10 Chili, 58; 11 Borja, 53; 12 Izutsu, 47; 13 Tamada, 45; 14 Pedercini, 39; 15 Martin, 33.

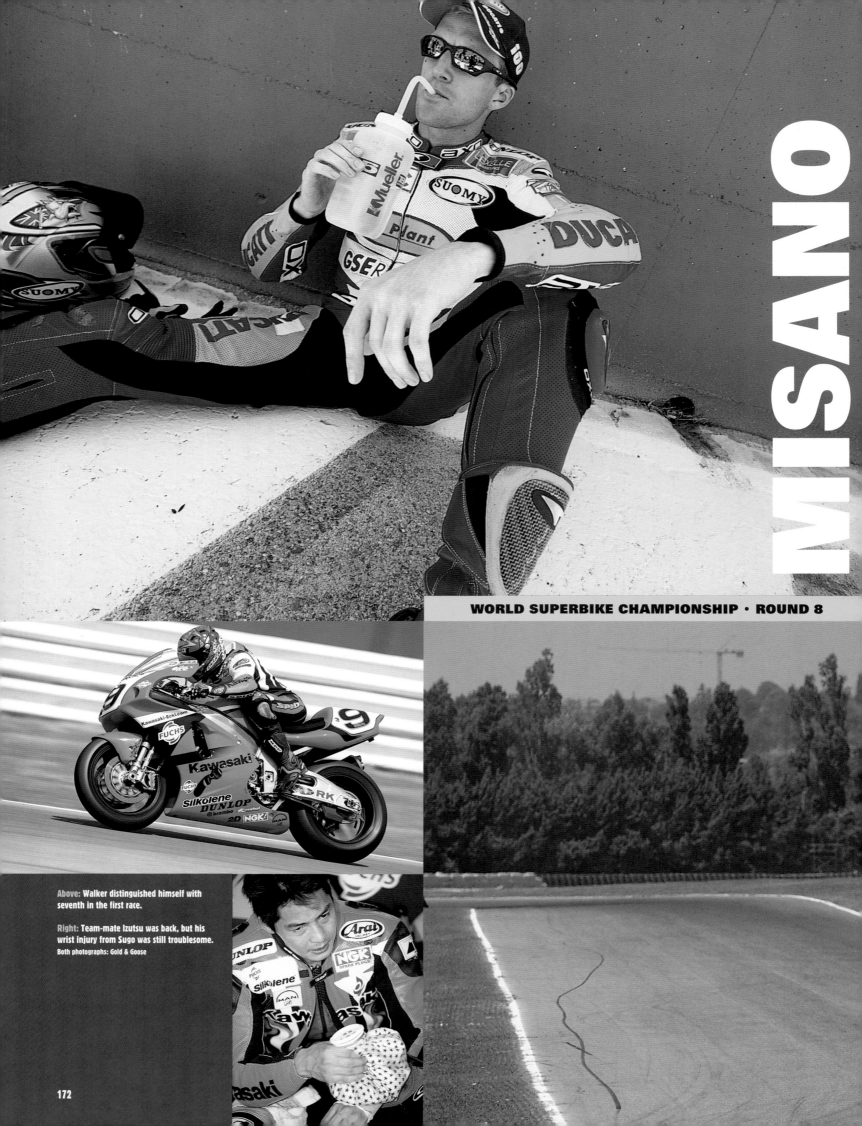

MISANO

WORLD SUPERBIKE CHAMPIONSHIP · ROUND 8

Above: Bayliss was unbeatable. Twice. Again.

Opposite page, top: Misano was baking hot. Hodgson seeks some relief.

Below: An only temporary situation... Edwards leads Bayliss and Hodgson in the early stages.
All photographs: Gold & Goose

AFTER Troy Bayliss won Superpole, the non-Italians at the seaside circuit of Misano heaved a sigh, shrugged and hoped for the best on race day. The best they hoped for was a four-rider fight for the wins and maybe some lessening of the gap back to second in the title for good measure. They got the best all right — the best man (so far) on the best bikes and the best able to maximise his tyre package.

Two wins, bling, bling: it was almost that easy.

The weather, blisteringly hot with a scorching breeze chaser, was really the biggest challenge to Bayliss. Track temperatures well over 50°C broiled tyres and riders, and were responsible for some of Edwards's by-now familiar problems of keeping pace throughout the races, despite riding better than he had ever done to win his title in 2000.

The usual relaxed pre- and post-race Bayliss was once more in excellent, near-faultless form on his way to scoring his sixth double of the year, even if he had to start one race warm-up lap from pit lane after a fault developed in his number one bike.

Second in both 25-lap races was again Edwards despite his best efforts to stay ahead of Bayliss, after two good starts and determined levels of riding aggression throughout.

In a strange twist during the second race, Edwards showed this by re-passing Bayliss as soon as he had the chance, then inexplicably letting him through, only for Bayliss to let him through again. It transpired that Edwards had accidentally passed Bayliss under a yellow at the end of the back straight, and had immediately let him through again as self-inflicted penance, only for Troy to join in the frivolity too.

This piece of mid-race kinetic badinage was only light-hearted on the outside, with Edwards fully aware that Bayliss could go past him at any time he pleased.

Neil Hodgson and Haga took turns to finish third on the podium, and also swapped fourth-place finishes, during a weekend in which Haga celebrated his 100th SBK race start.

A pair of fifth places was poor reward for previous Misano lover Ben Bostrom, his first race marred by a poor tyre choice.

Pierfrancesco Chili took sixth in race one but was beaten to the repeat sitting by the four-cylinder Suzuki of Gregorio Lavilla — a highly noteworthy performance from the Spanish rider, who was otherwise on a season-long hiding to nothing.

Chris Walker was almost as credit-worthy in race one, going seventh, after winning an up-close-and-personal fight with his countryman James Toseland.

Best of the conventional privateers proved to be Lucio Pedercini, running ninth times two at home, with Lavilla adrift of him in race one and Marco Borciani (Pedercini Ducati) in tenth in the second.

The anniversary of the appearance of Peter Goddard's factory triple was a tough birthday to take, with only one small prize of a point coming his way. A breakdown, mechanical not psychological, was the reason.

Goddard did, however, score one more point than double-crasher Ruben Xaus (Ducati Infostrada), who had his worst weekend of the season.

Bayliss was now 49 points ahead, but it felt like a million to everyone else.

Round 8 AUTODROMO SANTA MONICA, Misano, Italy
23 June, 2.523-mile/4.060-km circuit
2 x 25 laps, 63.075 miles/101.500 km

Race 1

Pl. Name Nat. (Machine)	No.	Time & speed	Laps
1 Troy Bayliss, AUS (Ducati)	1	40m 04.994s	25
		94.407 mph/151.934 km/h	
2 Colin Edwards, USA (Honda)	2	40m 07.900s	25
3 Neil Hodgson, GB (Ducati)	100	40m 19.089s	25
4 Noriyuki Haga, J (Aprilia)	41	40m 23.994s	25
5 Ben Bostrom, USA (Ducati)	155	40m 38.638s	25
6 Pierfrancesco Chili, I (Ducati)	7	40m 47.269s	25
7 Chris Walker, GB (Kawasaki)	9	40m 52.893s	25
8 James Toseland, GB (Ducati)	52	40m 54.879s	25
9 Lucio Pedercini, I (Ducati)	19	40m 58.539s	25
10 Gregorio Lavilla, E (Suzuki)	10	41m 02.198s	25
11 Marco Borciani, I (Ducati)	20	41m 08.065s	25
12 Mauro Sanchini, I (Kawasaki)	46	41m 15.067s	25
13 Steve Martin, AUS (Ducati)	99	41m 20.220s	25
14 Serafino Foti, I (Ducati)	28	41m 31.298s	25
15 Peter Goddard, AUS (Benelli)	6	41m 38.214s	25
16 Paolo Blora, I (Ducati)	113	40m 05.751s	24
17 Ivan Clementi, I (Kawasaki)	36	40m 11.251s	24
18 Alessandro Valia, I (Ducati)	50	40m 34.026s	24
19 Mark Heckles, GB (Honda)	5	40m 57.278s	24
20 Bertrand Stey, F (Honda)	68	40m 57.348s	24
21 Marjan Malec, SLO (Ducati)	61	41m 15.183s	24

DNF: Michele Malatesta, I (Ducati) 151, 5 laps; Broc Parkes, AUS (Ducati) 12, 4 laps; Giuliano Sartoni, I (Ducati) 40, 4 laps; Ruben Xaus, E (Ducati) 11, 3 laps; Juan Borja, E (Ducati) 33, 3 laps; Alessandro Antonello, I (Ducati) 30, 0 laps.

Fastest lap: Bayliss, 1m 34.913s, 95.687 mph/153.994 km/h.

Race 2

Pl. Name Nat. (Machine)	No.	Time & speed	Laps
1 Troy Bayliss, AUS (Ducati)	1	40m 07.599s	25
		94.305 mph/151.769 km/h	
2 Colin Edwards, USA (Honda)	2	40m 10.928s	25
3 Noriyuki Haga, J (Aprilia)	41	40m 16.046s	25
4 Neil Hodgson, GB (Ducati)	100	40m 21.688s	25
5 Ben Bostrom, USA (Ducati)	155	40m 29.083s	25
6 Gregorio Lavilla, E (Suzuki)	10	40m 43.765s	25
7 Pierfrancesco Chili, I (Ducati)	7	40m 44.143s	25
8 Chris Walker, GB (Kawasaki)	9	40m 52.365s	25
9 Lucio Pedercini, I (Ducati)	19	41m 07.851s	25
10 Marco Borciani, I (Ducati)	20	41m 14.117s	25
11 Mauro Sanchini, I (Kawasaki)	46	41m 22.150s	25
12 Steve Martin, AUS (Ducati)	99	41m 23.937s	25
13 Michele Malatesta, I (Ducati)	151	41m 32.894s	25
14 Broc Parkes, AUS (Ducati)	12	41m 35.667s	25
15 Bertrand Stey, F (Honda)	68	40m 58.997s	24
16 Marjan Malec, SLO (Ducati)	61	41m 20.484s	24
17 Giuliano Sartoni, I (Ducati)	40	41m 27.880s	24

DNF: Peter Goddard, AUS (Benelli) 6, 15 laps; Ivan Clementi, I (Kawasaki) 36, 14 laps; Paolo Blora, I (Ducati) 113, 10 laps; Mark Heckles, GB (Honda) 5, 8 laps; Serafino Foti, I (Ducati) 28, 6 laps; Ruben Xaus, E (Ducati) 11, 5 laps; James Toseland, GB (Ducati) 52, 4 laps; Alessandro Antonello, I (Ducati) 30, 2 laps; Juan Borja, E (Ducati) 33, 2 laps; Alessandro Valia, I (Ducati) 50, 0 laps.

Fastest lap: Edwards, 1m 35.451s, 95.148 mph/153.126 km/h.

Superpole: Bayliss, 1m 33.525s, 97.107 mph/156.279 km/h.

Lap record: John Kocinski, USA (Ducati), 1m 34.296s, 96.313 mph/155.001 km/h (1996).

Championship points: 1 Bayliss, 360; 2 Edwards, 311; 3 Hodgson, 194; 4 Haga, 182; 5 B. Bostrom, 165; 6 Xaus, 152; 7 Toseland, 107; 8 Walker, 97; 9 Lavilla, 84; 10 Chili, 77; 11 Borja and Pedercini, 53; 13 Izutsu, 47; 14 Tamada, 45; 15 Martin, 40.

LAGUNA SECA

WORLD SUPERBIKE CHAMPIONSHIP · ROUND 9

IF Colin Edwards had to choose one race meeting where wins were nothing less than essential for championship and personal reasons, then Laguna Seca, his home venue, would be the one. With Bayliss inexorably creeping ahead no matter what lengths Edwards had gone to to stop him, he simply had to win both races to have any chance of pressurising the 2001 champ as the season ran into its final third.

His disappointment at scoring only third in race one was an almost visible monkey on his back, and dropped him 58 points behind in the championship reckoning — a mountain that even Edwards knew was going to be impossible to climb without the oxygen of at least two Bayliss no-scores.

With Bayliss overcoming a painful pre-race crash on spilt oil to take his battling win (and with Xaus a team- and Michelin-pleasing second, at a track where they had enjoyed little prior success), the Aussie's Superman qualities drowned out even Edwards's one-off stars-and-stripes paint scheme. A significant blow for Edwards, and his normally bottomless cistern of self-confidence. 'After the first race I felt like going home,' he affirmed.

It was to be a temporary reversal, however, and he got his head and his set-up straight and scored a win in race two, followed home by Bayliss, who had a gladiatorial battle of wills and tyre suppliers with Hodgson, with audacious passes back and forth every other corner.

In fact, the second race was a particular classic, with all three leading riders in with a chance of the win and a lucky seven in the front group at the start of the 28-lap race.

One by one, Eric Bostrom, Edwards, Hodgson, Bayliss, Ben Bostrom, wild card Nicky Hayden and Noriyuki Haga were whittled down to the final three, Edwards, Bayliss and Hodgson, the lone Dunlop man on any Laguna podium.

Xaus had an eventful second outing, running off the track then crashing on the warm-up lap, and finishing an eventual 19th. A throttle stuck wide open took the blame.

Nicky Hayden (American Honda) enjoyed race one, holding off Hodgson to take fourth. Determined and motivated, the Southerner made wise tyre choices, as could be expected from a 'local'.

Hayden later showed his inexperience at this level by crashing in front of Noriyuki Haga (Aprilia) at turn 11 in race two, skittling both of them off the tarmac and ending Haga's day with a haul of nil points, the final result of a first-race crash and no-score. The American remounted to take 13th spot.

The Bostrom brothers, wild card Eric and regular Ben were sixth and eighth in race one, and fourth and fifth in the second. Eric was particularly impressive in the second, leading the best in the world in the early stages, while Ben was a pale reflection of the man who was a double winner at Laguna in 2001.

The Benelli triple of Peter Goddard scored two points for 14th place in race two, some reward for a team perennially plagued by reliability and speed problems.

Gregorio Lavilla (Alstare Suzuki), injured in a practice crash, elected not to ride, and neither did wild cards Anthony Gobert (Yamaha) or Miguel Duhamel (Honda).

Round 9 LAGUNA SECA, USA
14 July, 2.243-mile/3.610-km circuit
2 x 28 laps, 62.804 miles/101.080 km

Left: Special paint didn't help Edwards in the first race — he dropped behind Bayliss and Xaus.

Opposite page, top left: The Castrol Honda team joined Edwards in dressing the part for the US round.

Opposite page, centre left: Wild card Nicky Hayden had an impressive first race, crashed (and remounted) in the second.

Opposite page, top right: Bayliss delighted, Edwards smiles weakly while plotting revenge.

Top: Xaus savours a massive moment at the Corkscrew. He survived this time.

Above centre: Texan Tornado was a long way from home, but closer than usual.

Above: Star Wars star Ewan McGregor was a high-profile visitor to the race.

All photographs: Gold & Goose

Race 1

Pl. Name Nat. (Machine)	No.	Time & speed Laps
1 Troy Bayliss, AUS (Ducati)	1	40m 18.943s 28
		93.475 mph/150.433 km/h
2 Ruben Xaus, E (Ducati)	11	40m 19.282s 28
3 Colin Edwards, USA (Honda)	2	40m 20.994s 28
4 Nicky Hayden, USA (Honda)	69	40m 21.531s 28
5 Neil Hodgson, GB (Ducati)	100	40m 23.047s 28
6 Eric Bostrom, USA (Kawasaki)	32	40m 30.677s 28
7 Aaron Yates, USA (Suzuki)	120	40m 36.604s 28
8 Ben Bostrom, USA (Ducati)	155	40m 42.695s 28
9 James Toseland, GB (Ducati)	52	40m 45.380s 28
10 Mat Mladin, AUS (Suzuki)	101	40m 49.142s 28
11 Chris Walker, GB (Kawasaki)	9	40m 59.888s 28
12 Pierfrancesco Chili, I (Ducati)	7	40m 59.950s 28
13 Doug Chandler, USA (Ducati)	110	41m 02.140s 28
14 Steve Martin, AUS (Ducati)	99	41m 15.619s 28
15 Broc Parkes, AUS (Ducati)	12	41m 25.973s 28
16 Peter Goddard, AUS (Benelli)	6	41m 33.213s 28
17 Lucio Pedercini, I (Ducati)	19	41m 33.567s 28
18 Alessandro Antonello, I (Ducati)	30	41m 38.835s 28
19 Mauro Sanchini, I (Kawasaki)	46	41m 42.700s 28
20 Mark Heckles, GB (Honda)	5	40m 45.350s 27
21 Mark Miller, USA (Honda)	72	41m 04.870s 27
22 Bertrand Stey, F (Honda)	68	41m 09.892s 27

DNF: Ivan Clementi, I (Kawasaki) 36, 20 laps; Serafino Foti, I (Ducati) 28, 17 laps; Noriyuki Haga, J (Aprilia) 41, 14 laps; Marco Borciani, I (Ducati) 20, 9 laps.

Fastest lap: Haga, 1m 25.475s, 94.476 mph/152.044 km/h (record)

Race 2

Pl. Name Nat. (Machine)	No.	Time & speed Laps
1 Colin Edwards, USA (Honda)	2	40m 14.793s 28
		93.635 mph/150.691 km/h
2 Troy Bayliss, AUS (Ducati)	1	40m 15.879s 28
3 Neil Hodgson, GB (Ducati)	100	40m 16.465s 28
4 Eric Bostrom, USA (Kawasaki)	32	40m 19.836s 28
5 Ben Bostrom, USA (Ducati)	155	40m 26.636s 28
6 James Toseland, GB (Ducati)	52	40m 40.540s 28
7 Pierfrancesco Chili, I (Ducati)	7	40m 41.365s 28
8 Aaron Yates, USA (Suzuki)	120	40m 45.027s 28
9 Doug Chandler, USA (Ducati)	110	40m 54.137s 28
10 Chris Walker, GB (Kawasaki)	9	41m 02.466s 28
11 Steve Martin, AUS (Ducati)	99	41m 10.256s 28
12 Broc Parkes, AUS (Ducati)	12	41m 13.858s 28
13 Nicky Hayden, USA (Honda)	69	41m 21.789s 28
14 Peter Goddard, AUS (Benelli)	6	41m 29.634s 28
15 Mauro Sanchini, I (Kawasaki)	46	41m 33.856s 28
16 Lucio Pedercini, I (Ducati)	19	41m 37.660s 28
17 Serafino Foti, I (Ducati)	28	41m 38.149s 28
18 Marco Borciani, I (Ducati)	20	41m 39.173s 28
19 Ruben Xaus, E (Ducati)	11	40m 26.969s 27
20 Mark Heckles, GB (Honda)	5	40m 27.375s 27
21 Ivan Clementi, I (Kawasaki)	36	40m 38.545s 27
22 Mark Miller, USA (Honda)	72	40m 58.398s 27
23 Bertrand Stey, F (Honda)	68	41m 08.544s 27

DNF: Mat Mladin, AUS (Suzuki) 101, 14 laps; Noriyuki Haga, J (Aprilia) 41, 13 laps; Alessandro Antonello, I (Ducati) 30, 3 laps.

Fastest lap: Hodgson, 1m 25.597s, 94.342 mph/151.828 km/h.

Superpole: Edwards, 1m 24.888s, 95.129 mph/153.096 km/h.

Previous record: Troy Corser, AUS (Aprilia), 1m 26.317s, 93.743 mph/150.864 km/h (2001).

Championship points: 1 Bayliss, 405; 2 Edwards, 352; 3 Hodgson, 221; 4 B. Bostrom, 184; 5 Haga, 182; 6 Xaus, 172; 7 Toseland, 124; 8 Walker, 108; 9 Chili, 90; 10 Lavilla, 84; 11 Borja and Pedercini, 66; 13 E. Bostrom, 49; 14 Izutsu and Martin, 47.

WORLD SUPERBIKE CHAMPIONSHIP · ROUND 10

Top left: Christmas in mid-summer — Hodgson leads in front of the vast Brands crowd.

Top: Haga and Xaus locked in close combat. Later they would collide.

Above centre: Snap! Superpole winner Hodgson was the man of the moment at home in Britain.

Far left, above: Bayliss was hurt, but still defended his title lead.

Far left, below: Team Foggy Petronas's delayed triple ran demo laps, with Fogarty at the helm. The crowd was ecstatic.

Left: Edwards was styling for his first double of the season.

All photographs: Gold & Goose

T HERE was a Spaniard in the works at Brands Hatch, Xaus gaining another notch on his bedpost of doom and gloom as he and his team-mate collided pre-race, re-injuring Bayliss at the worst possible time. After clanging with Chili at Kyalami, and then going on to rub tyres at scary full chat with Haga on race day at Brands, Xaus was acquiring the sort of reputation any respectable factory rider would like to avoid.

The blame for this incident? No one attributed blame within Ducati but Bayliss paid the highest price come the end of race day, part of his double-defeat at the hands of a resurgent Edwards being put down to his pre-race scare and the pain from a newly cracked rib.

Even allowing for the pre-competition dramas for his main rival, Edwards was good value for his first double win of the year, especially after spinning his rear tyre on the rim from the line in the opener, undermining his feel for the machine somewhat. Edwards's wins took his personal Brands Hatch total to six, three more than any other rider in the history of the event in Kent.

For Edwards's Lincolnshire-based team Brands was a joy, and the temperamental English summer even behaved itself once more, with the mercury almost hitting 30ºC on occasion. The track went as high as 40ºC, which again appeared to be more of a challenge for the Dunlop runners to deal with, unless you were British and called Hodgson.

The winner of Superpole, Hodgson was up for his home cup, desperate to take at least one win from a season in which he was being outgunned, out-vulcanised and occasionally just plain outridden by the dynamic table-topping duo of Troy and Colin.

The big three of the 2002 season, Edwards, Bayliss and Hodgson had things their own way at Brands, with the track asking much of handling and suspension set-up, and only so much of the engine output. Hodgson and Bayliss, old adversaries in the GSE Racing team when it was based in the UK, exchanged top three places in each race.

Bayliss, despite his cracked rib and damaged foot (a legacy of his pre-race fall), took the new lap record, 1m 26.690s, in the first race, showing natural Aussie grit and acquired Monaco panache all in one.

Haga and Xaus had strong rides, if rather distant from the top three, and took fourth and fifth respectively in race one, despite a high-speed tyre-rubbing contact which saw smoke billowing from Haga's rear and Xaus's front on the haul out of Clearways.

With Chris Walker's Kawasaki sixth, Ben Bostrom went seventh in the opener and was a strong fourth in the second, working his way through a rolling maul involving Haga, Xaus and veteran Chili.

Haga was fifth in the second running — Xaus sixth.

The British wild-card riders, competitive in qualifying, had relatively hard races, with Renegade Ducati rider Shane Byrne finishing with a pair of tenths, and his team-mate Michael Rutter at first a faller and then ninth.

With no machine to race properly, the much-heralded Foggy Petronas FP1 team had to settle for a scheduled few laps of demos on Sunday to an uproarious welcome from the fans, as the three-cylinder machine ran in public for the first time.

Round 10 BRANDS HATCH, Great Britain
28 July, 2.623-mile/4.221-km circuit
2 x 25 laps, 65.575 miles/105.525 km

Race 1

Pl.	Name Nat. (Machine)	No.	Time & speed	Laps
1	Colin Edwards, USA (Honda)	2	36m 27.555s	25
			107.907 mph/173.660 km/h	
2	Neil Hodgson, GB (Ducati)	100	36m 28.728s	25
3	Troy Bayliss, AUS (Ducati)	1	36m 37.882s	25
4	Noriyuki Haga, J (Aprilia)	41	36m 49.798s	25
5	Ruben Xaus, E (Ducati)	11	36m 50.038s	25
6	Chris Walker, GB (Kawasaki)	9	36m 54.051s	25
7	Ben Bostrom, GB (Ducati)	155	36m 54.090s	25
8	Pierfrancesco Chili, I (Ducati)	7	36m 54.343s	25
9	James Toseland, GB (Ducati)	52	36m 59.877s	25
10	Shane Byrne, GB (Ducati)	55	37m 00.189s	25
11	Juan Borja, E (Ducati)	33	37m 05.747s	25
12	Alessandro Antonello, I (Ducati)	30	37m 14.510s	25
13	Hitoyasu Izutsu, J (Kawasaki)	14	37m 14.802s	25
14	Dean Ellison, GB (Ducati)	56	37m 16.340s	25
15	Gregorio Lavilla, E (Suzuki)	10	37m 17.445s	25
16	Marco Borciani, I (Ducati)	20	37m 25.207s	25
17	Mark Heckles, GB (Honda)	5	37m 35.097s	25
18	Peter Goddard, AUS (Benelli)	6	37m 35.784s	25
19	Steve Martin, AUS (Ducati)	99	37m 48.858s	25
20	Glen Richards, GB (Kawasaki)	57	37m 52.675s	25

DNF: Michael Rutter, GB (Ducati) 54, 20 laps; Mauro Sanchini, I (Kawasaki) 46, 12 laps; Broc Parkes, AUS (Ducati) 12, 8 laps; Lucio Pedercini, I (Ducati) 19, 6 laps; Bertrand Stey, F (Honda) 68, 4 laps; Ivan Clementi, I (Kawasaki) 36, 3 laps.

Fastest lap: Bayliss, 1m 26.690s, 108.918 mph/175.287 km/h (record).

Race 2

Pl.	Name Nat. (Machine)	No.	Time & speed	Laps
1	Colin Edwards, USA (Honda)	2	36m 27.655s	25
			107.902 mph/173.652 km/h	
2	Troy Bayliss, AUS (Ducati)	1	36m 29.981s	25
3	Neil Hodgson, GB (Ducati)	100	36m 30.403s	25
4	Ben Bostrom, USA (Ducati)	155	36m 40.785s	25
5	Noriyuki Haga, J (Aprilia)	41	36m 40.927s	25
6	Ruben Xaus, E (Ducati)	11	36m 40.948s	25
7	Pierfrancesco Chili, I (Ducati)	7	36m 42.619s	25
8	Chris Walker, GB (Kawasaki)	9	36m 49.579s	25
9	Michael Rutter, GB (Ducati)	54	36m 52.363s	25
10	Shane Byrne, GB (Ducati)	55	36m 57.485s	25
11	Juan Borja, E (Ducati)	33	36m 57.871s	25
12	Gregorio Lavilla, E (Suzuki)	10	36m 58.264s	25
13	Alessandro Antonello, I (Ducati)	30	37m 12.025s	25
14	Glen Richards, GB (Kawasaki)	57	37m 14.449s	25
15	Marco Borciani, I (Ducati)	20	37m 19.286s	25
16	Steve Martin, AUS (Ducati)	99	37m 22.034s	25
17	Hitoyasu Izutsu, J (Kawasaki)	14	37m 25.808s	25
18	Broc Parkes, AUS (Ducati)	12	37m 32.699s	25
19	Mauro Sanchini, I (Kawasaki)	46	37m 33.638s	25
20	Mark Heckles, GB (Honda)	5	37m 36.488s	25
21	Ivan Clementi, I (Kawasaki)	36	37m 41.682s	25

DNF: Dean Ellison, GB (Ducati) 56, 24 laps; James Toseland, GB (Ducati) 52, 14 laps; Lucio Pedercini, I (Ducati) 19, 3 laps; Bertrand Stey, F (Honda) 68, 3 laps; Peter Goddard, AUS (Benelli) 6, 0 laps.

Fastest lap: Edwards, 1m 26.711s, 108.892 mph/175.244 km/h.

Superpole: Hodgson, 1m 25.752s, 110.109 mph/177.204 km/h.

Previous record: Ben Bostrom, USA (Ducati), 1m 26.884s, 108.675 mph/174.895 km/h (2001).

Championship points: 1 Bayliss, 441; 2 Edwards, 402; 3 Hodgson, 257; 4 B. Bostrom and Haga, 206; 6 Xaus, 193; 7 Toseland, 131; 8 Walker, 126; 9 Chili, 107; 10 Lavilla, 89; 11 Borja, 63; 12 Pedercini, 53; 13 Izutsu, 50; 14 E. Bostrom, 49; 15 Martin, 47.

WORLD SUPERBIKE CHAMPIONSHIP · ROUND 11

Left: **Colin Edwards got an upgraded bike for Germany — and scored his second double in a row.**

Opposite page, centre left: **Lavilla fights off Walker in their four-cylinder battle for eighth.**

Opposite page, bottom left: **Xaus takes to the paint — he crashed again in the first race.**

Below centre: **Hodgson was getting firmly entrenched in third, with another pair of podiums.**

Below right: **Oscherslebensraum — plenty of space in the paddock.**

All photographs: Gold & Goose

N OBODY loves the well-appointed but soulless Oschersleben as a classic racing venue, probably not even its mum, but Colin Edwards loves what it does to his championship results.

This year he took both race wins, a new lap record and the full available complement of 50 championship points, even with a fully fit and race-ready Bayliss to contend with.

Edwards also had a few new magic props up his sleeves and under his hat. A re-vamped Honda VTR1000SP2 — a by-product of Honda's Suzuka Eight-Hour developments, complete with back-to-the-future twin cans, new throttle bodies and other small but significant alterations — was Edwards's new formula for the last six races of the season.

The Texan, having recently started turning his bronze and silver medals into gold, exploited his more powerful, better balanced and more useable VTR in swashbuckling style, striding across the results sheets unchallenged. The lone Castrol Honda rider's front-running performances in Germany were nothing short of untouchable. His new race lap record of 1m 26.549s compared well even with Hodgson's absolute circuit record of 1m 26.502s, achieved on his HM Plant Ducati during Saturday's Superpole competition.

The finishing orders in Germany proved to be a double interpretation of a familiar SBK arrangement, with Edwards twice the winner, Bayliss two times second and Hodgson bracing himself with thirds.

Best of the rest of the factory twins and Dunlop riders was arguably Ben Bostrom, who scored fourth- and sixth-place finishes but was none too happy about it, his season shuffling towards a void.

Haga, for his part, was a somewhat lowly seventh and then a fighting fourth, although he was unexpectedly turned over in race one by the ever-pugilistic Toseland.

Xaus's up-and-down season saw him crash in race one, and then reap 11 points for fifth place in the follow-up.

Chili was in sparkling form in race one, taking fifth and a similarly impressive seventh in race two, only giving way to the factory-supported machines.

The four-cylinder factory efforts were best represented by Gregorio Lavilla (Alstare Suzuki) and Chris Walker (Kawasaki Racing Team) with Lavilla winning both four-pot duels; the first in eighth, the second ninth. Walker's ninth in race one was contrasted with an eventual 15th in race two, blamed on technical problems.

In the lower points-scoring positions, the still-unfit Hitoyasu Izutsu (Kawasaki Racing Team) held off the factory Benelli of Peter Goddard in race one, but neither rider finished the second outing. For Goddard and the Benelli camp followers, 12th in race one was a new high-water mark, putting smiles on faces that had resembled the hue of the team's grey and green clothing.

Privateers Lucio Pedercini, Serafino Foti and Mark Heckles finished off the top 15 in the first competition, Ivan Clementi and Mauro Sanchini joining in the points-scoring fun in race two, at the expense of Heckles.

Edwards, now with the faint essence of Ducati's increasing nervousness drifting towards him on the winds of change, racked up Castrol Honda's 50th and 51st race wins at 'Oschers', and equalled Doug Polen's record of 21 podium finishes in a season.

Round 11 OSCHERSLEBEN, Germany
1 September, 2.279-mile/3.667-km circuit
2 x 28 laps, 63.812 miles/102.676 km

Race 1

Pl. Name Nat. (Machine)	No.	Time & speed	Laps
1 Colin Edwards, USA (Honda)	2	40m 55.744s	28
		93.528 mph/150.518 km/h	
2 Troy Bayliss, AUS (Ducati)	1	40m 57.485s	28
3 Neil Hodgson, GB (Ducati)	100	41m 00.061s	28
4 Ben Bostrom, USA (Ducati)	155	41m 19.459s	28
5 Pierfrancesco Chili, I (Ducati)	7	41m 22.267s	28
6 James Toseland, GB (Ducati)	52	41m 25.972s	28
7 Noriyuki Haga, J (Aprilia)	41	41m 26.102s	28
8 Gregorio Lavilla, E (Suzuki)	10	41m 38.270s	28
9 Chris Walker, GB (Kawasaki)	9	41m 38.471s	28
10 Broc Parkes, AUS (Ducati)	12	41m 44.577s	28
11 Hitoyasu Izutsu, J (Kawasaki)	14	41m 55.125s	28
12 Peter Goddard, AUS (Benelli)	6	42m 17.845s	28
13 Lucio Pedercini, I (Ducati)	19	42m 20.777s	28
14 Serafino Foti, I (Ducati)	28	42m 25.824s	28
15 Mark Heckles, GB (Honda)	5	41m 11.836s	27
16 Mauro Sanchini, I (Kawasaki)	46	41m 20.843s	27
17 Yann Gyger, CH (Honda)	70	41m 59.838s	27
18 Thierry Mulot, F (Ducati)	69	42m 09.576s	27

DNF: Ivan Clementi, I (Kawasaki) 36, 25 laps; Ruben Xaus, E (Ducati) 11, 22 laps; Marco Borciani, I (Ducati) 20, 21 laps; Jiri Mrkyvka, CZ (Ducati) 23, 7 laps; Alessandro Antonello, I (Ducati) 30, 0 laps.

Fastest lap: Edwards, 1m 27.007s, 94.278 mph/151.726 km/h (record).

Race 2

Pl. Name Nat. (Machine)	No.	Time & speed	Laps
1 Colin Edwards, USA (Honda)	2	40m 56.724s	28
		93.490 mph/150.458 km/h	
2 Troy Bayliss, AUS (Ducati)	1	41m 00.585s	28
3 Neil Hodgson, GB (Ducati)	100	41m 03.747s	28
4 Noriyuki Haga, J (Aprilia)	41	41m 05.021s	28
5 Ruben Xaus, E (Ducati)	11	41m 08.899s	28
6 Ben Bostrom, USA (Ducati)	155	41m 22.873s	28
7 Pierfranceso Chili, I (Ducati)	7	41m 27.869s	28
8 James Toseland, GB (Ducati)	52	41m 29.115s	28
9 Gregorio Lavilla, E (Suzuki)	10	41m 42.001s	28
10 Broc Parkes, AUS (Ducati)	12	41m 58.510s	28
11 Marco Borciani, I (Ducati)	20	42m 11.508s	28
12 Lucio Pedercini, I (Ducati)	19	42m 16.236s	28
13 Ivan Clementi, I (Kawasaki)	36	42m 26.530s	28
14 Mauro Sanchini, I (Kawasaki)	46	41m 12.177s	27
15 Chris Walker, GB (Kawasaki)	9	41m 21.510s	27
16 Mark Heckles, GB (Honda)	5	41m 43.573s	27
17 Thierry Mulot, F (Ducati)	69	42m 08.354s	27

DNF: Serafino Foti, I (Ducati) 28, 24 laps; Peter Goddard, AUS (Benelli) 6, 21 laps; Hitoyasu Izutsu, J (Kawasaki) 14, 21 laps; Jiri Mrkyvka, CZ (Ducati) 23, 9 laps; Yann Gyger, CH (Honda) 70, 6 laps; Alessandro Antonello, I (Ducati) 30, 2 laps.

Fastest lap: Edwards, 1m 26.549s, 94.777 mph/152.529 km/h (record).

Superpole: Hodgson, 1m 26.502s, 94.829 mph/152.612 km/h.

Previous record: Ruben Xaus, E (Ducati), 1m 27.669s, 93.566 mph/150.580 km/h (2001).

Championship points: 1 Bayliss, 481; 2 Edwards, 452; 3 Hodgson, 289; 4 B. Bostrom, 229; 5 Haga, 228; 6 Xaus, 204; 7 Toseland, 149; 8 Walker, 134; 9 Chili, 127; 10 Lavilla, 104; 11 Borja, 63; 12 Pedercini, 60; 13 Izutsu, 55; 14 E. Bostrom, 49; 15 Martin and Parkes, 47.

Above: Chili celebrated his podium finish by throwing his leathers into the crowd.

Right: Bayliss leads Hodgson, Haga and Chili — but his real target was out of reach.

Far right: Edwards can hardly believe the change of fortune; Toseland (right) and the Chili family likewise.

All photographs: Gold & Goose

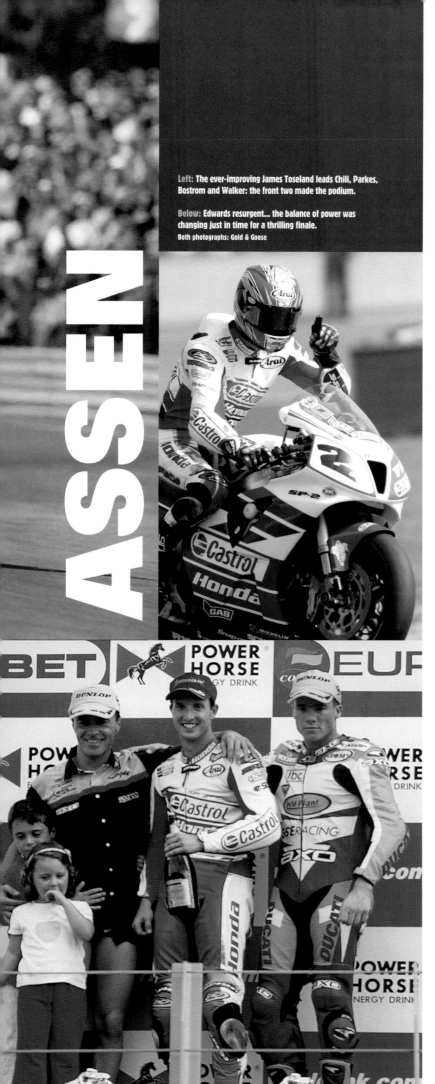

Left: The ever-improving James Toseland leads Chili, Parkes, Bostrom and Walker: the front two made the podium.

Below: Edwards resurgent... the balance of power was changing just in time for a thrilling finale.
Both photographs: Gold & Goose

ASSEN

THE previous year Assen proved to be the undoing of Edwards's championship season. The Texan Tornado blew himself off course with two less than perfect tyre choices and Troy Bayliss was awarded the title a race early.

Going into Assen this year the parallels between the 2001 and 2002 seasons were uncanny, with a similar margin of advantage for Bayliss on race eve.

If Edwards was dwelling on this aspect of the weekend he only demonstrated it on the last corner of Superpole, where he outbraked himself and ran over the dirt on the final corner, yet still took the best time. Despite a protest from Ducati his lap time of 2m 01.743s was maintained and therefore delivered Edwards a controversial pole position.

An omen of his impending good fortune?

It certainly turned out that way, as he held off Bayliss and Haga with seconds to spare in the first race, with Xaus, Chili and the ever-improving Toseland filling out the top six. Edwards closed the leading gap in the championship to 24 points with his maximum score, even if the ball was still very much in Bayliss's court. After race one the reigning champ only needed to follow Edwards in the remaining three races to win his second title in as many years.

The hard work Edwards had put into tyre testing through the year, at Michelin's own test track, had obviously paid off in one significant way, as the American stated that he could run one compound softer than any of his Michelin peers, allowing him to make best use of his heftier power output in both races.

Frustrated to be out of the running for the race win in the second 16-lapper, as Edwards waved say-onara to everyone by a final margin of seven seconds, Bayliss — quite astonishingly — crashed at the exit of de Strubben, a carbon copy, he said, of his earlier practice fall. The disbelief was palpable, as Bayliss succumbed to his own temper, rather than just the front-running pressure from Edwards. With one meeting to go, therefore, race two winner Edwards deposed Bayliss from the championship lead for the first time in all 24 races. By one point.

With Bayliss and Xaus non-finishers, and first-race retiree Hodgson and the disappointing Ben Bostrom off their oats once more, it was up to Chili and Toseland to fill the two vacant steps of the podium; the best result of the year for Frankie and the best of his career for an emotional Toseland were their just rewards.

The newly modified Assen was a fantastic backdrop for the unfolding dramas to be played in front of and some notable results went into the record books as well.

The four-cylinder riders, who may have looked at Assen as a happy hunting ground, within the limitations of their ever-decreasing circles of course, were to be disappointed again, as the last year of the 750 cc limit stuttered towards an overdue demise. Lavilla's Suzuki and Walker's Kawasaki took seventh places apiece. The Benelli Sport team approached the final curtain call of their triple's brave but ill-fated SBK adventure with a best-ever 12th and 11th.

All of the interest in any position other than the leading two was, however, lost in the waves of disbelief ebbing and flowing from pit garage to pit garage as the sun waned over the Dutch circuit's remodelled environs.

For the neutrals Assen was a dream, for Edwards the lifeline he had toiled so long for. And the brave-faced Bayliss? A mini disaster with great consequences for the champ.

Round 12 ASSEN, Holland
8 September, 3.745-mile/6.027-km circuit
2 x 16 laps, 59.920 miles/96.432 km

Race 1

Pl. Name Nat. (Machine)	No.	Time & speed	Laps
1 Colin Edwards, USA (Honda)	2	32m 58.601s	16
		109.023 mph/175.455 km/h	
2 Troy Bayliss, AUS (Ducati)	1	33m 02.207s	16
3 Noriyuki Haga, J (Aprilia)	41	33m 03.952s	16
4 Ruben Xaus, E (Ducati)	11	33m 06.342s	16
5 Pierfrancesco Chili, I (Ducati)	7	33m 14.863s	16
6 James Toseland, GB (Ducati)	52	33m 18.193s	16
7 Gregorio Lavilla, E (Suzuki)	10	33m 20.483s	16
8 Ben Bostrom, USA (Ducati)	155	33m 20.767s	16
9 Broc Parkes, AUS (Ducati)	12	33m 35.075s	16
10 Juan Borja, E (Ducati)	33	33m 42.728s	16
11 Marco Borciani, I (Ducati)	20	33m 45.237s	16
12 Peter Goddard, AUS (Benelli)	6	34m 03.117s	16
13 Mauro Sanchini, I (Kawasaki)	46	34m 03.637s	16
14 Serafino Foti, I (Ducati)	28	34m 37.457s	16
15 Jeronimo Vidal, E (Honda)	60	34m 49.714s	16
16 Thierry Mulot, F (Ducati)	69	34m 59.915s	16
17 Mark Heckles, GB (Honda)	5	33m 53.684s	15

DNF: Ivan Clementi, I (Kawasaki) 36, 13 laps; Lucio Pedercini, I (Ducati) 19, 9 laps; Steve Martin, AUS (Ducati) 99, 7 laps; Chris Walker, GB (Kawasaki) 9, 6 laps; Alessandro Antonello, I (Ducati) 30, 6 laps; Neil Hodgson, GB (Ducati) 100, 4 laps.

Fastest lap: Edwards, 2m 02.395s, 110.152 mph/177.272 km/h (record).

Race 2

Pl. Name Nat. (Machine)	No.	Time & speed	Laps
1 Colin Edwards, USA (Honda)	2	32m 59.881s	16
		108.952 mph/175.341 km/h	
2 Pierfrancesco Chili, I (Ducati)	7	33m 07.387s	16
3 James Toseland, GB (Ducati)	52	33m 10.923s	16
4 Neil Hodgson, GB (Ducati)	100	33m 17.971s	16
5 Ben Bostrom, USA (Ducati)	155	33m 23.576s	16
6 Noriyuki Haga, J (Aprilia)	41	33m 24.137s	16
7 Chris Walker, GB (Kawasaki)	9	33m 25.767s	16
8 Broc Parkes, AUS (Ducati)	12	33m 41.065s	16
9 Marco Borciani, I (Ducati)	20	33m 49.938s	16
10 Lucio Pedercini, I (Ducati)	19	33m 55.935s	16
11 Peter Goddard, AUS (Benelli)	6	33m 57.973s	16
12 Mauro Sanchini, I (Kawasaki)	46	34m 02.215s	16
13 Alessandro Antonello, I (Ducati)	30	34m 04.849s	16
14 Ivan Clementi, I (Kawasaki)	36	34m 05.363s	16
15 Mark Heckles, GB (Honda)	5	34m 13.405s	16
16 Serafino Foti, I (Ducati)	28	34m 34.311s	16
17 Thierry Mulot, F (Ducati)	69	34m 55.959s	16

DNF: Troy Bayliss, AUS (Ducati) 1, 9 laps; Jeronimo Vidal, E (Honda) 60, 7 laps; Ruben Xaus, E (Ducati) 11, 6 laps; Gregorio Lavilla, E (Suzuki) 10, 5 laps; Juan Borja, E (Ducati) 33, 1 lap.

Fastest lap: Xaus, 2m 02.502s, 110.055 mph/177.117 km/h.

Superpole: Edwards, 2m 01.743s, 110.741 mph/178.221 km/h.

Previous circuit record: Carl Fogarty, GB (Ducati), 2m 03.914s, 109.199 mph/175.738 km/h (1999).

Championship points: 1 Edwards, 502; 2 Bayliss, 501; 3 Hodgson, 302; 4 Haga, 254; 5 B. Bostrom, 248; 6 Xaus, 217; 7 Toseland, 175; 8 Chili, 158; 9 Walker, 143; 10 Lavilla, 113; 11 Borja, 69; 12 Pedercini, 66; 13 Parkes, 62; 14 Borciani and Izutsu, 55.

Above: The team had a new Number One plate ready for Edwards — but it will never race. Like Bayliss, the Texan has left Superbikes for GP racing.

Right: Bayliss fought like a champion, ended up an ex-champion.

All photographs: Gold & Goose

IMOLA

HISTORY repeated itself in an uncanny fashion at Imola, a circuit with both good and bad motor sports memories echoing around its impressive 4.933-km length. In some ways it proved to be 1983 all over again, with Edwards playing the part of Honda's GP boy wonder Freddie Spencer, Bayliss the part of Kenny Roberts and Xaus the role of the less experienced team-mate Eddie Lawson. Twenty years before, Kenny not only had to win but put Eddie between himself and Spencer, the new best American rider of his generation, to win the title; meaning Spencer had the luxury of merely sitting behind the best American rider of the previous generation to appoint himself the new boss.

The main difference is that the 2002 cast had two takes to perform their trickery, but after an exciting and closely contested first 21-lap race, which Edwards won from Bayliss and Xaus, the story was the same as '83 going into the title decider. Xaus had to beat Edwards to second place and hope Bayliss could win. With a six-point advantage, almost any other result would be good enough for Edwards.

Bayliss's tactics were the same in race two as the opener: win at the lowest possible speed to allow Xaus to catch up to the immaculate Edwards. Like race one, it was not to be, but a more dramatic and entertaining finale to a season would have been impossible to plan.

On the last laps of the year, on a track that proved slippery and unpredictable to the finish, Bayliss and Edwards stuck in pass after pass, locking horns and occasionally redefining the boundaries of competitiveness and racecraft. Edwards, pouncing on any chance to get by Bayliss and reduce the average lap times, was countered by the Ducati rider, diving under the American at every available opportunity to slow him down.

To their eternal and memorable credit, both top men still managed to ride the race to win it, their brinkmanship and sheer guts, all at a repeated lap-record pace, eliciting a standing ovation — even in the cynical press room — for the last lap and a half.

Just as in '83, five years before SBK was born, the Honda rider took the title, this time in even more impressive fashion, by winning both races, even though he had no need to.

Xaus, second behind Edwards in Superpole, could only manage third again in race two, and simply couldn't live with the pace at the front, despite some brave and selfless attempts to get on terms with Edwards.

The 20-odd other riders might as well not have been there at all, such was the focus of the world's attention on the front-runners. Nonetheless, Hodgson assured himself a clear third place in the final points table with a fourth and fifth place, Haga took fourth overall after rides to fifth and fourth, and Bostrom did enough with his lacklustre tenth and ninth places to keep Xaus off his fifth place.

The Benelli factory season ended in the most ignominious fashion possible, when Goddard's bike leaked oil onto his rear tyre and subsequently the race track when he crashed, causing the first race to be halted and re-started. The decision was made not to compete on an equally leaky spare bike in race two. A sad year's end for the classic marque, and the frustrated Goddard.

Left: A gruelling battle lasting all year long was finally resolved in favour of the persistent Edwards.

Below left: James Toseland — a star in the making.

Bottom left: Hodgson was already sure of finishing third overall. Next year he takes over Bayliss's Ducati.

All photographs: Gold & Goose

Round 13 AUTODROMO ENZO E DINO FERRARI, Imola, Italy

29 September, 3.065-mile/4.933-km circuit
2 x 21 laps, 64.365 miles/103.593 km

Race 1

Pl. Name Nat. (Machine)	No.	Time & speed	Laps
1 Colin Edwards, USA (Honda)	2	38m 17.324s	21
		100.870 mph/162.334 km/h	
2 Troy Bayliss, AUS (Ducati)	1	38m 17.838s	21
3 Ruben Xaus, E (Ducati)	11	38m 25.975s	21
4 Neil Hodgson, GB (Ducati)	100	38m 37.719s	21
5 Noriyuki Haga, J (Aprilia)	41	38m 38.137s	21
6 James Toseland, GB (Ducati)	52	38m 54.814s	21
7 Pierfrancesco Chili, I (Ducati)	7	38m 58.724s	21
8 Gregorio Lavilla, E (Suzuki)	10	39m 00.125s	21
9 Broc Parkes, AUS (Ducati)	12	39m 00.320s	21
10 Ben Bostrom, USA (Ducati)	155	39m 06.705s	21
11 Chris Walker, GB (Kawasaki)	9	39m 10.780s	21
12 Alessandro Antonello, I (Ducati)	30	39m 19.875s	21
13 Steve Martin, AUS (Ducati)	99	39m 22.286s	21
14 Lucio Pedercini, I (Ducati)	19	39m 22.797s	21
15 Hitoyasu Izutsu, J (Kawasaki)	14	39m 26.191s	21
16 Marco Borciani, I (Ducati)	20	39m 40.207s	21
17 Mauro Sanchini, I (Kawasaki)	46	40m 02.721s	21
18 Ivan Clementi, I (Kawasaki)	36	40m 11.727s	21
19 Alessandro Valia, I (Ducati)	50	40m 24.870s	21
20 Mark Heckles, GB (Honda)	5	40m 31.371s	21
21 Paolo Blora, I (Ducati)	113	40m 32.629s	21
22 Redamo Assirelli, I (Yamaha)	77	40m 44.346s	20

DNF: Jeronimo Vidal, E (Honda) 60, 13 laps; L. Pini, I (Ducati) 75, 11 laps; Peter Goddard, AUS (Benelli) 6, 9 laps; Michele Malatesta, I (Ducati) 151, 9 laps; Serafino Foti, I (Ducati) 28, 8 laps; Juan Borja, E (Ducati) 33, 6 laps.

Fastest lap: Edwards, 1m 48.717s, 101.500 mph/163.349 km/h (record).

Race 2

Pl. Name Nat. (Machine)	No.	Time & speed	Laps
1 Colin Edwards, USA (Honda)	2	38m 13.128s	21
		101.054 mph/162.631 km/h	
2 Troy Bayliss, AUS (Ducati)	1	38m 14.108s	21
3 Ruben Xaus, E (Ducati)	11	38m 19.311s	21
4 Noriyuki Haga, J (Aprilia)	41	38m 34.775s	21
5 Neil Hodgson, GB (Ducati)	100	38m 40.531s	21
6 James Toseland, GB (Ducati)	52	38m 47.315s	21
7 Gregorio Lavilla, E (Suzuki)	10	38m 54.737s	21
8 Broc Parkes, AUS (Ducati)	12	38m 54.947s	21
9 Ben Bostrom, USA (Ducati)	155	39m 02.514s	21
10 Hitoyasu Izutsu, J (Kawasaki)	14	39m 04.351s	21
11 Juan Borja, E (Ducati)	33	39m 04.546s	21
12 Chris Walker, GB (Kawasaki)	9	39m 36.342s	21
13 Lucio Pedercini, I (Ducati)	19	39m 39.908s	21
14 Steve Martin, AUS (Ducati)	99	39m 52.377s	21
15 Mauro Sanchini, I (Kawasaki)	46	39m 59.777s	21
16 Ivan Clementi, I (Kawasaki)	36	40m 01.968s	21
17 Alessandro Valia, I (Ducati)	50	38m 21.478s	20
18 Jeronimo Vidal, E (Honda)	60	38m 43.693s	20
19 Redamo Assirelli, I (Yamaha)	77	38m 26.225s	18

DNF: Serafino Foti, I (Ducati) 28, 19 laps; L. Pini, I (Ducati) 75, 18 laps; Pierfrancesco Chili, I (Ducati) 7, 17 laps; Marco Borciani, I (Ducati) 20, 16 laps; Mark Heckles, GB (Honda) 5, 12 laps; Michele Malatesta, I (Ducati) 151, 8 laps; Paolo Blora, I (Ducati) 113, 2 laps; Alessandro Antonello, I (Ducati) 30, 1 lap.

Fastest lap: Bayliss, 1m 48.389s, 101.807 mph/163.843 km/h (record).

Superpole: Edwards, 1m 49.021s, 101.217 mph/162.893 km/h.

Previous record: Troy Corser, AUS (Aprilia), 1m 49.398s, 100.868 mph/162.332 km/h (2001).

Final World Championship points: see page 185.

WORLD SUPERBIKE
CHAMPIONSHIP

Position	Rider	Nationality	Machine	Valencia/1	Valencia/2	Phillip Island/1	Phillip Island/2	Kyalami/1	Kyalami/2	Sugo/1	Sugo/2	Monza/1	Monza/2	Silverstone/1	Silverstone/2	Lausitzring/1	Lausitzring/2	Misano/1	Misano/2	Laguna Seca/1	Laguna Seca/2	Brands Hatch/1	Brands Hatch/2	Oschersleben/1	Oschersleben/2	Assen/1	Assen/2	Imola/1	Imola/2	Points total
1	Colin Edwards	USA	Honda	13	16	20	20	20	16	25	20	16	20	25	20	20	20	20	20	16	25	25	25	25	25	25	25	25	25	552
2	Troy Bayliss	AUS	Ducati	25	25	25	25	25	25	11	13	25	25	11	25	25	25	25	25	25	20	16	20	20	20	20	–	20	20	541
3	Neil Hodgson	GB	Ducati	10	11	11	13	11	13	13	16	20	13	16	10	–	8	16	13	11	16	20	16	16	16	–	13	13	11	326
4	Noriyuki Haga	J	Aprilia	20	20	–	10	–	10	16	11	–	16	20	6	13	11	13	16	–	–	13	11	9	13	16	10	11	13	278
5	Ben Bostrom	USA	Ducati	16	13	13	11	13	11	9	9	–	7	9	8	11	13	11	11	8	11	9	13	13	10	8	11	6	7	261
6	Ruben Xaus	E	Ducati	11	–	16	16	16	20	–	7	10	–	8	16	16	16	–	–	20	–	11	10	–	11	13	–	16	16	249
7	James Toseland	GB	Ducati	4	6	8	9	10	8	7	5	11	–	6	7	9	9	8	–	7	10	7	–	10	8	10	16	10	10	195
8	Pierfrancesco Chili	I	Ducati	7	–	–	–	–	–	–	–	13	–	13	5	10	10	10	9	4	9	8	9	11	9	11	20	9	–	167
9	Chris Walker	GB	Kawasaki	6	9	7	7	8	7	5	3	–	6	2	13	–	7	9	8	5	6	10	8	7	1	–	9	5	4	152
10	Gregorio Lavilla	E	Suzuki	8	–	9	8	–	5	4	4	9	11	–	2	8	–	6	10	–	–	1	4	8	7	9	–	8	9	130
11	Broc Parkes	AUS	Ducati	1	–	–	3	5	2	–	–	–	8	–	4	5	–	–	2	1	4	–	–	6	6	7	8	7	8	77
12	Juan Borja	E	Ducati	5	8	4	6	7	6	2	1	5	–	–	9	–	–	–	–	–	–	5	5	–	–	6	–	–	5	74
13	Lucio Pedercini	I	Ducati	2	5	6	–	–	4	–	–	–	10	–	6	6	7	7	–	–	–	–	–	3	4	–	6	2	3	71
14	Hitoyasu Izutsu	J	Kawasaki	9	10	10	–	9	9	–	–	–	–	–	–	–	–	–	–	–	–	3	–	5	–	–	–	1	6	62
15	Marco Borciani	I	Ducati	–	4	5	–	6	3	–	–	–	–	–	–	4	4	5	6	–	–	1	–	5	5	7	–	–	–	55
16	Steve Martin	AUS	Ducati	–	7	3	–	–	–	–	–	6	5	–	7	5	3	4	2	5	–	–	–	–	–	–	–	3	2	52
17	Eric Bostrom	USA	Kawasaki	–	–	–	–	–	–	3	2	7	9	5	–	–	–	–	–	10	13	–	–	–	–	–	–	–	–	49
18	Makoto Tamada	J	Honda	–	–	–	–	–	–	20	25	–	–	–	–	–	–	–	–	–	–	–	–	–	–	–	–	–	–	45
19	Mauro Sanchini	I	Kawasaki	–	1	1	4	3	–	–	–	4	3	1	–	2	2	4	5	–	1	–	–	2	3	4	–	–	1	41
20	Alessandro Antonello	I	Ducati	3	–	2	5	–	–	–	–	8	–	–	3	3	–	–	–	–	–	4	3	–	–	3	4	–	–	38
21	Shane Byrne	GB	Ducati	–	–	–	–	–	–	–	–	–	–	7	11	–	–	–	–	–	–	6	6	–	–	–	–	–	–	30
22	Peter Goddard	AUS	Benelli	–	–	–	–	–	–	–	–	2	–	3	1	1	1	–	–	–	–	2	–	4	–	4	5	–	–	23
23	Akira Yanagawa	J	Kawasaki	–	–	–	–	–	–	10	10	–	–	–	–	–	–	–	–	–	–	–	–	–	–	–	–	–	–	20
24=	Serafino Foti	I	Ducati	–	2	–	–	4	1	–	–	–	4	–	–	–	2	–	–	–	–	2	–	2	–	–	–	–	–	17
24=	Aaron Yates	USA	Suzuki	–	–	–	–	–	–	–	–	–	–	–	–	–	–	–	–	9	8	–	–	–	–	–	–	–	–	17
26=	Nicky Hayden	USA	Honda	–	–	–	–	–	–	–	–	–	–	–	–	–	–	–	–	13	3	–	–	–	–	–	–	–	–	16
26=	Wataru Yoshikawa	J	Yamaha	–	–	–	–	–	–	8	8	–	–	–	–	–	–	–	–	–	–	–	–	–	–	–	–	–	–	16
28	Mark Heckles	GB	Honda	–	–	–	2	–	–	–	–	1	10	–	–	–	–	–	–	–	–	–	–	–	1	–	1	–	–	15
29	Takeshi Tsujimura	J	Yamaha	–	–	–	–	–	–	6	6	–	–	–	–	–	–	–	–	–	–	–	–	–	–	–	–	–	–	12
30=	Ivan Clementi	I	Kawasaki	–	3	1	–	–	–	–	–	–	2	–	–	–	–	–	–	–	–	–	–	–	–	3	2	–	–	11
30=	Michael Rutter	GB	Ducati	–	–	–	–	–	–	–	–	–	–	–	4	–	–	–	–	–	–	–	–	7	–	–	–	–	–	11
32	Doug Chandler	USA	Ducati	–	–	–	–	–	–	–	–	–	–	–	–	–	–	–	–	3	7	–	–	–	–	–	–	–	–	10
33	Mat Mladin	USA	Suzuki	–	–	–	–	–	–	–	–	–	–	–	–	–	–	–	–	6	–	–	–	–	–	–	–	–	–	6
34=	Alexander Hofmann	D	Kawasaki	–	–	–	–	–	–	–	–	–	–	–	–	1	3	–	–	–	–	–	–	–	–	–	–	–	–	4
34=	Alessandro Valia	I	Ducati	–	–	–	–	–	–	–	–	3	1	–	–	–	–	–	–	–	–	–	–	–	–	–	–	–	–	4
36=	Michele Malatesta	I	Ducati	–	–	–	–	–	–	–	–	–	–	–	–	–	–	–	–	–	–	–	–	3	–	–	–	–	–	3
36=	Bertrand Stey	F	Honda	–	–	–	2	–	–	–	–	–	–	–	–	–	–	–	–	–	–	–	–	1	–	–	–	–	–	3
38=	Dean Ellison	GB	Ducati	–	–	–	–	–	–	–	–	–	–	–	–	–	–	–	–	–	–	–	–	–	2	–	–	–	–	2
38=	Glen Richards	GB	Kawasaki	–	–	–	–	–	–	–	–	–	–	–	–	–	–	–	–	–	–	–	–	–	2	–	–	–	–	2
40=	Youichi Takeda	J	Honda	–	–	–	–	1	–	–	–	–	–	–	–	–	–	–	–	–	–	–	–	–	–	–	–	–	–	1
40=	Jeronimo Vidal	E	Honda	–	–	–	–	–	–	–	–	–	–	–	–	–	–	–	–	–	–	–	–	–	–	1	–	–	–	1

RISING SONS

By GORDON RITCHIE

THE fastest growing form of international motor sport set its course for the heart of the rising sun once more in 2002.

World Supersport's fourth year of existence was to deliver a period of positive change and more than mere organic growth, as Honda (always the barometer of the importance of any individual race class it seems) became even more serious about the CBR600 racers than the VTR Superbike — early season at least. The other Japanese factories have been practising this favouritism for the less hefty second-born siblings for a while now.

Not everyone shares the same viewpoint of the middleweight locus, however. In fact, since its inception as a full World Championship class in 1999 a curious and unexplainable dichotomy has appeared.

Ducati, such a massive SBK power, have taken a back seat in the development of their 748 machines for the last three years, opting out of the race of the middleweights to concentrate on their Superbike. Hence the 2002 season rolled around with only two regular Dukes on the grids, regularly outpaced.

As if to prove that all the Japanese factories are equally interested in WSS now, each one has taken a turn to score a World Championship. Until this year, Honda was the missing link, and the season started with some controversy for Honda's great yellow hopes, Ten Kate Honda and Pere Riba.

The chance to run in MotoGP for the Antena 3 Yamaha team removed the pre-season favourite, promoting his team-mate Fabien Foret as the man-most-likely-to, and finding a new place for intended OPCM Yamaha runner Iain Macpherson. This in turn allowed unemployed double 2001 race winner Kevin Curtain to replace 'MacP'.

Foret, reckless and loose to the point of incredulity on occasions, an adrenaline-fuelled personality in every respect, did not disappoint. From the very first it appeared that he would be something new to WSS — a runaway winner; on a different plane compared to his rivals.

Foret outpaced the field on his Ten Kate team's favourite test track, Valencia, during round one, even though he made it hard for himself with a poor start. This followed a winter of tests spent frightening some of his rivals with his machine's power and his own swashbuckling corner speed, and there were already mutterings that he might win the title with races to spare. Stéphane Chambon (Alstare Suzuki) was Foret's Valencian shadow in second, with Christian Kellner (Yamaha Germany) third.

The Frenchman was in for an Ocker-shocker at round two, Phillip Island, when reigning champion Andrew Pitt (Kawasaki) took his first WSS race win. This dampened the dull and empty echo which followed him after his feat of winning a championship without ever having won a race.

His ride at Phillip Island was so assured that he looked like he would now be the man to give Foret a tussle, after early race leaders James Whitham (Yamaha Belgarda) and his team-mate Paolo Casoli each crashed out. Piergiorgio Bontempi (NCR Ducati) had an up-and-downhill struggle against the ever-refined machines from all four Japanese manufacturers, and took a praiseworthy second.

When Pitt followed his home win with another right on its back at Kyalami, it looked like his self-confidence and controlled riding style were about to net him a lot more than fleeting success. Winner of a three-way fight with Whitham and Chambon, and with Foret finishing fifth, Pitt eased into the championship lead, with only Chambon and Foret on his coat-tails.

Four races, three winners, as Chambon headed a Suzuki 1-2 at Sugo, his team-mate Katsuaki Fujiwara taking a fine second place after a career marked by bad luck and crashes at key moments. With Foret third, new series leader, Chambon, Pitt and Foret were already vying for overall honours.

Back in Europe, Foret used the speed of his official Honda to hold off young rider Chris Vermeulen (van Zon Honda) to win at Monza, by the very thinnest of margins. Fujiwara gave notice of his enhanced pace in third.

Atrocious conditions welcomed the first World Supersport race at Silverstone, the full F1 track proving treacherous. Whitham, in front of a sodden but enthusiastic home crowd, scooped the win in bizarre fashion when he fell but was still awarded the full 25 points. With six riders ditching it in one lap, the race was red-flagged and, as per the rules, the result taken from one lap prior to the stoppage. Whitham was thus the winner, from Casoli and Karl Muggeridge (Honda UK).

Chambon, Pitt and Foret seemed clear by this stage, but a rich seam of form, and a little good fortune for Fujiwara, saw him join the high flyers. His first-ever WSS win came as a result of the exclusion of some top names at Lausitz — Casoli, Whitham and especially Foret — for a technical infringement. Foret had taken the chequered flag first but lost all his 25 points after scrutineering discovered his bike had an over-light rear-wheel spindle. Casoli was in a similar position, but Chambon (third) and Pitt (second) capitalised on their rivals' misfortunes.

The San Marino round at Misano gave Foret his third 'real' win of the year, the ever-improving Fujiwara second, bringing him back into the game with some force. Whitham's luck returned and he rode hard for a third-place finish, but the biggest news was a bit higher up the table, with Foret retaking his championship lead.

Reconvening at Brands Hatch after the mid-season break (Supersport misses the Laguna Seca round of the SBK Championship) Fujiwara's points tally was increased still more by his win, with Foret second, Casoli third. More significantly Pitt and Chambon proved to be non-finishers. Now Fujiwara was Foret's closest rival.

Casoli secured a deserved win at Oschersleben, with Suzuki men Chambon and Fujiwara second and third, Pitt fourth. Proving that you need luck as well as speed to win titles, leader Foret crashed on the second-last lap, remounted and finished sixth — and even kept his championship lead.

With two races and a potential 50 points left, it looked like a Foret/Fujiwara shortlist for the crown, and the penultimate race at Assen proved almost decisive in that battle.

Foret's fourth and last 2002 win, the most ever scored in a single World Supersport season, took him 17 points clear of Fujiwara, who could only manage fifth. Macpherson took his only podium of the year in second place, with the resurgent Casoli third — fourth in the table after leap-frogging the non-finishing Kawasaki of Pitt.

At the final round of the year there were no dramas, and Foret kept his normally overheated cranium to score fifth (eventually fourth after Whitham was disqualified) and win the title for Honda by five clear points, despite Fujiwara's third race win of the year.

The day therefore belonged to the Japanese rider, but for Foret it was the war itself that composed the prize, not the latest battlefield.

Chambon, second at Imola and overall third, was once more scrapping to the end, Casoli stayed fourth in the table and Imola faller Pitt was eventually fifth after suffering a total of four no-scores.

Honda's win with Foret has seen a different make of machine take the title every year so far. With three completely new bikes from Honda, Kawasaki and Yamaha coming in 2003, and the usual six to ten potential champion riders firmly in place, the march of Supersport is becoming a swagger of self-confidence.

Opposite and below: Fabien Foret took a first title in the class for Honda.

Below centre: Finally a good season for Suzuki's Katsuaki Fujiwara, who ran Foret close with three race wins.

All Photographs: Gold & Goose

Above left: Stéphane Chambon (Suzuki) was an early contender for the title — it would have been his second.

Above: Paolo Casoli took the Yamaha to fourth.

Left: Defending champion Andrew Pitt (Kawasaki) salvaged his reputation by winning races this year.
All Photographs: Gold & Goose

SUPERPRODUCTION RULES!

By KEL EDGE

Above: Is a 200-miler a true endurance race? Looks more like a sprint as the Imola starters scramble away, led by the title-winning Zongshen 2 Suzuki of series star Nowland and Bussei.

Photograph: Paterlini Giovanni Communication

THE 2002 season was once again a period of transition for the World Endurance Championship. Series promoter and organiser Octagon ensured better television coverage and increased publicity for the championship, but for whatever reason the hard-core endurance fans largely stayed away. Part of the reason may have been that it had lost its three 24-hour classics — Le Mans, Spa and the Bol d'Or — which had been the mainstay of the championship for over a quarter of a century and home to the glory days of endurance racing. Indeed, many GP and Superbike stars tasted success in endurance — Raymond Roche, Christian and Dominique Sarron, Carl Fogarty, Doug Polen, Fred Merkel and Terry Rymer to name but a few. Other events — usually six- or eight-hour races (with the exception of the Suzuka Eight Hours) — have never really captured popular imagination in the same way.

In the Seventies, Eighties and early Nineties, thousands upon thousands of bike fans went to Le Mans, Spa and the Bol d'Or, often basing holidays round these events and spending at least three days at the track, enjoying the festival atmosphere of live rock concerts and funfairs. When the series briefly lost its World Championship status in 1989 and '90, it didn't matter — the fans still turned up anyway. This period also witnessed the emergence of a prototype class and the races were alive with home-grown specials like Nessie, or well-funded efforts like the Elf. It was this innovative machine that gave us the single-sided swing arm that is now so popular. In fact, much of today's current technology saw the first light of day at an endurance event somewhere.

This year the organisers of Le Mans, Spa and the Bol d'Or set up their own 'mini championship' (Masters of Endurance) after failing to agree terms with Octagon, running these 24-hour races on their own. Later in the year, though, the season was deemed illegal and no final results were posted. It was a pity because all three had enjoyed their usual substantial crowds as well as television coverage.

Perhaps the problems now being suffered by the World Endurance Championship are that the current races have not yet become 'classic' events — or is it because they are not viewed as a true test of endurance? There were six rounds in 2002, but only one 24-hour race — at Oschersleben. The other rounds comprised three 200-milers (Imola, Silverstone and Vallelunga), one six-hour race (Brno) and the Suzuka Eight Hours. Imola was in memory of the famous long-distance race of the Seventies and Eighties — an event sometimes referred to as the Daytona of Europe, and run over the same distance as its American counterpart. Fittingly an American — Jason Pridmore — won it in 2002.

For many people, though, a 200-miler is not really an endurance race — it's just a longish sprint! A World Superbike racer covers the same distance

on a Sunday afternoon — albeit in two races separated by a couple of hours. Also a 200-miler — which lasts just over two hours — favours the richer teams who can afford expensive quick-fillers and fast-change systems for wheels, brakes and tyres. The 24-hour races always gave the privateers, who rely on good organisation and steady riding, a chance to be competitive with their faster (but usually more fragile) opponents.

In 2001, only the teams in the Superbike category could be crowned World Endurance Champions, while the Superproduction bikes (such as the Suzuki GSX-R1000, Yamaha R1, Honda Fireblade, etc.) competed for the World Endurance Cup. The Superproduction bikes trounced the Superbikes in every round but one, however, and the writing was on the wall for 2002.

Before the 2002 season began teams were told that no matter which category they entered, only one would be crowned champion at the end of the year. For most, the Superproduction class was the only one worth considering. Russell Benney, team manager of Britain's most successful endurance team in recent years, QB Phase One, said, 'Superproduction is definitely the way to go for endurance. Because engine work is very limited, it means that we don't have expensive bills. We can modify the chassis and suspension as much as we like — to Superbike rules — so we have a relatively unstressed engine in a good rolling package.'

For the fans, the 2002 season will be remembered for one thing — the total domination of the Suzuki GSX-R1000 again. The bike controlled the championship in 2001 and was still *the* weapon to have in 2002. It won four out of the six races — losing out to the Endurance Moto 38 Yamaha of Frenchmen Cuzin, Hacquin and Morillon at Oschersleben and the formidable Cabin Honda of Colin Edwards and Daijiro Kato at Suzuka. The GSX-R1000 took 13 out of a possible 18 podiums, with the rest of the competition hardly getting a look in.

Undoubted star of the championship was Aussie Warwick Nowland, who piloted his Zongshen 2 Suzuki GSX-R1000 to the title. Nowland scored more points than any other rider in the series but, as the title is awarded to a team instead of a rider, it was Zongshen 2 from China which took the glory. Nowland was usually accompanied by former World Superbike star Stéphane Mertens, and these two recorded two wins, one runner-up spot and one seventh. In his two races without Mertens, Nowland took a fourth at Imola (with Bussei) and a second place at Brno (with Jerman) — to maintain his amazing record of finishing every endurance race this year. 'I would prefer it if the title were awarded to riders, not teams,' he said afterwards. 'People tend to remember riders. And also it's probably better for my personal sponsors if they know I am the champion. But that's the way it is at the moment. Team Zongshen are great to work with. They are professional and enthusiastic and have ambitious plans. You'll be seeing more of

Left: The prize went to the team not the riders: the France-based Zongshen 2 mob celebrate.

Below: Even at shorter races, the traditional Le Mans start was a regular spectacle. This is at Vallelunga.

Bottom: Victory at Oschersleben's sole 24-hour race went to the French Yamaha of Cuzin, Hacquin and Morillon.

All photographs: Paterlini Giovanni Communication

them in the future. I like this championship, but I think the balance of the calendar has to be thought about and sorted out. Maybe in a few years, some of the events we do now will become "classics" — just like the big 24-hour races in the past.'

Russell Benney echoed this view. 'We have had some great racing this year. The organisation has been good and there has been lots more publicity and coverage, but we haven't had the huge crowds to go with it. Maybe this is down to the nature of the calendar. I think most of the teams would probably be happy with two or three 24-hour races, two or three 6-, 8- or maybe 12-hour races and a couple of 200-milers. Seven rounds altogether would be just about right.'

Paris-based Zongshen sponsored two Suzuki teams in 2002, and by judiciously juggling their riders at the end of the season they also took second place in the championship. Third overall went to France's GMT 94, with regular riders Scarnato and Costes on a Suzuki, with the Yamaha of Endurance Moto 38 in fourth, just ahead of yet another Suzuki GSX-R1000, that of British team QB Phase One, whose riders included Mike Edwards and Pridmore.

The 2002 season saw fewer traditional long-distance races than ever before and many fans missed their passing. If the old 'classic' events like Le Mans, Spa and the Bol d'Or are not going to feature highly in the future, it will be up to the championship to re-invent itself and appeal to today's race-goers. It's not something that will happen overnight, but in a period when all three world road racing championships are undergoing changes, endurance — like the others — will have to get it right if it is to survive.

ABBOTT AT LAST

By JOHN McKENZIE

Above: After 20 years of trying and with a gush of flame, Steve Abbott finally won the championship.

**Opposite page, clockwise from top left:
Oschersleben start — Klaffenböck (1) has the inside line, and led the early laps; Abbott and Biggs... persistence (and a push) rewarded; Steinhausen and Hopkinson hug the ground; Klaffenböck and Parzer were out of luck this year.**
All Photographs: Gold & Goose

STEVE Webster and Klaus Klaffenböck have dominated the series over the last couple of years, with Jörg Steinhausen and Steve Abbott occasionally stealing some glory. With no line-up changes, more of the same was expected, but mid-season misfortunes for both Webster and Klaffenböck altered the chase to give the closest title finish ever. A seemingly insignificant (at the time) mid-season push home for an 11th place would be the act that sealed the title, hammering home the truism that every point counts.

Organisationally the most significant change from round three onwards was the scrapping of the Superpole session so that the race could take place late on Saturday afternoon to allow canned footage to be fitted into Sunday TV schedules, and hopefully guarantee coverage.

Round 1, Valencia, Spain, 10 March 2002

Reigning World Champion Klaffenböck surprised many by switching to Yamaha R1 power to defend his title. Whilst top-end performance was similar to his old 1200 Suzuki, mid-range power was lower, making twisty circuits hard work. Valencia would prove to be a tough debut. 'The course has simply too many curves for our motor,' said Klaffenböck after practice.

By lap two pole-starter Webster swept into the lead and quickly built a gap, but with just three laps to go, and a 13-second advantage, he was forced to slow after a cracked crankcase caused the ignition to loosen, cutting out two cylinders. Webster limped home to 11th place, and the race win was gifted to Steve Abbott and Jamie Biggs, first time out with the Maxsym-developed FZR motor, with Steinhausen second and Klaffenböck third.

Round 2, Kyalami, South Africa, 7 April 2002

Webster and Woodhead put on a dominant performance, fighting through traffic to take the lead on the sixth lap, relegating early pace-setters Klaffenböck and Steinhausen. From then, Webster was never headed to win by a controlled 4.98-second margin, setting a new lap record in the process.

'We came here to win — the bike was perfect, but the altitude made it very hard work. I had to really concentrate on breathing properly and not panting. Towards the end I was starting to suffer from a lack of oxygen and I even lifted my visor to try to get some more air. I was struggling to keep my concentration,' said Webster.

'We built a "safe" engine for reliability — particularly because of the altitude and we also needed as many points as possible after Valencia, so we had to ride pretty hard to catch Klaffy and then build up a lead. After we got the gap, we were able to back off a bit towards the end,' explained Webster.

Second place went to Klaffenböck, with Steinhausen making up the rostrum, whilst Valencia winner Abbott retired with a broken crank after having to use his spare engine.

Round 3, Monza, Italy, 11 May 2002

An audacious move by Klaffenböck on the final lap of the race foiled Webster with a dramatic last-corner bid for glory almost within sight of the chequered flag. The pair had fought a race-long battle, with eventual winner Klaffenböck sealing it by half a machine's length and just 0.142 seconds.

The race had been a classic sidecar battle — easily the best of the season so far — with Webster, Klaffenböck and Swiss rider Markus Schlosser all exchanging the lead until Schlosser's Suzuki motor expired with only one and a half laps to go.

That left Webster on Klaffy's tail, knowing that the best place to be on the very last lap was second on the superfast Monza circuit, and despite balking from back-markers Webster was poised. 'With about four laps to go I was where I wanted to be in second place, and the plan was to slipstream Klaffy down the straight and pass him going into the Parabolica.'

Klaffenböck had other ideas and managed to get past again by going on the outside to notch up his first win of the season, as the 10-kg weight advantage of his 1000 cc Yamaha R1 outfit showed under braking on the ultra-high-speed straights. An uneventful race for Steve Abbott gave him the final rostrum place.

Round 4, Silverstone, Great Britain, 26 May 2002

With Klaffenböck out after only three laps with an oil leak, Webster had built up a commanding 16-second lead with only three laps remaining when engine failure stopped him and threw the championship wide open.

With Webster and Klaffenböck out, the way was left clear for Abbott and Biggs to take their second win of the season, 20 seconds clear of fellow British pair Tom Hanks and Phil Biggs (brother of Jamie), recording their best-ever result. Steinhausen was a distant third.

The home win was a popular one for Abbott, who got a third place here back in 1982. Rostrum finishes at the same track 20 years apart must be some kind of record...

'After Webbo went out it was pretty straightforward for us, if a bit lonely,' said Abbott.

Round 5, Lausitzring, Germany, 8 June 2002

Despite being on pole again — for the 60th time — yet another engine failure robbed Webster of the win.

'We'd had a bit of a battle getting to the front, we'd just taken the lead and as we crossed the line at the end of lap seven the motor went. When we got back to the paddock and examined the bike it seemed that the problem was another cracked crankcase — exactly the same problem we had in Valencia in the opening round.'

Just before Webster's retirement, Klaffenböck's bid for glory also ended when he skidded on oil, catapulting Parzer from the sidecar platform, and breaking his ankle.

That left Abbott, Steinhausen and Hanks battling for the lead, with Abbott seemingly having the race won comfortably only for his battery to fail on the last lap, leaving his outfit dead almost within sight of the flag.

Steinhausen grabbed the lead, winning the race by five seconds from Hanks. Abbott pushed home for an 11th place.

Although Abbott and Biggs could never have imagined it at the time, the five points gained from their heroic lung-bursting push to the line

would eventually win them the title: 'I let it roll as far as possible, and not knowing who was still racing I thought we should push and hopefully get a placing and maybe even one point. It nearly killed me and I collapsed when we got to the line, but everyone in the pit lane was shouting us on so we couldn't give up. It was the hardest five points of my life,' said Steve.

And also the most precious as it was to turn out...

Five rounds down and four winners so far — at that point everyone realised it could go down to the last race.

Round 6, Misano, Italy, 22 June 2002

The 20-lap race ran in broiling 34-degree heat and, with track temperatures at a rubber-melting 52 degrees, it was eventually won by almost five seconds by Abbott, with the re-emerging Markus Schlosser in second. Abbott had battled to the front by half-distance and grabbed the lead from Klaffenböck when the Austrian's ignition momentarily cut out.

Championship leader Steinhausen was third, and saw his points lead eaten into by Abbott, who scored his third win of the season.

Klaffenböck, whose passenger Christian Parzer surely won the weekend's Hard-as-Nails award after racing with a broken ankle, eventually finished fifth.

Webster's third non-finish in a row saw his hopes of a ninth world title evaporate in a cloud of steam after six laps, when his 1200 Suzuki engine once more succumbed to problems, forcing him out.

Round 7, Brands Hatch, Great Britain, 28 July 2002

A solid month in the workshop paid off handsomely for Webster with a pole, lap record and comfortable race win first time out with his new Suzuki GB-supplied GSX-R1000 motor.

'After the troubles we'd had with the 1200 engine we decided to ditch the old motors and get straight on with the new engine,' said Webster.

'It's much easier to ride because it's at least 10 kg lighter — it's almost like going back to a two-stroke again. To win first time out with it is just

brilliant — and we know there is quite a bit more to go. It's got massive potential for us.'

By lap three Webster was in second, challenging the fast-starting Schlosser, and took the lead into Paddock bend; within two laps he was five seconds clear and pulling away:

'We wanted to get a good gap and defend it. It's important not to get boxed in here at Brands Hatch; you've got to take chances to get past,' said Webster.

Webster post-race vociferously denied mutterings from some corners that the engine must be bored out: he offered to show it stripped to prove its 1000 cc capacity. Clearly some were rattled.

Tom Hanks had a lonely ride to a third runner-up spot of the year: 'I hung back because I was worried I'd wreck my tyres like at Misano if I went hard too early. It was a mistake. I got held up behind Schlosser and by the time I got passed him Webbo was well gone.'

Behind Hanks, it was war: barely three-tenths of a second separated Klaffenböck, Abbott and Steinhausen as they crunched fairings and swapped paint with the apparent bad blood between Klaffy and Steinhausen coming to the fore once more.

'Steinhausen broke Christian Parzer's hand!' claimed Klaffy. (He hadn't as it turned out.) 'He made contact with us and Christian is injured because of that.'

Steinhausen saw the events differently: 'Klaffenböck was out to push us off the circuit, his behaviour made that obvious.'

In the end Klaffenböck took third ahead of Steinhausen, with Abbott fourth, after surviving a spectacular 120-mph grass-tracking excursion:

'We lost the brakes, so I adjusted the bias to get the front back but they went again. That's when we went off — it was scary,' said Abbott, oblivious of his powers of understatement.

Round 8, Oschersleben, Germany, 31 August 2002

An action-packed classic, this two-part thriller saw eventual victory go to Webster. It was Webster's 50th World Championship win.

'I said before the race that all we can do now is try to win all the races and see where we finish off,' said a delighted Webbo.

In the first race, Klaffenböck led the pack for five

laps until Bill Philp turned his outfit over, covering the track with debris and bringing out the red flags. The Karttiala brothers also flipped their outfit, which then started to burn.

In the second leg, Jock Skene, having the ride of his life, powered away to an early lead, which he held for two laps before Webster swept past and romped away to a 10-second winning margin over Klaffenböck.

A third for Hanks, who just pipped Abbott, was enough to give him the championship lead. Abbott had slowed towards the end of the race and later revealed that his engine had blown its head gasket early in the second leg. 'I noticed that the engine note had changed,' said Abbott. 'The motor felt short on power; to be honest, I'm surprised we finished.'

Round 9, Assen, Holland, 7 September 2002

After a poor start from pole, Webster was crowded in, and could only watch as Abbott swept into the lead at the first turn. By the second lap, though, Webster, on his 20th visit to the venue, had forced through to second place at the chicane and then set about lining up Abbott for the pass.

At the start of the third lap, Webster picked his spot and grabbed the lead, before getting down to some fast laps to build a defendable cushion on the pack.

Five straight laps in the 2m 11s bracket gave him the gap he wanted and from then on it was plain sailing for Webbo as he notched up his third successive win with the GSXR1000 motor, to take the flag with a six-second margin.

'I really enjoyed that,' admitted Webster. 'I love this circuit and racing here isn't work — it's fun!'

Abbott's comfortable and uneventful second place lifted him back to the championship lead. 'It feels great to lead the championship and now it's all on the last race at Imola; it could go any way, couldn't it?' said Abbott.

Third-placed Steinhausen raced minus his normal quickshift gear arrangement: 'Toward the end of the race I couldn't feel my leg and was really struggling to change gear,' explained Jörg.

With the top five teams covered by only 19 points the season was set for a memorable finale.

Round 10, Imola, Italy, 28 September 2002

And what a climax to an eventful season it proved to be.

After striving for the title for over 20 years, the 47-year-old Derbyshire rider's fifth place left him tying on points with German Jörg Steinhausen, but Abbott's greater tally of wins — three to one — gave him his first World Championship.

Going into the final round, any one of the top five had a fighting chance of landing the ultimate prize, but it was Abbott and Biggs (34) — who needed a fifth place and got it — whose game plan succeeded, despite struggling with a slipping clutch for most of the race.

Steinhausen had only just made the race after changing his engine — just 20 minutes before the start.

Whilst Abbott endured the longest race of his life, at the front it was another classic battle between Webster and Klaffenböck. With both paint and race lead swapped several times, Webster finally seemed to have got the upper hand with a couple of laps to go, and grabbed the lead.

However, the race was red-flagged to allow an ambulance onto the track to reach Bill Philp's passenger Mick Frith who had trapped his arm under the fairing, suffering nasty injuries.

With the race stopped but over 75 per cent of the race run, positions taken at the last lap gave Klaffenböck the win by 0.37s.

Steve Abbott and Jamie Biggs crossed the line in fifth completely unaware that this meant they had won the title. They soon found out when they pulled into the pit lane to be greeted by their entire team doing an ecstatic victory dance.

'I'd had a lot of sleepless nights over the last few weeks and stripped the bike and rebuilt it over and over again to make sure everything was OK. Then I destroyed the clutch on the startline! We had to ease round, but when Schlosser started to catch up I went quicker realising we could lose it — I did my fastest lap then.'

The race results meant that the championship had had its closest finish ever, just six points separating first from fifth.

Abbott and Steinhausen were joint on 151, Klaffenböck had 146, Webster finished fourth with 145 and Hanks rounded off a consistent season to also notch up 145, but with no wins to Webster's four, he ended the championship in fifth place.

Abbott's victory was a very popular result amongst his peers, and it was a well-deserved championship at last for a genuinely popular bloke who always seems to have a smile.

With three World Champions on the grid for 2003, sidecar racing just gets better!

BACK TO THE FUTURE

By **PAUL** **CARRUTHERS**

BACK in the good old days, Americans who won or had come close to winning AMA Championships would be snatched away by the strong lure of Grand Prix racing. The list is long, the names synonymous with success: Kenny Roberts (the original), Freddie Spencer, Eddie Lawson, Wayne Rainey, Kevin Schwantz... Of late, however, none have had the opportunity. Sure, there have been the triumphant stories of Americans in World Superbike racing (Fred Merkel, Doug Polen, Colin Edwards and Ben Bostrom to name a few), but only Kenny Roberts Jnr., a relative stranger to US racing fans because he seemed to grow up racing elsewhere, and most recently John Hopkins have been given the opportunity to go GP racing. And even Roberts Jnr. had first to prove his worth in 250 cc GPs and then on his father's Proton (actually Modenas at the time) before getting a crack at big-time factory-supported Grand Prix racing, while Hopkins went straight to MotoGP, albeit with the satellite Red Bull Yamaha team.

Enter Nicky Hayden, the young man who is taking us back to the days of old — an American taking his AMA title and going straight to the big time, to a spot in the most powerful team in MotoGP, HRC.

Why Hayden?

For starters, he truly wanted it, and he held his ground against the might of Honda. The 21-year-old racer from Kentucky said no to World Superbikes, and he said no to returning to the AMA series to defend his new title (more on that later). And since he said no while well armed with offers, including one that he almost took to ride as Carlos Checa's team-mate in the factory Yamaha team, Honda really couldn't refuse. And just like that, Hayden became an American Grand Prix racer — and one with the strongest dirt-track racing background of any American in Europe since Kenny Roberts (again, the original).

But before all the negotiating started, Hayden had to prove his worth on the race-track. And prove it he did. He won the AMA Superbike Championship because he was the best rider on the best bike over the course of the 16-round championship. As is usually the case with a champion, he was fast, smart and surrounded by a quality crew. He was also motivated and went into the year as the favourite to take the title. He ended it as the series champion, the culmination of a life-long dream.

'I'm just so happy to win this title,' Hayden said at the end of it all. 'People don't realise the kind of work that goes into winning this championship.'

Three-times (in a row) champ Mat Mladin realised it before and he definitely realises it now. The Australian's season unravelled early and stayed unravelled. His Suzuki wasn't as competitive as he'd hoped and truth be told he seemed to lose his drive and enthusiasm. From Daytona on, he wasn't close to the motivated, ride-your-guts-out racer that AMA series racing had come to know. The result: he went home to Australia without a win for the first time since his rookie AMA season in 1996. It wasn't until the final race of the season that we saw the Mladin of old, battling to the bitter end only to lose out to Eric Bostrom at Virginia International Raceway.

Daytona, as is the norm, got things rolling for the AMA Superbike Championship again in 2002. As always, they all showed up thinking they would be champions, or at least doing a good job of pretending they would be.

Hayden was no pretender and he came to Daytona full of confidence. Winter testing had gone well and the RC51 was the fastest motor cycle in the field. Obviously, he would fare well in 2002.

Hayden's team-mates for 2002 were grizzled veteran Miguel DuHamel and the always-confident Kurtis Roberts. They came to Daytona as equals, but from Daytona onwards this was clearly Hayden's team. To the winner go the spoils, and Hayden did the most winning.

As it turned out, however, DuHamel also won. After a slow start to his season, the French Canadian would end up winning both races at Road America in Wisconsin — and, quite remarkably, he managed to claw his way up to third in the championship point standings. A gritty effort, by a man who refuses to give up.

Roberts was a bust in 2002. He came to Daytona with his chest puffed out, qualified third after being the first man ever to lap the famed Speedway in the 1m 47s range, then proceeded to show that he wasn't quite ready for prime time. To win Daytona you have to be fast. But you also have to be smart. The bottom line: you have to make your tyres last while also going fast. Roberts could do one, but not the other. Trying to stay with Hayden, Roberts destroyed his rear tyre and was forced to make an extra pit stop or two. End of story. He would finish sixth and his season would actually go downhill from there, thanks to a severe knee injury suffered prior to the second round of the series.

The man expected to give Hayden his biggest fight was Mladin, back again with his Yoshimura Suzuki family. They knew Daytona would be difficult, but they also knew that the title wasn't necessarily won in Florida. Mladin's team-mates would be the returning Aaron Yates and Jamie Hacking, and all three would be mounted on Suzuki GSX-R750s.

Of the three, Yates would fare the best. Mladin's season fell apart right away when he crashed during practice on Friday morning at Daytona, a day after qualifying sixth-fastest for the 200. The crash was a big one — a highside in the International Horseshoe — and it left him with a badly damaged left elbow, an injury that required surgery. Tough to the end, Mladin tried to ride during the warm-up on Sunday morning but he simply couldn't do it. A dismal start to what would be a long season for the Australian.

Yamaha and Anthony Gobert came back for more in 2002, the Australian the only Superbike rider on the team. Unfortunately, they brought the dated,

never truly competitive Yamaha R7 with them. Gobert also brought the black cloud that seems to be following him. He won a race along the way and was competitive early. Then he crashed in practice at Road Atlanta and broke his leg, for the most part ending another season of hope for the talented but unlucky Australian.

'Talented' can sum up Eric Bostrom. Talented and determined. He came to Daytona as the lone Superbike man in the factory Kawasaki team, armed with the same ZX-7 that's been making the rounds for what seems like an eternity. Not a lot changed on the motor cycle, but Bostrom rode it like a man possessed all season long and in the end he was the only thorn in Hayden's side. The younger brother of Ben, Eric won four races during the season and was red hot when the year ended — no doubt helped along the way with his World Superbike outings for the Eckl team. Still, he ended the year in the giant Hayden shadow and then, quite surprisingly, re-inked with Kawasaki for what looks to be another season of AMA racing on the ancient ZX-7.

Ducati's racing effort started straight away with controversy. HMC Ducati was the semi-official team and started out with French Canadian Pascal Picotte as its rider. The team had problems at Daytona and a transmission failure meant that Picotte didn't finish the race, a typical result for the Italian bikes in the 200-miler. Apparently, the team had other problems, however, and after some 'he said–she said', Picotte was fired. Just as quickly, ex-Doug Chandler engine builder, tuner Gary Medley jumped ship from Bostrom's Kawasaki team to the HMC team and just as suddenly Chandler himself was lifted from the easy chair at his Salinas home to the Ducati's seat in time for the second round of the series. The former GP racer didn't set the world on fire, but he was consistent as always and ended up on the podium three times while finishing eighth in the final standings.

Ironically, he ended up being upstaged at most races by Picotte, who was taken from the unemployment line by the Austin/Bleu Bayou Ducati team after his ousting from HMC. Picotte and his Michelins (he was really the only Michelin runner in the Superbike class) ended up finishing fifth in lots of the races, and fourth overall in the series.

As for the rest of the factory or semi-factory teams in AMA Superbike racing... well, there weren't any. Three Hondas, three Suzukis, one Yamaha, one Kawasaki and two Ducatis. The lack of factory bikes meant that privateers on trusty GSX-R750s always filled the top ten, with some of them faring even better than that when the factory boys faltered. By season's end, privateer Brian Parriott put his Suzuki into sixth in the series standings — ahead of Mladin, Chandler, Hacking and Gobert.

Thus the season finished with talk of rule changes, aimed at making the class more competitive. At publication time, however, exactly what those changes would be still wasn't decided upon, though it is likely that there will be some sort of 1000 cc four-cylinder option in 2003.

But we can't get to 2003 without talking about 2002 — the season of Nicky, with a little bit of Eric thrown in for good measure.

It all started for Hayden at Daytona with a pole position and a new lap record (and a nasty crash right after the record-setting lap). Hayden was fortunate to escape with just bumps and bruises, and it did absolutely nothing to slow him in the 200. The race was his from the beginning as he just watched the demise of his would-be challengers on his pit board. With Mladin out before it started, Hayden's team-mates were thought to be his main competition

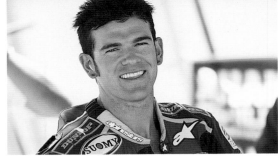

Above: Pascal Picotte switched from one Ducati to another in a muddled year, and was fourth overall.
Photograph: Tom Riles Photography

Above centre: Defending triple champion Mat Mladin had a thin and winless season on the Suzuki. Here he holds off Bostrom's Kawasaki.

Top left: Veteran Doug Chandler was called back mid-season to take over Picotte's Ducati.
Both photographs: Tom Hnatiw

Top right: Anthony Gobert won a race, but his Yamaha season was wrecked by injury.
Photograph: Gold & Goose

Several of the AMA Superbike events are now double-headers (a race on Saturday and another on Sunday) and such was the case for the debut race at the immaculate California Speedway in Southern California. Riding a four-race winning streak that dated back to 2001, Hayden's hot run was interrupted by Gobert in the first of two races at the Superspeedway. Following a rain delay, Gobert was on top form in defeating Yates, the Georgian shadowing the Australian for the duration. Hayden ended up third.

That third wasn't bad for the championship leader, but it set him and his team in motion. In a pattern that would oftentimes be repeated over the course of the season, when Hayden and his crew suffered defeat they fixed the problem and came back stronger the next day.

In Sunday's race, Hayden beat Bostrom by over six seconds — his motor cycle clearly better than it had been the day before. Third place went to Mladin, though it still left him 50 points behind Hayden in the championship race after just three races. And it wouldn't get much better for the Aussie.

Meanwhile, it couldn't get much worse for Roberts. The younger son of three-times World Champion Kenny Roberts, Kurtis was flicked off the highside of his factory Honda during qualifying and suffered a knee injury that would end up much more serious than anyone originally thought. Basically, it would cost him the majority of the season and we wouldn't see Kurtis Roberts until late in the championship.

If Roberts was the hard-luck rider on Friday, then that dubious honour definitely fell to Gobert on Sunday. Fresh from his win on Saturday, Gobert was never a factor on Sunday as one of his crew-members forgot to check the air pressure in his front tyre before the race. With a tyre pumped up harder than Chinese arithmetic, Gobert could only cruise to an eighth-place finish. Still, he was the closest man to Hayden in the title chase and he trailed by only 13 points — not nearly enough to dent his championship aspirations. Yet.

At the next double-header round at Sears Point, Gobert's demise began. Fourth in the first race and a non-finisher in the second, the Australian left the wine country of Northern California 60 points behind Hayden — though he was still in second place.

Hayden, meanwhile, had started another winning streak with a perfect double victory at Sears. Combined with his second race win at California Speedway, Hayden had won three in a row and showed no signs of letting up.

DuHamel fared second best at Sears Point, his second- and third-place finishes over the two races jump-starting his season after a sluggish start. Bostrom was third on Saturday and fourth on Sunday, but things weren't looking promising for the Kawasaki rider as he was still having problems getting the ZX-7 to his liking.

The Hayden steamroller gathered even more momentum at the following rounds in Atlanta with young Nicky securing two more victories. It was a good weekend for the team with DuHamel scoring second- and third-place finishes.

Road Atlanta spelled the end for Yamaha with its one and only rider, Gobert, suffering a broken leg in a practice crash — another season that had started full of promise coming to an abrupt end. We would see Gobert again, but he wouldn't be the same guy who'd shown up 100 per cent prepared for the 2002 season.

Hayden left Georgia having won his fifth straight race and his tenth of the last eleven. Bostrom rode hard all weekend and turned his season around with fourth- and second-place finishes to show for it. He also moved into second in the series standings — 80 points behind Hayden. It was early and the fat lady wasn't singing yet, but she was certainly riding shotgun on the Honda truck.

It's too bad for Bostrom that Pikes Peak wasn't a double-header. Always dominant at the tiny little 1.35-mile race track in the Colorado Rockies, Bostrom was again so in 2002. While Pikes put Bostrom's season in high gear, it also marked the first error of Hayden's year.

After not putting a wheel wrong in the seven rounds prior to Colorado, Hayden proved that no man is perfect when he tossed his RC51 down the road in the race. The crash was innocent enough, but the damage was sufficient as the bike burst into flames. It also gave Bostrom some hope, albeit slim, in the title chase. The lead was down to 42 points. Yates ended the day second after a heroic ride from the back following a stop-and-go penalty, and his team-mate Hacking was third.

Two races were held at Road America. And DuHamel won both of them. At home on the fast four-mile circuit, the French Canadian scored popular wins — the first over Bostrom and the second over Hayden. DuHamel's RC51 was the class of the field, but he still had to ride it, and ride it he did. The all-time leader in AMA Superbike victories added to that total with his 24th and 25th career wins — and they were close. Margin of victory? 0.356 of a second on Saturday, 0.007 of a second on Sunday.

With second- and third-place finishes in the two races compared to Hayden's fourth and second, Bostrom gained a bit more ground — but it would take more than that to catch up.

If Bostrom was unlucky not to have two races at Pikes Peak, he was fortunate that Brainerd International Raceway didn't host a double-header. There was no beating the RC51 on this ultra-fast circuit and Hayden got back on

as the RC51s were vastly superior on the high banks of Daytona. DuHamel, though, went out early with an engine failure and Roberts showed his immaturity by destroying a rear tyre early on while jousting with Hayden. Even those with little racing knowledge could see that Hayden was doing it easier, his bike more upright on the corner exits, while Roberts's rear tyre was puffing smoke rings on the exits. It was only a matter of time before it was destroyed, and Roberts was fortunate that it didn't occur at top speed. He was able to pit and ultimately finish sixth. Lesson learned. Hopefully.

Second place ended up going to Hacking on the Yoshimura Suzuki, some 18 seconds behind Hayden. Hacking ran down Gobert on the final lap for his best-ever finish in the 200.

'Don't count me out. If you count me out, you've done messed up,' Hacking said after the race. And to think the young man was born in England.

Hacking's team-mate Yates was fourth with Bostrom a disappointed fifth.

This one was all about Hayden and he became the youngest man to win the Daytona 200 since a 19-year-old by the name of Johnny Cecotto took victory in 1976.

But Daytona is Daytona and not everything that happens there means much in terms of the championship. The title is won elsewhere. Leave Daytona with some points and you're okay goes the theory.

track with a victory there, his first win in the last three races. But Bostrom had given him fits throughout and the Kawasaki rider came up just 0.188 of a second short. Those two were in a class of their own, with Chandler taking his first podium finish of the series in third place. The returning Roberts held fourth until the final lap when he waved his team-mate DuHamel past. Leaving Minnesota, Hayden's points lead was 42.

If one race in the AMA Superbike series is deemed more important than the rest, that race would be Laguna Seca. Held in conjunction with the World Superbike event, the world comes to Laguna and they come with eyes open — team managers looking for young Americans to steal away to the Big Series.

Last year was the first year for the race to be held side by side with the world round, and Bostrom was dominant. This year he was even more so. He gave Hayden a sound beating and made his mark on the race. He also gathered back a few points in the championship chase, though things were getting close to being over. With four races to run, Hayden led by 36 points. Third place at Laguna went to Chandler, his second such finish in a row.

We'd have to call Mid-Ohio a draw. After a stunning battle, Bostrom won on Saturday, Hayden was second. After another thriller, Hayden won on Sunday, Bostrom was second. The point for pole position went to Hayden, the two points for leading the most laps in both races went to Bostrom. The final tally: Bostrom 70 points, Hayden 69. The lead was 35 points with just two races left. Yates had finished third on the first day and that man Mladin was back with a third on Sunday, his first podium finish of the season — believe it or not.

The season came to a close at Virginia International Raceway in anti-climatic fashion. Bostrom crashed out of the first race and the title was Hayden's. He'd won the event, topping Chandler and DuHamel, and the series. And he was the youngest champion ever — at 21 years, 10 days.

Sunday's race was a mess and Hayden ended up making his second mistake of the season while trying to run with Bostrom and Mladin. The newly crowned champion crashed on lap seven and was left to watch a thrilling battle between his rival and the back-on-form Australian. It was a race that went to Bostrom, but just barely — 0.004 of a second. The parting shot went to Mladin. He didn't attend the rostrum ceremony or the post-race press conference.

'Everyone thinks I'm pissed off for coming second, but I'm not,' Mladin said after his best finish of the season. 'When I went across the finish line, all I thought about was the amount of work that we should have done, that should have been happening this year, and that shouldn't have happened. I don't care if I come second or fifth. It's not the point. Or if I win, I'd be happier I won because I won a race, and I didn't win a race all year. But I'd still be annoyed as I've been all year for the amount of effort my guys and myself have put in to get the results we got. I had nothing good to say, and I didn't want to get up there and make a dick of myself and my team and the rest of them.'

So with that the season ended. It was Hayden's year, but Bostrom was close — if not on points then definitely in the art of being a racer through and through. The rest would be back to start it all again at Daytona, their hopes and dreams somewhat revitalised with the departure of America's next Grand Prix hero.

As for the other classes, Yates made good on Suzuki's GSX-R600 to top the 600 cc Supersport series while Jimmy Moore successfully defended his 750 cc Supersport crown. In the big-bore Formula Xtreme class, Australian Damon Buckmaster lost a series title by just a handful of points for the third straight year, with Jason Pridmore doing the deed this season.

Aprilia-mounted Chuck Sorensen won the 250 cc Grand Prix Championship while Aussie Kirk McCarthy and his Ducati won what was the last AMA Pro Thunder title... the series is being banished for 2003.

Top left: Aaron Yates had a disappointing Superbike season, but he won the 600 series for Suzuki.

Above left: Jason Pridmore narrowly won the Formula Xtreme title.
Both photographs: Tom Riles Photography

Bottom: Eric Bostrom consistently impressed on the ageing Kawasaki ZX-7 Superbike.
Photograph: Tom Hnatiw

MASTER DJ

By MACMcDIARMID

Above: David Jefferies takes the GSX-1000R to 1000 cc Production victory — one of three wins for the record-breaker from Yorkshire.

Photograph: Dave Collister/www.photocycles.com

THEY call it the 'World's Greatest Road Race', which is certainly still true. This year, thanks to a 'one-off cash injection of around £200,000', plus a £5000 bonus to each TT winner, it was also the richest of all time.

But with each year that passes the TT becomes more of an anachronism in the greater racing scheme of things; 2002 was the year in which the races lost any pretence of running Grand Prix classes. With the 250 class dropped for 2003 and 125s hanging on principally because they offer racing at realistic cost, it was left more than ever for production-based machines to carry the show (despite the commentary's tone-deaf references to an Aprilia triple roaring round). But what a show they put on. Welcome to the World's Greatest Production Race, the sternest and most relevant test there is of real bikes on real roads.

PRACTICE

You can also define the TT by the weather. Last year, when there was no racing due to the UK foot-and-mouth epidemic, the Island enjoyed perfect racing conditions. For the month leading up to TT 2002, there was a near-drought. Saturday's opening practice session was held in a typhoon. Then the Island's notoriously fickle elements improved, which is to say that it was fine for most of the time, but rained the instant a racing bike even looked like roaring down Bray Hill.

The loss of meaningful practice time troubled many teams, and none more so than the sidecar crews. Lap record holder and seven times winner Dave Molyneux gave a miss to Monday's dry session since 'It looked like it was going to rain.' This was in contrast to all the other sessions, where it was already raining. It would be Friday morning before he got in a half-decent lap, albeit over 5 mph down on his 112.76 mph record. Many other teams, solo and sidecar, were in similar straits. Geordies Ian Bell/Neil Carpenter led the final sidecar standings at 110.10 mph, ahead of Rob Fisher/Rick Long, double winners at the last TT. Moly, reunited with 1989 passenger Colin Hardman, stood third at 107.64 mph.

If a bike is big and fast, David Jefferies would always take some beating. So it was in the Senior/F1 class, where DJ's final lap at 125.95 mph put him comfortably ahead of the Honda Britain duo of John McGuinness and Adrian Archibald. Fourth was Jim Moodie's V&M Yamaha, with Ronnie Smith and Richard Britton's Suzukis completing the top six.

In the 1000 cc Production class it was much the same story, with Jefferies way out on his own and Archibald's Fireblade almost 30 seconds behind. Some way back again was Ian Lougher, riding the other TAS Suzuki, followed by Britton, Iain Duffus and Kiwi Bruce Anstey.

Partly because riders had bigger fish to fry, and partly because the bikes were expected to work pretty much out of the crate, times in the new 600 Production class (replacing the Single-cylinder TT) gave a misleading picture. Moodie's V&M Yamaha topped the rankings at 115.51 mph, followed by the Suzukis of Britton, Mick Skene and Jefferies, and Paul Hunt and Gordon Blackley on a brace of Hondas.

A Honda Britain rider for the first time, lap record holder Archibald looked set to make amends on his Supersport 600, posting 120.02 mph. Shaun Harris, having lost his entire sponsorship package on the eve of the TT, somehow borrowed a Suzuki to put him into second place, ahead of Moodie's V&M Yamaha. Jefferies, McGuinness and Jason Griffiths completed the top six.

In a 250 cc field numbering just 17 machines, Anstey set the challenge with 115.87 mph on Monday evening, and no one came remotely close until Ronnie Smith jumped on Steve Manton's NS250 after Shaun Brown broke an ankle, lapping at 112.59 mph first time out. Third was Richard Coates's Honda at 108.38 mph.

Fittingly, in the first TT for 27 years not to be graced by Joey Dunlop, younger brother Robert topped the Ultra Lightweight 125 rankings at 108.07 mph, with Lougher second and Michael Wilcox third.

What the Lightweight 400 cc class lacked in outright power, it made up in sheer determination. With Nigel 'Cap' Davies's 108.59 mph already atop the field, Richard 'Milky Bar' Quayle found himself marooned at Black Hut when his RC45 expired. Miles away in Douglas his CBR400 awaited its first dry lap of the week, its gearing a total guess.

In full leathers on a hot evening, Milky ran almost two miles to the Bungalow only to be directed off the course by marshals. Undaunted, he managed to borrow a dirt bike, and set off across the moor, only to crash head-first into a bog, burying the front wheel and anointing himself with putrid slime. Abandoning the bike, he finally made it to Brandywell, where he scrounged a lift back to Douglas.

Then, 'wet through, knackered and covered in crap' he put himself second on the leaderboard, just 0.1 seconds ahead of McGuinness. Can you imagine Max going to such lengths?

FORMULA ONE

After all the misery of practice week, the opening race day brought the best weather of the week so far. If this proved a mixed blessing for the pit crews sweating into their newly mandatory fire-proof overalls, Jefferies relished the conditions, leading from start to finish at a race record 123.38 mph — 3.38 mph up on Steve Hislop's mark of 11 years before.

On the opening lap the first three riders smashed the lap record from a standing start, but the Yorkshireman was never pressed. The drama was more in the numbers than the contest: the fastest-ever TT race, with the fastest lap speed — Jefferies second, slowing for the pits, at 126.68 mph. DJ even found time for a spot of comedy during his second pit stop. As the TAS Suzuki crew changed his rear wheel, he was tentatively approached by Dave Moore, now the man with the mike in pit lane. DJ gave the nod to indicate that a mid-race interview was OK. After the race, Moore asked him why. Apparently he was bored. 'What else was I going to do for 30 seconds?' he asked.

What wasn't obvious until the post-race interviews was that, far from taking it easy, the winner's TAS Suzuki was stuck in third gear from Ramsey Hairpin on lap six, cutting his lead from 69 to 35 seconds. 'A big worry,' said DJ after the race. 'The Mountain Mile was really the Mountain Three Miles — it took so long for the bike to buzz its way along it.' The win was only Suzuki's second in the Honda-dominated F1 race, Graeme Crosby having won controversially in 1981.

Second, despite lapping no less than 27 seconds faster than he ever had before, was John McGuinness on the Honda Fireblade. With Archibald retiring on lap four after earlier lying third, the final rostrum place went to Jim Moodie's V&M Yamaha. Lougher, Quayle and Jason Griffiths filled the final leaderboard places.

SIDECAR 'A'

In taking his ninth TT win, Rob Fisher joined illustrious sidecar company in the record books, equalling the record tallies of Mick Boddice, Dave Saville and Siegfried Schauzu. After leading all the way for what looked a comfortable victory, the Cumbrian admitted that this was his toughest-ever TT win.

'I nearly ran straight on at Sulby Bridge, watching Molly and not noticing cement dust on the road. Then I had to stop real quick when a Frenchman crossed in front of me on the Mountain Mile.'

Ian Bell, 21 seconds behind in second place, had problems of his own, clipping the kerb violently at Laurel Bank on lap one, before taking things a little more steadily. Third were Gary Horspole and Kevin Leigh who narrowly missed their first 110 mph lap when they overshot into the gravel trap at Creg-ny-Baa.

Local hero Dave Molyneux had his dramas before the race when passenger Colin Hardman crashed a road bike, badly damaging a hand. Fourth place was the best the duo could manage.

ULTRA LIGHTWEIGHT 125

If there were an award for the most versatile and accomplished rider at the TT, it would surely go to Ian Lougher. Now resident near the heart of road racing in Ulster, the Welshman looks equally at home on 125 cc tiddlers as he does on the 1000 cc TAS Suzuki. With damp patches making riding conditions tricky, he took his third class win in Monday's 125 cc TT.

'That was a close one,' he admitted as he climbed off the RS125 Honda. 'I went flat out from the off but it was very wet on the run out of Ramsey Hairpin and I had a couple of slides, but nothing to worry about too much.' In fact 'Lucky' had had to work hard, and didn't overhaul James Crumpton to take the lead until the Glen Helen commentary position on lap three.

Crumpton, going all-out to celebrate his 33rd birthday, held on for a career-best second place, ahead of four-times 125 cc winner Robert Dunlop. Lougher, Crumpton and fourth-placed Chris Palmer all broke the lap record on their fourth and final lap, with 'Lucky' fastest at 110.21 mph.

LIGHTWEIGHT 400

If any mud stuck to Richard Quayle after his adventures in Friday's final practice session, it certainly didn't show as he became the first Manxman to win a solo TT since Neil Kelly in 1967. Riding a CBR400 Honda, no winner for years was more overjoyed than 'Milky' after his start-to-finish win. 'This is my dream,' the 29-year-old enthused afterwards, 'I've never wanted to do anything else in my life but win a TT, this is all I've ever dreamed of.'

Second, 22 seconds in arrears, was Jim Hodson's Yamaha, with Ulster's Richard Britton third on a Kawasaki.

Above: Ian Lougher conquered tricky mixed conditions for victory in the Ultra Lightweight TT.
Photograph: Dave Collister/www.photocycles.com

Below left: Manxman Richard Quayle (Honda CBR) realised a lifetime's ambition, winning the Lightweight 400 TT.
Photograph: Dave Purves

Bottom: Rob Fisher equalled the record with his ninth Sidecar TT win. He went on to set a new one with his tenth.
Photograph: Dave Collister/www.photocycles.com

Top: History man — Kiwi Bruce Anstey cruised to a maiden TT win in the last-ever 250 TT.
Photograph: Dave Collister/www.photocycles.com

Above: Ready to go — a classic TT scene. Yamaha-mounted Jim Moodie awaits the off before the 1000 cc Production TT.
Photograph: Dave Purves

1000 cc PRODUCTION

'There's not much difference between the F1 and Proddy bike,' said a tongue-in-cheek David Jefferies after practice week, 'just grip... suspension... brakes... and power. Apart from that, they're the same.'

A few days later he added, a little more seriously, that 'the proddy bike's so much easier to ride... a doddle, really. It's lots softer than the F1. The F1's a lot harsher... more grip but much harder work to ride.'

So his demolition of the rest of the field in ideal conditions during Monday afternoon's 1000 cc Production TT was little more than a spot of fast touring around the scenic Isle of Man. With not a single flying lap on the TAS GSX-R1000 he set a fastest of no less than 124.31 mph. His average, 122.64 mph, was faster than any TT race ever run prior to his own F1 victory of two days before. Some tour. Some bike.

Second place, 15 seconds in arrears, was Jefferies' TAS team-mate, Lougher — also faster than any pre-2002 TT race, with New Zealand's Bruce Anstey a further 27 seconds behind on yet another GSX-R. Moodie, Duffus and McGuinness completed the leaderboard.

Less happy was the accident befalling two race marshals, Jim Sutcliffe and John Cattle, who were struck by the GSX-R1000 of Llanelli's Nigel Davies, as he slid off at Glen Helen. Both were taken to Noble's Hospital, where Jim was treated for a broken leg and John for a fractured ankle — for which he was later seen taking additional medication in Peel's Creek Inn.

SIDECAR 'B'

Their race may have been sponsored by the Hilton Hotel, but the sidecar boys found their living conditions less than five-star. Prior to their second race they handed in a petition complaining about the state of paddock facilities, and particularly the bogs: 'disgusting... a Third-World set-up,' fumed one of them. Then the flag dropped and they got on with that special form of pink-misted discomfort that only the three-wheelers can bring.

Fisher, winner of Saturday's Sidecar 'A', started the race 10 seconds behind Molyneux but when he caught the Manxman on the road the two drivers treated spectators to the most stirring tussle of the week so far. At the finish Fisher took victory, by 14 seconds on corrected time, to put himself alone at the top of the all-time sidecar standings with ten wins — the last five on the trot.

Moly's second place was some consolation for his poor showing on Saturday. Ian Bell and Neil Carpenter placed third.

JUNIOR 600

Jim Moodie's eighth TT win, in what is usually the toughest of classes, turned out to be one of his easiest. Pre-race favourite David Jefferies retired at Sulby on lap one when his GSX-R600 Suzuki dropped a valve, while John McGuinness's CBR600 broke a piston at the Eleventh Milestone when lying second on lap two.

By the time DJ retired, however, the veteran Scot was already ahead, although it wasn't until the Gooseneck that he became aware his main rival's effort was spent. Lougher took full advantage to take another second place, with fellow Welshman Jason Griffiths in third, ahead of the Ulstermen pair of Richard Britton and Ryan Farquhar. Richard Quayle placed sixth, one ahead of Adrian Archibald.

JUNIOR 250

Bruce Anstey, way ahead on the practice leaderboard, comfortably won what was destined to become the last 250 cc, run alongside the 600 cc division. With only 18 starters (six of whom retired) the class is now a shadow of its former self.

The Kiwi's maiden TT win proved utterly untroubled, as he led by almost a minute after one lap, and by over three minutes at the end of the four-lap race. Second was Ronnie Smith, with Roy Richardson 43 seconds behind in third.

600 PRODUCTION

Although David Jefferies' exploits on the GSX-R1000 grabbed the headlines, Ian Lougher's blistering lap record in the inaugural 600 cc Production event was the one that most impressed his fellow racers. Riding a GSX-R600 Suzuki which was essentially stock but for race pads, revalved forks and a race can, and despite 'a few spots of rain', he lapped at 120.25 mph.

After a 75-minute delay due to low cloud, Lougher's lead was initially contested by Anstey, also GSX-R-mounted, but a visor change in the pits cost the Kiwi precious time. After three laps the Welshman won by 28 seconds, with Jim Moodie's V&M Yamaha a further 18 seconds adrift in third.

'I couldn't believe what I was seeing on the boards, because I thought I was on the limit,' was Moodie's response. Lougher said the 600 was 'similar to riding the 125... you just have to wring the neck of both of them all around this place. I just had to tuck in, nail it, and push as hard as I dared.'

With David Jefferies having to eke out his fuel on the final lap, another Kiwi, Shaun Harris, finished fourth, ahead of Archibald and Britton.

SENIOR

It wasn't so much a race as a mugging. Rarely can the TT course have suffered such a working over. If the TT is principally a contest between course and rider, maybe they should put in a few obstacles next year. For this was the TT in which the top eight finishers all averaged over 120 mph.

Way out in front of them all was that man Jefferies, recording his ninth TT win and, uniquely, his third consecutive treble. Slowing for his pit stop on lap two, he lapped at 127.29 mph, what turned out to be only one of three sub-18-minute laps. At 124.74 mph his race average speed was the fastest ever, and to cap it all no less a legend than Giacomo Agostini presented him with the Senior trophy. As the aggregate winner of both F1 and Senior, DJ also collected the Joey Dunlop trophy, plus an extra £10,000. For TAS Suzuki, it had been an equally astounding week. Team boss Hector Neill, exactly 20 years after tasting Senior victory with Norman Brown, wore a grin two decades wide.

Although Jefferies led throughout, they were not hanging about behind. After six laps and 226 miles, Lougher lay only 22 seconds behind despite a five-second penalty for overshooting the pit lane 'stop box'. Third was John McGuinness, followed by Quayle, Britton and Archibald, with Farquhar and Chris Heath rounding off the over-120-mph club.

Left: David Jefferies took his third win of the week — his third consecutive treble — with a Senior win that smashed an 11-year-old record. He's flanked by TAS Suzuki team owners Philip and Hector Neill.

Below: Junior 600 winner Jim Moodie chalked up an eighth TT victory on the Yamaha. It might have been his easiest yet.

Both photographs: Dave Collister/www.photocycles.com

HIZZY'S HOME RUN

By GARY PINCHIN

NOBODY, not even his rivals, begrudged Steve Hislop the 2002 *Motor Cycle News* British Superbike Championship. He was focused, he was fast and in three of the final four rounds of the year he was simply sensational.

Hislop had come so close to winning last year only to lose out after suffering a badly broken ankle in the penultimate round at Rockingham. This time, he went all the way. 'It's been a long, long time since I last won... uphill and down dale over the years. But after what happened last season I was determined,' said the man who bounced back and led on points all season. It was his first championship since winning the same series back in 1995.

And he did it in a manner that proved beyond any shadow of doubt that, even at 40, he's still one of the fastest four-stroke riders in the world.

The defining moment came in practice for the final round at Donington, when Hizzy lapped the 2.5-mile GP circuit faster than Rossi at the GP. Hislop left his rivals open-mouthed as he clocked 1m 31.45s in the first official session on Saturday, 0.11s faster than Rossi's pole time for the GP in July. To prove it was no fluke, he did a 1m 31.46s in the warm-up session just prior to the afternoon's Superpole — which he took at 1m 31.62s. Hislop's times were achieved on a production Ducati 998 with 40 less bhp and 17 kilos extra weight than Rossi's exotic, hand-built Honda V5. 'Imagine what I could have done with carbon brakes and a bit less weight on the bike!' he said.

Hislop's Donington finale mirrored his entire campaign. Most weekends he'd come out for the first Friday free practice and run close, or even under, the lap record. As the weekend progressed he'd perfect race set-up while his rivals would close the gap. Then he'd find an extra gear in the races. His season was similar. He led the points throughout after second and first in the opening Silverstone round. Then he went off the boil mid-term when Dunlop brought in high-profile tyres, which he took longer to get to grips with than anyone else. Then he kicked back into gear in the closing rounds, wrapping it up in the last.

There were times when his perceived fragility seemed to have surfaced. Critics persistently said he'd 'fall apart like a cheap watch'. The tyre problems started the talk, then came the second Knockhill race where Michael Rutter knocked him off at the Hairpin. Hizzy broke his collarbone and people counted him out again. Within days he was his usual chirpy self, with a four-week break to get himself fit for the next round at Thruxton. Then there was the second-last round at Mallory. He did struggle there, but it was more technical than psychological. He'd battled with the Hairpin all weekend, and that's what lost him the tow from the race leaders in traffic.

The next day he was talking about clinching the title at Donington. If that was a cheap watch, it was still ticking and keeping perfect time. As he proved. 'It's true I made winning the championship hard work for myself. The new tyres affected me for a couple of rounds, then I got skittled at Knockhill. None of it was really my fault, but I should have wrapped it all up at Mallory,' he admitted later.

There's no doubt Hislop had the best bike, even though the 2002 Testastretta wasn't the only one in the field. Renegade duo Rutter and Shane Byrne had identical bikes. It was Hislop's decision to run smaller-diameter factory forks to get more feel, fit smaller-diameter brakes to help turn the bike more quickly and extensively re-map the fuel system for his preferred power delivery — plus his own incredible feel for the bike — that gave him the edge.

But he had to work hard for it, in what was arguably the most competitive season in the history of the series. The title battle between him, Sean Emmett and Rutter was no less intense than the epic Walker/Hodgson clashes of 2000 — or last year's Reynolds/Hislop scrap. What was different about BSB 2002 was the massively increased depth of field brought about by the introduction of 1000 cc four-cylinder bikes to the grid.

For years British Superbike bosses gave special dispensation to the hugely popular, rotary-engined Nortons to run alongside traditional Superbikes but when the Duckhams team quit after winning the 1994 series, BSB adopted the FIM Superbike technical regulations to the letter. Series boss Jos Foulston was forced to make wholesale changes last winter. His grid had dwindled to an all-time low of just 14 bikes at Knockhill and he faced up to a massive set of problems. He couldn't wait for the FIM's new 1000 cc rules to come into effect in 2004. But he knew the fans were getting bored with what had become a 'Ducati cup' after Italian V-twins won every race bar one in 2001 (Rutter at Rockingham on a Kawasaki ZX7-RR).

The problems went deeper. The big teams were struggling to afford to lease genuine factory bikes capable of running with the best of the Ducatis. Privateers had even less chance. And too many good teams who might have enhanced the Superbike class were happier to run lower-cost programmes, to grab the Supersport and Superstock pickings. Foulston spent the second half of 2001 in consultation with manufacturers, teams, technicians and riders before coming up with a total revamp of the championship.

In Superbike 1000 cc four-cylinder machines were allowed Supersport-tuned engines in full Superbike chassis. The aim was competitive Superbikes at around the same cost as Supersport or Superstock. At the same time Foulston withdrew British championship status from the supporting classes, encouraging bigger Supersport and Superstock teams to move up. He also scrapped the dwindling 250 class. Foulston said: 'I know some of

the changes weren't popular, but what was I supposed to do: sit there and watch the championship die?'

History will show that he made the right calls. The BSB grid virtually doubled overnight but, more importantly, he was able to present the fans with a quality grid and racing intrigue. They responded: most tracks boasted record attendances — with Cadwell's 35,000 topping the lot.

The really smart thinking was to juggle the rules during the year. Suzuki had to rev their GSX-R1000 to get the power, but that stressed the stock rods to the point of failure. Expensive failures at that — and compromising safety. Mid-term after-market rods were allowed, of the same material as stock — in other words no titanium!

Both Suzuki and Yamaha embraced the new BSB rules with enthusiasm.

Paul Denning's Rizla-backed Crescent team started work on their new bike earlier than anyone else, completing their first GSX-R1000 test bike mid-way through 2001. The mule slotted the big engine into a works GSX-R750 chassis, but by the time defending BSB champion John Reynolds and British Supersport champion Karl Harris joined the team at year's end the final version was ready to roll.

Reynolds became the first to win a race with one of the 1000 cc fours when he took race one on the long circuit at Brands Hatch. But he struggled all year to get the Suzuki working well enough to let him repeat that victory. Chassis set-up with worn tyres was the biggest problem. It was common to see Reynolds challenging for the lead only to drop off the pace in the closing stages. It was a development year, explained the rider, 'and I was happy with the bike by the end. By then I'd run out of chances to prove it.'

It was a cruel first Superbike season for Harris after a crash at Oulton. He was in a pack of riders when, not for the first time, Reynolds's bike exploded, dumping oil all over the track. Reynolds escaped unhurt but his slick (which caused the meeting to be abandoned) claimed several riders including Harris, who suffered a badly smashed wrist. Even when he staged a comeback in the later half of the year, he was still far from fit and lacking confidence.

Another team to opt for a GSX-R1000 was ETI with John Crawford. He'd raced Crescent's works GSX-R750 Superbike the previous year, but never really got to grips with the new bike after a crash at Silverstone. Knocked unconscious, he suffered persistent dizzy spells, missing subsequent rounds. His problems also hurt development for the team.

Many expected Aussie Paul Young to have a big advantage on the GSX-R1000 after winning the 2001 Superstock title aboard one. He too crashed out of the first round and broke his arm; he too was behind all year. His plight wasn't helped by his untried Penske forks and shock, plus Pirelli tyres, so he had less data to work from than everyone else with the new bikes.

The closest Virgin Yamaha came to winning a race with the 750 cc R7 in three seasons of BSB was at Mallory in 2001. It was no surprise that team owner Rob McElnea was keen to try a race version of the R1. With this, McElnea's team was into uncharted territory, although Yamaha proffered plenty of technical advice.

McElnea thought he'd pulled off a coup by signing Kiwi Simon Crafar. The 1998 British 500 GP winner hadn't raced for virtually two seasons, but McElnea figured his previous exploits and experience of working as an Ohlins technician would help in the development of the new bike.

Crafar didn't win any races and was finicky to the point of obsession. He sent his crew wild with his wholesale changes from session to session, and never provided the results to reward their efforts. But team-mate Steve Plater often said that without Crafar's contribution to the development of the bike, he would have been lost.

Plater was closing a traumatic 2001 season when he signed for McElnea. Part of the official Kawasaki effort at the start of 2001, when promised sponsorship failed to appear he took a World Supersport ride, and endured some big crashes on an uncompetitive bike. McElnea plucked him from despair to ride the Virgin R7, and he finished the year on a high with third at Donington.

Plater went into 2002 with a reputation for too much aggression and too little consistency, but McElnea and the team moulded him into a polished performer. When he took the second race at Oulton in round 11 it was not just the first Superbike victory of his career, it was the first for Virgin Yamaha, and the first for McElnea's team since Hislop won the opening race at Brands at the end of 1998! A week later at Mallory he repeated the feat in the first race after a cracking scrap with new team-mate Sean Emmett, proving beyond any doubt the 1000s were capable of running with the Ducatis.

McElnea's gang were not fully ready for the start. At Silverstone their bikes handled the bumpy surface dreadfully and the team was forced to develop them as the season progressed. Ironically enough, the Yamaha package ended the year as the most desirable of the new 1000s. Kev Stephenson did engine development, the factory sending over a succession of update software for the fuel management system. The engines proved reliable and fast, though they were never revved beyond 12,200 rpm. When the rules were changed to allow aftermarket con-rods, Yamaha continued to use stock parts. Chassis development, carried out by Harris Performance,

Opposite page: Steve Hislop bounced back (again) in 2002 to wear the BSB crown (again).
Photograph: Clive Challinor Photography

Right: All action at Mallory, with Sean Emmett and Steve Plater locked in battle.

Below: Defending champion Reynolds had a hard year race-developing the 1000 cc Suzuki, but it was the first of the new one-litre Superbikes to win a race.

Bottom: Motor Cycle News backed the series, and staff reporters added a touch of glamour to the booming series.

All photographs: Clive Challinor Photography

came in three stages. Initially the frame was braced around the headstock, then around the swing-arm pivot and finally plates were wrapped around the outside of the main spars and welded in place — just like an R7.

Progress was difficult to judge until Oulton in late August. Plater admitted he was worried about going back, since the bike had been so out of control over the Cheshire circuit's undulations earlier in the year he'd had to use the back brake to keep the front wheel in contact with the ground. He needn't have worried. The handling had become totally predictable, and he won his first Superbike race. 'The bike handles as well as the R7, and next year [with high lift cams and more power] it'll be even better,' he said. Plater won't be there to ride it, however. He'll race the ex-Edwards title-winning SP2 for Honda Britain in BSB.

McElnea wasn't ready to park the old R7s though, and with Colin Appleyard's help assembled a 'junior' team with Paul Jones and South African Shane Norval. For Appleyard, a supporter of pure-bred racing two-strokes, it was a major shift of allegiance, but he was exactly the kind of team chief Foulston targeted when he revamped the series.

The team didn't enjoy the greatest fortunes with the pair: Jones kept up his own reputation for crashing, preserving the team record of Haydon, including a same-corner repeat of his predecessor's massive 2001 Silverstone high-side at the first round. He was even wearing Haydon's old Joe Rocket leathers. Eventually the team ran out of R7 spares and built him an R1 — which he also crashed.

Former 250 rider Norval didn't crash, but did not live up to Appleyard's high expectations, and when Sean Emmett was looking for a ride after his IFC Ducati team pulled out, McElnea snapped him to ride Jones's bike (more on that later). Jones was to share races with Norval for the remainder of the year — until he smashed the R7 at Oulton, finally exhausting the remaining stock of spares.

There was no direct Honda involvement. The 'big H' doesn't like to enter without even a chance of winning, and the 'Blade's 50 cc deficit didn't fit their remit. Honda's BSB presence was left to privateer Team MotoPower riders Matt Llewellyn and the inexperienced Gary Mason. They and less well-financed riders like Lee Jackson and Jamie Robinson (also on CBR900s) had to run their own development programmes.

Llewellyn broke his wrist early in the year at Brands but even when he came back he was far from happy with the power or handling of the bike. MotoPower wasn't too happy with his results either so the two parties agreed an amicable split after Rockingham.

Although the team drafted in the inexperienced Marty Nutt, they relied heavily on the Superbike rookie Gary Mason to develop the bike and he coped admirably, winning the plaudits of his peers after several stunning Superpole qualifying laps. But the 'Blade simply wasn't competitive and while MotoPower and Robinson saw out the year, Jackson dumped his at Thruxton in favour of a new R1.

Kawasaki's sports-tourer ZX-9 had no potential to become a Superbike so Hawk Racing opted to stick with their tried and tested (and old) ZX7-RRs

At Thruxton Emmett lined up on a Virgin Yamaha R1 — Jones's bike — and a couple of thirds proved he was able to run with the fast men on any bike. That kept his title hopes alive, and he scored heavily at Hislop's nightmare weekend at Mallory, taking the title battle to the last round. Emmett crashed out of the first race, breaking his wrist. Emmett said: 'It was a disappointing way to the end the season but at least I went out when I was in the lead and going for the title. I was still in with a chance of the championship even though I had to swap bikes mid-year.'

Emmett's team-mate Brown took longer to acclimatise to the V-twin but scored third and fifth places in the second round at Brands despite breaking two fingers in his right hand when he crashed in qualifying... during the same week that David Beckham hit the headlines with a broken bone in his foot that sidelined him for three months. After IFC withdrew Brown made ends meet working on a building site, and finished the season with a one-off outing on his bike clothed in D&B bodywork. He qualified strongly, but his race was blighted by brake problems.

Hislop was the undoubted star of the show. He bounced back from the massive blow of losing the 2001 series through no fault of his own to win the 2002 title in convincing fashion. His efforts didn't go unnoticed in the world championship ranks either. When his team boss Paul Bird opted not to renew his contract because he favoured a younger rider, Hislop was feted by WCM team boss Peter Clifford to ride a much-modified R1 or Ducati Testastretta in MotoGP. Hizzy turned him down, and signed for Virgin Yamaha instead. 'I always dreamed of going GP racing,' he said. 'But at this stage of my career do I really want to be off around the world? I'd sooner stay in the UK and defend my title. And riding the R1 is a whole new challenge to fire me up into doing even better things than I did this year. I can't wait for the season to start.'

Neither can we. With works Ducatis for Rutter and Emmett at Renegade, and for Byrne at Bird's team, plus the factory Honda SP2 for Plater, Hislop is going to have his hands full. It seems that after one of the best seasons in the history of BSB the prospects for 2003 are even better.

Below left: Australian Glen Richards caused a stir with his exceptional daring on the old 750 cc Kawasaki.

Below right: Steve Plater — the Virgin Yamaha team made a race winner out of him.

Bottom: When Michael Rutter got his Ducati going right, he equalled Hislop on race wins.
All photographs: Clive Challinor Photography

for new signing Aussie Glen Richards and Mark Burr. Richards, an ex-Supersport class rookie, was the sensation of the season and finished on a high note with two fourth places at Donington. The bike lacked grunt off the turns compared to the 1000 cc fours, let alone the Ducatis; Richards made up for it by rushing into corners at breakneck speed, so much so that his team boss couldn't bear to watch how hard he was pushing the front end going into Mallory's notorious Gerrards Bend in the penultimate round. But it was tough against the Ducatis — not just for Richards, but for everyone on four-cylinder bikes.

And there were so many V-twins out there.

One of the biggest surprises was the emergence of Renegade Racing. Team owner Mark Griffiths's company, Music and Video Campaign, had backed privateer Nigel Nottingham on R7s in 2001 but when rumours surfaced he was buying four new Testastrettas no one really took them seriously — except the racers. He was inundated with riders' CVs, and picked Michael Rutter and 2001 Privateer Cup Champion Shane Byrne. People scoffed too when his riders had to start the first race of the year from the pit lane after getting the timing wrong, but smiles were soon wiped off faces when Rutter and Byrne shared the wins in the third round of the series at Donington.

Rutter had raced Ducatis before (from 1994 to 1996) but admitted to being 'blown away' by the fierce power delivery of the new Testastretta — and with no one in the team to fine-tune the fuelling it took several races to come to terms with it. Likewise his confidence in the front end, but by Silverstone WSB weekend, the team had the bike dialled in. From then on, he was rocking, ending as runner up with eight wins, the same number as Hizzy, finishing more strongly with three wins in the last three races. He said: 'I thought it was going to be easy on a Ducati, but these things are so hard to set up. At the start of the year Hizzy was so strong and I was sat on the grid thinking, "I can't ride this thing." ' Byrne, after a season on a GSX-R750, struggled more to adapt, seeming to peak mid-year, finishing fourth overall.

Rutter's end-of-season drive nosed Sean Emmett out of second overall, although Emmett had actually looked a title contender on the IFC Racing Ducati, riding his old Red Bull bike (a 2000 model machine on which he had finished the season so strongly in 2001). The team, owned by Dave Copley and including Paul Brown, arrived at Silverstone with the paint barely dry on pristine white bodywork, and no testing at all. Massive backing had failed to materialise but was still promised, so they went racing anyway. As it turned out, the money never did come.

Incredibly, Emmett won the first race of the day and was third in race two, setting the tone for the first two thirds of his year. He even scored a double at Snetterton where he expected to struggle against the faster Testastrettas but floundered at Knockhill, his bike short of grunt out of the Hairpin against Hislop's. For the first time he complained that his bike wasn't good enough to win the title. But by that time the IFC team was in dire financial straights and the team didn't appear again.

MAJOR WORLDWIDE RESULTS

Compiled by Kay Edge

Endurance World Championship

200 MIGLIA DI IMOLA, Autodromo Enzo e Dino Ferrari, Imola, Italy, 28 April. Endurance World Championship, round 1. 66 laps of the 3.065-mile/4.933-km circuit, 202.290 miles/325.578 km

1 QB Phase One: Jason Pridmore/Mike Edwards, USA/GB (Suzuki GSXR), 2h 21m 42.046s, 85.662 mph/137.859 km/h.

2 Herman Verboven Racing 5: Michael Barnes/Michael Ciccotto, USA/USA (Suzuki 750), 66 laps; **3** Zongshen 9: Igor Jerman/Bruno Bonhuil, SLO/F (Suzuki GSXR), 66; **4** Zongshen 2: Warwick Nowland/Giovanni Bussei, AUS/I (Suzuki GSXR), 66; **5** Bolliger Team: Marcel Kellenberger/Roman Stamm, CH/CH (Kawasaki ZX9R), 65; **6** Dap Unisson Motomax: Stephane Gallis/Jean-François Cortinovis, F/F (Suzuki GSXR), 65; **7** Team 22 Police Nationale: Bertrand Sebileau/Jehan D'Orgeix, F/F (Kawasaki ZX9R), 65; **8** GMT 94: Sebastien Scarnato/William Costes, F/F (Suzuki GSXR), 65; **9** Endurance Moto 38: Bernard Cuzin/Christian Hacquin, F/F (Yamaha R1), 65; **10** QB Phase One Junior: James Hutchins/David Morillon, GB/F (Suzuki GSXR), 65; **11** Suriano: Andrea Giachino/Enrico Manara, I/I (Suzuki GSXR), 64; **12** Team Schäfer Endurance: Hans Herber/Martin Blug/Sandor Bitter, D/D/H (Suzuki GSXR), 64; **13** Nolden Racing: Erich Nolden/Markus Josch/Norbert Jansen, D/D/D (Suzuki GSXR), 63; **14** Bergamelli Racing 1: Paolo Bosetti/Bruno Bergamelli, I/I (Suzuki 1000), 63; **15** Jet Endurance: Claude-Alain Jäggi/Thomas Kausch, CH/CH (Suzuki GSXR), 63.

Fastest lap: Bussei, 1m 54.268s, 96.570 mph/155.414 km/h.

Championship points: 1 QB Phase One, 25; **2** Herman Verboven Racing 5, 20; **3** Zongshen 9, 16; **4** Zongshen 2, 13; **5** Bolliger Team, 11; **6** Dap Unisson Motomax, 10.

SILVERSTONE 200 MILES, Silverstone Grand Prix Circuit, England, 19 May. Endurance World Championship, round 2. 63 laps of the 3.165-mile/5.094-km circuit, 199.395 miles/320.922 km

1 Zongshen 2: Stephane Mertens/Warwick Nowland, B/AUS (Suzuki GSXR), 2h 02m 45.045s, 97.430 mph/156.798 km/h.

2 QB Phase One: Frédéric Moreira/Mike Edwards, F/GB (Suzuki GSXR), 63 laps; **3** GMT 94: Sebastien Scarnato/William Costes/Christophe Guyot, F/F/F (Suzuki GSXR), 63; **4** Zongshen 9: Igor Jerman/Bruno Bonhuil, SLO/F (Suzuki GSXR), 63; **5** Bolliger Team: Marcel Kellenberger/Roman Stamm, CH/CH (Kawasaki ZX9R), 62; **6** Endurance Moto 38: Bernard Cuzin/Christian Hacquin, F/F (Yamaha R1), 62; **7** Piazza Corse: Dario Marchetti/Marc Garcia, I/F (Ducati 998R), 62; **8** Wim Motor Racing Division: Laurent Naveau/Albert Aerts/Heinz Platacis, B/B/D (Honda SP2), 62; **9** Yamaha Austria Racing: Horst Saiger/Erwin Wilding/Manfred Kainz, A/A/A (Yamaha R1), 62; **10** Herman Verboven Racing 5: Michael Ciccotto/John Jacobi/Dave Estok, USA/USA/USA (Suzuki 750), 62; **11** Team 22 Police Nationale: Gwen Giabbani/Christophe Roche/Frank Gebelin, F/F/F (Kawasaki ZX9R), 61; **12** Sigma Corsa Superbikes: John Barton/Alex Buckingham, GB/GB (Ducati 998), 61; **13** QB Phase One Junior: James Hutchins/David Morillon/Olivier Ullman, GB/F/F (Suzuki GSXR), 61; **14** Jet Endurance: Dave Rollier/Regis Bosonnet, CH/CH (Suzuki GSXR), 61; **15** Bergmann & Söhne Racing: Klaus Schulz/Rüdiger Seefeldt, D/D (Suzuki GSXR), 61.

Fastest lap: Mertens/Nowland, 1m 53.232s, 100.630 mph/161.950 km/h.

Championship points: 1 QB Phase One, 45; **2** Zongshen 2, 38; **3** Zongshen 9, 29; **4** Herman Verboven Racing 5, 26; **5** GMT 94, 24; **6** Bolliger Team, 22.

6 HOURS OF BRNO, Autodrom Brno, Czech Republic, 16 June. Endurance World Championship, round 3. 164 laps of the 3.357-mile/5.403-km circuit, 550.548 miles/886.092 km

1 GMT 94: Sebastien Scarnato/William Costes/Christophe Guyot, F/F/F (Suzuki GSXR), 6h 01m 21.255s, 91.421 mph/147.128 km/h.

2 Zonghshen 2: Warwick Nowland/Igor Jerman, AUS/SLO (Suzuki GSXR), 164 laps; **3** Piazza Corse: Marc Garcia/Bernard Garcia/Dario Marchetti, F/F/I (Ducati 998R), 163; **4** Zongshen 9: Bruno Bonhuil/Pierrot Lerat, F/F (Suzuki GSXR), 163; **5** Replay Racing Team: Karl Truchsess/Michal Bursa/Janos Vegh, A/CZ/H (Yamaha R1), 162; **6** QB Phase One Junior: Frédéric Moreira/David Morillon/James Hutchins, F/F/GB (Suzuki GSXR), 162; **7** Endurance Moto 38: Bernard Cuzin/Christian Hacquin/Olivier Ulmann, F/F/F (Yamaha R1), 162; **8** Team 22 Police Nationale: Gwen Giabbani/Bertrand Sebileau/Christophe Roche, F/F/F (Kawasaki ZX9R), 161; **9** Team Schäfer Endurance: Cyril Fernandez/Sandor Bitter, F/H (Suzuki GSXR), 160; **10** QB Phase One: Jason Pridmore/Mike Edwards, USA/GB (Suzuki GSXR), 159; **11** Ducateam: Yann Sotter/Marc Dos Santos, F/F (Suzuki GSXR), 158; **12** Herman Verboven Racing 5: Dave Estok/Andrew Nobles/Andy Deatherage, USA/USA/USA (Suzuki GSXR), 158; **13** Bergmann & Söhne Racing: Klaus Schulz/Rüdiger Seefeldt, D/D (Suzuki GSXR), 158; **14** Jet Endurance: Claude-Alain Jäggi/Dave Rollier/Thomas Kausch, CH/CH/CH (Suzuki GSXR), 157; **15** Rookie Endurance: Thomas Roth/Jochen Schermuly/Christian Plantius, D/D/D (Suzuki GSXR), 156.

Fastest lap: Nowland/Jerman, 2m 08.460s, 94.085 mph/151.415 km/h.

Championship points: 1 Zonghsen 2, 58; **2** QB Phase One, 51; **3** GMT 94, 49; **4** Zongshen 9, 42; **5** Herman Verboven Racing 5, 30; **6** Endurance Moto 38, 26.

SUZUKA EIGHT-HOUR, Suzuka International Circuit, Japan, 4 August. Endurance World Championship, round 4. 219 laps of the 3.617-mile/5.821-km circuit, 792.123 miles/1274.799 km

1 Cabin Honda 1: Colin Edwards/Daijiro Kato, USA/J (Honda SP-W), 8h 02m 04.992s, 98.587 mph/158.660 km/h.

2 Cabin Honda 2: Makoto Tamada/Tadayuki Okada, J/J (Honda SP-W), 219 laps; **3** Team Sakurai Honda: Alex Barros/Yuichi Takeda, BR/J (Honda SP-W), 219; **4** YSP Racing: Wataru Yoshikawa/Takeshi Tsujimura, J/J (Yamaha R7), 217; **5** Team Challenger: Norihiko Fujiwara/Tekkyu Kayoh, J/J (Yamaha R7), 214; **6** Weider Honda: Osamu Deguchi/Hiroki Noda, J/J (Honda SP-2), 211; **7** Zongshen 2: Stephane Mertens/Warwick Nowland, B/AUS (Suzuki GSXR), 210; **8** Zongshen 9: Bruno Bonhuil/Igor Jerman, F/SLO (Suzuki GSXR), 210; **9** Corona Extra Ebsco Suzuki: Alex Fergusson/Jordan Szoke, AUS/CAN (Suzuki GSXR), 210; **10** Team 22 Police Nationale: Bertrand Sebileau/Takahurui Kishida/Gwen Giabbani, F/J/F (Kawasaki ZX9R), 205; **11** QB Phase One: Jason Pridmore/Mike Edwards, USA/GB (Suzuki GSXR), 204; **12** Garfield RSK: Hiroki Kobayashi/M. Furisawa, J/J (Suzuki 750), 203; **13** Honda Hamamatsu: Kaichi Nagura/H. Kuzuhara, J/J (Honda SP-2), 203; **14** Ambitious Racing: Hiroyuki Watanabe/Hayato Takada, J/J (Kawasaki ZX7RR), 201; **15** Sakurai Honda 95: Yukio Nukumi/Shinichi Nakatomi, J/J (Honda SP-W), 200.

Fastest lap: Barros/Takeda, 2m 07.844s, 101.855 mph/163.920 km/h.

Championship points: 1 Zongshen 2, 67; **2** QB Phase One, 56; **3** Zongshen 9, 50; **4** GMT 94, 49; **5** Herman Verboven Racing 5, 30; **6** Endurance Moto 38, 26.

24 STUNDEN VON OSCHERSLEBEN, Oschersleben Circuit, Germany, 10-11 August. Endurance World Championship, round 5. 778 laps of the 2.279-mile/3.667-km circuit, 1773.062 miles/2852.926 km

1 Endurance Moto 38: Bernard Cuzin/Christian Hacquin/David Morillon, F/F/F (Yamaha R1), 21h 52m 43.402s, 81.025 mph/130.397 km/h.

2 Zongshen 2: Stephane Mertens/Warwick Nowland/Igor Jerman, B/AUS/SLO (Suzuki GSXR), 768 laps; **3** Zongshen 9: Bruno Bonhuil/Fernando Cristobal/Pierrot Lerat, F/E/F (Suzuki GSXR), 767; **4** GMT 94: Sebastien Scarnato/Julien Da Costa/Bertrand Stey, F/F/F (Suzuki GSXR), 762; **5** Herman Verboven Racing 5: Kris Jennes/Jeff Vermeulen/Didier van Keymeulen, B/B/B (Suzuki GSXR), 757; **6** Nolden Racing: Heinz Platacis/Markus Josch/Karl-Heinz Hennemann, D/D/D (Suzuki GSXR), 756; **7** Yamaha Austria Racing: Horst Saiger/Erwin Wilding/Mirko Kalsek, A/A/SLO (Yamaha R1), 747; **8** Bolliger Team: Marcel Kellenberger/Roman Stamm/Tobias Nyström, CH/CH/F (Kawasaki ZX9R), 745; **9** Ducateam: Michael Goffinghs/Yann Sotter/Arnaud Larose, F/F/F (Suzuki GSXR), 739; **10** Rookie Endurance: Thomas Roth/Jochen Schermuly/Christian Plantius, D/D/D (Suzuki GSXR), 738; **11** Abbco K & W: Oliver Wagenführ/Thomas Schönfelder/Erich Freiberger, D/D/D (Suzuki GSXR), 737; **12** Racing Team Hepelmann: Hans-Josef Hepelmann/Reinhard Krächter/Oliver Wrede, D/D/D (Yamaha R1), 736; **13** PS Team: Dietmar Franzen/Jörg Schüller/Christian Kohlhaas, D/D/D (Suzuki GSXR), 727; **14** Herman Verboven Racing 6: Simon Tampaxis/Stavros Stavroulakis/Sinioris Alkiviadis, GRE/GRE/GRE (Suzuki GSXR), 750; **15** Elf Schäfer Motosport: Herbert Kaufmann/Stefan Nebel/Katja Poensgen, D/D/D (Suzuki GSXR), 722.

Fastest lap: Cristobal, 1m 31.842s, 89.315 mph/143.738 km/h.

Championship points: 1 Zongshen 2, 107; **2** Zongshen 9, 82; **3** Endurance Moto 38, 76; **4** GMT 94, 75; **5** QB Phase One, 56; **6** Herman Verboven Racing 5, 52.

200 MIGLIA DI VALLELUNGA, Vallelunga Circuit, Italy, 6 October. Endurance World Championship, round 6. 100 laps of the 2.015-mile/3.243-km circuit, 201.500 miles/324.300 km

1 Zongshen 9: Stephane Mertens/Warwick Nowland, B/AUS (Suzuki GSXR), 2h 21m 13.645s, 85.611 mph/137.778 km/h.

2 GMT 94: Sebastien Scarnato/William Costes, F/F (Suzuki GSXR), 100 laps; **3** Zongshen 2: Bruno Bonhuil/Igor Jerman, F/SLO (Suzuki GSXR), 100; **4** QB Phase One: Mike Edwards/Damien Cudlin, GB/AUS (Suzuki GSXR), 100; **5** Herman Verboven Racing 6: Didier van Keymeulen/Jehan D'Orgeix, F/F (Suzuki GSXR), 99; **6** Piazza Corse: Dario Marchetti/Marc Garcia, I/F (Ducati 998), 99; **7** Bolliger Team: Marcel Kellenberger/Roman Stamm, CH/CH (Kawasaki ZX9R), 99; **8** Herman Verboven Racing 5: Pierrot Larat/Michael Barnes, F/USA (Suzuki GSXR), 99; **9** Endurance Moto 38: Christian Hacquin/David Morillon/J. Devoyon, F/F/F (Yamaha R1), 98; **10** X-One: Andrea Perselli/Giuseppe Galie, Maurizio Bargiacchi, I/I/I (Suzuki GSXR), 98; **11** Yamaha Austria Racing: Horst Saiger/Erwin Wilding, A/A (Yamaha R1), 97; **12** QB Phase One Junior: James Hutchins/Heinz Platacis/Richard Cooper, GB/D/GB (Suzuki GSXR), 97; **13** Biassono Racing 2: Paolo Tessari/Alessandro Valia/Paolo Bentivogli, I/I/I (Ducati 998), 97; **14** Raser Racing: Andrea Giachino/Enrico Manara, I/I (Suzuki GSXR), 97; **15** Ducateam: Russell Baker/David Higgins, GB/GB (Suzuki GSXR), 97.

Fastest lap: Nowland, 1m 19.865s, 90.833 mph/146.182 km/h.

Final Endurance World Championship points

1	Zongshen 2, CHN	123
2	Zongshen 9, CHN	107
3	GMT 94, F	95
4	Endurance Moto 38, F	83
5	QB Phase One, GB	69

6 Herman Verboven Racing 5, B, 60; **7** Bolliger Team, CH, 47; **8** Piazza Corse, I, 35; **9** Yamaha Austria Racing, A, 30; **10** Team 22 Police Nationale, F, 28; **11** Cabin Honda 1, J, 25; **12** Nolden Racing, D and QB Phase One Junior, GB, 23; **14** Cabin Honda 2, J and Ducateam, F, 20.

Sidecar World Championship

VALENCIA, Spain, 10 March. 2.489-mile/4.005-km circuit. Sidecar World Championship, round 1 (18 laps, 44.802 miles/72.090 km)

1 Steve Abbott/Jamie Biggs, GB/GB (Yamaha), 30m 52.318s, 87.059 mph/140.108 km/h.

2 Jörg Steinhausen/Trevor Hopkinson, D/GB (Suzuki); **3** Klaus Klaffenböck/Christian Parzer, A/A (Yamaha); **4** Stuart Muldoon/Andy Peach, GB/GB (Suzuki); **5** Tom Hanks/Phil Biggs, GB/GB (Yamaha); **6** Markus Schlosser/Adolf Hänni, CH/CH (Suzuki); **7** Roger Lovelock/Gary Yendell, GB/GB (Suzuki); **8** Peter Schröder/Ueli Wäfler, CH/CH (Suzuki); **9** Rob Cameron/Ian Simons, GB/GB (Suzuki); **10** Gerhard Hauzenberger/Trevor Crone, A/GB (Suzuki); **11** Steve Webster/Paul Woodhead, GB/GB (Suzuki); **12** Sepp Doppler/Bernhard Wagner, A/A (Yamaha); **13** Chris Founds/Peter Founds, GB/GB (Yamaha); **14** Sebastien Delannoy/Jerome Vannier, F/F (Suzuki).

Fastest lap: Webster, 1m 39.817s, 89.753 mph/144.444 km/h (record).

Championship points: 1 Abbott, 25; **2** Steinhausen, 20; **3** Klaffenböck, 16; **4** Muldoon, 13; **5** Hanks, 11; **6** Schlosser, 10.

KYALAMI, South Africa, 7 April. 2.649-mile/4.263-km circuit. Sidecar World Championship, round 2 (19 laps, 50.331 miles/80.997 km)

1 Steve Webster/Paul Woodhead, GB/GB (Suzuki), 35m 02.112s, 86.192 mph/138.712 km/h.

2 Klaus Klaffenböck/Christian Parzer, A/A (Yamaha); **3** Jörg Steinhausen/Trevor Hopkinson, D/GB (Suzuki); **4** Stuart Muldoon/Andy Peach, GB/GB (Suzuki); **5** Markus Schlosser/Adolf Hänni, CH/CH (Suzuki); **6** Tom Hanks/Phil Biggs, GB/GB (Yamaha); **7** Martien Van Gils/Tonnie Van Gils, NL/NL (Suzuki); **8** Peter Schröder/Ueli Wäfler, CH/CH (Suzuki); **9** Gerhard Hauzenberger/Trevor Crone, A/GB (Suzuki); **10** Uwe Göttlich/Johannes Koloska, D/D (Suzuki); **11** Mike Roscher/Uwe Neubert, D/D (Suzuki); **12** Dieter Eilers/Helmut Engelmann, D/D (Suzuki).

Fastest lap: Webster, 1m 48.343s, 88.017 mph/141.650 km/h (record).

Championship points: 1 Klaffenböck and Steinhausen, 36; **3** Webster, 30; **4** Muldoon, 26; **5** Abbott, 25.

MONZA, Italy, 11 May. 3.600-mile/5.793-km circuit. Sidecar World Championship, round 3 (14 laps, 50.400 miles/81.102 km)

1 Klaus Klaffenböck/Christian Parzer, A/A (Yamaha), 27m 34.060s, 109.681 mph/176.515 km/h.

2 Steve Webster/Paul Woodhead, GB/GB (Suzuki); **3** Steve Abbott/Jamie Biggs, GB/GB (Yamaha); **4** Jörg Steinhausen/Trevor Hopkinson, D/GB (Suzuki); **5** Tom Hanks/Phil Biggs, GB/GB (Yamaha); **6** Martien Van Gils/Tonnie Van Gils, NL/NL (Suzuki); **7** Gerhard Hauzenberger/Trevor Crone, A/GB (Suzuki); **8** Uwe Göttlich/Johannes Koloska, D/D (Suzuki); **9** Tero Karttiala/Timo Karttiala, SF/SF (Honda); **10** Sebastien Delannoy/Jerome Vannier, F/F (Suzuki); **11** Chris Founds/Peter Founds, GB/GB (Yamaha); **12** Dieter Eilers/Helmut Engelmann, D/D (Suzuki); **13** Dan Morrisey/Mick Frith, GB/GB (Yamaha); **14** Barry Fleury/Jane Fleury, NZ/NZ (Suzuki).

Fastest lap: Klaffenböck, 1m 56.525s, 111.209 mph/178.973 km/h.

Championship points: 1 Klaffenböck, 61; **2** Webster, 50; **3** Steinhausen, 49; **4** Abbott, 41; **5** Hanks, 32; **6** Muldoon, 26.

SILVERSTONE, Great Britain, 26 May. 3.165-mile/5.094-km circuit. Sidecar World Championship, round 4 (16 laps, 50.640 miles/81.504 km).

1 Steve Abbott/Jamie Biggs, GB/GB (Yamaha), 30m 52.432s, 98.421 mph/158.394 km/h).

2 Tom Hanks/Phil Biggs, GB/GB (Yamaha); **3** Jörg Steinhausen/Trevor Hopkinson, D/GB (Suzuki); **4** Stuart Muldoon/Andy Peach, GB/GB (Suzuki); **5** Markus Schlosser/Adolf Hänni, CH/CH (Suzuki); **6** Jock Skene/Neil Miller, GB/GB (Suzuki); **7** Martien Van Gils/Tonnie Van Gils, NL/NL (Suzuki); **8** Peter Schröder/Ueli Wäfler, CH/CH (Suzuki); **9** Vincent Biggs/Robert Biggs, GB/GB (Yamaha); **10** Mike Roscher/Uwe Neubert, D/D (Suzuki); **11** Roger Lovelock/Garry Yendell, GB/GB (Suzuki); **12** Chris Founds/Peter Founds, GB/GB (Yamaha); **13** Sebastien Delannoy/Jerome Vannier, F/F (Suzuki); **14** Uwe Göttlich/Johannes Koloska, GB/GB (Suzuki); **15** Gerhard Hauzenberger/Trevor Crone, A/GB (Suzuki).

Fastest lap: Webster, 1m 53.741s, 100.183 mph/161.229 km/h (record).

Championship points: 1 Abbott, 66; **2** Steinhausen, 65; **3** Klaffenböck, 61; **4** Hanks, 52; **5** Webster, 50; **6** Muldoon, 39.

LAUSITZ, Germany, 8 June. 2.650-mile/4.265-km circuit. Sidecar World Championship, round 5 (19 laps, 50.350 miles/81.035 km)

1 Jörg Steinhausen/Trevor Hopkinson, D/GB (Suzuki), 35m 21.270s, 85.453 mph/137.524 km/h).

2 Tom Hanks/Phil Biggs, GB/GB (Yamaha); **3** Markus Schlosser/Adolf Hänni, CH/CH (Suzuki); **4** Uwe Göttlich/Johannes Koloska, D/D (Suzuki); **5** Rob Cameron/Ian Simons, GB/GB (Suzuki); **6** Peter Schröder/Ueli Wäfler, CH/CH (Suzuki); **7** Sepp Doppler/Bernhard Wagner, A/A (Yamaha); **8** Sebastien Delannoy/Jerome Vannier, F/F (Suzuki); **9** Chris Founds/Peter Founds, GB/GB (Yamaha); **10** Martien Van Gils/Tonnie Van Gils, NL/NL (Suzuki); **11** Steve Abbott/Jamie Biggs, GB/GB (Yamaha); **12** Roger Lovelock/Garry Yendell, GB/GB (Suzuki); **13** Vincent Biggs/Robert Biggs, GB/GB (Yamaha); **14** Gerhard Hauzenberger/Trevor Crone, A/GB (Suzuki); **15** Dan Morrisey/Mick Frith, GB/GB (Yamaha).

Fastest lap: Webster, 1m 46.216s, 89.822 mph/144.554 km/h (record).

Championship points: 1 Steinhausen, 90; **2** Hanks, 72; **3** Abbott, 71; **4** Klaffenböck, 61; **5** Webster, 50; **6** Schlosser, 48.

MISANO, Italy, 22 June. 2.523-mile/4.060-km circuit. Sidecar World Championship, round 6 (20 laps, 50.460 miles/81.200 km)

1 Steve Abbott/Jamie Biggs, GB/GB (Yamaha), 34m 19.837s, 88.181 mph/141.914 km/h.

2 Markus Schlosser/Adolf Hänni, CH/CH (Suzuki); **3** Jörg Steinhausen/Trevor Hopkinson, D/GB (Suzuki); **4** Tom Hanks/Phil Biggs, GB/GB (Yamaha); **5** Klaus Klaffenböck/Christian Parzer, A/A (Yamaha); **6** Martien Van Gils/Tonnie Van Gils, NL/NL (Suzuki); **7** Peter Schröder/Ueli Wäfler, CH/CH (Suzuki); **8** Gerhard Hauzenberger/Trevor Crone, A/GB (Suzuki); **9** Uwe Göttlich/Johannes Koloska, D/D (Suzuki); **10** Rob Cameron/Ian Simons, GB/GB (Suzuki); **11** Chris Founds/Peter Founds, GB/GB (Yamaha); **12** Sepp Doppler/Bernhard Wagner, A/A (Yamaha); **13** Dan Morrisey/Mick Frith, GB/GB (Yamaha); **14** Barry Fleury/Robert Biggs, NZ/GB (Suzuki); **15** Paul Steenbergen/René Steenbergen, NL/NL (Suzuki).

Fastest lap: Klaffenböck, 1m 41.251s, 89.697 mph/144.354 km/h.

Championship points: 1 Steinhausen, 106; **2** Abbott, 96; **3** Hanks, 85; **4** Klaffenböck, 72; **5** Schlosser, 68; **6** Webster, 50.

BRANDS HATCH, Great Britain, 27 July. 2.623-mile/4.221-km circuit. Sidecar World Championship, round 7 (19 laps, 49.837 miles/80.199 km)

1 Steve Webster/Paul Woodhead, GB/GB (Suzuki), 29m 24.446s, 101.675 mph/163.630 km/h.

2 Tom Hanks/Phil Biggs, GB/GB (Yamaha); **3** Klaus Klaffenböck/Christian Parzer, A/A (Yamaha); **4** Jörg Steinhausen/Trevor Hopkinson, D/GB (Suzuki); **5** Steve Abbott/Jamie

Biggs, GB/GB (Yamaha); **6** Markus Schlosser/Adolf Hänni, CH/CH (Suzuki); **7** Martien Van Gils/Tonnie Van Gils, NL/NL (Suzuki); **8** Paul Steenbergen/René Steenbergen, NL/NL (Suzuki); **9** Bill Philp/Ian Conn, GB/GB (Suzuki); **10** Gerhard Hauzenberger/Trevor Crone, A/GB (Suzuki); **11** Roger Lovelock/Dawna Holloway, GB/GB (Suzuki); **12** Peter Schröder/Ueli Wäfler, CH/CH (Suzuki); **13** Jock Skene/Neil Miller, GB/GB (Suzuki); **14** Chris Founds/Peter Founds, GB/GB (Yamaha); **15** Rob Cameron/Ian Simons, GB/GB (Suzuki).
Fastest lap: Webster, 1m 31.162s, 103.575 mph/166.688 km/h (record).
Championship points: **1** Steinhausen, 119; **2** Abbott, 107; **3** Hanks, 105; **4** Klaffenböck, 88; **5** Schlosser, 78; **6** Webster, 75.

OSCHERSLEBEN, Germany, 31 August. 2.279-mile/3.667-km circuit. Sidecar World Championship, round 8 (22 laps, 50.138 miles/80.674 km)
1 Steve Webster/Paul Woodhead, GB/GB (Suzuki), 34m 53.827s, 86.188 mph/138.706 km/h.
2 Klaus Klaffenböck/Christian Parzer, A/A (Yamaha); **3** Tom Hanks/Phil Biggs, GB/GB (Yamaha); **4** Steve Abbott/Jamie Biggs, GB/GB (Yamaha); **5** Uwe Göttlich/Johannes Koloska, D/D (Suzuki); **6** Roger Lovelock/Dawna Holloway, GB/GB (Suzuki); **7** Gerhard Hauzenberger/Trevor Crone, A/GB (Suzuki); **8** Dan Morrisey/Darren Harper, GB/GB (Yamaha); **9** Dieter Eilers/Patrick Homann, D/D (Suzuki); **10** Jean-Noel Minguet/Nicolas Bidaud, F/F (Suzuki); **11** Vincent Biggs/Roberts Biggs, GB/GB (Yamaha); **12** Baptist Kohlmann/Wilhelm Anderle, D/D (Suzuki).
Fastest lap: Webster, 1m 33.012s, 88.191 mph/141.930 km/h.
Championship points: **1** Hanks, 121; **2** Abbott, 120; **3** Steinhausen, 119; **4** Klaffenböck, 108; **5** Webster, 100; **6** Schlosser, 78.

ASSEN, Holland, 7 September. 3.745-mile/6.027-km circuit. Sidecar World Championship, round 9 (13 laps, 48.685 miles/78.351 km)
1 Steve Webster/Paul Woodhead, GB/GB (Suzuki), 28m 47.023s, 101.485 mph/163.324 km/h.
2 Steve Abbott/Jamie Biggs, GB/GB (Yamaha); **3** Jörg Steinhausen/Trevor Hopkinson, D/GB (Suzuki); **4** Klaus Klaffenböck/Christian Parzer, A/A (Yamaha); **5** Tom Hanks/Phil Biggs, GB/GB (Yamaha); **6** Markus Schlosser/Adolf Hänni, CH/CH (Suzuki); **7** Roger Lovelock/Dawna Holloway, GB/GB (Suzuki); **8** Paul Steenbergen/René Steenbergen, NL/NL (Suzuki); **9** Martien Van Gils/Collin Buyserd, NL/NL (Suzuki); **10** Gerhard Hauzenberger/Trevor Crone, A/GB (Suzuki); **11** Peter Schröder/Ueli Wäfler, CH/CH (Suzuki); **12** Dan Morrissey/Darren Harper, GB/GB (Yamaha); **13** Bill Philp/Mick Frith, GB/GB (Suzuki); **14** Mike Roscher/John Scott, D/USA (Suzuki); **15** Sebastien Delannoy/Ian Simons, F/GB (Suzuki).
Fastest lap: Webster, 2m 11.228s, 102.738 mph/165.340 km/h (record).
Championship points: **1** Abbott, 140; **2** Steinhausen, 135; **3** Hanks, 132; **4** Webster, 125; **5** Klaffenböck, 121; **6** Schlosser, 88.

IMOLA, Italy, 28 September. 3.065-mile/4.933-km circuit. Sidecar World Championship, round 10 (13 laps, 39.845 miles/64.129 km)
1 Klaus Klaffenböck/Christian Parzer, A/A (Yamaha), 26m 02.699s, 91.798 mph/147.734 km/h.
2 Steve Webster/Paul Woodhead, GB/GB (Suzuki); **3** Jörg Steinhausen/Trevor Hopkinson, D/GB (Suzuki); **4** Tom Hanks/Phil Biggs, GB/GB (Yamaha); **5** Steve Abbott/Jamie Biggs, GB/GB (Yamaha); **6** Markus Schlosser/Adolf Hänni, CH/CH (Suzuki); **7** Martien Van Gils/Tonnie Van Gils, NL/NL (Suzuki); **8** Peter Schröder/Ueli Wäfler, CH/CH (Suzuki); **9** Gerhard Hauzenberger/Trevor Crone, A/GB (Suzuki); **10** Roger Lovelock/Dawna Holloway, GB/GB (Suzuki); **11** Sebastien Delannoy/Ian Simons, F/GB (Suzuki); **12** Dan Morrisey/Darren Harper, GB/GB (Yamaha); **13** Chris Founds/Peter Founds, GB/GB (Yamaha); **14** Dominique Marzloff/Helene Marzloff, F/F (Suzuki); **15** Dieter Eilers/Helmut Engelmann, D/D (Suzuki).
Fastest lap: Klaffenböck, 1m 58.616s, 93.030 mph/149.717 km/h.

Final World Championship points

1	Steve Abbott, GB	151
2	Jörg Steinhausen, D	151
3	Klaus Klaffenböck, A	146
4	Steve Webster, GB	145
5	Tom Hanks, GB	145

6 Markus Schlosser, CH, 98; **7** Martien Van Gils, NL, 69; **8** Gerhard Hauzenberger, A, 61; **9** Peter Schröder, CH, 60; **10** Roger Lovelock, GB, 48; **11** Uwe Göttlich, D, 47; **12** Stuart Muldoon, GB, 39; **13** Chris Founds, GB, 29; **14=** Rob Cameron, GB and Sebastien Delannoy, F, 25.

AMA National Championship Road Race Series (Superbike)

DAYTONA INTERNATIONAL SPEEDWAY, Daytona Beach, Florida, 10 March 2002. 200.000 miles/321.869 km
1 Nicky Hayden (Honda); **2** Jamie Hacking (Suzuki); **3** Anthony Gobert (Yamaha); **4** Aaron Yates (Suzuki); **5** Eric Bostrom (Kawasaki); **6** Kurtis Roberts (Honda); **7** Andy Deatherage (Suzuki); **8** Brian Livengood (Suzuki); **9** Rich Conicelli (Suzuki); **10** Ricky Orlando (Suzuki).

CALIFORNIA SPEEDWAY, Fontana, California, 6-7 April 2002. 66.080 miles/106.345 km
Race 1
1 Anthony Gobert (Yamaha); **2** Aaron Yates (Suzuki); **3** Nicky Hayden (Honda); **4** Doug Chandler (Ducati); **5** Pascal Picotte (Ducati); **6** Mat Mladin (Suzuki); **7** Lee Acree (Suzuki); **8** Brian Parriott (Suzuki); **9** Brian Livengood (Suzuki); **10** Andy Deatherage (Suzuki).

Race 2
1 Nicky Hayden (Honda); **2** Eric Bostrom (Kawasaki); **3** Mat Mladin (Suzuki); **4** Doug Chandler (Ducati); **5** Pascal Picotte (Ducati); **6** Jamie Hacking (Suzuki) **7** Miguel DuHamel (Honda); **8** Anthony Gobert (Yamaha); **9** Brian Parriott (Suzuki); **10** Andy Deatherage (Suzuki).

SEARS POINT RACEWAY, Sonoma, California, 4-5 May 2002. 60.320 miles/97.076 km
Race 1
1 Nicky Hayden (Honda); **2** Miguel DuHamel (Honda); **3** Eric Bostrom (Kawasaki); **4** Anthony Gobert (Yamaha); **5** Pascal Picotte (Ducati); **6** Aaron Yates (Suzuki); **7** Mat Mladin (Suzuki); **8** Jamie Hacking (Suzuki); **9** Doug Chandler (Ducati); **10** Brian Parriott (Suzuki).

Race 2
1 Nicky Hayden (Honda); **2** Aaron Yates (Suzuki); **3** Miguel DuHamel (Honda); **4** Eric Bostrom (Kawasaki); **5** Pascal Picotte (Honda); **6** Mat Mladin (Suzuki); **7** Jamie Hacking (Suzuki); **8** Doug Chandler (Ducati); **9** Brian Livengood (Suzuki); **10** Thomas Montano (Ducati).

ROAD ATLANTA, Braselton, Georgia, 19-20 May 2002. 63.000 miles/101.389 km
Race 1
1 Nicky Hayden (Honda); **2** Miguel DuHamel (Honda); **3** Aaron Yates (Suzuki); **4** Eric Bostrom (Kawasaki); **5** Mat Mladin (Suzuki); **6** Pascal Picotte (Ducati); **7** Jamie Hacking (Suzuki); **8** Michale Barnes (Suzuki); **9** Brian Livengood (Suzuki); **10** Larry Pegram (Suzuki).

Race 2
1 Nicky Hayden (Honda); **2** Eric Bostrom (Kawasaki); **3** Miguel DuHamel (Honda); **4** Aaron Yates (Suzuki); **5** Pascal Picotte (Ducati); **6** Mat Mladin (Suzuki); **7** Jason DiSalvo (Suzuki); **8** Brian Parriott (Suzuki); **9** Vincent Haskovec (Suzuki); **10** Chris Caylor (Suzuki).

PIKES PEAK INTERNATIONAL RACEWAY, Fountain, Colorado, 2 June 2002. 64.800 miles/104.285 km
1 Eric Bostrom (Kawasaki); **2** Aaron Yates (Suzuki); **3** Jamie Hacking (Suzuki); **4** Mat Mladin (Suzuki); **5** Miguel DuHamel (Honda); **6** Pascal Picotte (Ducati); **7** Brian Parriott (Suzuki); **8** Ricky Orlando (Suzuki); **9** Vincent Haskovec (Suzuki); **10** Brian Livengood (Suzuki).

ROAD AMERICA, Elkhart Lake, Wisconsin, 7-8 June 2002. 64.000 miles/102.998 km
Race 1
1 Miguel DuHamel (Honda); **2** Eric Bostrom (Kawasaki); **3** Aaron Yates (Suzuki); **4** Nicky Hayden (Honda); **5** Mat Mladin (Suzuki); **6** Doug Chandler (Ducati); **7** Pascal Picotte (Ducati); **8** Jake Zemke (Honda); **9** Jason DiSalvo (Suzuki); **10** Brian Livengood (Suzuki).

Race 2
1 Miguel DuHamel (Honda); **2** Nicky Hayden (Honda); **3** Eric Bostrom (Kawasaki); **4** Aaron Yates (Suzuki); **5** Jake Zemke (Honda); **6** Doug Chandler (Ducati); **7** Pascal Picotte (Ducati); **8** Jamie Hacking (Suzuki); **9** Brian Parriott (Suzuki); **10** Craig Connell (Suzuki).

BRAINERD INTERNATIONAL RACEWAY, Brainerd, Minnesota, 30 June 2002. 63.000 miles/101.389 km
1 Nicky Hayden (Honda); **2** Eric Bostrom (Kawasaki); **3** Doug Chandler (Ducati); **4** Miguel DuHamel (Honda); **5** Kurtis Roberts (Honda); **6** Jamie Hacking (Suzuki); **7** Pascal Picotte (Ducati); **8** Robert Jensen (Suzuki); **9** Jason DiSalvo (Suzuki); **10** Brian Livengood (Suzuki).

MAZDA RACEWAY AT LAGUNA SECA, Monterey, California, 13 July 2002. 61.600 miles/99.136 km
1 Eric Bostrom (Kawasaki); **2** Nicky Hayden (Honda); **3** Doug Chandler (Ducati); **4** Aaron Yates (Suzuki); **5** Miguel DuHamel (Honda); **6** Pascal Picotte (Ducati); **7** Anthony Gobert (Yamaha); **8** Brian Parriott (Suzuki); **9** Craig Connell (Suzuki); **10** Jason DiSalvo (Suzuki).

MID-OHIO SPORTS CAR COURSE, Lexington, Ohio, 27-8 July 2002. 62.400 miles/100.423 km
Race 1
1 Eric Bostrom (Kawasaki); **2** Nicky Hayden (Honda); **3** Aaron Yates (Suzuki); **4** Pascal Picotte (Ducati); **5** Mat Mladin (Suzuki); **6** Kurtis Roberts (Honda); **7** Miguel DuHamel (Honda); **8** Jamie Hacking (Suzuki); **9** Brian Livengood (Suzuki); **10** Anthony Gobert (Yamaha).

Race 2
1 Nicky Hayden (Honda); **2** Eric Bostrom (Kawasaki); **3** Mat Mladin (Suzuki); **4** Kurtis Roberts (Honda); **5** Doug Chandler (Ducati); **6** Jamie Hacking (Suzuki); **7** Miguel DuHamel (Honda); **8** Brian Livengood (Suzuki); **9** Jason DiSalvo (Suzuki); **10** Robert Jensen (Suzuki).

VIRGINIA INTERNATIONAL RACEWAY, Alton, Virginia, 10-11 August 2002. 62.300 miles/100.262 km
Race 1
1 Nicky Hayden (Honda); **2** Doug Chandler (Ducati); **3** Miguel DuHamel (Honda); **4** Kurtis Roberts (Honda); **5** Pascal Picotte (Ducati); **6** Brian Livengood (Suzuki); **7** Vincent Haskovec (Suzuki); **8** Geoff May (Suzuki); **9** Andy Deatherage (Suzuki); **10** Brian Parriott (Suzuki).

Race 2
1 Eric Bostrom (Kawasaki); **2** Mat Mladin (Suzuki); **3** Aaron Yates (Suzuki); **4** Doug Chandler (Ducati); **5** Jason DiSalvo (Suzuki); **6** Robert Jensen (Suzuki); **7** Brian Parriott (Suzuki); **8** Brian Livengood (Suzuki); **9** Eric Wood (Suzuki); **10** Andy Deatherage (Suzuki).

Final Championship points

1	Nicky Hayden	488
2	Eric Bostrom	451
3	Miguel DuHamel	381
4	Pascal Picotte	350
5	Aaron Yates	345

6 Brian Parriott, 308; **7** Mat Mladin, 300; **8** Doug Chandler, 294; **9** Brian Livengood, 294; **10** Jamie Hacking, 260.

Isle of Man Tourist Trophy Races

ISLE OF MAN TOURIST TROPHY COURSE, 25 May-7 June. 37.73-mile/60.72-km course.
TT Formula One (6 laps, 226.38 miles/364.32 km)
1 David Jefferies (Suzuki), 1h 50m 05.1s, 123.38 mph/198.56 km/h.
2 John McGuinness (Honda), 1h 50m 41.6s; **3** Jim Moodie (Yamaha), 1h 51m 09.6s; **4** Ian Lougher (Suzuki), 1h 51m 14.8s; **5** Richard Quayle (Suzuki), 1h 53m 05.6s; **6** Jason Griffiths (Yamaha), 1h 54m 02.2s; **7** Richard Britton (Suzuki), 1h 54m 04.2s; **8** Simon 'Ronnie' Smith (Suzuki), 1h 54m 06.1s; **9** Iain Duffus (Yamaha), 1h 54m 15.2s; **10** Chris Heath (Yamaha), 1h 54m 27.2s; **11** Nigel Davies (Suzuki), 1h 54m 31.2s; **12** Gordon Blackley (Yamaha), 1h 55m 18.8s.
Fastest lap: Jefferies, 17m 52.2s, 126.68 mph/203.87 km/h (record).

125 Ultra-Lightweight TT (4 laps, 150.92 miles/242.88 km)
1 Ian Lougher (Honda), 1h 23m 20.4s, 108.65 mph/174.86 km/h.
2 James Crumpton (Honda), 1h 23m 40.7s; **3** Robert Dunlop (Honda), 1h 24m 35.7s; **4** Chris Palmer (Honda), 1h 25m 42.2s; **5** Garry Bennett (Honda), 1h 26m 44.8s.
Fastest lap: Lougher, 20m 32.4s, 110.21 mph/177.37 km/h (record).

400 Lightweight TT (4 laps, 150.92 miles/242.88 km)
1 Richard Quayle (Honda), 1h 22m 52.0s, 109.27 mph/175.85 km/h.
2 Jim Hodson (Yamaha), 1h 23m 14.1s; **3** Richard Britton (Kawasaki), 1h 23m 33.8s; **4** Nigel Davies (Honda), 1h 24m 27.2s; **5** David Madsen-Mygdal (Honda), 1h 24m 38.7s; **6** John Barton (Yamaha), 1h 24m 51.0s; **7** John McGuinness (Honda), 1h 25m 13.3s; **8** Ryan Farquhar (Kawasaki), 1h 25m 27.7s; **9** Brian Gardiner (Kawasaki), 1h 26m 16.8s.
Fastest lap: Quayle, 20m 28.4s, 110.57 mph/177.95 km/h.

Junior 600 TT (4 laps, 150.92 miles/242.88 km)
1 Jim Moodie (Yamaha), 1h 15m 56.9s, 119.22 mph/191.87 km/h.
2 Ian Lougher (Suzuki), 1h 16m 30.3s; **3** Jason Griffiths (Yamaha), 1h 17m 08.2s; **4** Richard Britton (Suzuki), 1h 17m 22.4s; **5** Ryan Farquhar (Kawasaki), 1h 17m 24.7s; **6** Richard Quayle (Honda), 1h 17m 30.6s; **7** Adrian Archibald (Honda), 1h 17m 30.8s; **8** Shaun Harris (Suzuki), 1h 17m 44.8s; **9** Brian Gardiner (Honda), 1h 17m 51.8s; **10** Iain Duffus (Yamaha), 1h 17m 55.5s; **11** Nick Jefferies (Suzuki), 1h 19m 11.1s; **12** Nigel Davies (Suzuki), 1h 19m 39.3s.
Fastest lap: Moodie, 18m 45.9s, 120.63 mph/194.14 km/h.

Junior 250 TT (4 laps, 150.92 miles/242.88 km)
1 Bruce Anstey (Yamaha), 1h 18m 31.1s, 115.32 mph/185.59 km/h.
2 Simon 'Ronnie' Smith (Honda), 1h 21m 34.7s; **3** Roy Richardson (Honda), 1h 22m 18.5s.
Fastest lap: Anstey, 19m 10.7s, 118.03 mph/189.95 km/h.

1000 Production TT (3 laps, 113.19 miles/182.16 km)
1 David Jefferies (Suzuki), 55m 22.5s, 122.64 mph/197.37 km/h.
2 Ian Lougher (Suzuki), 55m 38.0s; **3** Bruce Anstey (Suzuki), 56m 05.2s; **4** Jim Moodie (Yamaha), 56m 33.4s; **5** Iain Duffus (Suzuki), 56m 43.0s; **6** John McGuinness (Honda), 56m 55.8s; **7** Richard Britton (Suzuki), 57m 01.4s; **8** Richard Quayle (Suzuki), 57m 16.1s; **9** Adrian Archibald (Honda), 57m 18.2s; **10** Jason Griffiths (Yamaha), 57m 27.1s; **11** Shaun Harris (Yamaha), 57m 32.4s; **12** Chris Heath (Yamaha), 57m 38.7s; **13** Simon 'Ronnie' Smith (Suzuki), 58m 00.0s.
Fastest lap: Jefferies, 18m 12.6s, 124.31 mph/200.06 km/h (record).

600 Production TT (3 laps, 113.19 miles/182.16 km)
1 Ian Lougher (Suzuki), 57m 08.4s, 118.85 mph/191.27 km/h.
2 Bruce Anstey (Suzuki), 57m 36.9s; **3** Jim Moodie (Yamaha), 57m 55.4s; **4** Shaun Harris (Suzuki), 58m 08.6s; **5** Adrian Archibald (Honda), 58m 28.1s; **6** Richard Britton (Suzuki), 58m 35.2s; **7** David Jefferies (Suzuki), 58m 47.0s; **8** Gordon Blackley (Honda), 58m 58.0s; **9** Roy Richardson (Suzuki), 59m 03.5s; **10** John McGuiness (Honda), 59m 10.3s; **11** Chris Heath (Honda), 59m 10.5s; **12** Adrian McFarland (Suzuki), 59m 54.0s; **13** Davy Morgan (Yamaha), 59m 57.3s.
Fastest lap: Lougher, 18m 49.5s, 120.25 mph/193.52 km/h (record).

Senior TT (6 laps, 226.38 miles/364.32 km)
1 David Jefferies (Suzuki), 1h 48m 53.1s, 124.74 mph/200.75 km/h.
2 Ian Lougher (Suzuki), 1h 49m 15.2s; **3** John McGuinness (Honda), 1h 50m 01.3s; **4** Richard Quayle (Suzuki), 1h 51m 18.6s; **5** Richard Britton (Suzuki), 1h 51m 30.7s; **6** Adrian Archibald (Honda), 1h 52m 19.1s; **7** Ryan Farquhar (Yamaha), 1h 52m 27.0s; **8** Chris Heath (Yamaha), 1h 53m 05.1s.
Fastest lap: Jefferies, 17m 47.0s, 127.29 mph/204.85 km/h (record).

Sidecar TT: Race A (3 laps, 113.19 miles/182.16 km)
1 Rob Fisher/Rick Long (LMS), 1h 01m 25.9s, 110.55 mph/177.91 km/h.
2 Ian Bell/Neil Carpenter (Yamaha), 1h 01m 46.0s; **3** Gary Horspole/Kevin Leigh (Honda), 1h 02m 06.6s; **4** Dave Molyneux/Colin Hardman (Honda), 1h 02m 17.1s; **5** Roy Hanks/Dave Wells (Yamaha), 1h 02m 57.5s; **6** Ben Dixon/Mark Lambert (Honda), 1h 03m 05.3s; **7** Philip Dongworth/Stuart Castles (Kawasaki), 1h 03m 13.6s; **8** Steve Norbury/Andrew Smith (Yamaha), 1h 03m 44.5s; **9** Mick Harvey/Stephen Thomas (Yamaha), 1h 03m 55.4s; **10** Kenny Howles/Doug Jewell (Yamaha), 1h 04m 04.8s.
Fastest lap: Fisher/Long, 20m 25.8s, 110.80 mph/178.32 km/h.

Sidecar TT: Race B (3 laps, 113.19 miles/182.16 km)
1 Rob Fisher/Rick Long (LMS), 1h 01m 19.0s, 110.75 mph/178.23 km/h.
2 Dave Molyneux/Colin Hardman (Honda), 1h 01.33.2s; **3** Ian Bell/Neil Carpenter (Yamaha), 1h 01m 49.7s; **4** Roy Hanks/Dave Wells (Yamaha), 1h 02m 37.3s; **5** Gary Horspole/Kevin Leigh (Honda), 1h 02m 45.5s; **6** Philip Dongworth/Stuart Castles (Kawasaki), 1h 03m 20.4s; **7** Kenny Howles/Doug Jewell (Yamaha), 1h 04m 11.2s; **8** Tony Baker/Scott Parnell (Yamaha), 1h 04m 13.9s.
Fastest lap: Fisher/Long, 20m 17.3s, 111.58 mph/179.57 km/h.

British Championships

SILVERSTONE INTERNATIONAL CIRCUIT, 1 April. 2.252-mile/3.624-km circuit.
MCN British Superbike Championship, round 1 (2 x 22 laps, 49.544 miles/79.728 km)
Race 1
1 Sean Emmett (Ducati), 30m 26.668s, 97.49 mph/156.88 km/h.
2 Steve Hislop (Ducati); **3** Steve Plater (Yamaha); **4** John Reynolds (Suzuki); **5** Shane Byrne (Ducati); **6** Karl Harris (Suzuki); **7** Michael Rutter (Ducati); **8** Paul Brown (Ducati); **9** Simon Crafar (Yamaha); **10** Glen Richards (Kawasaki); **11** Paul Jones (Yamaha); **12** Jamie Morley (Suzuki); **13** Dean Ellison (Ducati); **14** Paul Young (Suzuki); **15** Gary Mason (Honda).
Fastest lap: Hislop, 1m 22.171s, 98.66 mph/158.78 km/h (record).

Race 2
1 Steve Hislop (Ducati), 30m 23.034s, 97.68 mph/157.20 km/h.
2 John Reynolds (Suzuki); **3** Sean Emmett (Ducati); **4** Michael Rutter (Ducati); **5** Paul Brown (Ducati); **6** Steve Plater (Yamaha); **7** Glen Richards (Kawasaki); **8** Simon Crafar (Yamaha); **9** Dean Thomas (Ducati); **10** Dean Ellison (Ducati); **11** Paul Jones (Yamaha); **12** Lee Jackson (Honda); **13** Mark Burr (Kawasaki); **14** Jamie Robinson (Honda); **15** Shane Norval (Yamaha).
Fastest lap: Hislop, 1m 21.707s, 99.22 mph/159.68 km/h (record).
Championship points: **1** Hislop, 45; **2** Emmett, 41; **3** Reynolds, 33; **4** Plater, 26; **5** Rutter, 22; **6** Brown, 19.

MB4U.com Supersport Championship, round 1 (18 laps, 40.536 miles/65.232 km)
1 Jim Moodie (Yamaha), 26m 27.729s, 91.74 mph/147.64 km/h.
2 Scott Smart (Honda); **3** Danny Beaumont (Yamaha); **4** Jimmy Lindstrom (Suzuki); **5** Jeremy Goodall (Suzuki); **6** Ben Wilson (Honda); **7** Douglas Cowie (Kawasaki); **8** Gary May (Yamaha); **9** Callum Ramsay (Suzuki); **10** Craig Sproston (Honda); **11** Tom Tunstall (Suzuki); **12** Richard Norris (Honda); **13** Juan Kinnish (Kawasaki); **14** Ian Campbell (Honda); **15** Chris Bishop (Honda).
Fastest lap: Moodie, 1m 27.248s, 92.92 mph/149.54 km/h.
Championship points: **1** Moodie, 25; **2** Smart, 20; **3** Beaumont, 16; **4** Lindstrom, 13; **5** Goodall, 11; **6** Wilson, 10.

National 125GP Championship, round 1 (16 laps, 36.032 miles/57.984 km)
1 Christian Elkin (Honda), 24m 06.092s, 89.51 mph/144.05 km/h.
2 Chris Martin (Honda); **3** Michael Wilcox (Honda); **4** Guy Farbrother (Honda); **5** John Pearson (Kawasaki); **6** Paul Robinson (Honda); **7** Steve Patrickson (Honda); **8** Andy Walker (Honda); **9** Leon Camier (Honda); **10** John Laverty (Honda); **11** Russell Hodgson (Honda); **12** David Mateer (Honda); **13** Sam Owens (Honda); **14** Paul Veazey (Honda); **15** Jon Vincent (Honda).
Fastest lap: Elkin, 1m 29.160s, 90.92 mph/146.33 km/h.
Championship points: **1** Elkin, 25; **2** Martin, 20; **3** Wilcox, 16; **4** Farbrother, 13; **5** Pearson, 11; **6** Robinson, 10.

Performance Bikes Superstock Championship, round 1 (18 laps, 40.536 miles/65.232 km)
1 Chris Burns (Suzuki), 25m 59.639s, 93.39 mph/150.30 km/h.
2 David Jefferies (Suzuki); **3** Dave Johnson (Suzuki); **4** Kieran Murphy (Suzuki); **5** Andi Notman (Suzuki); **6** Ross McCulloch (Suzuki); **7** Danny Beaumont (Suzuki); **8** Luke Quigley (Honda); **9** Simon Andrews (Honda); **10** Darren Mitchell (Suzuki); **11** Keith Amor (Suzuki); **12** Tommy Hill (Yamaha); **13** Andy Tinsley (Suzuki); **14** Steve McMillan (Suzuki); **15** Steve Brogan (Suzuki).
Fastest lap: John Crockford (Suzuki), 1m 25.663s, 94.64 mph/152.30 km/h (record).
Championship points: **1** Burns, 25; **2** Jefferies, 20; **3** Johnson, 16; **4** Murphy, 13; **5** Notman, 11; **6** McCulloch, 10.

BRANDS HATCH INDY CIRCUIT, 14 April. 1.226-mile/1.973-km circuit.
MCN British Superbike Championship, round 2 (2 x 30 laps, 36.780 miles/59.190 km)
Race 1
1 Steve Hislop (Ducati), 23m 25.264s, 94.28 mph/151.73 km/h.
2 John Reynolds (Suzuki); **3** Paul Brown (Ducati); **4** Sean Emmett (Ducati); **5** Shane Byrne (Ducati); **6** Steve Plater (Yamaha); **7** Michael Rutter (Ducati); **8** Karl Harris (Suzuki);

9 Simon Crafar (Yamaha); 10 Gary Mason (Honda); 11 Paul Jones (Yamaha); 12 Dean Ellison (Ducati); 13 David Jefferies (Suzuki); 14 Jamie Morley (Suzuki); 15 Shane Norval (Yamaha).
Fastest lap: Hislop, 46.192s, 95.56 mph/153.79 km/h (record).

Race 2
1 Steve Hislop (Ducati), 23m 58.976s, 92.07 mph/148.17 km/h.
2 Sean Emmett (Ducati); 3 John Reynolds (Suzuki); 4 Michael Rutter (Ducati); 5 Paul Brown (Ducati); 6 Steve Plater (Yamaha); 7 Shane Byrne (Ducati); 8 Dean Thomas (Ducati); 9 Simon Crafar (Yamaha); 10 Gary Mason (Honda); 11 David Jefferies (Suzuki); 12 Shane Norval (Yamaha); 13 Lee Jackson (Honda); 14 Phil Giles (Suzuki); 15 Jason Davis (Suzuki).
Fastest lap: Reynolds, 46.189s, 95.57 mph/153.80 km/h (record).
Championship points: 1 Hislop, 95; 2 Emmett, 74; 3 Reynolds, 69; 4 Brown and Plater, 46; 6 Rutter, 44.

MB4U.com Supersport Championship, round 2 (26 laps, 31.876 miles/51.298 km)
1 Stuart Easton (Ducati), 21m 25.846s, 89.31 mph/143.73 km/h.
2 Jim Moodie (Yamaha); 3 Pete Jennings (Kawasaki); 4 Douglas Cowie (Kawasaki); 5 Ben Wilson (Honda); 6 Jeremy Goodall (Suzuki); 7 Adam Redding (Kawasaki); 8 Scott Smart (Honda); 9 Simon Andrews (Honda); 10 Spencer Cook (Yamaha); 11 Sam Corke (Yamaha); 12 Tom Tunstall (Suzuki); 13 Daniel Fowler (Yamaha); 14 Richard Norris (Honda); 15 Gary May (Yamaha).
Fastest lap: Cowie, 48.767s, 90.51 mph/145.67 km/h.
Championship points: 1 Moodie, 45; 2 Smart, 29; 3 Easton, 25; 4 Wilson, 23; 5 Goodall, 22; 6 Beaumont and Jennings, 16.

National 125GP Championship, round 2 (24 laps, 29.424 miles/47.352 km)
1 Chris Martin (Honda), 20m 16.333s, 87.15 mph/140.25 km/h.
2 John Pearson (Kawasaki); 3 Russell Hodgson (Honda); 4 Christian Elkin (Honda); 5 Paul Robinson (Honda); 6 Guy Farbrother (Honda); 7 Leon Camier (Honda); 8 Steve Patrickson (Honda); 9 John Laverty (Honda); 10 Midge Smart (Honda); 11 Jon Vincent (Honda); 12 Kris Weston (Honda); 13 William Dunlop (Honda); 14 Chester Lusk (Honda); 15 Oliver Bridewell (Honda).
Fastest lap: Hodgson, 49.794s, 88.65 mph/142.67 km/h.
Championship points: 1 Martin, 45; 2 Elkin, 38; 3 Pearson, 31; 4 Farbrother, 23; 5 Hodgson and Robinson, 21.

Performance Bikes Superstock Championship, round 2 (26 laps, 31.876 miles/51.298 km)
1 John Crockford (Suzuki), 21m 16.174s, 89.98 mph/144.81 km/h.
2 Ross McCulloch (Suzuki); 3 Chris Burns (Suzuki); 4 Andi Notman (Suzuki); 5 Luke Quigley (Suzuki); 6 Dave Johnson (Suzuki); 7 Andy Tinsley (Suzuki); 8 Jon Kirkham (Suzuki); 9 Phil Giles (Suzuki); 10 Steve McMillan (Suzuki); 11 Steve Brogan (Suzuki); 12 Paul Sheehan (Suzuki); 13 Simon Andrews (Honda); 14 Kelvin Reilly (Yamaha); 15 Tommy Hill (Yamaha).
Fastest lap: David Jefferies (Suzuki), 48.133s, 91.71 mph/147.59 km/h.
Championship points: 1 Burns, 41; 2 McCulloch, 30; 3 Johnson, 26; 4 Crockford, 25; 5 Notman, 24; 6 Jefferies, 20.

DONINGTON PARK NATIONAL CIRCUIT, 28 April. 1.957-mile/3.149-km circuit.
MCN British Superbike Championship, round 3 (2 x 25 laps, 48.925 miles/78.725 km)
Race 1
1 Shane Byrne (Ducati), 29m 19.469s, 100.05 mph/161.01 km/h.
2 Steve Plater (Yamaha); 3 Steve Hislop (Ducati); 4 Michael Rutter (Ducati); 5 Sean Emmett (Ducati); 6 Glen Richards (Kawasaki); 7 Dean Thomas (Ducati); 8 Dean Ellison (Ducati); 9 Paul Brown (Ducati); 10 Paul Jones (Yamaha); 11 Jamie Robinson (Honda); 12 Phil Giles (Suzuki); 13 Shane Norval (Yamaha); 14 Jason Davis (Suzuki); 15 Marty Nutt (Suzuki).
Fastest lap: Rutter, 1m 09.479s, 101.41 mph/163.21 km/h.

Race 2
1 Michael Rutter (Ducati), 33m 19.098s, 88.06 mph/141.72 km/h.
2 Shane Byrne (Ducati); 3 Simon Crafar (Yamaha); 4 Sean Emmett (Ducati); 5 Paul Brown (Ducati); 6 Steve Hislop (Ducati); 7 Steve Plater (Yamaha); 8 Glen Richards (Kawasaki); 9 Dean Thomas (Ducati); 10 Dean Ellison (Ducati); 11 Shane Norval (Yamaha); 12 Karl Harris (Suzuki); 13 Neil Faulkner (Suzuki); 14 Marty Nutt (Suzuki); 15 Gordon Blackley (Honda).
Fastest lap: Emmett, 1m 17.581s, 90.82 mph/146.16 km/h.
Championship points: 1 Hislop, 121; 2 Emmett, 98; 3 Rutter, 82; 4 Byrne, 76; 5 Plater, 75; 6 Reynolds, 69.

MB4U.com Supersport Championship, round 3 (19 laps, 37.183 miles/59.831 km)
1 Stuart Easton (Ducati), 23m 21.903s, 95.41 mph/153.55 km/h.
2 Pete Jennings (Kawasaki); 3 Simon Andrews (Honda); 4 Scott Smart (Honda); 5 Tom Tunstall (Suzuki); 6 Gary May (Yamaha); 7 Douglas Cowie (Kawasaki); 8 Chris Bishop (Honda); 9 Jeremy Goodall (Suzuki); 10 Craig McLelland (Suzuki); 11 Craig Sproston (Honda); 12 Spencer Cook (Yamaha); 13 Mark Holton (Kawasaki); 14 Paul Chance (Suzuki); 15 Michael Laverty (Honda).
Fastest lap: Easton, 1m 13.137s, 96.34 mph/155.05 km/h.
Championship points: 1 Easton, 50; 2 Moodie, 45; 3 Smart, 42; 4 Jennings, 36; 5 Goodall, 29; 6 Andrews, 24.

National 125GP Championship, round 3 (18 laps, 35.226 miles/56.682 km)
1 Steve Patrickson (Honda), 23m 17.488s, 90.67 mph/145.92 km/h.
2 Chris Martin (Honda); 3 Paul Robinson (Honda); 4 Andy Walker (Honda); 5 Leon Camier (Honda); 6 Michael Wilcox (Honda); 7 John Laverty (Honda); 8 Paul Veazey (Honda); 9 Midge Smart (Honda); 10 Kris Weston (Honda); 11 Daniel Coutts (Honda); 12 Sam Owens (Honda); 13 Eugene Laverty (Honda); 14 David Mateer (Honda); 15 Ryan Saxelby (Honda).
Fastest lap: Martin, 1m 16.029s, 92.67 mph/149.15 km/h.
Championship points: 1 Martin, 65; 2 Patrickson, 42; 3 Elkin, 38; 4 Robinson, 37; 5 Pearson, 31; 6 Camier, 27.

Performance Bikes Superstock Championship, round 3 (15 laps, 29.355 miles/47.235 km)
1 Chris Burns (Suzuki), 20m 04.439s, 87.66 mph/141.08 km/h.
2 David Jefferies (Suzuki); 3 John Crockford (Suzuki); 4 Simon Andrews (Honda); 5 Dennis Hobbs (Honda); 6 Steve Brogan (Suzuki); 7 Jonti Hobday (Suzuki); 8 Andi Notman (Suzuki); 9 Steve Allan (Kawasaki); 10 Kieran Murphy (Suzuki); 11 Luke Quigley (Suzuki); 12 Douglas Cowie (Kawasaki); 13 Steve McMillan (Suzuki); 14 Kelvin Reilly (Yamaha); 15 Ross McCulloch (Suzuki).
Fastest lap: Burns, 1m 18.552s, 89.70 mph/144.36 km/h.
Championship points: 1 Burns, 66; 2 Crockford, 41; 3 Jefferies, 40; 4 Notman, 32; 5 McCulloch, 31; 6 Johnson, 26.

OULTON PARK, 6 May. 2.769-mile/4.456-km circuit.
MCN British Superbike Championship, round 4
Race 1 (18 laps, 49.842 miles/80.208 km)
1 Steve Hislop (Ducati), 27m 47.928s, 107.57 mph/173.12 km/h.
2 Michael Rutter (Ducati); 3 Sean Emmett (Ducati); 4 Paul Brown (Ducati); 5 John Reynolds (Suzuki); 6 Steve Plater (Yamaha); 7 Karl Harris (Suzuki); 8 Shane Byrne (Ducati); 9 Dean Ellison (Ducati); 10 Glen Richards (Kawasaki); 11 Simon Crafar (Yamaha); 12 Gary Mason (Honda); 13 Ross McCulloch (Suzuki); 14 Mark Burr (Kawasaki); 15 Shane Norval (Yamaha).
Fastest lap: Hislop, 1m 32.143s, 108.18 mph/174.10 km/h.

Race 2 (8 laps, 22.152 miles/35.648 km)
1 Michael Rutter (Ducati), 12m 25.313s, 106.99 mph/172.18 km/h.
2 Steve Hislop (Ducati); 3 Sean Emmett (Ducati); 4 Paul Brown (Ducati); 5 John Reynolds (Suzuki); 6 Karl Harris (Suzuki); 7 Shane Byrne (Ducati); 8 Dean Thomas (Ducati); 9 Glen Richards (Kawasaki); 10 Steve Plater (Yamaha); 11 Dean Ellison (Ducati); 12 Simon Crafar (Yamaha); 13 Gary Mason (Honda); 14 Shane Norval (Yamaha); 15 Jason Davis (Suzuki).
Fastest lap: Hislop, 1m 31.681s, 108.72 mph/174.98 km/h (record).
Championship points: 1 Hislop, 156; 2 Emmett, 122; 3 Rutter, 114.5; 4 Byrne, 88.5; 5 Plater, 88; 6 Reynolds, 85.5.

MB4U.com Supersport Championship, round 4 (15 laps, 41.535 miles/66.840 km)
1 Stuart Easton (Ducati), 26m 08.044s, 95.35 mph/153.45 km/h.
2 Scott Smart (Honda); 3 Pete Jennings (Kawasaki); 4 Michael Laverty (Honda); 5 Ben Wilson (Honda); 6 Tom Tunstall (Suzuki); 7 Callum Ramsay (Suzuki); 8 Spencer Cook (Yamaha); 9 Daniel Fowler (Yamaha); 10 Jeremy Goodall (Suzuki); 11 Craig Sproston (Honda); 12 Adam Redding (Kawasaki); 13 Les Shand (Honda); 14 Mark Brewster (Kawasaki); 15 Paul Chance (Suzuki).
Fastest lap: Easton, 1m 37.386s, 102.36 mph/164.73 km/h.
Championship points: 1 Easton, 75; 2 Smart, 62; 3 Jennings, 52; 4 Moodie, 45; 5 Goodall, 35; 6 Wilson, 34.

National 125GP Championship, round 4
Race postponed.

Performance Bikes Superstock Championship, round 4 (15 laps, 41.535 miles/66.840 km)
1 David Jefferies (Suzuki), 24m 07.405s, 103.30 mph/166.25 km/h.
2 Chris Burns (Suzuki); 3 Kieran Murphy (Suzuki); 4 Luke Quigley (Suzuki); 5 Steve Brogan (Suzuki); 6 Andy Tinsley (Suzuki); 7 Dave Johnson (Suzuki); 8 Steve McMillan (Suzuki); 9 Nigel Scott (Suzuki); 10 Kevin Falcke (Suzuki); 11 Scott Roper (Honda); 12 Jonti Hobday (Suzuki); 13 David Summerson (Suzuki); 14 Darren Mitchell (Suzuki); 15 Kelvin Reilly (Yamaha).
Fastest lap: Jefferies, 1m 35.447s, 104.43 mph/168.07 km/h.
Championship points: 1 Burns, 86; 2 Jefferies, 65; 3 Crockford, 41; 4 Quigley, 37; 5 Johnson and Murphy, 35.

SILVERSTONE GRAND PRIX CIRCUIT, 18 and 19 May. 3.165-mile/5.094-km circuit.
MB4U.com Supersport Championship, round 5 (10 laps, 31.650 miles/50.940 km)
1 Stuart Easton (Ducati), 19m 29.703s, 97.18 mph/156.40 km/h.
2 Tom Tunstall (Suzuki); 3 Simon Andrews (Honda); 4 Chris Bishop (Honda); 5 Pete Jennings (Kawasaki); 6 Jeremy Goodall (Suzuki); 7 Spencer Cook (Yamaha); 8 Richard Norris (Honda); 9 Edward Smith (Yamaha); 10 Daniel Fowler (Yamaha); 11 Adam Redding (Kawasaki); 12 Darren Fry (Suzuki); 13 Chris Platt (Yamaha); 14 Mark Holton (Kawasaki); 15 Ricky Chadwick (Honda).
Fastest lap: Easton, 1m 56.031s, 98.20 mph/158.04 km/h.
Championship points: 1 Easton, 100; 2 Jennings, 63; 3 Smart, 62; 4 Tunstall, 51; 5 Goodall and Moodie, 45.

National 125GP Championship, round 4 (12 laps, 37.980 miles/61.128 km)
1 Chris Martin (Honda), 24m 23.350s, 93.25 mph/150.07 km/h.
2 John Pearson (Kawasaki); 3 Christian Elkin (Honda); 4 Steve Patrickson (Honda); 5 Andy Walker (Honda); 6 Leon Camier (Honda); 7 Midge Smart (Honda); 8 Guy Farbrother (Honda); 9 Daniel Coutts (Honda); 10 Sam Owens (Honda); 11 Brian Clark (Honda); 12 James Ford (Honda); 13 Russell Hodgson (Honda); 14 Ryan Saxelby (Honda); 15 Paul Veazey (Honda).
Fastest lap: Elkin, 2m 00.670s, 94.42 mph/151.96 km/h.
Championship points: 1 Martin, 80; 2 Patrickson, 55; 3 Elkin, 54; 4 Pearson, 51; 5 Camier and Robinson, 37.

National 125GP Championship, round 5 (12 laps, 37.980 miles/61.128 km)
1 Christian Elkin (Honda), 24m 09.518s, 94.14 mph/151.50 km/h.
2 Chris Martin (Honda); 3 Leon Camier (Honda); 4 John Pearson (Kawasaki); 5 Howie Mainwaring (Honda); 6 Midge Smart (Honda); 7 Paul Veazey (Honda); 8 Sam Owens (Honda); 9 Guy Farbrother (Honda); 10 Kris Weston (Honda); 11 Brian Clark (Honda); 12 Russell Hodgson (Honda); 13 Daniel Coutts (Honda); 14 Jon Vincent (Honda); 15 James Ford (Honda).
Fastest lap: Camier, 1m 59.650s, 95.23 mph/153.26 km/h.
Championship points: 1 Martin, 100; 2 Elkin, 79; 3 Pearson, 64; 4 Patrickson, 55; 5 Camier, 53; 6 Farbrother, 38.

Performance Bikes Superstock Championship, round 5 (12 laps, 37.980 miles/61.128 km)
1 David Jefferies (Suzuki), 23m 17.585s, 97.64 mph/157.14 km/h.
2 Ross McCulloch (Suzuki); 3 Kieran Murphy (Suzuki); 4 Andy Tinsley (Suzuki); 5 John Crockford (Suzuki); 6 Tristan Palmer (Suzuki); 7 Simon Andrews (Honda); 8 Dave Johnson (Suzuki); 9 Warren Scott (Suzuki); 10 David Summerson (Suzuki); 11 Jonti Hobday (Suzuki); 12 Kelvin Reilly (Yamaha); 13 Douglas Cowie (Kawasaki); 14 Brett Sampson (Suzuki); 15 Malcolm Ashley (Ducati).
Fastest lap: Andi Notman (Suzuki), 1m 54.325s, 99.67 mph/160.40 km/h.
Championship points: 1 Jefferies, 90; 2 Burns, 86; 3 Crockford, 52; 4 McCulloch and Murphy, 51; 6 Johnson, 43.

SNETTERTON CIRCUIT, 3 June. 1.952-mile/3.141-km circuit.
British Superbike Championship, round 5
Race 1 (25 laps, 48.800 miles/78.525 km)
1 Sean Emmett (Ducati), 28m 48.986s, 101.60 mph/163.51 km/h.
2 John Reynolds (Suzuki); 3 Steve Plater (Yamaha); 4 Steve Hislop (Ducati); 5 Paul Brown (Ducati); 6 Simon Crafar (Yamaha); 7 Giovanni Bussei (Suzuki); 8 Dean Ellison (Ducati); 9 Dean Thomas (Ducati); 10 Adrian Coates (Suzuki); 11 Mark Burr (Kawasaki); 12 Jamie Robinson (Honda); 13 Shane Norval (Yamaha); 14 Marty Nutt (Suzuki); 15 Jason Davis (Suzuki).
Fastest lap: Emmett, 1m 06.330s, 105.94 mph/170.49 km/h.

Race 2 (20 laps, 39.040 miles/62.820 km)
1 Sean Emmett (Ducati), 22m 24.643s, 104.52 mph/168.21 km/h.
2 Steve Hislop (Ducati); 3 Michael Rutter (Ducati); 4 Steve Plater (Yamaha); 5 Shane Byrne (Ducati); 6 Paul Brown (Ducati); 7 Simon Crafar (Yamaha); 8 Glen Richards (Kawasaki); 9 Dean Ellison (Ducati); 10 Paul Jones (Yamaha); 11 Giovanni Bussei (Suzuki); 12 Adrian Coates (Suzuki); 13 Shane Norval (Yamaha); 14 Jamie Robinson (Honda); 15 Lee Jackson (Honda).
Fastest lap: Emmett, 1m 06.419s, 105.80 mph/170.27 km/h.
Championship points: 1 Hislop, 189; 2 Emmett, 172; 3 Rutter, 130.5; 4 Plater, 117; 5 Reynolds, 105.5; 6 Brown, 104.5.

MB4U.com Supersport Championship, round 6 (18 laps, 35.136 miles/56.538 km)
1 Stuart Easton (Ducati), 21m 11.598s, 99.47 mph/160.08 km/h.
2 Michael Laverty (Honda); 3 Scott Smart (Honda); 4 Jeremy Goodall (Suzuki); 5 Chris Bishop (Honda); 6 Ben Wilson (Honda); 7 Edward Smith (Yamaha); 8 Craig Sproston (Honda); 9 Douglas Cowie (Kawasaki); 10 Adam Redding (Kawasaki); 11 Darren Fry (Suzuki); 12 Spencer Cook (Yamaha); 13 Matt Layt (Suzuki); 14 Chris Platt (Yamaha); 15 Mark Davies (Kawasaki).
Fastest lap: Easton, 1m 09.748s, 100.75 mph/162.14 km/h.
Championship points: 1 Easton, 125; 2 Smart, 78; 3 Jennings, 63; 4 Goodall, 58; 5 Tunstall, 51; 6 Moodie, 45.

National 125GP Championship, round 6 (14 laps, 27.328 miles/43.974 km))
1 Midge Smart (Honda), 17m 35.205s, 93.23 mph/150.04 km/h.
2 Chris Martin (Honda); 3 Christian Elkin (Honda); 4 John Pearson (Kawasaki); 5 Guy Farbrother (Honda); 6 Leon Camier (Honda); 7 Andy Walker (Honda); 8 Paul Robinson (Honda); 9 Russell Hodgson (Honda); 10 Steve Patrickson (Honda); 11 Paul Veazey (Honda); 12 Brian Clark (Honda); 13 Howie Mainwaring (Honda); 14 John Laverty (Honda); 15 Kris Weston (Honda).
Fastest lap: Elkin, 1m 14.234s, 94.66 mph/152.34 km/h.
Championship points: 1 Martin, 120; 2 Elkin, 95; 3 Pearson, 77; 4 Camier, 63; 5 Patrickson, 61; 6 Smart, 57.

Performance Bikes Superstock Championship, round 6 (15 laps, 29.280 miles/47.115 km)
1 Chris Burns (Suzuki), 17m 29.325s, 100.45 mph/161.66 km/h.
2 Marshall Neill (Suzuki); 3 Steve Brogan (Suzuki); 4 Ross McCulloch (Suzuki); 5 Jonti Hobday (Suzuki); 6 Tristan Palmer (Suzuki); 7 David Summerson (Suzuki); 8 Andy Tinsley (Suzuki); 9 Mark Baldock (Suzuki); 10 Douglas Cowie (Kawasaki); 11 Graham Darracott (Suzuki); 12 John Crockford (Suzuki); 13 Donald MacFadyen (Suzuki); 14 Ian Hutchinson (Suzuki); 15 Malcolm Ashley (Ducati).
Fastest lap: Burns, 1m 08.603s, 102.43 mph/164.84 km/h.
Championship points: 1 Burns, 111; 2 Jefferies, 90; 3 McCulloch, 64; 4 Crockford, 56; 5 Murphy, 51; 6 Brogan, Johnson and Tinsley, 43.

BRANDS HATCH GRAND PRIX CIRCUIT, 16 June. 2.623-mile/4.221-km circuit.
MCN British Superbike Championship, round 6 (2 x 20 laps, 52.460 miles/84.420 km)
Race 1
1 John Reynolds (Suzuki), 29m 25.192s, 107.01 mph/172.22 km/h.
2 Steve Plater (Yamaha); 3 Michael Rutter (Ducati); 4 Paul Brown (Ducati); 5 Simon Crafar (Yamaha); 6 Glen Richards (Kawasaki); 7 Dean Ellison (Ducati); 8 Giovanni Bussei (Suzuki); 9 Shane Byrne (Ducati); 10 Dean Thomas (Ducati); 11 John Crawford (Suzuki); 12 Steve Hislop (Ducati); 13 Adrian Coates (Suzuki); 14 Jamie Morley (Ducati); 15 Mark Burr (Kawasaki).
Fastest lap: Byrne, 1m 27.359s, 108.08 mph/173.94 km/h.

Race 2
1 Sean Emmett (Ducati), 31m 50.803s, 98.96 mph/159.26 km/h.
2 Steve Hislop (Ducati); 3 Michael Rutter (Ducati); 4 John Reynolds (Suzuki); 5 Shane Byrne (Ducati); 6 Steve Plater (Yamaha); 7 Paul Brown (Ducati); 8 Giovanni Bussei (Suzuki); 9 Simon Crafar (Yamaha); 10 Dean Ellison (Ducati); 11 Glen Richards (Kawasaki); 12 Mark Burr (Kawasaki); 13 Paul Jones (Yamaha); 14 Jamie Robinson (Honda); 15 Shane Norval (Yamaha).
Fastest lap: Reynolds, 1m 26.878s, 108.68 mph/174.90 km/h.
Championship points: 1 Hislop, 213; 2 Emmett, 197; 3 Rutter, 162.5; 4 Plater, 147; 5 Reynolds, 143.5; 6 Brown, 126.5.

MB4U.com Supersport Championship, round 7 (16 laps, 41.968 miles/67.536 km)
1 Stuart Easton (Ducati), 24m 40.323s, 102.10 mph/164.31 km/h.
2 Simon Andrews (Honda); 3 Tom Tunstall (Suzuki); 4 Scott Smart (Honda); 5 Gary May (Yamaha); 6 Chris Bishop (Honda); 7 Douglas Cowie (Kawasaki); 8 Danny Beaumont (Yamaha); 9 Craig Sproston (Honda); 10 Pete Jennings (Kawasaki); 11 Jeremy Goodall (Yamaha); 12 Mark Davies (Kawasaki); 13 Ian Campbell (Honda); 14 Edward Smith (Yamaha); 15 Richard Norris (Honda).
Fastest lap: Easton, 1m 31.252s, 103.47 mph/166.52 km/h.
Championship points: 1 Easton, 150; 2 Smart, 91; 3 Jennings, 69; 4 Tunstall, 67; 5 Goodall, 63; 6 Andrews, 60.

National 125GP Championship, round 7 (14 laps, 36.722 miles/59.094 km)
1 Midge Smart (Honda), 22m 29.227s, 98.02 mph/157.75 km/h.
2 Chris Martin (Honda); 3 Christian Elkin (Honda); 4 Guy Farbrother (Honda); 5 John Pearson (Kawasaki); 6 Michael Laverty (Honda); 7 Andy Walker (Honda); 8 John Laverty (Honda); 9 Sam Owens (Honda); 10 Steve Patrickson (Honda); 11 Daniel Coutts (Honda); 12 James Ford (Honda); 13 Kris Weston (Honda); 14 Michael Wilcox (Honda); 15 Brian Clark (Honda).
Fastest lap: Farbrother, 1m 34.615s, 99.79 mph/160.60 km/h.
Championship points: 1 Martin, 140; 2 Elkin, 111; 3 Pearson, 88; 4 Smart, 82; 5 Patrickson, 67; 6 Camier, 63.

Performance Bikes Superstock Championship, round 7 (16 laps, 41.968 miles/67.536 km)
1 David Jefferies (Suzuki), 24m 25.195s, 103.15 mph/166.00 km/h.
2 Chris Burns (Suzuki); 3 John Crockford (Suzuki); 4 Ross McCulloch (Suzuki); 5 Kieran Murphy (Suzuki); 6 Andy Tinsley (Suzuki); 7 Steve Brogan (Suzuki); 8 Simon Andrews (Honda); 9 Tristan Palmer (Suzuki); 10 Steve McMillan (Suzuki); 11 Kelvin Reilly (Yamaha); 12 Stephen Thompson (Suzuki); 13 Brett Sampson (Suzuki); 14 Kevin Falcke (Suzuki); 15 Steve Allan (Kawasaki).
Fastest lap: Jefferies, 1m 30.706s, 104.09 mph/167.52 km/h.
Championship points: 1 Burns, 131; 2 Jefferies, 115; 3 McCulloch, 77; 4 Crockford, 72; 5 Murphy, 62; 6 Tinsley, 53.

ROCKINGHAM CIRCUIT, 23 June. 1.736-mile/2.794-km circuit.
MCN British Superbike Championship, round 7 (2 x 22 laps, 38.192 miles/61.468 km)
Race 1
1 Michael Rutter (Ducati), 27m 18.099s, 83.93 mph/135.07 km/h.
2 Steve Hislop (Ducati); 3 Sean Emmett (Ducati); 4 Shane Byrne (Ducati); 5 Dean Thomas (Ducati); 6 John Reynolds (Suzuki); 7 Glen Richards (Kawasaki); 8 Jamie Morley (Ducati); 9 David Jefferies (Suzuki); 10 Dean Ellison (Ducati); 11 Simon Crafar (Yamaha); 12 Paul Young (Suzuki); 13 Shane Norval (Yamaha); 14 Paul Jones (Yamaha); 15 Gary Mason (Honda).
Fastest lap: Rutter, 1m 10.485s, 88.66 mph/142.69 km/h (record).

Race 2
1 Michael Rutter (Ducati), 26m 01.047s, 88.07 mph/141.73 km/h.
2 Sean Emmett (Ducati); 3 Dean Thomas (Ducati); 4 Steve Hislop (Ducati); 5 Shane Byrne (Ducati); 6 Glen Richards (Kawasaki); 7 Jamie Morley (Ducati); 8 David Jefferies (Suzuki); 9 Mark Burr (Kawasaki); 10 Dean Ellison (Ducati); 11 Paul Young (Suzuki); 12 Shane Norval (Yamaha); 13 Jason Davis (Suzuki); 14 Paul Jones (Yamaha); 15 Marty Nutt (Suzuki).
Fastest lap: Hislop, 1m 09.961s, 89.33 mph/143.76 km/h (record).
Championship points: 1 Hislop, 246; 2 Emmett, 233; 3 Rutter, 212.5; 4 Reynolds, 153.5; 5 Plater, 147; 6 Byrne, 141.5.

MB4U.com Supersport Championship, round 8 (17 laps, 29.512 miles/47.498 km)
1 Scott Smart (Honda), 20m 57.081s, 84.51 mph/136.01 km/h.
2 Stuart Easton (Ducati); 3 Edward Smith (Yamaha); 4 Callum Ramsay (Suzuki); 5 Craig Sproston (Honda); 6 Jeremy

Goodall (Suzuki); 7 Richard Cooper (Suzuki); 8 Tom Tunstall (Suzuki); 9 Ben Wilson (Honda); 10 Chris Platt (Yamaha); 11 Pete Jennings (Kawasaki); 12 Mark Davies (Kawasaki); 13 Chris Bishop (Honda); 14 Juan Kinnish (Kawasaki); 15 Jason Boyle (Yamaha).
Fastest lap: Easton, 1m 11.429s, 87.49 mph/140.80 km/h (record).
Championship points: 1 Easton, 170; 2 Smart, 116; 3 Tunstall, 75; 4 Jennings, 74; 5 Goodall, 73; 6 Andrews, 60.

National 125GP Championship, round 8 (15 laps, 26.040 miles/41.910 km)
1 Chris Martin (Honda), 19m 08.759s, 81.60 mph/131.32 km/h.
2 Christian Elkin (Honda); 3 Guy Farbrother (Honda); 4 Midge Smart (Honda); 5 Russell Hodgson (Honda); 6 Leon Camier (Honda); 7 Daniel Coutts (Honda); 8 Michael Wilcox (Honda); 9 Andy Walker (Honda); 10 Sam Owens (Honda); 11 Oliver Bridewell (Honda); 12 Brian Clark (Honda); 13 James Ford (Honda); 14 Lee Longden (Honda); 15 Ryan Saxelby (Honda).
Fastest lap: Elkin, 1m 15.680s, 82.57 mph/132.89 km/h (record).
Championship points: 1 Martin, 165; 2 Elkin, 131; 3 Smart, 95; 4 Pearson, 88; 5 Farbrother, 78; 6 Camier, 73.

Performance Bikes Superstock Championship, round 8 (17 laps, 29.512 miles/47.498 km)
1 David Jefferies (Suzuki), 20m 50.156s, 84.98 mph/136.76 km/h.
2 Steve Brogan (Suzuki); 3 John Crockford (Suzuki); 4 Steve McMillan (Suzuki); 5 Kieran Murphy (Suzuki); 6 Andy Tinsley (Suzuki); 7 Phil Giles (Suzuki); 8 Tristan Palmer (Suzuki); 9 Jonti Hobday (Suzuki); 10 Tommy Hill (Yamaha); 11 Kevin Falcke (Suzuki); 12 Chris Burns (Suzuki); 13 Steve Allan (Kawasaki); 14 Brett Sampson (Suzuki); 15 David Summerson (Suzuki).
Fastest lap: Jefferies, 1m 12.816s, 85.82 mph/138.12 km/h (record).
Championship points: 1 Jefferies, 140; 2 Burns, 135; 3 Crockford, 88; 4 McCulloch, 77; 5 Murphy, 73; 6 Brogan, 72.

KNOCKHILL CIRCUIT, 7 July. 1.299-mile/2.091-km circuit.
MCN British Superbike Championship, round 8 (2 x 30 laps, 38.970 miles/62.730 km)
Race 1
1 Steve Hislop (Ducati), 26m 59.545s, 86.59 mph/139.35 km/h.
2 Sean Emmett (Ducati); 3 Michael Rutter (Ducati); 4 Paul Brown (Ducati); 5 John Reynolds (Suzuki); 6 Simon Crafar (Yamaha); 7 David Jefferies (Suzuki); 8 Glen Richards (Kawasaki); 9 Paul Jones (Yamaha); 10 Dean Ellison (Ducati); 11 Marty Nutt (Suzuki); 12 Jon Kirkham (Suzuki); 13 Jason Davis (Suzuki); 14 Mark Burr (Kawasaki); 15 Jamie Robinson (Honda).
Fastest lap: Hislop, 50.194s, 93.13 mph/149.89 km/h (record).

Race 2
1 Shane Byrne (Ducati), 25m 21.236s, 92.19 mph/148.37 km/h.
2 Paul Brown (Ducati); 3 Sean Emmett (Ducati); 4 John Reynolds (Suzuki); 5 Steve Plater (Yamaha); 6 Glen Richards (Kawasaki); 7 Steve Hislop (Ducati); 8 Dean Thomas (Ducati); 9 Simon Crafar (Yamaha); 10 Dean Ellison (Ducati); 11 Jamie Morley (Ducati); 12 Paul Jones (Yamaha); 13 Mark Burr (Kawasaki); 14 Paul Young (Suzuki); 15 Jason Davis (Suzuki).
Fastest lap: Hislop, 50.053s, 93.40 mph/150.31 km/h (record).
Championship points: 1 Hislop, 280; 2 Emmett, 269; 3 Rutter, 228.5; 4 Reynolds, 177.5; 5 Byrne, 166.5; 6 Brown, 159.5.

MB4U.com Supersport Championship, round 9 (26 laps, 33.774 miles/54.366 km)
1 Scott Smart (Honda), 23m 10.528s, 87.41 mph/140.67 km/h.
2 Michael Laverty (Honda); 3 Craig McLelland (Suzuki); 4 Callum Ramsay (Suzuki); 5 Ben Wilson (Honda); 6 Torquil Paterson (Suzuki); 7 Les Shand (Honda); 8 Douglas Cowie (Kawasaki); 9 Mark Davies (Kawasaki); 10 Chris Bishop (Honda); 11 Tom Tunstall (Suzuki); 12 Edward Smith (Yamaha); 13 Pete Jennings (Kawasaki); 14 Darren Mitchell (Suzuki); 15 Steve Allan (Kawasaki).
Fastest lap: Laverty, 52.804s, 88.53 mph/142.48 km/h (record).
Championship points: 1 Easton, 170; 2 Smart, 141; 3 Tunstall, 80; 4 Jennings, 77; 5 Goodall, 73; 6 Wilson, 62.

National 125GP Championship, round 9 (24 laps, 31.176 miles/50.184 km)
1 Christian Elkin (Honda), 22m 27.493s, 83.26 mph/133.99 km/h.
2 Guy Farbrother (Honda); 3 Leon Camier (Honda); 4 Chris Martin (Honda); 5 Midge Smart (Honda); 6 John Pearson (Kawasaki); 7 Russell Hodgson (Honda); 8 Daniel Coutts (Honda); 9 John Laverty (Honda); 10 Eugene Laverty (Honda); 11 Steve Patrickson (Honda); 12 Paul Veazey (Honda); 13 Michael Wilcox (Honda); 14 Kris Weston (Honda); 15 Simon Byrne (Honda).
Fastest lap: Farbrother, 55.054s, 84.91 mph/136.65 km/h.
Championship points: 1 Martin, 178; 2 Elkin, 156; 3 Smart, 106; 4 Farbrother and Pearson, 98; 6 Camier, 89.

Performance Bikes Superstock Championship, round 9 (24 laps, 31.176 miles/50.184 km)
1 John Crockford (Suzuki), 22m 30.661s, 83.07 mph/133.69 km/h.
2 David Jefferies (Suzuki); 3 Ross McCulloch (Suzuki); 4 Sandy Christie (Suzuki); 5 Andy Tinsley (Suzuki); 6 Donald MacFadyen (Suzuki); 7 Steve McMillan (Suzuki); 8 Tristan Palmer (Suzuki); 9 Kieran Murphy (Suzuki); 10 Dennis Hobbs (Suzuki); 11 Ian Hutchinson (Suzuki); 12 Douglas Cowie (Kawasaki); 13 Malcolm Ashley (Ducati); 14 Chris Burns (Suzuki); 15 Alan Bailey (Suzuki).
Fastest lap: Burns, 51.911s, 90.05 mph/144.93 km/h (record).

Championship points: 1 Jefferies, 160; 2 Burns, 137; 3 Crockford, 113; 4 McCulloch, 93; 5 Murphy, 80; 6 Tinsley, 74.

THRUXTON CIRCUIT, 11 August. 2.356-mile/3.792-km circuit.
MCN British Superbike Championship, round 9 (2 x 22 laps, 51.832 miles/83.424 km)
Race 1
1 Michael Rutter (Ducati), 28m 31.896s, 108.99 mph/175.40 km/h.
2 Steve Hislop (Ducati); 3 Sean Emmett (Yamaha); 4 John Reynolds (Suzuki); 5 Simon Crafar (Yamaha); 6 Shane Byrne (Ducati); 7 Steve Plater (Yamaha); 8 Glen Richards (Kawasaki); 9 Dean Thomas (Ducati); 10 John Crawford (Suzuki); 11 John Crockford (Suzuki); 12 Karl Harris (Suzuki); 13 Gary Mason (Honda); 14 Mark Burr (Kawasaki); 15 Dean Ellison (Ducati).
Fastest lap: Emmett, 1m 16.639s, 110.67 mph/178.10 km/h.

Race 2
1 Shane Byrne (Ducati), 28m 15.712s, 110.03 mph/177.08 km/h.
2 Steve Hislop (Ducati); 3 Sean Emmett (Yamaha); 4 Steve Plater (Yamaha); 5 Glen Richards (Kawasaki); 6 Karl Harris (Suzuki); 7 Simon Crafar (Yamaha); 8 Dean Thomas (Ducati); 9 John Crawford (Suzuki); 10 Mark Burr (Kawasaki); 11 Jason Davis (Yamaha); 12 Shane Norval (Yamaha); 13 Lee Jackson (Yamaha); 14 Paul Young (Suzuki); 15 Jamie Robinson (Honda).
Fastest lap: Byrne, 1m 16.328s, 111.12 mph/178.83 km/h.
Championship points: 1 Hislop, 320; 2 Emmett, 301; 3 Rutter, 253.5; 4 Byrne, 201.5; 5 Reynolds, 190.5; 6 Plater, 180.

MB4U.com Supersport Championship, round 10 (18 laps, 42.408 miles/68.256 km)
1 Michael Laverty (Honda), 23m 59.183s, 106.08 mph/170.72 km/h.
2 Simon Andrews (Honda); 3 Scott Smart (Honda); 4 Stuart Easton (Ducati); 5 Tom Tunstall (Suzuki); 6 Pete Jennings (Kawasaki); 7 Chris Bishop (Honda); 8 Gary May (Yamaha); 9 Callum Ramsay (Suzuki); 10 Douglas Cowie (Kawasaki); 11 Jeremy Goodall (Suzuki); 12 Ben Wilson (Honda); 13 Danny Beaumont (Yamaha); 14 Mark Rollin (Yamaha); 15 Mark Davies (Kawasaki).
Fastest lap: Laverty, 1m 19.149s, 107.16 mph/172.45 km/h.
Championship points: 1 Easton, 183; 2 Smart, 157; 3 Tunstall, 91; 4 Jennings, 87; 5 Andrews, 80; 6 Laverty, 79.

National 125GP Championship, round 10 (16 laps, 37.696 miles/60.672 km)
1 Guy Farbrother (Honda), 22m 03.537s, 102.53 mph/165.01 km/h.
2 Chris Martin (Honda); 3 Michael Wilcox (Honda); 4 Christian Elkin (Honda); 5 Midge Smart (Honda); 6 Leon Camier (Honda); 7 Eugene Laverty (Honda); 8 Russell Hodgson (Honda); 9 Daniel Coutts (Honda); 10 John Pearson (Kawasaki); 11 Andy Walker (Honda); 12 Paul Robinson (Honda); 13 Steve Patrickson (Honda); 14 Paul Veazey (Honda); 15 Brian Clark (Honda).
Fastest lap: Farbrother, 1m 21.748s, 103.75 mph/166.97 km/h.
Championship points: 1 Martin, 198; 2 Elkin, 169; 3 Farbrother, 123; 4 Smart, 117; 5 Pearson, 104; 6 Camier, 99.

Performance Bikes Superstock Championship, round 10 (18 laps, 42.408 miles/68.256 km)
1 John Crockford (Suzuki), 25m 00.414s, 101.75 mph/163.75 km/h.
2 David Jefferies (Suzuki); 3 Kieran Murphy (Suzuki); 4 Chris Burns (Suzuki); 5 Andi Notman (Suzuki); 6 Matt Llewellyn (Suzuki); 7 Jonti Hobday (Suzuki); 8 Steve McMillan (Suzuki); 9 Tristan Palmer (Suzuki); 10 Phil Giles (Suzuki); 11 Luke Quigley (Suzuki); 12 David Summerson (Suzuki); 13 Steve Allan (Kawasaki); 14 Douglas Cowie (Kawasaki); 15 John Nisill (Suzuki).
Fastest lap: Jefferies, 1m 18.430s, 108.14 mph/174.03 km/h.
Championship points: 1 Jefferies, 180; 2 Burns, 150; 3 Crockford, 138; 4 Murphy, 96; 5 McCulloch, 93; 6 Tinsley, 74.

CADWELL PARK CIRCUIT, 26 August. 2.173-mile/3.497-km circuit.
MCN British Superbike Championship, round 10 (2 x 18 laps, 39.114 miles/62.946 km)
Race 1
1 Steve Hislop (Ducati), 27m 03.104s, 86.75 mph/139.61 km/h.
2 Shane Byrne (Ducati); 3 Michael Rutter (Ducati); 4 John Reynolds (Suzuki); 5 Sean Emmett (Yamaha); 6 Simon Crafar (Yamaha); 7 Glen Richards (Kawasaki); 8 Karl Harris (Suzuki); 9 Gary Mason (Honda); 10 John Crawford (Suzuki); 11 Mark Burr (Kawasaki); 12 Dean Ellison (Ducati); 13 Paul Young (Suzuki); 14 Phil Giles (Suzuki); 15 Paul Jones (Yamaha).
Fastest lap: Hislop, 1m 25.056s, 91.97 mph/148.01 km/h (record).

Race 2
1 Steve Hislop (Ducati), 26m 01.046s, 90.20 mph/145.16 km/h.
2 Michael Rutter (Ducati); 3 Shane Byrne (Ducati); 4 John Reynolds (Suzuki); 5 Steve Plater (Yamaha); 6 Sean Emmett (Yamaha); 7 Karl Harris (Suzuki); 8 John Crawford (Suzuki); 9 Mark Burr (Kawasaki); 10 Dean Ellison (Ducati); 11 Paul Young (Suzuki); 12 Paul Jones (Yamaha); 13 Jason Davis (Yamaha); 14 Phil Giles (Suzuki); 15 Lee Jackson (Yamaha).
Fastest lap: Hislop, 1m 24.883s, 92.16 mph/148.31 km/h (record).
Championship points: 1 Hislop, 370; 2 Emmett, 322; 3 Rutter, 289.5; 4 Byrne, 237.5; 5 Reynolds, 216.5; 6 Plater, 191.

MB4U.com Supersport Championship, round 11 (13 laps, 28.249 miles/45.461 km)
1 Michael Laverty (Honda), 20m 47.382s, 81.52 mph/131.19 km/h.
2 Stuart Easton (Ducati); 3 Ben Wilson (Honda); 4 Edward Smith (Yamaha); 5 Kris Jennes (Yamaha); 6 Callum Ramsay (Suzuki); 7 Mark Davies (Kawasaki); 8 Scott Smart (Honda); 9 Jeremy Goodall (Suzuki); 10 Matt Layt (Suzuki); 11 Adam Redding (Kawasaki); 12 Jamie Green (Yamaha); 13 Pete Jennings (Kawasaki); 14 Les Shand (Honda); 15 Mark Jarvis (Honda).
Fastest lap: Laverty, 1m 29.911s, 87.000 mph/140.02 km/h.
Championship points: 1 Easton, 203; 2 Smart, 165; 3 Laverty, 104; 4 Tunstall, 91; 5 Jennings, 90; 6 Goodall, 85.

National 125GP Championship, round 11 (13 laps, 28.249 miles/45.461 km)
1 Christian Elkin (Honda), 22m 53.082s, 74.06 mph/119.19 km/h.
2 Eugene Laverty (Honda); 3 Midge Smart (Honda); 4 Leon Camier (Honda); 5 Chris Martin (Honda); 6 Brian Clark (Honda); 7 Howie Mainwaring (Honda); 8 Kris Weston (Honda); 9 Russell Hodgson (Honda); 10 Daniel Coutts (Honda); 11 Paul Veazey (Honda); 12 Sam Owens (Honda); 13 Chester Lusk (Honda); 14 Lee Longden (Honda); 15 Jon Vincent (Honda).
Fastest lap: Elkin, 1m 38.262s, 79.61 mph/128.12 km/h.
Championship points: 1 Martin, 209; 2 Elkin, 194; 3 Smart, 133; 4 Farbrother, 123; 5 Camier, 112; 6 Pearson, 104.

Performance Bikes Superstock Championship, round 11 (14 laps, 30.422 miles/48.958 km)
1 Chris Burns (Suzuki), 21m 41.161s, 84.17 mph/135.46 km/h.
2 John Crockford (Suzuki); 3 David Jefferies (Suzuki); 4 Kieran Murphy (Suzuki); 5 Dennis Hobbs (Suzuki); 6 Matt Llewellyn (Suzuki); 7 Jonti Hobday (Suzuki); 8 Steve McMillan (Suzuki); 9 Tristan Palmer (Suzuki); 10 Kevin Falcke (Suzuki); 11 Steve Allan (Kawasaki); 12 Tommy Hill (Yamaha); 13 Kris Jennes (Suzuki); 14 Kelvin Reilly (Yamaha); 15 Brett Sampson (Suzuki).
Fastest lap: Burns, 1m 30.679s, 86.26 mph/138.82 km/h.
Championship points: 1 Jefferies, 196; 2 Burns, 175; 3 Crockford, 158; 4 Murphy, 109; 5 McCulloch, 93; 6 Tinsley, 74.

OULTON PARK, 1 September. 2.769-mile/4.456-km circuit.
British Superbike Championship, round 11 (2 x 18 laps, 49.842 miles/80.208 km)
Race 1
1 Steve Hislop (Ducati), 29m 15.791s, 102.19 mph/164.46 km/h.
2 Shane Byrne (Ducati); 3 Michael Rutter (Ducati); 4 Steve Plater (Yamaha); 5 Karl Harris (Suzuki); 6 Glen Richards (Kawasaki); 7 John Crawford (Suzuki); 8 John Reynolds (Suzuki); 9 Sean Emmett (Yamaha); 10 Dean Thomas (Ducati); 11 Paul Young (Suzuki); 12 Adrian Coates (Suzuki); 13 Dean Ellison (Ducati); 14 Phil Giles (Suzuki); 15 Jamie Robinson (Honda).
Fastest lap: Hislop, 1m 31.652s, 108.76 mph/175.03 km/h (record).

Race 2
1 Steve Plater (Yamaha), 27m 48.010s, 107.57 mph/173.12 km/h.
2 John Reynolds (Suzuki); 3 Simon Crafar (Yamaha); 4 Karl Harris (Suzuki); 5 Michael Rutter (Ducati); 6 Sean Emmett (Yamaha); 7 John Crawford (Suzuki); 8 Dean Thomas (Ducati); 9 Paul Young (Suzuki); 10 Gary Mason (Honda); 11 Adrian Coates (Suzuki); 12 Dean Ellison (Ducati); 13 Phil Giles (Suzuki); 14 Jamie Robinson (Honda); 15 Lee Jackson (Yamaha).
Fastest lap: Hislop, 1m 31.532s, 108.90 mph/175.26 km/h (record).
Championship points: 1 Hislop, 395; 2 Emmett, 339; 3 Rutter, 316.5; 4 Byrne, 257.5; 5 Reynolds, 244.5; 6 Plater, 229.

MB4U.com Supersport Championship, round 12 (15 laps, 41.535 miles/66.840 km)
1 Stuart Easton (Ducati), 24m 22.360s, 102.25 mph/164.56 km/h.
2 Michael Laverty (Honda); 3 Scott Smart (Honda); 4 Jeremy Goodall (Suzuki); 5 Callum Ramsay (Suzuki); 6 Pete Jennings (Kawasaki); 7 Douglas Cowie (Kawasaki); 8 Ben Wilson (Honda); 9 Gary May (Yamaha); 10 Tom Tunstall (Suzuki); 11 James Buckingham (Yamaha); 12 Darren Mitchell (Suzuki); 13 Spencer Cook (Yamaha); 14 Craig Sproston (Honda); 15 Edward Smith (Yamaha).
Fastest lap: Laverty, 1m 36.324s, 103.48 mph/166.54 km/h.
Championship points: 1 Easton, 228; 2 Smart, 181; 3 Laverty, 124; 4 Jennings, 100; 5 Goodall, 98; 6 Tunstall, 97.

National 125GP Championship, round 12 (14 laps, 38.766 miles/62.384 km)
1 Chris Martin (Honda), 23m 53.429s, 97.35 mph/156.67 km/h.
2 Leon Camier (Honda); 3 Christian Elkin (Honda); 4 Michael Wilcox (Honda); 5 Daniel Coutts (Honda); 6 John Pearson (Kawasaki); 7 Russell Hodgson (Honda); 8 Kris Weston (Honda); 9 Howie Mainwaring (Honda); 10 Andy Walker (Honda); 11 Lee Longden (Honda); 12 Oliver Bridewell (Honda); 13 Ashley Beech (Honda); 14 Thomas Bridewell (Honda); 15 Brian Clark (Honda).
Fastest lap: Martin, 1m 41.538s, 98.17 mph/157.99 km/h (record).
Championship points: 1 Martin, 234; 2 Elkin, 210; 3 Smart, 133; 4 Camier, 132; 5 Farbrother, 123; 6 Pearson, 114.

Performance Bikes Superstock Championship, round 12 (12 laps, 33.228 miles/53.472 km)
1 David Jefferies (Suzuki), 19m 14.765s, 103.58 mph/166.70 km/h.
2 John Crockford (Suzuki); 3 Chris Burns (Suzuki); 4 Matt Llewellyn (Suzuki); 5 Andy Tinsley (Suzuki); 6 Steve Brogan (Suzuki); 7 Kieran Murphy (Suzuki); 8 Michael Laverty (Suzuki); 9 Steve McMillan (Suzuki); 10 Stephen Thompson (Suzuki); 11 Jonti Hobday (Suzuki); 12 Dennis Hobbs (Suzuki); 13 Tommy Hill (Yamaha); 14 Kelvin Reilly (Yamaha); 15 Carl Rennie (Suzuki).
Fastest lap: Burns and Jefferies, 1m 35.457s, 104.42 mph/168.06 km/h.

Championship points: 1 Jefferies, 221; 2 Burns, 191; 3 Crockford, 178; 4 Murphy, 118; 5 McCulloch, 93; 6 Tinsley, 85.

MALLORY PARK CIRCUIT, 15 September. 1.370-mile/2.205-km circuit.
MCN British Superbike Championship, round 12 (2 x 30 laps, 41.100 miles/66.150 km)
Race 1
1 Steve Plater (Yamaha), 24m 03.412s, 102.50 mph/164.96 km/h.
2 Sean Emmett (Yamaha); 3 Michael Rutter (Ducati); 4 Shane Byrne (Ducati); 5 Glen Richards (Kawasaki); 6 Steve Hislop (Ducati); 7 Karl Harris (Suzuki); 8 John Crawford (Suzuki); 9 Simon Crafar (Yamaha); 10 Dean Ellison (Ducati); 11 Paul Young (Suzuki); 12 Dean Thomas (Ducati); 13 Gary Mason (Honda); 14 Phil Giles (Suzuki); 15 Adrian Coates (Suzuki).
Fastest lap: Byrne, 47.319s, 104.22 mph/167.73 km/h (record).

Race 2
1 Michael Rutter (Ducati), 23m 58.072s, 102.88 mph/165.57 km/h.
2 Sean Emmett (Yamaha); 3 Steve Plater (Yamaha); 4 Shane Byrne (Ducati); 5 Steve Hislop (Ducati); 6 Glen Richards (Kawasaki); 7 John Reynolds (Suzuki); 8 Karl Harris (Suzuki); 9 John Crawford (Suzuki); 10 Simon Crafar (Yamaha); 11 Gary Mason (Honda); 12 Paul Young (Suzuki); 13 Adrian Coates (Suzuki); 14 Dean Thomas (Ducati); 15 Phil Giles (Suzuki).
Fastest lap: Rutter, 47.159s, 104.58 mph/168.30 km/h (record).
Championship points: 1 Hislop, 416; 2 Emmett, 379; 3 Rutter, 357.5; 4 Byrne, 283.5; 5 Plater, 270; 6 Reynolds, 253.5.

MB4U.com Supersport Championship, round 13 (26 laps, 35.620 miles/57.330 km)
1 Michael Laverty (Honda), 22m 19.168s, 95.75 mph/154.09 km/h.
2 Simon Andrews (Honda); 3 Stuart Easton (Ducati); 4 Pete Jennings (Kawasaki); 5 James Buckingham (Yamaha); 6 Ben Wilson (Honda); 7 Danny Beaumont (Yamaha); 8 Gary Haslam (Honda); 9 Tom Tunstall (Suzuki); 10 Craig McLelland (Suzuki); 11 Callum Ramsay (Suzuki); 12 Les Shand (Honda); 13 Craig Sproston (Honda); 14 Edward Smith (Yamaha); 15 Darren Mitchell (Suzuki).
Fastest lap: Laverty, 49.321s, 99.99 mph/160.92 km/h.
Championship points: 1 Easton, 244; 2 Smart, 181; 3 Laverty, 149; 4 Jennings, 113; 5 Tunstall, 104; 6 Andrews and Wilson, 100.

National 125GP Championship, round 13 (24 laps, 32.880 miles/52.920 km)
1 Midge Smart (Honda), 21m 24.799s, 92.13 mph/148.27 km/h.
2 Chris Martin (Honda); 3 Daniel Coutts (Honda); 4 Christian Elkin (Honda); 5 Leon Camier (Honda); 6 Michael Wilcox (Honda); 7 Russell Hodgson (Honda); 8 John Pearson (Kawasaki); 9 Oliver Bridewell (Honda); 10 Howie Mainwaring (Honda); 11 Kris Weston (Honda); 12 Thomas Bridewell (Honda); 13 Eugene Laverty (Honda); 14 Brian Clark (Honda); 15 Paul Veazey (Honda).
Fastest lap: Wilcox, 50.436s, 97.78 mph/157.37 km/h.
Championship points: 1 Martin, 254; 2 Elkin, 223; 3 Smart, 158; 4 Camier, 143; 5 Farbrother, 123; 6 Pearson, 122.

Performance Bikes Superstock Championship, round 13 (23 laps, 31.510 miles/50.715 km)
1 John Crockford (Suzuki), 18m 58.767s, 99.61 mph/160.31 km/h.
2 Chris Burns (Suzuki); 3 Jamie Morley (Suzuki); 4 Kieran Murphy (Suzuki); 5 Andy Tinsley (Suzuki); 6 Steve Allan (Kawasaki); 7 Michael Laverty (Suzuki); 8 Simon Andrews (Honda); 9 Steve McMillan (Suzuki); 10 Tommy Hill (Yamaha); 11 Malcolm Ashley (Ducati); 12 Alan Moreton (Yamaha); 13 John Nisill (Suzuki); 14 Ian Hutchinson (Suzuki).
Fastest lap: Crockford, 48.909s, 100.84 mph/162.28 km/h (record).
Championship points: 1 Jefferies, 221; 2 Burns, 211; 3 Crockford, 203; 4 Murphy, 131; 5 Tinsley, 96; 6 McCulloch, 93.

DONINGTON PARK GRAND PRIX CIRCUIT, 29 September. 2.500-mile/4.023-km circuit.
MCN British Superbike Championship, round 13 (2 x 20 laps, 50.000 miles/80.460 km)
Race 1
1 Michael Rutter (Ducati), 31m 23.476s, 95.50 mph/153.69 km/h.
2 John Reynolds (Suzuki); 3 Steve Hislop (Ducati); 4 Glen Richards (Kawasaki); 5 Simon Crafar (Yamaha); 6 John Crawford (Suzuki); 7 Karl Harris (Suzuki); 8 Dean Ellison (Ducati); 9 Dean Thomas (Ducati); 10 Gary Mason (Honda); 11 Phil Giles (Suzuki); 12 Lee Jackson (Yamaha); 13 Jon Kirkham (Suzuki); 14 Adrian Coates (Suzuki); 15 Simon Smith (Suzuki).
Fastest lap: Richards, 1m 33.531s, 96.22 mph/154.85 km/h.

Race 2
1 Michael Rutter (Ducati), 31m 27.367s, 95.61 mph/153.87 km/h.
2 Steve Hislop (Ducati); 3 Steve Plater (Yamaha); 4 Glen Richards (Kawasaki); 5 Shane Byrne (Ducati); 6 John Reynolds (Suzuki); 7 Dean Ellison (Ducati); 8 John Crawford (Suzuki); 9 Gary Mason (Honda); 10 Simon Crafar (Yamaha); 11 Dean Thomas (Ducati); 12 Paul Brown (Ducati); 13 Phil Giles (Suzuki); 14 Mark Burr (Kawasaki); 15 Lee Jackson (Yamaha).
Fastest lap: Hislop, 1m 32.830s, 96.95 mph/156.02 km/h (record).

MB4U.com Supersport Championship, round 14 (16 laps, 40.000 miles/64.368 km)
1 Scott Smart (Honda); 26m 22.692s, 90.91 mph/146.31 km/h.
2 John McGuinness (Honda); **3** Danny Beaumont (Yamaha); **4** Craig McLelland (Suzuki); **5** Pete Jennings (Kawasaki); **6** Tom Tunstall (Suzuki); **7** James Buckingham (Yamaha); **8** Jeremy Goodall (Suzuki); **9** Ben Wilson (Honda); **10** Les Shand (Honda); **11** Douglas Cowie (Kawasaki); **12** Darren Mitchell (Suzuki); **13** Callum Ramsay (Suzuki); **14** Craig Sproston (Honda); **15** Mark Jarvis (Honda).
Fastest lap: McGuinness, 1m 37.888s, 91.94 mph/147.96 km/h.

National 125GP Championship, round 14 (15 laps, 37.500 miles/60.345 km)
1 Chris Martin (Honda), 25m 43.796s, 87.37 mph/140.61 km/h.
2 Leon Camier (Honda); **3** Paul Veazey (Honda); **4** Daniel Cooper (Honda); **5** John Pearson (Kawasaki); **6** Andy Walker (Honda); **7** Michael Wilcox (Honda); **8** Howie Mainwaring (Honda); **9** Sam Owens (Honda); **10** Daniel Coutts (Honda); **11** Kris Weston (Honda); **12** Chester Lusk (Honda); **13** Steven Neate (Honda); **14** Thomas Bridewell (Honda); **15** Jon Vincent (Honda).
Fastest lap: Midge Smart (Honda), 1m 41.858s, 88.35 mph/142.19 km/h.

Performance Bikes Superstock Championship, round 14 (12 laps, 30.000 miles/48.276 km)
1 John Crockford (Suzuki), 19m 33.378s, 91.94 mph/147.96 km/h.
2 Steve Brogan (Suzuki); **3** David Jefferies (Suzuki); **4** Andy Tinsley (Suzuki); **5** Kieran Murphy (Suzuki); **6** Tristan Palmer (Suzuki); **7** Luke Quigley (Suzuki); **8** Danny Beaumont (Suzuki); **9** Dennis Hobbs (Suzuki); **10** Tommy Hill (Yamaha); **11** Marshall Neill (Suzuki); **12** Simon Andrews (Honda); **13** Jonti Hobday (Suzuki); **14** Kelvin Reilly (Yamaha); **15** Rhys Boyd (Yamaha).
Fastest lap: Brogan, 1m 36.720s, 93.05 mph/149.75 km/h.

Final MCN British Superbike Championship points

1	Steve Hislop	452
2	Michael Rutter	407.5
3	Sean Emmett	379
4	Shane Byrne	294.5
5	Steve Plater	286

6 John Reynolds, 283.5; **7** Glen Richards, 187.5; **8** Simon Crafar, 187; **9** Paul Brown, 163.5; **10** Dean Ellison, 131.5; **11** Dean Thomas, 130; **12** Karl Harris, 117; **13** John Crawford, 83; **14** Gary Mason, 56.5; **15** Paul Jones, 50.

Final MB4U.com British Supersport Championship points

1	Stuart Easton	244
2	Scott Smart	206
3	Michael Laverty	149
4	Pete Jennings	124
5	Tom Tunstall	114

6 Ben Wilson, 107; **7** Jeremy Goodall, 106; **8** Simon Andrews, 100; **9** Callum Ramsay, 78; **10** Douglas Cowie, 62; **11** Chris Bishop, 61; **12** Edward Smith, 54; **13** Danny Beaumont, 52; **14** Craig Sproston, 49; **15** Gary May, 46.

Final National 125GP Championship points

1	Chris Martin	289
2	Christian Elkin	223
3	Leon Camier	163
4	Midge Smart	158
5	John Pearson	133

6 Guy Farbrother, 123; **7** Russell Hodgson, 88; **8** Michael Wilcox, 87; **9** Daniel Coutts, 83; **10** Andy Walker, 78; **11** Steve Patrickson, 75; **12** Paul Veazey, 53; **13** Paul Robinson, 49; **14** Kris Weston, 48; **15** Sam Owens, 45.

Final Performance Bikes Superstock Championship points

1	David Jefferies	237
2	John Crockford	228
3	Chris Burns	211
4	Kieran Murphy	142
5	Andy Tinsley	109

6 Steve Brogan, 102; **7** Ross McCulloch, 93; **8** Steve McMillan, 77; **9** Tristan Palmer, 67; **10** Jonti Hobday, 62; **11** Simon Andrews, 52; **12** Luke Quigley, 51; **13=** Dave Johnson and Andi Notman, 43; **15** Dennis Hobbs, 39.

Supersport World Championship

VALENCIA, Spain, 10 March. 2.489-mile/4.005-km circuit. Supersport World Championship, round 1 (23 laps, 57.247 miles/92.115 km)
1 Fabien Foret, F (Honda), 38m 11.646s, 89.916 mph/144.706 km/h.
2 Stéphane Chambon, F (Suzuki); **3** Christian Kellner, D (Yamaha); **4** Chris Vermeulen, AUS (Honda); **5** Andrew Pitt, AUS (Kawasaki); **6** James Whitham, GB (Yamaha); **7** Alessio Corradi, I (Yamaha); **8** Paolo Casoli, I (Yamaha); **9** Antonio Carlacci, I (Yamaha); **10** Werner Daemen, B (Honda); **11** Piergiorgio Bontempi, I (Ducati); **12** Gianluca Nannelli, I (Ducati); **13** Robert Ulm, A (Honda); **14** Karl Muggeridge, AUS (Honda); **15** James Ellison, GB (Kawasaki).
Fastest lap: Foret, 1m 38.981s, 90.511 mph/145.664 km/h (record).
Championship points: **1** Foret, 25; **2** Chambon, 20; **3** Kellner, 16; **4** Vermeulen, 13; **5** Pitt, 11; **6** Whitham, 10.

PHILLIP ISLAND, Australia, 24 March. 2.762-mile/4.445 km circuit. Supersport World Championship, round 2 (21 laps, 58.002 miles/93.345 km)
1 Andrew Pitt, AUS (Kawasaki), 34m 18.694s, 101.427 mph/163.231 km/h.
2 Piergiorgio Bontempi, I (Ducati); **3** Stéphane Chambon, F (Suzuki); **4** Katsuaki Fujiwara, J (Suzuki); **5** Jörg Teuchert, D (Yamaha); **6** Christian Kellner, D (Yamaha); **7** Christophe Cogan, F (Honda); **8** Iain MacPherson, GB (Honda); **9** Fabien Foret, F (Honda); **10** Alessio Corradi, I (Yamaha); **11** Chris Vermeulen, AUS (Honda); **12** Kevin Curtain, AUS (Yamaha); **13** Robert Ulm, A (Honda); **14** Werner Daemen, B (Honda); **15** James Ellison, GB (Kawasaki).
Fastest lap: Bontempi, 1m 37.128s, 102.372 mph/164.752 km/h (record).
Championship points: **1** Chambon and Pitt, 36; **3** Foret, 32; **4** Kellner, 26; **5** Bontempi, 25; **6** Vermeulen, 18.

KYALAMI, South Africa, 7 April. 2.649-mile/4.263-km circuit. Supersport World Championship, round 3 (25 laps, 66.225 miles/106.575 km)
1 Andrew Pitt, AUS (Kawasaki), 44m 58.860s, 88.334 mph/142.160 km/h.
2 James Whitham, GB (Yamaha); **3** Stéphane Chambon, F (Suzuki); **4** Jörg Teuchert, D (Yamaha); **5** Fabien Foret, F (Honda); **6** Christian Kellner, D (Yamaha); **7** Paolo Casoli, I (Yamaha); **8** Iain MacPherson, GB (Honda); **9** Chris Vermeulen, AUS (Honda); **10** Alessio Corradi, I (Yamaha); **11** Piergiorgio Bontempi, I (Ducati); **12** Christophe Cogan, F (Honda); **13** Karl Muggeridge, AUS (Honda); **14** Werner Daemen, B (Honda); **15** Arushen Moodley, RSA (Honda).
Fastest lap: Whitham, 1m 46.975s, 89.143 mph/143.462 km/h (record).
Championship points: **1** Pitt, 61; **2** Chambon, 52; **3** Foret, 43; **4** Kellner, 36; **5** Bontempi and Whitham, 30.

SUGO, Japan, 21 April. 2.322-mile/3.737-km circuit. Supersport World Championship, round 4 (25 laps, 58.050 miles/93.425 km)
1 Stéphane Chambon, F (Suzuki), 39m 07.182s, 89.037 mph/143.291 km/h.
2 Katsuaki Fujiwara, J (Suzuki); **3** Fabien Foret, F (Honda); **4** Paolo Casoli, I (Yamaha); **5** Christian Kellner, D (Yamaha); **6** Karl Muggeridge, AUS (Honda); **7** Andrew Pitt, AUS (Kawasaki); **8** Werner Daemen, B (Honda); **9** Kevin Curtain, AUS (Honda); **10** Jörg Teuchert, D (Yamaha); **11** Alessio Corradi, I (Yamaha); **12** David de Gea, E (Honda); **13** James Ellison, GB (Kawasaki); **14** Stefano Cruciani, I (Yamaha); **15** Antonio Carlacci, I (Yamaha).
Fastest lap: Foret, 1m 33.015s, 89.872 mph/144.635 km/h (record).
Championship points: **1** Chambon, 77; **2** Pitt, 70; **3** Foret, 59; **4** Kellner, 47; **5** Fujiwara, 33; **6** Bontempi, Casoli, Teuchert and Whitham, 30.

MONZA, Italy, 12 May. 3.600-mile/5.793-km circuit. Supersport World Championship, round 5 (16 laps, 57.600 miles/92.688 km)
1 Fabien Foret, F (Honda), 30m 42.007s, 112.560 mph/181.148 km/h.
2 Chris Vermeulen, AUS (Honda); **3** Katsuaki Fujiwara, J (Suzuki); **4** Andrew Pitt, AUS (Kawasaki); **5** Stéphane Chambon, F (Suzuki); **6** Paolo Casoli, I (Yamaha); **7** Piergiorgio Bontempi, I (Ducati); **8** Iain MacPherson, GB (Honda); **9** Jörg Teuchert, D (Yamaha); **10** Werner Daemen, B (Honda); **11** Matthieu Lagrive, F (Yamaha); **12** Gianluca Nannelli, I (Ducati); **13** Diego Giugovaz, I (Yamaha); **14** Antonio Carlacci, I (Yamaha); **15** Sébastien Charpentier, F (Honda).
Fastest lap: Foret, 1m 54.082s, 113.590 mph/182.805 km/h (record).
Championship points: **1** Chambon, 88; **2** Foret, 84; **3** Pitt, 83; **4** Fujiwara, 49; **5** Kellner, 47; **6** Vermeulen, 45.

SILVERSTONE, Great Britain, 26 May. 3.165-mile/5.094-km circuit. Supersport World Championship, round 6 (13 laps, 41.145 miles/66.222 km)
1 James Whitham, GB (Yamaha), 28m 15.649s, 87.362 mph/140.595 km/h.
2 Paolo Casoli, I (Yamaha); **3** Karl Muggeridge, AUS (Honda); **4** Jörg Teuchert, D (Yamaha); **5** Iain MacPherson, GB (Honda); **6** Katsuaki Fujiwara, J (Suzuki); **7** Fabien Foret, F (Honda); **8** Stéphane Chambon, F (Suzuki); **9** Diego Giugovaz, I (Yamaha); **10** Matthieu Lagrive, F (Yamaha); **11** Christian Kellner, D (Yamaha); **12** Stefano Cruciani, I (Yamaha); **13** Gianluca Nannelli, I (Ducati); **14** Chris Vermeulen, AUS (Honda); **15** John McGuinness, GB (Honda).
Fastest lap: Whitham, 2m 07.994s, 89.027 mph/143.275 km/h (record).
Championship points: **1** Chambon, 96; **2** Foret, 93; **3** Pitt, 83; **4** Casoli, 60; **5** Fujiwara, 59; **6** Whitham, 55.

LAUSITZ, Germany, 9 June. 2.650-mile/4.265-km circuit. Supersport World Championship, round 7 (23 laps, 60.950 miles/98.095 km)
1 Katsuaki Fujiwara, J (Suzuki), 40m 03.477s, 91.298 mph/146.930 km/h.
2 Andrew Pitt, AUS (Kawasaki); **3** Stéphane Chambon, F (Suzuki); **4** Christian Kellner, D (Yamaha); **5** Chris Vermeulen, AUS (Honda); **6** Jörg Teuchert, D (Yamaha); **7** Kevin Curtain, AUS (Yamaha); **8** Stefano Cruciani, I (Yamaha); **9** Piergiorgio Bontempi, I (Ducati); **10** Iain MacPherson, GB (Honda); **11** Alessio Corradi, I (Yamaha); **12** Robert Ulm, A (Honda); **13** Christian Zaiser, A (Yamaha); **14** Karl Muggeridge, AUS (Honda); **15** David de Gea, E (Honda).
Fastest lap: Fujiwara, 1m 43.644s, 92.051 mph/148.142 km/h (record).
Championship points: **1** Chambon, 112; **2** Pitt, 103; **3** Foret, 93; **4** Fujiwara, 84; **5** Kellner, 65; **6** Casoli and Teuchert, 60.

MISANO, Italy, 23 June. 2.523-mile/4.060-km circuit. Supersport World Championship, round 8 (23 laps, 58.029 miles/93.380 km)
1 Fabien Foret, F (Honda), 38m 24.180s, 90.655 mph/145.895 km/h.
2 Katsuaki Fujiwara, J (Suzuki); **3** James Whitham, GB (Yamaha); **4** Christian Kellner, D (Yamaha); **5** Paolo Casoli, I (Yamaha); **6** Andrew Pitt, AUS (Kawasaki); **7** Christophe Cogan, F (Honda); **8** Chris Vermeulen, AUS (Honda); **9** Robert Ulm, A (Honda); **10** Alessio Corradi, I (Yamaha); **11** Kevin Curtain, AUS (Yamaha); **12** Stefano Cruciani, I (Yamaha); **13** Stéphane Chambon, F (Suzuki); **14** Piergiorgio Bontempi, I (Ducati); **15** Camillo Mariottini, I (Yamaha).
Fastest lap: Chambon, 1m 38.856s, 91.870 mph/147.851 km/h (record).
Championship points: **1** Foret, 118; **2** Chambon, 115; **3** Pitt, 113; **4** Fujiwara, 104; **5** Kellner, 78; **6** Casoli and Whitham, 71.

BRANDS HATCH, Great Britain, 28 July. 2.623-mile/4.221-km circuit. Supersport World Championship, round 9 (23 laps, 60.329 miles/97.083 km)
1 Katsuaki Fujiwara, J (Suzuki), 35m 09.441s, 102.951 mph/165.683 km/h.
2 Fabien Foret, F (Honda); **3** Paolo Casoli, I (Yamaha); **4** Iain MacPherson, GB (Honda); **5** Jörg Teuchert, D (Yamaha); **6** Christian Kellner, D (Yamaha); **7** Alessio Corradi, I (Yamaha); **8** Chris Vermeulen, AUS (Honda); **9** Kevin Curtain, AUS (Yamaha); **10** Stuart Easton, GB (Ducati); **11** Stefano Cruciani, I (Yamaha); **12** Werner Daemen, B (Honda); **13** James Ellison, GB (Kawasaki); **14** Sébastien Charpentier, F (Honda); **15** John McGuinness, GB (Honda).
Fastest lap: MacPherson, 1m 30.095s, 104.802 mph/168.662 km/h (record).
Championship points: **1** Foret, 138; **2** Fujiwara, 129; **3** Chambon, 115; **4** Pitt, 113; **5** Kellner, 88; **6** Casoli, 87.

OSCHERSLEBEN, Germany, 1 September. 2.279-mile/3.667-km circuit. Supersport World Championship, round 10 (28 laps, 63.812 miles/102.676 km)
1 Paolo Casoli, I (Yamaha), 42m 42.079s, 89.646 mph/144.271 km/h.
2 Stéphane Chambon, F (Suzuki); **3** Katsuaki Fujiwara, J (Suzuki); **4** Andrew Pitt, AUS (Kawasaki); **5** Kevin Curtain, AUS (Yamaha); **6** Fabien Foret, F (Honda); **7** Jan Hanson, S (Honda); **8** Alessio Corradi, I (Yamaha); **9** James Ellison, GB (Kawasaki); **10** Jürgen Oelschläger, D (Honda); **11** Laurent Brian, F (Honda); **12** Matthieu Lagrive, F (Yamaha); **13** Sébastien Charpentier, F (Honda); **14** John McGuinness, GB (Honda); **15** Gianluca Nannelli, I (Ducati).
Fastest lap: Kellner, 1m 30.591s, 90.548 mph/145.723 km/h (record).
Championship points: **1** Foret, 148; **2** Fujiwara, 145; **3** Chambon, 135; **4** Pitt, 126; **5** Casoli, 112; **6** Kellner, 88.

ASSEN, Holland, 8 September. 3.745-mile/6.027 km circuit. Supersport World Championship, round 11 (11 laps, 41.195 miles/66.297 km)
1 Fabien Foret, F (Honda), 23m 37.444s, 104.626 mph/168.380 km/h.
2 Iain MacPherson, GB (Honda); **3** Paolo Casoli, I (Yamaha); **4** Kevin Curtain, AUS (Yamaha); **5** Katsuaki Fujiwara, J (Suzuki); **6** Karl Muggeridge, AUS (Honda); **7** James Whitham, GB (Yamaha); **8** Jörg Teuchert, D (Yamaha); **9** Stéphane Chambon, F (Suzuki); **10** Christian Kellner, D (Yamaha); **11** Christophe Cogan, F (Honda); **12** Robert Ulm, A (Honda); **13** Piergiorgio Bontempi, I (Ducati); **14** Alessio Corradi, I (Yamaha); **15** Werner Daemen, B (Honda).
Fastest lap: Foret, 2m 07.497s, 105.744 mph/170.178 km/h (record).
Championship points: **1** Foret, 173; **2** Fujiwara, 156; **3** Chambon, 142; **4** Casoli, 128; **5** Pitt, 126; **6** Kellner, 94.

IMOLA, Italy, 29 September. 3.065-mile/4.933-km circuit. Supersport World Championship, round 12 (21 laps, 64.365 miles/103.593 km)
1 Katsuaki Fujiwara, J (Suzuki), 40m 15.186s, 95.947 mph/154.412 km/h.
2 Stéphane Chambon, F (Suzuki); **3** Chris Vermeulen, AUS (Honda); **4** Fabien Foret, F (Honda); **5** Jörg Teuchert, D (Yamaha); **6** Antonio Carlacci, I (Yamaha); **7** Iain MacPherson, GB (Honda); **8** Stefano Cruciani, I (Yamaha); **9** Christophe Cogan, F (Honda); **10** Robert Frost, GB (Yamaha); **11** James Ellison, GB (Kawasaki); **12** Robert Ulm, A (Yamaha); **13** Matthieu Lagrive, F (Yamaha); **14** Paul Young, GB (Honda); **15** Michael Laverty, GB (Honda).
Fastest lap: Vermeulen, 1m 54.064s, 96.743 mph/155.692 km/h.

Final World Championship points

1	Fabien Foret, F	186
2	Katsuaki Fujiwara, J	181
3	Stéphane Chambon, F	162
4	Paolo Casoli, I	128
5	Andrew Pitt, AUS	126

6 Christian Kellner, D, 94; **7=** Jörg Teuchert, D and Chris Vermeulen, AUS, 90; **9** Iain MacPherson, GB, 83; **10** James Whitham, GB, 80; **11=** Alessio Corradi, I and Kevin Curtain, AUS, 56; **13** Piergiorgio Bontempi, I, 51; **14** Karl Muggeridge, AUS, 43; **15** Christophe Cogan, F, 34.